TUSCANY
AND
UMBRIA

THE COLLECTED TRAVELER

ALSO EDITED BY BARRIE KERPER

Istanbul: The Collected Traveler

Barrie Kerper

TUSCANY AND UMBRIA

Barrie Kerper is an avid traveler and reader who has lived abroad. She has over a thousand books in her home library—and an even greater number of file clippings—and has filled up four passports.

TUSCANY
AND
UMBRIA

THE COLLECTED TRAVELER

Edited by Barrie Kerper

An Inspired Companion Guide

Vintage Departures
Vintage Books
A Division of Random House, Inc.
New York

Owing to limitations of space, all acknowledgments to reprint previously published material can be found on pages 614–16.

Grateful acknowledgment is made to the publisher for permission to reprint the following recipes: "La Panzanese Grilled Steak" contributed by Dario Cecchini, "Chickpea Purée with Shrimp" contributed by Fulvio and Emanuela Pierangelini, and "Broccoli and Cauliflower Sformatino" contributed by Benedetta Vitali, from *Adventures of an Italian Food Lover: With Recipes from 254 of My Very Best Friends* by Faith Heller Willinger. Copyright © 2007 by Faith Willinger. Reprinted by permission of Clarkson Potter/Publishers, an imprint of the Crown Publishing Group, a division of Random House, Inc.

All photographs by Peggy Harrison (www.peggyharrison.com) with the exception of those that appear on pages xxiv, 172, 210, 223, 310, 317, 324, 366, 396 (all courtesy of the Italian Government Tourist Board North America, Fototeca ENIT—ENIT Photo Archive Ver. 1.8.1, photos by: Vito Arcomano); pages 2 and 46 (courtesy of the Italian Government Tourist Board North America, Fototeca ENIT—ENIT Photo Archive Ver. 1.8.1, © De Agostini Picture Library; page 304 (courtesy of the Italian Government Tourist Board North America, Fototeca ENIT, © Turismo Torino, photo by: Giuseppe Bressi); and page 328 (courtesy of the Italian Government Tourist Board North America, © Fototeca ENIT, photo by: Vito Arcomano). The photos of Laurie Albanese, Charles Darwall, Dianne Hales, Lisa McGarry, and Laura Morowitz are reproduced courtesy of their subjects.

Library of Congress Cataloging-in-Publication Data
Tuscany and Umbria : the collected traveler / edited by Barrie Kerper.
    p.   cm.—(The collected traveler) (Vintage departures)
            "An inspired companion guide."
        "A Vintage departures original"—T.p. verso.
        Previous ed.: New York : Three Rivers Press, 2000,
            with title Central Italy, Tuscany & Umbria.
            Includes bibliographical references.
                ISBN 978-0-307-47490-2
    1. Tuscany (Italy)—Description and travel—Sources.   2. Umbria (Italy)—Description and travel—Sources.   3. Travelers' writings.   4. Tuscany (Italy)—Biography.
    5. Umbria (Italy)—Biography.   6. Interviews—Italy—Tuscany.   7. Interviews—
Italy—Umbria.   8. Tuscany (Italy)—Social life and customs—Sources.   9. Umbria
(Italy)—Social life and customs—Sources.   10. Cookery, Italian.   I. Kerper, Barrie.
            II. Central Italy, Tuscany & Umbria.
                    DG734.23.T87 2010
                    914.5'504—dc22
                        2010010183

Book design by Jo Anne Metsch

www.vintagebooks.com

Printed in the United States of America
10 9 8 7 6 5 4 3 2 1

Once again, to my mother, Phyllis,

who always believed my boxes of files

held something of value,

and to my father, Peter,

the most inspiring person in my life

Italy is both [wonderful and awful] because it is a real country, and not fairyland (even though, now and again, it is just possible to believe that it might be fairyland).

—DAVID LEAVITT AND MARK MITCHELL,
Italian Pleasures

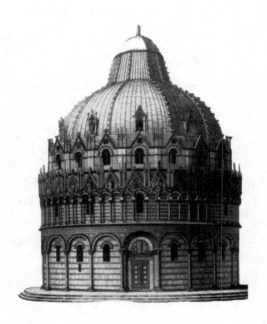

CONTENTS

INTRODUCTION

For most of us, Tuscany is the quintessence of Italy, the distillation of all those elements of the country that we think of as being most specifically Italian.

> —John Julius Norwich, from the foreward to
> *Tuscany: An Anthology,* by Laura Raison

The more leisurely visitor, especially if he has a motorcar to putter about in, soon learns how much his hurried compatriot has missed. He finds that a wealth of hill towns beckon him closer. By the time he has seen such miniature Carcasonnes as Spello, Spoleto, Cascia, and Gubbio, he realizes that this Umbrian region is one of the neglected treasures of Italy. Though he may have found a dearth of fashionable spots for the skier, the casino hound, and the sun worshiper, he has encountered good food and wine, and comfortable places to stop overnight—almost everything, in fact, except his fellow tourist.

> —Samuel Chamberlain,
> *Italian Bouquet: An Epicurean Tour of Italy* (1958)

TUSCANY IS WITHOUT doubt one of the most visited regions of Italy and is the region many people think of first when they think of Italy. And with good reason: the treasures and pleasures of Florence alone could easily hold one's attention for years. Umbria, often known as "the green heart of Italy," exists somewhat in Tuscany's shadow, but happily within the last dozen or so years many visitors have discovered that it, too, offers world-class gems of art and architecture, and its cuisine and landscapes are the equal of its neighbor's.

Some people feel that Tuscany, Florence especially, is too clichéd and too popular for its own good, and too much like anywhere else. (Often visitors complain excessively about the problems tourism creates, about Italian corruption and bureaucracy; but I like to remind them of a remark made many, many years ago by Lord Byron: "There is, in fact, no law or government at all [in Italy]; and it is wonderful how well things go on without them." But those who think Italy isn't exotic enough to be travelworthy are simply mistaken: things *are* different in Tuscany and Umbria.

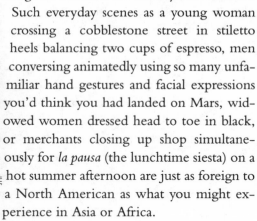

Such everyday scenes as a young woman crossing a cobblestone street in stiletto heels balancing two cups of espresso, men conversing animatedly using so many unfamiliar hand gestures and facial expressions you'd think you had landed on Mars, widowed women dressed head to toe in black, or merchants closing up shop simultaneously for *la pausa* (the lunchtime siesta) on a hot summer afternoon are just as foreign to a North American as what you might experience in Asia or Africa.

Florence, like other cities throughout Tuscany and Umbria, is filled with much that is old but also plenty that is new. Unfortunately, some American fast-food chains have found a foothold here and many international stores are the very same ones we find in North America; still, it is mostly the older sites we come to see. I for one will never forget the day I first saw Santa Maria del Fiore, Florence's Duomo: as I walked down a narrow street, the name of which I no longer remember, I saw a sliver of it suddenly; as I approached it and discerned the different colors and patterns of marble, I was filled with a warmth and a happiness to be alive I've rarely felt again. Over the years, no matter how crowded Florence be- comes, the Duomo will never fail to impress.

Part of the reason Florence can feel completely overrun with tourists is that it's quite a compact city and you can run repeatedly into the same visitors. But it is also the remarkable repository of a huge number of the world's greatest works of art. It's easy to suc- cumb to Stendhal Syndrome, named for French novelist Stendhal, who felt physically sick after he visited Santa Croce; it refers to the feeling of being completely overwhelmed by your surroundings. (My translation: seeing and doing way too much.) Visitors to Flo- rence who arrive with too long a list of must-sees are prime can- didates for the syndrome. Author and Italian expert Fred Plotkin counsels against falling into this trap in his foreword to Claudio Gatti's *Florence in Detail* (an excellent guidebook) by advising, "Like it or not, one must adopt a policy of '*Poco, ma buono*' (loosely translated as 'Do less, but do it really well') to experience what Florence has to offer. A mad dash through a gallery will leave you with only fleeting impressions. Spend ten minutes in front of one painting and you will see remarkable things that a two-minute look could not reveal; spend an hour in front of that same painting and your life will be changed. To really pause and reflect, whether in front of a sculpture or a dish of gelato, is to find the presence of art and genius in all things." I would add that by creating more reasonable itineraries, you actually give yourself

the opportunity to acquire more than a superficial understanding of a place. I particularly enjoy simply sitting at a café table, looking, listening, and wondering. What is life like in the beautiful apartment building off the piazza, the one the young boy has just entered carrying a purchase from the *panificio*? I am curious about the elderly man in his shoe repair shop, and the fruit vendor at the Mercato Centrale, who talks nonstop and greets everyone as though she's known them all her life. And, enviously, I wonder where the two office girls breaking for a cigarette bought their beautiful suits. "Slow" is a good word to keep in mind when visiting Italy.

In addition to maintaining a reasonable schedule, the other single most important word of advice I have for travelers setting off for any place around the globe is to adjust to daily life. One of the fastest ways to do this in Italy is to abandon whatever schedule you observe at home and eat when the Italians eat. Mealtimes in Italy are generally well established, and if you have not purchased provisions for a picnic or found a place to eat by one o'clock, most restaurants will be full and most shops closed. Likewise, dinner is not typically served at six, when Americans are accustomed to eating, an hour that is entirely too early for anyone in a Mediterranean country to contemplate his or her evening meal. Frances Mayes, in *Under the Tuscan Sun,* addresses this issue well in writing that many tourists make "the mistake of eating two wedges of great sausage pizza at eleven and now have no inclination to eat anything. Instead, they wander under the unbearable sun, peeking through metal grates covering shop windows, pushing at the massive doors of locked churches, sitting on the sides of fountains while squinting into miniscule guidebooks. Give it up! I've done the same thing. Then, later, it's hard to deny yourself the luscious *melone* ice cream cone at seven, when the air is still hot and your sandals have rubbed your heels raw. Those weak ones (*mea culpa*) who succumb possibly will have another wedge, artichoke this time, on the way to the hotel; then, when Italy begins eating at nine, the foreign stomach doesn't even mumble. That happens much later, when all the good restaurants are full." Adjust your schedule and you'll be on Italian time, doing things when the Italians do them, eliminating possible disappointment and frustration and the feeling of being utterly out of step.

ABOUT THIS BOOK

> **A traveler without knowledge is a bird without wings.**
> **—Sa'adi, Persian poet,** *Gulistan*

The Collected Traveler editions are meant to be companion volumes to guidebooks that go beyond the practical information that traditional guidebooks supply. Each individual volume is perfect to bring along, but each is also a sort of planning package—the books guide readers to many other sources, and they are sources of inspiration. James Pope-Hennessy, in his wonderful book *Aspects of Provence,* notes that "if one is to get best value out of places visited, some skeletal knowledge of their history is necessary. . . .

Sight-seeing is by no means the only object of a journey, but it is as unintelligent as it is lazy not to equip ourselves to understand the sights we see." Immerse yourself in a destination and you'll acquire a deeper understanding and appreciation of the place and the people who live there, and, not surprisingly, you'll have more fun.

This series promotes the strategy of staying longer within a smaller area so as to experience it more fully. Susan Allen Toth refers to this in one of her many wonderful books, *England as You Like It,* in which she subscribes to the "thumbprint theory of travel": spending at least a week in one spot no larger than her thumbprint covers on a large-scale map of England. Excursions are encouraged, as long as they're about an hour's drive away.

I have discovered in my own travels that a week in one place, even a spot no bigger than my thumbprint, is rarely long enough to see and enjoy it all. For this reason, most of the books in *The Collected Traveler* series focus on either cities or regions, as opposed to entire countries. There will not be a book on all of Italy, for example. I am mindful that Italy is a member of two communities, European and Mediterranean, and an understanding of both is essential to understanding Italy. I have tried to reflect this wider-world sense of community throughout the book, which covers two regions that can be seen together manageably. Some travelers may fly into or out of Rome or may be heading south from Emilia-Romagna, Milano, or Venezia, but each of these areas deserves to be covered in a separate book and is too far outside this particular thumbprint.

The major portion of this book features a selection of articles and essays from various periodicals and recommended reading relevant to the theme of each section. The articles and books were chosen from my own files and home library, which I've maintained for more than two decades. I often feel I am the living embodiment of a comment that Samuel Johnson made in 1775, that

"a man will turn over half a library to make one book." The selected writings reflect the culture, politics, history, current social
issues, religion, cuisine, and arts of the people you'll be visiting.
They represent the observations and opinions of a wide variety of
novelists, travel writers, and journalists. These writers are typically
authorities on Tuscany, Umbria, or Italy, or all three; they either
live there (as permanent or part-time residents) or visit there often
for business or pleasure. I'm very discriminating in seeking opinions and recommendations, and I am not interested in the remarks of unobservant wanderers. I am not implying that
first-time visitors to Italy have nothing noteworthy or interesting
to share—they very often do, and are often keen observers. Conversely, frequent travelers are often jaded and apt to miss the finer
details that make Italy the exceptional place it is. I am interested
in the opinions of people who want to *know* Italy, not just *see* it.

I've included some older articles because they were particularly
well written, thought-provoking, or unique in some way, and because the authors' views stand as a valuable record of a certain
time in history. Even after the passage of many years you may
share the emotions and opinions of the writer, and you may find
that *plus ça change, plus c'est la même chose.* I have many, many more
articles in my files than I am able to reprint here. Though there
are a few pieces whose absence I very much regret, I believe the
anthology you're holding is comprehensive.

A word about the cuisine and restaurant sections, "La Cucina
Italiana" and "A Tavola!" I have great respect for restaurant reviewers; though their work may seem glamorous—it sometimes
is—it is also very hard. It's an all-consuming, full-time job, and
that is why I urge you to consult the very good cookbooks I recommend as well as guidebooks. Restaurant (and hotel) reviewers
are, for the most part, professionals who have dined in hundreds
of eating establishments (and spent hundreds of nights in hotels).
They are far more capable of assessing the qualities and flaws of a

place than I am. I don't always agree with every opinion of a reviewer, but I am far more inclined to defer to their opinion over that of someone who is unfamiliar with Tuscan and Umbrian food or someone who doesn't dine out frequently enough to recognize what good restaurants have in common. My files are filled with restaurant reviews, and I could have included many more articles, but that would have been repetitive and ultimately beside the point. I have selected a few articles that give you a feel for eating out in Tuscany and Umbria, alert you to some things to look for in selecting a truly worthwhile place versus a mediocre one, and highlight notable dishes visitors will encounter in these regions.

The recommended reading for each section is one of the most important features of this book; together they represent my favorite aspect of this series. (My annotations are, however, *much* shorter than I would prefer—did I mention that I love encyclopedias?—but they are still nothing less than enormously enthusiastic endorsements and I encourage you to read as many of these as you can.) One reason I do not include many excerpts from books in my series is that I am not convinced an excerpt will always lead a reader to the book in question, and good books deserve to be read in their entirety. Art critic John Russell wrote an essay, in 1962, entitled "Pleasure in Reading," in which he stated, "Not for us today's selections, readers, digests, and anthologizings: only the Complete Edition will do." Years later, in 1986, he noted that "bibliographies make dull reading, some people say, but I have never found them so. They remind us, they prompt us, and they correct us. They double and treble as history, as biography, and as a freshet of surprises. They reveal the public self, the private self, and the buried self of the person commemorated. How should we not enjoy them, and be grateful to the devoted student who has done the compiling?" The section of a nonfiction book I always turn to first is the bibliography, as it is there that I learn something about the author who has done the compiling, as well as about other notable books I know I will want to read.

When I read about travel in the days before transatlantic flights, I always marvel at the number of steamer trunks and the amount of baggage people were accustomed to taking. If I were traveling back then, however, my trunks would have been filled with books, not clothes. Although I travel light and seldom check bags, I have been known to fill an entire suitcase with books, secure in the knowledge that I'll have them all with me for the duration of my trip. Each of my bibliographies features titles I feel are the best available and most worth your time. I realize that "best" is subjective; readers will simply have to trust that I have been extremely thorough in deciding which books to recommend. It disappoints me, however, that there are undoubtedly books with which I'm unfamiliar and that therefore do not appear here. I would be grateful to hear from you if a favorite of yours is missing. I have not hesitated to list out-of-print titles because some very excellent books are out of print (and deserve to be returned to print!), and because many of them can be found easily, through individuals who specialize in out-of-print books, booksellers, libraries, and online searches. I also believe the leisure reading you bring along should be related in some way to where you're going, so these lists include fiction and poetry titles that feature characters or settings in Tuscany or Umbria or highlight aspects of Italy and the Italians.

Sprinkled throughout this book are the musings of a number of visitors to Tuscany and Umbria—ranging from bestselling writer Frances Mayes to noted chef Mario Batali—briefly describing their most memorable sight or experience from their visits.

An "A to Z Miscellany" appears at the end of the book. This is an alphabetical assemblage of information about words, phrases, foods, people, themes, and historical notes that are unique to Tuscany, Umbria, and Italy. Will you learn of some nontouristy things to see and do? Yes. Will you also learn more about the better-known aspects of these regions? Yes. The Uffizi, the Ponte Vecchio, San Gimignano, Siena, Deruta, Assisi, the picture-postcard landscape of the Tuscan countryside, the rolling green hills of Umbria, a glass of Chianti, a cup of *caffè,* an artisan's workshop in the Oltrarno, and the local trattoria are all equally representative of Tuscany and Umbria. Seeing and doing them *all* is what makes for a memorable visit, and no one, by the way, should make you feel guilty for wanting to see some famous sites. They have become famous for a reason: they are really something to see, the Uffizi and the Duomo included. Canon number eighty-four in Bruce Northam's *Globetrotter Dogma* is "The good old days are now," in which he wisely reminds us that destinations are not ruined even though they may have been more "real" however many years ago. " 'Tis a haughty condescension to insist that because a place has changed or lost its innocence that it's not worth visiting; change requalifies a destination. Your first time is your first time; virgin turf simply is. The moment you commit to a trip, there begins the search for adventure."

Ultimately, this is the compendium of information that I wish I'd had between two covers years ago. I admit it isn't the "perfect" book; for that, I envision a waterproof jacket and pockets inside the front and back covers, pages and pages of accompanying maps, lots of blank pages for notes, a bookmark, mileage and size conversion charts . . . in other words, something so encyclopedic in both weight and size that no one would want to carry it, let alone read it. I envision such a large volume because I believe that to really get to know a place, to truly understand it in a non-superficial way, one must either live there or travel there again and again. It seems to me that it can take nothing short of a lifetime of studying and traveling to grasp Italy. I do not pretend to have completely grasped it now, many years and many visits later, nor do I pretend to have completely grasped the other destinations that are featured in *The Collected Traveler* series, but I am trying, by continuously reading, collecting, and traveling. And I presume readers like you are, too. That said, I am exceedingly happy with this edition, and I believe it will prove helpful in the anticipation of your upcoming journey, in the enjoyment of your trip while it's happening, and in the remembrance of it when you're back home.

Buon viaggio!

ITALY

Italy is a dream that keeps returning for the rest of your life.

—Anna Akhmatova

Maybe it's a small world, maybe we're in a global economy, and maybe we're slowly melting into one pot, but everyday life is still radically particular in rural Italy. Cut a slice anywhere: It remains purely *Italian*.

—Frances Mayes,
Bella Tuscany: The Sweet Life in Italy

Italia! oh Italia! thou who hast
The fatal gift of beauty.

—Lord Byron, *Childe Harold*

Italians live in a land with many layers of history. They walk on stones worn smooth by the feet of Etruscans, Romans and Saracens who came before them. They think nothing of it. They live with centuries of history piled up visibly in the walls and stone cathedrals of every little town.

—Carol Field,
Celebrating Italy

Avrai tu l'universo,
Resti l'Italia a me.

You may have the universe,
But let Italy remain mine.

—Giuseppe Verdi

My Italy

ERICA JONG

RECENTLY, AFTER I returned from a trip to Naples and the Amalfi Coast, I told my brother-in-law Gordon, who knows how fond I am of France, that if someone informed me I could travel only to Italy for the remainder of my life I would not be entirely unhappy. (Well, sort of.) I love that writer Erica Jong made up her mind years ago to simply travel again and again to Italy and be done with it.

ERICA JONG is the author of more than twenty works of poetry, fiction, and memoir, including *Fear of Flying* (Holt, Rinehart & Winston, 1973), *Fear of Fifty* (HarperCollins, 1994), *Parachutes and Kisses* (NAL, 1984), *Love Comes First* (Tarcher, 2009), and *Serenissima* (Houghton Mifflin, 1987; republished as *Shylock's Daughter,* Norton, 2003). She is also the author of a children's book, *Megan's Two Houses* (Dove Kids, 1996), originally published as *Megan's Book of Divorce* (1984).

WHENEVER I GO anywhere but Italy for a vacation, I always feel as if I have made a mistake. All too often I have changed my plans and left—from a ski resort in the French Alps, a mountain town in Switzerland, a country house in Provence—to get to Italy as soon as possible. Once across the border I can breathe again. Why bother to go anywhere, I think in those first ecstatic moments of reentry, but Italy?

What do we find in Italy that can be found nowhere else? I believe it is a certain permission to be human that other countries lost long ago. Not only is Italy one of the

few places left where fantasy runs unfettered (as Luigi Barzini said in *The Italians,* "even instruments of precision like speedometers and clocks are made to lie in Italy for your happiness"); it is also one of the few places that tolerate human nature with all its faults. Italy is the past, but it is also the future. It is pagan, but it is also Christian and Jewish. It is grand and tawdry, imperishable and decayed. Italy has seen marauding armies, Fascists and Communists, fashions and fripperies come and go. And it is still, for all its layers of musty history, a place that enhances existence, burnishes the moment.

Consider the Italian art of making the small transactions of life more pleasant. On my first visit to Italy, when I was nineteen, I was mistakenly riding in a second-class carriage with a third-class ticket. Upon discovering this, the train conductor refused to accept the *supplemento* I readily proffered. He said (in Italian it sounds even better than in English), "Signorina, you have given Italy the gift of your beauty. Now let Italy give this small gift to you." The conductor wasn't coming on to me; rather, it was Italian charm at work. And Italian charm is often a delicious combination of rule-bending and harmless flirtation.

The seven deadly sins seem somewhat less deadly in Italy; the Ten Commandments slightly more malleable. This is a country that not only accepts contradictions; it positively encourages them. The Italian shrug embodies this philosophy. It says, "Things have been this way forever and always will be this way. Why buck *la forza del destino?*"

And even the rigid northern Italian relaxes and has another glass of wine.

Your trip here will never quite go as planned. This is part of the *avventura*. There may be strikes, mixed-up reservations, maddening *imbrogli* of all sorts. But they will be charming *imbrogli* because the Italian people are charming, down to the whimsical tone of their language. A lost reservation in Germany is a Walpurgisnacht; in Italy it is an opera buffa.

Being in Italy is rather like being in love. So what if people have been in love before? So what if Italy has been a tourist trap for at least a thousand years? So what if everything you say in criticism—or praise—of Italy has already been said? Writers and travelers yet unborn will say it all again, blissfully unaware that anyone has uttered the same thoughts before.

🐝   🐝   🐝

The first place I knew in Italy was Florence—or, more specifically, Bellosguardo, a lovely hilltop section of the city looking down on the Duomo from a yew-studded prominence. As a college junior, I lived in the Torre di Bellosguardo, a thirteenth-century tower adjoining a fifteenth-century villa. I studied Italian and Italians and fell in love with Italy.

The moon was brighter in Italy. The geraniums were pinker and more pungent. The wine was more intoxicating. The men were handsomer. Italian had more rhymes than English. It was the language of love, the language of poetry.

I thought my impressions were original. I filled notebooks, aerograms, and sheets and sheets of something we then called "onionskin" with my banal musings. If I had known at nineteen what I know now—that a thousand years of similar musings by similar young musers had preceded me—I would have felt diminished. Thank God I *didn't* know. I felt special, chosen. Italy has the power to confer this sense of chosenness.

I went back to Bellosguardo a few years ago and stayed in the same villa (now a lovely small hotel owned by the erudite Amerigo Franchetti). I was with my daughter, Molly, who was at the *least* charming age of teenage daughters: thirteen going on fourteen. Because she knew I had wonderful memories of this part of Italy, Molly whined in the car from Arezzo to Florence, whined while passing through beautiful hill towns, whined at gas stations, whined as we threaded our way past the congestion of a procession in honor of Nostra Signora del Autostrada. She hated Florence, our room in Bellosguardo, the swimming pool, the restaurant, and of course her mother—until I had the inspiration to empty a bottle of icy San Pellegrino on her head. Whereupon she threw her arms around me and said, "Mommy, I love you!"

Trips like that have taught me a lesson. For me, the secret of being happy in Italy now is to live life *all'italiana*: to stay in one place and follow the eminently sensible Italian schedule, walking in the morning and evening, eating and resting in the middle of the day.

During the last few years, I have concentrated on two particular sections of Italy: Lucca, in Tuscany, and Venice and the Veneto.

I discovered Lucca almost by accident. My friends Ken and Barbara Follett had rented a place called Villa Michaela, outside Lucca in the town of Vorno, and they invited us to stay. Since the Follett clan never goes on summer holidays without having room for their five grown daughters and sons, various pals and partners, cousins, siblings, and work colleagues, they have to rent enormous houses. Molly and I joined this happy throng; later my husband sprang himself from New York and met us.

To reach Lucca you drive west of Florence on the *autostrada,* past Montecatini, the spa town, and stop just east of Pisa and Livorno. Lucca is a walled and gated city; you first see it from a ring road, with bicyclists cruising the wide parapets and cars parked outside the impressive walls of the town's historic center. There is a lovely restaurant on the walls called Antico Caffè delle Mura; a Roman colosseum turned into a honeycomb of dwellings during the Middle Ages; medieval streets; a glorious duomo. Nearby is a cluster of small country towns with some delightful places to stay, from modest *pensioni* to entire twelve-bedroom villas, such as the one the Folletts rented that summer.

Villa Michaela is entered through narrow gates. It's a sprawling eighteenth-century villa, once a ruin, with gorgeous views and an ample swimming pool. Hills covered with vineyards rise around it.

The joy of vacationing in Italy is in *far niente*: doing nothing. The teenagers slept till noon every day; the grown-ups—if you can call us that—wrote, faxed, and telephoned in the morning, then lazed by the pool after lunch. If we went to Lucca to bike around the walls or shop or see works of art, it was never until three thirty or four. I remember one lunch that ended at six in the evening. I remember passionate political discussions while we all sat topless around the pool. I finished a chapter of *Fear of Fifty*, called "Becoming Venetian," while sitting near that pool with a yellow legal pad balanced on my knee. I remember a cruise we took to snorkel and swim in the Golfo dei Poeti. When we stopped for lunch at Portovenere we looked out over Carrara, where Michelangelo's white marble was quarried. The joy of Italy often consists of doing ordinary things in extraordinary settings.

Lucca has the layers of history characteristic of Rome and Verona. It was founded in 180 BC as a Roman encampment; it evolved into a medieval village and then a Renaissance city. The arches of its colosseum were long ago filled in with houses; the central stage remains as a vast piazza. Lucca reached its zenith as a trading town during the eleventh, twelfth, and thirteenth centuries. Between the fourteenth and eighteenth centuries it remained an independent city-state like Venice—until Napoleon conquered them both.

Perhaps the most beautiful thing in Lucca is the white Carrara marble sepulchre, in the Duomo, of Ilaria del Carretto, done by Jacopo della Quercia in 1408. Ilaria was the young wife of Paolo Guinigi, one of the fifteenth-century bosses of Lucca. I forget how she died; I'm sure I deliberately blank out her story because I loathe tales of women who die at tender ages. I would rather see monuments to women who survived their first loves and went on to have several more.

Lucca has a taste for luxury. The food is excellent even in little *pizzerie*. Posh jewelry shops, displaying antique and modern treasures, seem to be everywhere. And there are wonderful shoemakers—one of whom, Porselli, makes slippers for the dancers of La Scala; I never leave without ballerina flats in half a dozen colors. How can you go wrong in a town with good shoe shops?

We enjoyed that first time with the Folletts so much that the next summer we rented a house up on a promontory just outside Lucca, in a town called San Macario al Monte. Molly and I both invited friends to stay with us. It was a comfortable farmhouse rather than a palazzo, but it was spacious, with lots of bedrooms and dazzling sunrise and sunset views. (I've found that such houses are often reached by spectacularly tricky roads, and this one was no exception. The road fell away in places to resemble the corniche along the Dalmatian coast—after the shelling.)

The grounds held a swimming pool beside a vine-shaded pergola, silvery olive trees, and dark cypresses. It was a ten-minute drive to Lucca, fifteen minutes to the Folletts at Villa Michaela, and half an hour to Pisa.

Between Lucca and Pisa, there are sweet country inns, restaurants in gardens, restaurants on terraces both splendid and modest. The jolliest meal we had was at a hilltop trattoria whose kitchen had closed when we arrived. With great panache, the obliging *padrone* laid out cheeses and salami and prosciutto for us. This out-of-the-way trattoria is nowhere near as famous as Vipore or Il Giglio or the other starred restaurants around Lucca—again, it was the kindness of the people that made it so exceptional.

Molly is a Leo, born on August 19, so she has spent almost every birthday in Italy. Her fifteenth summer was one of our best times; we celebrated with the Folletts, their guests, and our guests at Villa La Principessa, a beautiful country hotel with a garden restaurant surrounded by huge chestnut trees. We sat at a horseshoe-shaped table: the teenagers captured the middle and the grown-ups commanded the ends.

Surrounded by our crowd of friends, we rarely stirred without twenty people. Fortunately, Italians find that normal: they, too, rarely stir without twenty people. Parties of family, friends, big kids, little kids, are not only tolerated, they are considered simpatico—which makes Italy the ideal spot for a family vacation. There are few places where children are not treated as full-fledged guests.

A villa on a hill about five minutes from ours sold excellent local wine; the simple meals we made at home were as memorable as the ones in restaurants. Sitting on our terrace under the rising moon, eating prosciutto and *melone* and grilled local fish, drinking inexpensive wine, playing charades—this was as magical as any evening out.

What is this fatal charm of Italy? Why does it reflect us like a mirror that obliterates wrinkles, subtracts pounds, and gives our

eyes a devil-may-care sparkle? Why does Italy remain the country
of the Saturnalia—the feast when everything was permitted? Is it
because the pagan past is still alive in Italy and Christianity is just
a thin veneer that scarcely covers?

To wake up on a Sunday morning in Italy, to hear the roosters
crowing and the bells pealing, is one of life's greatest pleasures. To
take a walk or a run in that tintinnabulation is even better. The
mornings are cool, the birds swoop from hill to hill, and the bells
seem to have been created not to draw worshipers to church
but—like so many things here—for your particular pleasure.

If you stay long enough to transform yourself from tourist to
habitué, the headwaiters will also call you *maestro* or *contessa* or
dottore or perhaps even *commendatore*. To Italians, this flattery is almost meaningless; only Americans take it semi-seriously. Typically, we at first fall madly in love with this overstatement;
somewhat later we pronounce Italians liars and fakes when we
discover it is only a form of social lubrication. Actually, both re-
actions are wrong. Naked truth, the Italians believe, can always do
with some enhancement. No wonder we fall in love with Italy;
we believe the whole country is in love with us!

THE FACTS: ITALY

Hotels

Torre di Bellosguardo (Via Roti Michelozzi 2, Florence/+39 055
229 8145/torrebellosguardo.com).

Villa La Principessa (Via Nuova per Pisa 1616, Lucca/+39 0583
370 037/hotelprincipessa.com).

Restaurants

Antico Caffè delle Mura (Piazzale Vittorio Emanuele 2, Lucca/+39
0583 47 962).

Ristorante Giglio (Piazza del Giglio 2, Lucca/+39 0583 494 058/ristorantegiglio.com).

Vipore (Via della Pieve Santo Stefano, Lucca/+39 0583 394 065).

I met Dr. Ellyn Berk because we are both enormous fans of the jewelry designs of Leslie Genninger, an American who has been living in Venice for many years (genninger studio.com). Leslie was in New York for a trunk show, and she introduced me to Ellyn, whom I liked immediately. Since that first meeting, Ellyn and I meet periodically for lunch (always at an Italian restaurant) to talk about our shared passion: Italy. Actually, Italy is Ellyn's greatest passion, and she, like Erica Jong, decided some years ago that she was going to travel to Italy every year, forever. And she does.

I asked her to share some of her Tuscan and Umbrian favorites:

Florence and Tuscany offer myriad pleasures to be savored throughout one's traveling life. As a lucky one, who has made dozens of trips to the region, I now enjoy deepening each Tuscan experience by seeking challenging connections and contrasts. Here are a few suggestions, suitable even for a first-time visit:

An Artistic Adventure

While nothing could equal the wonderment of one's first glimpse of Michelangelo's David, *an intriguing way to view the artistry of this son of Florence is to wander through the city to study some of his sculptures as benchmarks in his creative development. I suggest* Madonna della scala *(c. 1490), in the*

Casa Buonarroti, created when the artist was a young teenager; David *(c. 1501–4), in the Accademia, which offers an unforgettable example of male beauty; the four Slaves (1520–3), also in the Accademia, which compellingly demonstrate the artist's struggle to wrest emotion from marble;* Night, Day, Evening *and* Morning, *on the tombs of the Medicis in the Basilica of San Lorenzo (1520–34), which personify the timelessness of eternity; and the* Florentine Pieta *(c. 1550), in the Museo dell'Opera del Duomo—this demonstrates by its powerful, angular style the distance Michelangelo traveled to artistic maturity. For even more Michelangelo, visit three of his "residences": Caprese Michelangelo, near Arezzo, the village where he was born—there's a small Michelangelo museum here; Casa Buonarroti, now a Florentine museum, originally owned by the artist; and Santa Croce in Florence, which houses his tomb.*

A Tuscan Adventure

Engaging all five senses is key to visiting the fifteenth-century Abbazia di Monte Oliveto Maggiore in southern Tuscany. It's incredibly relaxing to stroll across the monastery's drawbridge into the grounds, feeling the crunch of the cypress needles underfoot while inhaling their pungent fragrance. Wander through the Chiostro Grande (cloister) with its amazingly colorful frescoes. If you're lucky, you might hear the Gregorian chant of the Benedictine monks in the Gothic abbey; they pray musically three times daily. And in the gift shop, the deliciously rich honey, gathered by the monks, is available. We couldn't resist trying some right away.

And on the Subject of Eating

My husband and I enjoy restaurants that have the added value of a memorable experience beyond delicious food. In Florence, Il Latini provides the fellowship of sharing an abundant, multicourse Tuscan feast with other diners at communal tables. Another Florence treat is La Giostra, a restaurant owned by a colorful Austrian prince and his family who serve historic Tuscan cuisine in a charmingly idiosyncratic setting. Finally, a trip to the southern Tuscan village of Montefollonico brings you to La Chiusa, where you will enjoy a memorable meal cooked by the enchanting Dania. Ask to visit her in the kitchen of this beautiful restaurant and try the duck with fennel . . . I dream of it.

Welcome to Our Rented Nightmare

MARY-LOU WEISMAN

I LAUGHED OUT loud when I read this piece, which serves as a reminder to ask a lot of questions before you agree to a rental. Among the questions to ask: Is there someone who can be contacted locally if there are problems? Is there a gas station nearby? Is there a weekly market day? Are towels and toilet paper provided? Where is the nearest shop to buy bottled water? If there is a fireplace, does it work? If you're renting between October and April, are there blankets? And perhaps most important, if you're renting in warm weather, are there screens in the windows? (The answer to this is almost always no, even if you're told yes. Mosquito coils—the ones that burn slowly—and repellent are therefore good items to bring along.)

As rented accommodations in Italy are very popular, I've devoted a section of my blog (thecollectedtraveler.blogspot.com) to this subject, so be sure to read it if you are thinking of renting an apartment, farmhouse, villa, or castle during your stay.

MARY-LOU WEISMAN is a freelance writer who has written a number of articles about travel. This piece originally appeared in the travel section of the *New York Times* and later was included in her book of essays, *Traveling While Married* (Algonquin, 2003).

Dear New Tenants:

Benvenuto! We are the Weismans, the people who rented this villa for the two-week period just before yours. We hope you didn't have any trouble finding the house. Did you get a kick out of the agent's directions—"left at the tennis courts and a right at the statue of the Madonna"? We imagine that you too fell in love with the place when you saw a photograph of the villa and read the description in a catalog of rentals—"a renovated mill, in the heart of Chianti Classico, only two kilometers from the center of San Gimignano, a hill town famous for its beautiful towers. A perfect base for exploring Tuscany." Are you paying the same rent we did: $3,500 for two weeks?

We had been thinking for years about renting in Italy. We imagined rosemary growing in the garden and cozy rooms filled with rustic, family heirlooms. We would hang ropes of garlic and a Parma ham in the sunny kitchen, and dip crusty bread into a terra-cotta bowl filled with redundantly chaste, extra virgin olive oil. For once we would not be tourists, always on the outside of life, moving from hotel to hotel, packing and unpacking, collecting tiny bottles of shampoo. We would shop only at farmers' markets: spaghetti, pomodoro, pecorino, porcini—*no problema*. We'd go on picnics in vineyards. We would not feel the typical tourist compulsion to see everything. We would not stand in line at the Uffizi. We would stay home, curled up in a cozy armchair and read all day if we wanted to. We would stay home and make love all day if we wanted to. And we would see the Piero della Francescas, too.

Welcome to Villa Potemkin. Right about now you must be wondering why the house is so dark, what happened to the furniture, why there are no rugs on the floors, no spoons in the kitchen, soap in the soap dish, hangers in the closets, or toilet paper in the bathroom; and why the only art in the house, which hangs over the kitchen table, is a pen-and-ink drawing of a headless man in a business suit, holding his own entrails.

Take a look at the loose-leaf notebook on the kitchen table, next to the flashlight. It is packed with troubleshooting advice and the phone numbers of people to call in an emergency. The book was written by the owner of Villa Potemkin, Nigel Potemkin, who is also a well-known architect in London and the man responsible for this renovation. Mr. Potemkin is a member of the postmodernist, deconstructionist school of architecture known as New Brutalism.

Paola is the housekeeper. She comes every other Saturday to hose down the floors, strip the beds, and change the batteries in the flashlights. Paola has mixed feelings about New Brutalism. "This is easy place to clean," she says, "but hard place to live in."

Don't bother to read page three, "How to Operate the Cappuccino Machine." The machine does not *va bene* anymore, having blown up several rentals ago.

On the other hand, "Electrical Fault Finding" on page eight will prove particularly important if you are renting the villa during the rainy season, which you are. Although the guidebooks say September and October are ideal months to visit Tuscany and the Italian rainy season begins in early November and lasts through December, Paola says that for the last few years the rainy season has come in September and October.

The Italian rainy season is very impressive, very operatic. *Che tempo orribile!* (What awful weather!)—very vivace, very fortissimo, and with molte, molte blown fuses. Start reading at the bottom of the page. "If electrical supply cuts out, set restart button on incoming supply. If electrical supply cuts out to ground floor only, set internal restart button." The instructions are fine as far as they go, but they will not help you when you have an Italian electrician on the phone.

An ordinary tourist can get by on *grazie* (thank you), *per favore* (please), and *Dov'e il gabinetto?* (Where is the bathroom?). You, however, will need to know how to say, *Dov'e la valvola?* (Where is the restart button?) All Italian appliances have valvolas. At any time, any one of them may be hit by lightning. Don't be surprised if you find yourself asking *Dov'e la valvola?* with metronomic regularity. Try it to the tune of "La Donna È Mobile."

🦎 🦎 🦎

Because the house book leaves so much out, Larry and I have attempted to anticipate some of the questions that might arise during your stay.

Where is the view? Not everyone who rents a villa in a hill town in Tuscany automatically gets a view. Somebody's got to live in the valleys. Villa Potemkin is at the bottom of a valley, at the end of a two-kilometer rutted dirt driveway, so steep, winding, and narrow that it must be tackled in first gear, and then only under dry, daytime conditions. Learn how to time your arrivals and departures. Step outside, holding a mirror in the palm of one hand. Tilt it to and fro and see if you can deflect any sunlight. If it isn't raining, there is usually a window of opportunity between eleven a.m. and two p.m. You will get used to life in a hole. So, you do not have a view of acres of rolling vineyards, rows of stately cypress trees, and the charmingly scabby ocher farmhouses with their red tile roofs. You are a part of somebody else's view. You are somebody else's red tile roof! You knew you were renting a converted mill. You know that mills use water power. You know that water does not flow uphill. You have only yourself to blame.

Why is there an echo? What else would you expect from a virtually unfurnished, renovated mill with barrel-vaulted ceilings as high as major duomos, thirty-two stone steps, a living room the size of the Roman Forum, a fireplace in which you could roast a wild boar—if it weren't bricked over—and no drapes. A cast-iron sofa, slate kitchen table, two folding chairs, two metal beds, and a broken cappuccino machine do not provide much acoustic relief under those conditions. You should have asked the agent to send you pictures of the inside of the house.

Furniture, the more upholstered the better, would absorb sound and act as a wind barrier as well. Some rugs on the terra-cotta tile floors and a few unicorn tapestries on the gray plaster walls would also help to cut down the echo. Or you could just stop talking to one another. That's what we did.

Why is the underside of my rental car making that funny noise? See "Where is the view?" above.

Are there screens for the windows, to keep out flies and those long, gray things that have wings and jump? No.

Where is the nearest garden market? There isn't one. There's an A&P about twelve kilometers from San Gimignano (not counting the driveway). It costs 500 lire (about 35 cents)—that's the silver coin with the copper center—to rent a shopping cart. *Risotto ai funghi porcini* comes in a plastic bag with directions to drop the contents into *acqua in ebollizione*. It's *pronto in 15 minuti*. (So many of the words are the same.) The Parmesan is grated. The tomatoes are green. The bakery sells croissants. Take a number.

Why does the shower fill up and pour under the bathroom door and run down the hallways? Because there is hair in the drain.

Why does our hair feel so thin and lifeless? Because the house has its own well and there are chemicals in the water. That's your hair in the drain.

🦂 🦂 🦂

What do we do when we finish all the books we brought? There are rainy-day activities available at Villa Potemkin, even if you forget to bring your traveling Scrabble set. (To be perfectly fair, Larry brought the board. He just forgot the letters.) We considered making letters out of shirt cardboard until we were diverted by the entertainment possibilities of the washing machine. It has a porthole in the door, like old-fashioned American washers used to have. It's got two channels: with and without clothes. Watching will help you unwind.

After that, we drank a lot of Chianti Classico.

Buon Viaggio
A Bouquet of Reminders

KATE SIMON

❧❀❧

THIS IS THE final chapter of Kate Simon's wonderful book *Italy: The Places in Between* (Harper & Row, 1970). The chapter is nothing more than a list of reminders, but it is so good and so appropriate to the spirit of *The Collected Traveler* that I feel it is indispensable to this volume. Though this was written more than thirty years ago, it remains true today in many ways (even the note about coins—these days in euros, not lire—as no one ever seems to have enough, or enough of the right kind).

Remember that everything is subject to change—museum hours, and price, which are rising steadily. If there were rigidity it wouldn't be Italy. Don't fret; don't set tight limits of time or lire, don't eat your heart out if some art goal or other is closed on your day, or most days, for lack of personnel. Normally, closing days are either Monday or Tuesday and safe times are 9:30 to 12:30, 3:00 to 5:30.

Remember that no one ever has any change. When you pay a gas attendant, he will ask you for *spiccioli* (coins). The girl in the small chain department store will leave her register and a group of customers to run from one co-worker to another for change from one hundred lire you have given her for a seventy-five lire purchase. She returns with ten-lire pieces—no fives—after a long absence, and one or the other of you has to be sporting about the difference between twenty and thirty lire.

Remember that Italians find standing in line an absurdity. Learn to push and, an advantageous spot conquered, gyrate in it like an animal marking out its territory.

Remember that the recoil on a salesgirl's face doesn't mean that she dislikes you; she is afraid to cope with your English— or worse still, your Italian.

Remember, when you ask directions, that one of the national characteristics is to point right as one says left (*sinistra*) and to point left when speaking of right (*destra*). Make sure whether it is gesture or word that counts.

Remember that a little learning can be a pleasant thing. Italy gives much, in beauty, gaiety, diversity of arts and landscapes, good humor, and energy—willingly, without having to be coaxed or courted. Paradoxically, she requires (as do other countries, probably more so) and deserves some preparation as background to enhance her pleasures. It is almost impossible to read a total history of Italy. There was no united country until a hundred years ago [1861], no single line of power, no concerted developments. It is useful, however, to know something about what made Siena run and stop, to become acquainted with the Estes and the Gonzagas, the Medicis, and the Borgias, the names that *were* the local history. It helps to know something about the conflicts of the medieval church with the Holy Roman Empire, of the French, Spanish, and early German kings who marked out large chunks of Italy for themselves or were invited by a nervous Italian power. Above all, it helps to turn the pages of a few art and architecture books to become reacquainted with names other than those of the luminous giants. The informed visitor will not allow himself to be cowed by the deluge of art. See what interests you. There is no Italian Secret Service that reports on whether you have seen *everything*. If you try to see it all, except as a possible professional task, you may come to resist it all. Relax, know what you like and don't like, and let the rest go.

By moving ruminatively, all antennae out and receptive, you may learn—in the gesture of an old woman's finger stroking the arm of a baby as if he were the Infant Jesus, in the warmth and pleasure of friends meeting on a street, in the loud rumble of angry café voices when a father boxes his young son's ears, in the infinite bounty of concern among the members of a family, in the working-class coins that drop into the cap of a beggar—more about living, and Italy, than in miles of magniloquent buildings and seas of paint.

RECOMMENDED READING

NONFICTION

Cento Città: A Guide to the "Hundred Cities & Towns" of Italy, Paul Hofmann (Henry Holt, 1988). This is one of the most treasured books in my Italy library, and Hofmann, for many years the *New York Times* bureau chief in Rome, is one of my favorite writers. The one hundred *città* (a word that is both singular and plural—one of the exceptions in Italian grammar—meaning city or town) featured in this book are his personal favorites, and it would be ridiculous to disagree with his selections. They are sensational. The Heartlands section, which is devoted to Emilia, Romagna, and Tuscany, highlights Arezzo, Chiusi, Cortona, Fiesole, Lucca, Montepulciano, Pienza, Pisa, Pistoia, Porto Ferraio, San Gimignano, Sansepolcro, Siena, and Volterra. The bigger cities—Rome, Florence, Venice,

Milan, etc.—are not included. This is a book for those who want to get off the predictable circuit and better understand *regions* of Italy. The appendix contains practical information, such as postal and telephone codes, recommended hotels and restaurants, museums, much of which might be outdated, but the distances and traveling times by car or train are still applicable. With seventy-four black-and-white photographs. *Essenziale.*

The Civilization of the Renaissance in Italy, Jacob Burckhardt (Modern Library, 1954, 2002). In his afterword, Hajo Holborn refers to this definitive and much-quoted work as "the greatest single book ever on the history of Italy between 1350 and 1550." If the title sounds dry, it's misleading. This is an endlessly fascinating and brilliant book, *essenziale* for *all* visitors to Italy.

Culture Shock! Italy: A Survival Guide to Customs and Etiquette, Raymond Flower and Alessandro Falassi (Marshall Cavendish, 2008, second edition). Each *Culture Shock!* edition is authored by a different writer(s) and each is eminently enlightening. The Italy edition covers such topics as language (including the enormous variety of hand gestures), the pervasiveness of religion in daily life (a helpful hint to be mindful of is that in Italy the week begins on Monday and ends on Sunday; you'll see that Italian calendars are printed this way), home life and attitudes, doing business in Italy, superstitions, gifts and tips, art and literature, and restaurant dos and don'ts. Although some of the information is directed at people who plan to be in Italy for an extended stay, this is a useful, basic guide that I consider to be *essenziale,* even for a short visit.

The Dark Heart of Italy: An Incisive Portrait of Europe's Most Beautiful, Most Disconcerting Country, Tobias Jones (North Point, 2003). Jones, who wrote for the *London Review of Books* and the

Independent on Sunday before moving to Parma in 1999, has written a book that is about Italy's "livelier and stranger sides" and that goes well beyond the happier topics of art, climate, and cuisine. He notes that someone once wrote that "history begins when memory ends," and he describes his book as being on the cusp between the two. At the time Jones moved to Parma, Italy was involved in a collective debate as "people tried to remember or forget what had gone on in Italy only a few years, or decades, before." Jones is knowledgeable, fond of Italian literature, and witty; he attended trials, interviewed people, followed Italian football and politics and daily life, and the portrait (to borrow from the title) he paints is one that will surprise most readers. I think a very accurate description of this book appeared in a review in the *Herald* of Glasgow: "[He is] an acute, open-minded, cultured observer, and his enduring attachment to Italy combined with his deep anger at the wrongs perpetrated on Italians [gives] him a critical perspective denied both the casual visitor and the native resident."

D. H. Lawrence and Italy, D. H. Lawrence (Penguin Classics, 2007, new edition). None of the three essays that make up this volume ("Twilight in Italy," "Sea and Sardinia," "Etruscan Places") are exclusively about Tuscany or Umbria, but I include this collection here for "Etruscan Places," as Volterra, one of the Etruscan places featured, is in Tuscany. Anthony Burgess, in his introduction, notes that the Etruscan tombs have not changed much over the years, but the Italy that Lawrence knew, in the first decades of the 1900s, "is different in so many respects from the Italy of today that, entering his books, we enter a remote world which, to use a paradox, touches modernity only through its perennial antiquities." Burgess also tells us that Lawrence originally envisioned a larger Etruscan book, but he recognized that he couldn't rival the authoritative works by D. Randall-MacIver (*Villanovans and*

Early Etruscans), Pericles Ducati (*Etruria Antica*), or a major survey by George Dennis. No matter. I have felt for many years that this piece is one of the best ever written about the Etruscans, and I consider it *essenziale*.

Henry James on Italy (Grove, 1988). A handsome hardcover package with color reproductions of period paintings matched with text from James's *Italian Hours*. I am not typically fond of book excerpts, and certainly *Italian Hours* deserves to be read in its entirety, but this is such an appealing collection and I have enjoyed it so much that I am happy to include it here. Relevant to Tuscany are three chapters, and Umbrian towns featured include Perugia, Narni, Spoleto, and Assisi. Great to keep or give as a gift.

Image of Italy, edited by William Arrowsmith, with photographs by Russell Lee (special issue of *Texas Quarterly*, Summer 1961, volume IV, no. 2). Although it's an edition of the *Texas Quarterly*, this is actually a hardbound book with unforgettable photos and superb text. The fact that it was published in 1961 is irrelevant. Today's image of Italy is just as varied and complex as it was then. As stated in the foreword, our image of Italy is occasionally distorted in part because of Italy's "staggering diversity" of people and landscape:

> Her politics have been polarized by the Cold War, her Communist party is proportionally the largest in Europe, while her economic policies vacillate between state socialism and uncontrolled laissez-faire capitalism. Add to this war (and the civil war which was its consequence), overpopulation, underemployment, a growing gap between rich and poor and South and North, the flight of the peasantry from unproductive farms to cities, continual emigration, the desuetude of old ways and old customs, and

the violent alterations in landscape and living, and the impression is utterly variety and change. In a half hour's drive out of almost any city in Italy you can pass through three or four successive centuries, all of them simultaneously alive and even competitive, each one with its distinctive way of being Italian, and its Italian hunger for change.

This is not a record of contemporary Italian culture, nor a venue for representative Italian writing. Rather, it suggests how the ideas of Italy and of being Italian are formed and how they are shaped by the work of Italian writers and thinkers. Some of the contributors are Carlo Cassola, Cesare Pavese, Carlo Levi, Paolo Volponi, Gabriella Parca, and Elena Croce. An outstanding collection.

In Love in Italy: A Traveler's Guide to the Most Romantic Destinations in the Country of Amore, Monica Larner (Rizzoli, 2006). I got no farther than the first page of this lovely little book when Larner had me with her dedication: "To my father, Stevan Larner, who died as this book was being written and who loved my mother in the most profound way I have ever seen." Above it is a great color photograph, and above that a quote: "*Un bacio al giorno toglie il dentista di torno*" (A kiss a day keeps the dentist away). I mean, seriously, how can you not be inspired? Larner has been

spending time in Italy since childhood—she's also the coauthor of *Living, Studying, and Working in Italy* (Henry Holt, 2003) and *Buying a Property: Italy* (Cadogan, 2006)—and has chosen some of the most gorgeous and intoxicating places for romantic trips; there's a chapter on Tuscany but not one on Umbria. I don't think this is a book for lovers only (though there is a section devoted to getting married in Italy)—every traveler appreciates beauty, and this guide is useful for anyone who wants to create a memorable trip.

Italian Days, Barbara Grizzuti Harrison (Grove/Atlantic, 1989). My enthusiasm for this superb, beautifully written book, no matter how many times I reread it, is endless. I am incapable of praising it sufficiently. In an endorsement from the *Washington Post Book World,* a reviewer wrote that it "will be the companion of visitors for years to come." I hope this has become true since it was published two decades ago, and hope that it remains true. I cannot imagine going to Italy without reading it, can't imagine anyone with a serious interest in Italy not reading it, can't imagine my life without having read it. Only one chapter, the third, is relevant to Tuscany, "Lovely Florence," which includes "San Gimignano: City of Fine Towers." But don't let that stand in the way of reading the entire book. You won't regret it. *Essenziale.*

Italian Dreams, photographs by Steven Rothfeld (Collins, 1995). With writings about Italy and the Italians to accompany the dreamy photographs by Rothfeld, this is a special treat to buy for yourself (but it also makes a nice gift for your favorite Italophile). The images—handmade Polaroid transfers—are not the predictable pictures of Italy one sees in so many other books. A beautiful package for those who appreciate beautiful things.

Italian Hilltowns, Norman F. Carver, Jr. (Documan, 1979). I cherish
this book. Carver, an architect, has also spent a considerable
number of years photographing folk architecture in the Mediterranean region as well as Japan and Mexico. It's not only that
these color and black-and-white photographs are exquisite, but
that Carver is passionately concerned with preserving Italy's hill
towns and sharing what we can learn from them. He highlights
many towns throughout Italy that are hardly mentioned in
guidebooks: Pierele, Grisolia, Sorano, Caprancia, Archidosso,
Postignano (which is featured on the cover), Castelvecchio
Calvisio, and the Val di Fafora, a valley west of Florence where
there are seven tiny villages perched on hilltops, none of which
overwhelm the environment. He writes in the preface, "Though
I have included a few of the larger and more famous towns, such
as Siena and San Gimignano, which have adapted well to modern life, most photographs are of small anonymous towns that
retain most of their original character. To convey as much as possible the original ambiance of these medieval places, the photographs lie a little by what they leave out. You will see few
contemporary signs, shops, electrical poles, though TV antennas
appear with rather more frequency than I would have liked." He
adds that cars posed less of a problem for his photography as the
narrow streets are not suitable for motor vehicles, which are
parked and used on the outskirts of each village. There is a map
at the back of the book indicating the whereabouts of each hill
town, and a great number are in Tuscany and Umbria. *Essenziale.*

Italian Hours, Henry James (many editions of this classic are available). There are twenty-two essays in this wonderful book,
which James wrote during the 1870s. Those pertaining to Tuscany and Umbria include "A Chain of Cities," "Siena Early
and Late," "The Autumn in Florence," "Tuscan Cities," and
"Other Tuscan Cities." *Essenziale.*

Italian Journeys, W. D. Howells and with illustrations by Joseph
Pennell (Marlboro/Northwestern University Press, 1999; first
published in 1867). Howells (1837–1920) was the American
consul in Venice for four years and was also editor of the *Atlantic Monthly* and *Harper's.* His travels in Italy took him
throughout the country, but Pisa is the only town in central
Italy in this book (it was raining too hard while he was in
Bologna to cross the Apennines to Florence). However, it is
such an insightful book that I felt I should include it here.

*The Italian Way: Aspects of Behavior, Attitudes, and Customs of the
Italians,* Mario Costantino and Lawrence Gambella (Passport
Books, 1996). One of my favorite books, this is a slim, handy
A to Z guide to a multitude of key traits of the Italians. Costantino and Gambella have compiled an interesting and useful list
including abbreviations and acronyms tourists will need to recognize; the numerous ways the Italians have of attracting attention; the finer points of compliments, appreciation, criticism,
and gallantry; a brief history of Carnevale; Italian films; sports;
ways of conveying information; and women. *Assolutamente essenziale.*

*The Italians: A Full-Length Portrait Featuring Their Manners and
Morals,* Luigi Barzini (Atheneum, 1964). *Still* the classic, *still*
the best book of its kind. If I were to recommend only one
book, this would be it. Don't bother trying to understand Italy
or grasp the Italian character without reading this, or rereading
it if it's been a while since you picked it up. Each chapter is well
written and thought-provoking, but a few that really stand
apart are "The Problema del Mezzogiorno," "Illusion and
Cagliostro," and "Sicily and the Mafia," which might be the
best essay I've ever read on the history and influence of both
the mafia (defined by Barzini as a state of mind, a philosophy of

life, a conception of society, and a moral code, prevalent among *all* Sicilians) and the Mafia (the illegal organization that makes headlines). *Essenziale.*

The Italians: History, Art, and the Genius of a People, edited by John Julius Norwich (Harry Abrams, 1983). A wonderful, wonderful book I include in the *essenziale* category. Norwich is an engaging historian and also the distinguished author of *A History of Venice, The Normans in Sicily,* and a three-volume history of Byzantium. He has gathered an impressive bunch of authors to answer the question, how did the qualities of "Italianness" that make Italy unique arise in history? With an equally impressive collection of color and black-and-white illustrations.

Italians First!: An A-to-Z of Everything First Achieved by Italians, Arturo Barone (Renaissance Books, UK, 1999, third edition). The only book of its kind I've ever seen, this is a handy and truly amazing cross-indexed listing of Italians and the areas in which they achieved "firsts," such as: Giorgio Vasari became the first art historian in 1550. The first newspaper was published in Venice in 1563. In 1871, Antonio Meucci applied for a telephone patent (Alexander Graham Bell's application came in 1876). In 1889, Giuseppe Pirelli made the first motor car tire. In 1350, gold wire was first made in Italy. Venice established the first coffeehouse in the western world in 1645. The list is endless (or at least more than eight hundred entries). Barone also provides commentaries for some topics that are an interesting diversion from the entries.

Letters from Italy, J. W. von Goethe (various editions of this classic are available). Even more so than Henry James and D. H. Lawrence, Goethe and his writings on Italy are *essenziale* in any library of Italian books. Readers will notice that Goethe's letters are referenced in a great number of sources, and with good reason: they are a delight to read, filled with the sorts of observations and insights that make such good quotations.

One Hundred & One Beautiful Small Towns in Italy (2004), *One Hundred & One Beautiful Towns in Italy: Food & Wine* (2005), and *One Hundred & One Beautiful Towns in Italy: Shops & Crafts* (2007), text and photographs by Paolo Lazzarin, all published by Rizzoli. I've recommended this trio of books so often to friends, relatives, and colleagues that I've run out of adjectives to properly describe how wonderful they are. These fully illustrated hardcover books were originally written by and for Italians (and translated into English), but they wouldn't be worth mentioning if they were merely coffee-table books. They're packed with information on a hundred and one towns in all twenty regions of Italy, and each features a directory at the back of the book with contact information for hotels, tourist offices, shops, studios, restaurants, artisans, wineries, bakeries, craft workshops, food markets, etc. Best of all is that the hundred and one towns featured include a great mix of famous towns and cities and lesser-known places. As each volume costs about forty-five dollars, buying all three is an investment (though your local library may have them), but because these are also books you'll page through again and again, potentially planning many other trips, it's an investment that's very worthwhile.

The Mediterranean

The grand object of traveling is to see the shores of the Mediterranean.

—Samuel Johnson, *Diary*, April 11, 1776

A Mediterranean day is like a dream whose effect persists after its substance has been forgotten.

—Sean O'Faolain, *A Summer in Italy* (1949)

Italy is often the first country people think of when they hear the word "Mediterranean," and with good reason: Italy has long held a dominant position in the region, and she utterly depends upon it. Here are some books I highly recommend about the history, culture, natural history, architecture, and uniqueness of the Mediterranean; Italy is featured in each:

The Cruise of the Vanadis, Edith Wharton, with photographs by Jonas Dovydenas (Rizzoli, 2003).

The First Eden: The Mediterranean World and Man, David Attenborough (Little, Brown, 1987).

The Inner Sea: The Mediterranean and Its People, Robert Fox (Knopf, 1993).

Mediterranean, photographs by Mimmo Jodice and essays by George Hersey and Predrag Matvejević (Aperture, 1995).

The Mediterranean, Fernand Braudel (first published in France, 1949; English translation of second revised edition, HarperCollins, 1972). A definitive classic.

Mediterranean Color: Italy, France, Spain, Portugal, Morocco, Greece, photographs and text by Jeffrey Becom (Abbeville, 1990).

Mediterranean: A Cultural Landscape, Predrag Matvejević (University of California Press, 1999). A beautiful, unique book that combines personal observations with history, maps, maritime details, people, and language.

Mediterranean Living, Lisa Lovatt-Smith (Watson–Guptill, 1998).

The Mediterranean in History, edited by David Abulafia (Getty Publications, 2003). Abulafia reminds us that "it was around the shores of the Mediterranean that many of the great civilizations of antiquity developed: Egyptians, Minoans, Mycenaeans, Greeks, Etruscans, Romans, to mention the most obvious, while from its Levantine shores spread out not merely the merchants of Phoenicia, from whose writing system the alphabet in which these words are written is descended, but the belief in one God which originated with the ancient Israelites and forms the core of Judaism, Christianity and Islam."

The Mediterranean: Lands of the Olive Tree, Culture & Civilizations, text and photographs by Alain Chenevière (Vilo, 1997). Text and gorgeous photos.

Mediterranean Vernacular: A Vanishing Architectural Tradition, V. I. Atroshenko and Milton Grundy (Rizzoli, 1991).

On the Shores of the Mediterranean, Eric Newby (Little, Brown, 1985).

The Phoenicians, edited by Sabatino Moscati (Rizzoli, 1999). I include this volume—with essays contributed by a number of scholars—here because, though the Phoenicians remain mysterious, they are nothing if not Mediterranean.

The Pillars of Hercules: A Grand Tour of the Mediterranean, Paul Theroux (Putnam, 1995).

Playing Away: Roman Holidays and Other Mediterranean Encounters, Michael Mewshaw (Atheneum, 1988).

The Spirit of Mediterranean Places, Michel Butor (Marlboro, 1986).

The Sun at Midday: Tales of a Mediterranean Family, Gini Alhadeff (Pantheon, 1997). Even though Alhadeff's life was and remains partly Italian, this is a full Mediterranean story. Neither her mother's nor her father's families were very religious, but she was raised Catholic, not discovering until she was almost twenty that her family was Sephardic. (She was raised Catholic because her father decided it would be a good idea, shortly after his brother was taken by the Germans in Rome.) This is a beautifully written, cosmopolitan memoir with a unique Italian touch. Alhadeff writes, "It is one of the effects of Italy that even people who have been transplanted as often as Jews have, tend to feel Italian before they feel Jewish. And to feel Italian is to feel a little Catholic, after all."

Villages in the Sun: Mediterranean Community Architecture, Myron Goldfinger (Rizzoli, 1993, second edition).

World War II in the Mediterranean, 1942–1945, Carlo d'Este (Algonquin, 1990). One of the only books to deal exclusively with the war in the Mediterranean; events in Italy—on Sicily and at Anzio, Rome, and Monte Casino—are all well documented.

Out of Italy: 1450–1650, Fernand Braudel (Flammarion, 1991). I
   had only known Braudel as the author of *The Identity of France*
   and *The Mediterranean* before I ran across this beautiful and
   fascinating book, illustrated with color reproductions by
   Michelangelo, Raphael, Titian, Ghirlandaio, Van Eyck,
   Rubens, Poussin, and others. Braudel examines Italy's dominant position in Europe and around the Mediterranean and analyzes the interaction between art, science, politics, and
   commerce in terms of how they contributed to Italy's influence abroad during the two centuries of the Renaissance,
   Mannerism, and Baroque periods. This is Braudel's specialty—
   looking at history simultaneously with other social studies—
   and readers will find this to be *essenziale.*

That Fine Italian Hand: A Wry Close-up of a Resourceful People, Paul
   Hofmann (Henry Holt, 1990). Another wonderful book by
   Hofmann (see *Cento Città* above). This title covers topics such
   as pasta, pizza, and espresso; red tape and anarchy; the Mafia; the
   two Italies; the *carabinieri;* the family; etc.: all subjects having
   "that fine Italian hand," which "has long meant the particular
   way Italians like to do things, preferring adroitness to sheer
   force." *Essenziale.*

Towns of the Renaissance: Travellers in Northern Italy, David D. Hume
   (J. N. Townsend, 1995). I am very fond of this book although
   it is not written by someone who is a noted historian or scholar
   in Italian studies. Hume has one quality, however, that is
   equally important: a sincere love and enjoyment of Italy, which
   translates into an insatiable curiosity about things Italian. He
   writes about Italy and travel very much in the spirit of *The Collected Traveler,* and I immediately liked him when I read his author's note, in which he writes, "My wife Cathy and I learned
   a lot about that wonderful country while we were there and
   perhaps twice as much by reading about it both before and after

we went on these visits." He presents a good bibliography at the end of the book, offers lots of practical tips for traveling, and includes quite a lot of interesting observations and thoughts. The book features Renaissance towns from Venice to Rome, but there are individual chapters on Cortona, Siena, Florence, and Orvieto. The chapter titled "Understanding Italian and Italians" is an excellent encouragement for *anyone,* of any age, to learn a foreign language. Very highly recommended.

A Traveller in Italy, H. V. Morton (Dodd, Mead, 1964, 1982). Morton has been described as "a fine traveling companion," and I would agree that it would be difficult to find a better one. His books on Rome, Spain, and Southern Italy are among the best ever published, although they're all, including this one, out of print. Chapters ten, eleven, and twelve cover Florence and a number of hill towns in Tuscany and Umbria. Wonderful and *essenziale.*

A Traveller's History of Italy, Valerio Lintner (Interlink, 1994). This edition is one in a great series for which I have much enthusiasm. I'm not sure what the editors' vision for the series is, but *my* idea of it is to give readers a compact, historical overview of each place, highlighting the significant events and people with which every visitor should be familiar. Each edition is a mini "what you should know" guide, a minimum of milestones to help you really appreciate what you're seeing. The eight chapters in this volume cover the major periods in Italian history, from the Stone Age, Etruscan civilization, and the Rinascimento to Fascism and postwar and contemporary Italy. Additionally, there are charts of emperors, popes, Venetian doges, Italian artists, prime ministers, and the Chamber of Deputies; an A to Z historical gazetteer can be used to cross-reference towns, sites, and buildings of historical importance.

FICTION

All Our Yesterdays (1989), *The Little Virtues* (1989), and *The Things We Used to Say* (1999), all novels by Natalia Ginzburg, published by Arcade. This last is especially interesting because Ginzburg asked that it be read as a novel, but it's actually autobiographical. In it, she makes the single best short observation about World War II in Italy that I've ever read: "We thought that the war would immediately turn everyone's lives upside down. Instead, for years many people remained undisturbed in their own homes and went on doing the things they had always done. Then just when everyone thought that in fact they had got off lightly and that there would not be any devastations after all, nor houses destroyed nor flights nor persecutions, then all of a sudden bombs and shells exploded everywhere and houses collapsed and the streets were full of rubble and soldiers and refugees. And there was no longer a single person who could pretend that nothing was happening and close their eyes and stop their ears and bury their head under the pillow, not one. That is what the war was like in Italy."

The English Patient, Michael Ondaatje (Knopf, 1992).

Italian Fever, Valerie Martin (Knopf, 1999).

Italian Folktales, selected and retold by Italo Calvino (Harcourt, 1980).

Partisan Wedding, Renata Viganò (University of Missouri Press, 1999). Though this story collection is fiction, it's based on the true efforts of women who were members of the Italian resistance in World War II, the author included.

The Road to San Giovanni, Italo Calvino (Pantheon, 1993).

The Secret Book of Grazia dei Rossi, Jacqueline Park (Scribner, 1997).

Where Angels Fear to Tread, E. M. Forster (originally titled *Monteriano;* several editions available, separately as well as in Forster collections). I'm not sure when the title of Forster's well-known book changed, but the new title was borrowed from a line in Alexander Pope's "An Essay on Criticism" of 1709: "For fools rush in where angels fear to tread." (Pope's essay, by the way, is quite long, and you don't discover this line until more than halfway through.) The most oft-quoted line from Forster's novel is one that Philip Herriton says to his sister-in-law, Lilia: "Love and understand the Italians, for the people are more marvelous than the land." Taken alone, it can sound as if it's unassailably true. But it's more complicated than that, as David Leavitt and Mark Mitchell so accurately note in *Italian Pleasures* (Chronicle, 1996): "Italians are a marvelous people, as Forster and we and many others have experienced, but they also can be as rude and in-sular and self-interested and hypocritical and xenopho-bic as anyone else. Some-times, then, with apologies to Forster, the land *is* more wonderful than the people. And whatever the Italians are, they are not 'simple.' "

Re-creating the *Bel Paese*

> When it comes to Italy, we are never quite satiated; we
> always want more. We want her leather, her gold, her
> art, her music, and her sensuality. But perhaps what we
> need most of all is her ability to relish life.
> —Raeleen D'Agostino Mautner, *Living La Dolce Vita*

A trip to anywhere in the world can be transforming, but
there's no doubt about it that a trip to Italy is on a short list
of most inspiring destinations. When my friend Carol S. returned from a three-month stay in Florence, where she also
enrolled in Italian language classes, she informed us that we
were now to call her Carola, that we were to drink no other
wine but Italian, and, please, learn when it's appropriate to
use the phrase *va bene*. Italia is seductive, and many people
(myself included) have a great desire to incorporate many
Italian lifestyle details into our lives. Happily, there are some
great resources to help us Italophiles re-create an Italian
spirit in our homes:

*Bringing Italy Home: Creating the Feeling of Italy in Your Home
Room by Room,* Cheryl MacLachlan, with photographs by
Bardo Fabiani (Clarkson Potter, 1995). MacLachlan, who
traveled frequently to Italy for many years, covers not only
rooms but everything else from stucco walls, weaving, lighting, linens, and setting the table to terra-cotta tiles, food and
wine, brewing coffee, oil and vinegar, and displaying collections.

Italianissimo: The Quintessential Guide to What Italians Do Best,
Louise Fili and Lise Apatoff (Little Bookroom, 2008). This
great little hardcover is more about those eclectic things that

are quintessentially Italian—or, *Italianissimo*—than things you can create in your home or life, things the authors say "intrigue, endear, and inspire all devotees of Italy." They include such *cose* (things) as *le autorità, bellissimo, le ceramiche, il giardino all'italiana, il gelato, la mezzaluna, i patroni,* and, of course, the Vespa.

La Bella Cucina: How to Cook, Eat, and Live Like an Italian, Viana La Place (Clarkson Potter, 2001). Though mostly a book about food—it's filled with great recipes (La Place is coauthor of *Cucina Fresca* and *Cucina Rustica,* and author of *Verdura: Vegetables Italian Style*) and the book's first chapter begins, "The kitchen is the soul of the Italian home"—this is inspiring on a larger scale, too. La Place's essays on such topics as "Life in the Piazza and the Double Kiss," "The Big Sunday Lunch," and "Cena" round out the recipes, some of which are inspired by her neighbors and friends in the Salento, the southernmost part of Puglia, where she has a house.

Living La Dolce Vita: Bring the Passion, Laughter and Serenity of Italy into Your Daily Life, Raeleen D'Agostino Mautner (Sourcebooks, 2003). This is actually classified as a self-help book because the author believes the idea of *la dolce vita* can do nothing less than change one's life. I think she's absolutely right, and absolutely inspiring. As Mautner notes, Italy's centuries-long history has included "battle, starvation, plague, domination, and natural disaster. Consequently it produced a people who learned not only how to survive unthinkable hardship, but also how to sing, paint, make love, and pray as if each day was a personal gift. The indestructible spirit that characterizes Italian life baffles observers. We long for a bit of this magic to rub off on ourselves. Americans may very well love Italy because in her we find a connection to all of mankind."

Tuscany Interiors, Paolo Rinaldi (Taschen, 1998). If looking at pictures of houses, inside and out, inspires you, you will want a copy of this book—a volume in the Taschen *Interiors* series—immediately. It's filled with beautiful and unique abodes, from *palazzi,* apartments, and farmhouses to former castles, art studios, and villas, both rural and urban, in styles that are modern and antique. Some of the properties are owned by such notable figures as Wanda Ferragamo, Matthew and Maro Spender, and Piero and Francesca Antinori, and one is an inn, Villa Vignamaggio in Chianti.

TUSCANY

Close your eyes and pronounce the word Tuscany. It summons up associations of earthly perfection, of images sprinkled with happiness, daubed with ocher and marble (white from Carrara, green from Prato, pink from Maremma), and a Cyprus-lined path that leads nowhere, an infinity of hills bathed in clear light blessed by the gods, a honey-colored villa glimpsed from a baroque garden, the perfume of olive oil, faded frescos in silent cloisters—and a long procession of great men: Leonardo da Vinci, Machiavelli, Galileo, Michelangelo, Lorenzo de' Medici, Giotto, Petrarch, Dante, Pinocchio.

—SONJA BULLATY AND ANGELO LOMEO,
Tuscany

For my grandparents' generation it was Berenson and the Sitwells, for my parents' it was the Pieros at Borgo Sansepolcro, but for me it was a melon and raspberry ice cream outside Vivoli's in Florence that first convinced me that Tuscany was the place to be.

—LAURA RAISON,
Tuscany: An Anthology

One by one we emptied the bottles of wine in our tiny cantina, and little by little we learned about Tuscany—its hills, its light, its art, its food and wine, and most importantly its simple, passionate, in-love-with-life people. And, almost in spite of ourselves, we learned to live and enjoy life as the Tuscans do—*piano, piano, con calma.*

—FERENC MÁTÉ,
The Hills of Tuscany

The Trouble with Tuscany

FRED PLOTKIN

"FOR MOST OF US," writes John Julius Norwich in his foreword to *Tuscany: An Anthology,* "Tuscany is the quintessence of Italy, the distillation of all those elements of the country that we think of as being most specifically Italian." This is utterly true, and it isn't always a positive, as the writer notes in this piece. And yet . . . somehow Tuscany continues to be remarkable.

FRED PLOTKIN is the author of *La Terra Fortunata: The Splendid Food and Wine of Friuli-Venezia Giulia* (Broadway, 2001), *Recipes from Paradise: Life and Food on the Italian Riviera* (Little, Brown, 1997), *Italy for the Gourmet Traveler* (Kyle Books, London, 2006, revised edition), and *Opera 101* (Hyperion, 1994), among others. He is an all-around Italy expert and divides his time between New York City and Italy.

As a WRITER who is fortunate enough to devote his life to discovering the pleasures of Italy, I frequently receive calls from readers seeking the inside scoop about the country's best as they plan trips there. Ironically, though, most of these callers have already decided what they want to do and are only seeking my approval. Almost without exception, all roads now lead not to Rome, but to Tuscany.

Although the country is divided into twenty different regions, Tuscany has become synonymous with what most people think of as Italy. There are its exquisite works of art, but you can find those in most regions. The architecture is solid and reassuring, but it seldom rivals the grandeur of Rome or Venice. The truth is that Tuscany's weather is overrated, its shoreline flat and unremarkable. Florence chokes with air pollution. Pisa is a tourist trap, and the fabled "Chiantishire" is a theme park for foreign holiday makers.

Chefs and nutritionists outside of Italy tend to extol the superiority of everything Tuscan without really knowing the rest of the country. They fall into a familiar trap, the same one as the people who call me: the image of Tuscany is so extraordinary that every good Italian thing must be from there. There *are* amazing "super-Tuscan" red wines. In fact, they outclass the region's rustic, rather simple food. Countless restaurants in the States claim to serve Tuscan cuisine, when what they really offer is a blend of dishes from Campania, Liguria, Puglia, and Sicily. In other words, these American menus include lightly grilled vegetables and fish, portions of meat the size of a deck of cards, and pasta with a few slivers of vegetables and a toss of fresh herbs.

The Tuscans, a lusty and pleasure-loving people, do not eat as we imagine. Their cooking is often referred to by other Italians as burnt meat and baby food. They are some of Italy's biggest carnivores, regularly gnawing on vast amounts of beef, hare, pork, veal, wild boar, and various livers, spleens, and other organ meats. The "mad cow" and foot-and-mouth scares of recent years frightened Tuscans more than most other Italians.

People there dote on mushy foods: soups and salads made of leftover bread; overcooked vegetables; and *castagnaccio,* a dreary pudding made of chestnut flour, olive oil, and rosemary. Tuscans douse everything with olive oil so thick and peppery that it obliterates all that it covers. Baking is notable primarily for *panforte,* a chewy, dense, Sienese cake of honey, candied fruit, and nuts. *Cantuccini* are dry almond cookies that are dipped in *vin santo,* a dessert wine that pales against comparable ones from Friuli-Venezia Giulia, Veneto, and Sicily.

And yet, I never discourage anyone from going to Tuscany, because I adore it too, for the Tuscans themselves. If you ignore the stereotype of smiling peasants who give birth to geniuses, you will discover why other Italians regard them with grudging respect. These people cling tenaciously to beliefs that refuse to be globalized. When you are in Tuscany, you can't mistake it for anywhere else. People from this region are warm, as all Italians are, but famously contentious. A Tuscan may understand the language of Dante, but will likely pepper his speech with jaw-dropping scatology that makes other Italians blush. Tuscans passionately argue about politics, literature, sex, soccer, and the state of the world. Militantly out of step with the rest of the nation, Tuscany has now surpassed Emilia-Romagna as the most left-wing region of Italy. Americans think Tuscans are mellow, when really they are rambunctious and idiosyncratic.

These traits can be found in the food. The seemingly pallid salt-free bread is a divine vessel for everything it carries, whether it is that aggressive olive oil, lusty fennel-scented salami, or a warm sheep's milk ricotta topped with organic fig preserves. Tuscany defiantly produces a greater variety of organic foods than anywhere else in Italy, and the flavor of these fruits, vegetables, and herbs is extraordinary. The pecorino cheese is second only to Sardinia's in quality. The region's red wines are among the world's best because the feisty Tuscans go their own way, rather than copy other styles. These flavors are not fancy, but they are honest and uncompromising—truly Tuscan characteristics.

As in all of Italy, Tuscany gives us a different sense of time, one in which modern history spans the past five hundred years and the pursuit of physical and intellectual pleasures is more important than earning money or having countless possessions. What Tuscany asks from us is to recognize the best part of ourselves; that which admires audacity, creative genius, education, and respect for nature.

So when you go to Italy, first visit regions you have never heard of, take the road less traveled, and rekindle your sense of daring and that natural human predilection for sensuality. Then, and only then, go to Tuscany, and you will understand what makes it sublime: nowhere else has man elevated nature to the degree that nature has elevated man. It must be something in that wine.

Market Day in a Tuscan Town

FRANCES MAYES

❧❧

THIS PIECE ORIGINALLY appeared in the travel section of the *New York Times* in 1992. Later, it became part of a chapter titled "A Long Table under the Trees" in *Under the Tuscan Sun.* I decided to include it because it existed first as an article, and it's a wonderful depiction of one of the essential aspects of life in the Tuscan countryside. After the piece appeared in the *Times,* a reader wrote a letter to say that she, her husband, and two friends were inspired to visit Camucia, which she described as "an experience we all relished and continue to enjoy. It just goes to show that filing information away for future reference is worthwhile even if the article is four years old by the time we use it." Hear, hear!

FRANCES MAYES is the author of more than a dozen books, including *Under the Tuscan Sun* (Chronicle, 1996), *Bella Tuscany: The Sweet Life in Italy* (Broadway, 1999), *A Year in the World: Journeys of a Passionate Traveller* (Broadway, 2006), five books of poetry, and, most recently, *Every Day in Tuscany: Seasons of an Italian Life* (Broadway, 2010).

MARKET DAY IS Thursday in Camucia, the lively town at the bottom of Cortona. Most tourists in Tuscany pass right through Camucia; it's just the "modern" spillover from the venerable and dominant hilltown above. But "modern" is relative. Among the *frutta* and *verdura* shops, the hardware and seed stores, you happen on a couple of Etruscan tombs. Near the butcher I like are remnants of a villa, an immense curly iron gate and swag of garden wall. Camucia, bombed in World War II, has its share of chestnut trees, photographable doors and shuttered houses.

On market day, a couple of streets are blocked to traffic. The vendors arrive an hour or so early, at about seven a.m., unfolding what seems like whole stores or supermarket aisles from specially made trucks and wagons. One wagon sells local pecorino, the sheep's milk cheese that can be soft and almost creamy, or aged and strong as a barnyard, along with several grades of parmesan. The aged parmesan is crumbly and rich, wonderful to nibble as I walk around the market. I'm hunting and gathering food for a dinner for three new friends.

My favorite wagons belong to the two *porchetta* maestros. The whole pig, parsley entwined with the tail, apple—or sometimes a big mushroom—in its mouth, stretches across the cutting board. Sometimes the decapitated head sits aside at an angle, eyeing the rest of its body that has been stuffed with herbs and bits of its own ears, etc. (best not to inquire too closely), then roasted in a wood oven. You can buy a *panino* (a crusty roll) with nothing on it but slabs of *porchetta,* or you can buy pork to take home, lean or with crispy, fatty skin.

One of the lords of the *porchetta* wagons looks very much like his subject: little vacant eyes, glistening skin and bulbous forearms. His fingers are short and porky, with bitten-down nails. He's smiling, extolling his pig's virtues, but when he turns to his wife, he snarls. Her lips are set in a permanent tight half smile. I've bought from him before and his *porchetta* is delicious. This time I buy from the milder man at the next stand. I ask for extra *sale* (salt), which is what the indefinable stuffing is called. I like it but find myself picking through to see if there's something peculiar in it.

Though the pig is useful and tasty in all its parts and preparations, the slow-roasted *porchetta* must be its apogee. Before I move on to the vegetables, I spot a pair of sandals and balance my pock-

etbook and shopping bag while I try on one. Perfect, and less than ten dollars. I drop them in with the *porchetta* and Parmesan.

Scarves and tablecloths float from awnings, toilet cleaners, tapes and T-shirts are stacked in bins and on folding tables. Besides buying food, you can dress, plant a garden and stock a household from this market. There are local crafts for sale but you have to look for them. The Tuscan markets aren't like ones in Mexico, with wonderful weaving and pottery. It's a wonder these markets continue at all, given the sophistication of Italian life and the standard of living in this area.

The ironworking tradition is still somewhat in evidence. Occasionally I see good andirons and handy fireplace grills. My favorite is a holder for whole prosciutto, an iron grip with handle mounted on a board for ease in slicing; maybe someday I'll find I need that much prosciutto and buy one. One week I bought handwoven baskets made from dark supple willow twigs, perfect for the peaches and cherries. One woman sells table and bed linens, some with thick monograms, all of which must have been gathered from farms and villas. She has three mounds of old lace. Perhaps some of it was made on the nearby island, Isola Maggiore in Lake Trasimeno. Women still sit in the doorways there, hooking lace in the afternoon light.

I find two enormous square linen pillowcases with miles of inset lace and ribbons. Ten thousand lire (about nine dollars), same as the sandals, seems to be the magic number today. Of course I will have to have the pillows especially made. When I buy some striped linen dish towels, I notice several goatskins hanging from a hook. I have in mind that they would look terrific on the *cotto,* the old brick floors at my house. The four the man has are too small but he says to come back next week. He tries to convince me that his sheepskins would be better anyway, but they don't appeal to me.

I'm wending my way toward the produce, but walk up to the bar for a coffee. Actually, I stop with an excuse to stare. People from surrounding areas come not only to shop but also to greet friends, to make business arrangements.

The din around the Camucia market is a lovely swarm of voices, many of them speaking in the local Val di Chiana dialect; I don't understand most of what they're saying but I do hear one recurring habit.

They do not use the *ch* sound for *c,* but slide it into an *s* sound. "Shento," they say for *cento* (hundred), instead of the usual "chento." Once I heard someone say "cappushino," for *cappuccino,* though the usual affectionate shortening of that is "cappuch." Their town is not "Camuchia," but "Camushea." Odd that the *c* is often the affected letter. Around Siena people substitute an *h* sound for *c*—"hasa" and "Hoca-Hola."

🦂   🦂   🦂

Whatever the local habit with *c,* they're all talking. Around the bar, groups of farmers, maybe a hundred men, mill about. Some play cards. Their wives are off in the crowd, loading their bags with tiny strawberries, basil plants with dangling roots, dried mushrooms, perhaps a fish from the one stand that sells seafood from the Adriatic. Unlike the Italians who take their thimbleful of espresso in one quick swallow, I sip the black, black coffee.

A friend says Italy is getting to be just like everywhere else, homogenized and Americanized, she says disparagingly. I want to drag her here and stand her in this doorway. The men have the look of their lives—perhaps we all do. Hard work, their faces and bodies affirm. All are lean, not a pound of extra fat anywhere. They look cured by the sun, so deeply tan they probably never go pale in winter. Their country clothes are serviceable, rough—they don't "dress," they just get dressed. They wear, as well, a natural dignity. Surely some are canny, crusty, cruel, but they look totally present, unhidden and alive.

Some are missing teeth but they smile widely without embarrassment. I look in one man's eyes and the left one is milky white with veins only, like an exploded marble. The other is black as the center of a sunflower. A retarded boy wanders among them, neither catered to nor ignored. He's just there, living his life like the rest of us.

At home I plan, though I frequently alter the menu as I shop. Here, I only begin to think when I see what's ripe this week. My impulse is to buy too much. At first I was miffed when tomatoes or peas spoiled when I got around to cooking them a few days later. Finally I caught on that what you buy today is ready to eat immediately. This also explained another puzzle; I never understood why Italian refrigerators are so minute until I realized that they don't store food the way we do. The Sub-Zero giant I have at home begins to seem almost institutional compared to the toy fridge I have here. The habit I have comes from buying produce at home that is picked before it's ripe.

This week the small purple artichokes with long stems are in. There's my first course. Steamed, stuffed with tomatoes, garlic, yesterday's bread and parsley, then doused with oil and vinegar. The slender beans are irresistible. I'll slice some fennel into them, add a few dry olives. Can I have two salads, because the beans also would be good with raw vinaigrette? Why not? I buy white peaches for a recipe with macaroons and white wine I've been meaning to try. But for tonight's dessert, the cherries are perfect. I take a kilo, then set off to find a pitter back in the other part of the market.

Since I don't know the word I'm reduced to sign language. I do know *ciliegia* (cherry), which helps. I've noticed in French and Italian country desserts, the cooks don't bother to pit the cherries but I like to use the pitter when they're served in a dish. These I'll steep in Chianti with a little sugar and lemon. When I buy bread, I'll pick up some biscotti to go with them. I decide on some tiny yellow potatoes still half covered with dirt. Just a dribble of oil and some rosemary and they'll roast in the oven.

I could complete my shopping for this meal right here. I pass cages of guinea hens, ducks and chickens, as well as rabbits. If my friend Paul, a chef, were here, I know we'd be going home with some trembling creature in the trunk. Since I had a black Angora rabbit as a pet once, I can't look with cold eyes on the two spotted ones nibbling carrots in the dusty Alitalia flight bag. I intend to stop at the butcher's for a veal roast. The butcher's is bad enough. I admit it's not logical. If you eat meat, you might as well recognize where it comes from. But the drooped heads and closed eyelids of the quail and pigeon make me stop and stare. Rooster heads, chicken feet (with nails like Mrs. Ricker's, my grandmother's rook partner), the clump of fur to show the skinned rabbit is not a cat, whole cows hanging by their feet—all these things make my stomach flip. Surely they're not going to eat those fluffy chicks. I love roast chicken. Could I ever wring a neck?

I have as much as I can carry. The other stop I'll make is at the cooperative *cantina* for the local red and white wine. If I had a demijohn, I could back the car up and get the wine hosed in from what looks exactly like a gasoline pump.

Near the end of the sinuous line of market stalls, a woman sells flowers from her garden. She wraps an armful of pink zinnias in newspaper and I lay them under the straps of my bag. The sun is ferocious and people are beginning to pack up for siesta. A woman who has not sold many of her striped lime and yellow towels looks weary. She dumps the dog sleeping in her folding chair and settles down for a rest before she begins to fold.

On my way out, I see a man in a sweater, despite the heat. The trunk of his minuscule Fiat is piled with black grapes that have warmed all morning in the sun. He offers me one. The hot sweetness breaks open in my mouth. I have never tasted anything so essential in my life as this grape on this morning. The flavor, older than the Etruscans and deeply fresh and pleasing, just leaves me stunned. Such richness, the big globes, the heap of dusty grapes cascading out of two baskets. I ask for *un grappolo,* a bunch. The taste will stay with me all summer.

"In Panzano there is a must-stop for any serious meat lover at the butcher shop of a great friend of mine, Dario Checchini. His shop, Antica Maccelleria Checchini, is a fantasy of salted, cured, and fresh meats with a theatrical setting and with the very handsome and fascinating man himself presiding over the counter with advice and tastes for anyone with a smile. His torpedo-sized *soppressata* lies on the counter, tempting you to take some for the road for a vineyard picnic. Submit . . . resistance is useless. Dario now also runs two *trattorie* in Panzano. The one called "*ciccia*" is just meat, and bring your own wine is the new rule: pick up some older vintages of Castello di Ama or Montevertine at the winery or at the *enoteca* in Radda and head over for a feast. As long as there is a glass for Dario himself, the experience is unparalleled."

—Mario Batali, owner/co-owner of fifteen restaurants, including the award-winning Babbo Ristorante e Enoteca in New York City, Food Network chef, and author of nine books, including, most recently, *Molto Gusto: Easy Italian Cooking* (Ecco, 2010)

Italy's Best-Kept Secret

DAVID LEAVITT

❀❧❀

FERENC MÁTÉ, IN *The Hills of Tuscany,* reminds us that "one seldom thinks of the sea when one thinks of Tuscany, conjuring instead its inland sea of hills, forgetting the long coast on the Tyrrhenian, with vast uninhabited stretches, dark pine forests, cliffs, and the medieval harbors of sailboats and fishing boats with their bows anchored to sea." In my own travels along the Tuscan coast—notably in Porto Ercole, Orbetello, La Feniglia, Isola Giglio, and Monte Argentario—I have rarely encountered many North Americans. The pace here is wonderfully slowed down, even more so in the region known as the Maremma, just a few miles inland, and it is the Maremma that is topping more and more people's lists of favorites.

DAVID LEAVITT is the author of *The Indian Clerk* (Bloomsbury, 2007), *Florence: A Delicate Case* (Bloomsbury, 2002), and, with Mark Mitchell, *In Maremma: Life and a House in Southern Tuscany* (Counterpoint, 2001) and *Italian Pleasures* (Chronicle, 1996), among others.

SOMETIMES IN THE morning, on the way to Semproniano to buy groceries or cappuccinos, we'll encounter a sheep jam. Sheep have a way of appearing when you least expect them, and in the most inconvenient of places—say, on the other side of a hairpin turn. I screech to a stop. Our fox terrier,

Tolo, agitated by the rich odor of manure, begins to bark madly, then tries to dig his way through the back window. Meanwhile we idle. What else can one do when faced with a flock of forty ewes along with a ram or two, their backs draped with coils of yellowing wool, like dreadlocks? Sometimes the sheep are alone; more often someone's leading them—an elderly farmer, say, driving an equally elderly Ape, or "bee," one of those curious three-wheeled vehicles so popular in rural Italy, halfway

San Gimignano - Il nuov Palazzo del Podestà (XIII secolo)

between a motorcycle and a truck. His pace is glacial. With a smile he signals me forward—to drive not around but into the herd.

Although it seems dangerous, I do as bidden. Gritting my teeth, anticipating with every inch I move forward the moment when lamb legs will flatten under the wheels, wool will fly, and the farmer will scream, I edge the car directly into the flock, which parts, as the Red Sea parted for Moses.

This is what passes for traffic here, in this valley where not a stoplight is to be found for miles and miles.

WHERE WE LIVE

"Here" is the Tuscan Maremma, a region roughly corresponding to the province of Grosseto and comprising the southern corner of Tuscany. From the vineyards and noble villas of Chianti, forested mountains alternate with plains and hills husbanded since Etruscan times all the way to the sea. Along the coast are the posh resorts of Monte Argentario where rich Romans spend their summers, the fishing villages of Porto Ercole and Orbetello (with an isolated lighthouse in the middle of its lagoon), and the beach of La Feniglia, where we go to eat spaghetti topped with clams tinier than your fingernail. Drive inland a few miles and the Maremma proper begins. *Maremma* means "marshland," and for centuries that's exactly what the area was: a marshy cluster of fiefdoms, each controlled by a single family. *Butteri,* the Italian version of cowboys, tended herds of horned white Maremma cattle. Boars and roebuck roamed the woods. The people were poor and accustomed to hardship.

Even in the age of the Grand Tour there was little tourism: the threat of malaria dissuaded all but the most adventurous travelers. Nor was the zone spared anything of Fascism or the Second World War. Bombs destroyed much of Grosseto, the principal city. Teracle, the real estate agent who sold us our house (many Tuscans have Magna Graecian names), recalls witnessing at thirteen the shooting of an entire family by the Blackshirts, because they had given refuge to an English soldier. The father of our friend Brunella was beaten for refusing to sing Fascist hymns at school.

Things started to change in the 1930s, when the government instituted a land-reclamation scheme and began building a series of canals and drains to clear the marshes. By the fifties malaria was eradicated, and more land was habitable. The government then made an effort to revitalize the region by buying up land from feudal owners and distributing it among the tenant farmers whose families had been working it for generations. This program, called the Ente Maremma, not only provided funding for hospitals and schools but built houses for the farmers, cobbled together from a mixture of tufa and stone. Today the countryside is punctuated with dozens of these houses, all more or less identical, with animal stalls downstairs and an apartment for the farmer upstairs. Recently they've started to come on the market. We bought and restored one, making it look older than it was. Now American friends take for granted that its origins are medieval, when in fact it was built in the early sixties.

These days the Maremma is a prosperous zone. Most of the farmers own immense American tractors, with radios and air-conditioning. In summer they thresh the wheat with huge machines that recall the mechanical dinosaurs in *Star Wars*. It was not always this way, of course. In the old days the *trebbiatura,* or threshing, was a ritual, and required thirty men. Afterward, to celebrate a job well done, everyone would feast and dance outdoors. Now each summer, in homage to their less affluent past, the people of our village, Semproniano, drag out an ossified exemplar of the old threshing machine, set it up in a field, thresh a few bales of wheat, and then eat a big lunch while admiring it.

TRATTORE! TRATTORE!

"Traffic and sheep!" our friend Giampaolo complained to us when we first decided to move to this part of Tuscany. "That's all anyone thinks about here!" Giampaolo himself is Roman. Like many Italians, he owns substantial quantities of real estate elsewhere, which is why he and his wife, Pina, can afford to open their country restaurant only on weekends. It was partly so their children could profit from a rural upbringing—fresh air and animals and no risk of getting run over—that they first moved here. But now, like many urban immigrants, they sometimes seem a bit restless. A few Christmases ago a neighbor gave their son, Martino, a toy tractor, and as the boy ran gleefully through the restaurant shouting "*Trattore! Trattore!*" I couldn't help but notice a look of worry pass over his mother's face.

Sometimes Pina and Giampaolo talk about closing down the restaurant, selling their house, and moving back to Rome. On days like this—usually winter days—the new multiplex cinema near EUR, a neighborhood in southwest Rome, is always mentioned. Still, they stay. It is my theory that living in the country alters both one's expectations and one's needs in a way that living in the city does not: true, I may miss Chinese restaurants and bookstores, but I don't need them the way I need the smell of hay in the spring, and lavender in the summer, and olives in the fall, when they are gathered in glossy green-black heaps at the *frantoio,* or olive press.

The views besot me. From the high road that connects the main villages, fields of hay, wheat, and sunflowers, olive groves, and patches of forest spread out in every direction—as if a god had woken from a nap and hurled his quilt down from the sky. On clear days you can even see the Mediterranean, crisp and still as a sheet on a tightly made bed. For this is an agricultural region, unsullied by the small industry that blights Umbria. In July, when the afternoon temperature often reaches a hundred degrees, farmers work by moonlight. Even after midnight we can hear the cool hum of their tractors, watch the patient progress of these slow, majestic animals as they move over the fields.

OUR VILLAGE

The house we live in is on top of a softly proportioned ridge, at the base of which a little creek—dry in summer—runs between borders of oak and pine. Drive five miles southwest, and you arrive in Saturnia, famous for its thermal baths. On windy days their rising steam fills the air with the potent perfume of sulfur.

The village we consider our own, however, is Semproniano. This town of about six hundred souls sits high above the valley of the Fiora, the principal river of the region. The oldest part of Semproniano is medieval, a clutter of dark stone houses piled on their hill like luggage at a station. Then, beyond the piazza, a flattening occurs. There's the Bar Sport, and the bread shop, and

Carlucci's, where we get our groceries; and then there are the houses, mostly of tufa, that were built in the thirties; and just outside the defensive ramparts of the Old Town the clutch of tidy apartment blocks built from poured concrete and covered in plaster, in which most of the Sempronianese actually live.

Semproniano has no sights of great historical interest, which is why I like it so much. There are no churches containing rare frescoes of Carlo Dolci, no Madonnas weeping blood: just a bar, a newsstand, one restaurant, one hotel, three groceries, a hardware store, and a housewares store. Oh, and a doctor. (No dentist.) For a long time Semproniano did have one tourist attraction, the *olivone,* an immense olive tree rumored to be more than two thousand years old. Before our house was finished Mark and I visited it twice, sitting for a few minutes under its capacious and maternal branches. We spoke of how, when we lived here, we would bring all our friends to see the *olivone.* Then in May of last year— the evening of Mother's Day, in fact—someone torched it; burned it to the ground. The town went into mourning, especially the children, who had a tradition of walking to the *olivone* for a picnic on the last day of school. Ettore, the nine-year-old son of Sauro, our stonemason, asked if he could borrow my computer to write an essay called "L'Olivone, Ormai Bruciato" (The *Olivone,* Burned and No More).

Though life here is a dangerous business for olive trees, in summer the children roam the streets alone, and well into the night. Everyone knows whose are whose, and keeps an eye out. Sometimes we'll see Silvia, the stonemason's wife, peripatetic in her pumpkin-colored Fiat 500, waiting to pick up Ettore after a soccer game. Or perhaps she'll be at the Bar Sport, buying her lottery ticket from Alberto, the handsome barman, while near the espresso machine our doctor, Rosaria, chats with Aldo the grocer. Or Giampaolo will be talking with Idia, the tiny and vigorous old lady in whose garage we stored our furniture for a year, about the imminent August return of the . . . who? It sounds like "arshai."

In fact they are talking about Hershey, Pennsylvania, to which vast numbers of Sempronianese emigrated just before the Second World War.

That I myself have never even been to Hershey surprises some of the older residents of Semproniano, all of whom have a Hershey connection. Rosaria, for instance, recalls how her grandmother, who worked at the chocolate factory, would return every few years bearing umbrellas filled with chocolate kisses. In those days such sweets impressed less for their flavor than for the novelty of their shape; after all, at the *gelateria* that Idia used to run you could get chocolate ice cream made with sheep's milk. "So rich!" Rosaria says nostalgically. "Of course you can't do it now. The law. Pasteurization." No doubt as a doctor she has no choice but to approve of such sensible regulations, and yet: "You should have tasted it," she says. "So *cremoso*. Really, you haven't tasted ice cream at all until you've tasted ice cream made from sheep's milk. . . ."

ILVO AND DELIA

Ilvo and his wife, Delia, have lived on the same farm for most of their adult lives. During the Second World War Ilvo left for a time: he fought in Sicily, where he met several Americans, then spent years in a British prisoner-of-war camp near Banbury. They are and always have been a remarkably self-sufficient couple. Every winter they kill a pig, which gives them enough meat not only to stock their freezer but to make prosciutto, salami, and *ammazzafegato,* a local liver sausage said to be so fatty that it "kills the liver" of anyone who eats it. Each spring they plant an enormous vegetable garden: carrots, potatoes, onions, garlic, basil, and parsley. The sheep they tend with their son, Fosco, produce enough manure to fertilize their olive trees, which give them plenty of oil, and their grapevines, which give them plenty of wine. (Also a delicious sweet grappa flavored with the peel of mandarin oranges.)

In the spring Delia walks up and down our road, gathering thin stalks of wild asparagus, which she pickles.

Her intimacy with the natural world amazes me. She always knows exactly when—and how—to plant things: garlic in March, a few centimeters under the ground; tomatoes in late spring; cauliflower at the end of summer. Plants we have left for her to water while we've been away on trips, even if they were at death's door when we gave them to her, come home in a state of vigor. Roses bloom vividly under her aegis, as do gigantic hydrangeas, geraniums, even the tiny hot peppers—red and yellow and in a few cases pale purple—that by summer's end are spilling over the edges of the big clay planter near her front door.

Later, Delia harvests these peppers and hangs them in bunches from the ceiling to dry. She will give us some if we ask for them, for she is never less than generous with food. Whenever I go over to "borrow" some eggs (amazingly fresh, and with shells so frail the merest pressure of a finger will break them) she never fails to invite me in for a glass of grappa or a slice of jam *crostata* warm from the oven. Usually I leave with more than I came for: not just three dozen eggs, but also several pounds of zucchini, a handful of parsley, and some fresh garlic. (The shoots are as delicious as the heads.)

Ilvo and Delia's house is typical of the residences in this area, in that it has no living room. Instead, it consists of a highly ceremonial dining room (used only on special occasions), two bedrooms, a bathroom, and a big, dark kitchen that is cool in summer and warm in winter, thanks to the wood-burning stove on which Delia does her cooking. And what cooking she does! One Wednesday morning, when I stroll over to pay Fosco for pruning our olive trees, and find her standing at the kitchen table rolling out dough for gnocchi, she invites us to lunch. I'm surprised, as Italians—despite their reputations to the contrary—are rarely spontaneous.

Though it's a hot day, Delia serves up big bowls of gnocchi

with a meat *ragù,* as well as grilled pork chops (which the Italians call *bistecchine di maiale;* literally, "little beefsteaks of pork") and slices of fried liver. Next comes a salad of cucumbers from her garden. When I compliment the salad, she gives me about twenty: small and as fancifully serpentine as calligraphy, softer than their supermarket counterparts, run through with a watery pulp of sweet seeds.

Though in all probability Delia has been to Rome, at the very most, half a dozen times, she is in her own way worldly. Her assessment of local politics is always subtle and acute; nor is there much in world politics that escapes her ken, thanks to the television news, which she watches assiduously and analyzes trenchantly. Thus when Milosevic's wife appeared in her kitchen one morning (this was in the middle of the war in Kosovo), Delia turned to me and said, "I don't like that woman. She looks mad." As it happened, the *International Herald Tribune* had reported the same thing that very morning.

It is to Delia that we turn when something of a local nature perplexes us: for instance, the mosquitoes so tiny they can actually fit through the holes in our window screens. "What are they?" I ask her. "Where do they come from? How long will they last?"

"Oh, the little ones—*piccini piccini*? We call them *cugini.*"

"*Cugini?*" I repeat. Cousins?

Delia smiles. "Now you see what we really think of our relatives."

AT THE *FRANTOIO*

Of the many agricultural rituals that define the Maremman year—hay cutting in April, wheat threshing in July, the *vendemmia* (or grape picking) in October—none means more than the November pressing of the new olive oil. Oil, after all, is the essential underpinning of Maremman life; unlike their neighbors to the north, the people here almost never use—indeed, barely know—

butter, which perhaps explains their longevity. The arrival of the new oil brings an element of pageantry: the people of Semproniano greet it with the sort of exuberance that the French show their Beaujolais nouveau.

To preserve its peppery kick, the young oil is never cooked (heaven forbid!) but instead poured over simple salads of tomato and spicy ruffled greens. Or it is drizzled as a final touch onto a bowl of *acquacotta* ("cooked water"), the most famous dish of the region, and a source of great dispute among our neighbors, each of whom claims to possess the real recipe. (So far as we have been able to ascertain, the basic ingredients for this soup are bread, carrots, onions, and the green tops of celery; it is on ancillary matters such as whether one ought to add spinach, or top each bowl with a poached egg and a palmful of grated pecorino, that our friends become apoplectic.)

The most classic way to serve the new oil, however, is simply to drip some onto a piece of grilled Tuscan bread that has been rubbed with garlic: this is the famed bruschetta, so commonly imitated and so rarely gotten right, even in Tuscany. For bruschetta must be a delicate dish, which is the point that many chefs seem to miss. (The fact that the Florentine version is known as *fettunta*—or "greasy slice"—attests to its comparative coarseness.)

No wonder the Sempronianese regarded the burning of a two-thousand-year-old olive tree not merely as an act of vandalism but of murder! In a town where oil is life, this great mother of a tree was looked to not merely for sustenance but as a force for good. When Pina, in her restaurant, offered us oil made from the olives of the *olivone,* I accepted it with an almost mystic wonderment, not because the oil tasted different from any other local oil—after all, the trees here are more or less of the same variety—but because it came from the *olivone* and was older than Christ.

Today I try to console myself with the knowledge that each of our own trees, though mere striplings, has the potential to grow into an *olivone.* At the moment we have thirty-eight—last spring a cold snap killed two—which is just enough to produce a year's worth of oil for two hungry people and a dog. As is the local custom, we harvest the fruit in November, picking it by hand just at the moment when the green has begun mottling into black. (Umbrians, by contrast, wait for the fruit to fall before they gather it, with the result that their oil is far more acidic.) Then we pack the olives in plastic crates and take them to the *frantoio* in Semproniano.

In November the *frantoio* is a busy and sociable place. In the first room you enter, olives wait to be weighed and pressed, mounds of them, either loose or in burlap bags through which a little moisture is already seeping. Usually there is a truck parked outside, bearing the immense crop of one of the larger companies. Beside their thousand kilos, our five crates seem paltry, almost embarrassing. Still, I give them to the *frantoiano* to weigh, and he tells us how much oil we're entitled to, basing his calculations on a mysterious formula that takes in not only the quantity of olives but their relative juiciness in comparison with other years. When I nod acceptance, he takes our olives and throws them onto the pile with all the others. Generally, only huge crops are pressed individually; in the case of smaller harvests, the olives of several different families are mixed together, which means that one can never say truthfully, "This oil is mine," though of course I say it anyway.

After depositing our olives, we follow the *frantoiano* into the next room, where the machinery is located. This consists of a huge tub and a stone-grinding wheel, operated not by hand, as in the last century, but by a sophisticated system of gears. For sheer scale it is daunting—the wheel is easily twice the size of the Bocca della Verità in Rome; as for the tub, if you fell into it you would be crushed in seconds. (I'm reminded of Charlie Chaplin trying to negotiate the mammoth cogwheels in *Modern Times*.) At the bottom of the tub a muddy sludge of olive residue shifts and churns, while from its side a stainless-steel pipe leads to a series of

what appear to be distillation tubes, and then to a tap that is never turned off, and from which a stream of deep green oil perpetually pours. As with Guinness, you cannot see light through it. It gives off a slightly pungent, mulchy odor that is nonetheless compelling, like the smell of sulfur at the thermal baths. This is the cold-pressed extra virgin oil for which Tuscany is famous.

The *frantoiano* (I know him as Paolo; in summer he works at the bar and in spring he does construction) asks me if I want to take my oil now or wait until "my" olives are pressed. I think for a moment, then tell him that now would be fine. He takes the stainless-steel container I've brought and proceeds to fill it. As he does so, one of our neighbors, a farmer with a lot of land, walks in and greets us. Behind him I see his sons hauling in huge sacks of olives, and I would feel intimidated (this is the curse of masculinity) were it not for the tiny old man who has followed him in. This old man is so clear-eyed, has such a broad, winning smile, that instantly I want to know him, to talk to him, to hear what he thinks about Milosevic's wife. In his right hand he holds a straw basket containing, at most, twenty olives; in his left, a baby bottle—what Italians call a *biberon*.

"*Buongiorno.*"

"*Salve.*"

"*Buongiorno.*" Jovially the old man greets my neighbor, Paolo, us. (Like the *olivone,* he is indiscriminate in his beneficence.) And who is he? I ask myself. An inmate of the town's *casa di riposo* (rest home), tending for memory's sake a single, potted tree? Perhaps.

I can't know. Instead I admire the ease with which he passes his basket to Paolo, who weighs the olives before throwing them onto the heap. In a few hours they will lose all identity, they will be ground along with ours and my neighbor's and those of a dozen other people, pulp and stone into the great democracy of oil. The old man hands Paolo his *biberon* to be filled: just a few drops, mind you, yet enough.

THE MAREMMA

This part of Tuscany is rich in Etruscan archaeological sites, most of them outside the beautiful village of Sovana. The synagogue in nearby Pitigliano is among the oldest in Italy. Roman ruins can be seen in Saturnia (take particular note of the Porta Romana). Tiny Poggio di Capanne has a beautiful Renaissance church. Museums are few, and modest; one of the most curious, in Sovana, is dedicated to snails.

Hotels

Terme di Saturnia (Saturnia/+39 0564 600 111/termidiSaturnia .it). Offers immediate access to the thermal pools.

Villa Clodia (Via Italia 43, Saturnia/+39 0564 601 212/ hotelvillaclodia.com). A friendly and cheerful hotel in the center of the village, with beautiful views and a swimming pool. Be sure to sample the cakes at breakfast.

Villa Acquaviva (Strada Scansanese, Montemerano/+39 0564 602 890/relaisvillaacquaviva.com). Rooms, each named after a different flower, are divided between the main villa and a farmhouse. Acquaviva also produces an excellent version of the local wine, the Morellino di Scansano.

Albergo Scilla (Via del Duomo 5, Sovana/+39 0564 616 531/ albergoscilla.net). The eight-room inn was restored recently.

As an alternative to traditional hotels, stay at an *agriturismo* (farm bed-and-breakfast). Among the nicest in this region are **Tenuta La Parrina** (Km. 146, Via Aurelia, Albinia/+39 0564 862 626/parrina.it), where you stay on a working farm, and the **Aia della Colonna** (Usi, Santa Caterina/+39 0564 986 110/aiacolonna.it), whose three charming rooms and one small apartment all come with private bathrooms. To find out about other *agriturismi,* contact **Il Consorzio l'Altra Maremma** (Via Mazzini 4, Saturnia/+39 0564 601 280/laltramaremma.it).

Restaurants

Il Mulino (Via Roma 112, Semproniano/+39 0564 987 117). Open only on weekends except in August, when it is open daily. Chef Pina Pinghi takes the orders herself, wearing a toque. The menu changes seasonally; in spring, order the *braciola di maiale al salsa d'aglio,* a grilled pork chop served with a surprisingly sweet marmalade of fresh young garlic.

Ristorante da Michele (Piazza Vittorio Veneto 26a, Saturnia/+39 0564 601 074). Closed Tuesdays. A good place to try the *cucina tipica* of the Maremma: *acquacotta, tortelli,* and dishes made from *cinghiale* (boar).

Braccio (Feniglia, Orbetello/+39 0564 834 210/braccio.org). Open April to October. The best of the simple restaurants lining the beach at La Feniglia (a forty-minute drive from Saturnia).

Shopping

Tenuta La Parrina (Km. 146, Via Aurelia, Albinia/+39 0564 862 626/parrina.it). In addition to the *agriturismo,* this small estate has a large nursery and a shop selling the farm's produce: cheeses (most made from sheep's milk), sheep's- and goat's-milk yogurt, wine, olive oil, and fresh vegetables.

Enoteca Bacco e Cerere (Via Mazzini 4, Saturnia/+39 0564 601 235). A tempting assortment of wines, jams made on the premises, hams, salami, and *sottoli* (wild asparagus, porcini mushrooms, and artichoke hearts preserved in olive oil), as well as locally made crafts.

Fabio Parenti and Brunella Anzidei (Via Roma 22, Semproniano/+39 0564 986 164). Fabio, a superb carpenter and restorer, and his wife, Brunella, sell mirrors, frames, boxes, desk accessories, and furniture, most of it made from olive and chestnut wood that Fabio cuts and seasons himself.

Enrico and Marco Vincenti (Via del Duomo 17, Sovana/+39 0564 614 443/emvincenti.it). The Vincenti brothers offer a wide range of excellently restored Tuscan, French, and Colonial furniture, as well as works in iron by local craftspeople.

It's really due to my friend Charles that I went to the Argentario and Porto Ercole at all. Within the first half hour of meeting him, in 1983, I learned that he'd spent many summers in Porto Ercole, and he spoke of it with so much passion that there was no doubt I'd find myself there one day. Armed with the names of his family friends from childhood Robin and Katie Coventry, who established Marina di Cala Galera there after World War II, my husband and I arrived unannounced on a hot July day and were immediately and warmly welcomed. Porto Ercole is a pretty, pleasant coastal village with a refreshing lack of sites to see, though it's noteworthy for the fact that Michelangelo Merisi—Caravaggio—

died here in 1610. And when the Argentario area came under the control of Spain in the late 1500s, Philip II had the Forte Stella ("star fort") built, seeking advice on the fort's design from Cosimo de' Medici, who recommended Bernardo Buontalenti and Giovanni Camerini. The Argentario was described as "scarcely undiscovered, but neither is it a byword among Mediterranean resorts" by writer Doone Beal in *Gourmet* (July 1988), and I think this is still accurate.

The Coventrys treated us to a great seafood dinner at La Lampara (Lungomare Andrea Doria/+39 0564 833 024), which I'm happy to say is still thriving in Porto Ercole, as are some noteworthy places to stay: Il Pellicano, a Relais & Châteaux property voted "first among the 100 Best Southern European Hotels" by *Condé Nast Traveler*, 2008 (+39 0564 858 111/pellicanohotel.com); and Hotel Don Pedro (+39 0564 833 914/hoteldonpedro.it). More recent hotels include the Argentario Golf Resort & Spa (+39 0564 182 8400/argentariogolfclub.it) and the Bi Hotel (+39 0564 833 055/bi-hotel.it). Tuttomaremma.com, in English and Italian, is also a good resource.

I asked Charles to share some of his wonderful memories of Porto Ercole and the Argentario region:

The faint glow of a sunrise served as a reminder that we'd been up all night partying at La Strega del Mare, the witch of the sea, nightclub above Porto Santo Stefano. La Strega was an outdoor venue surrounded by blossoming bougainvillea and overlooking the Tyrrhenian Sea, on the southwestern corner of Tuscany. It was frequented by Romans, or Romani, and a community of Americans and Brits with summer homes on the Monte Argentario, a peninsula that includes Porto Santo Stefano and Porto Ercole. Spaniards heavily fortified the two

*ports in the late sixteenth century,
two hundred years before the beginning of the unification of Italy.
Ruins of these fortifications remain, serving as great places to
play hide-and-seek as children or
make out as teenagers.*

*The club was run by an eccentric
British expatriate. He staffed it
with a motley crew of lads from
east London who were a stark contrast to the Roman male
clientele sporting cashmere sweaters wrapped fashionably into
cummerbunds around the waist and shirts unbuttoned to reveal
a forest of black chest hair and gold chains. They oozed sex.
At least they did in their own minds. Barry Manilow, Donna
Summer, and Abba were local favorites as this was the late
1970s. The lads enjoyed "mixing it up a little" by slipping in
gritty British rockers including Ian Dury and the Blockheads
("Wake up and make love with me"), Pink Floyd, and Deep
Purple. It was eclectic and we loved it. I was sixteen.*

*As the sun began its ascent over the hills of the Maremma,
we would board our Vespas and head toward la Marina di
Cala Galera for our day jobs as deckhands. But the prospects
of hot bomboloni alla crema (Italian doughnuts with custard) in Orbetello offered a tempting diversion. Orbetello has
a rich history dating back to 500 BC and still remains largely
unspoiled. Its Communist mayor wasn't fond of American
and Brit teenagers banging nosily against the roll-up door of
the bakery on Piazza Garibaldi demanding hot buns at five
thirty a.m. The baker would yell profanities and threats to get
us to leave until we shoved a ten-thousand-lira note under his
door. Thirty years later I can still smell the salty air of the La-*

guna di Orbetello, and taste the sugar crystals and warm custard.

For our second breakfast we would gather at a small bar at the end of the yacht-lined *Marina di Cala Galera,* or prison cove, named after the ruins of the Spanish prison looming overhead, and inhale cappuccini doppi con Vov and Italian brioche, washed down with a Jägermeister. The local fishermen mocked us for not ending with a raw egg shooter. My career as a deckhand on private yachts included a couple summers on the Miss Two, a seventy-one-foot sailing ketch skippered by Steve, a Vietnam-era Green Beret double my size who slept with a loaded handgun under his pillow. My job required me to balance myself on a heaving foredeck while breathlessly grinding winches and taking buckets of salty waves in my face.

A favorite sailing destination was the nearby island of Isola del Giglio, where we ate a local adaptation of the Sicilian spaghetti alla baronessa. The traditional recipe calls for capers, anchovy fillets, chopped vine-ripened tomatoes, basil, cubes of tuna, and local first-press olive oil tossed with warm angel hair pasta. On Giglio they substitute the anchovies and capers with fresh mozzarella di bufala, which melts gently under the heat of the pasta. Insalate di riso, or rice salad, was another favorite. They offered seasonal variations of the traditional recipe calling for parboiled rice served cold with black olives, cooked peas, mushrooms in oil, pickled artichoke hearts, hard-boiled quail eggs, capers, minced parsley, olive oil, and a tablespoon of lemon juice. The oil came from the fattore in town who pressed the olives by hand from his own oliveto, or olive grove. I enjoyed the vitello tonnato, which sounds less romantic when you describe it as chilled veal in a creamy tuna sauce. Ingredients include anchovies, egg yolks, cayenne pepper, and lemon juice. This is not something you want to serve to impress a first date. For dessert we'd have a simple macedonia di frutta, a fruit salad macerated in white wine and sugar featuring locally available figs, peaches, and cantaloupe melon. My afternoons were generally spent diving to ear-popping depths to unhinge a stuck anchor or recover car keys dropped overboard by an inebriated guest. Everyone else slept off the meal by spreading themselves on deck in various stages of nudity.

Back at Marina di Cala Galera we'd convene at Bilbo's American Bar to exchange exaggerated stories of the day, with rounds of fizzy Trebbiano served by MacKay, a trilingual German-American artist with bleached white hair. No one knew or cared about legal drinking age. Cocktails were part of our Italian experience.

A Vespa ride along La Strada Panoramica at dusk was a wonderful way to end the day, inhaling wild fennel and sage and watching the sun melt behind the ruins of Forte Stella. To our left we watched fishing boats returning to Porto Ercole loaded with swordfish, sea bass, and snapper. We were thrilled to come across Prince Bernard, the husband of Queen Juliana of Holland, in his yellow dune buggy playing catch-the-leader with his security detail of carabinieri. The officers clearly did not enjoy entertaining his highness at their expense on .the windy country roads. We'd join in on the chase and be shooed away with angry fists and profanities. The prince thought we were a hoot.

My favorite dinner spot over the twenty summers I spent in Porto Ercole was at the town of Capalbio, on the Maremma hills behind the community of Ansedonia. Capalbio is a classic Tuscan hilltop town. A favorite dish at La Torre di Capalbio in the old town was handmade fettuccini served with a rich *sauce of* ragù di cinghiale *made from the herds of wild boar visible from the road winding up to the walled town. For dessert we would shove wine-soaked blackberries into our faces, which turned our teeth black.*

Days ended with the difficult decision of where to go for evening entertainment. We predictably mounted our bikes and headed back to La Strega for another night of revelry and hot bomboloni *at sunrise.*

Only in Tuscany

DAN HOFSTADTER

As the writer notes in this piece of memorable vignettes, Tuscany "is an idea as well as a place."

DAN HOFSTADTER has translated a number of books from Italian to English and is the author of *The Earth Moves: Galileo and the Roman Inquisition* (Norton, 2009), *Falling Palace: A Romance of Naples* (Knopf, 2005), and *Goldberg's Angel: An Adventure in the Antiquities Trade* (Farrar, Straus & Giroux, 1994), among others.

Last April, on the eve of the Italian general election, I set out on a search for something elusive. This something was what you might call the Tuscan sense of life—the Tuscan temperament. It was to be a brief ramble, and I was concerned that I'd do meager justice to such a rich topic; the consolation was that brevity might concentrate my thoughts. Tuscany, like very few other places—Paris, for instance—is an idea as well as a place. It gave its language to a country. Its most gifted mathematician invented modern science. Its artists redesigned Rome. Its grand dukes had nineteen palaces. There is even a "Tuscany" perfume, as if the local breezes were unfailingly aromatic. Until recently, the national language was not properly spoken by very many people, the gifted mathematician was shut up in his house, the artists who redesigned Rome didn't talk to one another, one of the grand dukes and his wife were poisoned in their palace, and the Tuscan breezes, laden with wild thyme, mint, sage, and juniper, were redolent of the kitchen, not the boudoir. But the myth of Tuscany persists, for the simple reason that it is based very largely on fact.

Ever since international travel on a large scale was invented, by the English in the eighteenth century, huge numbers of people have come to Tuscany every year, including some very famous people, like Byron and Shelley and, a little later, Dickens. Dickens was startled to discover that in the port of Livorno "there was an assassination club, the members of which bore no ill-will to anybody in particular, but stabbed people (quite strangers to them) in the streets at night, for the pleasure and excitement of the recreation." This jolly pastime has gone by the board, and nowadays the visitors, many of them Italians, come to Tuscany for the art, the architecture, the food, the universities, the shopping, the beaches. The region includes not only the great medieval and Renaissance centers of Florence, Pisa, Siena, Lucca, and Arezzo but also seldom-visited cities that long ago became industrial, like Pistoia, or were badly damaged during World War II, like Livorno; and even these have great treasures.

Tuscany—more than any other area, with the possible exception of the Amalfi Coast—corresponds to our conception of what Italy ought to be. The traveler who first arrives in the Florentine countryside, with its parasol pines, its alleys of cypresses, its villas and crenellated towers, may feel that he has seen it somewhere before. The hills to the north and south of Florence are surmounted by manors, castles, and formal gardens that, though by no means necessarily old, do not give a theatrical or dreamlike impression, as they might along the Rhine, but rather one of conscious, serene, and elegant organization. This is not so much a romantic as a classical landscape, and therein lies its magnetism.

I have lived in Tuscany on several occasions over the past thirty years. Although I have a certain fondness for the lesser-known littoral of the Maremma and the uplands of the Casentino, this time I set myself the task of revisiting only the provinces of Siena, Pisa, Lucca, and Florence. I began with the Sienese countryside, and if anyone were to wander about its rolling hills as I did last spring, slipping in and out of the cloud shadows, peering at arrangements of vineyards so perfect that they might have been composed by Sassetta or Pietro Lorenzetti, at castles festooned by clotheslines and abandoned abbeys wanting only a chorus of hooded friars to complete the picture, they could be forgiven for thinking that here, at last, is the eternal Italy. The panorama is unremittingly tempting: on any unpaved road, you find yourself bouncing past huge fortified farmhouses, sheepfolds guarded by scrambling dogs, ancient olive orchards climbing up hillsides. Beware of easy conclusions, however, for this is a land of illusions and paradoxes.

One thing is certain: the province of Siena is one of the most unspoiled on the Italian peninsula. Of course, these slopes were modeled by nature, not by man, but as I dodged the rainstorms, spiral notebook in hand, I found myself resorting to the language of art to describe the harmony of the agricultural shadings and hatchings running over their surfaces, these washes and stipplings of orchard and tilled field: they had the quality of expert drawing in their revelation of the underlying geological form. So only after much dawdling did I come to Siena itself, city of sweet vowels and brutal horsemen, which I entered in a blaze of sunshine that modulated at once to twilight amid the nearly meeting cornices and alleylike streets, from which cars are mercifully banned. Unchanged since my last visit, a distillation of the late medieval, Siena insists on turning you now to the left and now to the right, on marching you up and marching you down: its variety of levels, stairways, and sudden curves, its narrowings and widenings of passage, and the arcs of shadow that its massive palazzi describe on the streets during the course of a day's bemused excursion—all this makes for terrific entertainment. It's a warrant of bygone majesty that such a small, steep city holds so many pugnacious noble residences, their lower windows barred with grilles, as if to remind you that whatever tales are unfolding inside, whatever rich gifts or vows of love, they are not yours to know of. And over this dense procession of edifices, the impossibly slender tower of the Palazzo Pubblico leaps into the sky.

But the eternal Italy? Cesare Brandi, the great Sienese apostle of historic preservation, devoted many pages to blasting insensitive changes to the city's Gothic fabric. For immemorial beauty there is the Val d'Orcia, south of Siena, with its sweeping cadences of hillside and simple travertine architecture, its Romanesque churches guarded by inscrutable stone monsters, its remote abbeys where I had to stand at the door, begging admittance; this valley seems the sure embodiment of something that has always been. Yet actually nothing here is as it was only a few decades ago. A quasi-wasteland in 1900, it was largely colonized in the twenties according to the then-standard Tuscan sharecropping system, which was abolished after World War II; again abandoned, it was eventually resettled by Sardinian sheepherders, who helped create a pecorino sold all over Italy. The most famous product of the area is the wine known as Brunello di Montalcino; yet the Brunellos appeared on the market as a group of recognized vintages only about thirty-five years ago.

And consider this: ever since the late forties, the province of Siena has voted for the Communists or, more recently, their ideological descendants. One of the most pleasant of Tuscan customs is the summertime Festa dell'Unità, which brings rollicking families together in meadows and pavilions all across the region, from the Tyrrhenian Sea to the Apennines, in the name of working-class solidarity. I have often joined in these festivities myself, listening to live bands and filling my plate with pasta; nobody has ever asked me my political views.

It almost always happens, however, that ideological expectations meet unexpected results. So it is that the planned workers' and peasants' paradise of Siena has led instead to something quite different: the tourist state—for Siena Province today depends for its livelihood largely upon tourism, essentially a luxury industry, and its most notable product is very expensive wine. As for those picturesque *castelli* punctuating the horizon, don't imagine that they were there in Garibaldi's day. Oh, the vine was surely cultivated here at various times in the past, and the ancient fortresses surely existed in a different, more dilapidated form. But most of the

estates in this area are no more than fifty years old, and the castles housing the vintners' *cantine* were usually restored in a similar span of time; the same can be said of many grand villas in the more northerly Chianti region, which followed the lead of the Castello di Brolio, rebuilt in the 1830s in the Gothic Revival style. As one Brunello winemaker, the proprietor of a tiny but lovely *terroir* with a stunning view of Monte Amiata, put it to me, "This place was so overgrown that we had to hack our way through to it after we bought it."

🐝   🐝   🐝

The little Brunello estate is in the neighborhood of Montalcino. I am sitting with charming company on a sunny afternoon, eating fresh fava beans with homemade ricotta and drinking the house wine. The family speak of knowing this *terroir* yard by yard, of lovingly coaxing along each slope, and of how that has little in common with "knowing wines" as oenologists do. The buildings, small enough to feel very domestic, actually belong to a ruined *borgo,* brought back to life by the winemaker and his family; there is even a deconsecrated church. Wherever I look, I see flowers, and creeping vines on warm stone walls, and brief passages of horizon that seem to watch over me. From my position, I contemplate a fine old stone tower, ruined but slated for restoration, which I will later explore with some risk to life and limb. It occurs to me that with so much that is new and yet also old— new-old, you might say—the genuine Tuscan temperament, that abiding sense of life transmitted down the centuries, can sometimes prove rather hard to come by.

Then the winemaker tells me a story. He remembers meeting a Tuscan farmer who began to praise his village and its land, adding that if you walked over to a nearby hill town, which you could see outlined against the sky, you'd find that it too was beautiful and productive, if admittedly a little less so. The only trouble with that other village, the farmer said, suddenly scornful, was the way they sounded when they spoke. Their Italian was truly dreadful.

Later, when I think about this story, it seems to me that the farmer was incidentally elucidating two distinct but related elements of the Tuscan identity. One is that the Tuscan at his most elemental lives at the center of the world. The other is that one's degree of social status is defined here largely by precision of speech. It was because of Dante's poetry that the Tuscan dialect, one of numerous offshoots of low Latin spoken in the fourteenth century, was adapted as Italy's national language, and many Tuscans, including those of humble birth, can recite long passages of Dante by heart. Correct, clearly enunciated Italian always carries prestige in Tuscany, even when spoken by hucksters or paupers. Older Tuscans recall shepherds whiling away the time reciting the tales of Paolo and Francesca, Farinata and Cavalcanti.

꒰   ꒰   ꒰

A certain respect for proportion, which conjoins aesthetics and mathematics, is another chief component of the Tuscan sense of life. You feel it almost anywhere in Tuscany—people seem to pick it up by constant exposure to thoughtful design—but a good place to start is in Pienza, a hill town in the Val d'Orcia and the first truly Renaissance town center in Italy.

I arrive in Pienza with friends, and we decide to have lunch at Sette di Vino, a tiny but excellent *osteria*. Its owner, Luciano, a wiry, hyperenergetic man and the gadfly of village political councils, regales us with his opera buffa reasons for voting for Silvio Berlusconi, the television magnate and conservative leader; Luciano's performance could be set to music, with a lot of sixteenth notes. Then we walk over to the Piazza Piccolomini. Pienza was the brainchild of Enea Silvio Piccolomini, a poet and libertine who, after an adventurous youth of pleasures and disasters, got himself elected pope. As Pius II, he decided to transform this village, his birthplace, into a model miniature city, and around 1459 entrusted the task to a brilliant disciple of Leon Battista Alberti named Bernardo Rossellino. I have never gotten over the magic of this place: each time I come, I feel that I'm standing in a sort of diminutive Rome that is mercifully free of traffic, an ideal townscape for a pontiff steeped in humanistic studies. The streets meet at right angles, as they might in a metropolis, but bend slightly as they progress outward, preventing one from perceiving how soon they end at the village gates, and the two buildings on either side of the main piazza diverge somewhat, reversing the effect of perspective and appearing to enlarge and define the piazza. It's a triumph of design, but it doesn't end there—it encompasses the entire outlying landscape as well.

I have often had the oddest sense, walking around a Tuscan hill town, that my gaze as I look through the gaps between houses does not stray out toward the horizon amid a loose, discordant smattering of vineyards and hamlets, but is somehow bound to a picture—a picture formed perhaps by a road winding up to a convent, or an alley of poplars flanking the carriageway to a manor. In Pienza, this correspondence between hill town and surrounding countryside is no matter of lucky accident or superimposed desire but was clearly conceived at a stroke. I notice that my vision—channeled through the openings on either side of the duomo, or, later, through the three round-arched doors in the hanging gardens behind the Palazzo Piccolomini—is pinned to specific points on the horizon, such as the fortress of Radicofani, lair of a thirteenth-century gentleman-bandit immortalized by Dante in *Purgatory*. The feeling that one has wandered into a painting or stage set, a somewhat fortuitous characteristic of other hill towns like Volterra or Montepulciano, became fully conscious in Rossellino's extraordinary mind.

🦁   🦁   🦁

Tuscany has been on the map as a recognizable cultural entity for almost three thousand years, but it's hard to say how much of the Tuscan sense of life really harks back to antiquity. Ancient Etruria, a federation of Etruscan city-states, was folded into the Roman Empire in the third century BC, creating the fundamental mix, and it's arguable that something in the ancestral identity never wholly disappeared—one thinks of the olive tree and the cypress, of travertine construction, of certain habits of speech—and in the later Middle Ages roughly the same entity was reunified under Florentine rule. Florence's power grew out of the wool trade, banking, and the acquisition of Pisa and Siena; her great prestige in the arts and sciences lasted roughly from 1300 to 1550. The Medici, a banking family that came to dominate the city, managed to get itself ennobled in the mid-sixteenth century and governed Tuscany as a grand duchy until the reunification of Italy in 1861. But Tuscany has changed greatly over the centuries, and even the townsfolk of closely linked cities such as Pisa and Livorno are given to merrily disparaging one another.

One feels, all the same, that certain people, ideas, and monuments produced by this land could not possibly have been produced anywhere else. It belongs to the genius of the Italian city to possess some emblematic attraction that enchants and amazes visitors, like the Palio, Vesuvius, or the Grand Canal, and Pisa has the greatest of them all, the Leaning Tower. More than any other symbol, this one also memorializes an abiding aspect of the Tuscan genius: the spirit of mathematical inquiry and its happy conjunction with the art of design. When I arrived in the city last spring, I made my way straight to the aptly named Piazza dei Miracoli—home of the tower, the duomo, the baptistry, and the *camposanto,* or cemetery. Pisa has preserved all the attributes of a small European university town—the bookshops, the crowded cafés, the flocks of students on bicycles—and as I hurried toward my destination, relishing this stream of life pursuing its traditional path, I almost forgot to look ahead. All at once, floating over the roofline of the Piazza Arcivescovado, slanting improbably into the heavens like a storybook Tower of Babel, ringed by the most delicate rows of white arches imaginable, was the greatest architectural delight the world has to offer.

Virtually all Renaissance church towers are pierced with progressively more windows as they rise, to lighten the load, but this one soars upward in the form of an almost unperforated cylinder. Defying gravity, it looks weightless, a miraculous column; any monotony in the design is mitigated by the rings of white arches. And yet it leans, and it started to lean—because of subsidence— by the time the builders reached the third story: It was, to the permanent astonishment of architectural historians, built leaning. In that sense, although it defies gravity, it becomes, paradoxically, evidence for gravity and a sort of popular sign of the earth's gravitational field. Like human beings, who have something angelic about them but who often behave like animals, it delicately conjoins two opposing qualities. I believe it is for this reason that Galileo's disciple Vicenzio Viviani, in his biography of his master, had the great Pisan physicist prove the law of falling by dropping weights off the Leaning Tower. We know that he didn't do it, not like that and not here; but here, poetically, is where we feel it had to happen.

🦁 🦁 🦁

I have noticed, now and again, passing by a Tuscan playground, that although the toddlers and young women there cannot be readily distinguished from the population at large, they are seldom speaking Italian. I do not really know what they are speaking—I suppose it may be Romanian or Albanian, or some North African dialect of Arabic. The new immigrants look very contented to be where they are, and I do not hesitate to ask them for directions or advice. It was one of these, a Peruvian au pair, who urged me to visit a place I'd never even heard of—the Villa di Corliano.

About a half hour north of Pisa, I passed through a monumental gate into an overgrown park dominated by ornamental palm trees. It had just stopped raining. The park had a romantic, self-sequestered feeling, enlivened by the caroling of hundreds of melodious songbirds. No one seemed to be about. I moseyed around behind the handsome ocher villa, where verdant meadows slanted away into the hills. As I mounted the rear stairway, a smiling lady who introduced herself as Countess Agostini Venerosi della Seta—we took this in stages—came out and explained that her house served as an inn in the summer months but that she would be happy to show me the decorations inside, which dated from about 1590.

The interior was almost entirely frescoed, in colors that had lost nothing of their richness. Extravagant illustrations of Ovid, in a Mannerist style, covered the ceiling of the main salon and wandered out into the vestibule, where Atalanta and Hippomenes could be seen racing each other in successive lunettes. Soon their exertions wearied me, and I felt like sinking into one of the big downy beds upstairs and falling asleep. But the villa was not yet receiving guests.

Lucca, just northeast of Pisa, has its own string of villas. After a short drive, I found the grandiose Villa Torrigiani, with its monstrous Rococo façade like shelving overburdened with Meissen statuettes. Everything else about this house is wonderful. The Torrigiani family, who furnished ambassadors to Versailles from the minuscule Republic of Lucca, were much preoccupied with camellias and engaged Le Nôtre as a garden designer. Camellia trees, blooming from March through November, encircle the villa; carmine was out in force on the day of my arrival. As if that were not enough, a decorative painter named Pietro Scorzini was hired to paint camellia gardens on every ceiling of the main floor, to stupendous effect. Not the least impressive achievement of the family was embroidery (which, you will recall, along with clock making and floriculture, was one of the great pursuits of the enlightened European aristocracy of the eighteenth century). Carlo Luca Torrigiani embroidered the coverlets for a daybed and matching ottoman here, a pastime that fully occupied him for twenty-one years. The daybed is indeed a chef d'oeuvre, and no doubt he was blissfully contented.

🐿   🐿   🐿

Florence is a city that, more than any other in Tuscany, reinforces your feeling of being terribly late to the table. It was nicer twenty years ago, people tell you; or thirty, or forty. They are right. Largely returned to its condition before the great flood of 1966, the city is still flooded with tourists, students, and scholars to the point where its personality (though not its beauty) is submerged. It is, of course, the best place in the world to look at art and architecture, but also the best place to marvel at the resilience of the *panino* as a repellent streetside snack, and at the perseverance of the huge English colony, with its spinsterish Italian patois and its self-projection into a past rather too encumbered with Ruskin, the Brownings, and E. M. Forster. Oh, there are indeed Italian quarters in Florence, but they are found toward the outskirts of the city.

The problem here is seeing anything with an innocent eye. An architect who has trained with Richard Rogers tells me how maddeningly hard it is to get anyone interested in anything new in the land of Bramante and Alberti. Even if you can, you are hampered by codes and bureaucratic restrictions. On the other hand, watch what happens if you tell someone you were born and bred in Florence. There's an instant assumption that the highest social polish and the subtlest aesthetic discriminations are yours.

I am staying at a hotel called the Loggiato dei Serviti, which was carved out of quarters built in 1537 for the Servite Fathers, a monastic order suppressed in 1808. I have picked this place—which turns out to command very pretty rear views of a labyrinth of courtyards, terraces, and domes—because it was built by Antonio Sangallo the Elder to match Brunelleschi's Ospedale degli Innocenti, on the other side of the Piazza Santissima Annunziata. I come and go at all hours, traversing the world of my antecedent life, remembering with regret the days when I could stroll into the forecourt of the Annunziata to look at Jacopo Pontormo and Andrea del Sarto's frescoes without paying a cent.

It is useful, I believe, if you have an interest in painting, to think of Florence as the site of great conventual orders—Dominican, Franciscan, Carmelite—because they all once owned vast tracts of land inside the city walls and commissioned frescoes for their principal churches. These great temples often feature painters whose murals may be found elsewhere in Tuscany, but so do less imposing churches. The Chiesa di Santa Felicità, just across the Ponte Vecchio from the Piazza della Signoria, has, among other treasures, a large *Deposition* in a brilliant color scheme of dissonant blues and pinks; by Pontormo, it is a picture like none other fashioned in the Renaissance. This is hardly the last the Pontormo-lover need see, however, because a well-informed trek through the southern Florentine countryside—through Bellosguardo, with its dramatic view of the dome of Santa Maria del Fiore, and the pretty hamlet of Arcetri, where Galileo spent his last years—might lead the devotee to the palatial Charterhouse of Galluzzo. Here an indulgent monk, unlocking a huge door, allowed me to contemplate Pontormo's great *Passion* cycle for as long as I liked. These lunette-shaped frescoes have been mildly damaged by moisture, but not enough to prevent the viewer from enjoying Pontormo's rather Matisse-like painterly strategy, which consisted of muting all chiaroscuro in the interests of vast fields of rare and brilliant color. And how pleasant it was, this time, not to be subjected, as I often have been in the past, to fierce Carthusian scolding for having brought a noisy child, or tried to take a photograph, or failed to offer a sufficiently liberal donation to the handful of cowled residents of this vast establishment.

🦂   🦂   🦂

The abbey of Passignano, half an hour south of Florence in the Val di Pesa, is an island of sun-dappled masonry and arboreal luxuriance; it is also a prime instance of the sort of over-restoration that would have excited Cesare Brandi's ire. At its portal, I am for some reason turned away.

"It's the Taliban," says Tonino Salvatori, when we meet at his bakery, Il Forno Macucci, in nearby San Casciano, a pretty village leveled during the war and recomposed brick by brick. Tonino and his wife, Silvia, are old friends of mine who were married in the abbey; "the Taliban" is an Italian colloquialism for zealous or conservative clergy.

The bakery, which Tonino and Silvia own together with their friend Luca Macucci, is celebrated in this area, particularly for its *schiacciata,* or flatbread: pensioners line up outside at six in the morning to buy *schiacciata* or brioches to have with their coffee. Curiously, Tonino chose to go in with Luca only a few years ago, after a long time in another occupation. I suppose that something like this had to happen, however, because his interest in food was always intense. When I lived outside Florence, he would sometimes drive us to remote farms in the hills where cheese or *salumi* were made; liberal samples were always bestowed upon us, and I would emerge as the proud owner of, let us say, an entire prosciutto. (In Tuscany, I have often found myself escorting around far more food than I know what to do with.)

Schiacciata has to be crisp on top and soft underneath and is baked in broad, bumpy sheets. You can consume considerable acreage out of a sheet of Tonino and Luca's *schiacciata* before you know what you're up to. "We make it out of the rest of the previous day's dough mixed with new dough," Tonino tells me as he closes up shop. "The question is—how much of each? That depends on your microclimate and on other conditions, like your oven. We have a tube oven that maintains a constant temperature, and we use only extra virgin olive oil and no yeast—our only leaven comes from the old dough. I suppose our prize item is *schiacciata all'uva,* which has local grapes baked inside. But that's available only from the middle of August to November, and not everyone likes it because of the seeds."

We drive over to the San Casciano Soccer Club to pick up the couple's twelve-year-old son, Matteo. Waiting for him to change, we get a drink at the bar and look down over this neck of the Val di Pesa, with its windswept parasol pines and groups of red-tiled cottages. "When I was a kid, I used to knock about all over this area," says Tonino, with a hint of nostalgia. "That was before people started leaving the land—by thirty years ago or so, it was practically empty. Now they're coming back in droves, of course, but for new reasons, not usually connected to farming. Maybe they want a country cottage, or they set up a small business."

I think about this later in the evening, as we're all sitting in a trattoria called Mamma Rosa, which has served us enough good, robust pasta and steak to feed a battalion of Etruscan troops. I realize what extraordinary changes a Tuscan in his or her mid-eighties has seen in a lifetime: the cruelties of war, the fall of Fascism (Mussolini was extremely unpopular here), entire landscapes forsaken and revitalized, a dramatically declining birthrate. At the same time, mass consumerism has arrived, and with it the marketing of the Tuscan artistic and culinary heritage for purely commercial purposes. I have to square the Tuscany of today with memories stretching back four decades, memories of a much quieter, less crowded, more tradition-bound place. I remember eccentric friends calling down to me out of their tiny windows, indigent but welcoming old folks, long walks to fetch oil from the mill press, summer meals based on fresh tomatoes, stale bread, and basil—*pappa di pomodoro,* a so-called poverty food. I remember being turned out of a house I had rented from a choleric *vetturale,* a man with a van, because he claimed that I had designs on his girlfriend, whom in fact I had never met. I remember calling on vast, tumbledown medieval villas filled with families so large that they seemed to go on forever—what, another *nonna!*—everybody milling about in rooms that smelled only of cat. The Tuscan sense of life . . . oh, it endures, of that I am sure, in whatever guise it chooses to assume.

TUSCAN TREASURES

Tuscany is one of the largest and most varied of Italy's regions, encompassing Renaissance Florence and medieval Siena, as well as a vibrant coast, a host of small hill towns, and famous vineyards. The months of September, October, May, and June are the most beautiful and also the best time to sample local produce such as truffles and porcini (in fall), and zucchini flowers and fava beans (in spring). During the peak months of July and August, huge numbers of travelers are vying to get into the same museums, hotels, and restaurants. To help plan your time, consider booking a trip through **Insider's Italy**—Marjorie Shaw lives in Rome and tailors itineraries for foodies, oenophiles, architecture buffs, and families (insidersitaly.com).

The country code for Italy is 39.

Florence and Chianti

Florence has an unparalleled concentration of Renaissance art and architecture—including icons such as the Duomo, the Uffizi, and the Pitti Palace—all within an easily navigated city center. Hence the tourist crush. Book tickets to galleries and museums in advance through your hotel concierge or travel agent. Nearby Chianti was one of the first wine areas to make Tuscan red a household staple and has since become a favorite of British expats.

After a seven-year renovation, the **Four Seasons Florence** reopened this summer. The grand property joins two palazzi in one of the city's largest gardens (055 26 261). In the Piazza di Santa Maria Novella, **J.K. Place** has a modern design (055 264 5181). **Residence Hilda,** a two-minute walk from the Duomo, has spacious rooms and competitive prices (055 288 021). The Ferragamo group owns a number of fashionable properties, including the **Gallery Hotel Art** and the **Lungarno Suites** (055 2726 4000). Across from the Piazza Santissima Annuziata, the **Loggiato dei Serviti,** in a palazzo built by Antonio da Sangallo the Elder, has large, pleasant rooms at modest rates (055 289 592). The intimate **Casa Howard Florence** feels like the home of a well-connected local, but services are scant (06 6992 4555).

If you prefer to stay a little out of town, the **Villa Mangiacane** has wonderful views of Florence, plus three pools, a spa, a vineyard, and some Michelangelo frescoes (055 829 0123). The painstakingly restored sixteenth-century **Villa Bordoni,** near Greve, has a good restaurant (055 884 0004).

In Pisa, the **Relais dell'Orologio** is a remodeled ancient tower five minutes from the Duomo and across the street from the house where Leopardi wrote his famous verses about Silvia. The lovely if pricey inn also has an excellent restaurant (050 830 361).

Florence is still one of Italy's top dining cities; avoid the tourist traps and stick to simple trattorias where you'll find better, and cheaper, food. Since 1869, locals have flocked to **Sostanza-Troia** for its excellent *bistecca alla fiorentina* and unpretentious, bustling atmosphere (Via del Porcellana 25r/055 212 691). Settle onto the long benches at **Alla Vecchia Bettola** and follow your waiter's recommendations on the daily specials (Viale Luigi Ariosto 34r/ 055 224 158). The city's most famous chef, Fabbio Picchi, has a formidable empire of restaurants, where he delivers modern takes on Tuscan classics: **Cibrèo** (Via Andrea del Verrocchio 8r/055 234 1100), **Trattoria Cibrèo** (Via dei Macci 122r/055 234 1100), **Cibrèo Caffè** (Via dei Macci 122r/055 234 5853), and **Teatro della Sale** (Via dei Macci 111r/055 200 1492).

Siena and Southern Tuscany

Siena is a mecca for medieval buffs, with most of the action concentrated around the huge Campo. Nearby Montalcino, Pienza, Montepulciano, and Cortona are exquisite hill towns with lovely countrysides and vineyards. South of Montepulciano, the gardens of La Foce, established by Iris Origo in the 1920s, are historically interesting and gorgeous. The estate has a few lovely houses available for short stays. It recently opened the **Villa La Foce** for weekly rentals—a fifteenth-century three-story former tavern with period furnishings that can sleep twenty-one people (057 869 101/lafoce.com).

Most of Siena's best hotels actually fall outside its wall. **Borgo Santo Pietro,** thirty-five minutes to the southwest, near the spectacular Abbey of San Galgano, is a renovated thirteenth-century villa with six bedrooms (soon to be twelve), landscaped gardens, a bocce court, a pool, and orchards (0577 751 222). Within the walled city of Cortona, **San Michele** is an imposing sixteenth-century palazzo with comfortable rooms at reasonable rates (0575 604 348). Near Pienza, the contemporary-styled **La Bandita,** which has views of the Val d'Orcia, is an eight-room inn (also available for weekly rental) owned by *Condé Nast Traveler* contributing editor Ondine Cohane's husband (333 404 6704). In the center of Montepulciano, **La Locanda di San Francesco** has a few well-priced rooms with views, plus a wine bar with local *vino nobiles* and Montalcino's Brunellos (0973 664 384).

Montepulciano's **Acquacheta** is owned by a zany Tuscan who likes his steak rare and won't cook yours any other way. The place is so popular that he often has to take three seatings a night (Via del Teatro 22/0578 758 443).

Luciano, the owner of Pienza's **Sette di Vino,** has a similarly impassioned approach, warning tourists as they walk in that there is "no pizza, no pasta, no Diet Coke." At lunch he serves lighter dishes such as grilled meats, pecorino sampling platters, and salads (Piazza di Spagna 1/0578 749 092). **Latte di Luna,** also in Pienza, has an outdoor terrace and local dishes such as *pici al cinghiale,* or wild boar, and *maialino,* or suckling pig (Via San Carlo 2/4/0578 748 606). **Il Rossellino,** the fanciest (and tiniest) joint in town, is run by a husband-and-wife team (Piazza di Spagna 4/0578 749 064).

In the small town of Monticchiello, famous for its Teatro Povera, **La Porta**'s highlights include *taglioni al tartufo, tagliata,* and the owner, Daria Cappelli, who knows her wines (Via del Paino 1/0578 755 163). In a former pharmacy right off Siena's Campo, the well-known **Le Logge** is still one of the city's best restaurants (Via del Porrione 33/0577 48 013). Most people don't think of eating fish in Tuscany, but **Tre Christi** reminds visitors that they are just forty-five minutes from the Mediterranean. Try the excellent *crudo* (Vicolo di Provenzano 17/0577 280 608).

Vineyards

The best way to explore Tuscan vineyards is by sampling vintages. In Montepulciano, **Avignonesi** has one of the best *vino nobile* blends (0578 724 304/avignonesi.it). In Chianti, the wine trail is well marked; stop by **San Giusto a Rentennano** (0577 747 121/fattoriasangiusto.it) or **Isole e Olena** (055 807 2767). Brunellos are Italy's superstars; visit the medieval fortress in Montalcino for a Brunello overview—after walking up the ramparts for marvelous views—and then head to **Castello di Argiano** for a taste of Sesti Brunello, an authentic version of the Sangiovese grape (0577 844 037/argiano.net). **Casanova di Neri** is an example of a more modern take on the wine (0577 834 455/casanovadineri.com), and **Ciacci Piccolomini d'Aragona** is one of the oldest and most established producers (0577 835 616/ciaccipiccolomini.com).

Reading

The classic modern Tuscan novelist is Aldo Palazzeschi, whose *Materassi Sisters* tells the story of two spinsters who grow besotted with their unusually handsome (and unscrupulous) nephew (out of print). Vasco Pratolini, a left-wing, working-class Florentine novelist who also wrote screenplays for Luchino Visconti, left a number of affecting novels, most notably *The Naked Streets,* a coming-of-age story set in a poor quarter of Florence (out of print). *War in Val d'Orcia,* Iris Origo's dispassionate World War II diary, culminates in her marching orphans to safety through Tuscany (David R. Godine). Eve Borsook's *Mural Painters of Tuscany: From Cimabue to Andrea del Sarto* is the best guide to the Tuscan art of the fresco (out of print); also recommended is her *Companion Guide to Florence* (out of print). Italian speakers will want *Aria di Siena* by the great Cesare Brandi (Progaton).

Coming Home to Chianti

GINI ALHADEFF

HERE'S A GREAT piece on Chianti, complete with recommendations for places to stay and rent, restaurants, food shops and markets, wine, and kilns where you can buy terra-cotta pots, tiles, and olive oil urns.

GINI ALHADEFF is the founder of two literary reviews, *Normal* and *XXIst Century,* and is a contributing editor at *Travel + Leisure,* where this piece originally appeared, in 1994. She is also the author of *The Sun at Midday: Tales of a Mediterranean Family* (Pantheon, 1997) and the novel *Diary of a Djinn* (Pantheon, 2003).

IT WAS IN Tokyo, at the terrible age of thirteen, that I first heard of Strada in Chianti. What I heard came in the form of stories. They were told to us by a genuine Tuscan called Franco Innocenti. My father was then working for Olivetti, and Franco, a surrealist painter in his spare time, had come to train some young Japanese in the art of selling typewriters. He was far from home, and from his American wife and two children, and he came to dinner often. There was only one Italian restaurant in Tokyo then, Antonio's, and an Italian could easily have felt homesick. "Poor thing," my father would say, "he doesn't know anyone here." But we were the "poor things," starved as we were for any news of our faraway country, for any particulars that could make the abstraction of our Italian nationality less abstract.

Franco lived in Strada in Chianti, a small town fifteen minutes from Florence, set among the hills that produce Chianti wine and the best olive oil in Italy. The town began as four houses built in the 1500s on either side of the old Via Chiantigiana, hence its name, which means a "street in Chianti." Along the rectangular piazza, one finds Roberto's car repair shop, a pharmacy, a newsstand, and the *carabinieri*. About three thousand people live here, most of whom know each other, as their parents and their parents' parents did before them, and there is usually one person, and no more than three, for every profession—an electrician, a plumber, a builder, three butchers, three greengrocers (if one includes Gastone, who sells his vegetables door-to-door from a van). The one supermarket is the size of a shoebox, and so is the *latteria,* which sells dairy products. The town is not picturesque, like Greve some twenty kilometers away, or Radda or Gaiole, but the landscape is.

The first story Franco told of Strada was of a family friend, an Englishwoman, who had arrived to spend a fortnight. She was very round, milky-skinned, and pink-cheeked, with stocky legs, and Mario, the *fattore*—the man who tended the vines and olive groves—on the Innocentis' land, said, sizing her up in admiration, "What lovely legs the signorina has, lovely as a pig's." It was a compliment, of course. Franco himself painted a picture in which a slice of *prosciutto crudo* was unfurled on a pole like a proud flag in the wind.

Years later Mario's brother Terzilio came to work for us, when my parents bought a piece of land in Strada between two castles, neither medieval, one pompous, one pretty, the pretty one imposing from a distance but a one-room affair close up. The land had a ruined farmhouse on it—a *casa colonica* with a lovely big arched entrance and a Madonna nestled in a sky blue niche above it—some rows of vines and ancient twisted olive trees, and a great deal of dry stony earth. All around was the silvery green of olive trees, spiky dark points of cypresses, hills combed with rows of vines, a barn here and there, and the idea of Florence nearby: on the horizon, on crisp evenings, the city's sprinkling of lights cast a rosy yellowish haze on the sky. The house was known as La Casa Nova, and that is the name it has kept.

🦂   🦂   🦂

What better place to write about the Chianti region than from a kitchen, in Chianti, where I am sitting at a long wooden table. Some thirty years ago, when this house was converted from a farm for animals to a house, my brothers and I were instructed to "weather" the kitchen table by denting the surface here and there with a hammer so it wouldn't look so new. A few real dents have been added to those first impatient ones. On the table is a bottle containing a green, somewhat cloudy olive oil, from the very olives grown on this small property, and a bottle of our 1992 Chianti La Casa Nova—fermented, bottled, and labeled in the garage and stored in the cellar beneath the kitchen. Farther down the table is a mound of hand-cut ribbons of pasta made this morning and laid out to dry by a woman who could have stepped out of a Piero della Francesca painting: Peppina has vivid black eyes, a round face, curly black hair that seems to want to escape from her scalp and into the heavens, a voice that travels on gusts of air making its way triumphantly from the lungs through the vocal cords into the surrounding countryside, with every hard *c* Tuscanized into an *h* so that *casa* becomes "hassa."

Strada in Chianti is a place of voices such as hers, of opinions fit to be spoken out loud, unequivocally. In the haze of jet lag, when eight in the morning is two a.m. for me and I struggle with the injustice of the hours lost during the journey from New York, voices tell me I have arrived in Strada—the voice of Peppina when she comes in and those of Franca and Bruno who live in a house next to ours. They have always made their living as they do now: he takes care of the land, tends the olive trees, the vines, the orchard, and the animals, makes the wine and the olive oil; she cooks. Before coming here, they worked at one of the larger wineries in the region belonging to the Frescobaldis; then, on a remote estate five times the size of ours. Even so, Bruno took care of all the vines and olive trees himself. Their daughter, Marilla, studies at the Liceo Classico in Florence. Emilio, their eldest child, works at a Ford dealership in a nearby town. It seems unlikely that either will want to apply what they may have learned from their father about the making of wine and oil. It is unlikely they will even live here: this place is not exotic to them as it is to me, who lives so far from it and misses it.

🦎　　🦎　　🦎

For years, even after La Casa Nova was restored and the vines and olive trees had had the earth dug up around their roots and more fertile earth deposited on them, the place looked quite barren. In three decades, the three pines on the front lawn have grown so tall that their branches intertwine on top to form a single cloud of fragrant shade under which the dogs like to lie on summer mornings and crack pinecones between their teeth. The larch, the magnolia, and the horse chestnut are at least twenty times the size they were when they were planted.

At the end of the garden, by the vines, there is a coop, with chickens, guinea hens, ducks, and rabbits, and a cement sty with a green roof on it where pigs used to be kept—two a year, till none of us could stand to see them led to slaughter anymore. Still, as Count Niccolò Capponi intoned when I visited his family estate, Calcinaia, "The pig is fundamental to the countryside. As they say around here, a pig is like a woman: you throw none of it away." He proceeded to enumerate the animal's various uses: "The bristles are used for brushes, the flesh for cured meats—*salame,* prosciutto, bacon, sausage . . ." He mentioned the uses of the snout, too, and of the hoofs, but now I forget what they were. We dove into a passageway and emerged, festooned in cobwebs, in Bluebeard's locked chamber, only with the pig as victim: from the ceiling hung four whole hams, myriad *salami* and *finocchione* (soft salami with fennel seeds), and many hunks of bacon, all of which were encrusted with grains of pepper, salt, and dust.

Since we gave up keeping pigs, we buy the meat and make our own *salame* in the cellar. Most people in Chianti have a cellar, or know someone who does who will sell them good unadulterated wine and olive oil—though the latter is harder to find, and few can really tell the difference between average and excellent oil. But it's a far cry from our cellar, where the wine vats compete for space with the Fiat and the garden furniture, and the Capponis' high-vaulted cellar, with its rows of gleaming oak barrels from Slavonia where the only creature you might encounter is a toad. And though our respective wines might taste quite different, they are both good. With small quantities it's possible to add only a small amount of sulfites compared with more commercial wines, which have to endure storage, changes of temperature, and transport. Every town in Chianti has an *enoteca,* a store that sells wines from the surrounding estates. The thing to do is to taste a few wines there, choose one, then buy a supply directly from the vineyard's retail outlet, usually located at the entrance to the winery or not far down the road.

I'll take any pretext to get into the car and drive into one of the nearby towns. The choice is between Strada in Chianti; the smallest; Impruneta, the most impersonal; or Greve, the farthest from us—though it takes only twenty minutes to get there—but my favorite. During the ritual of morning coffee around the kitchen table, the day's menu is discussed. The contents of the freezer—chickens, ducks, guinea fowl—are taken into consideration, as is what the garden has to offer: in the summer, tomatoes, eggplant, radicchio (which in Tuscany is a dark green bitter lettuce that is sliced like cabbage), string beans, zucchini. The chickens lay eggs, too, bless them. But if there are no white beans to go with the *bistecca* or black cabbage to make *ribollita* (a vegetable soup ladled over slices of bread) or mushrooms to go into the sauce for the tagliatelle, I take off. Going shopping is the peculiar form of sightseeing I have developed here.

It is a visit to stories and conversations I have heard, to the people who have told them to me and who tell me new ones every time I see them. I take the breathtakingly pretty Chiantigiana that winds its way from Florence to Siena, through the hills and vineyards of Chianti, to the town of Greve. It doesn't matter how many times I've driven through it. I'm always thrilled when I go up a steep incline and come upon a certain stretch of fields and farms, always amused to see the hedges in front of the church at Giobbole which the eccentric priest has clipped in the shape of swans and doves. I always remember, too, the sermon I heard him give, about a girl possessed by demons who spoke Greek though she was Italian—a proof of her possession, he said. A Tuscan is incapable of telling a story without adding salt to it; something unsalted is *sciocco*—stupid. No transaction, no matter how trivial, takes place without words leaping about on the flat field of the everyday. Everything is made funny.

The piazza at Greve, which began to be built in the 1400s to serve as a marketplace, is like a triangular stage, with arcades of shops on two sides, where one feels that one's every move is for the entertainment of an audience who sit on their terraces above the arches and survey the action through fronds of pink and red geraniums. I have never seen a single outsider, let alone a foreigner, among them. Sometimes they appear not to be looking and set the table for lunch under a beach umbrella or go about hanging laundry on the clothesline. They themselves are on a stage enacting their own curiosity and their everyday existence.

The piazza, which is dedicated to Verrazzano, has all one needs: La Formicola, the bookstore, which also stocks books in English, a newsstand, food shops, an *enoteca,* real estate offices, an information center, and, as in all self-respecting Italian piazzas, two competing cafés—La Loggetta, for a glass of wine, and the Caffè Lepanto (also known as Caffè Centrale), for ice cream and a complete view of the square. At the entrance to Falorni, the butcher, there is a farouche stuffed boar that bears a marked resemblance to the one I almost collided with one evening while driving down a road through the woods. The preservation of boars has been so successful, certain areas are overrun with them—the property of a woman who did not allow boar hunting is ravaged by hoof marks. Chiantigiani do not approve of this form of preservation, and they mind, too, when they are not hired to cultivate lands they have always known and now see lying fallow. One palpable instance of an ecological conscience is in the signs lining most roads that say optimistically, "This is a denuclearized zone"—in intention, that is, if nothing else.

Politics is nobody's pastime anymore. Just over a year ago a loudspeaker on the roof of an Italian Socialist Party van cruising through the piazza incited the inhabitants to gather on the following Sunday evening at seven. A punctiliously dressed old *contadino* in a gray suit, white shirt, and black felt hat was heard to comment acidly, "That's when they give us all our money back." Until recently, most farmers in the area were Socialist or Communist, and those who were known to have been active Fascists— such as the now defunct carpenter of Strada, who, it was rumored, forced cod liver oil down the throats of partisans from whom he wanted information—were shunned. But since the corruption scandal that involved political parties in Italy two years ago and brought down, first and foremost, the Socialist Party for accepting millions in bribes, people have been scouring the newspapers for the names of the latest victims of their bloodless revolution. In the evening, after supper, Bruno dons wide beige

cotton trousers and a short-sleeved shirt with a blue and white di-
amond pattern, gets into his pewter-colored Fiat Uno, and rides
off to Strada to play bocce at the Christian Democrat court. He
doesn't care what party the court belongs to, he says, as long as it
is properly maintained.

One Tuesday morning I went with him and his daughter to the
market in Strada; the goal of our expedition was to buy canvas
shoes and anchovies. On the way, at the crossing in Martellina,
where there is a grocery with good pecorino and a restaurant
overlooking the hills, Bruno caught sight of the mailwoman—a
gaunt young creature in blue overalls straddling a bicycle, a black
mailbag slung across her chest. "There's my little treasure!" Bruno
exclaimed, putting on the brakes.

There was another *postina* before her who had asked to be
transferred. Bruno said that a German shepherd had pinched
her—in Tuscan "pinching" means biting; it is something that
snakes, bees, dogs, mosquitoes do. When the wisteria was in
bloom by our front gate, in May, the new *postina* complained to
Bruno of the bumblebees, afraid she'd get bitten. Bruno confided
that he had told her, "The *calabroni* won't touch you, but I will,
I'll give you pollen." From the backseat, his daughter, who is experiencing the first stirrings of a feminist conscience, implored,
"Papà!" An American feminist might encounter many instances
of apparent "sexual harassment," but in Chianti the harassment, if
it can be termed that, is reciprocal and a way of giving an edge to
an otherwise uniform social climate: one would have to go all the
way to Florence or Siena to meet a stranger.

Bruno carries on verbal courtships with attached and unat-
tached women of spirit, but only those who are an equal match.
He asks Beppina news of her husband, for instance, and inquires
whether old age has impaired his performance. This is an ongoing
skit: Beppina's husband, Giotto (so nicknamed because he worked
as a housepainter for a while), is Bruno's best friend and a peer.

Beppina's repartee is always something along the lines of "You'll keep still when the rats start gnawing on you." The exchange usually takes place in the presence of Bruno's wife. Here, as everywhere, there is real adultery, too. But because no one has a pied-à-terre or knows of a hotel that isn't owned by someone's relative, it's usually carried out in the fields, often in daylight, and so doesn't remain clandestine for long. I am sorry to return to the subject of sex so often, but it is pertinent to the spirit of the region, where women are described in the same language used for wine—harsh when too young, perfect in their prime, and known to be affected by the moon. The people of Chianti generally have a low opinion of physical exertion for its own sake. Once when Bruno and I were driving up from Florence, we saw a group of runners carrying flags and Bruno remarked that youthful energy—something he stressed he no longer had—should not be wasted this way but lavished on a *ragazza* under a tree.

At the Strada market, we looked for the *acciughino,* the anchovy man, also known as "*povero* Marchino," poor little Mark, because he shouts, comically, "Come buy anchovies, I need money to get married." We immediately ran into Giotto, almost as all-knowing as his wife when it comes to the affairs of the region, who told us "*povero* Marchino" hadn't come because he was actually getting married, at last. We bought the anchovies instead from a shop called Bussotti, on the square at Strada, and they came out of a vat-size tin: coarse, silvery, beheaded, and a bit larger than one would have wished, but Bruno eyed them approvingly. One of his favorite dishes consists of anchovies mixed with chopped red onions, oil, and pepper. This is for initiates. I understand him better when he talks about his passion for bread and figs, a combination he indulges in at sunrise sitting by himself in the shade of one of the three fig trees in our garden.

As we drive back over the Chiantigiana I am reminded of a story told to me by Tebaldo, the mechanic and taxi driver of

Strada, who has now retired and been replaced by his son. He had taken an Englishwoman on a drive to see the countryside, which the English call Chiantishire, and at every turn in the road she gasped, "We have nothing like this in England!" They passed Castellina and reached Radda, and there, too, she exclaimed, "We have nothing like this in England!" They drove to Passignano, had lunch below an abbey set in an oval clump of cypresses as in a Renaissance landscape, and she repeated, "We have nothing like this in England!" Finally, Tebaldo, who had been to England once in his life, saw her point; he confided, thinking to himself, "But is it fair that we should have everything and the others nothing?" He had nothing to be modest about.

THE CHIANTI REGION

A sixty-five-square-mile stretch of vineyards and hill towns between Florence and Siena, Chianti is an ideal area to rent a villa or a room in a farmhouse hotel and revel in the pleasures of the Tuscan countryside. Days can revolve around visits to markets, piazzas, and wineries; hiking and biking trips; and pilgrimages to historic sites—the romantic Badia a Coltibuono (the abbey of San Lorenzo), the fortified town of Montefioralle—and museums (Florence's Uffizi is about a fifteen-minute drive from Strada in Chianti). Eating and sleeping are also respected as serious pursuits in these parts.

The easiest way to get to Chianti is by flying to Florence and renting a car at the airport. You can also fly to Pisa or Rome and take an Alitalia train from either airport to Santa Maria Novella station in Florence.

Chianti is prettiest in spring and summer. Even on the hottest days a breeze floats in by afternoon. And the hills are always cooler than the streets of Florence. The big draw in September and October is the grape and olive harvest.

Hotels

Since agriculture rather than tourism is the mainstay of the region, there are more lodgings in the vicinity of Siena or Florence than in the heart of the wine country. The following hotels, however, are well situated for travelers who want to see—and taste—Chianti.

Castello di Spaltenna (Via Spaltenna 13, Gaiole in Chianti/+39 0577 749 483/spaltenna.it). A twenty-one-room hotel and restaurant on the premises of a thirteenth-century monastery. Local gourmets flock here for sophisticated Tuscan cuisine. Breakfast and drinks are served by a well in the cloister garden.

Hotel Tenuta di Ricavo (Castellina in Chianti/+39 0577 740 221/ricavo.com). Lovely gardens and two swimming pools at a farmstead inn, with pleasant walks in the area. The restaurant is a good place to sample regional wines and dishes, such as *ribollita,* a thick vegetable soup served over slices of toasted bread.

Villa Belvedere (Via Senese, Colle di Val d'Elsa/+39 0577 920 966/villabelvedere.com). A seventeenth-century villa, with fifteen rooms, overlooking a formal Italian garden. The food extends beyond the Tuscan basics, and in summer, meals are served in the garden with views of San Gimignano. Lake fishing, riding, and tennis in the vicinity.

Hotel Villa La Montagnola (Via della Montagnola 110–12, Strada in Chianti/+39 055 858 485). No-frills accommodations in a prime location.

Villa Le Barone (Via San Leolino 19, Panzano in Chianti/+39 055 852 621/villalebarone.com). A sixteenth-century villa surrounded by parkland, olive groves, and vineyards. Pool on the grounds and tennis and golf nearby. Breakfast is served on a terrace.

Villa Sangiovese (Piazza G Bucciarelli 5, Panzano in Chianti/+39 055 852 461/villasangiovese.it). A Swiss-German couple, who have lived in Italy for years, run this simple shipshape hotel with terra-cotta tiled floors and beds under beamed ceilings. An Italian cook is in residence, and tables are set on an enclosed courtyard during the summer.

Villa Scacciapensieri (Strada di Scacciapensieri 10, Siena/+39 0577 41 441/villascacciapensieri.it). Located in the countryside just north of Siena, this eighteenth-century villa has formal gardens with clipped hedges, a pool, and tennis court.

Villa Vignamaggio (Via Petriolo 5, Greve in Chianti/+39 055 854 661/vignamaggio.com). Doubles, villa apartments, house for two, cottage for four. The setting for Kenneth Branagh's *Much Ado About Nothing,* this estate has guest rooms and apartments in the villa, as well as two small houses and a cottage on the grounds. There's a tennis court, a pool, and a glorious garden.

Villas

The following agencies will help you find a house or apartment rental in Italy. Most are affiliated with Italian companies and issue catalogs of properties that range from cottages to estates. Inquire about rates, but note that they decrease by as much as 45 percent during off-season. Radda in Chianti, Castellina in Chianti, and Gaiole in Chianti are particularly charming locales.

At Home Abroad, New York (212 421 9165/athomeabroadinc .com).

Italian Rentals, Washington, D.C. (202 237 5111/italrentals.com).

Vacanza Bella, San Francisco (415 554 0234/vbella.com/daniel @vbella.com).

Vacanze in Italia, Great Barrington, MA (800 533 5405 or 413 528 6610/homeabroad.com).

Restaurants

Badia a Coltibuono (Gaiole in Chianti/+39 0577 749 498). This first-rate trattoria has wonderful views of the abbey of San Lorenzo. During the summer, tables are set up in a courtyard. The excellent wine is from the nearby estate of Badia a Coltibuono.

Borgo Antico (Via Case Sparse 115, Lucolena/+39 0550 851 024). Fresh pasta is the thing to order here. There's also satisfying grilled pork and chicken.

Da Antonio (Via Fiorita 40, Castelnuovo Berardenga/+39 0577 355 321). The place in Chianti for fresh fish. Everything is impeccably prepared, from the seafood hors d'oeuvres to the charbroiled red snapper.

Da Padellina (Corso del Popolo 54, Strada in Chianti/+39 0550 858 388). The dining room may be uninspiring, but the kitchen turns out wonderful Chianti cuisine: charbroiled T-bone steak, white beans, *ribollita,* and *pappa al pomodoro* (a summer soup).

Il Papavero (Barbischio/+39 0577 749 063). No credit cards. One of the few restaurants where you won't be expected to order a three-course meal. This is a nice spot for a light evening meal of *panzanella* (a tomato-based soup made with bread) and a *salame* sandwich.

Cafés

Bar Italia (Piazza Buondelmonti, Impruneta/+39 0550 201 1046). This is a classic stand-up coffee bar. In the summer there are a few tables on the sidewalk. The gelato is especially good (the hazelnut and the coffee are favorites); so is the tiramisu.

Caffè Le Logge (Piazza Matteotti, Greve in Chianti/+39 0550 853 038). A café with wooden benches and marble tables, where locals go for a cappuccino or a glass of wine and a sandwich.

Caffè Lepanto (Piazza Matteotti, Greve in Chianti/+39 0550 853 040). The other café in Greve attracts tourists, who come for the views of the square, and children, who come for the staggering selection of gelato. The newsstand next door carries the area's largest assortment of foreign-language newspapers, magazines, and guidebooks.

Shopping

If you're planning to spend some time in the area, here's where to stock your kitchen, Chiantigiana style.

GROCERIES

Alimentari Piccini (Via Mazzini, Impruneta). Recommended for basic staples, as well as olives, fresh pasta (including potato gnocchi), and cheeses. Piccini's delicious locally made ricotta should be mixed with black currant jam and eaten as a dessert.

La Martellina (Via della Montagnola 39, Martellina/+39 0550 858 051). On the main road between Impruneta and Strada in Chianti, this general food store is notable for its cold cuts, such as *finocchiona* (a soft *salame* flavored with fennel seeds), pecorino cheese, and breads. The restaurant in back has a terrace overlooking the hills.

MARKETS

Fruit and vegetables, canvas shoes, cotton sheets and tablecloths, and vats of anchovies. Hours: about eight a.m. to two p.m. **Impruneta,** Piazza Buondelmonti, Saturday. **Strada in Chianti,** Piazza del Mercato, Tuesday. **Greve in Chianti,** on the piazza, Saturday. All of these markets are open year-round.

MEAT

Antica Macelleria Falorni (Piazza Matteotti 69, Greve in Chianti/ +39 0550 858 039). A renowned establishment, grander and more commercial than Secci. A highlight is the array of *prosciutti: crudo dolce* comes from the north and is sweet; *crudo nostrano,* the salty, hard local variety, goes well with unsalted Tuscan bread. Falorni also has perfect round thin slivers of *bresaola,* a sliced dried beef that, like carpaccio, is served with oil, lemon, and pepper.

Secci (Borgo Baldassare Paoli 1, Strada in Chianti/+39 0550 858 039). Like his father before him, Pier Francesco Secci is the best butcher in the area, especially for Florentine T-bone steak and rabbit.

BREAD

Falciani (Via Cassia 245, Falciani/+39 0550 202 0091). This bakery makes traditional thick-crusted Tuscan bread, which Chiantigiani prefer to eat when it's a day old. In August and September, look for *schiacciata all'uva,* a sort of sweet focaccia covered with grapes.

VEGETABLES

Donatella (Strada in Chianti). Next to Secci, the butcher, this Strada shop sells *verza* (the Savoy cabbage for making *ribollita*), tomatoes, white beans, and zucchini flowers, which, dipped in batter and lightly sautéed, make a wonderful appetizer. Fresh porcini mushrooms are always in supply after a rain.

TERRA-COTTA

Chianti is famous for its pots, tiles, and olive oil urns. These shops sell pieces straight from the kiln.

La Fornace Manetti (Via del Ferrone 50A, Impruneta/+39 0550 850 631).

Urbano Fontana E Figlio (Castellina in Chianti/+39 0577 740 340).

WINE AND OIL

Most towns in Chianti have an *enoteca*—a liquor store stocked with local wines (which can be sampled) and olive oil. Take note: Vineyards sell their own products at 30 to 40 percent less than *enoteca* prices.

Best Books

The House of Medici: Its Rise and Fall, Christopher Hibbert (William Morrow, 1975). This chronicle of the Florentine banking family from obscurity to preeminence as art patrons and power brokers, and then its inglorious descent, exemplifies the best in popular history.

Philip's Travel Guides: Tuscany, Jonathan Keates, with photographs by Charlie Waite (George Philip, London, Scribner, 1991). Dazzling color images capture the attractions of the area while the text explores its culture and past.

Tuscany and Umbria, Dana Facaros and Michael Pauls (Cadogan Guides). An exceptional combination of sightseeing and practical information. Detailed maps, paths to hidden cultural treasures, and tips on finding local delicacies round out the best book on the region.

On Screen

Much Ado About Nothing. The Chianti countryside never looked lovelier than in Kenneth Branagh's enchanting version of Shakespeare's comedy.

Lucca
A Tuscan Treasure

LORRAINE ALEXANDER

❧

LUCCA IS NOT always included on visitors' grand tour of Tuscany, which I suppose is because it is not the home of a great many art masterpieces or museums. Its impressive walls, however, are alone worth a detour, and I would indeed refer to the town itself as a treasure.

LORRAINE ALEXANDER wrote for many years for *Gourmet*, where this piece originally appeared, in 1996, and she has also contributed to *Saveur* and the *New York Times*.

RECENTLY A FRIEND from out of town was staying with me for a couple of days and began leafing through a book of photographs of Lucca. "Now this," she said with sudden feeling, "looks exactly the way Italy is *supposed* to look."

If there is something inherently convincing about going straight to the center of an issue, then Lucca's nomination as Italy-writ-small is only bolstered by its location in a quiet corner of Tuscany, the country's geographic and historic bull's-eye. Meanwhile Lucca itself is so self-effacingly off-center that tourists, wearing the topsoil thin between Florence and Siena, barely know it exists. (Opera lovers may be the exception, for Lucca was Giacomo Puccini's native city.) Taken as a whole, this ironic situation is, for the resident and traveler alike, equivalent to having your *torta* and eating it, too.

Lucca has never eluded attention entirely, of course. With the sea to the west and mountains to the north, it was Julius Caesar's favorite winter resort (marshland to the south toward Pisa—which is why the Leaning Tower leans—made it undesirable in summer). One of Tolstoy's characters in *War and Peace* mentions Lucca, however briefly ("*Eh bien, mon prince,* so Genoa and Lucca are now no more than private estates of the Bonaparte family"). The writer who really "discovered" Lucca, though, was the brilliant, eccentric art critic and social reformer John Ruskin, initially traveling there in 1845. He would return a half dozen times, but it was this first trip that set his course.

> Here in Lucca I found myself suddenly in the presence of twelfth-century buildings . . . so incorruptible that, after 600 years of sunshine and rain, a lancet could not now be put between their joins . . . I took the simplest of façades for analysis . . . and thereon literally began the study of architecture.

Ruskin eventually became associated more with Venice than with Lucca, just as Henry James, who admired Lucca's "charming mixture of antique character and modern inconsequence," wrote mostly about Rome and Florence in his *Italian Hours*. Still, even James fell under her spell: "I remember saying to myself . . . that no brown-and-gold Tuscan city could *be* as happy as Lucca looked . . . [seeming] fairly to laugh."

Not that the city hasn't had to withstand difficult times in the usual way of history. Her advantage was really that during the Middle Ages, when the growing pains of Tuscany's other city-states were ending in seizures of villainy and violence, Lucca concentrated on trade with northern Europe and used her wealth wisely, once purchasing ninety years of peace from the pope's functionaries for two thousand gold pieces. Profits from silk, wool, and banking financed expansion of Lucca's defensive wall and employment for stonemasons and sculptors as they built—or rebuilt on ancient sites—her finest churches.

By the time Napoleon arrived in 1805, Lucca was edging up to her "modern inconsequence," and the new emperor, his attention fixed more in the vicinity of Lord Nelson, gave the city to his sister Elisa, who set about widening the streets and adding neo-classical touches to Piazza Napoleone. When Marie Louise de Bourbon was given Lucca by the Congress of Vienna, she, perhaps not to be outdone, planted double rows of horse chestnut trees along its wall, creating two and a half miles of what James called a "circular lounging-place of a splendid dignity." Today the wall's garden path is where the fortunate Lucchesi take their evening *passeggiata,* and the churches where they worship and make *musica lirica* comprise one of Italy's great concentrations of Romanesque architecture.

🦁   🦁   🦁

The handful of hotels inside the city wall are relentlessly ordinary, perhaps because Lucca is so precisely not on the tourist track, and for this reason visitors often prefer to make their base in the near countryside. To the west, on the way to Puccini's villa at Torre del Lago and the popular beach resort of Viareggio, is Villa Casanova, the chief attributes of which are the view from its tree-shaded terrace of Castello di Nozzano's crenellated tower; the modest price; and the main house itself, "roomy and stony, as an Italian villa should be," in the words of James. In the converted fieldworkers' dwellings, rooms are smaller, sparer, but equally—and not unpleasantly—evocative of past centuries' rural life. Do have dinner elsewhere, however; this is not the Tuscan table to write home about.

To the south of town is a cluster of grander houses converted to hotels. The newest and prettiest by far is the ten-room Locanda l'Elisa, a mauve and white villa that, glimpsed through its surrounding greenery, looks like a debutante who's strayed from the ballroom into the conservatory. The rooms are cocoons of sumptuous fabrics, and the elegant glassed-in Gazebo restaurant brings the garden indoors to complement chef Antonio Sanna's cuisine, the most refined of the region.

Across from the Elisa is the parent Villa La Principessa, an impressive house, with loggias giving into parkland, that was originally built by the general who saved Lucca from the Pisans in the fourteenth century (and, some say, was Machiavelli's model prince). The main salon is ornate—coffered ceiling, enormous stone fireplace, and handsome circa 1750 console made in Lucca—but it can seem a battlefield of dueling decoration as the plaid carpet squares off against the floral wallcovering. The unusual décor takes another twist in the guest rooms; ours was spacious, comfortable, and electric blue from bedspread to baseboard.

Villa San Michele once belonged to a Luccan prior, and if you imagine him as I did—with a weakness for intrigue and old *vin santo*—the Rococo reception room looks the perfect set piece. Our room was a tight fit (the one to try for, number 109, has a *baldacchino* bed and a window aimed straight at Lucca's medieval towers), but from its tiny balcony I could see the sun rise to wake the swallows and filter through the villa's somewhat neglected olive grove, at that hour still touched by a silvery dignity.

Other countryside options for lodging, ones that bring opportunities for a closer experience of both people and place, are Fattoria Villa Maionchi and Tenuta di Valgiano, both *agriturismi* (farms with tourist lodgings) in the beautiful olive- and vine-planted hills to Lucca's northeast. The owners live in the "big house," while guests stay in the former fieldworkers' stone quarters, which come with kitchens and most of the comforts and quirks of home. Maria Maionchi and Roberto Palagi offer, in addition, umbrellaed garden tables and tubs of flowers, the charms of their pet donkey (an enchantment for children), and a friendliness that is at the heart of "farm vacations." The excellent

Maionchi wines and olive oil can, of course, be purchased by guests and passersby alike. This is the case, too, at Valgiano, where Laura di Collobiano and Moreno Petrini rent out the four apartments that sit atop their wine cellars. Spread over the estate's 260 acres are three thousand olive trees, their rows stitching the hillsides, and up near the guests' lodgings a swimming pool has been added. When I visited, Laura, Moreno, and winemaker Saverio Petrilli were bottling their white Giallo dei Muri '94, and last fall Valgiano's was one of only three Tuscan olive oils honored by the World Olive Conference from a field of a hundred.

The one night I spent in town, to attend a late jazz concert in Lucca's Roman-era *anfiteatro,* I chose the Universo, where, having read that Ruskin had favored it, I hoped to find an art-historical cobweb or two. Only the reception area hinted nostalgically at the long ago, but here-and-now amenities included CNN, wake-up calls, and a porter who was not someone's grandmother. Location is a plus, too: across from the Teatro del Giglio, where Rossini's *William Tell* overture premiered in 1831 and Lucca's opera season unfolds each September; and one piazza away from San Martino, the city's cathedral.

🎋   🎋   🎋

As you enter Lucca's narrow streets, you will find yourself tracing a pleasant grid (the Roman plan survives) of cobblestoned streets broadening here and there into piazzas, most of which are named for the churches that dominate them. Roman columns (removed from the amphitheater) punctuate San Frediano's nave, though nothing inside compares, for effect, with the magnificent gold-grounded Ascension mosaic spread over the top third of the twelfth-century church's otherwise plain façade. Unless, that is, you count the mummified remains of Saint Zita, patron saint of servants, which nearly sent me spinning for the exit. But, as creepy as her glass cubicle is, her legend of food smuggled to the poor and miraculously transformed into flowers so that she might escape detection by her masters is touchingly evoked each April 26, when flowers are brought to fill the piazza in her honor.

At Piazza San Giusto you can stop by the café across from the church for housemade frozen yogurt or, on Saturday mornings, rummage through the crafts/flea market, which leads around San Giusto to tables of books and finally, facing Via Beccheria, a permanent stall of Pucciniana: sheet music, libretti, and sepia photos of the maestro. For me this cache was irresistible, especially the glimpses of Puccini-at-play, debonair in his roadster, at the wheel of a speedboat, and hoisted on the shoulders of his hunting pals.

Reminders of Puccini are around every corner, nowhere more so than at San Martino. Appointment as cathedral organist was an honor handed down in an unbroken line from Giacomo, Sr. (1722–81) to "our" Giacomo (1858–1924), when he was six, and held for him in trust by an uncle. The church's façade, a masterpiece of carved marble; a strikingly Mannerist *Last Supper* by Tintoretto; even the relic of the Holy Countenance, supposedly modeled by Nicodemus immediately after the Crucifixion, though this one is an eleventh-century copy, are no more significant to many Lucchesi than the double organ on which those generations of Puccinis played. The sole exception might be the exquisite tomb of Ilaria del Carretto, sculpted by the Sienese Jacopo della Quercia, which Ruskin called "the loveliest Christian tomb in Italy." On my last visit it was *in restauro,* but perhaps you'll be luckier, for this is no formulaic sepulchral stone; seek it out for Ilaria's serene beauty, and for the adoring dog at her feet.

The church in Lucca I return to first and last is inevitably San Michele in Foro (its adjacent piazza was the site of the Roman forum), at the very center of town now, as then. This fact alone is worth a moment's pause, used as we are to ever-altering urban plans. In Lucca, though, the wall has kept things orderly—and growth outside its bounds—so that when present-day Lucchesi buy flowers at the piazza's stalls or step into Farmacia Massagli for a sip of *china* (pronounced *kee*-na, the Italian word for quinine), the city's specialty herbal liqueur, they are walking with similar purpose literally in the footsteps of their ancestors.

San Michele, begun in 1070, is most famous for its remarkable façade, the base a strictly Romanesque series of rounded blind arches, above which rise four levels of intricately carved pillared galleries. This delicate elaboration distinguishes the church (and its contemporary, San Martino) as Pisan-Romanesque, after the cathedral complex only twenty miles south, which embodies so gloriously the late medieval Tuscan desire to balance weight with grace and decorative innovation. By the time Ruskin happened upon San Michele the marble sculptures and intarsia were "in such a state of abandon that I felt obliged to draw them if only for fear that they would soon disappear." Restoration began in the 1860s, with heroes of the Risorgimento, including the anticlerical Garibaldi, replacing the antique elements that are now displayed at Lucca's Museo Nazionale at Villa Guinigi.

San Michele's interior is as somber as the exterior is joyous. There is a beautiful painting of four saints by Filippino Lippi and a Madonna and Child medallion by Andrea della Robbia. But, if you must choose between inside and out, consider spending a quiet half hour before that magnificent façade—perhaps to sketch as Ruskin did, or just to imagine Giacomo Puccini, as a boy, making his way down Via di Poggio to choir practice there and then, years later, composing the choirboys' Te Deum for *Tosca*.

The obvious next step is to accompany young Giacomo back along that single block from San Michele to his childhood home, today's Casa Puccini museum. Here you will find the family tree of Lucca's great musical dynasty; letters and original scores; photographs and portraits (including one of an ancestor who surely married for love and not the name when she became Angela Maria Piccinini Puccini); and drawings of costumes and sets. There is also the Steinway on which Puccini composed *Turandot*, his final opera—unfinished at the time of his death, in fact, but completed by one of his pupils.

Anyone as intrigued as I was by the Casa will want to make the detour to nearby Torre del Lago, where Puccini's lakeside villa was built after his first popular success, *Manon Lescaut* (1893), mainly to indulge his passion for duck hunting. The house contains some Liberty touches, thanks to Puccini's friendship with Galileo Chini, who was Italy's leading exponent of Art Nouveau—and later designed the exotic sets for *Turandot*. The mosaic floor and fireplace tiles in the sitting room are Chini's work, and when sun shines through the colored glass of the doors and windows, the room fairly glows. Its focal point is the simple upright piano on which Puccini wrote the music for nine of his twelve operas, among them *La Bohème, Tosca, Madama Butterfly,* and *Turandot*. Preferring to spend his days hunting on the lake and socializing in Lucca or Viareggio, he composed through the night, having fitted the piano with dampers to avoid disturbing his household.

In some ways, though, as our guide recounted with spirited affection, the family was quite regularly disturbed, in particular by Puccini's (inordinate, in his wife's view) love of women. Puccini's life does seem to have been marked by tragic overtones worthy of, well, grand opera. Restless after years of living with Elvira—mother of his only child but still married to someone else—the composer was about to run away with a singer when he wrecked his car on the road to Lucca and was taken home ("Where *else* can you go when you're not well?" pleaded our guide, every syllable weighted with the subtext of destiny) to Elvira . . . whose husband had died that very day, freeing her to marry the stunned maestro. Which is what happened.

We were all hanging on our guide's every word by now, but the most dramatic hush descended when he moved to his next subject: "The big problem of Puccini was without doubt [not his love life but] his smoking—sixty to seventy cigarettes a day." He died at sixty-six, before anyone knew the dangers, of course, from throat cancer.

Finally came the moment just before the curtain is lowered.

Did any of us know, we were asked, Puccini's last words, scribbled in pencil on a scrap of paper (and displayed at the villa)? It was as if Butterfly were about to disappear behind her screen, as if we could hear Scarpia's firing squad climbing the castle steps. *"Elvira, povera donna, finita."* (Elvira, poor lady, it's finished.) Nothing could be more affecting, and, though the visit is conducted in Italian, it may hardly matter if you don't speak the language—you will understand a great deal by simply walking through the villa's rooms and catching your guide's inflections.

A half day at Torre del Lago can be completed by an excursion on Lake Massaciuccoli or a gelato at Ristorante Antonio, where Antonio's brother, Sergio, has his own Puccini collection. I discovered this quite by accident when I noticed, above the bar, the program for the New York premiere of *Madama Butterfly,* February 11, 1907, with Enrico Caruso as Pinkerton. "If you wish, I have more about Puccini," said Sergio somewhat timidly before showing me to a back dining room where, lovingly preserved, were drawings of the costumes from *Manon Lescaut,* among other memorabilia. Before leaving Torre, you may want to consult the program for July's Puccini Festival, part of which takes place at Torre's open-air theater.

🐝   🐝   🐝

Lucca's charms do not exist in isolation, and striking out in any direction inevitably means stumbling upon some treasure. A short drive northeast into the hills toward Tofori is Villa Torrigiani, once the home of Lucca's ambassador to the court of Louis XIV. Restored in the Baroque style beginning in the 1660s, the villa boasts fine frescoes and furnishings but is most famous for its Le Nôtre designed gardens and, not least, the fountains' water games, which have become a tradition and which the present count still delights in setting in motion—just as he did as a child when the Duke of Windsor came to call . . . and, startled by a sudden spouting, landed, linen suit and all, in the mud. The villa's façade is as busy as its owner, but with statues rather than pranks, as if an entire house party decided long ago to stay on, perpetually roaming the balustrades and ducking into the niches.

To prolong a pleasant day in the country, a particularly satisfying plan might include a meal at La Mora, where Angela Brunicardi and her mother-in-law, Assunta, cook such local fare as citrus-sauced salmon trout (fresh from the Serchio, which flows nearby) and lamb chops with artichokes. Fattoria Maionchi's luscious red Cintello, a blend of Sangiovese and Canaiolo grapes aged in Luccan chestnut, accompanies both the fish and meat perfectly.

If you haven't a car or simply prefer to inhabit the spell within Lucca's wall, try not to miss Palazzo Mansi's frescoed ballroom and sumptuous "bridal chamber," every inch covered in golden Luccan silk. Or you may choose to sip something cool and people-watch in late afternoon sun at the café across from San Paolino, where Puccini's first composition, "Mass for Four Voices," premiered in 1881. Should you stop by Panificio Chifenti, on the same street, for a slice of Lucca's specialty vegetable tart with "birds' beaks" (for the pastry points decorating the crust), you'll recognize the two owners, sisters with silver hair in shining marcelle waves, as the *nonne* of your dreams.

And finally—or firstly—there is Lucca's astonishing Guinigi Tower. Broad, shallow steps lead to its roof garden, a shaded nest beneath which the city extends: plains of tile roofs, stonemasons' plots cultivated nearly a millennium ago; ancient streets, dark as old mortar; the massive wall, proud and blossoming; and, at every turn, Lucca herself, still laughing.

DINING WITHIN LUCCA'S WALL

Lucca lies in a fertile plain, reclaimed centuries ago from swampland and given over to the cultivation of *cereali* (grains). Within the city's wall the best menus reflect this, and none more authentically than Da Giulio in Pelleria, on the site of a former tannery, where first-course pastas and *ribollita,* the bread soup found else-where in Tuscany, are supplanted by thick, grain-based dishes. Such characteristic, unfussy food is exemplified by this popular restaurant's hearty, delicious *farinata* (cornmeal cooked with veg-etables).

For excellent seafood in sophisticated surroundings, lunch might be scheduled at Puccini, across from Casa Puccini. The *fritto misto alla retina* ("from the fisherman's net") is noteworthy not only for its shrimp and mullet but also for the light-as-air bat-ter. *Branzino al cartoccio* (sea bass in a foil envelope), boned at table, is perfection for the purist. For such exemplary fish a wine equal to the task was Fattoria del Buonamico's Vasario '93, named for the author of *Lives of the Artists.*

Too-strong salt cod at the Buca di Sant'Antonio was, on the other hand, disappointing, but the *farro,* combining spelt, vegeta-bles, and cranberry beans; salmon trout "carpaccio" on arugula with only salt, pepper, and Lucca's renowned olive oil; and *tordelli lucchesi* (meat-stuffed and -sauced pasta) were splendid, especially with Fattoria Maionchi's 1994 red. Such dishes and the cozy at-mosphere—copper hung from the ceiling, lamps and bouquets on the tables—make this restaurant a favorite among Lucchesi for special occasions, and you may well see a wedding or confirma-tion party convening here, as it is only steps from San Michele.

On the street behind San Michele, by the way, is the Antica Botega di Prospero—sacks of rice, beans, and pastas propped against the walls; dried mushrooms and figs, nuts and oils on the shelves—a shop that is a window into Lucca's agricultural and culinary life. Also nearby, on Via Fillungo, the main shopping street, is Caffè di Simo, an Art Nouveau gem. This, Puccini's pre-ferred café, was before and after him a gathering place for artists and litterati, among them the Nobel-honored poets Carducci and Quasimodo.

Other possibilities for casual meals—with greater selection—are Gli Orti di Via Elisa and Il Tabarro, the former a cheery neighborhood place near Via del Fosso (what remains of the Roman moat). Lunch offerings include a salad bar, especially good *polpette* (meatballs, called *porpette* in Lucca), a cold plate of fava beans with shrimp, and a "Tuscan milk shake" of gelato, red fruits, and grappa. Il Tabarro, named for a lesser-known Puccini opera, is a restaurant-pizzeria at Piazza del Giglio, where students stand around en masse on Friday nights. When we asked what the draw was, the chef said good-naturedly, "They come to the piazza to talk, just to talk. That's what we do in Italy," and, with that and a gesture worthy of the Giglio theater's stage, he ushered us inside for the best spaghetti (*al raddicchio*) of our trip.

Finally, a restaurant actually *on* Lucca's wall is the Antico Caffè delle Mura, a monument to the Belle Epoque good life. Salads here are noteworthy, and the calf's liver in red wine sauce with pears was excellent, but the most memorable dish of all was *tordelli scuri* (meat-filled pasta made with unsweetened cocoa—an idea as old as the Renaissance—in cream sauce). A *dolce* worth scaling the wall for is *panna cotta al caffè*, a coffee custard under a delicately crisp glaze.

Hotels

Albergo Villa Casanova (Via di Casanova 1600, Lucca/+39 0583 36g 000/albergocasanova.com).

Fattoria Villa Maionchi (Località Tofori, San Gennaro, Lucca/+39 0583 978 194/fattoriamaionchi.it).

Locanda l'Elisa (Via Nuova per Pisa 1952, Massa Pisana, Lucca/+39 0583 379 737/locandalelisa.it).

Tenuta di Valgiano (Via di Valgiano 13, Valgiano, Lucca/+39 0583 402 271/valgiano.it).

Villa La Principessa (Via Nuova per Pisa 1616, Massa Pisana, Lucca/+39 0583 370 037/hotelprincipessa.com).

Siena in Three Acts

WILLIAM ZINSSER

"I HAD ALWAYS believed, and continue to believe, really, that there is no more beautiful square in the world than the one in Siena." Those are the words of Gabriel García Márquez, from his work "Watching the Rain in Galicia." The fact that he continues on to say that the only place that made him doubt that statement was the plaza in Santiago de Compostela is irrelevant: one is allowed to feel that more than one public place is not only beautiful but extraordinary, as I believe Siena's Piazza del Campo to be.

Only a little over an hour from Florence, Siena is perceived by some visitors as merely a day trip. I think this is a mistake, as Siena and its surrounding countryside are worthy of much more than a day (walking around the Campo and looking at the paintings by Ambrogio Lorenzetti and Simone Martini in the Museo Civico easily occupy a full day for me). It is unlikely that many of us can claim as personal an odyssey with Siena as the author of this piece, but we can at least agree that Siena is one of the most exceptional places in the world.

WILLIAM ZINSSER is a writer, editor, and teacher, and began his long career with the *New York Herald Tribune*. He taught writing at Yale, and from 1979 to 1987 he was general editor of the Book-of-the-Month Club. Zinsser is also the author of more than a dozen books, including *On Writing Well* (HarperCollins, 2006, thirtieth anniversary edition), *Writing to Learn* (Harper & Row, 1988), *Easy to Remember: The Great American Songwriters and Their Songs* (David Godine, 2001), *Spring Training* (Harper & Row, 1989), *American Places: A Writer's Pilgrimage to Sixteen of This Country's Most Visited and Cherished Sites* (Paul Dry, 2007), and, most recently, *Writing Places: The Life Journey of a Writer and Teacher* (HarperCollins, 2009). In this last work, Zinsser won a place in my heart forever when he explains that he does not use e-mail, because he doesn't need it in his work and he doesn't want to be its captive. " 'But how can I *reach* you?' friends say. Their tone suggests that I have entered a Trappist monastery." He suggests they give him a call, as he enjoys "the human pulse of a phone conversation." His final words in the book are worth repeating a thousand times over: "And yet, stuck with my traditional skills, I'm not feeling obsolete. Language is still king, writing still the supreme conveyor of thoughts and ideas and memories and emotions. Somebody will have to *write* all those Web sites and blogs and video scripts and audio scripts; nobody wants to consult a Web site that's not clear and coherent. Whatever new technology may come along, writers will continue to write, going wherever their curiosities and affections beckon. That can make an interesting life."

IN EARLY MAY of 1945 my army unit was stationed in an Italian seaside town south of Leghorn. World War II was ebbing to a close, and talk of Germany's surrender was in the air. For GIs like us, far behind the lines, there was nothing to do. I remember that we played a lot of baseball. I also remember that I kept hearing about a town called Siena, two or three hours' drive away. It

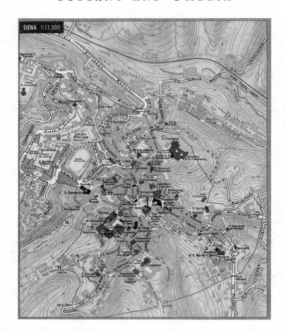

was one of those names that travelers listen for, like Kyoto or Fez, and I persuaded three of my friends—we were all sergeants—that we should try to go see it. We got permission to take a company jeep for one day, and on the morning of May 7 we set out.

The gravel road left the coast and climbed across a landscape of hills and farms and brought us to Volterra, an old Etruscan town, hunched like a fortress on a hilltop. It was famous for its alabaster, and with the fervor of all tourists coming upon a local specialty of unsuspected beauty, we bought alabaster cigarette boxes and ash-trays for our unsuspecting families back home. The ancient city held us with its power, and it was midday before we pushed on. Later, far off to the left, we saw a sight so fanciful, an illustration from a child's fairy tale, that I thought if I blinked it would go away. It was a cluster of stone towers rising out of a village on a hill. After the war I would learn that it was San Gimignano, a relic of the many Tuscan towns that once had such towers, built for defense and long since fallen down. But on that afternoon it was only a teasing apparition; there was no time to go chasing mirages.

If San Gimignano was the perfect miniature, Siena was the master painting. Announcing itself to us from a distance, it looked both proud and playful, arrayed across three hills and sprawling down the sides, all contained within a medieval wall. Bestriding the city from its highest ridge was an immense white cathedral. Inside, I was struck by the city's remarkable harmony. The prevailing color was pale red brick, the prevailing architecture was Gothic, and the geometry was uniformly random: all curves and inclines. Yet such was Siena's gravitational logic that the streets from all three hills funneled down into one large public square, the Piazza del Campo.

It was the most beautiful square I had ever seen, partly because it wasn't square; it was shaped like an open fan. Anchoring the Campo was the handsome Palazzo Pubblico, or city hall, built around 1300, which had a bell tower so slender and audacious, so much taller than anyone would expect, that it set a tone of high civic enjoyment. The square sloped upward, and all the buildings around its rim were consistent in their height and sensibility. It was a collective work of art, and we sat at an outdoor café and had lunch, our goal achieved, hardly believing our good luck.

The square had the serenity of well-proportioned space, but it was also alive with people; obviously it had always been the emotional center of Sienese life. At that time I hadn't even heard of its most famous event, the horse race called the Palio, held every summer since 1659 amid much medieval pageantry and hysteria. The nags that clomp around the perimeter of the Campo represent Siena's contentious political districts, and the event takes its passion from the fact that it's much more than a horse race. It's a ritual acting out of an arcane system of municipal governance by seventeen highly territorial tribes.

After lunch we walked up to the cathedral, which, along with a jaunty striped campanile, regally occupied the city's high ground. But nothing about the exterior of the church prepared me for its interior. All I could think when I stepped inside was, "How wonderful!" I was amazed that an isolated Italian town in the early 1200s had found the energy to raise such an exuberant house of God. The nave was a fantasia of zebra stripes—alternating bands of black and white marble that formed not only the walls of the church but two rows of massive columns, which supported two rows of Romanesque arches, which supported two higher rows of Gothic arches and windows, which in turn supported a blue ceiling with gold stars and a vaulted dome. Other wonders gradually revealed themselves: a mosaic floor that covered the entire area of the church, a superb marble pulpit by Nicola Pisano, a haunting *Saint John the Baptist* by Donatello, and a profusion of other works tucked into every niche. From there we went next door to a small museum, where Siena sprang its final marvel on me: Duccio's group of small paintings of the life of Christ that had been part of the duomo's original altarpiece.

All those Duccios completed our crash course in Sienese art, and we began to think about heading back. Just then we noticed a stone stairway that a guard said would take us to a panoramic view. The museum, it turned out, was housed within the walls of a new nave that the city started adding to the cathedral in 1339 but had to abandon, and our stairs, spiraling up and up, deposited us on top of its unfinished façade. From that catwalk we could look down on the entire city. The time was around four-twenty. I remember that it wasn't on the hour or the half hour, because we were startled when the bells in the campanile began to ring. It was a jubilant, spread-the-news kind of ringing, and suddenly it dawned on us what news was being spread. The war was over!

Below us the city exploded into life. Men and women and children came running from every direction down the streets that emptied into the Campo. We scrambled down to join them. The square was a shifting sea of happy people, and it already had an air of pageantry—heraldic banners were hanging from the windows of the Palazzo Pubblico. We seemed to be the only Allied soldiers there; Siena had been skirted by the retreating and pursuing armies, and whatever troops may have once been stationed in the city were gone. Later it occurred to me that all four of us had German names: Helmuth Gerbich, Herbert Myers, William Schramm, and William Zinsser.

Now, seeing four GIs, the people of Siena hugged us and shouted "*Viva America!*" and lifted us onto their shoulders and carried us around the square. We didn't feel like conquering heroes—none of us had seen combat. But we had lived with the smashed towns and smashed lives that were the residue of that bloody campaign up the Italian peninsula, and on behalf of its real heroes we acted as happy as we felt, bobbing above the crowd. Darkness had fallen by the time we got back to our jeep. But we weren't allowed to leave; little bands of musicians and revelers kept falling in ahead of us and behind us as we inched our way through the crowded streets. Finally we broke away, reached a gate through the wall, and found our road to the coast.

The night was black and the countryside was asleep. But the villages were awake, and when the people heard our jeep they ran out to shout "*Viva la pace!*" One old man handed a bottle of Chianti into our jeep and we all joined him in a drink. At one point we saw a bonfire on a hill far ahead. Eventually our road took us past that bonfire, which was being tended by some farmers, and from there we could see another bonfire on another hill, and when we reached that bonfire we saw still another one, far away. Only after three or four bonfires did we make the connection: the country people were spreading the news. Many hills later, around midnight, we got back to our base. The next morning we learned that nobody else had been allowed off the base. When the end of the war was announced on Armed Forces Radio, all passes were suspended.

But that wasn't the end of Siena in my life. After V-E Day the army faced the problem of keeping its men occupied, not having enough troopships to bring us home. As one solution, it started a college in Florence, recruiting its faculty from officers and enlisted men who had been teachers in civilian life. My unit had moved back to a dismal region of southern Italy; months of tedium stretched out ahead of us. One day I saw in the *Stars and Stripes* an item announcing the new college. Only one man per unit would be admitted. Being whisked off to Florence was the ultimate fairy godmother's intervention, and I ran to the adjutant to be the first to apply. My lifelong newspaper-reading habit was rewarded, and on the first of July I went off to college.

Our campus was a former Italian air corps academy just outside Florence. My dormitory window had a perfectly framed view across the red tile roofs to Brunelleschi's soaring cathedral dome and Giotto's campanile. I decided to sign up for art history courses, never having taken any, and they became my passport into the Renaissance. In the morning I could look at slides of Ghiberti's baptistery doors and then go see the doors on my own; our afternoons were free, and we were the only tourists in town. The city had just begun to bring its masterpieces out of hiding, and sometimes I caught one of them being hauled through the streets or hoisted back onto its pedestal—I looked Cellini's *Perseus* in the eye. That summer was a re-Renaissance—art again belonged to the Florentine people, as it had when the statues were first put up. By September the city was in my bones. I found myself dropping in on statues and paintings that had become old friends, or hiking across the Ponte Vecchio—every other bridge across the Arno had been blown up—and climbing up to my favorite church, San Miniato, and my favorite view of Florence, lying below me in the palm of my hand.

When the summer was over I reported to an embarkation depot at Naples to wait for a troopship to take me home. There I had plenty of time to think about returning to civilian life. Everything depended on whether I would have to go back to college. When I left Princeton to enlist in the army I had a grab bag of wartime credits that almost added up to a B.A. degree. Now I had three more credits, which Princeton granted just for serving in the armed forces, plus some certificates for the courses I took at Florence. Originally I had thought I would want to go back to Princeton to round out my fragmented college years. Now I only wanted to get on with whatever I was going to do next.

In November a troopship finally brought me home, and I went to Princeton for an interview. I was nervous as I walked toward Nassau Hall, its walls clothed in two hundred years of historic ivy; the army certificates I was clutching suddenly looked crude. Worst of all, I learned that my interview would be with Dean Root. Robert K. Root, dean of Princeton's faculty and guardian of its academic honor, was then in his late sixties, the prototype old professor: stern and dry and dour. As a sophomore I had taken his lecture course in eighteenth-century English literature and had listened, week after week, as he rained on our unappreciative heads the pearls of his lifelong scholarship, excavating with dry precision the buried ironies of Jonathan Swift and the unsuspected jests of Alexander Pope, which even then we continued not to suspect. It never occurred to me that he and I would ever meet, and I was appalled to be meeting him now. He looked just as stern up close.

Dean Root studied my Princeton transcript and then looked at my army certificates. He said he had never seen anything like them; my impression was that he didn't think I had spent the summer at Oxford. He examined my Princeton transcript again and took another look at the certificates and made some notes. I could see that he was adding up my credits and that they weren't coming out right. He went over his figures one more time. Finally he shook his head and mumbled that I seemed to be a little short. I told myself I was a dead duck.

Then, abruptly, I was no longer being interviewed by a dean.

A real person was sitting across from me, his features not unkindly, and he was asking me what I had done during the war. I found myself talking to him about my year in North Africa and how it had opened my eyes to the Arab world. I told him about my trips to Rome, and about seeing *La Bohème* in the Naples opera house, and about my Renaissance summer in Florence, and about the weekend jaunts I made to Pisa and Lucca and Siena. A clouded look came over Dean Root's face.

"Tell me," he said, "I suppose Siena was mostly destroyed during the war." I realized that I was the first returning veteran to bring him news of the city. Suddenly I understood what Siena would mean to this quintessential humanist; probably he had first visited Siena as a young man himself. Suddenly it was possible to understand that Dean Root had once been a young man. I told him that Siena hadn't been touched by the war and that the great duomo was still there on the crest of the hill.

Dean Root smiled fleetingly and saw me to the door. He said Princeton would inform me of its decision soon. Two weeks later he wrote to say that I had met Princeton's requirements for a B.A. degree and that I could receive my diploma at a special winter graduation for returning servicemen. I was quite sure he had waived one or two credits to make the total add up. In the middle of my interview, I think, he decided to stop counting. Numbers weren't as important to him as learning, and he freed me to get on with my life. But I also think that if Siena had been destroyed I would have had to go back to college for one more term.

🦂   🦂   🦂

In the fall of 1992 I watched the steady approach of my seventieth birthday and wondered how to contend with it when it arrived. Then one day I knew what I wanted to do. "Let's go to Siena for my birthday," I said to Caroline. I would celebrate the day by going back to the place where I spent the most celebratory day of my life. I didn't want to relive that distant moment; I just wanted to make a connection with its emotions—to borrow its essential joy. Whether such emotions were transferable across the decades I wouldn't know until I made the journey.

Over the years I had been back to Tuscany several times, but always as part of a longer trip, not as a destination, and always in summer. Florence was then so swollen with tourists that I could hardly find the city I remembered. But now it was fall, and I made a one-week itinerary that would take Caroline and me to Siena by way of Florence, starting in Rome. There was no question of starting anywhere else. My Italy begins and ends in Rome—and has since I was a schoolboy, when my Latin teacher kept plaster statues of the Roman gods on his desk. He knew that the icons that inhabit the classrooms of our youth can exert a lifelong spell, and in my case he was right. As soon as the war landed me in Italy I fidgeted to see Rome, though I was stationed in far-off Brindisi, in Italy's heel. When I finally wangled a five-day pass I hitchhiked to Rome in a truck, over the Apennines in midwinter, taking two days to get there and two to get back. But the day in between was one I've never forgotten.

Since then I've stopped off in Rome whenever I could. I go to Rome the way other people go to the Bahamas and lie in the sun—to be renewed. Friends try to warn me; the traffic, they say, is "impossible." But it's never any more impossible than it was the last time, and it wasn't impossible when Caroline and I arrived there on a Friday morning in October of 1992. After twenty-four hours of walking all over the city I felt young again.

On Saturday afternoon we took a train to Florence and headed out into the streets to get reacquainted. I was wary, recalling my earlier sense of loss. But the summer hordes were gone, and Florence was no longer their captive. The city had a mercantile bustle, going about its old business. Money was still its lubricant—the shops were elegant and expensive—and the Medicis were still around every corner. I had forgotten what a serious face Florence presents to the world, its color relentlessly brown, its grid flat and rectilinear, its buildings massive in their stonework—just the opposite of gay, red, undulating Siena. No wonder the two medieval city-states, so unalike in temperament, were such enemies for so many centuries.

Now, rediscovering Florence, I felt fresh respect for the city. If it was serious, as many serious people are admirable without necessarily being much fun, it insisted that I take it seriously, and I did. It had the earnest familiarity of an old college roommate. So did the other guests at our hotel: professorial men and tweed-skirted women ensconced under reading lamps. They looked as if they had been coming there every year since the 1920s—sent by, or perhaps invented by, E. M. Forster.

On Sunday my feet took me all over Florence; they still knew the way. Ghiberti's baptistery doors were still "worthy to be the gates of paradise," as Michelangelo described them. His own statue of David in the Galleria dell'Accademia and Giotto's frescoes in the church of Santa Croce were no less worthy, and Fra Angelico's frescoes in the convent of San Marco had lost none of their unassailable purity. Caroline let me follow my inner compass, and when it pointed to San Miniato I warned her that we were in for a climb. Walking across the Ponte Vecchio, I was back in my army boots: left along the Arno, then a right turn, then through the old wall, then up the long penitential steps. San Miniato was waiting for me at the top.

I remembered the church as being so likable, almost toylike in its gaiety and in the daring of its split-level nave—it was begun in 1013—that I was afraid my older self would find it too likable, too ingratiating; my naive soldier self had undoubtedly been seduced by it. But that fear evaporated as soon as I walked in, and when my art-wise wife pronounced it a gem and my guidebook pronounced it "one of the finest Romanesque churches in Italy" I felt that my pilgrimage to Florence was complete, the circle full.

On Monday we rented a car and headed south for Siena, first

stopping at San Gimignano, whose phantom towers had hailed me so long ago. It turned out to be real, a medieval jewel. Beyond it I found the country road my friends and I had taken on the day the war ended, and I followed it toward the coast. But the road hadn't improved much since 1945, and I decided to turn south to Siena.

"I thought this was a return trip," Caroline said. "Keep going to Volterra." I told her that Volterra was quite a push. "I want to see it," she said, and after quite a push we sighted it in the distance, silhouetted on a hill behind its armament of walls. The brooding city held me again, and I was glad I had come—another memory nailed down. When at last we did head for Siena we ran out of daylight and ended up driving in the dark. No bonfires kept us company; in 1992 any news worth spreading would be spread by television. But otherwise I imagined life on those Tuscan farms to be not much different. For the grandchildren of the villagers who cheered our jeep through the night with bottles of Chianti it was probably still 1945.

At Siena our hotel was outside the wall, as most of Siena's hotels are, and we spent Tuesday visiting some of the hill towns, like Pienza and Montepulciano, that give the region its distinctive flavor. I was saving Siena for my birthday, and the next morning Caroline and I went into town. We entered by the Porta Romana and walked up a meandering street that I had no doubt would bring us to the Campo. When it did, the square looked exactly as I remembered it; nothing had changed. I felt a surge of gratitude that such a place existed in my life, always available, no appointment necessary. I strolled over to the restaurant where I wanted to have lunch and reserved an outdoor table for four. Just before leaving New York I had run into old friends, Rosa and Al Silverman. They happened to mention that they would be vacationing in Perugia, and I asked if they would drive over to Siena on October 7 to help us celebrate. They said they would, and we set a rendezvous for one-thirty at the restaurant.

Caroline and I lingered in the Campo, but I could feel the cathedral pulling me up the hill, and I didn't resist. As soon as I stepped inside I thought, "How wonderful!" It, too, was unchanged. We spent an hour marveling and then went to the museum next door to see the Duccios. But I also kept an eye out for my stairway, and when I found it I knew what I had to do. At the summit my view was intact—no postwar buildings, as in London or Paris, impinged on a remembered skyline. Far below, the Campo spread its fan, and I mentally filled it with crowds pouring into it from every direction. Except for the vertigo I felt terrific.

By then it was almost one-thirty, and we made our way back down to the Campo. Rosa and Al were there, and the four of us settled down to an unhurried lunch. As the October sun moved across the sky, the buildings around the Campo turned in subtle gradations from red to rose to pink. In the square, people came and went, meeting and separating. Toddlers played, mothers watched, teenagers lounged, old men and women gossiped. Watching the reality of the Campo, I was struck by how much it meant to me to be with good friends from my own real life. None of us talked about tourist things—where we had been or what sights we had seen. We talked about the same things everyone in the square was talking about: children and grandchildren, food and drink, work and play. Things got said that we hadn't known about each other.

Ordinarily I seek change—it has always been a tonic to me. But on that October 7 in Siena I was at ease, slipping over into my next decade without regret. The connection I had hoped to make was made; the joyful emotions of May 7, 1945, did turn out to be transferable. But mainly I was contented because I was in a place where values that are important to me had endured for a thousand years: the humanity of urban space, the integrity of architecture, the magnificence of Christian art.

Dean Root's rueful question came back to me. The thought

that Siena might have been destroyed seemed unthinkable now, as it hadn't when the dean was old and I was young, home from the war that destroyed so much. Now the continuity of the city mattered just as deeply to me. Siena had survived, and so had I.

RECOMMENDED READING

NONFICTION

The Arts of Tuscany: From the Etruscans to Ferragamo, Marina Belozerskaya (Harry Abrams, 2008). This unique book by art historian Belozerskaya is a journey through a handful of notable Tuscan corners from the perspective of their arts, including Etruscan bronzes and frescoes in Tarquinia and Volterra; Christian architecture in Lucca and Pisa; the marble quarries of Carrara; *quattrocento* Florence; the gardens of Boboli, Castello, and Pratolino; resort architecture in Viareggio and Montecatini; the shoes of Ferragamo; the fashion designs of Emilio Pucci; and the cuisine and theater of chef Fabio Picchi. The photographs and reproductions of artworks are numerous and exceptionally beautiful—Abrams books are consistently of high quality, and this edition was published in association with the prestigious Scala Group in Florence, making for a special volume. Belozerskaya reminds us that "layers of history are palpable here, and have always provided inspiration. The extraordinary richness of Tuscan arts results from conscious cultivation of the past, and the desire to surpass what came before."

Exploring Tuscany's Chianti Countryside: Four Excursions Out from Radda and Gaiole in Chianti, Nancy Shroyer Howard and Richard Mello (Mandragora, 2003). This must-have little paperback, with reproductions of Mello's delightful color paintings and prints, is really the finest companion I know to Chianti. After having lived in the southern hills of Chianti for a number of years and being asked by visitors to suggest "pleasant half-day drives or all-day outings," the authors decided to put all of this between two covers. The first part of the book is devoted to the itineraries; the second half, "Along the Way," includes commentary on the area's unique features, like old stone walls, olive groves, walking in the Chianti countryside, and, of course, vineyards. Some practical information is included as well, such as advice for using gas stations. If you show up at a station and it's closed but the self-service pumps are turned on, "at a machine near a pump, insert a bill, exactly as it shows you, into the slot with the number that matches the pump you select. At the top of the machine, a message tells you if the bill is accepted. Squirt the hose into your tank. Cross your fingers. If it works, risk a bigger bill."

The Hill Towns of Italy, photographs by Richard Kauffman and text by Carol Field, (Dutton, 1983; Chronicle, 1997). The title of this lovely and interesting book is a bit misleading as it actually refers only to the hill towns of Tuscany and Umbria; but, no matter, this single volume on "the heart-stopping beauty of this part of Italy" is terrific. Field is the respected author of *The Italian Baker, Celebrating Italy,* and *Italy in Small Bites,* among others. She's long been one of my favorites—and she knows much more about Italy than just its cuisine (see page 340). The towns featured in this volume include Siena, San Gimignano, Montepulciano, Pienza, Volterra, Cortona, Arezzo, Perugia, Assisi, Orvieto, Todi, Spoleto, and Gubbio, and Kauffman's photographs are among the most unique I've ever seen of these much-photographed regions. He admits that he is a romantic, delighting in the past, "in the picturesqueness of a vanishing (or a vanished) civilization. . . . With my camera, I avoid the roofs bristling with television antennas, the piazzas filled with Fiats (no easy task), and I strive to re-create, as best I can, the hill towns I saw some thirty years ago."

Tuscany:Wandering the Back Roads, volume I, photographs by Paula Chamlee, and volume II, photographs by Michael Smith, with text by Ferenc Máté and Robert Sobieszek (Lodima, 2004). These two gorgeous hardcover volumes—one in a long-format, panoramic size—are without doubt the most beautiful photography books on Tuscany I've ever seen. The photographs are black and white, and they are amazing, unique, and wonderful. They were taken on three trips, in 1999, 2000, and 2001, by the husband-and-wife team of Chamlee and Smith, who "had seen the usual 'coffee-table' books on Tuscany and felt confident it was a place where we would be stimulated by the visual possibilities and feel at home in the culture." Máté's beautifully written foreword comments on these photographs far better than I can: "The spectacular photography of Paula Chamlee and Michael A. Smith, with its powerfully composed and delicately lit black-and-white images, captures the eternal soul of Tuscany. Through the serenity of their vast landscapes, the melancholy of their brooding black cypresses, the peeling plaster of the churches, the *venatura* of her everlasting marble, the frailty of her bowers, they seem to say, 'This is a gentle land. Walk softly. And leave nothing behind that would not speak well of you down through the ages.' "

The Venus Fixers: The Remarkable Story of the Allied Soldiers Who Saved Italy's Art During World War II, Ilaria Dagnini Brey (Farrar, Straus & Giroux, 2009). I loved *The Rape of Europa: The Fate of Europe's Treasures in the Third Reich and the Second World War,* by Lynn Nicholas (Knopf, 1994), so when I learned there was a book on the same subject but devoted exclusively to Italy, I couldn't wait to read it (and Brey acknowledges that Nicholas's book was among those that inspired her own work).

It's immediately clear that though many Italian cities and villages, from Sicily to the Alps, played a role in this story, Florence and Tuscany had the dubious honor of playing the lead. As Brey notes, "Between the fall of 1942 and the summer of 1943, Florence was emptied of its art. The exodus was unprecedented, the effort to carry it out monumental. Thirty-seven of the one hundred art deposits in Italy contained Florentine and Tuscan works of art." To read of how many of the world's most famous masterpieces were transferred from the Uffizi alone to countryside locations; how a few art superintendents and a sympathetic German consul desperately tried to convince the Nazis not to dynamite the Arno bridges; and how at noon on July 30, 1944, the streets of Florence were filled with thousands of people leaving their homes, "carrying their mattresses and what little food they had and their pots, pans, and pets," is akin to reading a thriller, except that you already know how it ends. (And by the way, Brey informs us that some of those Florentines leaving their homes ended up at the Palazzo Pitti, which sheltered "an estimated four to six thousand people.")

The men chosen to serve on the Allied Subcommission for the Protection and Salvage of Artistic and Historic Monuments in War Areas—"Venus Fixers" is certainly an easier name!—all spoke and read Italian and brought their own expertise to the job. Among them was Frederick Hartt (1914–1991), who'd written his master's thesis on Michelangelo and who later authored more than a dozen books, including *The History of Italian Renaissance Art* (revised edition edited by David Wilkins, Prentice Hall, 2006), which remains the unrivaled classic in its field. Brey relates that a colleague said that Hartt "breathed and lived Tuscan art for the U.S. Army." Hartt continued to visit Florence over the years after the war, and he showed up two days after the flood in 1966 to help out; he was named an honorary citizen of the city, and is buried in the cemetery on the hill of San Miniato. The main task of the Venus Fixers was to render the damaged buildings and works of art into such shape that restoration could begin after the war was over. "A bittersweet measure of their success," notes Brey, "is how invisible their work is in today's beautifully restored churches and palaces of Italy."

City Secrets: Florence, Venice & the Towns of Italy, Robert Kahn, series editor (Little Bookroom, 2001). It's not entirely clear from the title that Tuscany (outside of Florence) and Umbria are included in this book, but they very much are, and I know you will find this to be *essenziale*. The *City Secrets* series is a gem— the subtitle is *Artists, writers, architects, curators, historians and gourmets reveal their favorite discoveries in the ultimate insider's guide*—and I can't begin to count all the fantastic suggestions and wonderful detours I've learned from this volume (as well as those on Rome, New York, and London).

Tuscany 360°, photographs by Ghigo Roli (Random House, 2000). This is another oversized coffee-table book that is so much more. The photographs are beautiful, and a number of them fold out, so you really get a panoramic, 360-degree view (Roli specializes in geographic, panoramic photography). A section at the back of the book includes interesting notations about each photograph. This—along with companion volumes on Rome and Venice—is a great gift, for yourself or for another Tuscany enthusiast.

Tuscan Country: A Photographer's Journey, Wes Walker, with an introduction by Piero Antinori (Welcome, 2007). "Tuscany," Antinori writes, is "a magnificent name and a picturesque place. Every time I travel, I realize the magic this region evokes and the emotions it arouses." This is a great keepsake hardcover that will help you to relive the Tuscan magic every time you open it. Photographs are not the typical shots, and there are accompanying quotations and explanatory text. I've actually gleaned some great tips about places to see from this book that I hadn't come across previously. The resource guide at the back is also useful.

The Tuscan Lifestyle, Pier Francesco Listri (Mandragora, 2002). This is one of my favorite books on Tuscany, and it is not at all similar to any other. Rather than extol the usual attributes of art, culture, and landscape, the author ties together these and other characteristics to create "a style of life, an existential *unicum.*" Some of Tuscany's lesser-known aspects are emphasized, namely, "its productive skills, traditional artifacts, flair for research, capacity for agriculture renewal, and the achievements of sophisticated technology combined with the intelligence of an ancient tradition." That said, it is filled with gorgeous, inviting photographs and insightful text, and is a "small Baedeker of the spirit."

Views from a Tuscan Vineyard, photographs by Carey More and text by Julian More (Henry Holt, 1987). I find it hard to describe exactly why I love this book (and its companion volume by the same authors, *Views from a French Farmhouse,* Henry Holt, 1985) but not hard to find the enthusiasm to press it into someone's hands. I love the shape of it—sort of a square the size of a large paving stone—and I love the photographs, which are not typical. The writing reveals so much about Tuscany that isn't repeated in other books. At the time of its publication, in the 1980s, More wrote, "Tuscany is responding to its latest foreign invasion with a typical shrug of the shoulders. It is, after all, a much-needed injection of new blood rather than the shedding of blood in the wars of the past. And it takes a lot more than either to threaten Tuscany's independence. Its well-being, like its sunshine, is soaked up gratefully by the foreigners—artists, writers, farmers, dreamers, lovers and lushes who have made it their home. And many others like us lucky enough just to visit this radiant, strong country." This is a really nice book that would also make a nice gift, except that I couldn't bear to part with it.

The Vinegar of Spillamberto and Other Italian Adventures with Food, Places and People, Doris Muscatine (Shoemaker Hoard, 2005). Food, wine, and cultural history writer Muscatine tells delightful stories of her adventures in Italy, which began when her husband was awarded a Fulbright scholarship in Rome in 1958. "Italy," she notes, "changes the lives of most Americans who go there—the effects of overwhelming friendliness, landscape, sea, Umbrian light everywhere, primary colors, rhythms, music, flowers, markets, an abundance of gratifying food—sensual pleasures that easily overtake the puritan spirit that seems to be part of our baggage." Many corners of Italy are covered in this book, and Florence and Tuscany are among them.

FICTION

Miracle at St. Anna, James McBride (Riverhead, 2002). Though this is a novel, McBride bases the story around a true horrific incident that took place on August 12, 1944, in the village of St. Anna di Stazzema, in the Apuan Alps north of Pietrasanta in Tuscany, involving the Buffalo Soldiers of the 92nd Division. On that day, 560 villagers were killed, mostly women, children, and elderly men.

Tomato Rhapsody: A Fable of Love, Lust & Forbidden Fruit, Adam Schell (Delacorte, 2009). This novel is set in a Tuscan village in the Middle Ages, and is a love story between Davido, a Jewish tomato farmer, and Mari, a Catholic olive farmer, as well as a story of life's passions, dreams, and schemes. When *parte uno* opens, tomato sauce has yet to be discovered.

INTERVIEW

Barbara Milo Ohrbach

Barbara Milo Ohrbach is the author of more than twenty trendsetting lifestyle books, including The Scented Room, Tabletops, Simply Flowers, *and* A Passion for Antiques, *as well as the bestselling inspirational books* All Things Are Possible— Pass the Word *and* If You Think You Can . . . You Can. *She is one of North America's most noteworthy Italophiles, and also one of the most inspiring human beings in my life. In 2006, Rizzoli published her great book* Dreaming of Tuscany, *a book that is utterly* essenziale—*it's a 9¼ × 11 inch hardcover, but I hesitate to call it a coffee-table book because it's so eminently practical and useful. As the cover states, it includes thorough information on "where to find the best there is" with her recommendations for "perfect hilltowns, splendid palazzos, rustic farmhouses, glorious gardens, authentic cuisine, great wines, intriguing shops, astounding art, luxurious hotels, and hidden discoveries." Barbara is someone who isn't content until she's uncovered every stone, and the minor miracle of this Tuscany book is that she managed to do that without actually moving to Italy. For her most recent book,* Dreaming of Florence *(Rizzoli, 2009), which is, in a way, the book she was meant to create her*

whole life, she knew she had to move in, so she rented an apartment right
on Piazza del Duomo, which is where I caught up with her.

Q: How did the idea for these *Dreaming of . . .* books come
   about?

A: For years I've included travel information in my books—rose
   gardens to visit and where to stay in *Roses for the Scented Room;*
   where to go antiquing in fifteen cities from Paris to Hong
   Kong to Dublin in *A Passion for Antiques;* where to shop for
   great stuff in *Tabletops.* As I traveled around the U.S. speaking to
   groups and showing slides from my books, I found I got more
   questions, by far, about where I went and traveled than I did
   about the books. Everyone wanted to know about insider
   places to stay, eat, shop, and visit. I determined that people who
   loved a beautiful lifestyle and read my books also loved to travel
   in style. My husband and I love Italy, so we decided to start
   there, a country we love that was always a joy to travel through.
   Rizzoli, being an Italian publishing group, seemed a natural
   choice for publisher. Our first, *Dreaming of Tuscany,* is a look
   at one of the bounteous regions of Italy, always filled with
   wonderful surprises—vineyards to visit, family restaurants,
   generational artisans, new *agritur-*
   ismi, beautiful countryside, precious
   treasures. It just has everything!

Q: When you decided to move to Florence temporarily, did you have a
   preference for certain neighborhoods of the city? And how did
   you decide upon your apartment
   on Piazza del Duomo?

A: During the making of *Dreaming of*
   Tuscany we were always on the

move, and quite exhausted. So we decided to try to find a place to hang our hats while we worked on the second volume, *Dreaming of Florence.* We had met so many wonderful Tuscans and Florentines working on the first book, and we put out the word. A friend had an apartment that had just become available in her palazzo, just behind the Duomo, and it was a dream come true for us. It was in the center of town with a view of the Duomo from its terrace, quiet, and near all the markets. Having it made our experience just extraordinary!

Q: You described *Dreaming of Tuscany* as a vade mecum (literally, "go with me," used to refer to a guidebook) on the true Tuscany; *Dreaming of Florence* is an extension of the same. Can you elaborate on this definition?

A: I'd worked in the fashion industry for years and spent so much time during trips to the collections in Italy, France, and England searching out not only fashion trends, but great places to stay, eat, and, of course, shop. I was in my early twenties and was staying in the best hotels. It was a wonderful education and I fell in love with the lifestyle. We have three large file cabinets filled with our travel information. I take cards from everywhere I love and pass them on to friends. People are always calling us for suggestions on where to stay and eat. I'm a teacher at heart and love sharing information, especially if the place is a gem or a new discovery. I think travel should be romantic, in the sense that all is new and discoveries are continually being made. Everything is becoming mundane and cookie-cutter—not my idea of what travel should be.

Q: What are some of your longtime favorite things in Florence that you've been returning to over the years?

A: In this rapidly changing world, Florence is unique in that there are so many places we visited years ago that are still

there, being run by the same family, just another generation. The great museums are still there, of course, but spruced up, like the Bargello, La Specola (the science museum)—their essence has not changed. Trattorias like Camillo, Buca del Orafo, and Sostanza have been there for generations and are still good and delicious, maintaining the traditional Tuscan cuisine. Rivoire and Gilli are still the most popular *caffès*. The shop Loretta Caponi with its luxurious handmade lingerie, baby clothes, and table linens is still going strong and run by her daughter. Officina di Santa Maria Novella is more popular than ever. We loved it in the 1980s when our shop, Cherchez, was the only shop in the world that carried its skincare products and scents outside of Florence—and we still love it. Artisans are thriving now with centuries-old *occhi* still making and repairing crystal, and Pampaloni and Paglia still crafting exquisite silver objects, just to mention a few. The hotel scene, on the other hand, has changed. Pensione Hermitage, where I stayed decades ago, is still there but restored and more expensive. Boutique hotels like J.K. Place and the Continentale are very chic, and historic residences like Palazzo Niccolini enable people to feel that they live in the city. The Four Seasons has just reopened and has a spectacular garden, centuries old.

Q: What are some of your favorite things that are relatively new in Florence?

A: There are lots of new "old" things going on in the city. The Bardini Gardens were restored and reopened last year, with quite spectacular plantings and views way above the city— lovely. Then, surprise of surprises, the Bardini Museum was reopened after being closed for almost thirty years! The exhibits have been redesigned very beautifully using a vivid blue wall paint that Stefano Bardini felt showed the works off to great advantage. Both are just across the Ponte alle Grazie in the Oltrarno. A new science museum is set to open soon, dedicated to Galileo—it promises to be noteworthy. The Palazzo Strozzi has been restored and holds museum-quality exhibits on a rotating schedule, including lectures and seminars. The Museo dell'Opificio delle Pietre Dure moved a few years ago to new quarters, and its precious, glittering treasures of the Medici never looked better. There are some new restaurants, including Ora d'Aria on Via Ghibellina and Nanamuta on the Corso Italia—both good. And, of course, new shops including perfume scent specialists Dr. Vranjes and Lorenzo Villoresi, handmade shoemaker Saskia Wittmer, and costume jeweler Aprosio.

Q: You now know so many people in Florence. Is there someone you'd most like to meet whom you don't currently know?

A: I'd dearly like to meet some of the incredible geniuses I encountered writing this book, starting with the amazing Dante to Galileo to Donatello . . . Fra Angelico and Raffaello—just to name a few. What a golden age in one small city!

Q: You've spoken at length about how you first visited Italy as a college student, were smitten with the country, and vowed to return. Can you say more about your passion for Italy?

A: When I first visited Italy, I was in college, and it was then that I vowed to return. And I did: when I first started working in the fashion industry, I got myself transferred to our Florence office. As vice president of Vogue Patterns, I covered the collections in Europe. The couture shows were held in the opulent Pitti Palace's White Room—absolutely unforgettable! But before I ever set foot in Italy I was introduced to it through my father's books, which included a first edition of *The Stones of Florence* by Mary McCarthy, Time-Life's *Foods of Italy, Italian Hours* by Henry James, *Italian Food* by Elizabeth David, and the *Divine Comedy* by Dante Alighieri.

Q: What will your next book be?

A: At this point in the process, I can barely think of what comes next. All I know is, I'm not done traveling yet and I still love Italy!

TUSCAN MEMOIRS

In my previous Tuscany and Umbria edition, I wrote long and, sometimes, lovingly, about a number of Tuscan memoirs. Even then, every time one was published, I wondered, "Do we really need *another* Tuscan memoir?" Other memoirs have been published since, and I still wonder, but I admit that most of them are not at all the same and are very worthwhile. However, due to the sheer number of these books, I can't devote the same amount of space to their descriptions as I did previously or it would result in something the size of a separate volume. So I've given short descriptions here in order to include all of them (and hopefully to inspire you to read some of them), but please see my blog (thecollectedtraveler.blogspot.com) for more thorough reviews (and reasons to read them all!).

The Hills of Tuscany: A New Life in an Old Land (1998) and *A Vineyard in Tuscany: A Wine Lover's Dream* (2007), both by Ferenc Máté, published by Norton. I appreciated Máté's honesty when, in his first book, he wrote, "When I started this memoir I swore I would not clutter it with dissertations about food, but I soon realized that writing about Tuscany without talking about food is like writing about the *Titanic* without mentioning that it sunk." His pair of books is great, and each reads like a dream, a dream of moving to Tuscany (even if only temporarily). "Few things in life are as wonderful as spending lazy afternoons in the hills of Tuscany looking for a ruin," Máté notes early on in his second book, which recounts how he and his wife, Candace, came to buy Il Colombaio, outside of Montalcino. And—*bellissima fortuna!*—they had as neighbors noted vintners Angelo Gaja and Gianfranco Soldera. I won't spoil the details, but *vini* Máté (matewine.com) have been praised by noted wine experts Jancis Robinson, James Suckling, and Steven Spurrier and have received points ranging from 88 to 92 by *Wine Enthusiast* and *Wine Spectator.*

In Maremma: Life and a House in Southern Tuscany, David Leavitt and Mark Mitchell (Counterpoint, 2001). Podere Fiume—a truly dilapidated and abandoned farmhouse dating from the 1950s—officially became a possession for Leavitt and Mitchell on the first day of spring 1997. Their home is not only in a part of Tuscany little known to North Americans but is near a small town, Semproniano, with "no Caravaggios, no Giottos, no Della Robbia babies. Brunelleschi never worked here; neither did Leonardo. And yet the town has sat on its hill for a long time, and at certain times of the day it looks as if it might have been painted by De Chirico." The authors' reflections and opinions—on not only the Maremma but also Florence, the countryside, and other corners of Tuscany and Umbria—are refreshing, exact, and celebratory.

Isabella Dusi

Bel Vino: A Year of Sundrenched Pleasure Among the Vines of Tuscany (2004) and *Vanilla Beans & Brodo: Real Life in the Hills of Tuscany* (2002), both published by Simon & Schuster (UK). Isabella Dusi's pair of books is really fantastic, and I urge readers to read them both. (I ordered my copies from Amazon .com since they are published in the UK.) She and her husband, Luigi, left Australia nearly twenty years ago and settled in Montalcino, and they patiently watched, listened, and paid close attention to the way things were done in this world-famous yet insular village. Their fellow citizens identify themselves as not only Tuscan but Montalcinesi, "while those whose ancestors were born on the hill, whose unbroken genealogy goes back many centuries can claim to be and are referred to as Ilcinesi, an ancient label that harks back to the 1200s, or even earlier." Perhaps because they live inside the walls of Montalcino, Isabella and Luigi are now fully accepted by the villagers, or at least, as accepted as *stranieri* (foreigners) can ever be. They are invited for dinner to other villagers' homes and vice versa; they participate in the village's annual festivals, traditions, and rituals; and they travel to other parts of Italy with another Montalcino couple. But this acceptance has been hard-won, and has not been without its perplexing and embarrassing moments, which are revealed in these books. In *Vanilla Beans,* Dusi mostly recounts the history of the village through the seasons. In *Bel Vino,* she continues with her seasonal stories but also tries to solve the somewhat mysterious and legendary beginnings of Brunello di Montalcino.

Much as I was engrossed in the tale of the wine (especially the chapter about John Mariani and Banfi), it was the clarification of the curious rhyme she kept hearing—"What Siena could not do in a decade, the monks of Sant'Antimo did in half a morning"—that I was especially keen on understanding (I won't spoil the answer here). Additionally, her depiction of local traditions is wonderful and valuable, since most visitors do not have the opportunity to experience them. About an Easter procession, Dusi notes, "I marvel that it is conceivable, in this day and age, to find young so attached to the traditions of Montalcino, even religious ones, that they are moved to tears by their own participation."

And if one had any doubt that ancient rivalries still exist in Tuscany, Dusi confirms it in a chapter devoted to an archery contest (that had me sitting on the edge of my seat waiting to hear the outcome) and the preparation for a *sagra* (festival). Maurelia, a Montalcinesi mother, announces to the team of cooks that her son Carlo is to be married to a girl from Montepulciano. "Carlo is *not* marrying someone from the enemy village across the hill? It took a full minute before Maurelia could regain her audience because the women, each turning to another, were tutting and clucking over the awful scenario Carlo will face having to eat barbarian food and dwell among Florentines!"

Significantly, in another chapter, Mayor Massimo makes a speech pointing out to the villagers that Montalcino is not a tourist town. What he means is that tourists are most welcome, and plenty of them come, but when a town's economy is based firmly on agriculture, it doesn't have to rely solely on tourism to survive. Montalcino thrives whether tourists are there or not. "Nothing is put on, there is no façade, no pretence of *Italy for tourists.* . . . A few visitors wander into the piazza and stay for an hour, not able to comprehend why they are here; others understand, receding into the background, watching, sipping wine and listening to the daily exchanges. They visit the churches, the museums and walk around the gardens; they linger because Montalcino exudes its enigmatic Italian-ness. . . . All those paradoxical signals that lure them to Italy are here."

The Dusis also operate a tour and holiday company they founded in 1994 (see Tourstravelitaly.com for more information on the personally designed and escorted trips they coordinate, focusing on art, history, wine, culture, food, architecture, sculpture, cuisine, opera, archaeology, and village festivals). They are not mere spectators in their adopted village: at the end of *Bel Vino,* Isabella invites readers to help her and her fellow residents of the Quartiere Pianello restore its Church of San Pietro (you'll read about its damage in the book). Readers who contribute become Friends of San Pietro, and you are offered the unique opportunity to take up honorary membership of Quartiere Pianello. Contributions small and large are gratefully accepted, and your name can be permanently recorded in San Pietro. You can learn more about the Quartiere Pianello by visiting Montalcino -tuscany.it. I can't think of a better way to show your appreciation for this wonderful village than by doing so in this very meaningful way.

Pasquale's Nose: Idle Days in an Italian Town, Michael Rips (Little, Brown, 2001). Fifth-generation Nebraskan Michael Rips, his wife, and their infant daughter moved to the town of Sutri, equidistant from Viterbo and Rome in an area known popularly as the Tuscia—Romans referred to the Etruscans as Etrusci or Tusci. Rips, "an oddity in Sutri," notes that "the absence of tourists, American or otherwise, is endemic to the area," which nonetheless is as beautiful as any other region of Italy, Rips assures us, with "medieval towns perched on hilltops, volcanic lakes, abandoned beaches, and mountains forested with chestnut and oak trees." The residents of Sutri are among the most unusual I've ever read about, and some of Rips's tales are laugh-out-loud hilarious.

Rosemary and Bitter Oranges: Growing Up in a Tuscan Kitchen, Patrizia Chen (Scribner, 2003). I mostly liked this memoir because of its focus on the coastal town of Livorno, about which few people write anymore and in which the author grew up. Chen notes that the word that best describes the characteristic traits of the residents of her nonaristocratic natal town is *beceri* (boorish): "And the Livornesi have almost managed to convert this admittedly insulting adjective, used strictly in Tuscany, into a term of affection. Yes, loud and boorish we definitely are, and we take pride in the countless tales of pirates and brigands indissolubly linked to our history." Recipes and descriptions of food are woven into this book, and one of my favorites is when Chen boasts about the most famous example of Livorno's "magnificent" street food: *la torta di ceci,* a razor-thin pancake made of chickpea flour and olive oil, "nothing more, nothing less." Chen says this specialty of Livorno is "impossible to replicate successfully in other cities or regions. " '*La vera torta di ceci la si trova solo a Livorno!*' as any Livornese worth his name will cry." I'm not sure this is entirely true, as I've had something extremely similar and delicious in Nice (*socca*), but I don't doubt that *la torta di ceci* is unique.

Songbirds, Truffles, and Wolves: An American Naturalist in Italy, Gary Paul Nabhan (Pantheon, 1993). Nabhan is also the author of another favorite book of mine, *The Desert Smells Like Rain* (North Point, 1987), about the southwestern United States. In this work he sets out on a walk across the Tuscan and Umbrian countryside to *really look* at the land from the perspective of the people who use it, learn from it, and depend upon it. In talking with farmers, bakers, truffle dealers, and others, he discovers what still has merit for us today in the old ways of working the land.

A Thousand Days in Tuscany: A Bittersweet Adventure, Marlena de Blasi (Algonquin, 2004). On the heels of *A Thousand Days in Venice: An Unexpected Romance,* de Blasi and her husband, Fernando, move to San Casciano dei Bagni, in Tuscany proper but very close to Umbria and Lazio. In this book readers learn much more about the people of this village, especially Flori and Barlozzo, and it is their relationship that forms part of the "bittersweet" in the book's title. As de Blasi was a chef, restaurant critic, and food and wine consultant before she moved to Italy, there is much here about Tuscan culinary specialties and the many festivals that honor them, as well as recipes galore.

Too Much Tuscan Sun: Confessions of a Chianti Tour Guide (Globe Pequot, 2004), *A Day in Tuscany: More Confessions of a Chianti Tour Guide* (Globe Pequot, 2007), and *Too Much Tuscan Wine* (self-published, 2008), all by Dario Castagno. It would be hard to find another person who is as passionate about Chianti as Dario Castagno, who, though British-born, was raised in Chianti and has lived there all his life. For twenty years Castagno has been leading visitors (mostly Americans) on personal tours of Chianti, and in his first book he shares some of his favorite places in Chianti as well as details about some of his more colorful, quirky clients. His second book takes readers through a full day in Tuscany, from 4:08 a.m. to midnight; the third is about wine but also about a correspondence with an American woman, with a surprise ending. With good reason, after his first book was published, Castagno suddenly became wildly popular—I tried to confirm a full-day appointment with him much in advance, but was unsuccessful (although Castagno referred me to one of his colleagues, Francesco, who turned out to be terrific). Castagno visited the States for a book tour, but I was out of town when he was in New York, so I still have not met him. I was glad to read an interview with him in the *Dream of Italy* newsletter (with Laura Cimperman), since it seems he is as nice in person as I'd imagined. Though Castagno doesn't say so, I believe the reason he no longer leads tours is because of the stricter rules governing licensed guides, which require passing a number of tests, and he may feel he doesn't need to prove officially how well he knows Chianti. Whatever the reason, visitors may meet him for lunch at Relais Borgo Scopeto in Vagliagli (borgoscopetorelais.it), a traditional Tuscan estate overlooking Siena, or at the Villa Dievole winery (dievole.it), where he accompanies a winery guide through the cellars every Tuesday at five p.m. and imparts historical background on the region and on Chianti Classico. Castagno's Web site (dariocastagno.com) contains lots of information about him and the region, including his recommendation for a place to stay: Antico Casale San Lorenzo (casalesanlorenzo.com), B&B accommodations consisting of three apartments furnished in traditional Tuscan country style, near Siena for a *buon rapporto prezzo/qualità,* a good price-quality ratio.

A Tuscan Childhood, Kinta Beevor (Pantheon, 1999). This is both a book about Beevor's youth and a memoir about Tuscany in a specific time period, namely, the years between the two world wars. Beevor (1911–1995) was the daughter of the painter Aubrey Waterfield and the writer Linda Duff Gordon, who moved to the Tuscan village of Aulla, way up in the northwest corner of the region, the Lunigiana (closer to La Spezia in Liguria than any other large Tuscan town). Beevor also spent time at fourteenth-century Poggio Gherardo, in the hills of Fiesole outside Florence, which was owned by her aunt, Janet Ross. Her parents' friends included many personalities of the day, such as D. H. Lawrence, Bernard Berenson, Rex Whistler, Kenneth Clark, Iris Origo, and Virginia Woolf; but the real story Beevor tells is that of the mountain people of Aulla, whose "bravery could never be doubted after what they had been through—including those years of emigration before the First World War, when many had tried to walk to England to find work, not knowing that there was a stretch of sea to cross on the way. But the real trial by fire came during the Second World War, when they were dragged into a conflict they did not want, by a regime they had come to detest."

The Tuscan Year: Life and Food in an Italian Valley, Elizabeth Romer
(Atheneum, 1985; North Point, 1989). This wonderful, beautifully written book appeared years before *Under the Tuscan Sun*
but for reasons that I can't fathom, it's not nearly as popular.
Much of it, as its title suggests, is about food, but it's really
about far more. Filled with the seasonal recipes of Romer's
neighbors, the Cerotti family, in a "green and secret valley
joining Umbria and Tuscany," Romer takes readers through
the calendar year relating each month's typical tasks and activities, nearly all of which have to do with food. As she notes,
"Tuscan cuisine is inextricably bound to the culture and personality of Tuscany and its people. I do not mean by Tuscan
cuisine the elaborate food that one might eat in one of the region's many grand and elegant restaurants; I mean the sort of
food that the waiter will eat when he goes home, the recipes
that the grandmother of the chef might cook every day." Silvana Cerotti's recipes emphasize the single most important
tenet of Italian cooking in general and Tuscan cooking in particular: fresh ingredients in their season, which ensures they
will be of the best quality (and this includes cheese and olive
oil, both of which have seasons). This remains an essential element of cooking that many Americans seem to ignore. Some
of Silvana's recipes couldn't be simpler to make, but their success is wholly dependent on the quality of each ingredient. If
you try to replicate Tuscan recipes at home and try to cut corners with out-of-season produce and second-rate olive oil,
you'll wonder what all the fuss is about. *The Tuscan Year* remains
one of my favorite books and deserves more admirers.

Within Tuscany: Reflections on a Time and Place, Matthew Spender
(Penguin, 1993). Sculptor Matthew Spender and his wife went
to Tuscany over twenty years ago ostensibly to escape the London weather. They ended up moving there, and had two chil-

dren along the way. Spender blends historical details with his personal observations to create a portrait of the "ordinary" Tuscans he has encountered.

Eric and Wanda Newby

Readers may already be familiar with Eric Newby (1919–2006), who wrote a number of travel classics (notably *A Short Walk in the Hindu Kush* and *Slowly Down the Ganges,* both reissued by Lonely Planet), was travel editor of the *Observer* in London from 1964 to 1973, and was named a CBE (Commander of the British Empire) in 1994. Perhaps less well known (but I think even better) are his books about his experiences in Italy during and after World War II: *Love and War in the Apennines* (Picador, 1983) and *A Small Place in Italy* (HarperCollins, 1994; Lonely Planet, 1998). Newby was a captured officer of the British Army who served time as a POW at Fontanellato in the Po Valley near Parma in 1942–43. Like Iris Origo, he shared a desire to write about the Italian peasants who repeatedly, in the face of danger we can hardly imagine today, helped them and countless others survive the war.

Newby states that he finally decided to write *Love and War in the Apennines* because he felt that "comparatively little had been written about the ordinary Italian people who helped prisoners of war at great personal risk and without thought of personal gain, purely out of kindness of heart. The sort of people one can still see today working in the fields as one whizzes down the Autostrada del Sole and on any mountain road in the Apennines." *A Small Place in Italy* recounts the Newbys' experience with buying I Castagni, near the villages of Fosdinovo and Caniparola in northwest Tuscany in 1967, which they owned until 1991. At the time the New-bys arrived, they were the first foreigners ever to live in the area. What really sets this memoir apart is Eric's enormous respect for the *contadini* (country people) and his gratitude to them, especially the men, women, and children who helped hide and feed him during the war.

The story of Wanda Newby deserves to be better known, and in *Peace and War: Growing Up in Fascist Italy* (Picador, 1992), she reveals the details of her life before she met Eric. She was born Wanda Skof in a small Slovenian village near Trieste. But in the early 1930s, Mussolini issued an order that removed civil servants of Yugoslav origin, who were employed in parts of Yugoslavia ceded to Italy after 1918, from their posts and relocated them among Italians, as he did not trust their loyalty. As Wanda's father was a schoolteacher, the Skof family had to move, and they ended up in a village called Fontanellato. Though her life during this period did not take her to Tuscany or Umbria, she did marry Eric in Santa Croce in Florence after the war.

INTERVIEW

Frances Mayes

I love it when a book inspires people to travel to a particular place, and there is no question that Under the Tuscan Sun: At Home in Italy *(Chronicle, 1996; Broadway, 1997) is one of the most inspiring of all time in this regard. Many, many people have visited Tuscany because of this book, as well as because of* Bella Tuscany: The Sweet Life in Italy *(1999) and, most recently,* Every Day in Tuscany: Seasons of an Italian Life *(2010), both published by Broadway Books. In between these titles Mayes wrote* A Year in the World *(2006) and three illustrated books:* Shrines: Images of Italian Worship, *with photographs by Steven Rothfeld (Doubleday, 2006);* In Tuscany, *with her husband, Edward Mayes, and photographs by Bob Krist (Broadway, 2000); and* Bringing Tuscany Home: Sensuous Style From the Heart of Italy, *also with Edward Mayes and photographs by Steven Rothfeld (Broadway, 2004). Not only are these last two books interesting to read and beautiful to browse, but the final chapter of* In Tuscany *("Dove") and that of* Bringing Tuscany Home *("Belle Cose per la Casa"—Beautiful Things for the Home) include dozens and dozens of Mayes's recommendations for places to eat and drink, gardens, shops, antiques, books, hotels, and culinary specialties throughout Tuscany. One of the specialties is olive oil from groves on Mayes's property, Bramasole. The oil is labeled IGP—*Indicazione Geografica Protetta, *certified for both origin and processing in Tuscany—so when they say the olives are handpicked under the Tuscan sun, they really mean it! I've not yet tried Bramasole oil, though I would very much like to. Her daughter imports it, but it is only sold by the case (about $285 for twelve 500 ml. bottles, including delivery in the United States) and can only be purchased by joining the Bramasole Convivium, which simply means you have to commit in advance to purchase at least one case of oil for the year. Learn more by visiting Thetuscansun .com.*

What I especially like in Bella Tuscany *is that when Mayes is asked about why she is so smitten with her Tuscan corner of the world, she replies with some of the best remarks I've ever read about why life is different in Italy and why we have much to admire about the Italians. She notes that despite such ills as prostitution, pollution, and strikes, the Italians have generally managed the twentieth century better than Americans. "Everyday life in Tuscany is good," she writes. "There's very little violent crime, people have manners, the food is so much better, and we all know the Italians have more fun." Mayes also elaborates that her expatriate friends, most of whom have lived in Tuscany longer, talk of how much Cortona has changed. "But," she adds, "the changes were rapid—and needed— after the war. Now they have slowed. The life of the town is intact, they've taken the right measures to protect the countryside, the cultural life of this tiny town puts to shame most good-sized American cities. I think of the younger generation . . . bringing along all the good traditions. When our adored Rita retired from her* frutta e verdure *last year, a young man took over. Unlike many rural towns, this one hasn't lost its young to the cities."*

I had the great honor and pleasure to meet Mayes at Bramasole, her house, which she refers to in Every Day in Tuscany *as "a place-in-time that took over my life" and also as "the place without price," adding "I could no more sell it than I could place my firstborn in a basket in the bulrushes." I met her a short while after she had completed the manuscript for* Every Day in Tuscany *in early May. There were gorgeous flowers in bloom and Bramasole—the word means "yearning for the sun"—looked exactly as she'd so often described it. If you've read her books and have formed a kindly opinion of Mayes, I can assure you that you're right, except that she's even kinder than you may imagine, as well as thoughtful, funny, and extremely gracious. Also, as much as she loves Bramasole, she loves to travel, and she prepares for each trip in the same way I do. In an interview with* BookPage, *she noted, "I love to read the poetry and the history, hear the music, and do all of the things that people who live there actually do."*

Q: In your newest book, which your editor Charlie Conrad has told me is your best yet, do you simply relate more of your experiences in Italy or is there another focus?

A: Well, the book is definitely about my continuing experiences, which to me are still wonderful, but it's also about the painter Luca Signorelli. Piero della Francesca is *the* painter of Tuscany, and everybody rightfully worships him, but I think that Signorelli (Piero's student) is a *great* painter and has been very much in the shadow of his teacher. He's very interesting to me because I think he was the first modern Renaissance painter. He doesn't frame what he's painting—he paints around it. His paintings go out beyond the edges, they are literally hanging over, and he has a lot of energy in his work. Signorelli is such a presence to me in Cortona—he was born here in Cortona, he grew up here, there's a piazza named for him, there's a bust of him, there's the Signorelli Theater, there's the Bar Signorelli, and it kind of seems like he's still here. Most of his work is right here, and the work he did in Cortona has never traveled. It's such a great legacy for Cortona to have his works here—they're in the Diocesan Museum, the Church of Saint Niccolò, the Church of Saint Dominic, and the Museum of the Etruscan Academy and of the City of Cortona (MAEC); plus his frescoes, considered masterpieces, are in the Cathedral of Orvieto. I really wanted the title to be *Afternoons with Luca,* because his work is kind of a leitmotif throughout my book, but my editor told me the

book had to have Tuscany in the title, which I suppose is right. This book is much more about people, much more about life in the piazza, more about the changes that I've seen since moving here. And there are fifty recipes. They're good, too—a lot are from chefs.

Q: I have an article in my files that you wrote for the travel section of the *New York Times* years ago (November 27, 1988) entitled "Wearing Out the Leather Looking at Shoes in Florence," in which you reveal an interesting fact: when Mussolini was trying to flee Italy at the end of World War II, he was disguised as a German soldier, but partisans spotted him among the troops because he was wearing neatly polished and elegant boots. You also, of course, noted that Italians "have a fixation on shoes," and that this fixation must be contagious because you did, too. Do you still love shoes?

A: I've always had a shoe problem, like Imelda Marcos, and a passion for shoes is a problem in a Tuscan house because in the old houses there were no closets. So if you accumulate a lot of shoes, you're in real trouble because there's nowhere to put them! I brought over from America a lot of those things with pockets you hang inside an armoire. I buy a lot of shoes at the Prada outlet. My favorite pair I ever bought there has velvet heels—they look like something a Venetian courtier would have worn. I've found that the outlet is a great place to buy shoes. I also buy a lot of handbags there. In Florence I still like Ferragamo (Via de' Tornabuoni), Luisa (Via Roma 19/21r), and Mantellassi (Via della Vigna Nuova 62–66).

Q: Do you get many visitors who randomly show up at Bramasole?

A: People actually come to Bramasole all the time—my house appears on the map tourists get. Sometimes I chat with visitors if I'm outside. Often universities who have programs in

Italy, especially the University of Georgia, which has had a wonderful program here for more than forty years—the University bought a beautiful old convent here, and grandchildren of the original students are now enrolled—get in touch to ask if students can paint here, and I love that. They paint the garden and the house. Occasionally, someone tries to come up to the house—a man once tried to crawl over the fence. But it's been ten years since that happened.

Q: When you turned in the manuscript for *Under the Tuscan Sun*, did you have any inkling that it would be so popular?

A: No. It's one of those strange books that took on a life of its own. Chronicle Books, my first publisher, projected an initial print run of five thousand copies, which seemed about right to me at the time. They were amazed when it started selling— I think they thought it would sell like a book of poetry. They kept running out of books, and I thought it was dying, because when you run out you have to reprint, and I thought, well, that's the end of that because they couldn't print it fast enough. I still publish an *Under the Tuscan Sun* engagement calendar with Chronicle every year, and Steven Rothfeld, who is a great photographer, takes the photos. We both love religious art—Steven's Jewish but particularly loves Mary Magdalene— and we love folk art, the hand of the saint, and other iconic images, which is why we teamed up to do *Shrines*.

Q: Did the illustrated hardcover books prove popular, too?

A: Yes. *Bringing Tuscany Home* sold about 150,000 copies, and *In*

Tuscany sold extremely well, too. My Drexel Heritage furniture line, At Home in Tuscany (drexelheritage.com), also sold extremely well until the whole U.S. economy started tanking and it tanked with it. We have fifteen new pieces, and it's really fun to work with the people there—they make a lot of things happen much easier and faster than in the academic world. Some pieces have been designed from original antique pieces I own.★ It's so nice to have a house in Italy because you can take a drawing of something to a craftsman and he'll make it. That kind of thing happens here so easily, while other things don't, like when someone says it will take five minutes—translation: one hour. I took friends who were visiting recently to the Church of Saint Mary of Graces in Calcinaio, and we called a friend to ask when the priest would be back to open the door. He came down himself with the key and said, "The priest just said to leave the key under the mat." You've just got to love a place where things like that happen—a lot of things happen here through personal contacts. One thing that doesn't happen so easily is whenever we go back to the States, any work that was under way here stops. When we return, hoping the work would be finished, they say, "Oh, signora, you're back!" as if we've arrived ahead of schedule.

Q: Do you feel that work here at Bramasole is finally done?
A: Oh, no, it's been so long we need to redo it! We have in the meantime restored a little stone house—kind of a Little Red

---

★Note to readers: This furniture line is wildly appealing, with bedroom, dining room, and accent pieces, and a pewter rack for thirty bottles of wine. I haven't yet informed my husband that I am lusting after the sideboard, originally found in an Arezzo antique shop, with its *mano di vernice* ("hand of varnish"), an expression Mayes says she's always liked "because it strongly reflects my sense of everyday Tuscan life. We bought our house, Bramasole, with a handshake, not a contract."

Riding Hood house—nearby. We bought it as an investment but got too involved with it and too attached to it and now we can't sell it! We built a writing studio, too.

Q: Since you retired from teaching at San Francisco State ten years ago and write full time, where is "home" in the States now?

A: Durham, North Carolina, where my daughter lives. And you probably know, since you are a graduate of Hollins, that there are so many people from Hollins who are in Durham—Lee Smith, for one, is my neighbor. And my husband, Ed, received his MFA from Hollins.

Q: Like me, you are probably often asked to prepare itineraries for friends planning to visit Tuscany. What suggestions would you include for a five-to-seven-day itinerary for both first-time and repeat visitors to Tuscany?

A: After Florence and Siena, just wander. Get lost, see where you end up, take unpaved roads. The most beautiful road I know is the tiny one leading to Monticchiello. I love the Maremma area and the Mugello above Florence. Buy a guide to gardens and visit several because you also get to see the villas. A lunch with a fine bottle of Brunello in Montalcino, followed by vespers at Sant'Antimo, will be unforgettable. Buying ceramics in the little towns around Montelupo is great fun, as is the antique market in Arezzo on the first weekend of the month, and a weekend at Il Falconiere—a divine country inn outside Cortona—would be wonderful. Sansepolcro and Anghiari are two of my favorite towns.

Q: Is there some place that you really want to visit that you've not yet been to?

A: After I did all that traveling for *A Year in the World,* I really didn't want to travel for a while, but India and Egypt are two places I very much want to visit.

To view details of Frances Mayes's U.S. tour for *Every Day in Tuscany*, log onto randomhouse.com.

INTERVIEW

Charlie Conrad

I always think it's interesting to meet the people behind the people, so to speak, and one of the people behind Frances Mayes is her editor, Charlie Conrad, at Broadway Books. (He also holds the positions of vice president and deputy editorial director, previously worked at Anchor Books and Doubleday as editor in chief, and has held editorial positions at Warner Books, Newmarket Press, and New American Library.) Over the years he's edited a number of books that reflect his many interests—travel, food, wine, current affairs, history, world affairs, investigative journalism, adventure, historical fiction—and just a few of the other writers he's worked with include: Jon Krakauer (Into the Wild, Under the Banner of Heaven), *Tony Cohan* (On Mexican Time, Mexican Days), *Geraldine Brooks* (Nine Parts of Desire), *Steven Pressfield* (The Afghan Campaign, Killing Rommel), *Jo Tatchell* (The Poet of Baghdad), *Don and Petie Kladstrup* (Wine and War), *Alan S. Cowell* (The Terminal Spy), *Anthony Bourke and John Rendall* (A Lion Called Christian), *and Eric Clapton* (Clapton: The Autobiography). *I feel fortunate to know Charlie, who has also been bitten by the Italy bug.*

Q: You edit not only books by Frances Mayes but also those by Beppe Severgnini (*La Bella Figura: A Field Guide to the Italian Mind* and *Ciao, America!: An Italian Discovers the U.S.*), Sergio Esposito (*Passion on the Vine*), David Shalleck (*Mediterranean Summer: A Season on France's Côte d'Azur and Italy's Costa Bella*), and Robert Clark (*Dark Water*, an account of the 1966 Florence flood), as well as an upcoming book about the Amanda Knox trial in Perugia. Is it accidental that you have a number of authors who write about Italian themes?

A: It actually is a kind of accident. When I arrived at Broadway Books in 1996, the first meeting I had was with a literary agent who said I should consider a book by one of his clients published by Chronicle Books in San Francisco for our paperback reprint list. This turned out to be Frances Mayes's *Under the Tuscan Sun*. I loved everything about the book from its literary quality and its look at everyday life in Italy to its story of how Italy changed Frances's life. That book inspired me to explore Italy for myself and that, in turn, inspired me to publish more books about Italy.

Q: How frequently do you travel to Italy?

A: Since 2003 my wife, son, and I have visited Italy every summer. We always visit different regions, and some years our journeys have begun or ended in France, but every year we make it a point to visit Cortona, the setting of Frances's Tuscan memoirs and, to us, the ideal town in Tuscany. We love visiting Frances and her husband, Ed, and seeing the locals with whom we've become friendly over the years.

Q: What's on your short list of favorites in Tuscany and Umbria?

A: We've loved these restaurants in Tuscany: Osteria del Teatro and Trattoria La Grotta (Cortona); Il Vescovino (Panzano) and Badia a Coltibuono (Gaiole) in Chianti; and Da Ventura in Sansepolcro; Trattoria Gigi in Lucca. In Umbria, lunch on the terrace of Bosone Garden (Gubbio); dinner at Fattoria di Vibio (fourteen kilometers from Todi); and Giglio d'Oro (Orvieto). Classic Tuscan Homes is a great agency for house rentals in Tuscany (classictuscanhomes.com), and we loved our stay at Dario and Giusi's. We also had an amazing stay at Todi Castle in Umbria, and the property there has very nice rental houses (todicastle.com).

Q: Are you working on any upcoming books that have something to do with Italy?

A: In addition to the book on the Amanda Knox case, I'm really excited about an upcoming book titled *The Lion of Tuscany,* which is a biography of Gino Bartali, the Italian cycling champion, who holds the record for the longest time span between wins of the Tour de France. He won in 1938 and 1948, and his 1948 win played a role in unifying politically troubled postwar Italy.

UMBRIA

The widely observable fact is that many Umbrians in dealings with outsiders—non-Italians and Italians alike—are reserved and often taciturn. Ask a dozen of their countrymen from other parts of the nation how they would characterize Umbrians in one word, and the term you will hear most often is *chiusi* (closed). . . . Many people in the landlocked region seem at first standoffish or even defensive—like their ancient settlements, built on steep hills and ringed with stout walls. Whatever such apparent restraint may betray, timidity or diffidence, it will eventually melt if one proves to deserve trust.

—PAUL HOFMANN,
Umbria: Italy's Timeless Heart

The more leisurely visitor, especially if he has a motorcar to putter about in, soon learns how much his hurried compatriot has missed. He finds that a wealth of hill towns beckon him closer. By the time he has seen such miniature Carcasonnes as Spello, Spoleto, Cascia, and Gubbio, he realizes that this Umbrian region is one of the neglected treasures of Italy. Though he may have found a dearth of fashionable spots for the skier, the casino hound, and the sun worshiper, he has encountered good food and wine, and comfortable places to stop overnight—almost everything, in fact, except his fellow tourist.

—SAMUEL CHAMBERLAIN,
Italian Bouquet

Perugia

NADIA STANCIOFF

꿏

THERE ARE MANY special features and unique sites to see in Umbria's towns and villages, but to my mind none have as many as Perugia, and none can match the energy of Perugia. For a town of its size (about 150,000), there's a lot going on here year round, as Samuel Chamberlain noted in *Italian Bouquet:* "Few provincial cities reward the wandering sightseer as bountifully as Perugia. He can spend from two days to a week in this hilltop town in the heart of Umbria without exhausting its treasures." Henry James, too, in *Italian Hours,* opined that "I should perhaps do the reader a service by telling him just how a week at Perugia may be spent. His first care must be to ignore the very dream of haste, walking everywhere very slowly and very much at random, and to impute an esoteric sense to almost anything his eye may happen to en-counter." I am particularly fond of both these remarks as each writer refers to staying in Perugia for a week—not long enough to really see it, but at least better than trying to see it in a day, which is what many people do. A few towns in Umbria can be reasonably glimpsed in a full day, but Perugia is deserving of so much more of your time.

NADIA STANCIOFF, the daughter of a Bulgarian diplomat, wrote for many years for *Gourmet,* where this piece origi-nally appeared in 1989. She was assistant producer for *Peter Ackroyd's Venice,* a four-part television series that aired on Sky Arts in the UK in 2009, and she is the author of *Maria Callas Remembered: An Intimate Portrait of the Private Callas* (Dutton,

1987; Da Capo, 2000), which has been translated into eight languages. Stancioff has lived, for nearly forty years, in various Italian locales—including the beautiful Umbrian town of Todi—and currently lives in Rome. Because it was written in 1989, Nadia and I updated this piece, including only the restaurants, shops, and hotels she originally recommended that are still very much thriving.

OUR AIM WAS to reach Perugia before sunset. We were eager to settle in at the Hotel Brufani in time to admire the commanding view that Goethe, Tolstoy, and Henry James had marveled at. But as we approached the Umbrian capital, a menacing black cloud burst over the city. Blindly, we drove through the downpour to the top of the hill, parked in front of the Brufani, and made a dash from the car to the hotel's Art Deco lobby. We arrived soaked through.

When I got to my room, I opened the window facing the valley in hope of a miracle, but visibility was zero. "*This* is sunny Italy in June?" I exclaimed. Well, at least the room was comfortable and agreeably furnished. I discarded my dripping clothes and reached for a hanger. There in the closet, as if in jest, was a splendid umbrella with a tag that read: "Provided for the guests of the Hotel Brufani." I had to laugh at the irony of it but thought it was a wonderful touch that would be welcome in any hotel room. Of course, by then it was of little comfort to me, so I turned my attention to the well-stocked *frigo-bar* and consoled myself with a Bacio, the chocolate and hazelnut "kiss" for which Perugia is famous.

The storm was as short as it was violent. All at once the gray curtain rose to reveal a glistening landscape gilded by the afternoon sun: towns dotted on the hills; fertile fields seamed together by sinuous streams.

From her rock one thousand feet above the Tiber Valley, Perugia dominates a serene Umbria. But it hasn't always been so. Her history, in fact, is one of conflict and bloodshed. In the sixth century BC the town was an important Etruscan stronghold, but in 310 BC she fell into the hands of the Romans and subsequently became a *municipium*. Reduced to ashes in 40 BC during the bitter war between Mark Antony and Octavian and then rebuilt, the city became known as Augusta Perusia only to be taken, lost, and taken again by the Goths in the sixth century AD. As a Lombard duchy and then under a series of despots, she fared little better. In the fifteenth century Perugia became mistress of most of Umbria but even then was torn by internal contests for her rule. The *condottiere* Braccio Fortebraccio da Montone rose to power and controlled the city from 1416 to 1424; after much tumult and violence between the ruthless Oddi and Baglioni families, the latter won out and held sway from 1488 to 1534. The reign of fear ended at last when Pope Paul III took over the city in 1540 and declared it a pontifical domain.

🦅 🦅 🦅

Perugia, unlike many Umbrian towns of cone-shaped neatness, lacks definition. She sprawls in untidy fashion over ridges and hills, resembling the open claws of her emblem, the griffin. Her houses and churches jump one above the other, sometimes clinging to an apron of garden and at other times pierced through by steep streets tilting upward to the old walled city or plunging downward to the modern suburb in the plain below.

Raindrops were still trickling down the marble noses of the city's forefathers when we ventured out, but the town had already resumed its activity. The outdoor cafés along the Corso Vannucci were crowded with Perugini having their predinner *aperitivi,* and local teenagers and university students in trendy Benetton colors window-shopped or sat chatting on the steps of the Piazza IV Novembre. Students are a familiar sight in Perugia. They have been part of daily life here since the fourteenth century, when the university was founded, and in the last sixty years the Università Italiana per Stranieri (Italian University for Foreigners) has attracted an international spectrum of students.

We joined the strollers down the *corso,* pausing to look at Luisa Spagnoli's knitwear, which is designed and made in Perugia, and then stopping to admire the hand-smocked baby clothes and dainty lingerie in B. Paoletti's window. Signor Paoletti's shop is famous for its hand-embroidered linens and bridal trousseaux, we discovered. "Look at this exquisite workmanship," said the shop owner, lovingly stroking an embroidered tablecloth. "This tells you why my family has served Perugia's nobility for three generations. The embroidery is still done locally, but it won't last much longer. The average age of the women who do this work is between seventy-five and eighty-five. Once they go, it's finished." His hand cut the air in a gesture of finality. "This is a labor of love," he added, "and today's youngsters are only interested in quick money."

Perhaps that is true, but in Umbria devoted artisans still exist who carry on their forefathers' crafts. The ironmongers of Città di Castello, the potters of Deruta, the carpenters of San Nicolò di Celle, and the weavers of Assisi and Perugia are around to safeguard these ancient traditions. You'll find samples of their work at Perugia's Bottega d'Arte.

Adjacent to the *bottega* is the Caffè Sandri, where the window display was spectacular. Large fruit tarts patterned with strawberries, kiwis, peaches, and blackberries formed a colorful contrast to the golden brioche-shaped cheese bread, *crescia al formaggio.* A handwritten label listed the ingredients: flour, yeast, eggs, butter, and Parmigiano-Reggiano—Parmesan from Reggio. In the side window on the right were four *torciglioni* cakes, which are molded to look like eels, with almond fins and fiery, candied-cherry eyes. This Umbrian specialty, which can be traced back to antiquity, represents the eels of Trasimene lake.

Sandri is Perugia's landmark *caffè* and, judging from the crowd of businessmen and young couples, a favorite meeting spot. Here time seems to have stopped. The *caffè* has retained a nineteenth-century ambiance and the excellence on which it built its reputation. Everything, including its special blend of coffee, is still made on the premises. The frescoed ceiling remains intact, and descendants of the Swiss Schucan family, who founded the *caffè* 129 years ago, own it yet.

After a cappuccino and *pinocchiata,* a local sweet made with pine nuts, we crossed the Corso Vannucci to the Collegio del Cambio, or Exchange Guild. The Cambio was established in 1452 by the noblemen of Perugia. Here in a wing of the grandiose Palazzo dei Priori, Pietro Vannucci, better known as Perugino, painted his most important work—with the help of his pupils, Raphael among them. On the left wall of the frescoed Audience Hall, Prudence and Justice, Fortitude and Temperance sit among the clouds, looking down on heroes and sages of antiquity who embodied those virtues. On the far wall are depicted the Transfiguration and the Nativity. In the latter, the Holy Family, serene and still, is surrounded by angels poised in dancelike attitudes. Their choreographed movement can also be found in the postures of the pagan divinities on the ceiling. It's as if music accompanied the artist as he worked. From within a trompe l'oeil frame on a pilaster, the plump, red-capped Pietro Perugino, whose manner of painting greatly influenced the Umbrian school of Renaissance art, sternly scrutinizes his masterpiece.

While at the Palazzo dei Priori we also visited the National Gallery of Umbria on the third floor. With the finest collection of Umbrian paintings anywhere, as well as works by artists from farther afield, it's the kind of gallery we could have spent hours in. Perugino, Pinturicchio, Piero della Francesca, and Fra Angelico are all well represented here. Our visit to this wonderful museum was unfortunately cut short when repeated flickering of the lights signaled it was closing time, and we returned to the hotel to make our sightseeing plans for the following morning. At the top of the list was the Fontana Maggiore (Great Fountain) in the Piazza IV Novembre.

🦂   🦂   🦂

The Fontana Maggiore is Perugia's most glorious work of art. The Perugini declare that it is unique not only in Italy but in the entire world. Sculpted by Nicola and Giovanni Pisano in the thirteenth century, this fountain has been the focal point of Piazza IV Novembre and the city for centuries. Visitors never tire of photographing it and the dense flock of pigeons that wheels around it, while people sit on the cathedral steps watching life go by.

Though I admired the exquisite craftsmanship of the panels representing astronomy, philosophy, and rhetoric along the lower basin of the fountain, I had difficulty reconciling the gentle, mystic artistry of this work with the violent history and treachery of the period. How could it be that the same people who built an aqueduct and established one of Italy's first universities could have had so little respect for human life? Blood flowed freely here, and it was customary to engage in the most horrifying forms of entertainment. In one game—a form of training for soldiers—teams stoned each other, often to death. Enemies were sometimes thrown from the city's great towers and sometimes decapitated and their heads affixed to stakes outside the Palazzo dei Priori.

The Gothic Cathedral of San Lorenzo on the Piazza IV Novembre was never finished, and today its façade retains a makeshift appearance. Only the lower part, facing the fountain, gives us an idea of how it was originally conceived. (In fact, the diagonal rose-colored slabs of marble that cover part of its exterior were stolen from the cathedral in Arezzo in 1335.) Inside are some paintings of special interest. As one enters, in the first chapel on the right hangs Federico Barocci's 1569 depiction of Christ being lowered from the cross. Farther on, in another side chapel, a painting attributed to Berto di Giovanni gives us an idea of what the city looked like in medieval times. The skyline is clustered with thrusting towers, the highest of which belonged to the Baglioni family.

As we left the cathedral, we noticed two attractive shops right on the piazza. Rufini Mobili has a large selection of antique rings and earrings, as well as a mixed bag of pillboxes and Art Deco objects. Bianconi, in contrast, offers handsome contemporary silver frames, trays, and other articles that are very suitable as gifts.

Before going to lunch at Dal mi' Cocco, a restaurant recommended by a friend who lives in the area, we took a look at the Pozzo Etrusco (Etruscan well) adjacent to the Piazza Piccinino. The way there is somewhat slippery underfoot, but it's worth the visit. Built around 400 BC, the well is over a hundred feet deep and still functions. It somewhat diminishes today's technological feats by comparison.

There is nothing pretentious about Dal mi' Cocco. It is a rustic Umbrian trattoria with a cozy atmosphere and good food. The dining room has arched ceilings and chocolate- and white-checked table linen, and the food is served in local earthenware dishes by cheerful young people. The trattoria is always crowded with university students and a few out-of-towners like ourselves, lucky enough to have discovered its specialties and reasonable prices. It's advisable to reserve a table for dinner.

Dal mi' Cocco offers three seasonal menus, one each for spring, summer, and winter. The variations on these themes are printed in Perugian dialect, which is not easy to make out; even Italians have a hard time with it. But Giacomo Calderoni, the owner, and his staff are more than willing to help solve the puzzle. "Everything we serve is homemade and cooked on wood-burning stoves," Calderoni told us. "As a starter, I'd like to bring you three typically Perugian appetizers. Trust me, okay? One is a bread pizza topped with onions and sage. It's called *schiacciatina con salvia e cipolla*. The next is tomato crostini; and then *panzanella*, a specialty made with left-over dry bread. You crumble the bread, add chopped onions, tomatoes, and cucumbers, and dress it with olive oil and a touch of wine vinegar. It is tastier if allowed to sit for a while, so that the flavor of the juices can be fully absorbed by the bread."

The starters were followed by a thick chickpea soup to which diced cooked pasta was added just before serving. Then came a mixed grill of lamb, duck, rabbit, and pork, accompanied by a garden salad. For dessert Mr. Calderoni suggested a light sponge cake smothered in dark, sweet Vernaccia wine. As for the table wine, we had a carafe of white from the Trasimene lake region. We truly enjoyed our meal.

We retraced our steps through the Piazza Fortebraccio and past the Università Italiana per Stranieri to the Etruscan gate known as the Arch of Augustus: two monumental towers of granite blocks rise to an arch topped by a Renaissance loggia. We passed under the arch and sluggishly climbed up the almost vertical Via Ulisse Rocchi back to the hotel. A siesta was called for after such a generous meal.

🐾   🐾   🐾

Later that afternoon we drove to Perugia's Church of San Pietro, which dates back to AD 966 and was the site of frequent conflicts between church and city. In 1398 the church was set on fire by the townspeople, who rose against the Abbot Francesco Guidalotti to avenge his conspiracy against Biordo Michelotti, the leader of the popular party. Today the only remains of the ancient basilica are the thirteenth- and fourteenth-century frescoes on either side of the main entrance. On the left there is an Annunciation: a winged figure with a stern expression, arms crossed in a strikingly unangelic pose, delivers her message to the Virgin Mary. On the right the image of a three-headed woman with multiple halos aroused my curiosity. I found a monk arranging flowers at the main altar and asked him for an explanation.

"Oh," he said with a dismissive air, "that is supposed to be the

Trinity, but, as you can see, the figure is a woman. The Holy
Ghost can't be represented by a wo—" He caught my glance. "By
a controversial figure." The old man had laid the ground for an
interesting discussion, but I knew we'd never get to see the
church if we embarked on it.

The rich interior is decorated with canvases and frescoes by
artists ranging from the fourteenth to the seventeenth centuries.
Many are by Antonio Vassilacchi, a pupil of Tintoretto who was
commissioned to paint scenes from the Old and New Testaments.
An offering "for the maintenance of the church" opened the sacristy to us. There the old monk showed us four small paintings by
Perugino. "You are Americans?" he asked without awaiting an
answer. "Well, these cupboards were carved before Columbus
discovered your country. And now, if you follow me, I'll show
you the most beautiful choir in all of Italy. It was started in 1525
by Bernardino di Luca Antonili of Perugia. With the collaboration of skilled artists from many countries, it was completed ten
years later." The carving is indeed exquisite, as is everything in
the church. It was a pleasure to sit on a beautifully carved bench
and admire the works of art within the refreshing coolness of the
medieval walls.

From San Pietro we went on our way to the fifteenth-century
Oratory of San Bernardino, where we wanted to see Agostino di
Duccio's ornamented façade. Much to our surprise, we found it
quite quickly. There, sculpted in pale pink marble, were angels
playing different instruments. Our surprise was caused by the fact
that we rarely got to the destination of our choice on the first try.
We usually got lost and gravitated toward the train station, where
we would circle a statue of Garibaldi while trying to decide
which road to pick. What complicates getting around in Perugia
is the fact that traffic to the center of the old town is closed between seven and eleven in the morning and from about three to
five in the afternoon. It's a great idea, but we had not been fore-
warned.

Actually, our meandering paid off. Thanks to Garibaldi, we discovered the system of escalators that are the means of transportation most frequently used by the Perugini to reach the center of town. After trying it, I strongly recommend that other visitors do the same. We parked at the ramp on the Piazza dei Partigiani, which can be entered from Via L. Masi (not far from Garibaldi), and took the *scala mobile* from there. Soon the concrete walls on either side change to old brick, and you find yourself in a sixteenth-century underground city with mysterious vaulted passages, remnants of houses, streets complete with drainage, and an atmosphere reminiscent of the film *The Third Man*. You have entered the Rocca Paolina, the fortress built by Pope Paul III on the ruins of the Baglioni palaces when the papacy triumphed in 1540. In this fascinating underworld ghost town, part of the Baglioni family mansion still stands, a grim reminder of Perugia's most hated citizens. It was truly a touch of genius to have put the Rocca Paolina, the most imposing fortress of its time, to such intelligent contemporary use. This city within a city links Perugia's distant past to its present.

🦂   🦂   🦂

Because June had redeemed her sunny reputation, we decided that an outing to Lake Trasimene was called for. We drove to the medieval village of Passignano sul Trasimeno, twenty kilometers northwest of Perugia, and boarded a *traghetto,* or ferryboat, for Isola Maggiore. Although the most populated of the three islands on Trasimene, Isola Maggiore is not the largest. One can walk around it in less than an hour, and its present population numbers only fifty-five.

The old stone houses along the main street are perhaps not as lively as when the island had five hundred inhabitants, but a handful of children still attend the one-room schoolhouse, and, while fathers fish, mothers and grandmothers sit in front of their well-kept gardens chatting and making lace. On the hill behind them, dark cypress trees and yellow broom reach toward the abandoned castle of the Guglielmi family. Despite its tranquillity, this island, its residents tell us, was once the scene of a fierce battle. So much blood was spilled here and elsewhere around Trasimene when Hannibal routed the Romans in 217 BC that the bones of ancient soldiers still surface occasionally with the deep spring plowing. One town is named Ossaia—heap of bones—and a local wine carries the name Sangue dei Romani, or Blood of the Romans.

Lace-making is a tradition on Isola Maggiore, a tradition started three generations ago by Marchesa Isabella Guglielmi as a means for the island women to augment their husbands' modest earnings. According to the islanders, the Marchesa returned from a trip to Ireland with a lace-maker, who taught her craft to the local women. They learned quickly, and before long their work was being sold abroad. The lace made by islanders today still incorporates shamrocks and other Irish designs.

We lunched at Sauro, the island's only restaurant, named for the family that has run the restaurant-cum-hotel for more than twenty years. The Sauros were born on the island, and Signor Sauro, like his forefathers, is a fisherman. "We rarely leave the island," the pink-cheeked Signora Sauro said as she brought us an array of starters. "We have no desire to go elsewhere. Food establishes an important link of communication between the island and the rest of the world, and through tourism we share a lot with people of different lands." We were impressed by Signora Sauro's wisdom but even more so by her culinary talents. The assortment of spreads served on thinly sliced homemade bread were unusually delicate. The different pâtés were made of liver, mushroom, fish roe from the lake, and olive paste from island-grown fruit.

For the first course we had *pasta alla chittara:* freshly made, hand-cut pasta served with a barely cooked tomato sauce and grated Parmesan. For our entrées one of us tried the *fritto misto del lago,* a tasty "sampler of small fry" from the lake, which was served with a side dish of sliced carrots, olives, and peppers. The other had *anguilla,* eel from Trasimene. Of the two, I preferred the tender eel, with its rich, meaty consistency that seemed unusually nourishing. It had been simmered in a spicy tomato sauce and seasoned with wild herbs and garlic. In fact, for the sake of harmony, this is a dish best shared with one's companion.

Dessert was incredible. Actually, that should be *desserts,* for Signora Sauro brought us *two* of her specialties. The first could be described as Isola Maggiore's version of a chocolate sundae—ice cream made with deliciously creamy, whipped mascarpone cheese, its velvety whiteness covered with a hot chocolate sauce. The second sweet, *salame al cioccolata,* or chocolate salami, is a favorite with the Sauro children. Made with sweet biscuits, eggs, cocoa, chocolate, sugar, and a dash of liqueur, it can best be described as a Swiss roll dotted with pieces of chocolate.

🐾   🐾   🐾

We returned to Perugia in time to dine with Franco and Raymonda Buitoni, with whom we shared an account of our day. The visit also gave us the opportunity to learn about the origins of the famed Buitoni company, which is now owned by Nestlé.

"It all started with Nonna Giulia, five generations ago," Franco told us. "She was from Borgo Sansepolcro, the birthplace of Piero della Francesca. She was married to the local barber and had lots of children. To help provide for the family, Nonna Giulia pawned her gold jewelry, rented a roadside stand (for a lira a month), and sold her homemade pasta. In those days, pasta was made with soft-grain wheat. To make good pasta, Nonna Giulia realized that *semolino di grano duro*—hard-grain wheat—was essential, but it could not be found locally.

"That didn't faze the enterprising lady," continued Franco. "She organized a forty-mule caravan to bring the grain from Abruzzi and the south."

In 1827 this remarkable woman founded a pasta factory in Sansepolcro; some sixty years later, her grandson, Francesco Buitoni, established a second pasta factory, this one in Perugia, which quickly flourished. In 1907 he helped create Perugina, the company that makes such sweets as Baci—"the chocolate kiss with a message"—and *confetti*, the sugarcoated almonds tradition- ally given at christenings and weddings in France and Italy.

The evolution of *confetti*, or *dragées*, as they're known in France, can be traced to ancient Rome. In those days family and guests marked a birth, puberty, or marriage by showering the celebrants with rice, grain, or almonds, which symbolized fertility. By 1475 those who were feted did the throwing; after the wedding of Camilla D'Aragona and Costanzo Sforza that year, *confetti* were showered on their townspeople. By the seventeenth century French and Italian kings, courtiers, and noblemen were giving "tokens of rose, violet, or moss flavored almonds in gold boxes encrusted with precious stones" to their loved ones. At weddings, too, *confetti* filled *bomboniere*, those precious little boxes of mother- of-pearl, ivory, or gold that were distributed by the bride and groom to their guests in remembrance of the occasion and as a gesture of thanks for gifts received. It wasn't until the beginning of the eighteenth century that the custom became more wide- spread.

Today the making and selling of *confetti* and *bomboniere* are thriving businesses in Italy. Every town has a *bomboniere* shop. The one on Via Dottori Gerardo in Perugia, La Casa del Confetto, has an impressive variety of the boxes. Of course, they are no longer made of gold and precious stones, but there is something for every taste and pocketbook: Limoges and Ginori china, crystal, silver, wood, and terra-cotta.

Browsing through the shop, we were drawn to large glass jars filled with brightly colored *confetti*. Because I was only familiar with the white ones, I asked the owner what significance the others had. "In our country," she replied, "*confetti* are not limited to weddings. They are given to family friends and guests at a child's christening. The colors symbolize the occasion. Some of these have been influenced by paganism and others by Christianity. For instance, white *confetti* are for christenings, first communions, and weddings. Red ones are given at puberty or when a youngster has finished high school. Then we have green—the color of hope— for engagements and silver and gold for the respective anniversaries. After the gold anniversary, we abandon our clients," the lady said with a smile. Then she added: "We are great traditionalists in Italy. In some parts of the south, it is still customary to throw *confetti* at the bride and groom, as was done in Roman times."

In addition to their warm hospitality, the Buitonis gave us some valuable suggestions. Having listened to the enthusiastic chronicle of our visit to their city and its surroundings, they felt we might enjoy a couple of days at Le Tre Vaselle (The Three Jugs), a Relais & Châteaux inn in Torgiano, a small village not far from Perugia. They were confident that we would appreciate the inn's good food and the remarkable Museo del Vino, the wine museum nearby.

🎋 🎋 🎋

We waved good-bye to Garibaldi more than once as we vainly circled Perugia looking for the Torgiano exit. Thanks to our poor sense of direction, we ended up on a delightful country road that took us through vineyard-clad hills toward the twelfth-century walled village of Torgiano and Le Tre Vaselle, on Via Garibaldi. A sixteenth-century building with thick walls and vaulted ceilings, the inn has been restored and decorated with great taste by Giorgio Lungarotti and his wife, Maria Grazia. Their excellent restaurant and their winery, Cantine Lungarotti, have brought international attention to Torgiano.

The restaurant at Le Tre Vaselle offers Umbrian cuisine, and the menu varies according to the season. The freshest produce is used, all of it grown on the Lungarotti farms. During our stay, we tried a few of the *specialità della casa*. One of my favorites is the *insalata di zucchine*: a zucchini salad that is childishly simple to prepare yet has a wonderfully refined flavor. The zucchini are blanched for one minute, finely sliced, tossed with slivers of Parmesan, and dressed with olive oil and Lungarotti's Salsa Balsamica di Uva—an aromatic sauce aged in a succession of casks made of oak, chestnut, cherry, ash, robinia, mulberry, and juniper—a condiment so special that I brought some home for friends. The risotto is also quite delicious. It is prepared with a variety of fresh vegetables—zucchini, asparagus, artichokes, mushrooms, and spinach—and diced prosciutto, a hard-boiled egg, butter, and wine. Grated Parmesan and a dusting of nutmeg are added just before the risotto is served. For our main course, we ordered the beef marinated in olive oil and herbs. After the meat has absorbed the flavors of basil, marjoram, juniper berries, mint, and garlic, thick slices of it are grilled over a fire. Finally, we ended our meal with sliced peaches in Buffaloro wine and a sprinkling of sugar.

The secrets of these and other recipes can be learned on the premises. Le Tre Vaselle holds cooking classes in English, French, and German at different times of the year. For those interested in wine, an exciting international wine tasting takes place in Torgiano every fall.

Among the Lungarottis' numerous activities, winemaking is probably the most important to them. I dare say that, over time, their interest has grown into a passion. On their five-hundred-acre estate, the vines are tended with the traditional methods that established the reputation of Torgiano wines centuries ago. The estate's limestone-rich soil and good exposure to sunlight have favored the Lungarotti wines, which are enjoying a rapidly growing renown. Their Rubesco and Torre di Giano were among the first Italian wines to be denominated by origin. They also make a very good Pinot Grigio, a rosé called Rosato di Brufa, and a sparkling Lungarotti Brut. All these and other Lungarotti products, such as a Vino Santo (a sweet wine), honey, extra virgin olive oil, and the Salsa Balsamica di Uva, are for sale at the Osteria del Vino.

In addition to these achievements, the Lungarottis have created the impressive wine museum, a historic tribute to the importance of wine in Umbria. With a nod to the origins of vine cultivation in the Middle East, the museum goes on to create a meticulously documented picture of the history of wine in the area, from the Etruscan period to the present. The collection is exquisitely displayed and organized. Of special interest are the kylix (a footed drinking cup) of Phrynos and the Roman wine amphorae. Equally fascinating is the room with a huge seventh-century winepress and a manuscript of instructions showing its use. If you are partial to crafts, don't miss the early majolica amphorae signed by Giovanni Della Robbia and the antique tools connected with winemaking. We found the museum remarkable and had difficulty tearing ourselves away.

After the tour we stopped in at the Osteria del Vino for a refreshing glass of Torgiano white and then strolled around the village to have a look at the local handicrafts at La Tavola, a shop near the old mill. Some of the terra-cotta cachepots and glazed bowls were hard to resist, but the thought of lugging them home kept me in check. I told myself that I could succumb to temptation next time—yes, next time, because we long to return to these blue-green hills and discover other towns and treasures, stopping in *trattorie* along the way for good Umbrian meals.

Hotels and Restaurants

Hotel Brufani Palace (Piazza Italia 12, Perugia/+39 075 573 2541/brufanipalace.it).

Dal mi' Cocco (Corso Garibaldi 12, Perugia/+39 075 573 2111/ closed July 25–August 15).

Caffè Sandri (Corso Vannucci 32, Perugia/+39 075 572 4112/pasticceriasandri.it).

Sauro (Isola Maggiore, Tuoro sul Trasimeno/+39 075 826 168).

Le Tre Vaselle (Via Garibaldi 48, Torgiano/+39 075 988 0447/3vaselle.it).

Guida alle Botteghe Artigiane: Perugia

This small hardcover, a guide to artisans' workshops, is a neat little book to look for before you set out exploring Perugia— it's available at all the bookstores in town. It comes with an accompanying map that's in Italian, English, and German and features a number of wonderful artisans (including some of my favorites—Bottega d'Arte Ceccucci, Sposini Tessuti Umbri, Luciano Fioriti, Bottega Mancini, and Giuditta Brozzetti) as well as major historical sites of the town. The book also includes artisans in neighboring Ponte San Giovanni, Sant'Andrea delle Fratte, and Ponte Felcino. This last one is where the studio and shop of Valentina, La Bottega delle Ceramiche, is located (Via Giacomo Puccini 122/valentinaceramica.it). I was introduced to Valentina by Joan and Roger Arndt, of Le Vigne (see page 233), as she painted a great number of ceramic pieces available for guests'

use in the rental apartment at Le Vigne, including the coffee mugs, plates, bowls, and serving pieces. Valentina studied the art of ceramic painting in Deruta, and in her shop she stocks some pieces with traditional Deruta designs as well as some of her own signature patterns (I am partial to the pomegranate design). She will also create original designs upon request, though it's best to speak to her early in your visit about this. Careful packing and shipping are provided.

Spoleto
A Town for All Seasons

NADIA STANCIOFF

❦

SPOLETO IS WORTH a detour at any time of year, but it is perhaps at its best during the Festival dei Due Mondi (Festival of Two Worlds), held every summer and founded in 1958 by composer Gian Carlo Menotti. (For details on each year's events, visit Festivaldispoleto.it, as well as Visitspoleto.it, which is a good general site for Spoleto and its surroundings.) In 1977, Spoleto Festival USA (spoletousa.org) was founded in Charleston, South Carolina, as the American counterpart to the festival in Italy. Like the previous piece on Perugia, this piece originally appeared in *Gourmet,* in 1986, and Nadia and I again fact-checked her recommendations. Everything remains accurate, and it's somewhat remarkable that very few places are no longer around.

NADIA STANCIOFF, also the author of the previous piece, was for many years *Gourmet*'s Italy expert. I've had the great pleasure of meeting her several times, the most memorable being when we spent the day together in Ravello, one of the most stunning places on earth, on the Amalfi Coast, the subject of an upcoming *Collected Traveler* book.

LIKE A BEAUTIFUL woman Spoleto was always in demand, and often conquered. In some cases her resistance came as a surprise, as it did to Hannibal, when he violently—and unsuccessfully—attacked her in 217 BC. But at times the pursuer got the best of her, and she was hardly able to recover from her last devastation before she was singled out again. Choosing Spoleto for her strategic position, the Lombards, in the eighth century, made her the capital of their important and feared duchy and the principal seat of feudal papacy. It was one of the city's most brilliant and grandiose periods. However, in July 1155, Barbarossa arrived and ruined her. Her famed one hundred towers fell, and all the archives telling of her splendor and glory were burned. Alas, that was not the end of her strife, as for years to come she was the cause of constant dispute and war between the Guelfs and the Ghibellines. Through the ages, she has had her share of light and darkness.

Almost thirty years ago, when Maestro Gian Carlo Menotti visited Spoleto, she was in a bad way. Her prominence and glory had faded. The hidden charms of the has-been beauty no longer lured admirers. She had slowly slipped into lethargy and was forgotten. Her funds were dissolving, and she offered little or no industry. Even the young abandoned her, being forced to emigrate. In 1958 all that changed. Composer Menotti's genius and love of challenge gave the city a morale boost followed by a face-lift. With a small band of talent and a great deal of enthusiasm he breathed life back into her by creating his internationally famous Festival of Two Worlds. Menotti's potion of folly and insight put Spoleto back on the map and revolutionized her economy.

When asked why he was prompted to embark on what then seemed a madman's dream, Menotti answered with simplicity and artistic integrity: "For its own sake"—a concept initially met with skepticism by the townspeople and the national press. With time, success and pride have replaced doubt. There is an awareness of what has been and what can be achieved. The Spoletini have realized the potential of their town and have followed the Pied Piper, determined to play their trump cards: art, beauty, culture, and the fruits of their land.

Today, Spoleto is a center for the arts—a year-round meeting place for scholars, art lovers, and tourists. It bustles with activity, creating its own life. The cottage industries; the craft-training schools; the restoration of La Rocca, the citadel; and plans that will further enhance the city's international development in the arts now assure a future for the youngsters. Although the summer explosion of music, theater, and dance is still awaited with great expectation, the city no longer relies on the festival to pull it out of the inertia and desolation of thirty years ago.

🦎   🦎   🦎

Those who come in search of luxury hotels and three-star restaurants will be disappointed. As Menotti says, "Spoleto doesn't offer a night life, trendy beaches, or gambling. Only those who are interested in the arts will feel comfortable among us and enjoy themselves here." A traveler disposed to take pleasure in art, history, and beauty amid peaceful surroundings will be happy in Spoleto, even if he hasn't a touch of the contemplative in him. It is a town that leaves space for the imagination and for dreams.

But let's be practical for a minute. How do you get to Spoleto? Getting there is part of the pleasure of being there. If you choose to set out from Rome by train, make sure you board a *rapido* so as to avoid changes and endless stops: it is approximately a two-hour ride. By car it is a beautiful hour-and-a-half drive on the four-lane highway in the direction of Florence. Exiting at Orte, you follow the SS 3 Flaminia, which passes by picturesque hill towns peering out of Umbria's renowned olive groves. Leaving Narni and the rapidly growing industrial city of Terni behind, you will start a climb into the cool, wooded hills of the Somma mountains, where in the spring and autumn it is common to see women selling wild asparagus and freshly picked mushrooms by the roadside. As the Sommas dip into a narrow valley and curve around a hamlet of scattered stone houses, you will be confronted with a radiant surprise—Spoleto, rising on a hillside, crowned by the monumental La Rocca.

The city faces the oak-covered Monteluco, "sacred mountain," where the Romans venerated Saturn, Jupiter, and Minerva. Later, with the coming of Christianity, the pagan divinities were replaced by anchorites. Monteluco is both divided from and united to the town by the fourteenth-century viaduct Ponte delle Torri, "bridge of towers," which passes over a deep gorge near the citadel.

Spoleto is a city with a view within a view. As you glance northward, the valley opens up onto a landscape that voluptuously stretches its meadows in the direction of Perugia. Spoleto was built on ruins. You can still find fine examples of the walls that surrounded the city; they were built in the fifth century BC and joined the ancient acropolis on the highest strategical point, where La Rocca now stands. Other representative pre-Roman walls and arches are those of Porta Fuga and Via Cecili and on the road leading to the Ponte delle Torri below La Rocca. The best way to capture the city's atmosphere and past is by walking. For comfort's sake, a pair of low-heeled shoes or sneakers is advisable for the cobblestone streets and slippery steps. A sweater or jacket is essential: Spoleto is eleven hundred feet above sea level and gets quite chilly after sunset. It is not unusual to sleep under a light wool blanket in midsummer.

The most convenient place to leave your car as you enter the town from the south side is Piazza della Libertà, the first large square that you encounter. The local tourist office on the square will provide you with a map and a helpful list of hotels and restaurants. Before leaving the piazza, lean over the railing by the café: Framed by fields and wooded hillsides is the imposing Roman amphitheater built in the first century AD. It seats two thousand spectators and in the early days was often adapted for aquatic performances. Restructured by the city a few years ago, the amphitheater is now used by the festival for outdoor concerts and ballet performances. This is one of the many architectural surprises Spoleto offers.

The map gives several easy-to-follow itineraries, but you may elect to just wander because Spoleto is a city that should be looked at from various angles. Walking through the shady streets and alleyways, you will find that a good part of the time you are climbing upward, head inclined, body tilted, while your feet grip the ground for balance. You are immersed in a medieval flashback that without warning changes from black and white to Kodachrome as you are thrust onto sun-drenched, animated piazzas with their churches and fountains. While making your way through the tightly coiled streets you are unaware of these spectacles of color that are about to open up and dazzle you.

A visit by car is of course possible, but you will not experience the profound delight of discovery that accompanies a walking tour. And your patience might wear thin in one-way streets that force you to circle the town only to find yourself back where you started. If you have a good-sized car, beware of getting stuck in perilously narrow streets in the upper part of the old town.

Richard Nixon visited Spoleto during his vice presidency. I was working for the festival at the time and recall observing his arrival from my office window overlooking Piazza della Libertà. An immense blue Cadillac invaded the piazza. After a moment's hesitation the car took a right and vanished in the direction of the Arch of Drusus. It didn't take long for the car to reappear as it laboriously backed down the narrow hill. The next fruitless attempt was through the Corso, the main street, closed to traffic during the festival. So, back to Piazza della Libertà they rolled. I felt it my duty to inform Maestro Menotti of our important visitor. The Nixon family watched me slip into my tiny Fiat 500 and sail through the narrow street that they had tackled unsuccessfully earlier.

The shutters of Palazzo Campello, Menotti's residence, were closed: it was siesta time. I knocked gently on the maestro's bedroom door. "Gian Carlo? Nixon is here." Silence. With growing unease I repeated my message. "Who? Nixon who?" said a sleepy voice from within. I had barely finished my explanation before Menotti came out of the dark room fully dressed. He returned with me to Piazza della Libertà only to find that the colossal Cadillac had left town in defeat.

🦁   🦁   🦁

Spoleto's natural commodities represent an important part of its new image. Of particular interest are black truffles, extra virgin olive oil, and Trebbiano Spoleto wines. The black truffle, *Tuber melanosporum,* is described in my dictionary as "subterranean fungus used for seasoning." In no way does this give you an inkling of the extraordinary aroma and refined taste of these succulent black morsels. Truffles are found underground primarily in the roots of oak trees. One legend has it that their formation is a result of the energy released by thunder and lightning during summer storms. Others maintain that truffles grow because of the composition of the soil around the tree's roots. One thing is certain: no truffle hunter will disclose the area in which he gathers his crop. The treasure hunt is a closely guarded secret, and the region is plentiful in black treasures.

Spoleto prides itself as the producer of the best olive oil in the world. Its production is not comparable in quantity with that of southern Italy, but the quality is far superior. About 90 percent of the oil made by the small, manually run cooperative in Spoleto has been classified as extra virgin. In comparison, only 75 percent and 27 percent, respectively, of the oil from the Latium and Apulia regions are classified as extra virgin. By law extra virgin olive oil must have less than 1 percent acidity. The Spoleto product boasts an acidity content of one-tenth of a percent.

The rigorous climatic conditions—winter mornings in Umbria can be bitter—and the rocky soil are responsible for the large Macciano olive. The olives, first planted by the Benedictine monks in the eighth century, yield especially pure oil. A report by Ancel Keys, director emeritus of the epidemiology department at the University of Minnesota, stresses the importance of extra virgin olive oil in the diet. Among other things, it has been sustained that olive oil–consuming populations are less likely to suffer cardiovascular illnesses. A peasant woman from the Spoleto valley told me that in the spring and autumn her father, who lived to a ripe old age, religiously swallowed a tablespoonful of extra virgin olive oil, on an empty stomach, each day for three weeks. He maintained that the cleansing regimen was the cause of his good health.

As in the case of olives, the grapes grown around Spoleto are not commercially abundant, but the wine they produce stands up to some good foreign wines. The best known is the slightly fizzy white Trebbiano Spoletino, which had an appreciative audience in Roman times and was exported to Germany in the seventeenth century. The aromatic, ruby-colored wines from the fertile hillsides of Montefalco are known as Montefalco Rosso and Sagrantino. Their velvety texture and heightened perfume are wonderfully suited to roasts, game, and truffle dishes. These wines have not had the widespread recognition they deserve; they have remained a local product.

🦎   🦎   🦎

Most of the hotels and restaurants in Spoleto are somewhat improvised; nonetheless, they have a refreshing simplicity and lack of pretense about them. A number of restaurants, such as Sabatini,

Del Quarto, and Panciolle, offer shaded gardens for alfresco meals from May through October and crackling, wood-burning fireplaces in the colder months.

You might want to try Il Tartufo or Sciattinau in the lower part of town for truffle specialties. They serve a variety of flavorful dishes prepared with indigenous, fresh ingredients. The ideal season for truffles is late autumn. A Spoleto favorite, which can be found in most restaurants, is *strengozzi,* a pasta cut in rough, uneven strips resembling tagliatelle and served with black truffles, seasonings, and olive oil. Another local specialty is the autumn *sanguinacci* mushroom. The "blood red" mushrooms—grilled with a touch of olive oil, garlic, and a sprinkle of parsley—are quite delicious.

If sightseeing takes you as far as the Torre dell'Olio, "tower of oil," from which boiling oil was poured on the advancing enemy during times of attack, stop in at the Pecchiarda restaurant. This reasonably priced spot caters mostly to locals who, between courses under the grape-covered pergola, play endless games of bocce, which still thrives in rural centers of Italy. In the summer Pecchiarda becomes the meeting place for musicians on a tight budget, such as youngsters from the States, many of whom discover for the first time the joy of food that goes beyond the sacred hamburger and milk shake.

Piazza del Duomo is to Spoleto what Piazza San Marco is to Venice—the heart and showroom of the city. One cannot leave Spoleto without having lingered in its piazza. The time of day and the seasons bring constant change to the beautiful milieu: the early morning playground gradually becomes the meeting place, then the eating place, and to some, at times, a spiritual retreat.

The best way of approaching Piazza del Duomo is from the Via Saffi above. A wide staircase sweeps down toward the façade of the Romanesque Duomo with its Renaissance porch. It is a breathtaking sight. Prolong the pleasure by feasting your palate as well as your eyes. Relax at the Tric Trac restaurant on the piazza, facing the Duomo, and sip a Campari and soda or local wine with a snack of country *prosciutto crudo* or crostini with game pâté. The Tric Trac, which serves an international menu in addition to local specialties, is a pleasant choice for a light luncheon or a more elaborate evening meal. It is by far the most sophisticated of Spoleto's restaurants.

A visit to the Duomo to admire Fra Filippo Lippi's celebrated frescoes of the "Life of the Virgin" is a must for art lovers. Lippi came to Spoleto seeking refuge from Cosimo Medici after having abducted the beautiful Lucrezia Buti. Buti, a nun from the convent of which Lippi was chaplain, then became the mother of Lippi's son, artist Filippino, as well as his model for several frescoes. Lippi was poisoned at the age of sixty-three by a jealous Spoletino who had become infatuated with the lovely Lucrezia, and his tomb lies in the cathedral near the frescoes.

🦋   🦋   🦋

The Teatro Caio Melisso, to the left of the piazza, gives no indication of its function on first sight. The three-hundred-seat, horseshoe-shaped theater stands on part of the unfinished Palazzo della Signoria, where in 1660 there already existed an area dedicated to theatrical performances. Eight years later three tiers of boxes were added, making the Teatro dei Nobili, as the theater was known, one of the oldest tiered playhouses in Italy. Rossini's *L'Italiana in Algeri* was performed there in 1817. On that occasion the composer joined the orchestra in the small pit and played the contrabass.

In 1819 the theater underwent renovation by Florentines who in the process destroyed the beautiful seventeenth-century décor. The townspeople, in their disappointment and rage, set fire to the building in an attempt to have a new theater constructed to their liking. That attempt failed, but in 1880 the theater was rebuilt and redecorated as we see it today. The theater's museum is the repository of fascinating documents that give an insight into life in the

early eighteenth century. For instance, a letter from the apostolic
delegate laying down the rules of behavior for the public while at-
tending theatrical performances, unpublished letters of Rossini's
ordering Spoleto truffles and wine signed "ex-Maestro di musica," and photographs of famous singers in exaggerated theatrical poses, including Roberto Stagno, Carlo Cotogni, and the
great Beniamino Gigli, are reminders of the creative level of the
Spoleto lyric theater.

At the turn of the century the city was alive with painters,
writers, and printers of beautiful art books (using handmade
paper), who mingled in the salons held by the local gentry. But
the wrath of World War II brought a lull to Spoleto's artistic
growth. Then, in 1947, Adriano Belli, a concert pianist and music
master, whose mother was from Spoleto, founded the Experimental Opera Theater. His dream was to put on productions of
high artistic quality in his provincial town, giving young voices
that could not make their way into the Rome opera a chance.
Some of the careers initiated with Belli's blessing at Spoleto's
Teatro Nuovo were those of Cesare Valletti, Antonietta Stella,
Anna Moffo, and Franco Corelli. Belli's work served as the musical aperitif for the festival that was to follow.

🦁   🦁   🦁

The musical revival stirred the artistic cognizance of the town,
encouraging the return of artisanal activity. The medieval *botteghe*
on Via dei Duchi have reopened. It is now chic to own a boutique. Antiques, jewelry, ceramics, and fashion have replaced the
garages and storage facilities of yesterday. Business once again
flourishes across the stone trading counters of the shops, attracting weekend out-of-towners and browsing locals.

Upon entering Mastro Raphael's shop you are enveloped by
the unexpected mix of artisanal intimacy and the elegance belonging to an international world. The unusual designs and gentle hues of the fabrics are created by Mario Arcangeli, who credits

the festival's productions for his inspiration. His cottage industry, started in the 1960s, has grown into a business of worldwide importance, and architects and decorators from all over Europe use his collections. His New York exhibition in 1983 caused a great deal of interest in the textile world. A number of big names in the trade were eager for a United States exclusive, but Arcangeli's wisdom and artistic values prevailed. "If I expand," he says, "I will not be able to maintain the excellent craftsmanship I started out with. I am not interested in mass production. Today you find that everywhere. What I provide is distinguished by design and quality."

Just off Via dei Duchi is Piazza del Mercato (the marketplace), where it's fun to stop in at the grocery stores on either end and pick out unusual presents to take home: a can of the "best olive oil in the world," fresh black truffles (in season), olive paste (for pasta and hors d'oeuvres), or, at Easter, the traditional panettone-shaped cake called *pizza di Pasqua*. This breadlike cake with its strong pecorino cheese flavor shares no similarity with the pizza we know. At Easter it is customary for the parish priest to offer his parishioners slices of the cheese pizza with salami, hard-boiled eggs, and a generous glass of Trebbiano Spoletino as a chaser following morning mass.

Making your way through town, you will come across a number of carpentry shops in which, during the winter, the antiques dealers keep busy with restoration work. Good restorers being hard to come by, those in Spoleto are finding themselves patronized by dealers from Rome and Florence.

🐉　　🐉　　🐉

As you walk down Corso Mazzini, leaving Piazza della Libertà behind you, keep your eyes open for a small antiques shop on the right. If your search takes place between one and six p.m., forget it! The store blind is down, and no name or number indicates its existence. Even when it is open (from ten to one and six to eight) you need the eyes of a hawk to notice the business card stuck on the upper right of the store window—it reads, Nanni Antichita, Corso Mazzini, 59. The store, once found, is certainly worth a visit. Nanni has a wonderful choice of eighteenth-century English and Sèvres porcelain, jewels from the 1920s and 1930s, enamel boxes, perfume containers, vinaigrettes, antique rings, and a splendid array of nineteenth-century Neapolitan earrings. These low-karat gold baubles have a peasant origin. The gold is called *oro d'agosto,* "August gold," for after the harvest in August the peasants could afford to give their wives and sweethearts pins or earrings made of this lightweight metal. Roberta, who once used to assist Nanni, bought the store after Nanni died some years ago. She said that since Nanni never put a sign up, she would follow his tradition. The place is still like a tiny, intimate club. Townspeople stop by to pass the time of day on their way to the corner café or just to catch up on the local news. Prices are moderate, and the quality is excellent.

Professor Bruno Toscano, author and scholar of medieval history, is the mentor behind the new school for handicrafts, which is channeling young Spoletini into art-oriented careers. He and his collaborators have established a department for the restoration of frescoes and paintings as well as a specialized laboratory where antique fabrics can be cared for and meticulously brought back to pristine beauty. As they develop their skills, the young trainees will be able to maintain in perfect condition the thousands of costumes designed by world-famous artists for the Festival of Two Worlds.

The safeguard of the city's historic monuments is also part of Toscano's plan. The school, subsidized by government funds, will offer the technical, historical, and artistic background that students will need to master before confronting the upkeep or renovation of landmark buildings. Students graduating from this highly specialized school will, without a doubt, be sought after beyond their national boundaries.

At present the town's attention and funds are focused on the restoration of its most imposing monument, La Rocca. This fourteenth-century castle erected for use by papal rectors was converted to a prison during the nineteenth century, and now it is to become the Museum of the Duchy of Spoleto. In 1499, Lucrezia Borgia spent a brief period of pious meditation between husbands at La Rocca. Later, its function as a security prison separated it from the town. The severe old fortress will now take on a gentler guise: a living museum in which to browse, study, listen to music, rendezvous, or even sunbathe while admiring the view. During our stay we were granted special permission to visit La Rocca, which was in the early phase of its massive restoration. Under layers of grim, gray paint, valuable, brightly colored frescoes were being uncovered although not yet in Lucrezia Borgia's bedchamber and private chapel. If she could revisit them, she surely would not recognize them. No indication is left of their previous beauty. The graffiti-covered walls cry out with messages of hope and frustration left by the later occupants.

$$\text{\ding{264} \qquad \ding{264} \qquad \ding{264}}$$

Spoleto is a constant joy for those fascinated by architecture. It boasts exceptional examples of early Christian churches such as the Basilica of San Salvatore, built in the fourth century after the edict of Constantine. The church is a marvelous fusion of forms and influences—Roman, Christian, Eastern, and Western—and is of special value to those interested in the history of architecture. Other churches to include in your agenda are San Pietro, adorned with twelfth- and thirteenth-century reliefs, and Sant'Eufemia, with a façade and interior of simple, pure lines.

The choice of things to see and do is vast. What was once a dying museum town is now alive and kicking. Each season brings with it a new arts program and further growth. The Lyric Experimental Theater performs in the autumn; the traditional Carnival, which has been in existence for 160 years, can be attended in the winter; organ concerts can be heard in various churches around town in the spring; and the Festival of Two Worlds is held during the summer.

The better hotels such as the Gattapone and the Duchi are now booked throughout the year. There is talk of building a large, luxury hotel to meet the demand for rooms, and a group of young Spoleto businessmen intend to create an international dance and drama school that will operate year round. Spoleto has returned to being a center for the arts—for all seasons.

"We decided to check out Todi because the *New York Times* referred it as 'the most livable city in the world.' They were so right. The beauty of the landscape is breathtaking and the colors of the hills always spectacular and changing. Todi is probably the most beautiful medieval town in the world. It's perched over a steep hill (1,200 feet elevation) with unbelievable views and winding streets to the top, where two cathedrals, the Duomo and the Tempio di San Fortunato, are located. They are five hundred feet apart and date back to the year 1200, and there are many ruins dating back to the Etruscans.

"There is a large group of expatriates living here, mostly from the United States, the UK, Germany, and Holland. They are sculptors, painters, journalists, writers . . . and food is the main topic of conversation! We enjoy Sagrantino, a fabulous red wine, and Grechetto di Todi, a great white. Not to mention many others, which can still be purchased at the vineyards very reasonably. The drive from Todi to Montefalco is like driving through Napa Valley—just enchanting! It's best to visit between May and September.

"A new museum of archaeological findings, built underneath churches and buildings in Todi, was just inaugurated, and the library has about four hundred manuscripts hand-written on parchment paper. Many are beautifully illus-trated, and they all date back to the years 800 and 900. Incredible. See you in Todi!"

—Alberto Vitale, former chairman
Random House, Inc.

The Hills of the Sublime

G. Y. DRYANSKY

❧

HERE IS A very good little tour of Umbria, taking in Assisi, Baschi, Perugia, San Gemini, Spello, Spoleto, Toriano, and Tuoro sul Trasimeno.

For many years, G. Y. DRYANSKY has been a contributing editor of *Condé Nast Traveler,* where this piece originally appeared. I have saved nearly every article he's written as they are always insightful and filled with great tips. Just one of these tips I gleaned from this piece can be found on the reading list accompanying the article, which was compiled with Frederick Vreeland: the *Knopf Traveler's Guides to Art* series. As they note, the two-page "Painting in Umbria" tour is excellent. (Vreeland, by the way, is a former U.S. ambassador, also a *Condé Nast Traveler* contributing editor, and author of positively the very best guide to Rome, entitled *Key to Rome,* Getty Publications, 2006.)

THE ROAD MOST travelers take north from Rome is the Tuscan road. Tuscany, like Provence, has become the world's paradigm for heaven in a stylish Mediterranean setting. Next time, though, bear east and take the pilgrims' road. It leads to a region of landlocked green mountains knotted around a valley. Pilgrims have been heading there for centuries, because it is the homeland of Saint Francis, humble friend of all creatures,

who held silence and nature above buzz and ostentation. His shrine is the basilica in Assisi, but the entire region around it—the navel of Italy called Umbria—is very much his kind of country.

Everywhere these days, of course, there are more people traveling for pleasure than there are pilgrims. Yet even now, on a bright late spring afternoon in Assisi, you can walk along the narrow Via Giorgetti toward the basilica, pass no one on your way, and hear nothing but the rustle of leaves in the breeze from Mount Subasio. In the basilica, which houses "The Life of Saint Francis," one of the world's most astounding series of paintings, there's the murmur of a reasonable-sized crowd. Until, every few minutes, an appointed monk says into a microphone: "*Shhh. . . . Silenzio!*"

Muted splendor—it's not stretching the point to see this as the title for whatever little chapter in your life Umbria might come to represent. This is also the homeland of Perugino, hailed in his time as the finest painter in Italy, the one artist whose signature appears in the Sistine Chapel. As his career went forward after the turn of the sixteenth century, he gave away his riches as a painter, just as

Francis of Assisi did. Perugino's achievements are rooted in the elegance of understatement. He was quintessentially Umbrian.

In Umbria you're in the most cheerful mountain country I know. Trendsetters moving on from Tuscany are beginning to adopt this wispy Perugino landscape, where villas and an abundance of farmhouses with breathtaking views are for sale or rent. But the sprouting of real estate agencies in the walled towns that climb the lower ridges of the Apennines hasn't yet brought about great change. Perugia, Assisi, Spello, Foligno, Spoleto, Todi—the towns still look much as they do in Renaissance paintings. So, too, do the smaller villages whose treasures are locked away in tiny churches, until you find the villager with the key. "*Professore!*" I recall one of them once declaiming appreciatively, as he handed me a big iron key that opened the door to what I remember as a flaking Perugino *Madonna and Child Enthroned,* the fresco that is the pride of his village. In the etiquette of Italy, calling a stranger *professore* is the most polite form of address. Was that in Fontignano? It was long ago. On this latest trip, I didn't allot any time for searching villages for keys. It would still be very rewarding, but with all the looting Italy has known, the reception might be less warm and respectful.

On this trip, I thought my wife and I would get it all in during a reasonably leisurely week. But I had forgotten that in Umbria you can make a list of what you want to visit and wind up seeing only half of it. Wherever you go, your eyes, so to speak, don't want to leave the table in full feast. Sure enough, having looked at only half of what I'd intended, I now see sufficient material in my notes for a sizable book.

I came in from the north. I wanted to visit the shores of Lake Trasimeno, where I'd never been before, and from there drive through the region in a loop.

Observing Trasimeno, the fourth-largest lake in Italy, through a heat-generated haze, you get the same panorama of blue-green water that thrilled Goethe and that Perugino probably painted

into the background of his *Portrait of Francesco delle Opere*. But unlike Goethe, you'd be looking at it from a superhighway or from
one of the undistinguished villages on the shoreline. For me, what
made the area hard to leave was a country manor fifteen minutes
away, in Tuoro sul Trasimeno. An Australian whose family had
owned the memorable George Hotel in Melbourne had married
a woman from a line of Roman innkeepers and together they'd
restored the Villa di Piazzano and made it an inn. Once a ruin, it
doesn't have the asset of generations of accumulated décor, but
the owners are very hospitable, and I will forgive them the disappointing restaurant that they sent me to down the road. If history
thrills you, you might get goose bumps in Tuoro. It was on this
plain that the Roman army was camped when Hannibal the
Carthaginian, having crossed the Alps on his elephants, descended upon them. First he ambushed the Romans at a place
since appropriately called Sanguineto. The bones of the Romans,
who were slaughtered by the tens of thousands, ended up in a
nearby village called Ossaia.

The villa overlooks a French-style formal garden and green to-
bacco fields, not far from the border with Tuscany, where the
town of Cortona is perched. Tuoro seemed a languorous place to
spend time, but we hurried down the *autostrada* to see Orvieto.

Pope Clement VII fled to Orvieto when Rome was sacked by
Emperor Charles V's army in 1527, and you can see why he ran
here for protection. The walled city is on a plateau a thousand feet
above the valley. The streets, with their enclosed gardens and balconies hung with roses, geraniums, and petunias, are full of
charm. And they slope down from the Piazza del Duomo in such
a way that—through their interstices in the square—you can see
nothing but distant green hills. In the piazza, it's as if there were
no city—just this platform for one jewel of civilization, the cathedral, to sit on among the accomplishments of nature. The white-
and-gray-striped duomo pairs elaborate Gothic ornament with a
blunt Romanesque form. A more momentous aesthetic con-

frontation happens inside. It might be compared to having the British painter Francis Bacon complete a series of portraits begun by John Singer Sargent.

Fra Angelico, the rightly nicknamed friar who had begun to add to his decorative, sweet style a realistic plasticity at the turn of the fifteenth century, had completed two sections of the vault in the duomo's Cappella Nuova before he was summoned back to Rome. He had also started work on the *Last Judgment* that was to fill the chapel, lavishly using the gilding he loved, which harked back to Byzantine mosaics. Half a century later Luca Signorelli arrived to finish the task, and in swept a drastically new world view. Signorelli, who learned his anatomy by studying flayed corpses, covered the walls with human bodies in all their allure and repulsiveness. Flesh *matters,* he seemed to be insisting, provocatively thrusting penises, breasts, and buttocks in your face. Right there in God's house.

Half a millennium later, we hear Wallace Stevens saying something along the same lines, in poetry: "What is divinity if it can come / Only in silent shadows and in dreams? / Shall she not find . . . In any balm or beauty of the earth / Things to be cherished like the thought of heaven?"

Signorelli might not have really cherished the things of the earth that fascinated him. His work is saturnine, but it matters immensely. "Michelangelo," the art historian Frank Jewett Mather wrote, "fed his dream of a heroic world of splendid nudity from the drastic vision of Signorelli." In the cathedral of Orvieto, we meet Modern Man: heroic, pathetic, exalted, and in anguish.

🦁   🦁   🦁

You will think of Michelangelo again in Todi, where the church of Santa Maria della Consolazione overlooks handsome parkland at the edge of a town graced equally by its fine Piazza del Popolo and the hillside church of San Fortunato. Compact and impeccably proportioned, Maria della Consolazione seems like a badge of

Renaissance self-confidence. It was designed by Bramante, who conceived St. Peter's Basilica in Rome, which Michelangelo completed.

On a map, Spoleto looks like it's a stone's throw from Todi, but you have Mount Martani to cross, and although the high, winding road will treat you to some memorable vistas, you can easily miss lunch while trailing a truck.

Our schedule got us, by dinnertime, to the Eremo delle Grazie, an old monastery in the woods of Monteluco that overlooks Spoleto. It was for years the country house of Dr. Lalli Pio, who was Pope Pius XII's dentist. Dr. Pio turned it into an inn in the 1990s, and he is still there, a spry, courtly eighty-four-year-old innkeeper. The Eremo, somber but impressive, with lots of antiques and plunging beds far too soft for monks, is a place of great character. As night brought out a full moon, we drank in the mountain air with our aperitif of local white wine, then went inside to attack a meal to remember. We were the only guests that evening in late May, but the food seemed like a banquet for provincial Italian notables: an array of antipasti to start with, including fried fresh sage leaves and zucchini blossoms; two kinds of local pasta—ravioli in black truffle sauce and *strangozzi,* an eggless fresh pasta typical of Spoleto; roast pork in a wine and juniper berry sauce; fruit and an assortment of wicked, nutty, creamy cakes of the region; and a bottle of full, fruity Rosso di Montefalco. We would sample contemporary, internationally influenced Italian cooking on this trip and also the simple felicities of modest trattorias, but this meal, reminiscent, in its refined heartiness, of the *cuisine bourgeoise* we know at home in Paris, stands out in our memories as particularly special.

The Eremo has expensive room rates for the region, which perhaps explains why it had no other guests that night. But being alone within that patinaed souvenir of history and tradition was part of what made it worthwhile. Dr. Pio told us that Michelangelo also enjoyed his stay in the quiet woods of Monteluco, among the monks.

Although the annual music festival has placed Spoleto on the world's cultural map for about half a century, the city still seems quite poor. The backstreets are lined with darkened and worn buildings. Yet they keep their medieval dignity intact below the grime, and there are many Roman remnants of interest as well.

Spoleto is hell to get around in with a car, but the cathedral and its square will repay your frustration. Go into the apse of the cathedral, directly to the frescoes by Fra Filippo Lippi. I first saw an image of them at an imitation-Gothic campus in New Jersey, in the library of a building named for a farm machinery tycoon and designed to look like an Italian villa. The reading room had the spicy smell of old books, and pigeons cooed under the eaves. Opening a book to those astonishing pictures was a treat I can still remember. It would be many years before I stood in front of the real thing, and it was worth the wait. Filippo Lippi's frescoes from "The Life of the Virgin" in Spoleto's cathedral are his masterpiece, among the most appealing works of the Italian Renaissance. The narrative skill is profoundly humane. There is a powerful grace and an elegant sensuality. All the new techniques of plasticity and perspective were applied with an assurance that left no room for ostentation. Filippo Lippi worked in the duomo from 1467 until his death in 1469 and was buried there by his son.

Yes, his son. I said that the friar was a sensual painter, and so it seems he was in life. He seduced a nun, eloped, and married her. It is sometimes said that the Virgin of the frescoes is his lovely wife. He painted himself and his son, Filippino, into the scene of the transition of the Virgin. Filippo Lippi's ornate marble tomb, ordered by Lorenzo the Magnificent and designed by Filippino, is on a wall of the right transept.

Before leaving the cathedral, spend a euro to illuminate Pinturicchio's *Madonna and Child* in the Eroli Chapel. It's a handsome picture proving him a skilled decorator, but it's not as good as what you'll see of Pinturicchio in Spello.

Empty under the full moon and washed by rain, Spoleto's Piazza del Duomo seemed a real-life composition to match any painting. Nowhere can I remember having seen a lovelier polyphony of architectural shapes. The duomo itself deftly marries the ornateness of its Renaissance porch to a Gothic façade and a tall, martial-looking campanile. In front of the cathedral, the long piazza curves gently, and on each side the buildings form a double enfilade of complementary shapes and sizes from different periods. The low, rectangular Teatro Caio Melisso, the three high cones that form the apse of the Romanesque church of Sant'Eufemia, the vast flat façade of the sixteenth-century palazzo across from it: these varied existences in stone seem to be in the right place for elegant conversation with one another. And behind all of this, there's a splash of nature that is typical of the towns—a beech-covered hillside.

🦋   🦋   🦋

Spello, though a fortress-village, is a more cheerful place than Spoleto. I've always found it so because, on a sunny day long ago, I'd managed to have a delicious lunch under the ocher awning on the terrace of Il Molino, a trattoria on a street lined with the honey-colored old stone buildings that form the village. This time, we lingered over late spring's first sweet melon with local ham, some fresh pasta with thin wild asparagus, and the wine that had become our dependable friend, Montefalco red. After downing dark bullets of espresso, we saw the people at the neighboring tables dipping *tozzetti* cakes into sweet Sagrantino wine. With faint regret, we passed on that customary coda to a good lunch.

Just down the street is the *collegiata* (collegiate church) of Santa Maria Maggiore, where a couple of tourists were waiting for someone else to put a euro in the box to illuminate the frescoes in the Baglioni Chapel. These cheerful Renaissance masterpieces by the lavish Pinturicchio teem with life beyond their didactic purpose.

We chose to walk down the nave to the two frescoes in the choir, the *Pietà with Mary Magdalene and Saint John* and the

Madonna Enthroned Between Saint Catherine of Alexandria and the Bishop Saint Blaise, both late works of Pietro Vannucci, known as Perugino. They were painted in 1521, two years before he fell victim to the plague.

Perugino had a good life: fame came to him early, and his workshop, which was full of assistants, had more assignments than it could handle. Toward the end of his life, his classic compositions became repetitive, and his reputation began to fade in favor of that of more naturalistic painters—although Perugino was lucky, in a way, to have as an assistant Raphael, who updated his later style with softness and sentiment. During his final years, Perugino retreated to the light mysticism of his early work, achieving a momentous feeling without sentimentality. These two greatly overlooked choir frescoes say all that.

Spello is a modest mountain town that never hoped to rival Florence, Rome, or even Perugia, and yet here we have this work of a star. Poking around in Umbria, you get a sense of the matter-of-fact way in which the church could order brilliant art everywhere. Masters were less self-conscious in those days, when painters called their studios boutiques—before the line between art and artisanship was clearly drawn. But every church, no matter where, was a prestigious venue. One of Perugino's most important paintings, *The Adoration of the Magi,* is in Madonna delle Lacrime, a church on the outskirts of the town of Trevi, in the middle of nowhere—and, unfortunately for us, closed for repairs during our trip. Churches were everywhere and awesome. And yet, as the Renaissance progressed, attachment to the secular world, the here and now, increased. Luca Signorelli's fascination with flesh is matched, in Spello, by the glow of everyday activity in Pinturicchio's famous frescoes of the birth and childhood of Christ. Behind the subject of *The Adoration of the Magi,* the well-mastered perspective leads the eye to boats on a lake, warriors, peasants coming in from fields, camels. The Baglioni Chapel, which Pinturicchio finished painting in 1501, is a brilliant, celebratory embellishment of the real world, displaying mastery of line and color and structure. Don't wait for someone else to drop a euro in the light box to be able to admire it.

In Gubbio, we gave our eyes a rest from paintings and let a sunny afternoon roll by, punctuated by cheers, church bells, drums, and the fanfare of horns. We sat in the bleachers set up for the Palio at the Piazza Grande, a handsome square that seems to hang like a platform in the sky, at the edge of the mountain-hugging Via XX Settembre. The Gubbio Palio is a good-natured event. It has nothing like the time-honored bribery, jockey-beating, and horse-poisoning that animate the Palio of Siena. In Gubbio, the *palio,* or banner, is contested not in a horse race between sincerely hostile neighborhoods but in a civil crossbow match between Gubbio and the Tuscan town of Sansepolcro. The bowmen are fantastic. The arrows fired across the long plaza by both teams were all so close to the bull's-eye that they pierced each other. But there was even more glory for the spectator in the acrobatic banner-twirling by the teams from each city. All of this was performed in vastly varied, beautifully sewn medieval costumes. If you're tempted to think of Gubbio's Palio della Balestra as some Disney-like attraction, bear in mind that it's been going on year after year since the fifteenth century. I think it looked as brilliant and festive that afternoon, under the sun, with the same green mountains as a backdrop, as it must have back then. The costumed figures might have stepped out of a Pinturicchio.

We had not seen the Basilica of Saint Francis in Assisi since the earthquake of 1997. We found the restoration so skillful that only a number of holes in the Cimabue frescoes of the Crucifixion, in the left transept of the upper basilica, were a strong reminder of the disaster. These Cimabues, painted between 1277 and 1285, had already been in dire shape for centuries, having unfortunately been executed using lead white instead of lime white. After hurrying through the lower basilica, visitors rush past them to see Giotto's celebrated scenes from the life of Saint Francis, which run along both sides of the nave in the upper basilica. Giotto's stardom, consecrated by nineteenth-century art historians, persists—even though those Giottos look a lot more flat and pale than when I first saw them, before they were scrubbed several years ago.

We were told in college that art took a giant step forward with Giotto's attention to the everyday world. With that in mind, you come up from the darkness of the lower basilica, which is dominated by late medieval art, to where the Giottos bathe in daylight. And the sudden change might seem a felicitous metaphor for the dawn of the Renaissance. But in recent times, we have become more and more sure that the term "dark ages" is a misnomer. The metaphor doesn't really work.

This time in the basilica, my admiration was drawn to Cimabue, who found the shepherd boy Giotto sketching on a rock and made him his apprentice, and to that other brilliant contemporary, Pietro di Lorenzetti, whose work is poorly illuminated in the lower basilica. Lorenzetti's depiction of Christ being taken down from the Cross, the Cimabue Crucifixions, and Cimabue's *Madonna Enthroned,* all downstairs, are works that speak to our own age with more power than the congenial Giotto's empirical scenes. They embody awe and terror drawn from natural representation. I see Anselm Kiefer learning more from Cimabue than from Giotto.

Giotto captured the spirit of Saint Francis. In what is now the Piazza della Repubblica in Foligno, a plaque above a candy store commemorates where Francis sold his cloak and his horse in that square. He turned his back on materialism, but he loved the material world of nature. After Assisi, do not fail to take the mountain road to the Eremo delle Carceri, the caves where the saint and his disciples meditated. All you can hear there is the music of thousands of birds. Direct descendants, perhaps, of those you can still see Saint Francis preaching to in Giotto's famous fresco at the basilica.

The most important reason to visit Perugia, the high, elegant capital city of the region, is the National Gallery of Umbria in the

Palazzo dei Priori. One of the handsomest and finest museums in the country, it was closed for repairs when we arrived. In Italy, it seems, something you want to see is often locked up. Maybe it's the Italians' way of making you return. With me, they don't have to try that hard.

A HIGH ON EVERY HILLTOP

For a long time, the towns of Umbria were part of the Papal States, with distant and sometimes inept rulers. Consequently, they never achieved the power and glory—and importance to the Renaissance—of such independent cities as Florence, Venice, and Milan. They remain small and quiet to this day, but their intact medieval architecture is handsome and the churches, in this region of so many saints, contain some of the most important late medieval/early Renaissance art in Italy. A rare bonus is that you are often able to be alone or nearly so in front of some of these masterpieces, which have all the more resonance because they are not in some crowded museum but, rather, where the masters created them.

May is a good month to go, but June is drier, as are September and October. I love Umbria even in February, despite the wind that ruffles the smoke coming from the chimneys of trattorias where game birds are being cooked.

The towns are often very close together, yet each has so much to see that you can't swing through them quickly. Below is a selection of highlights.

The country code for Italy is 39.

Assisi

The venerable, old-fashioned **Hotel Subasio,** just a few steps from the basilica, recently underwent repairs for damage caused by the 1997 earthquake (075 812 206). In the mountains not far from the caves where Saint Francis meditated, **Le Silve di Armenzano,** once a farm, is now a comfortable hotel with breathtaking mountain views and a pricey and unmemorable restaurant (075 801 9000/lesilve.it).

A fine lunch bet is the simple and inexpensive **Taverna de l'Arco,** where the platter of grilled vegetables is as good as it gets (075 812 383). I heard positive things about **La Fortezza,** on the Piazza del Commune (075 812 418).

Baschi

Many Italians swear that the best restaurant in their country is **Vissani,** and Michelin gives it two stars (which it is loath to do outside France). The dishes are a little overweighted with foie gras and truffles—the danger of having Michelin stars is that the chef tends to favor Frenchified food—but there is enough authentic cucina to justify a trip to (and a reservation at) this gustatorial heaven on the shores of man-made Lake Corbara (074 495 0396).

Bevagna

You could spend the night at **L'Orto degli Angeli,** an eighteenth-century manor, but I found it cool and perfunctory and the fancy restaurant unimpressive. The **Hotel Palazzo Brunamonti,** simpler and less expensive but still with character, is a better choice (074 236 1932/brunamonti.com). The night I ate an insipid chicken at L'Orto's restaurant, everyone in town seemed to be at the inexpensive **Osteria del Podesta** (074 236 1832).

Gubbio

When I stayed at the understaffed (and rudely staffed) **Hotel Relais Ducale,** I switched to a suite after having been shown a dark little room. You can see Gubbio easily without staying overnight, but stop for lunch at **La Fornace di Mastro Giorgio.** Its cavelike candlelit atmosphere is a bit sad by day, but the food is delicious (075 922 1836).

Lake Trasimeno

On the north shore of this historic lake, the village of Passignano has several good restaurants, the best of which is **Fischio del Merlo,** "Whistle of the Blackbird" (075 829 283). A couple of miles south of the lake is a tiny jewel of a town, Panicale, and its diadem restaurant **Lillo Patini.** Specialties start with simple homemade pasta and build up with splendid sauces based on wild boar, pheasant, or lake fish (075 837 771). Be sure to visit the nearby Church of San Sebastiano to see Perugino's arrow-splattered *Martyrdom of Saint Sebastian.*

Orvieto

An excellent trattoria, **La Volpe e L'Uva** embodies the basic purity of Italian cooking. I recall a carpaccio of sliced fresh zucchini, although a *strangozzi* with preserved truffles was overwhelmed by bitter almonds (076 334 1612). We didn't stay at the **Hotel Maitani,** but a quick look revealed a pleasant, not overly luxe place with some history (076 3342 0112).

Perugia

The renovated **Hotel Brufani Palace** is probably the most luxurious in the entire region. Ask for room 112, where Charlie Chaplin stayed (075 573 2541/brufanipalace.it). The **Sandri** pastry shop, at Corso Vannucci 32, has excellent coffee and killer cakes and is a smart place for a light lunch.

San Gemini

Smaller versions of Rome's Colosseum and temple ruins have been unearthed at two-thousand-year-old **Carsulae,** forty-five

minutes southwest of Spoleto. Viewing is easier here than in the
bustling capital, and both the food and the service are pleasant at
the nearby **Antica Carsulae** (074 463 0163).

Spello

The **Hotel Palazzo Bocci,** across the street from the Church of
Santa Maria Maggiore, is a former palace and well maintained
(074 230 1021/palazzobocci.com). For lunch, try the pasta with
wild asparagus—if it's in season—at **Il Molino,** down the street
from the church (074 265 1305).

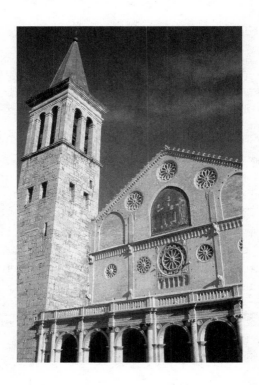

Spoleto

Eremo delle Grazie, a former monastery with rare character in Monteluco, in the wooded hills above Spoleto, is a nice place to stay and dine (074 349 624/eremodellegrazie.it). In town, on the Via del Duomo, the **Palazzo Dragoni** needs a little sprucing up but has pleasant service and will find you parking—if you can find the hotel (074 322 2220/palazzodragoni.it).

Torgiano

A dozen miles south of Perugia, the venerable **Hotel Le Tre Vaselle** has large, comfortable rooms in its ancient wing (075 988 0447). Best of all, however, is its restaurant, **Le Melagrane,** which has a charming old fireplace.

Tuoro sul Trasimeno

All is peaceful and languorous at the **Villa di Piazzano,** near Lake Trasimeno (075 826 226/villadipiazzano.com).

Reading

Jacob Burckhardt's nineteenth-century classic, ***The Civilization of the Renaissance in Italy,*** remains unequaled as the best take on the period in a single volume (Modern Library). *Italy,* in the **Knopf Traveler's Guides to Art** series, devotes two pages to a tour entitled "Painting in Umbria," which leads you to lesser Renaissance works in the medieval churches and palaces of tiny hill towns (out of print). **Blue Guide'**s *Umbria* is a dependable standby. Scala, an Italian publisher, produces beautifully illustrated and inexpensive monographs on all the major painters (available in many local bookstores). Highly recommended, too, is **Condé Nast Traveller'**s *Umbria,* which, although it requires a reading knowledge of Italian, has information on everything from art to food (abbonamenti.travelleritalia.it).

Assisi

"This twofold temple of St. Francis," Henry James wrote in
Italian Hours, "is one of the very sacred places of Italy, and it
would be hard to breathe anywhere an air more heavy with
holiness." There is no doubt that a visit to Assisi really feels
spiritual, and the frescoes in the lower basilica of San
Francesco—by Giotto and Simone Martini—are for many
visitors the highlight in all of Umbria.

Some good reads are "Mass Appeal," by Jan Morris (*Travel
+ Leisure,* November 1989), written eight years before the
September 26, 1997, earthquake; "Resurrection in Assisi,"
by Manuela Hoelterhoff (*Condé Nast Traveler,* October 1998),
written a little less than one year after the quake; and "The
Shock of the Old," by Jane Kramer (*The New Yorker,* February 8, 1999), written in the aftermath of an earthquake on
May 12, 1997, in the Umbrian town of Massa Martana, not
far from Assisi, where Kramer lives. Kramer has been European correspondent for *The New Yorker* for many years, and I
have long enjoyed her dispatches, many of which are investigative pieces. In this one about the Massa Martana earthquake, she shares that in Massa—which wasn't built to
withstand earthquakes—the people felt very let down that
the world utterly ignored Massa's devastation while pouring
money into and attention on Assisi. In 1998, $40 million of
the Italian government's $150 million earthquake budget
went to Assisi, even though the basilica there belongs to the
Vatican, not Italy. So Italy paid the restoration bills for Vatican
property, while none of Massa's churches made the first-
priority list (though later three Massa churches were included
on an updated list). Kramer argues in this very interesting
piece that the politics of restoration are about class, specifi-

cally an upper class that appreciates art and history more than people, and she claims that Saint Francis of Assisi would have saved a grandmother before ever thinking about the basilica.

Another good read is *On the Road with Francis of Assisi: A Timeless Journey through Umbria and Tuscany, and Beyond,* by Linda Bird Francke (Random House, 2005). Francke reminds us that approximately five million people visit Assisi every year (a good reason to rise early and arrive there before the tour buses), and that it is second only to Rome as an Italian pilgrimage destination. She and her husband set off on an unusual journey: to follow in Saint Francis' footsteps on his way to sainthood in the thirteenth century, using medieval texts as guidebooks, including the first official biography of the saint, dating from 1229.

RECOMMENDED READING

Living in a Foreign Language: A Memoir of Food, Wine, and Love in Italy, Michael Tucker (Atlantic Monthly Press, 2007). Actor Michael Tucker and his wife, actress Jill Eikenberry, bought a 350-year-old *rustico* (farmworker's cottage) near Spoleto, more or less on impulse, but one that has paid them back in spades. To say it changed their lives is an understatement. Tucker says the main piazza in their little town (the only one, actually) "is not a postcard-worthy town square the likes of Trevi, Bevagna, or Montefalco. Our town is not on the tourist trail. It's strictly for the locals, and I must say I prefer it that way. There are three bars, two butchers, two *alimentari,* a fruit and vegetable shop and a number of various other retailers—but if you didn't know they were there, you wouldn't be able to find any of them. We lived there a year and a half before we knew that the doorway next to the church—the one with the beads hanging down to keep the flies out—was Gloria's *orta-frutta* shop, the best and freshest local produce in the area. There's no sign, nothing. If Karen hadn't told us about it, we'd still be walking right past it without a clue. But once you know about it, you know. The same with Ugo's. There's no ad in the paper telling you that he makes the best prosciutto in the world. You just have to know."

Frankly, I sure wish *I* knew exactly where this only-for-the-locals little village is, but since I don't, and an invitation doesn't seem likely to materialize, I take solace in the fact that at least I can read about it, which is great fun. There are passages that are laugh-out-loud funny and others that are quite moving, and Tucker's descriptions of meals are delicious—he is, after all, also the author of *I Never Forget a Meal: An Indulgent Reminiscence* (Little, Brown, 1995).

Umbria: Italy's Timeless Heart, Paul Hofmann (Henry Holt, 1999). Before his passing in 2009, Hofmann, as noted previously, was bureau chief in Rome for the *New York Times* and the author of *Cento Città, That Fine Italian Hand,* and *The Seasons of Rome.* Hofmann was also quite an extraordinary human being: he fled his native Vienna for Rome after German troops occupied the country, but was later drafted into the German army and posted to Rome. He served as personal interpreter for two Nazi commanders, but also befriended some of Rome's anti-Fascist Resistance members. According to his obituary, Hofmann passed information to the Resistance about the deportation of Jews from Rome and the killing of 335 Italians at the Ardeatine Caves on Rome's outskirts, which occurred on March 24, 1944. This massacre was in retaliation for an attack by Italian Resistance fighters that killed thirty-three members of a Nazi military police unit. Hofmann eventually deserted, hiding his family in a convent and later in a safe apartment. In November 1944, he was tried in absentia by a German military court and sentenced to death for desertion and treason. After the war, he was a news assistant for the *Times'* Rome bureau, and remained with the newspaper for nearly a half century before his retirement in 1990.

It certainly was difficult, a dozen years ago, to have found a better companion to Umbria, and this is still an essential read, filled with his personal observations and historical anecdotes gleaned from his four decades of visiting the region. In the chapter entitled "Three Umbrian Gems," he shares that his three favorite towns in the region are Gubbio, Montefalco, and Todi. The book's appendix is an Umbria directory, organized alphabetically by town and featuring specifics on altitude (this might seem odd, but remember that the terrain is hilly), places to stay and eat (many of which are still around and recommended), sights to see, and directions.

Unforgettable Umbria: A Guide to 100 Masterpieces, Giovanna Mariucci (Scala, 2007). I bought this great book in the *Unforgettables* series at a bookstore in Perugia, at the suggestion of Marco, one of Italy's best guides (see page 234, 544). Scala Books is an arm of Scala Archives, which was founded in Florence in 1953 and has at one time or another served as the official archive for many of the collections in Italy's museums as well as a number outside of Italy. Scala Books (scalabooks.com) in turn is a publisher for art and cultural tourism, and its books are of very high quality. The hundred masterpieces of this title are found in seventeen Umbrian locales, and there are descriptive text, photographs, and itineraries for each one. The author writes, "In the Middle Ages new buildings were constructed over the remains of earlier settlements, creating the enchanting towns and villages for which Umbria is famed. Perched on rock, surrounded by turrets, a maze of twisting street opening onto

lovely squares, these hill towns capture the imagination and recall a way of life long past. The beautifully preserved towns of
Gubbio, Todi, Spello, Bevagna, Montefalco, and Assisi offer an
unrivalled opportunity to explore the Middle Ages." To my
mind, this is a perfect book for travelers as it's both a planning
resource and souvenir.

A Valley in Italy: The Many Seasons of a Villa in Umbria, Lisa St.
Aubin de Teran (HarperCollins, 1994). After she and her husband had bought Villa Orsola, outside of Città di Castello, but
before they moved in, St. Aubin de Teran told her two Irish au
pairs that there was still an enormous amount of work to be
done. She suspected that "the term 'enormous' did not ade-
quately describe the task ahead," which turned out to be an
understatement. The work is eventually (mostly) completed,
but before it is readers are introduced to all the characters in the
village, notably Imolo, Nunzia, Signora Maria, Don Annibale,
and Regina, as well as the Irish Beauties, and all in time for the
arrival of new baby Florence (Orsolana born and bred) and a
wedding. The family is a bit eccentric, but it's a story worth
reading.

INTERVIEW

Joan and Roger Arndt

*Joan and Roger Arndt can see one of the most superb vistas in all of Um-
bria from the windows of Le Vigne, the home they restored outside of Perugia and now operate as an inn. "The terrain is a postcard come to life"
is how Joan describes it in* Italian Lessons, *the book she self-published
(2008). "The patchwork hillsides change daily—from unplowed fields*

with a hint of green from winter wheat. It's no wonder Umbria is called 'The Green Heart of Italy.' " I can attest to the panoramic view—not only from the windows of Le Vigne but from anywhere on the property— and all that green. I was introduced to the Arndts by art historian Alessandra Marchetti, and I spent a few days with them in early spring at their hilltop home. But before I met them, I read Italian Lessons, and I was charmed by many of Joan's stories about their life in Umbria and impressed by their determination to relocate to Italy.

For the first few years, Joan did all the communicating because she'd studied Italian and Roger hadn't. Roger's skills have improved greatly: Joan notes that his favorite words are "domani, tomorrow—when he wants work done; caro, too expensive—when he's told the price; and sconto, discount—used at all times." But she, too, has had to learn all sorts of esoteric words needed for a restoration project, such as zoccolo, the desirable toe space beneath kitchen cabinets not typically found in Italian kitchens, and trave, the heavy, rough-hewn wooden beams that cover much of the apartment ceilings. She writes: "When is a gate not a gate? When in Italy and it's a cancello. When is a remote, either for the television or the cancello, not a remote but a telecomando? When is the *new faucet we've ordered a* rubinetto? *Same reason. While Roger and I speak English to each other, certain Italian words pepper our conversations replacing their English equivalents without a second thought. We're strad-dling two worlds; sometimes we speak in meters and kilograms, sometimes feet and pounds. Less English is spoken in Italy than in any other Euro-pean country. It's taught in school along with French or German but not put into regular practice. English speakers can get by just fine in the big, tourist-filled cities of Rome, Venice, or Milan but that's not the case in rural Italy. . . . In Italy, Italians speak Italian. They might also speak a dialect and there are hundreds of those throughout the country, but our focus is on Italian and the burden is on us."*

While we walked all around the grounds of Le Vigne, I had a chance to learn more about how they landed in this beautiful spot.

Q: Why Umbria, and why here?

A: We were initially drawn to Tuscany, mostly from having read Frances Mayes. But when we started looking in Tus-cany, we quickly learned how popular and expensive it was, and after many months we were very discouraged. We ex-panded our search to include Umbria and we found to our surprise that Umbria was less discovered, less expensive, less crowded . . . and it's just as beautiful and less spoiled than Tuscany. We came very close to buying something in Tus-cany and even signed a contract, but at the last minute it fell through, and we couldn't be happier about that now.

Q: How old is Le Vigne?

A: We know from a book we were given that the property eas-ily dates from 1727, but when we first visited the property, we were told the building was a former twelfth-century con-vent. We're told we can research the official historical records in the state archives or land registry offices to confirm this,

and someday, after we've brushed up on our ancient Italian and have a full second to breathe, we'll begin the research.

Q: You refer to your *località,* Colombella, as a "speck of a town." Just how small is it?

A: Colombella has a population of about two thousand, so it really is a speck! Some say the name is derived from *colle* and *bella,* meaning "beautiful hill," and others say it's from *colomba,* or "dove," of which there are plenty. Even though we live in Colombella, our address says we live in the town of Bosco—meaning "woods"—the next town to the south. We're told the reason we officially live in Bosco is because that's where our post office is located, but we're not convinced. There's also a post office in Colombella. Why isn't that one ours?

Q: In addition to the olive grove, what else do you grow on the property?

A: We have fig trees, and we grow asparagus and tomatoes, and it all tastes incredibly fresh. You know, when we moved to Italy we carried Joan's three-ring notebook filled with her favorite recipes on the plane—it was such a treasure that we wouldn't trust it to the shipping company or checked luggage. And we never opened it. We eat and cook differently here and we live differently here.

Q: Do you feel you've become part of the community?

A: Yes, finally, we do. We're still the Americans, but now after eight years people notice if we don't stick to our routine, to which they've become accustomed. Our mechanic, Paolo, has a few sheep, and before Easter he killed a lamb for us and his mother cooked an entire meal for us—that may not sound special, but really, it's very traditional and it was very kind of Paolo to offer. When we offered to pay the next day, Paolo said we owed him twenty-five euros—this was for a meal nearly fit for a king. Valentina, who makes all of our ceramic items at Le Vigne, has made us feel a part of her family, and her father, who is a hunter, often brings us something. The defining moments of acceptance continue to evolve, but the first one was when we held a party to mark the completion of the restoration and to thank everyone in the community who helped us. That was the first time we knew for sure that we were appreciated and welcome here. But another memorable moment was when Antonella, our friend who is a baker, visited one day to collect rosemary to use for some baking, and she looked around admiringly and said, "*Avete seminato bene qui in Italia*"—You have been planted well, you are rooted in Italy.

Q: When you leave here what do you miss?

A: We *love* our house. It has a great feel in the summer and winter, and we love the grounds, the views—we never tire of the views—the fire pit in the back . . . these are the things we miss. We *both* wanted to move to Italy—it wasn't an idea only one of us had—and we weren't interested in spending a few months a year here. We decided it was going to be a complete relocation or nothing, so all of these things—our house, the food, the people, the terrain, the weather—are the things that make up our life now, so of course they're what we miss when we leave. Each time we go back to the States to visit, we realize there are fewer and fewer things we admire, and we feel our Le Vigne experience has been life-changing.

Q: What are a few must-dos you feel Le Vigne guests should have on their Umbria itineraries?

A: We really only have one thing we feel is an absolute must-do: tour Perugia with Marco Bellanca. He's an outstanding guide who can tell you about every stone, every building, every work of art, every place to eat, every inch of Perugia. And we always tell our guests not to try and do too much, which they always want to do. Most people just don't understand the time it takes to get from place to place, and the afternoon siesta, and then to enjoy it fully and really get the most of a visit. . . . Well, in a week you scratch the surface, but less than that you can't really see and do much at all.

Q: What do you find most rewarding about being innkeepers?

A: We love it when we hear from guests that they had a great time, that the children want to come back, and that we may have played a small part in helping someone have an amazing experience.

"While life in Italy is now our norm, in no way has it become wallpaper. We understand how blessed we are to occupy sixteen heavenly acres with every view being postcard perfect. The steepled images of Perugia, seen from our bedroom window morning and night, remain striking. The seasonal changes revealed during my daily walks remain life-affirming. The sunsets over Perugia in winter and the northern hills in summer are majestic. I open my eyes and my heart daily to this beauty; none of it taken for granted. There was a time when both feet remained firmly on American soil and we peeked at life in Italy. Then there came a day when we straddled the ocean. After a while, both feet landed in Italy and the peek was back at America and the footprints we left behind."

—Joan Arndt,
Italian Lessons

FLORENCE

On my first morning in Florence I resolved not to enter a museum or a gallery, but just to walk about and recognize places. Florence is a city most people have known at second-hand all their lives. Stendhal was delighted to find himself perfectly at home there from the moment of his arrival; and I think this is not an uncommon experience.

—H. V. MORTON,
A Traveller in Italy

I was born in Florence many years ago. To be born in Italy and in Florence is good fortune: you have only to raise your eyes and Art and Beauty come to meet you. And you are fortunate not only for the wealth of works of art and cultural messages that rise unexpectedly from everywhere and that are not only a part of but actually constitute the very fabric from which this country is made. You are also fortunate for the traditions, for the many civilizations that have woven together, have mixed, have looked around them and have decided to stay here forever. For this, Italy is the most beautiful country in the world.

—FRANCO ZEFFIRELLI,
from the introduction to Italian Dreams, by Steven Rothfield

The First Time I Saw Florence

SALLIE TISDALE

SOMETIMES IT SEEMS that Florence's beauty and success have conspired against her—with over two million visitors a year, almost everything's crowded, almost all the time. It's noisy, and tour groups abound. Despite all this, however, Firenze is irresistible, as this piece attests, and the presence of lots of tourists is not a reason to deter you from visiting what is arguably one of the world's most special cities. Even on cloudy days (and there *are* gray and rainy days in Florence), "the warm colors many of the buildings are painted—cream, mustard, saffron, butterscotch, egg yolk, zabaglione—give the impression of sun upon them," as Mark Mitchell has noted in *Italian Pleasures*.

In a special issue of *Wine Spectator* (February 28, 1995), writer Thomas Matthews presented some sensible approaches to visiting the city in an essay titled "Why Visit Florence?" His first rule is to avoid large groups, and second, he believes one should be prepared, for although Florence is a small city, it's dense with significant things to see. He also notes that the cuisine of Tuscany is equally noteworthy, and he recommends planning your meals with as much care as the rest of your itinerary. Matthews then suggests that a good way to incorporate all of the above is to concentrate on a particular theme or neighborhood. Having a theme "helps put the city's treasures in context, gives you a way to link and interpret what you see. And there's almost always a trattoria or wine bar nearby that will satisfy your hunger and soothe your tired feet. All it takes is planning." I couldn't agree more.

SALLIE TISDALE is the author of numerous books on numerous subjects, including *Women of the Way: Discovering 2,500 Years of Buddhist Wisdom* (Harper, 2006), *The Best Thing I Ever Tasted: The Secret of Food* (Riverhead, 2000), *Talk Dirty to Me: An Intimate Philosophy of Sex* (Doubleday, 1994), and *The Sorcerer's Apprentice: Medical Miracles and Other Disasters* (McGraw-Hill, 1986; Beard, 2002). She has also written for *Harper's, Tricycle,* the *Antioch Review, Portland,* and *Condé Nast Traveler,* where this piece originally appeared in March 1997.

WHEN I TELL people I am going to Florence soon, I hear two things in reply. The first is always said a little wistfully, quietly: "I went to Florence once." And after a pause, comes the gleam in the eye, and the list: "You must do . . ." You must do/go/see—this and this and that. The tone of that second sentence is a little aggrieved. Do it for me, is the unspoken phrase—because I'm not there to do it for myself.

I have an armchair quarterback's knowledge of Florence. When I was seventeen, without warning, I became infatuated with Michelangelo. I collected copies of his work and read some of the history of his place and time, of that particular Florence, resilient and enduring in the mind: the Florence of the Medicis, Savonarola, intrigue, genius, and war. Florence is a place I know only through the wistful memories of friends, and through reading. My images are of old photographs and engravings, and I see the city filled with sober palaces, casually great museums, magnificent churches; a city of neighborhoods and alleyways; and, in my mind's eye, a labyrinth of empty, echoing avenues free of urban fuss.

I know better, of course. Stendhal, in 1817, called Florence "nothing better than a vast museum full of foreign tourists." John Ruskin was bitter about the number of hackney coaches crowding the squares. Henry James, a few years later, complained about the "crush" of winter traffic along the Cascine, the public park that skirts the Arno. Mary McCarthy, who lived in Florence in the 1950s, called it "a terrible city, in many ways, uncomfortable and dangerous to live in, a city of drama, argument, and struggle." When I

OPERA DI SANTA MARIA DEL FIORE
Via della Canonica 1 - 50122 Firenze
www.operaduomo.firenze.it

came across this last quote, I shut the book. Firenze is believed to be from the Italian *fiore,* for flower; one of the city symbols is the lily; it has a bloody, brilliant, unmistakably urban history; it has always been densely populated and heavily visited; the surrounding Tuscan hillsides are famously green and bucolic. Yet to me, Florence remains canvas and stone, a monotype all shades of white and gray, a grave and silent place, a private dream. My first view of the city is by way of a careening taxi ride through busy, narrow streets; my first, jet-lagged impression is a mess of noise and cars. For what seems a long time for such a small city, the taciturn driver (who speaks only English obscenities) screeches and squeals through dim alleys, past scooters and cars parked every which way, without an inch to spare.

He leaves me on a narrow sidewalk in front of my unprepossessing hotel; through its dark foyer is a happy maze of common rooms and winding stairways, dark paintings and plush armchairs. The shuttered windows of my tiny clean room look out over a courtyard full of blooming shrubs and birdsong and mosquitoes that have had a lot of experience with shutters. I fall into linen sheets until my traveling companion arrives.

She has come to join me in Florence on her way from Rome to Venice. She is rested, cheerful, acclimated; I am in a fragile, dazed state of sleep deprivation. We walk through the crowded

twilight streets, dodging bellicose scooters and manic cars, heading vaguely west through dimming stone-walled ways. There is
no logic to the streets that I can see; the lingerie and shoe and
clothing and paper and music shops all seem to be ten feet square
with seven individual items for sale, all jumbled up with trattorias,
pizzicherie, pastry shops, tiny bars, newsstands, pharmacies. Coffee
and liquor are for sale everywhere; so are postcards of Michelangelo's *David* with sunglasses on.

Then my companion nudges me, says, "Look," and I turn to
see above me the sweep of the Duomo, its rust red dome looming over the narrow walk in maternal splendor. Henry James
knew this fractured view, the way the cathedral is seen "from the
deep street as you greet the side of a mountain when you move in
the gorge . . . content with the minor accidents." Any number of
visitors have noted, with varying degrees of complaint, that there
is no other way to see it. The Duomo anchors the city; it is buried
in the city, and only a portion can be seen at a time—one gets little glimpses of a corner, a gable, an arch, or a sidelong look at the
wedding cake façade. It seems altogether less a whole object than
the sum of its highly fantasized parts, a gigantic sum for that, a
continual, impossible, surprise.

We walk under the mild, delicate twilight sky, with crescent
moon and clouds in a pink vault, across the River Arno. Above us
rise towering cypress trees. As we cross back across the Ponte alle
Grazie, I lean over the sluggish, turbid water and see giant rodents
below—sleek, dark rodents, several feet long, swimming content-
edly along in the midst of my
imaginary city.

The next day, we set out into
the daytime chaos. The streets are
ravines of stone and fluttering
laundry, winding just enough to
confuse, slipping shyly between
battlemented medieval buildings

and the somber cliffside walls of *palazzi*. The avenues are crammed with traffic: with scooters, taxis, cars, buses, bicycles; with mobs of people trying simply to cross the road. One short stretch of road is suddenly, disconcertingly, empty, and then a single turn reveals a honking, screeching river of cars. Every corner echoes with horns and the squeal of brakes, with rapid, argumentative conversation and the unmuffled roar of the internal combustion engine, with heels ticking on cobblestones and radios bursting from behind shutters.

We pedestrians are routinely forced off the narrow walks into the streets, taking turns letting each other pass; walking becomes a rhythm of stepping up and down, looking forward and back, listening, double-checking at corners, waiting an extra beat for safety's sake. The drivers seem quite mad. I begin to see Mary McCarthy's point.

In the center of the city, near the Duomo, where cars and scooters are limited or prohibited at different times of the day, the wide avenues stream with people: half a million Florentines, dressed breathtakingly well, and visitors—Italians from out of town, Japanese in large groups and Germans in small ones, Australians in pairs and South Asians in extended families, Irish and Filipino and Ethiopian and Mexican. I see two young Hawaiians, dressed to surf. Many Americans, alone and in pairs, pushing baby strollers, folding and unfolding maps, in groups, taking pictures, holding hands, looking lost. The steps of the Duomo are covered with people, the steps on every building around the Duomo are covered with people, people line the sidewalks, lean against the walls. People walk with purpose, stand without reason, hawk cheap jewelry, smoke, read the paper, eat, talk, talk, talk. A well-dressed man carefully brushes his teeth; a *carabiniere* chats up three girls; a waiter walks up the center of the pavement carrying a silver tray, two fizzing glasses of champagne upon it.

We walk east through the crowd to the Church of Santa Croce, skirting bleachers in its piazza, which is filled with sand for a

beach volleyball tournament.
Inside the door of the grand
church is a big white arrow
with the word MICHELANGELO,
pointing to his tomb, where a
sad angel perches, chin in
hand. Next to Michelangelo is a memorial to Dante, another to
Machiavelli; across the center of the church, which is filled with
enormous scaffolding like a metal cobweb, is the tomb of Galileo.

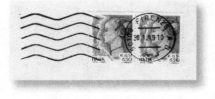

Pure Gothic, this echoing space of distant arches and delicate
tracery. The chancel, with its stained glass, giant crucifix, and
elaborate altar, seems to wait at the end of a tall tunnel in which I
am as small as a mouse, as quiet as a mouse. Chapels on both sides
rest in darkness; I find a 200-lira coin for the "illumination" machine in a far corner and buy one minute of light on the frothy
gold leaf décor of devotion. Heavy pews are lined up on a floor
of tombs, the status symbols of wealthy patrons. The stone figures
underfoot are so old and worn in places that their features are
gone; they are marble ghosts.

I pass among large, milling groups, hearing snatches of tour
lectures in four languages, watching the coordinated movement
of faces gazing roofward all at once. The illumination machines
click on, people turn and look upon Giotto, the lecture ends, the
machine clicks off again. Outside, I watch people in shorts walk
in past the sign saying NO SHORTS. The bare-chested volleyball
players jump and slap and grunt by pairs, in the blare of speakers
playing old American rock and roll.

In midafternoon, the shops and restaurants and museums close
with a definitive bang and the city is almost quiet. I go to my
hotel and watch *Matlock,* for the subtle pleasure of Andy Griffith
dubbed by a young Italian on too much espresso.

The outdoor marketplace by the Church of San Lorenzo is a
rabble of intense shoppers, full of deals and Whitney Houston yo-
deling out of powerful speakers. We are going up Via Cavour to

the Galleria dell'Accademia so I can see *David,* a central player in my dream time. I enter with a playful sense of anticipation. "When you go to see the *David,*" my friend Nancy wrote to me a few weeks ago, "wear cotton panties."

And yet I'm not prepared. I turn the first corner, and there is *David,* awash in soft light at the end of a long, vaulted hallway, with people swirling about his enormous feet. The four unfinished *Slaves* line the wall of the long gallery like guests at a wedding.

Behind me, alone and by twos and threes, other visitors turn the corner. A few gasp or murmur, surprised, suddenly whispering, in a half-dozen languages.

I take my time getting there, examining the strange, accidental *Slaves.* They are largely ignored. One can get quite close to them, and quite close to the enormous *David,* too. Close enough to stare straight up his smooth torso, close enough to see the obvious repair marks on the left forearm, the right middle finger. Close enough to see the carved MN on his right calf and the tiny white sticker on his bottom. I am startled to see that *David* is dusty. *David* has not been washed in a long time. *David,* in fact, has cobwebs.

I stand back a while, looking at the immensely pleasing lines of this sculpture I've longed to see, soaking up the subtle color of the marble and the complexity of expression in the face. Next to me, a stout British matron in a shocking pink suit stares, too, in a long silence, and finally says, without turning her head to her friend, "His chest is just super."

We find, at La Maremmana on Via de' Macci, a polite oasis of quiet and an antipasto buffet that haunts me for weeks afterward—pickled eggplant, juicy anchovies, roasted peppers, grilled zucchini, slabs of whitefish in an oily peppercorn marinade. At Maremmana I begin to see just how hard it can be to get a cup of plain black tea in Italy. "*Tè caldo, per favore.*" "*Tè caldo? Freddo?*" "*No, caldo.*" The waiter is dubious, shakes his head. "*Con latte? Zucchero?*" "*No, niente.*" I have only phrase book Italian, and he clearly thinks I've got the wrong words. *"Niente." "Con pesca, o limone?" "No, niente, per favore."* When my tea arrives, it is luke-warm, pale, and filled with lemon. I repeat this conversation many times, in many cafés, with the same result.

The evening is gelato time in the busy, bright tile of Vivoli's. We choose between strange flavors—mascarpone and white rice and rum crisp. Strolling away from Vivoli, through the small groups with their tiny cups and tiny white plastic spoons, I see so many stunned foreigners, so many subdued Italians from down south, so many teenagers with their golden brows and restless feet, that I know I'm watching the gates of the famous Florentine summer season swing open wide.

I wake early, a few days after my arrival, to the joyful noise of low thunder, and lie drowsily in the dark for some time while the rain waxes and wanes against the shutters. The bass shout of thunder in the valley is so abrupt and demanding it makes the heart sit up and take notice; it makes me want to stand on the bed and sing. Its echoes roll down the streets even as the next bolt flashes by above.

Rest and motion—so much to do: The Museo di Storia della Scienza, with room after room of polished brass armillary spheres and painted globes and strange machines for measuring electromagnetics, and the bones of Galileo's left middle finger. *Farmacie* and herbalists selling everything from incense and perfume to restorative unguents. The museum at the Pietre Dure Workshop, cele-brating the half-forgotten and slightly weird art of painting with colored stones. The Boboli Gardens, a bit dusty and ragged, with feral cats darting from hedge to hedge.

On one corner of the ugliest piazza in town, the ill-begotten parking lot of the Mercato Centrale, we find a tiny trattoria called, simply, Mario. It has the typical trattoria's stadium seating, cramped tables of strangers keeping track of their water and wine and ignoring each other's conversations. We order bowls of an exquisite ravioli and tart mixed salads. In the ordered chaos, the food comes quickly, brought by stout, middle-aged waitresses in white aprons and little soft white caps and red lipstick; they remember everything, write nothing down. We rest, and eat, without room to cross our legs, and in the dull roar of conversation overhead is the constant murmur of the staff skirting by, "*Permesso, permesso,*" balancing bowls of soup and pasta, whispering, "*Permesso.*"

The Campanile, the frosted bell tower of Giotto, stands with the Duomo like a soaring cliff beside the mountain's dignified peak. In Florence, much is lovely that needn't be lovely; much is breathtaking when lovely would do. The grand loggia of the Uffizi—the Uffizi, with its absurd wealth of art—is far grander than required. Its stairs are preposterously wide, the corridors ridiculously long. Even the Bargello, the old prison, with its history of torture and executions, is filled now with fine ivory carving, tapestries, armor, the resting bronze birds of Giambologna. And from every angle, the exquisite marblework and soaring lines of the Campanile beckon the eye upward.

Dire warnings about the effect of the climb on the ill and the weak are posted at the ticket window, where the plump, despairing guard sits in judgment on us all. We who climb become spelunkers, following the wavering bottoms of strangers up worn, narrow, and spiraling stairs, balancing against dank walls covered with cosmopolitan graffiti. At the top, winded travelers catch their breath in several languages and linger over the grand view—the sea of red tile roofs and television antennas, the cavernous streets, the distant hills of pine and olive. People take each other's pictures, trading cameras.

In the evening, we find our way to Osteria dei Cento Poveri, west of Santa Maria Novella. We scrutinize its fancy, handwritten menu, lost in the elaborate colloquialisms of Tuscan cuisine, and the fussy, baby-faced waiter finally brings us a basket of dead fish, insisting we pick our favorite. With a flourish, with distant curiosity, he brings us spaghetti with raw tomatoes and green beans and shreds of hard ricotta, good Tuscan wine, the grilled fish, and shot glasses of *vin santo* in which to dip hard almond cookies. The room is narrow, dim, and fragrant, and over the slow, intoxicating dinner we listen to Michael Jackson and bad British pop. Eventually our dimpled waiter, who speaks no English, brings a plate of pasta to our table and joins us without waiting to be invited, and we scribble on the tablecloth with pencils, drawing our conversation back and forth.

We buy gelato, quite late at night—kiwi, and *torroncino,* a kind of nougat, hazelnut and banana, and chocolate—and walk through the deserted square of San Lorenzo, by the silent, dark, comfortable church, with cups of ice cream in our hands. It begins quite suddenly to rain. We stop in a lighted shoe store doorway to wait, under the narrow roof and up against the glass, halos of light and shoes around our heads. The rain falls in white streaks through the empty dark, and four people run toward us, laughing, darting vainly, and when they reach the pedestrian rails by the empty street, they simply leap over them like so many gazelles and run on.

When we pass the Duomo, people are streaming in and out, and we enter to find a choir singing, lit only by a hundred candles burning in the shadowy space.

The next day my companion leaves for Venice; I take my happy solitude for an early morning hike to the Piazzale Michelangelo. Swifts dart like little dark arrowheads in the pale, fragrant sky, in front of fluffy bits of cloud. I cross the Arno, seeking giant rodents. In one of my city guides I have found a terse and curious reference to escaped coypu, and nothing more. The water is empty; there is nothing there.

I expect the *piazzale* to be a little park with a famously good view. The short, steep climb up Poggi's pretty steps brings me to a big parking lot filled with a sickly green copy of *David,* tour buses and souvenir carts, street artists, and flocks of people gazing at the skyline. The city's repeating tints of red and rust, dry yellow, and dark, wet green are like quiet water with only a few stark waves to break the surface. Florence is an uncompromisingly horizontal place these days; it's safer this way. In medieval Florence, every major family had a tower from which to toss pitch and garbage on their enemies.

I ask a woman from Washington, D.C., to take my picture. She tells me that her daughter studied here and has brought the whole family over to show them her adopted home. I stand before the Duomo, of course, and smile. Yes, I'm alone, I tell her; my traveling companion has gone to Venice for a few days. I wanted to stay.

"Venice is nice," she agrees. "But this place has class."

Casa Buonarroti is an unassuming, almost anonymous building on the corner of Via Ghibellina and Via Michelangelo Buonarroti. The airy, nourishing space was owned by Michelangelo and is now his museum—all small, tall, whitewashed rooms opening one into the other, with long windows and slim arches. His earliest sculptures are here, the *Madonna of the Steps* and the *Battle of the Centaurs.* A small group of lovely Italian teenagers with hardly any clothes on are carefully copying into big artists' pads; they lean against each other and whisper. One room is filled with the memorabilia of anniversary celebrations, the pomp and circumstance of intense civic pride. An entire wing of the house consists of Rococo tribute rooms done by Michelangelo's nephew after his death. I feel a funny melancholy here, missing a man dead almost five hundred years, a man famously unpleasant, with little regard for women. Wandering the overdecorated memorial rooms, finding his cup, his brush, his shoes, all encased and labeled, I begin to see that there is nothing untoward in my feeling for Michelangelo. It is only reasonable here. It is simply Italian, peculiarly Florentine. For the frantic lunchtime rush, for the spaghettini with shellfish, for the *panzanella*—and because it is near the *David.*

This time, I wait in line for forty minutes, snaking down the sidewalk past the Senegalese poster and belt and necklace salesmen working the crowd, pushing pictures of *David,* on special today. *David* is everywhere in the city—on postcards, T-shirts, neckties, watch bands, handbags, miniaturized by the thousands. Botticelli's *Venus* is everywhere too, and certain sappy cupids, an occasional *Mona Lisa,* fragments of the Sistine. One never sees copies of the subtle, decrepit *Bacchus,* though, or the stunning *Rape of the Sabines,* or Donatello's creepy *Maddalena.* Faith in tourists is a conservative religion.

The multiple repetitions of *David* have no lasting impact; the real thing is beyond imitation. He stands there, his mind on other things, and one expects to look away for a moment and turn back to find he has changed position—to find him looking at you, serene, arrogant. To wander in *David*'s shadow is to wander in a crowd of cheerful neophytes, people frankly amazed, moved without having expected to be moved. I feel completely contented here for a long time.

The crowds ebb and flow, festive, pleased. Two Irishmen sit beside me in the gallery. "Don't bother with the camera," says one. "The postcards are better." But the thickset, balding man continues to adjust his focus. "I want it in me photo album," he says, and takes the picture.

So much to do. The paper shops, glassmakers, shoe stores. The Santa Croce cloister, with its surprise Henry Moore. Maremmana again, for the much-desired antipasto buffet, the same tepid, pale tea. The Cappella dei Principi, a kind of Mad Hatter's fever dream of precious stone—oversize, overwrought, the giant crypts like big boats of crusted jewels, the dome florid with the Greatest Hits of the Bible.

The New Sacristy, containing the tombs of Lorenzo de' Medici and his hapless son and grandson, is a small room of monochromatic intensity. Michelangelo wrote, as he worked on these statues, "here we still are crushed / by doubt of joy." There is no color but the varied grays and creams and off-whites of Carrara marble, *pietra dura, pietra serena*. On two sides are the representations of time. They are not to everyone's liking, large and naked and preoccupied as they are. *Dawn* is drowsy, and her belly and thighs are full of possibility; her bluntly erotic lines disconcert on a grave. *Dusk* is rough and entwined in the rock, at ease, disdainful. *Night* ignores us, lost in memory. *Day* is monstrous, all back and thigh and benign command. They rest among the simplest angles and most perfect curves, promising and melancholy, more the Florence of my imagination than anything I've seen. It is a room resigned to loss, to the slow descent into self-examination. A room destined for solitude.

Four downy, slouching Italian teenagers perch on the crypt railing, talking, their backs to the marble. A Paraguayan couple repeatedly shoo people away from their examination of the statues to take long, involved photographs. A guard chases the teenagers off the rail, and then berates a woman to the point of tears for using a flashbulb. A large Italian tour group arrives and piles themselves up against the simple altar, listening halfheartedly to a lecture. An American woman behind me says to her friends, over and over, "We've got to keep moving."

In Florence, Mary McCarthy wrote, the past is "near and indifferently real." The grand and rare is an everyday thing; the things of everyday are treated with the same offhand manner as the grand and the rare. This is my great surprise: not that my grave and silent Florence, my dreamed Florence, is a riot of human beings, or that it smells of exhaust and sweat and sewage, or that it rumbles with noise night and day. The surprise is that I like this peopled Florence so much more than the dream; the multitudes animate the ghostly past with their fleshy presence. Like the city's history, they—we—are dignified and cruel, cynical and innocent, full of misery and of cheer. This human swell, this rolling, mammalian river of people, is the same swell, the same people, that has been here for centuries of contentious civic debate, assassinations, festivals, plague, flood, and massacre, Raphael and Botticelli and Masaccio, olive groves and wine so good it seems to spring from the well of soil.

What better response to the noble disregard of *Dawn* and *Dusk* than to sit on their rail and talk? How else to react, confronted with Brunelleschi's improbable Dome, than to stand and stare with craning neck? And what better thing to do next than eat?

I can barely resist the Chinese restaurants scattered around town, especially after seeing a large Japanese tour group march into one, silent and single file. Hard to resist, for that matter, the lone Japanese restaurant, called Eido, off the Piazza della Signoria, which offers, among other things, *zuppa di miso.* There is an Indian curry joint, a Brazilian disco club, an Irish pub. But I choose Sasso di Dante, near Dante's putative house, a rectangular room full of French people. I am the only person alone. The Florentines, I've decided, are mad behind the wheel because they are alone then; being alone makes them uncomfortable; driving is the tense and serious affair of getting as quickly as possible to the company of others. The handsome men at Sasso di Dante bring *spaghetti alla puttanesca* and grilled vegetables and water and wine to my little table under the kitchen window, where they seated me so I wouldn't feel lonesome.

Zubin Mehta is coming to give a free concert in the Piazza della Signoria, a spacious square filled with riotously varied sculpture: Cellini's bronze *Perseus,* Giambologna's *Hercules and the Centaur* and his magnificent *Rape of the Sabines,* a lumbering *Neptune,* another copy of *David,* a loggia of distant, writhing figures. Tiered steps of the Palazzo Vecchio were the traditional site of Florence's innumerable public debates—*arringare,* from which we get our word "harangue." Here the fanatic Savonarola burned books and paintings on the Bonfire of the Vanities; here he was burned himself. Here, Mary McCarthy relates in a long catalog of horrors, a man was eaten by an angry crowd. Here, wrote D. H. Lawrence, is "the perfect center of the human world."

The thunderstorms have passed, and the famous summer heat of the Arno valley is pouring in. For two days, I've watched the orchestra stage go up, the sound and television trucks come in, the electrical cables being connected. The scene is attended by self-conscious, chain-smoking classical music roadies, and even more people have arrived. All over town the mood just says, "Holiday!" The steps of the Palazzo Vecchio are covered with tired travelers politely watching the show they put on for each other. The square is sunny and fresh and crowded and loud, the roadies do a sound check—"*Uno, due, tre.*" The square swells with violins, with the roll of timpani, filling the air and startling the pigeons.

I have done what Stendhal did when he came here—"grown incapable of rational thought . . . surrendered to the sweet turbulence." When you go to Florence, you must see . . . this and this and that. You must hear a Rachmaninoff sound check on a sunny day. See a midnight choir in the Duomo. Eat gelato by a shoe store late at night, in the rain.

I return for dinner at a terrace restaurant in the piazza. The

breeze is cool; my wine and water, too. Behind me the waiters jabber like a flock of big, deep-voiced birds. The square is a slow simmer of people and pigeons, streams going every which way, shifting, sifting, changing direction, changing their mind. The bell of the Palazzo Vecchio begins to ring—a tenor gong tolling the hour for a long time, fading very slowly, sliding its sound invisibly into my dreams, into the myth I am making of Florence.

DIVERTIMENTO

The list of must-see sights in Florence is exclusively artistic and historical, with a single exception. A friend said I mustn't miss a little-known museum called La Specola, which means "observatory." No casual visitor would stumble upon the place, located on a side road south of the Pitti Palace, through a dark, dirty courtyard, and up three flights of stairs. The museum is open mornings a few days a week, and, from day to day, certain floors and rooms are closed.

The surpassingly weird La Specola is the best antidote in town to an overdose of gorgeous Crucifixions. It is part of the University of Florence's Natural History Museum and contains a tribute room to Galileo, though its main attraction is zoology. La Specola is not for the squeamish or for small children, but it is not to be missed by the curious.

The zoological floor is divided into two sections—natural history and waxworks. The natural history rooms have everything from a hollowed-out elephant foot to a disconcertingly long tapeworm and a ratty-looking gorilla. Room after windowless room form a maze of brightly lit glass display cases containing hundreds of taxidermied specimens: corals and insects, sharks and land tortoises, emus and quetzals and eagles, a white rhinoceros, a hippopotamus, a Tasmanian wolf, an echidna. I wandered these eerie, hypnotic rooms, which smell faintly and constantly of preservative, in solitude; the only other visitors I saw in two hours were a mother with her two small, wide-eyed children.

But those who go to La Specola do so for the human corpses most of all. Passing out of the animal rooms and into the waxwork section is a step through the looking glass, from natural history to nightmare. In perfect realism, chickens and turtles, human fetuses and pregnant women, spinal cords and skulls, genitalia and whole bodies fill the rooms. Each is dissected in a different way—for these are teaching models. Grand Duke Pietro Leopoldo of Lorraine, who founded the museum, and Felice Fontana, the first director, wanted to find a way to teach anatomy without the distasteful use of human corpses. An elaborate series of models was developed, from 1771 until the mid-1800s, into a collection of more than fourteen hundred pieces.

The Grand Duke's plan misfired dramatically. The effect of the models is one of continual vivisection; a walk through these strange rooms is a walk through a disturbingly violent fantasy world. The brilliant waxwork artists weren't content to make body parts according to drawings. They created sculpture, and all the models look alive in the midst of their evisceration. A young woman, gazing serenely, reclines on a soft bed, holding her braid in her hand, her chest and abdomen exploded into Technicolor butchery. Half-dissected heads in cases have their eyes open and a bit of goatee showing. A large man made to demonstrate the lymph system seems to rise in agony off his pallet, eyes wide and shocked by the brutality of his torture; he is called by local people *lo scorticato*, "the skinned." One room contains the lifework of a modeler famous in his time, Gaetano Zumbo—four brilliant dioramas of macabre plague scenes, a series depicting the effects of syphilis, and a decomposing head.

I mentioned my visit to the desk clerk at my hotel. He looked wistful and smiled in memory. "Ah, La Specola," he said. "I have not been to La Specola since I was a child."

PERSONAL BEST

My ideal travel guide to a city I've not visited before has a little of the historical and cultural context, the best hours to get into the most interesting museum, how to make a telephone call and where to get my linen trousers dry-cleaned, the location of every public toilet in town, how to buy a bus ticket, and a number of useful phrases for restaurants, shops, and getting around. ("I'll be thirty-three years old on July 16, 1967" is not a useful phrase. Neither is "I would like to buy a can of balls." Both of these are in my Italian phrase book.) My imaginary guidebook also has a complete and logical index and a good map. It does not exist.

As an experiment, Tisdale took four guides to Florence: *Knopf Guides: Florence;* Dorling Kindersley's *Eyewitness: Florence & Tuscany;* Fodor's *Exploring Florence & Tuscany;* and *Insight Guides: Florence.* She explained that: "Although the soberingly thorough three-hundred-page *Blue Guide: Florence* (Norton) is *the* definitive paperback reference to art and culture, I do not include it because it has only twelve pages of practical advice." Due to the passage of years, as well as changes that have since been made to these guidebook series, I've omitted her original critiques (at the time she recommended bringing the Knopf guide "for its art history" and the Eyewitness guide "for its cheerful information," though she noted that "both require a certain amount of patient sifting"). More relevant is Tisdale's general comment: "A city like Florence, with its complex and dramatic history and immense wealth of art, really requires more than one guide," and her final observation: "Don't go without a phrase book, as well—you may need to say, 'Please forward my mail to Venice.'"

The Other Side of the Arno

JO DURDEN-SMITH

No matter which bridge you cross to get there, the Oltrarno *is* different—bustling yet less frenetic, quieter, less touristy. In addition to the neighborhood's historic riches, such as the Palazzo Pitti and the Brancacci Chapel, its numerous artisan studios and handcrafted wares are riches of another kind.

JO DURDEN-SMITH was a British filmmaker and television documentary producer, notably of rock music programs with the Doors, the Rolling Stones, and Johnny Cash. He was the author of *A Complete History of the Mafia* (Metro, 2003) and *Russia: A Long-Shot Romance* (Knopf, 1994), among others. Durden-Smith also contributed numerous articles on Italian subjects to *Departures,* where this piece originally appeared, in 2003.

Every day Florence wakes to thousands of visitors trekking through the city toward the Pitti Palace, in what remains one of the world's most beautiful—and popular—secular pilgrimages. But as the crowds pour southward off the Ponte Vecchio, few among them are aware that they're entering the city's historic New Town. Kicked into life in the twelfth century when the old Roman settlement outgrew its borders, this southern addition, Oltrarno—"the other side of the Arno"—spilled out over land that had hitherto been home to vineyards, olive groves, and market gardens (as well as a few scattered religious communities). Merchants, squeezed out of their old quarters, found plenty of space in Oltrarno, and the district was soon populated by them and the people whose

livelihood depended on their patronage: servants, laborers, shopkeepers, and most importantly, skilled artisans.

The move to Oltrarno coincided with both a trade boom and a lifestyle revolution. Newly rich merchants who had once been content to live simple lives now wanted to live like princes. And for this they needed furniture, frescoes, bedding, tableware—everything to deck out their new single-family *palazzi*. So a vast number of artists and craftsmen decamped to nearby tenements and workshops and began to create everything their socially ambitious customers desired. They've been here ever since, very often in the same hole-in-the-wall ateliers, practicing their same trades. Although these days their customers aren't merchants but rather their contemporary equivalents: interior decorators, film designers, movie stars, and stylists, not to mention museums, hotels, and luxury department stores.

🦂   🦂   🦂

Take the **Luciano Ugolini & C.** bronze-working shop, for instance. Here the titular brothers, Luciano and Guido Ugolini (along with their sons, Daniele and Francesco) work in a garage-like space near the Church of Santo Spirito. Like many ateliers in Oltrarno, theirs is an old family business, one which has been producing exquisite bronze door handles and lamps since the end of the nineteenth century. Today the Ugolinis also produce hand-hammered copper amphorae and basins that are virtually indistinguishable from those that were made by Bernardo Buontalenti for the Medicis' Pitti Palace. "We design everything ourselves," says Luciano proudly. "Lamps, vases, urns, everything; and we still use the lost-wax method—we start with a wax model, then make a cast from it with holes drilled in for pouring the metal through."

Across the street from the Ugolinis' atelier is that of **Ivan Bardi,** who works with his daughter Consuelo and two friends in a streetside sprawl of little workshops. Bardi, a goateed man in his fifties, decorates and paints headboards, bureaus, and tabletops in a tradition that dates back to the fifteenth century. The raw material for his work he procures from the furniture markets or from individual clients. After having been stripped to the wood, it's coated with thin layers of gesso, onto which are painted layers of ornamentation—anything from floral motifs and decorative grisaille patterns to full-blown pastoral scenes. Bardi's warren of workshops is a chaos of furniture and bookcases, but out of the clutter emerges breathtakingly elegant furniture, all of it mellow and lustrous with varnish and wax. Touching their smooth, sheeny surfaces, I am reminded that both Sandro Botticelli and Filippino Lippi once moonlighted in *botteghe* exactly like this one, painting *cassoni* (hope chests) to earn extra money.

In medieval and Renaissance Oltrarno, little distinction was made between art and the sorts of crafts produced by the Ugolinis and the Bardis. Andrea del Verrocchio, after all, made terracotta figurines, and Luca della Robbia created wall tiles for kitchens. The whole quarter was in effect a factory whose artisans produced whatever was in demand, whether it was wall hangings or decorated tabletops. In the fifteenth and sixteenth centuries—Oltrarno's heyday—the workshops, which opened directly onto the street, functioned as ur-storefronts of sorts: Passersby had the opportunity to inspect the artisan's wares while witnessing their production. The workday began early in the morning. For lunch, errand boys would be dispatched to the great slaughterhouse on Via Bartolini, near the easternmost of the four gates in the city wall (which was erected in the fourteenth century to protect

Oltrarno from the army of the rapacious Holy Roman emperor Henry VII). Slaughterhouse workers would haul enormous vats of tripe soup onto the street, and the errand boys would hurry back to their workshops, their flasks filled with steaming liquid.

Today, the slaughterhouse is long gone, but in its place is a relatively new arrival, **Brandimarte,** a silver shop established in 1955 by Brandimarte Guscelli, a silversmith from Bologna. Like many ateliers in the Oltrarno, Brandimarte is a multigenerational effort; today it's run by the founder's son, Stefano, and sister, Giada. The atelier's twenty-five-person staff produces hand-worked silver, using, in Stefano's words, "Renaissance technology" to create "modern items," from goblets and candelabra to stunning silver pots and pans. The melted and molded silver is embossed and engraved in a clutch of small workshops ringing with the sound of hammers beating out patterns onto metal: stalks of wheat, olive branches, lilies, grapes, and oak leaves. "We can do anything a customer wants here," says one of the engravers, Fabrizio Aquafresca, a young cousin of the Guscellis'. He shows me a photograph of a vast solid-silver bath decorated with four gold-plated bronze fish. "It was one of a pair designed by Stefano," he says, "for an extremely rich Russian client."

Just down the street from the Brandimarte's shop is **Antico Setificio Fiorentino,** the great-grandmother of all Oltrarno's ateliers. After the city's golden age, in the fifteenth and sixteenth centuries, commercial silk production virtually died out, becoming the domain of aristocratic families, who considered silk making a prestigious—and exclusive—industry. In the mid-eighteenth century, six of these families decided to pool their looms and pattern books in a bid to consolidate their power; Antico Setificio is a descendant of that early conglomerate. "The company came to where we are now in 1786," says the managing director, Sabine Pretsch, "but our archives date back to 1492, the year of the death of Lorenzo the Magnificent!"

With this, Pretsch, who is passionate and brisk, leads me across a little gardened courtyard to a workshop where a cluster of local women—"from the parish of San Frediano, that's the silk guild's rule"—are busy weaving beautiful iridescent silks and hand-knotted damasks on eighteenth- and nineteenth-century looms. "The patterns are determined by a punched pattern-block system that dates back to the eighteenth century," says Pretsch, a one-time architect and journalist, over the constant clacking of the looms. "But the threads have to be knotted by hand, up to thirty-three thousand of them for the most complicated textiles." Against one wall is an odd-looking wooden machine resembling a bobbin (used for warping) "which was invented by Leonardo da Vinci."

The Setificio, which was once—and is now again—the most famous silkworks in Europe, was given a new lease on life after World War II, when Count Emilio Pucci di Barsento (a descendant of one of the founding families) bought a controlling interest in the company. Now Antico Setificio, which is a favorite among couturiers, filmmakers, and interior designers, also spe-

cializes in restoring and reproducing old silks for churches, museums, and European royal families. Setificio's showroom is filled with the results of what Pretsch calls "the luxury of going slowly": walls are ablaze with bales of hand-dyed silks in an astonishing range of textures and lusters and custom pillows. There are hand-woven damasks and brocades originally made for Renaissance aristocrats and re-creations of centuries-old designs. When the Russian government recently needed over 3,720 yards of silk for copies of wall hangings and furniture covers in the Kremlin, it entrusted the job to Setificio's looms.

The Russian project involved the re-creation of two nineteenth-century halls that were virtually destroyed under Stalin. The job, which took several years to complete, was overseen by another Oltrarno workshop, **Bartolozzi e Maioli,** which sits on Via Maggio. Via Maggio was once a dirt track used for hauling produce into the city, but today it is home to the city's best antiques shops, and at first glance Bartolozzi e Maioli looks like any other of the street's charming cluttered stores. But tucked away behind its plate-glass façade is a series of workshops and display areas crammed to the rafters with furniture and decorations in every shape and form: chairs, tables, chandeliers, and cupids.

The store, which is one of the most famous woodworking shops in the world, was founded in 1938 by two men who after the war spent a dozen years restoring the sacristy and choir of the famous bombed monastery in Monte Cassino, and later went on to decorate palaces in Brunei and Qatar, villas in Beverly Hills and San Francisco, the Holland Village in Nagasaki, and the Kremlin halls. For the Kremlin re-creation, the company employed over a hundred woodworkers, including apprentices from all over Europe. "About thirty-five different kinds of wood were used," says Gaia Bartolozzi, the late cofounder's granddaughter, who now runs the shop with her mother.

🐾   🐾   🐾

While Bartolozzi e Maioli and Antico Setificio may be among Oltrarno's most famous ateliers, every one of the neighborhood's workshops contains its own delights and surprises. On Via Toscanella, for example, **Giancarlo Giacchetti** and **Paolo Rossi** are hard at work on a sixty-yard-long wrought-iron staircase— which costs about $1,000 per yard—for a house in San Francisco. On Via de' Serragli, in a shop front dating back to the 1850s, *bronzista* **Lamberto Banchi** and son Duccio are making gold-plated brass candlesticks and picture frames for Neiman Marcus. And just off Santo Spirito Square, **Giuliano Ricchi** is packing up *objets de vertu*—enameled jewel boxes and pillboxes, gold-plated mirrors, and tortoiseshell-backed compacts—to send to luxury stores in London, Paris, and Hong Kong.

But unlike many owners of these small, family-owned businesses and shops, Ricchi will not be handing down his business to the next generation: "I have no son to take over from me," he says with a shrug, "and even if I could get an apprentice I couldn't afford to pay him what I'd have to while he trained."

This is a common complaint these days in Oltrarno. "Many of the ateliers have gone out of business because of it," says **Fabiola Lunghetti,** who operates from a small workshop directly opposite Pitti Palace. Like Picchi, Lunghetti, who is fifty-four years old, has no heir apparent. Twenty years ago she single-handedly revived the sixteenth-century art of *scagliola:* the use of gypsum stucco, transparent stone, rabbit-skin glue, and natural pigments to create a beautifully modulated marblelike surface for tabletops, boxes, and frames. "Others do an imitation," she says, "but they use synthetic resin, which can't be restored or polished." Today she occasionally restores old *scagliola* items for museums and for the antiques trade on Via Maggio, and laments the disappearance of many of Oltrarno's artisans. "There used to be a lot of coppersmiths here, for example," she says, "but very few survive."

And although Lunghetti, like all the artisans in this close-knit neighborhood, would like to see Oltrarno's traditions continue to the next generation, she too has neither the time nor the money to pass her skills on. "If I teach, I can't work," she says simply.

🦎   🦎   🦎

But Oltrarno's artisans are a practical lot, and for all the importance Lunghetti and her neighbors place on tradition, they also understand the importance—the necessity—of innovation, of change. Their predecessors, after all, developed their crafts in response to the changing tastes of their customers (not to mention the Medicis and the Grand Dukes of Lorraine, who over three centuries beautified Pitti Palace).

That progressive spirit still energizes the denizens of this ancient neighborhood. Thirty years ago, for example, **Stefano Ficalbi,** who has a studio and shop on Via Romana, was an Expressionist painter. Now he's a specialist in trompe l'oeil and grisaille. Twenty-five years ago, **Anna Anichini** at **Il Torchio,** on Via de' Bardi, was "a woman with a house full of books and a certain manual dexterity," when she began producing exquisite bindings for diaries, albums, and notebooks "the traditional way," using leather, handmade paper, and parchment. Ten years ago, **Christian Bernabé** and **Martina Fagorzi** were students at the Florence Academy of Art. Now they sit behind a shop front near the Specola museum, dabbing egg tempera and gold leaf on gessoed poplar to create modern versions of thirteenth-century masters. It might not be apparent, but change is everywhere you look.

Visiting the Workshops

The best introduction to Oltrarno is via a three-hour guided tour ($28; in English) by **Walking Tours of Florence,** which is part theatrical production and part wandering city seminar. (Piazza Santo Stefano 2/+39 055 264 5033 or +39 329

613 2730/artviva.com). All the ateliers below are open to the public, but call first to make an appointment:

- Luciano Ugolini & C. (Via del Presto di San Martino 23r/ +39 055 287 230)

- Ivan Bardi (Via del Presto di San Martino 4, 6, 8, 10, and 18r/+39 055 287 967)

- Brandimarte (Via L. Bartolini 18r/+39 055 239 381/ brandimarte.com)

- Antico Setificio Fiorentino (Via L. Bartolini 4/+39 055 213 861)

- Bartolozzi e Maioli workshops (Via de' Vellutin 5/+39 055 281 723; showroom, Via Maggio 13r)

- Giancarlo Giacchetti and Paolo Rossi (Via Toscanella 3–5r/+39 055 239 8088, by appointment)

- Lamberto and Duccio Banchi (Via de' Serragli 10r/+39 055 294 694)

- Giuliano Ricchi at Carlo Cecchi (Piazza Santo Spirito 12r/+39 055 214 942)

- Fabiola Lunghetti at La Scagliola (Piazza de' Pitti 14r/+39 055 211 523)

- Stefano Ficalbi (Via Romana 49r/+39 055 233 7697)

- Il Torchio (Via de' Bardi 17r/+39 055 234 2862)

- Christian Bernabé and Martina Fagorzi (Via Romana 47r/+39 055 219 879/bernabefagorziart.com)

- Pitti Mosaici (Piazza de' Pitti 23r/+39 055 282 127/ pittimosaici.it)

- Alessandro Dari (Via San Niccolo 115r/+39 055 244 747/alessandrodari.com)

- Stefano Bemer (Borgo San Frediano 143r/+39 055 211 356/stefanobemer.it).

So, also, is modernization: Ilio de Filippis, the owner of **Pitti Mosaici,** has assembled a fourteen-person team of craftsmen skilled in *pietra dura,* in which semiprecious stones and colored marble are used to create luminous patterned tabletops, clocks, and jewelry. De Filippis, an architect whose family has been selling marble and other stones since the 1890s, began his business by purchasing the workshops, archives, and sketches of a venerable *pietra dura* company called Menegatti, and has been expanding ever since. In the showroom on Pitti Square are sumptuous reproductions of tabletops made for the palace opposite, and in a workshop in a nearby alley, amid heaps of raw malachite, jasper, and turquoise, workmen are carefully assembling for a Japanese customer a twenty-foot-long landscape of Mount Fuji, all in lapis lazuli. Later, in his office, de Filippis shows me computer-generated images of works in progress: an extraordinary frescoed and columned Roman bathroom for a client in Laguna Beach and a twenty-three-foot-long *pietra dura* panel with life-size models for a fashion university in Tokyo. "A new technology in service to an old one," he says, smiling. "You see?"

But of all Oltrarno's remarkable workshops and artisans, two—to me, anyway—epitomize that balance of ambition and humility, modernity and tradition, adaptability and consistency that make this neighborhood what it is: not an anachronistic relic, but rather a vibrant, breathing community where artistic integrity and commercial practicalities coexist in relative harmony. The first is one of the most extraordinary of them all: the studio of **Alessandro Dari,** where the long-haired proprietor creates objects that almost defy description and dazzle the imagination.

Dari is a jeweler, but only in the sense that Cellini was one (and Picasso a maker of plates). For this fortyish Sienese, who trained in pharmacology, creates *objets d'art*—some wearable, some not—which are suffused with a profound knowledge of ancient jewelry-making techniques, as well as alchemic ideas and symbols. "I feel very strongly within me," he says, "the need to transform ephemeral and intangible emotions into matter."

Dari's pieces, which include Gothic sculpted rings, talismans, and pendants, are provocative meditations on the nature of love and power. One series of heavy gold rings, inspired by the four seasons and the work of Luca and Andrea della Robbia, are topped with tiny plates loaded with individually sculpted fruit, each not much larger than a nailhead. Another, inspired by the music of Mussorgsky, features mystical castles. These are museum-worthy pieces, and as the tall, dark Dari sits bowed over his workbench in a high-ceilinged fifteenth-century room, lute music quietly playing in the background, it's not hard to imagine him as the reincarnation of a Renaissance artist—of Donatello, say, who began his career not far away as a goldsmith.

On the other end of the Oltrarno triangle at the Borgo San Frediano is the atelier of **Stefano Bemer,** who appears to be the exact opposite of Dari: Bemer is short, fair, and cheery, his simple, welcoming shop a sharp contrast to Dari's magnificent cathedral-like space. But what unites the two men is an obsessive love for their craft and its traditions. Twenty years ago, the thirty-nine-year-old Bemer was a village shoe repairer. But then, just as Dari was studying metallurgy in Siena, Bemer apprenticed himself to an old Florence shoemaker, and later spent a year at night school learning pattern making. "I was driven. Almost from the beginning," he says, precisely echoing a remark of Dari's, "I knew that *this* was what I wanted to do."

Today Bemer hand-makes two hundred pairs of men's shoes a year according to strict nineteenth-century protocols. "The construction is entirely leather," he says. "I make my own wax for finishing. I use vegetable glues, and there's no rubber anywhere—except for rubber soles." The leathers can be arcane: from kudu and elephant to hippopotamus and shark, and in one case cured reindeer hides recovered from an eighteenth-century Russian shipwreck. The results, though, are seen by connoisseurs as the ultimate expression of the shoemaker's art. And like many of the craftspeople in Oltrarno, Bemer is both a purist and a pragmatist. Every year his atelier attracts apprentices from the world over—including the actor Daniel Day-Lewis.

"He came for a fitting in the late nineties, pursued by paparazzi," remembers Bemer, "and he took refuge in the workshop for a while. And then he said, 'You know, I'd like to learn this. Is it something I could learn?' Well, in the end, he stayed. He rented an apartment and he worked here for eleven months, very serious and talented. He was a very fast learner. In the last two weeks," Bemer continues, "he said to me, 'Make a pair of shoes for me and I'll make one for you.' See?" He points down to the pair of brown shoes on his feet and beams. "Look. I'm wearing them still."

We linger at the doorway of the workshop where five apprentices, one a woman from Japan, are crouched around a low table. Then Bemer says thoughtfully—and he could be speaking for all the artisanal workers of Oltrarno, from Dari and Fabiola Lunghetti to the Ugolinis and the Guscellis—"I think what attracted him was the passion. You know, when you make something with your hands, when you hold

it for hours at a time, you transfer to it all your energy and your love." After visiting this remarkable neighborhood, you understand exactly why Day-Lewis wanted to stay.

NAVIGATING OLTRARNO

North of the river is tourist country. South of the river is where the city lives and trades and works. The quarter's heart, the place to see and be seen, is Piazza Santo Spirito, which hosts a daily farmers' market, a buzzy night scene (be sure to check out the **Caffè Ricchi,** the **Borgo Antico,** and the **Cabiria Bar**), and on the last Sunday of the month, a crafts fair.

Where to Stay

The most luxurious hotel in Oltrarno is the **Lungarno,** which is owned by the Ferragamo family and has seventy-four rooms, some offering spectacular views over the Arno and Ponte Vecchio (Borgo San Jacopo 14/+39 055 27 261/lungarnohotels.com). Much more modest—though more atmospheric—are the **Pensione Annalena,** housed in a quiet fourteenth-century convent (Via Romana 34/+39 055 222 402/hotelannalena.it) and the tiny **Pensione Sorelle Bandini,** whose kitchen was used for the film *Tea with Mussolini* (Piazza Santo Spirito 9/+39 055 215 308). You could also stay on the north side of the river. The **Hotel Savoy** on Piazza della Repubblica (+39 055 27 351/roccofortehotels.com) is a bit farther afield, but it's the friendliest and finest—and my favorite—boutique hotel in Florence.

Where to Eat and Drink

Virtually all the restaurants south of the river are family businesses, offering hearty Tuscan home cooking. Recommended are the unassuming **Osteria Antica Mescita San Niccolo,** which offers a fine wine list (Via San Niccolò 60r/+39 055 234 2836); **Da**

Ruggero, owned by the Corsi family and much favored by Florentines (Via Senese 89r/+39 055 220 542); and just south of Florence, in the village of Arcetri (where Galileo spent his final years), Omero (Via Pian de' Giullari 11r/+39 055 220 053).

Wine Bars

Try the tiny Le Volpi e L'uva, in the equally tiny square behind Santa Felicita (Piazza de' Rossi 1r/+39 055 239 8132); and Fuori Porta, with an astonishingly deep list of six hundred or more wines, which includes rare vintages of Chianti Classico (Via del Monte alle Croci 10r/+39 055 234 2483).

Must-Sees in Oltrarno

Between atelier visits, stop by San Miniato al Monte, the most beautiful church in Italy; Brancacci Chapel in Santa Maria del Carmine, where you can gaze at the breathtaking frescoes by Masolino, Masaccio, and Filippino Lippi; Brunelleschi's great Santo Spirito Church; the museums of Pitti; and the Boboli Gardens.

Florence, Then and Now

ADAM BEGLEY

✿❀✿

A TERRIFIC AND brilliant series called the *Traveler's Literary Companion,* published by the Whereabouts Press, brings together an assortment of works of fiction in a number of individual volumes, including *Italy* (see page 292). As Isabel Allende notes about the series, "We can hear a country speak and better learn its secrets through the voices of its great writers." I completely agree, and why *not* see Florence with only a copy of *A Room With a View*?

ADAM BEGLEY is books editor of the *New York Observer* and the author of *Literary Agents: A Writer's Guide* (Penguin, 1993). His book reviews have also appeared in the *New York Times,* the *Guardian,* and the *Los Angeles Times,* among others.

HERE'S WHAT YOU do first in Florence: complain about the tourists. It's a time-honored tradition and there's no avoiding it—or them, as they squeeze down the narrow streets. They choke the majestic Piazza Signoria; they overwhelm the Uffizi Gallery—so go ahead and get the grumbling over with. Hordes of them! A year-round blight! Why can't they just stay home! Or, if you're like E. M. Forster's "clever" lady novelist in *A Room With a View,* the one who exclaims in dismay over the bovine "Britisher abroad," admit that you'd like to administer an exam "and turn back every tourist who couldn't pass it."

Snobbery is part of the sophisticated traveler's baggage—that hasn't changed at all in the one hundred years since Forster, in his charming novel, skewered the supercilious "good taste" of those who look down on the "ill-bred people whom one does meet abroad." Nowadays, when everyone in the ill-bred crowd is snapping photos of the Duomo with a cell phone, or swarming the Ponte Vecchio, plastic water bottle in hand, the urge to override touristic self-loathing by claiming for oneself a spurious superiority is pretty much irresistible; Forster, were he still around, would poke fun at that snobbish impulse with puckish glee. (But don't let that stop you from grousing about the sheer number of bodies blocking the view of the Arno.)

The next thing to do in Florence, according to Forster, is throw away your guidebook. Chapter two of *A Room With a View* is called "In Santa Croce with No Baedeker," and it's a gently comic interlude every honest visitor to that great Franciscan basilica will recognize as a mocking portrait of himself. Or herself, in the case of our young heroine, Lucy Honeychurch, who winds up alone in the vast interior of Santa Croce without her *Handbook to Northern Italy.*

On the way in she noted "the black-and-white façade of surpassing ugliness" (the marble was added in the nineteenth century—paid for by an Englishman, by the way); now she's rattling around in the vast nave, wondering which of all the tombs was "the one that was really beautiful," the one most praised by Ruskin. With no cultural authority to tell her what to think, she thinks for herself: "Of course it must be a wonderful building. But how like a barn! And how very cold!"

And then, just like that, her mood changes: "The pernicious charm of Italy worked on her, and, instead of acquiring information, she began to be happy." We all want to be happy tourists, so here's the question: is Forster's early twentieth-century advice— toss the guidebook aside and let the pernicious Florentine charm seduce you—still viable early in the twenty-first?

Enjoying *A Room With a View* is easy. A love story that begins and
ends in Florence, with complications in England sandwiched in
between, it's short, cheerful, and delightfully sly. Besides, there
are two excellent and generally faithful film adaptations, the classic 1986 Merchant-Ivory production starring Helena Bonham
Carter and Daniel Day-Lewis and a PBS version released just this
year with enticing shots of Florence and a weird, unwarranted
twist at the end. Once Lucy Honeychurch and George Emerson
have kissed in a field of violets in the hills above the city (near
Fiesole, about which more later), you know (spoiler alert) you're
going to hear wedding bells at the end, no matter how many plot
twists the crafty author engineers.

Enjoying Florence—a hard, forbidding city ("a city of en-
durance," Mary McCarthy called it, "a city of stone"), handsome
but not pretty, a challenge even if you could siphon off the
tourists and replace them with picturesque Italians energetically

engaged in producing local color—enjoying Florence takes more time and more effort. But if you have with you your copy of *A Room With a View,* you'll find it easier to get along. Forster's supple, forgiving irony, his ability to satirize lovingly, combined with his firm but regretful insistence on not confusing art and life, is exactly what you need if you plan to share this intensely urban town with tens of thousands of sightseers for the five or six days it will take you to do just like them and see the sights.

Forster reminds us that though Florence is a capital of art (is it ever!), it's not just an overcrowded museum. When Lucy leans out of her window in the Pensione Bertolini and gazes out across the Arno at the marble churches on the hill opposite, and watches with dreamy curiosity as the world trips by, the author notes approvingly, with his usual mild irony, "Over such trivialities as these many a valuable hour may slip away, and the traveler who has gone to Italy to study the tactile values of Giotto, or the corruption of the Papacy, may return remembering nothing but the blue sky and the men and women who live under it." He's not suggesting that you ignore Giotto or the magnificence of the city's turbulent history, but that the hours spent soaking up the dazzling Florentine sunshine with no cultural agenda may be valuable after all.

When Forster himself first came to Florence in October of 1901, he stayed as Lucy did in a pensione on the Lungarno delle Grazie, with a view over the Arno to the Basilica di San Miniato al Monte and the dark hills beyond. He was on a grand tour, traveling with his mother, and was a dutiful sightseer. He wrote to a friend back home, "the orthodox Baedeker-bestarred Italy—which is all I have yet seen—delights me so much that I can well afford to leave Italian Italy for another time." He was back the following year, at the same pensione, and by the time he'd finished *A Room With a View,* he'd struck a happy balance.

In and around the Basilica di Santa Croce is everything that's delightful and appalling about Florence today. The neo-Gothic façade is still ugly, the long square in front of it dusty, bland, pigeon-infested, and lousy with tourists. The interior is still cavernous, austere, and chilly, impressive but somehow dispiriting. Even if you've ditched your guidebook, you're reminded at every step of the city's vast cultural riches: here are the tombs of Michelangelo and Galileo and Lorenzo Ghiberti, whose bronze baptistery doors opposite the Duomo were so perfect, according to Michelangelo, they could have been the gates of paradise; here are the memorials to Dante and Machiavelli. Crowds are waiting to get into the small, high-ceilinged chapels to the right of the high altar—that's where you can admire the tactile values of Giotto, whose early fourteenth-century frescoes grace the walls. Just outside the basilica in the main cloister is the Pazzi Chapel, a perfectly proportioned Renaissance gem designed by the great Florentine architect Filippo Brunelleschi (who gave the Duomo its dome). The chapel, its white walls decorated with glazed terracotta medallions by Luca della Robbia (one of young Lucy's favorite artists), looks best when it's empty, filled to its noble height with nothing but chalky light from the lantern and the oculi in the dome. In other words, if a tour guide and his flock are in there, wait till they've gone.

The nature of those tours has changed dramatically since Forster's day. In 1901—and until very recently, in fact—the tour guide pronounced on art and architecture in a booming or piercing voice, mostly in English but possibly also in German or French, while his flock huddled close to catch the echoing words of wisdom. In *A Room With a View,* Forster had fun with the solemn pronouncements of the Reverend Cuthbert Eager, who steered an "earnest congregation" around Santa Croce, lecturing all the while on the fervor of medievalism ("Observe how Giotto is . . . untroubled by the snares of anatomy and perspective"). Today, technology has shushed the tour guide: he or she whispers into a microphone, which broadcasts the lecture soundlessly, piping the flow of factoids into the earphones of the audience, who can now stray a little (and there are more languages represented: Spanish, Greek, Polish, Russian). Some familiar props remain— the retractable antenna with a ribbon tied at the tip, a rallying sign for the group as it migrates from one artistic treasure to the next—but the new quiet is disconcerting, as though these clumps of tourists with headphones and wireless receivers hung around their necks were part of some sinister silent conspiracy.

🦎   🦎   🦎

If you stroll a few dozen yards past the Pazzi Chapel, you'll find yourself in a second cloister, also designed by Brunelleschi, in 1446, the last year of his life. It's a place of great beauty and calm, usually deserted, and you don't need to know a thing about it to fall in love. The simple, elegant two-story cloister with its slender columns shelters you from the rigors and confusions of Florence and gives you instead the tranquil harmony of the Renaissance without pomp or grandeur, washed by bright Tuscan sun. I like to imagine, though Forster doesn't suggest it, that Lucy loitered here without her Baedeker, and that's why she began to be happy. At the very least, a quiet moment in the cloisters will give you strength to confront the multitudes and the immortal works of art remaining on your list.

And so will loitering over lunch. And dinner. One eats very well in Florence, and in general the simpler the restaurant, the better the food. If you can visit one church and one museum before lunch and one more church or another museum after lunch (whatever you do, don't miss the wealth of paintings piled higgledy-piggledy in the Palatine Gallery of the Palazzo Pitti), and then take a nap (Tuscan wine is cheap and abundant), and then stroll to dinner, perhaps along the Via de' Tornabuoni, under the looming, illuminated façades of great, stern palazzos, and stroll some more after dinner when the crowds have thinned and Florence seems gentler and the multicolor Duomo seems less garish but just as huge and astonishing—you'll find that after a few days of this routine, all your complaints will be forgotten, replaced with amazement and gratitude.

Unless of course you stray into the Piazza Signoria, where the replica of Michelangelo's giant David attracts a sizable contingent of art lovers with camera phones night and day. This is where Lucy wanders one evening, unaccompanied:

> "Nothing ever happens to me," she reflected, as she entered the Piazza Signoria and looked nonchalantly at its marvels, now fairly familiar to her. The great square was in shadow; the sunshine had come too late to strike it. Neptune was already unsubstantial in the twilight, half god, half ghost, and his fountain plashed dreamily to the men and satyrs who idled together on its marge. The Loggia showed as the triple entrance of a cave, wherein dwelt many a deity, shadowy but immortal, looking forth upon the arrivals and departures of mankind. It was the hour of unreality—the hour, that is, when unfamiliar things are real. An older person at such an hour and in such a place might think that sufficient was happening to him, and rest content. Lucy desired more.

And then something does happen to her: two Italians quarrel, one stabs the other in the chest, and Lucy, who sees the blood come trickling out of the fatally wounded man's mouth, swoons—into the arms of George Emerson, as luck would have it.

Nothing so dramatic is likely to occur to the twenty-first-century visitor. But if it does, head for Fiesole, the little hill town no more than a few miles from the Piazza Signoria. Along with the far reaches of the Boboli Gardens, this is the city's escape hatch, a chance to breathe deeply and see some greenery, plant life being notably absent from the historic center. Forster sends his contingent to Fiesole by horse and carriage (it's nearby that Lucy

and George first kiss); now it's a fifteen-minute ride on a boxy orange municipal bus. But once you've arrived you realize that the
chief virtue of this modest town, aside from the fresh air, is the
panoramic view of the Arno Valley and the extraordinary, maddening city you've just left, its Duomo vast and proud even at this
distance. And the wisdom of the structure of *A Room With a View*
is suddenly as clear as the bright Tuscan sky: you will return to
Florence, and next time it will be a honeymoon.

BEAUTY, STONES, AND HANGING HAMS

Getting There

There are no nonstop flights from New York to Florence. A
number of airlines offer daily flights with connections through
various European capitals; of those, the easiest is Alitalia, which
offers several daily flights via Rome. The small Florence airport is
only a few miles from the city; a bus service runs to the train station in the center of town and there are taxis, too. Once you have
reached Florence, everything is within easy walking distance except Fiesole, which can be reached by taxi or bus.

Where to Stay

If you are staying in the center of Florence, what you want is an
oasis, and despite the tacky name, **Hotel Monna Lisa** (Borgo
Pinti 27/+39 055 247 9751/hotelmonnalisaflorence.com) provides exactly that. A converted fourteenth-century palazzo five
minutes by foot from the Duomo, it's handsomely decorated and
blessedly calm.

If you must have a room with a view, go to Fiesole. **Pensione
Bencistà** (Via Benedetto da Maiano 4/+39 055 59 163/bencista
.com) is shambolic and charming—and affordable.

Also in Fiesole is the **Villa San Michele** (Via Doccia 4,
Fiesole/+39 055 59 451/villasanmichele.com), which will bank-

rupt you—but you will be coddled and cosseted in a gorgeous setting.

Where to Eat

Meals are important in Florence, not just because the food is so good, but also because the rest of the time you're on your feet. Lunch for two, with wine, of course, should cost you about sixty euros; dinner, with more wine, about one hundred euros.

For lunch, especially Sunday lunch, **Il Latini** (Via de Palchetti 6r/+39 055 210 916/illatini.com) is a must. Don't bother with a menu (the waiters don't like to give them out, and anyway they know better than you what's good). Help yourself to the big bottle of red wine you'll find at your table. Admire the hundreds of hams hanging overhead. Eat!

Quiet, relatively tourist-free, pleasantly traditional, and equally delicious is **Del Fagioli** (Corso Tintori 47r/+39 055 244 285), just a few blocks from Santa Croce.

If you want a little atmosphere at night and you're willing to pay a premium for the buzz and the funky décor, try **Trattoria Garga** (Via del Moro 48r/+39 055 239 8898/garga.it).

And if you're in Fiesole at night and don't want to engage in the enforced sociability of the pensione, **Trattoria i' Polpa** (Piazza Mino 21/22/+39 055 59 485) is cozy and friendly and inexpensive.

What to Read

Fifty years after the publication of *A Room With a View,* E. M. Forster wrote a short essay in the *New York Times Book Review* called "A View Without a Room," in which he speculated on the fate of the characters in his novel—not quite dessert, more like a tasty petit four. It has been printed as an afterward in the Penguin Classics edition of *A Room With a View.*

P. N. Furbank's massive two-volume biography of Forster was

first published three decades ago; now available in a one-volume Faber paperback, it's still the best account of a long, remarkable life.

If you want a critic's perspective on *A Room With a View*, see the chapter on it in Lionel Trilling's excellent *E. M. Forster: A Study*, first published in 1943 but available in paperback from New Directions.

Learning to Live with Arrivederci

SUSAN JACOBY

❧

THIS HAS BEEN a favorite in my files since its appearance as the back-page essay in the travel section of the *New York Times* (October 12, 1997). Like the author, it saddens me when I realize I "won't see Florence again for a span of time I cannot bear to estimate or contemplate," and I love to "incorporate some of the small, portable pleasures of Florence into my New York life."

SUSAN JACOBY is the author of *The Age of American Unreason* (Pantheon 2008), *Freethinkers: A History of American Secularism* (Metropolitan, 2004), *Half-Jew: A Daughter's Search for Her Family's Buried Past* (Scribner, 2000), and *The Possible She* (Farrar, Straus & Giroux, 1979), among others.

IT HAS BEEN exactly six weeks since I closed the door of my small rented apartment in Florence and headed home to New York. I know that because my final memento of the trip—a majolica jar adorned with a gaily dancing putto—arrived intact, meticulously packaged, in today's mail. For twenty-five years, on each visit to Florence, I have been buying china in the same small, utterly reliable shop on the Via Guicciardini. And each time, as if there were no postal, airport, or customs snafus on either side of the Atlantic, my purchases have arrived, give or take a day, in six weeks. Now, once again, I must come to terms with the fact that I am truly here and won't see

Florence again for a span of time I cannot bear to estimate or contemplate.

Travel books never discuss the end of the journey. People are always trying to convince themselves, and everyone else, that "it was great to get away but it's great to be home." I've even felt that way myself, after trips to places I don't love as much as I love Tuscany.

But Florence feels like home, or rather, like what might have been home had I chosen a very different life when I was young. I know Florence well enough to know where to buy paper towels and cheap flowers, well enough to face a dental emergency with equanimity, well enough to be greeted with recognition (or feigned recognition, which amounts to the same thing) by certain shopkeepers and restaurant proprietors. I have never spent an uninteresting day in this city, never experienced small vicissitudes or deeper sorrows that could not be ameliorated by contact with the noble civilization of these stony streets.

In the past, each return from Florence followed a predictable, dispiriting pattern. I would unpack immediately. (Out of sight, out of mind?) Reverting to a modus operandi best suited to the aftermath of a love affair, I then plunged straight back into work—more work than I really needed to accomplish during the first few weeks of readjustment. I rarely talked about my trip, reminding myself that there is no worse bore than a travel bore.

Above all, I stayed away from museums, on the premise that they would only arouse a most painful longing for the feast that had been mine for the gorging only a few weeks earlier. No more statues of David, in either Donatello's or Michelangelo's version. No Giottos, no Masaccios, no Leonardos. I also avoided my art books because their reproductions only made me yearn more intensely for the real masterpieces I had left behind.

When these avoidance tactics failed—as they inevitably did—I would succumb to tears, self-pity, and something approaching genuine depression.

This year, I tried to handle my homecoming in a different and less dour manner. First, I told everyone I wouldn't be back until two days after I really intended to arrive. The white lie gave me time to catch up on my sleep and set my house in order before anyone could reasonably expect me to return a phone call or answer a fax. More important, it gave me breathing room to think about how to incorporate some of the small, portable pleasures of Florence into my New York life. I decided to follow the advice of a new friend acquired on the journey, who told me she always tries to bring back at least one new foreign habit from each trip abroad.

During this stay in Florence, I developed a taste for something I never used to like: biscotti dipped in *vin santo*. Not the assortment of weirdly flavored, oversized American biscotti (cousins to those humongous breakfast muffins), but the trim, plain almond Italian version. On my second day back, I scoured my neighborhood for the right sort of biscotti and, this being New York, found them in only the second gourmet store I tried. There sat distinctive orange-colored boxes of cookies, labeled I Famosi, made in Florence itself and selling for a fraction (these are, after all, the Oreos of Italy) of what the same store was charging for its mutant American-made monsters.

I easily slipped back into the vacation habit of finishing dinner by dipping five or six (or ten or twelve) of the crusty cookies into a double shot glass of *vin santo*. Drinking down the dregs with the crumbs is the best part, now an everyday routine rather than a memory of a no-longer-attainable treat.

I made a more significant change by spending a considerable

sum enlarging and framing some of the best photographs I took on the trip. Instead of stowing them away in a box, I made room for them on the walls in spots that catch my eye several times a day. I used to tell myself that putting away the photos was part of not boring others with vacation tales, but I now realize that I was trying to lock away my own yearning for everything Florence represents.

The presence of these new pictures on my walls may mean that I am ready to pay more attention to the part of me that comes alive most fully in the golden-ocher light reflecting off the façades along the Arno. To that end, I have been devoting more time, not less, to the pursuit of art in New York.

I had seen the Metropolitan's dazzling exhibit on the art of Byzantium before I went away, but it took on new meaning when I discovered its riches for the second time after my return. I focused on certain connections I had marked only in passing the first time around, felt the full power of the Byzantine influence in the West.

Gazing for the second time upon the remarkable icon from the Egyptian Monastery of Saint Catherine, with demons gloating over souls losing their precarious footing on a ladder to heaven, I found myself mentally comparing them to assorted Florentine devils lurking and cavorting in the Church of Santo Spirito, the Baptistry, and the museum of the Duomo.

In that moment, I realized I was no longer struggling to contain my beloved Florentine apparitions in a box.

I am learning to let the images breathe, as Charles Dickens advised in his own *Pictures from Italy*. How exceptionally horrid it must have been to return from the Mediterranean world to the dank London of the 1840s! "What light is shed upon the world, at this day," Dickens wrote, "from amidst these rugged Palaces of Florence! . . . Here, the imperishable part of noble minds survives, placid and equal, when strongholds of assault and defence are overthrown; when the tyranny of the many, or the few, or both, is but a tale; when Pride and Power are so much cloistered dust. . . . Let us look back on Florence while we may, and when its shining Dome is seen no more, go travelling through cheerful Tuscany, with a bright remembrance of it; for Italy will be the fairer for the recollection."

Let me look back on Florence while I may, for New York will only be the fairer for it.

RECOMMENDED READING

NONFICTION

The City of Florence: Historical Vistas & Personal Sightings, R. W. B. Lewis (Farrar, Straus & Giroux, 1995). A very special, wholly enjoyable and engaging book by award-winning writer and biographer Lewis, who has lived in Florence much of the year for over fifty years. Though a personal story of Florence, Lewis includes much historical material, and whether he is pondering the Via Lamarmora or how he was trapped behind enemy lines in 1943, you never want it to end. It's also a beautiful book, with numerous black-and-white reproductions and photographs. At the end of the book there are very helpful and fascinating notes on the maps and illustrations, some scholarly and literary sources, and a contemporary bibliography.

The Civilized Shopper's Guide to Florence, Louise Fili (Little Bookroom, 2007). This chunky little (4 × 4 inch) paperback is small enough to pack and small enough again to carry around Florence with you. Fili is a former art director of Pantheon Books and head of her own graphic design firm, Louise Fili Ltd., and in 2004 she was inducted into the Art Directors Hall of Fame. She has coauthored, with Steven Heller, a number of design books, including *Italian Art Deco* (Chronicle, 1993), and she's also the author, with Lise Apatoff, of *Italianissimo* (Little Bookroom, 2008). I've been following Fili's work for a number of years, and when she compiled this book I knew it would be a must-have. The book is divided into eight walks through various neighborhoods, with a map and recommendations for shops and food and drink for each one. The thing is, even if you come across a particular shop and you're not sure you're interested in what it specializes in, it is never ordinary: every single choice in this book is unique in some regard, and you will come home with fantastic, one-of-a-kind *ricordi* (souvenirs) by following her suggestions—and likewise, you'll eat and drink well. Do not go to Firenze without this book in your bag. (And make sure you have a copy of the Rome guide if you're going to the Eternal City.)

The Dante Plaques: A Florentine Itinerary from the Divine Comedy, Foresto Niccolai (Coppini Tipografi, Florence, 2007). This small, slender paperback, which I bought at Paperback Exchange (Via delle Oche 4r, Florence/+39 055 293 460/papex .it), is essential for those who are Dante aficionados, but it's even noteworthy for those who are only mildly curious about the Florentine places and people named in the *Divine Comedy.* Niccolai informs us that in 1900, the Comune di Firenze decided to create plaques to mark the real places in Dante's text, and in 1907 they were installed. Today visitors can see them on the walls of buildings throughout the city, and they record facts and events in Florence's history. Because the plaques may be vague or incomprehensible to nonscholars, Niccolai aims to provide some background on them for everyone else. He's done a great service to many by providing the Italian that's featured on the plaques, its English translation, the location of the plaques, and explanatory notes.

Florence Explored, Rupert Scott (New Amsterdam, 1988). This is one of my favorite books. It's very much of a companion volume to *Venice for Pleasure* by J. G. Links; the books are the same size and shape and follow the same format. Scott writes, "Florence is and always has been a city that gives most pleasure to those who take their pleasures seriously. The single most compelling reason for coming here is

to see Florentine art. Thus it is in galleries and churches that users of this guide will spend the greater part of their days. Since Florence has possibly a denser concentration of beautiful works of art than any other city in the world, this can hardly be seen as an insupportable burden." There is a thought-provoking passage on nearly every page, such as this one:

> Though untouched by the First World War, Florence suffered badly in the Second. It is ironic that one of Hitler's few recorded acts of cultural clemency—a personal order that the Ponte Vecchio, which he had seen and admired in 1938, be spared—should have resulted in a much worse loss, the destruction of the *borghi* at its either end, which were mined in order to block its access roads. Appalling disaster though this was, permanently scarring the core of the city, and transforming its most beautiful streets into its worst eyesores, Florence was fortunate not to be damaged more badly and has been just as fortunate since then in having a local government that has rebuilt the Ponte S. Trinita as a perfect facsimile and preserved most of the wonderful country immediately to the south from speculative building. The contado still sweeps right up to the walls of Forte del Belvedere and S. Miniato, which permits the delectable and rare sensation of being able to move in a single step from the city gates to the country, as if in a medieval town.

This small paperback fits easily into a small bag and is organized by neighborhoods, more or less. With lots of black-and-white illustrations, photos, and maps. *Essenziale*.

Florence in Detail: A Guide for the Expert Traveler, Claudio Gatti and the writers of the *International Herald Tribune* (Rizzoli, 2008, revised edition). This is simply among the very best guidebooks to any part of Italy ever published, with maps, walking tours, fundamentals, historical and practical information, "Best of" listings, and the editors' "Our Pick" sites. The detail is in-depth and wonderful—Claudio Gatti notes in the introduction that this is specifically geared to the "background traveler"— and there are color photographs throughout. In his foreword, author and Italian expert Fred Plotkin reminds us that "the ambitious traveler who ventures off the well-worn paths to sites will be richly rewarded: admire the unsurpassable Pontormo painting in Santa Felicità, the Casa Buonarroti (dedicated to the life and work of Michelangelo), the church of Santo Spirito, and the gorgeous Teatro della Pergola." (Note that there is a sister volume, *Rome in Detail,* also essential.)

Florence: The Biography of a City, Christopher Hibbert (Norton, 1993). Historian Hibbert, who is also the author of more than twenty-five books—including *Rome: The Biography of a City* and *Venice: The Biography of a City*—is a British authority on Italy. This book is as much a guidebook as a lively history book, and also includes hundreds of black-and-white photos, engravings, and line drawings, and sixteen color reproductions. *Essenziale.*

The Stones of Florence, Mary McCarthy, with photographs by Evelyn Hofer (Harcourt Brace Jovanovich, 1959; Harcourt, 2002). Even in 1959, McCarthy wrote, "Everyone complains of the noise; with windows open, no one can sleep. . . . In truth, short of leaving Florence, there is nothing to be done until fall comes and the windows can be shut again." Anyone who has ever visited Florence in the summer knows this to be unequivocally true (to say nothing of the mosquitoes!). Absolutely *essenziale,* and you positively must get the large, 8½ × 11 inch edition with the superb photos (128 black-and-white images and twelve color plates). Do not even *think* of reading only the significantly smaller edition. I would never have been inspired to visit the wonderful Tuscan town of Pistoia were it not for the photos in the large edition, and I would not really have understood the Guelph–Ghibelline conflict without the opportunity to see how architecture was defined by politics. A parting passage:

> The Florentines, in fact, invented the Renaissance, which is the same as saying that they invented the modern world—not, of course, an unmixed good. Florence was a turning-point, and this is what often troubles the reflective sort of visitor today—the feeling that a terrible mistake was committed here, at some point between Giotto and Michelangelo, a mistake that had to do with power

and megalomania or gigantism of the human ego. You can see, if you wish, the handwriting on the walls of Palazzo Pitti or Palazzo Strozzi, those formidable creations in bristling prepotent stone, or in the cold, vain stare of Michelangelo's *David,* in love with his own strength and beauty. This feeling that Florence was the scene of the original crime or error was hard to avoid just after the last World War, when power and technology had reduced so much to rubble.

A Traveller's Companion to Florence, selected and introduced by Harold Acton and Edward Chaney (Constable & Co., UK, 1986; Interlink, 2002). I received this book as a gift from my friends Jesse and Barbara, who bought it at one of the English-language bookshops in Florence. My husband and I visited them one summer when they were renting an apartment in the Oltrarno, and with the help of this wonderful book, we made daily in-depth discoveries in Florence. The selected essays include topics such as "A pro-Brunelleschian view of how Lorenzo Ghiberti won the competition to produce the bronze reliefs on the north doors of the Baptistery," "The 21-year-old Ruskin climbs the Campanile for the first time in November 1840," "The colours of the Lungarno," "The Mercato Vecchio in the fourteenth century," "An eye-witness account of the installation of the 'David' outside the Palazzo Vecchio in 1504," "The courtyard of Palazzo Pitti in the summer of 1944," and they are extracted from books, letters, diaries, and memoirs. In his introduction, Sir Harold Acton writes that since rivers of ink have flowed on the subject of Florence it is difficult to say anything new, "but from the majority who have recorded their impressions and opinions we have selected those extracts which form a mosaic of its long history and illustrate changes of taste. It is still intensely alive as a capital of the arts and crafts." With black-and-white contemporary and period drawings, photographs, and engravings.

FICTION

The Birth of Venus (2004), *In the Company of the Courtesan* (2007), and *Sacred Hearts* (2009), all by Sarah Dunant, all published by Random House in both hardcover and paperback editions. This trio of novels has as its setting Renaissance Florence. See my blog for more details about these works of historical fiction and more from the author, who lives in London and Florence.

Indian Summer, William Dean Howells (New York Review Books, 2004). The title of this 1886 novel reveals not at all that it takes place in Florence, yet as Wendy Lesser writes in the introduction, "The title is perfect for the novel. For one thing, there is a great deal of talk about the weather in this book: how it feels to be in Florence in the late winter, the spring, the early summer. . . . (How it feels to be an American in Florence at *all*—to be answered in English when you try to speak Italian; to meet up only with other Americans; to admire but feel somewhat removed from the architectural monuments—is part of what Howells, with his realistic eye for detail, is capable of offering us. And Florence being what it is, and was, Howells's city of 1884 is still recognizably itself twelve decades later.)"

Italy: A Traveler's Literary Companion, edited by Lawrence Venuti (Whereabouts, 2003). With stories arranged geographically, this paperback (lightweight enough to bring along) features fiction by some of Italy's best-known writers and rising stars, including Natalia Ginzburg, Luigi Pirandello, Alberto Moravia, and Antonio Tabucchi.

Up at the Villa, W. Somerset Maugham (Vintage, 2000). This 1940 novel, which was made into a movie I haven't seen, opens with this sentence: "The villa stood on the top of a hill." And, of course, from the hill there is a magnificent view of Florence. But those are the first and last simple details about this engaging story.

INTERVIEW

Lisa McGarry

The Piazzas of Florence

It's obvious that I love books. What might not be quite *as obvious is that I especially love hardcover books—and I love nice bindings and good, quality paper. I like books that are beautiful, which is one reason why I treasure the antique editions in my library. It's a rare and special event when a book is published today that has even an ounce of the kind of elegance and beauty of books published long ago, so I was over the moon when I received a copy of* The Piazzas of Florence: Mapping a Renaissance Spirit, *by Lisa McGarry (Pier 9/Murdoch, 2008). Lisa, an American who's been living in Florence for more than ten years, has created a book that's interesting to read and filled with great tips and trivia* but is also beautiful. *It's a hardcover that feels as if it were bound in hand-tooled leather; the endpapers are gorgeous, marbleized paper; there's a silk ribbon bookmark; and it includes watercolor maps of each piazza. This is a work of art in itself, and I urge readers to make the effort to find this book—it's not available in North America, but can be easily ordered from Amazon.co.uk.*

As McGarry relates, she'd fallen in love with Florence from afar, when she was studying for an architecture degree. Six years later, she finally went to Florence, and not only did she feel immediately at home, but the city was everything she'd imagined. "People often ask if I came to Florence to write the book. It was really more a case that I wrote the book so I would have a good excuse to continue visiting Florence. That, and the fact that I simply love this city." The book McGarry initially set out to write differed quite a bit from the book that was eventually published. Like me, she had difficulty finding the "right" travel journal and the "perfect" guide, and she concluded that the ideal journal or guide "would be the one we each designed for ourselves." After much feedback, she and an editor came up with the idea to focus on the piazzas but also to inspire readers through narratives of her own experiences in Florence. It's a winning formula, and I think you will agree.

I was unable to meet McGarry when I was last in Florence, but we've communicated by e-mail a lot over the last year—and I feel she is a friend I simply haven't met yet.

Q: When and why did you decide to stay in Florence?

A: The process was gradual. After only "knowing" Florence secondhand (mainly through studies for my architecture degree), I finally visited in 1996. I don't think I had ever been so prepared for a trip, in terms of reading and research. I was very enthusiastic about Florence—it already felt familiar to me—but the firsthand experience sparked an even deeper passion for the city. I knew that I wanted to live in Florence from my first visit, but it wasn't practical to pick up and move at the time. So I returned each year, studied the language, and continued to pursue my independent research, which eventually went into the book, between visits.

My British husband and I had decided to relocate from the United States to Europe. He was working on a variety of international contracts for a British aerospace company, and we planned to spend four months in Florence as an interlude while choosing where to settle, based on what contracts were available. We arrived in September 2004. My goal during that time was to complete the research for the book I had been working on (which ultimately became *The Piazzas of Florence*). After a few months, we decided that our daughter should have the opportunity to finish the school year there, and then, when my husband and I decided to go our separate ways, there was no question in my mind that my daughter and I would remain in Florence. The everyday life here has felt so natural from the beginning. Not needing a car has such a profound and positive impact on our everyday lives, and I love the intimacy and contact with the city and the people that come from being able to walk everywhere. I feel comfortable—at home—yet my senses are continuously stimulated by the very urban fabric (the streets, the buildings, the piazzas) and the rhythm of the days and the seasons. It feels natural, "right."

Q: Piazza Pitti—or rather Pitti Beach as you refer to it—is your neighborhood piazza. What are some of your favorite things about it?

A: Piazza Pitti is certainly not Florence's most charming piazza—it's very monochromatic with all that stone, and the scale is too grand—but I have developed a real fondness for it. I like how the space invites people to pause, to picnic, to sunbathe, to gather—it's always full of people, which creates a good energy—and I think it's amazing to feel so comfortable in such a monumental setting. I like how the palazzo, with *rondò* (wings) on either side, embraces the square: the sloping surface that's like theater seating, the generous expanse of sky overhead. The sun interacts beautifully with the palace's stone—my favorite time is the late afternoon, when it turns golden. I appreciate the square's changing role each season: in spring it's a wonderful place to absorb the first warmth of the year; in summer we go out there to enjoy early morning breezes or look for the evening's first stars (it's essentially empty during the intense heat of midday); and in autumn we enjoy the precious last warmth of the year.

Q: I love when you say, "I appreciate being inspired each time I open my front door." Is this something you feel because you live opposite the Pitti and in the Oltrarno or about Firenze in general?

A: I notice this sensation of being inspired in the course of repeating my regular routes through the city, whether I'm walking along the palazzo-lined Via Maggio, following the narrow streets that lead into Piazza Santo Spirito, crossing the River Arno, passing through Piazza della Signoria—or walking down a new street for the first time. I suppose that comment was my way of saying that the visual stimulation begins the moment I pass through my *portone* into the city. But it's true that, the longer I live in the Oltrarno, the more fond I grow of this neighborhood. I think it has something to do with experiencing the comfort of familiarity while at the same time continuing to encounter surprises—like glimpsing a private courtyard through a momentarily opened *portone* as I walk along a street, noticing a corner tabernacle that I haven't seen before, passing an antiques store and spotting an oil painting by an artist whose monograph I just checked out of the library. It's the way the sun plays on the rich architectural details, or looking down a long street and appreciating how the same elements—windows and shutters, roof overhangs and angles—repeat in slightly different ways.

Q: What were some things that inspired you to write the book?

A: First and foremost: Florence itself—everything I read, heard, then ultimately experienced. But it was also a love of books—of the very form of a book, and the potential inherent in a book's design. Ideas often unfold from unexpected sources, and it was literally a piece of paper that got me thinking about creating a physical book about Florence. I had bought some wonderful creamy-colored Rives paper at the art store, with a slightly toothy texture and deckled edges, and one day I found myself daydreaming about different ways to use it. I started experimenting with designing miniature booklets, considering conceptually how to lay out content. I was interested in a design with pages that folded out—my original plan for the book included historical and background information about Florence on the first pages of each chapter, and then pages that would unfold to reveal different types of increasingly more "personal" information: excerpts from the writings of a number of past travelers, watercolor maps (which could then be personalized by the reader), "invitations" (jumping-off points to inspire drawing, writing, and collaging), as well as blank space for the reader to use as she or he wished.

As I began to address the content itself, I played with a number of ideas for structuring the book. I was especially interested in Florence's physical features—the natural and built (the Arno River, the hills that enclose the valley; and the city walls, towers, *palazzi,* churches, and *piazze*)—so I began by considering these as a possible way to organize the material. Eventually this led me to the idea of structuring the book according to the piazzas, which was the urban feature I found most fascinating. The book concept changed considerably once I finally found a publisher—becoming narrative as opposed to what I called "interactive"—but since I had by that time been living in Florence for a few years, and the piazzas had become an integral part of my life, I felt comfortable weaving in my personal experiences. I'd say it was the whole physical experience of the city that inspired the book, then experiencing the everyday life that allowed it to grow—and the piazzas gave me a great way to tell the story. (A final note about that Rives paper: of course, it wasn't used for the book—too expensive—but I did use it for the mock-up chapters I produced as part of my proposal.)

Q: You note in the book's first chapter that there are more than one hundred piazzas in Florence, and "with their varied shapes, sizes, and characters, Florence's piazzas create necessary pauses, allowing breathing space within the compact urban fabric." You also note that of all Florence's diverse features, the piazzas are your favorite. So I have to ask: if forced to choose just one, which piazza would you choose as your favorite?

A: When asked to name my favorite piazza, I knew the answer immediately, but your question prompted me to run through the list again. On the one hand, choosing a favorite piazza isn't easy—they are all unique, and each one plays a different role in my life here—but Piazza Santo Spirito stands out as my clear favorite for as far back as I can remember. My associations with the other squares tend to be fairly specific: for example, I go to Piazza della Repubblica for the Thursday plant market, a cappuccino at Gilli's bar, and a visit to the bookstore; to Piazza della Signoria so I can spend some time sitting in the Loggia dei Lanzi; to Piazza San Lorenzo to reach the church's peaceful cloister; to Piazza Santa Croce for the chance to watch Sunday afternoon unfolding. And I regularly pass through a number of piazzas on my way to other destinations—one of the best things about living here and being able to walk everywhere.

But Piazza Santo Spirito is an *everyday* piazza, one that offers so much and satisfies a number of needs and wishes. Many times I have tried to define what I like so much about it. A number of reasons come to me quickly: the daily morning market; countless cafés and restaurants with patios encircling the square; shops filled with interesting things (baskets; seeds and grains; or school, office, and art supplies). And then there's the church of Santo Spirito, with its unusual curvy façade and a Renaissance interior by Brunelleschi—I still find it amazing that this inspiring example of architecture sits just a two-minute walk from my home, and that I can just wander in anytime. I love how people congregate around the octagonal fountain in the center of the piazza, along the stone benches that sit beneath the generous canopy of trees, or on the sunny steps in front of the church. Yet it's something more than these identifiable attributes. Piazza Santo Spirito is a comfortable piazza, like a big outdoor family room. You see a variety of people here, doing a variety of different activities, from grandparents minding toddlers to artists or students with sketch pads, schoolchildren chasing each other, residents and visitors enjoying a civilized lunch or a Prosecco in the evening, as well as the homeless who call this piazza home—it's a very real sample of life in a city. As I wrote in my book, it's not always "beautiful" per se, but it is authentic and alive and endlessly interesting. And, knowing it as I do, I find much beauty in this square.

Q: You also are a painter and a photographer—is your work represented in a gallery and if so, where is it? Or do people contact you for an appointment?

A: I am not represented in a gallery, but rather work through word of mouth. I haven't had as much time to paint as I've focused more on writing these past few years, though I'm always adding to my collection of notes, photos, and sketches for a rainy day—too many ideas, not enough time. But translating the way I experience the world into words and colors and patterns is inevitable for me. The cost of the paintings depends on the size, the medium, and the subject. I haven't tried to sell my photos, though I do hope to put a selection on a commercial site at some point, or maybe even produce a collection of cards or calendars.

Q: Does your daughter attend a bilingual school? She must be fluent in Italian by now—is she as inspired by Italy as you are?

A: Ella attends a local public school, with all of her classes in Italian (except the minimal gesture of an English class). She was about to enter first grade when we arrived in Florence, so was fortunate to be able to start at the very beginning. It was the perfect age to pick up the language, and the locals tell me she speaks like a Fiorentina now! On the one hand, it's been a very low-key education (reminding me a lot of the similarly small, simple elementary school I attended in Brazil), but, at the same time, I have been impressed by what she's had exposure to. Vasari's anecdotes about the artists seem to be part of the general knowledge even at this age. Her class read the original *Pinocchio* in the Florentine dialect, which apparently they got quite a kick out of! The local history they are taught comes alive through field trips to museums and the very piazzas where Florence's history was written. I love when she calls my attention to details I never knew or noticed as we walk through the city together. It's hard to know how much Italy itself has influenced her. It seems to be part of who she is now—she reads as easily in

Italian as English, and is as likely to write stories, poems, or songs in Italian as English.

🦁 🦁 🦁

Lisa McGarry may be reached through her Web site (lisa -mcgarry.com), where there is more information about *The Piazzas of Florence* and her other works of art.

LA CUCINA ITALIANA

"Italian" cooking is a concept of foreigners—to Italians, there is Florentine cooking, Venetian cooking, the cooking of Genoa, Rome, Naples, Sicily, Lombardy and the Adriatic coast. Not only have the provinces retained their own traditions of cookery, but many of their products remain localized.

—ELIZABETH DAVID, *Italian Food*

Behind each wine there is the story of communities large and small, the story of an Italy only recently united, and the story of an historical and venerable culture. Many people still feel a sense of belonging to a particular locality, to a particular region, and the winemaking reflects this.

—DANIELE CERNILLI AND MARCO SABELLICO, *The New Italy*

Flavor is what I miss whenever I leave Italy and what I seek as soon as I come back. It is a hard thing to describe; still, when something tastes the way it ought to, you recognize it instantly—authenticity always being a self-defining experience. Arugula and olive oil, cherries and figs, prosciutto di Parma sliced into transparent sheets, then draped over a wedge of melon: such foods announce themselves quietly, with assurance; then, just as quietly, they amaze the tongue. Even the Italian flag pays homage to this principle, for what do the red, green, and white stripes represent, if not tomato, basil, and mozzarella?

—DAVID LEAVITT, *Italian Pleasures*

I believe there is much happiness in people who are born where good wines are to be found.

—LEONARDO DA VINCI

Beaneaters & Bread Soup

LORI DE MORI

BEANEATERS & BREAD SOUP is the title of a very good book (Quadrille, UK, 2007) that I first read about in an issue of *The Art of Eating* (artofeating.com), one of my favorite culinary publications. The book sounded so appealing to me that I knew I had to have it right away, and I thought I showed great restraint by waiting a whole day before I went to Kitchen Arts & Letters in New York to buy a copy. When I arrived, Matt Sartwell, the manager, told me he had only a few copies left, which were slightly damaged and he was going to return, but he would sell me a copy if I really wanted one. The damage wasn't such that the book was unusable, so I took it, and I'm so glad I did.

I was already familiar with Lori De Mori's work—she's the author of two Williams-Sonoma books, *Foods of the World: Florence* (2004) and *Savoring Tuscany* (2001), and has written excellent articles for, among others, *Saveur* ("The Flavors of Home," about the trattorias of Florence, and "Mangia Fagioli" about the white beans of Tuscany). I urge readers to track these down as she shares many great recommendations. In *Beaneaters,* she emphasizes the kind of cooking unique to Tuscany and introduces us to the culinary artisans who are dedicated to it. We meet Tuscans who are there by birth or choice, and who are as different as beekeepers and countesses, potters and fishermen. Their dedication blurs the line between work and life, and they all share some essential qualities:

A kind of personal integrity that can be confused with eccentricity: "however strange it may seem to you, this is the way I do things."

Pride without arrogance: a sincere belief in the excellence of their work.

Humility and steadfastness: the ability to light the woodstove, milk the ewes, coax the bees out of their hives—quietly, without pretense—day after day, year after year.

The belief that their work is not a means to something else, but one of the ways to give meaning to their lives.

Genius: the brilliance that comes to those driven by their personal vision rather than by a desire for success, money, or fame.

Generosity: they have no secrets. If you appreciate what they do, they'll tell you everything they know . . . and usually set a place for you at their table.

IT WOULD BE tempting to romanticize the postcard-perfect version of Tuscany—olive groves, vineyards, and woodlands spread out like a patchwork over a sea of rolling hills; stone farmhouses shimmering in the Mediterranean sunshine— were it not for the fact that Tuscans refuse to romanticize themselves. They still remember a time, not so long ago, when the day's main meal was nothing more than *pane e companatico*—bread and "something to go with the bread."

The quintessential "something" was *fagioli* (beans)—*la carne dei poveri* (the poor man's meat)—usually dried white cannellini cooked overnight in an old wine flask nestled among the dying embers in the kitchen fireplace. The humble white bean—boiled with a sprig of sage, a clove of garlic, and a few peppercorns, then scattered into soups, ladled onto toasted bread and doused with olive oil, or simmered with crushed tomatoes—was such a fixture in the Tuscan kitchen that Toscani were nicknamed *mangiafagioli* by their fellow Italians: "beaneaters."

The bread half of the *pane e companatico* equation was, and remains, a curious thing. The heavy golden loaves with their thick crusts and dense, chewy crumbs have everything you'd expect from a naturally leavened, hearth-baked bread. Everything but salt. The story goes that when Italy was still an unruly collection of city-states, Pisa's neighbors responded to the maritime republic's imposition of a salt tax by baking their daily bread without it. *Pane sciocco* ("insipid" bread) balanced the earthy flavors of the Tuscan table so well that the habit of saltlessness evolved into an enduring tradition.

Of course, sometimes the "something that went with the bread" was more bread. The laws of frugality in those lean days meant that nothing from the kitchen could ever be wasted or thrown away. And so, scraps of dry, stale bread would be revived from their petrified state into a soup or a salad of sorts. Tuscan standards like *ribollita* ("reboiled" bread, cabbage and bean soup), *panzanella* (bread salad), and *pappa al pomodoro* (bread and tomato soup) owe their existence to two of the defining features of unsalted Tuscan bread: it can go hard without turning moldy, and absorb liquid without becoming gluey. They owe their abiding popularity to the fact that they are far more delicious than they sound on the page.

The truly remarkable thing about the Tuscan kitchen of those times is that however unrelenting the need for parsimony, it was never greater than the twin beliefs that there should be flavor— even, or perhaps especially, where there was not abundance—and that creativity and resourcefulness would do more to satisfy the family's appetite than the grim-faced determination simply to provide sustenance.

The end of World War II brought unthinkable prosperity to Italy. *La campagna toscana* was virtually abandoned as farmers poured into the cities looking for jobs. The kind of cooking that wasted nothing, chose *nostrale* (local) over exotic, and stayed faithful to the seasons was no longer a necessity. It was a matter of common sense. And so Tuscans still eat their beans. Not because they have to, but because there is no better vehicle for their beloved *olio di oliva;* because *fagioli* are, after all, delicious; and finally, because there's nothing wrong with eating beans—or for that matter, being called a Beaneater.

Italy's Original Garlic Bread

S. IRENE VIRBILA

❧

IT'S WORTH EMPHASIZING once again that it's all local when it comes to food in Italy. Burton Anderson, in the introduction to his wonderful book *Treasures of the Italian Table* (William Morrow, 1994), notes that one shouldn't muddle all the cuisines of Italy into one generic stew. The people of Italy have been separated by mountain ranges and bodies of water, and never supported one monarch or ruler long enough to set aside their regional identities. "Even now, long after former kingdoms, principalities, duchies, and Lilliputian republics metamorphosed into twenty regions comprising nearly a hundred provinces, ethnic peculiarities remain in customs, speech, and cooking. The local flavors of Italy's *trattorie, osterie, locande, taverne, pizzerie, pasticcerie, botteghe,* and *mercati* are often imitated but rarely duplicated elsewhere. In more than thirty years of dining in the country, the meals I've most savored invariably told a story of a people and a place." Even something as simple as bread and olive oil goes by a different name depending on where you are in Italy, as this piece explores. (And interestingly, in the Catalonia region of Spain and on the island of Mallorca, bread and oil—with salt or not, or with tomato—is known as *pa amb oli.*)

True Italian "garlic bread" is perfection. The American predilection for slathering copious amounts of butter and minced garlic on poor-quality bread misses the point. Bruschetta (one of the most mispronounced words in America—for some reason, many people want to make it French and come out with broo-*SHetta,* when in fact it is pronounced broo-*SKetta*), *fettunta,* and *soma d'aj,* in all their variations, are most delicious and satisfying antipasti, and easy to make at home. Although not mentioned in this piece, *panunto* is yet another name for a similar antipasto found in Tuscany.

S. IRENE VIRBILA, restaurant critic for the *Los Angeles Times,* writes frequently about food, wine, and travel for a number of newspapers and magazines, including the *San Francisco Chronicle, Saveur,* and *Departures.* She was the recipient of a James Beard Award for newspaper restaurant criticism in 1997, and has lived in San Francisco, Paris, northern Italy, and Los Angeles.

WHEREVER OLIVE OIL is produced in Italy, it's traditional to celebrate the olive harvest and the pungent new oil with a feast of bruschetta. This is the original garlic bread, made with thick slices toasted over a fire, rubbed with fresh gar-

lic, and saturated with intense green olive oil. This simple yet superb dish is known by various names all over Italy—*bruschetta, fettunta, soma d'aj*—depending on the region.

Alfredo Mancianti, a producer of *cru* olive oils in Umbria, said, "bruschetta was born in Umbria, and from there diffused first to neighboring Tuscany and Lazio, and then to other regions of Italy that produce olive oil." Until relatively recently, he explained, fuel was scarce and bread was baked just once a week in the countryside, so country people developed a repertory of dishes to use bread that was no longer fresh.

Thick vegetable soups ladled over a slice of toasted bread at the bottom of the soup bowl was one solution. Another was the toasted, thick slices of bread, vigorously rubbed with garlic.

"But the true bruschetta," Mr. Mancianti said, "was a little different than they make now. Instead of pouring the oil from a cruet or bottle over the toasted bread, originally the bread was actually immersed in the oil." And it was especially good during the winter toasted over an open fire, and immersed in new oil, just as it came from the *frantoio,* or olive mill.

Each year during the olive oil season (November and December), there is a celebration at Mr. Mancianti's cold-press mill in San Feliciano, on Lake Trasimeno near Perugia. Everyone who helped with the picking—all their workers, clients, and friends— are invited to a feast of bruschetta made with the new oil. The bruschetta is accompanied by the year's new young wine, scarcely out of the cask, and simple grilled food such as sausages or *spiedini di fegato,* laurel leaves and pieces of pork liver threaded on skewers.

Romans will tell you the name *bruschetta* is derived from *bruschato,* which is Roman dialect for the Italian word *bruciato,* scorched or burned. To prepare in the old way, you take a *pagnotta,* or big loaf of country-style bread (preferably baked in a wood-fired oven to give it a thick, chewy crust), and cut it into inch-thick slices. Then you toast it in the fireplace or over charcoal. It should be a little scorched or blistered. While the bread is still hot, you rub it with a cut clove of garlic, pour the best olive oil available over it, and sprinkle it with salt.

Romans and southern Italians are also fond of a summer version called *bruschetta al pomodoro*. It's made the same way, and topped with chopped, ripe tomatoes. Sometimes the tomatoes are marinated with a little garlic and oil, or chopped fresh basil.

In Lazio, the region around Rome, the dish is eaten as an appetizer, washed down with one of the fresh white wines from the region. Often you don't even have to order it: bruschetta will show up on the table as part of the standard antipasto, along with sausage, prosciutto, and olives. Pizzerias generally offer it at night with their full panoply of pizza and calzone. And this is where you might find untraditional toppings, such as minced porcini or fried eggplant. The place to get Roman bruschetta is not in the city, but in one of the many trattorias on the periphery of Rome, on the road to towns like Frascati and Nemi. These are down-to-earth places with open fireplaces, where you can eat outside in warm weather or inside at long tables covered with paper. At such restaurants they bring bruschetta throughout the meal, which might include specialties such as pasta with tomato sauce or roast lamb with rosemary.

Without ever having tasted an authentic bruschetta, it may be hard to understand just how delicious such seemingly meager fare can be. Bruschetta has its passionate devotees, in the United States and in Italy.

The San Francisco chef Carlo Middione includes bruschetta in *The Food of Southern Italy* (William Morrow, 1987). Mr. Middione's favorite variation is chopped tomatoes, fresh basil, oil, and vinegar. In his view, bruschetta is an unrecognized delicacy: "If you have good bread and good olive oil and good tomatoes, what could be simpler than this to show off the quality of those ingredients?"

🦁   🦁   🦁

In Tuscany and Lazio, it turns up all through the year as a first course or as a snack. Tuscan schoolchildren like bruschetta (sometimes dribbled with a little vinegar, too) at their midmorning or afternoon break. In Tuscany, where some of Italy's most prized olive oils are produced, it's called *fettunta,* slang for anointed or oiled slice. At the Chianti estate Badia a Coltibuono, the food writer and cooking teacher Lorenza de' Medici, who, with her husband Piero Stucchi-Prinetti, produces estate-bottled olive oil, explained how they make *fettunta*. She starts with day-old country-style bread. "It should be sliced quite thickly, generally an inch to an inch and a half, so that when the bread is grilled it will be crusty outside, yet remain soft inside." Traditionally, the bread is grilled over the embers in the fireplace. She also said that in the Tuscan countryside bread is baked from an unsalted dough so that the bread keeps longer. She sprinkles a little coarse salt over the toasted bread, then takes a peppery, sharp green olive oil and pours it lavishly over the bruschetta.

🐝 🐝 🐝

That's the classic, but variations abound. When tomatoes are in season, Ms. de' Medici might top the bruschetta with a slice or two of ripe tomato—an idea borrowed from country people, she said, who rub a tomato into stale bread in order to soften it. In yet another variation, *fagioli,* stewed white beans, are heaped on top. In still another version very typical of Chianti, the toasted bread is topped with boiled *cavolo nero,* the black cabbage of the region.

While bruschetta is more common in central and southern Italy, where much olive oil is produced, you can find it in northern Italy as well. In Piedmont, home of white truffles and red wines from Nebbiolo grapes, Barolo and Barbaresco, the dish is known as *soma d'aj.*

The name means "brushed with garlic" in the local dialect, according to Luciana Vietti Currado of Cantina Vietti, a wine producer in Castiglione Falletto. Though it can be made with thick slices of bread, as in Tuscany and Lazio, in Piedmont, bread sticks, or *grissini,* are often used. These are not the typical yard-long *grissini* that arrive at your table as soon as you sit down in a restaurant, but a fatter, shorter bread stick called *rubata.*

In this case, the bread won't be sliced or toasted since the stick is already crisp. A plate with a generous pool of virgin olive oil is set out for each diner, who takes a clove of peeled garlic, dips it in the oil, and rubs the bread stick with the oil-impregnated garlic.

Ms. Currado's husband, Alfredo, explained that in Piedmont they'll even eat *soma d'aj* for breakfast. Because the farmworkers leave at five or six in the morning to go to the fields, they take a loaf of bread, a flask of oil, and a clove of garlic with them. At about eight, they'll break for *soma d'aj.* Out in the fields, they don't usually make a fire. They simply rub the crust of the bread with garlic, and garnish with oil and salt. And they eat it with grapes from the vineyard and drink a little Barbera.

A SAMPLER'S GUIDE TO BRUSCHETTA

Country restaurants in Tuscany or Umbria might offer it as a first course, even if it's not on the menu.

Badia a Coltibuono (Gaiole in Chianti/+39 0577 74 481/ coltibuono.com). The restaurant at this wine estate features *fettunta* made with Badia's olive oil, as well as ravioli with butter and sage, *stracotto,* or beef stew with dried wild mushrooms, white beans with a drizzle of deep green olive oil, and other Chiantigiana specialties. A good selection of Badia a Coltibuono wines is available by the glass as well as by the bottle.

Cantinetta Antinori (Piazza Antinori 3, Florence/+39 055 23 595/antinori.it). The menu of simple Tuscan fare at this restaurant featuring Antinori wines includes *fettunta;* in the summer one can order it topped with tomato. Other specialties are *ribollita,* a kind of minestrone; *trippa fiorentina,* tripe stewed in fresh tomato sauce;

and *panzanella,* a salad of torn bread, sweet onions, tomato, and cucumber, tossed with sweet basil and mint, and olive oil.

Frantoio Faliero Mancianti (Via della Parrocchia 20, San Feliciano in Perugia/+39 075 847 6045/frantoiomancianti.com). Mornings, you can visit this Umbrian olive oil mill, where they'll explain (in Italian) how the artisanal *frantoio* works, and if they're not too busy, they may offer you bruschetta so you can taste their olive oils from specific microclimates and types of olives. Call first.

If no bruschetta is forthcoming, you can repair to Da Settimio (Via Lungolagol/+39 075 847 6000), also in San Feliciano, for lunch, where the proprietors will make you bruschetta with Mancianti oil.

Tuscan Olive Oils

FAITH WILLINGER

NEARLY A THIRD of the world's olive oil is produced and consumed in Italy (Spain is the next-biggest producer, followed by Greece). Olive oil differs, of course, throughout Italy, and each variety pairs perfectly with each region's local specialties. Extra virgin Tuscan oils, for example, tend to be green and peppery, which complement traditional Tuscan dishes. Umbria is equally endowed with olive trees, and its oil pairs especially well with one of its local delicacies, truffles. Perhaps surprisingly, some elements of producing high-quality olive oil in Italy haven't changed much in centuries. Chemicals aren't used in the processing, and olives are still picked by hand.

There are dozens and dozens—perhaps hundreds—of Tuscan and Umbrian oils that never leave the regions. Just one that I've read about is from Il Picciolo, a farm outside the walled village of Montisi, near Siena, produced by an American named Ruth McVey. According to an article in *Saveur,* No. 8, McVey's harvest doesn't produce more than about eight hundred liters in a good year, too little to export. She was quoted in the article as saying, "Olive oil for me isn't about making money. It's about quality, and whether that still matters anymore"—a statement that could also have been made by any number of Tuscans who believe, as I do, that it does indeed still matter. Burton Anderson, in *Treasures of the Italian Table,* notes that making extra virgin oil is so labor intensive that "even the most expensive oils are in a sense underpriced." Quality oils like these are an obvious choice to bring back home, for gifts or for yourself—I've brought back many,

many bottles of olive oil in my checked bags by wrapping them carefully within my clothing, and never once has one broken.

FAITH WILLINGER is the author of *Adventures of an Italian Food Lover: With Recipes from 254 of My Very Best Friends* (Clarkson Potter, 2007), *Red, White & Greens: The Italian Way with Vegetables* (HarperCollins, 1996), and *Eating in Italy: A Traveler's Guide to the Hidden Gastronomic Pleasures of Northern Italy* (William Morrow, 1998). She also writes for *Gourmet* and is an "Abroad" contributor to Theatlantic.com's "Corby's Fresh Feeds," an outstanding online food column created by Corby Kummer, referred to as "a dean among food writers in America" by the *San Francisco Examiner* (and one of my own longtime favorites).

I GREW UP thinking that olive oil—transparent, yellowish, and labeled "pure"—was used only by sophisticated Americans in salad dressings, by Europeans in cooking. Then I moved to Italy and met and married a Florentine who

brainwashed me about superior Tuscan oil—green, cloudy, peppery, and tasting of olives. My husband informed me that butter, too sweet and too fatty, was for unevolved palates. I learned that first-rate extra virgin olive oil is the reason food tastes so terrific in Tuscany, adding a lusty vegetal flavor to everything it encounters. Listening to locals, I noticed that no one bothered to say *extra vergine* or even *oliva,* just *olio nuovo* (when the oil is first pressed and at its most piquant), then *olio* (after a month or two, when flavors calm down). I began to try oils from all over Tuscany, each with its own complex taste, and was hooked. I attended *degustazioni* (learning how to "schlurp" alongside the professionals) and went to nurseries, groves, mills, and seminars, meeting professors and producers. The olive oil story is complicated—almost as complicated as the process of making a great oil.

In a good year only 5 to 7 percent of the olive oil consumed in Italy is produced in Tuscany, which amounts to around twenty million liters (think of a liquid liter as roughly a quart), most of it extra virgin but not all *super-Tuscan*—my term for top quality—extra virgin. Local demand for quality oil exceeds the supply, and so the quantity of great estate oil that is exported amounts to a drop in the bucket compared to Tuscany's total yield.

Super-Tuscan extra virgins are the Maseratis of lipids. Ordinary extra virgin olive oil is defined by law as having no serious defects and an acidity of less than 1 percent. What I call super-Tuscan extra virgins are more virtuous, with acidity of less than 0.5 percent and bigger, spicier flavors. In the marketplace, producers of small-quantity, high-quality oils compete against industrial giants who bottle extra virgins and what used to be labeled "pure" from elsewhere (Spain, North Africa, Greece, or southern Italy); political attempts to define the best zones of Tuscan olive oil production have met with little success due to the financial clout of the industrial bottlers.

Many factors contribute to the production of a super-Tuscan extra virgin olive oil, and any one of a minefield of disasters—

from the dreaded oil fly to freezing weather—can destroy an entire year's efforts or, worse, the trees themselves. (Every twenty-
five to thirty years, freezes kill Tuscany's olive trees; in 1985,
seventeen million of twenty-two million were leveled.) Each
grower deals with the risks as well as the unique circumstances of
olive variety, soil, and climate, producing an oil that expresses a
particular *terroir*—a term usually applied to wine, meaning a combination of soil and site—and possesses its own particular taste.

More than a hundred different olive varieties thrive in Italy's
central, southern, and coastal regions, but the Tuscan hills are
dominated by *frantoio, moraiolo, leccino, pendolino,* and *coreggiolo.*
With the approach of winter about mid-November, these
olives—ranging in color from just-beginning-to-ripen green to
purply black—are harvested, destined to become fruity oils with
zesty flavors and low acidity (the latter a protection against rancidity). An olive oil made only of ripe olives may have a more delicate flavor and a higher yield, but it also has higher acidity and,
besides, only regions with temperate climates can wait long
enough for all their olives to ripen. The danger of frost in the Tuscan hills dictates an earlier harvest.

At harvesttime, pickers on ladders strip the branches of their
fruit with handheld rakes so that the olives fall into nets spread
under the trees. Each tree yields enough olives for one to three
liters of oil. The olives are then hurried to the mill, or *frantoio,* to
be stored in well-aerated crates—not sacks, in which fermentation could occur, ruining the oil before it's made—and pressed
within a day or two. For anyone curious to see the oil-making
process close up, mills are open at least sixteen hours a day during
the November–December pressing season, but appointments are
essential (see "Milling Around" at the end of this article).

🦂   🦂   🦂

All the mills I visited begin by washing the olives and removing
the leaves. Typically they crush around six hundred pounds of

olives at a time with *molazze,* or rolling granite wheels, in a large granite tub for thirty to forty-five minutes, then knead the resulting pulp for up to an hour and a half.

Three main techniques are used to extract oil from this pulp, each method having its adherents. Outside Castelnuovo Berardenga, east of Siena, the mill at San Felice, which presses for Castello di Ama, still follows traditional practice. First an inch of olive pulp is piped onto circular woven mats interspersed with metal plates for reinforcement. Stacked on a spindle, the mats are then pressed, yielding a brownish mixture of oil and vegetable water, called *mosto,* which is lightly centrifuged to separate them.

The mill at Tenuta di Capezzana, twenty-four kilometers west of Florence, uses what is known as the continuous method of extraction: traditional granite wheels still do the crushing, but the pulp is then passed directly into a horizontal centrifuge that separates the oil and the residual water from the *sansa* of leftover solids. The mats of the old method are bypassed entirely. At some mills—but rarely artisanal operations—stainless steel hammers or rollers do the crushing, but they can heat the paste, and heat is the great enemy of an excellent olive oil. Any procedure that warms the pulp will diminish the flavor; this is the reason first-rate oils are always "cold-pressed." At Capezzana, flavor is additionally protected by the estate's practice of filling its centrifuge with only half the amount of pulp allowed by law at a single time and *no* yield-boosting hot water.

Super-Tuscan expert Maurizio Castelli works at the mill of Castello di Volpaia, south of Florence in Radda in Chianti, employing the new extraction technique known as *sinolea.* The equipment is expensive and therefore not widely used, but it is said that this method produces the finest oil. Why? Because no pressure is applied to the fruit. Instead, thousands of stainless-steel blades are plunged into the olive pulp, and the oil that adheres to them is then scraped off with a kind of rubber comb.

As much as 80 percent of the olive's oil is collected off the blades alone; then the paste that's left is centrifuged to extract the remaining oil. The bright green centrifuged oil has desirably low acidity but is not as fine as the first extraction; some producers blend the two, some allocate the centrifuged oil for cooking. The pulp residue is sold to large-scale industrial producers, who add solvents to it to extract the last of the oil, which is so unpalatable that it must be deodorized and deacidified. This final extract, virtually stripped of all flavor and color, is then mixed with a small amount of extra virgin oil to put back some taste and create what is called olive pomace oil—a product of no worth whatsoever to any serious cook.

Whichever oil extraction technique is favored at a given *frantoio,* cleanliness in the mill is of the utmost importance. Traditional mills such as the one at San Felice must press constantly because their oil-impregnated mats acidify with prolonged air contact. Defective olives—overripe or damaged by disease or hail—are another danger: they not only make poor oil but can also contaminate succeeding oils when machines or mats are not carefully washed.

Before bottling, the oil is stored in a cool, dark room, as exposure to light (which provokes oxidation) can be as damaging to oil as heat. Traditionally the storage receptacles of choice have been large terra-cotta urns called *orci,* although nowadays many producers prefer stainless-steel tanks. Most oil is filtered prior to bottling to remove any sediment that might harm the oil as it ages.

What I like to call home care for a fine oil is another, often overlooked consideration. Just as a cool, dark environment is key before bottling, so too is it important at home. Do not keep your prized Tuscan oil in a cupboard above the stove in the kitchen! Super-Tuscans are capable of lasting for two years or more if stored correctly—as you would a fine wine; that is, in a cellar or closet, not the refrigerator—although they taste best within a year of production.

🦁　　🦁　　🦁

Tasting all the subtleties of an olive oil isn't easy. Professional tasters take their oil neat, without distractions. They begin with a spoonful and, like a wine taster, a few noisy schlurps, a motion that aerates the oil while coating the taste buds on the back of the tongue and palate. Harmonious fruity aromas and flavors, green color, and density are the qualities desired in a super-Tuscan extra virgin oil. Tasters look especially for such merits as freshness, spiciness, and balance; such flavors as artichoke, almond, apple, or freshly cut grass. Serious defects in an oil include persistent bitterness, excess fattiness, yellow-to-orange color (which denotes rancidity), and flavors of ripe melon, tropical fruit, metal, or mud.

Each year's release of super-Tuscan *olio nuovo,* or just-pressed oil, is a cause for rejoicing in Tuscany. Served uncooked as a condiment to enhance the appreciation of its unique properties, this "new oil" is almost luminescent, green with chlorophyll, peppery and aggressive, with some slightly bitter overtones. After a few months the flavors soften and the oil becomes, simply, *olio,* ready for cooking, including deep-frying, and continued use as a condiment.

The best super-Tuscan extra virgins come from the hills in the province of Florence, extending to the Chianti Classico, Montalbano, Rufina, Pratomagno, and Arezzo-Cortona zones. Dedicated high-quality producers exist elsewhere, but they're in the minority. Industrial bottlers in Lucca have attained a position of prominence in the marketplace, but it's not easy to find fine artisanal oils from the area. Look for super-Tuscans made by Capezzana, in the Montalbano region; Castello di Ama, Castello di Volpaia, Jiachi, Podere Le Boncie, and Castellare in the Chianti Classico zone; Selvapiana from Rufina; I Bonsi and Frantoio di Santa Tea from Pratomagno; Grattamacco, from the hills near the coast between Livorno and Grosetto; Tenuta di Valgiano, in the hills above Lucca; Grappolini from the Arezzo-Cortona district; and Castello Banfi and Col d'Orcia from Montalcino.

Tuscany's regional government hasn't been able to agree about where to draw the lines for the official zones of quality olive oil, but eventually a DOC status (a controlled appellation of origin designation, as is now applied to wine) will probably cover all of Tuscany without distinguishing the best areas. For now, the only guarantee of quality on the label is the phrase *prodotto e imbottigliato* (produced and bottled), which means that the oil comes from an estate's own olives. (Equivalent phrases are *imbottigliato all'origine* and *prodotto e confezionato*.) The word *prodotto* or *imbottigliato* alone offers no guarantee of origin; it means only that the oil was bottled at an estate—any estate anywhere. Super-Tuscans will proudly display their year of harvest on the label.

The finest olive oils are never inexpensive. Bulk oil in Tuscany sells for around ten dollars a liter. Add to that the cost of bottling, shipping, and profits for producer, importer, distributor, and retailer—and the purchase price of a super-Tuscan can rise to at least twenty-five dollars for a 0.75 liter bottle. A difficult harvest can mean higher prices still. If used sparingly, a bottle of excellent oil can last for weeks, a shortcut to enhancing many foods. Cheap oil is never a bargain, ruining everything it comes into contact with.

MILLING AROUND

Readers who would like to stop by a working *frantoio* on their next visit to Italy—and possibly purchase oil at the source—are welcome at the following mills, though it is essential to be in contact a few weeks in advance to request an appointment. Accompanying the list of mills are suggestions of nearby hotels and restaurants for travelers who want to linger in the countryside rather than merely pass through.

FRANTOIO DI CASTELLO DI VOLPAIA

Agricola San Felice (Località San Felice, Castelnuovo Berardenga/+39 0577 39 91/agricolasanfelice.it).

Borgo San Felice (Località San Felice, Castelnuovo Berardenga/ +39 0577 39 64/borgosanfelice.com). Comfortable, rustic gentrification is the style of this Relais & Châteaux hotel and its restaurant, Poggio Rosso. Some dishes are quite elaborate, while others remain simple, and all are beautifully prepared and presented. Atypically for Tuscany, desserts receive much attention here.

Da Delfina (Via della Chiesa 1, Artimino/+39 055 871 8074/dadelfina.it). In the 1940s and 1950s Delfina was the cook at the nearby hunting lodge of the Artimino Medici villa. Her son, Carlo Cioni, has moved her now-legendary reputation and recipes to his restaurant on the confines of the village, where his passion for the best local ingredients—wild greens, herbs, mushrooms in season—gets full play. His super-Tuscan oil (from the Montalbano area) is, however, used parsimoniously: "I serve peasant food, and oil has always been precious to people who live and work in the country," Carlo explains. His version of *ribollita* is the best I've ever encountered, the *ghirighio* (an unsweetened chestnut-flour tart) is worth the voyage, and the wine selection is wonderful.

Frantoio della Tenuta di Capezzana (Via Capezzana 100, Carmignano/+39 055 870 6005/capezzana.it).

Hotel Paggeria Medicea (Viale Papa Giovanni XXIII 1, Artimino/+39 055 875 141/artimino.com).

Il Borgo di Vescine (Radda in Chianti/+39 0577 741 144/vescine.it).

Il Vescovino (Via Ciamiolo da Panzano 9, Panzano/+39 055 856 0152). Traditional dishes and innovative cooking share space on the menu at Il Vescovino, but super-Tuscan extra virgin oils are an integral part of almost everything. The wine list is stellar and well-priced, inviting diners to drink big as they settle in on the terrace overlooking the countryside of olive trees, vineyards, villas, and farmhouses.

Volpaia (Località Volpaia, Radda in Chianti/+39 0577 738 066/volpaia.it).

Italy's Vin Santo
A Sip of Hospitality

S. IRENE VIRBILA

Biscotti dipped in *vin santo* is divine, and as *vin santo* is not widely available in the United States, it makes a good choice for a *ricorda* (souvenir). It's also, as the writer notes in this piece, a *ricorda* unique to Tuscany and Umbria.

S. IRENE VIRBILA, introduced earlier, has been the restaurant critic of the *Los Angeles Times* since 1993, and has contributed a great number of articles about food and wine to a great number of periodicals. She has trained as a sommelier in Paris, worked as a restaurant cook, wine buyer, and cookbook editor, and won the James Beard Award for newspaper restaurant criticism in 1997.

In Tuscany and neighboring Umbria, *vin santo* is the wine of hospitality. Whatever the time of day, a guest is offered a small glass of the amber dessert wine. "It's the wine of hospitality, the wine of friendship and of courtesy," explains Giacomo Tachis, winemaker for the 650-year-old Tuscan firm Antinori. At one time, every family in the Tuscan countryside made some *vin santo* and had a prized barrel or two squirreled away in the attic. Chianti they made for sale, but *vin santo* was strictly for family use.

Though the tradition in Tuscany goes back for centuries, no

one seems to agree on how *vin santo* got its name. Some say it's because the grapes are sometimes not pressed until Christmas or as late as Holy Week.

Others insist the wine is "holy" because it was often used in the mass. But the more generally held theory is that the name dates from the Ecumenical Council held in Florence in 1349, when a Greek bishop commented that the wine served tasted like the sweet wine made on the Greek island of Xantos—and the name *vin santo* stuck.

Every farm and estate has a slightly different system of making *vin santo,* which produces wines in distinctly different styles. One may be rich and honeyed, tasting of dried apricots, figs, and prunes. Another is almost dry on the palate, with an aroma of hazelnuts and almonds. Whatever the style, the wine is generally 14 to 17 percent alcohol. The wine is made from partially dried grapes that are slowly pressed to yield a thick, concentrated juice. The must (unfermented grape juice) is sealed in small barrels, and then left, contrary to all normal winemaking practice, to weather extremes of hot and cold in an attic or other uninsulated structure for a minimum of three years. The fermentation can continue on and off for two or three years, starting up with the warm weather in spring, and shutting down in the cold.

Every winemaker creates a variation on the theme. The grape bunches may be strung in dramatic cascades from the rafters, or the grapes may be laid out to dry on cane mats stacked from floor to ceiling (with space between for the air to circulate). The grapes are usually local white wine varieties, but *vin santo* can also be made partly with red grapes. And the shriveled raisinlike grapes may be pressed anytime from late November to as late as February or March. Once the grapes are pressed, the wine is aged in barrels ranging from the traditional fifty-liter casks, called *caratelle,* to standard French oak *barriques* or old whisky barrels. The casks can be sealed with cement or sealing wax for three to six or more years before they are opened and the wine is bottled.

🦁   🦁   🦁

Until recently, most *vin santo* was made only for family consumption and to present as gifts. Now a growing number of wine estates in Tuscany are making *vin santo* for sale in limited quantities. One outstanding example is produced by Avignonesi, a Montepulciano firm known for its red Vino Nobile di Montepulciano. When the winemaker Ettore Falvo first tasted his father-in-law's *vin santo,* he was astounded. Aged twelve years, "it was dark and thick as tamarind syrup with a perfume so intense it lasted a week in an empty glass . . . and so concentrated, a forty-liter barrel might yield only five or six liters of *vin santo.*" It was not something he could make in any quantity.

For Mr. Falvo, Avignonesi's real treasure was the ancient *madre,* or mother, the dark, mucilaginous concentration of wild yeasts that had developed in the *vin santo* barrels through the generations the family had been making it. Carefully nurturing and dividing the mother at most by half each year, after twenty years he can now produce about fifty barrels a year, which he ages six, rather than twelve, years. His *vin santo* is lush and concentrated with a perfume of toasted almonds, plums, prunes, and dried fruit.

At his estate in Valiano, a few miles from Cortona, he has just finished building and restoring a *vinsantaia* (the place where *vin santo* is made and aged). Opening the door with a fist-sized key, he showed off the rows of cane mats covered with grape bunches to make a tapestry in shades of pale green and rose. Farther back

were carpets of red and purple grapes for the rare *vin santo* called *occhio di pernice* ("eye of the partridge"). Windows on either side of the room help the drying process. In damp weather ingenious wooden shutters close tight.

As Mr. Falvo explained, only the handsome, healthy grape bunches are selected for *vin santo*. Here they are mainly Grechetto (a local white grape) with a little Malvasia. As the grapes dry, water evaporates, and the sugar, extracts, and flavor become more and more concentrated. By mid-February, the sugar content is high enough that Mr. Falvo decides to press. Meanwhile he opens the barrels of wine sealed six years before, empties them, and prepares them for this year's wine. He fills each of the *caratelle* with a small quantity of *madre* and pours in the thick, syrupy must to within a few inches from the top. The bunghole is closed with red sealing wax. Here they'll stay, stacked four high in the uninsulated *vin santaia* for six years.

Because each barrel develops on its own, there can be remarkable differences in perfume, sweetness, and concentration, but in the end the barrels are blended to produce that year's wine, just eighteen hundred half bottles and about four hundred half bottles of *occhio di pernice*. Most of it is shipped to top wine shops and restaurants in Italy.

Fontodi, a Chianti estate in Panzano, produces an excellent *vin santo* in half bottles in very limited quantities. This one is half Malvasia and half red Sangiovese grapes, dried on mats until Christmas and aged four years in four different kinds of wood: oak, chestnut, cherry, and juniper. The deep golden wine is vinified dry and has an appealing perfume of honey and hazelnuts.

Another good example in the drier style is Badia a Coltibuono's *vin santo* with subtle overtones of apricot and hazelnut. Made from Trebbiano and Malvasia grapes pressed in early December, this one is aged in two-hundred-liter former whisky barrels in a room over the estate's olive press. A restaurant on the grounds of the thousand-year-old abbey offers *vin santo* after a

typical country meal. And the small retail shop sells the estate's
Chianti Classico and other wines, plus *vin santo,* and its own vinegar, extra virgin olive oil, and honeys.

Another very good producer in Gaiole is Francesco Martini di
Cigala at San Giusto a Rentennano. The small *vin santaia* in the
villa's attic looks much as it did a hundred years ago, with grapes
hanging from the beams to dry and the old chestnut *caratelle* set all
in a row. Fine and complex, with layers of flavor, this *vin santo* is
made from Trebbiano and Malvasia, and aged five years before
bottling.

Northwest of Florence, in the historic red wine region called
Carmignano, Count Ugo Contini Bonacossi is an old hand at
vin santo. His family has been making *vin santo* at Tenuta di Capezzana for five generations, but the *madre* they inherited with the
centuries-old estate is much older. The blend of Trebbiano, Malvasia, and San Colombano grapes now includes a small amount of
Chardonnay, and is aged four to five years in French oak *barriques.*
His father and his father's father set aside a good quantity of wine,
so Count Bonacossi is able to open bottles from the forties and
fifties to prove that *vin santo* can age.

While *vin santo* is also made in the regions of Trentino and Alto
Adige, it is most characteristic of Tuscany and parts of Umbria.

People from Umbria, the tiny region in the heart of Italy
halfway between Rome and Florence, are proud of their *vin santo*
tradition. Teresa Lungarotti, enologist in Torgiano for Lungarotti,
Umbria's best-known winery, explained that in the region *vin
santo* is almost always sweet and made entirely with Grechetto
grapes dried until February. The wine is aged four or five years in
very old chestnut barrels and, just before bottling, is fortified by
adding a *mistela,* a concentrate of must and alcohol made from
grapes.

Here, too, she says, *vin santo* is usually served with *torcolo di San*

Costanzo, a dry ring-shaped cake studded with raisins and candied fruit named for the protector of Perugia; the flat cookies called *mostaccioli;* or the hard little almond cookies known as *brutti ma buoni* ("ugly, but good").

🦂   🦂   🦂

One room of the Lungarotti wine museum in Torgiano is devoted to *vin santo.* Here you can see baskets, presses, and barrels used in its production. Most interesting are the ornate *cialde* irons, used to cook round anise-scented wafers from a flour and egg batter moistened with *vin santo.* They're supposed to cook in the time it takes to say an Ave Maria. And among the museum's collection of medieval and Renaissance faience is a seventeenth-century jar decorated with grape bunches, vines, and birds, once used to store *vin santo.*

Around the corner is Le Tre Vaselle, the country inn where the Lungarotti family offers regional dishes like *frittata alla menta* (with mint), risotto cooked in Rubesco wine, *pappardelle* (wide ribbon noodles) with black truffle sauce, and grilled wild boar, followed by *vin santo* served with pastries, cookies, and anise-scented *cialde.*

Order a glass of *vin santo* at a Tuscan restaurant and it is likely to show up at the table with a small plate of biscotti, crunchy "twice-cooked" cookies studded with toasted almonds. The shape is an elongated oval, flat on one side, and perfect for dipping in the narrow glass of dessert wine. Aficionados say that one particular type of biscotti—*cantuccini di Prato*—from the Mattei bakery in Prato, ten miles northwest of Florence, makes the best match.

At Cantinetta Antinori in Palazzo Antinori at the foot of Via de' Tornabuoni, in Florence, you can finish off a meal of simple Tuscan food with a glass of Antinori *vin santo* and a plate of authentic *cantuccini* and *brutti ma buoni* from Mattei.

Winemakers have discovered lots of uses for *vin santo* in cooking, too, from dousing roasted chestnuts along with a little sugar or deglazing the pan when making a pork roast. Contessa Lisa Contini Bonacossi adds a little *vin santo* to the chestnut purée for her Monte Bianco, a dessert composed of mounded chestnut purée topped with softly whipped cream to resemble the Alpine peak.

And at Badia a Coltibuono, Lorenza de' Medici, who teaches cooking at the Chianti estate she owns with her husband, Piero Stucchi-Prinetti, makes a soup with *vin santo,* pouring beaten egg mixed with lemon juice, lemon rind, and a glass of *vin santo* into a rich broth. When she roasts pigeons, she stuffs them with bread crumbs, prosciutto, and their livers, and glazes the birds with honey and *vin santo.*

THE WINE OF HOSPITALITY

Wine Estates

Most wine estates in Tuscany and Umbria produce their own *vin santo* and may have limited quantities for sale. Several estates have restaurants where their *vin santo* can be sampled following a meal. *Badia a Coltibuono* (Gaiole in Chianti/+39 0577 74 481/colti buono.com).

Cantinetta Antinori (Piazza Antinori 3, Florence/+39 055 23 595/antinori.it).

Le Tre Vaselle (Via Garibaldi 48, Torgiano/+39 075 988 0447/3vaselle.it).

Wine Shops

These wine shops have impressive collections of *vin santo* for sale. Very cheap *vin santos* are rarely a good bet; true *vin santo* is costly to make.

Enoteca la Fortezza (Piazzale Fortezza, Montalcino/+39 0577 849 211/enotecalafortezza.com). *Vin santo* from producers of Brunello di Montalcino, the wine region just southwest of Siena, can be tasted by the glass.

Enoteca del Gallo Nero (Piazzetta Santa Croce 8, Greve in Chianti/+39 055 853 297/chianticlassico.it). More than two dozen *vin santos* from Chianti Classico producers.

Enoteca Italica (Fortezza Medicea, Siena/+39 0577 228 811/enoteca-italiana.it). This *enoteca,* the first in Italy, collects wines from all over the country. Order a bottle of *vin santo* to enjoy on the outdoor terrace or in a room in a sixteenth-century fortress.

Wine Museum

Museo del Vino, Lungarotti Foundation (Corso Vittorio Emanuele 31, Torgiano/+39 075 988 0200/vino.lungarotti.biz).

NACH WAXMAN AND MATT SARTWELL'S FAVORITE FOOD BOOKS

An Interview

Though I am a fairly accomplished home cook and baker, and read cookbooks with as much relish as I read novels, I am in no way a culinary expert. But I'm fortunate to know two people who are: Nach Waxman, owner of the wonderful store Kitchen Arts & Letters in New York (1435 Lexington Avenue, between 93rd and 94th Streets/212 876 5550/kitchenartsandletters.com), and Matt Sartwell, manager, who's been at the store since 1991. Kitchen Arts opened in 1983 and is the largest store in the United States devoted exclusively to books on food and wine, with more than eleven thousand titles in English and other lan-

guages. Nach worked previously in book publishing for seventeen years and had long thought about opening a specialized store; Matt also worked in publishing. Both Matt and Nach are extremely knowledgeable about cookbooks and all books about food and beverages, and their opinions are regularly sought after by customers, chefs, culinary professionals, book and periodical editors, and journalists. Beginning with this Tuscany and Umbria edition, Nach and Matt will present their best recommendations for cookbooks and reference books about the cuisine of each Collected Traveler destination.

We decided not to include works of fiction or memoirs, though Nach and Matt could talk for hours about these, too. Nach says some of the food descriptions in Frances Mayes's Under the Tuscan Sun are forever burnished in his memory, like the time Mayes is at her local outdoor market and is hungry, so she goes to a little stand and orders a thin steak that's grilled and put on top of a bed of arugula. "That, to me, is such an inspirational account, such a statement about the way a particular kind of people eat, and she reveals more of this in some ways than an entire 288-page cookbook could."

MEDITERRANEAN

Nach: The Mediterranean is not always as happy a subject as it might be. The food picture has been dominated by so-called promises of glowing health—what's wrong with it being just good food?

Matt: The Mediterranean is such a big subject, and though there is a great deal that unites Mediterranean cookbooks, I think sometimes when someone says "Mediterranean" what they're essentially saying is "Italian and Provençal"—certainly a lot of people mean that when they come into the store.

Nach: All of this said, Nancy Harmon Jenkins is someone who is very serious about her cooking. You see this immediately in her *New Mediterranean Diet Cookbook: A Delicious Alternative for Lifelong Health* (Bantam, 2008) and *The Essential Mediterranean: How*

Regional Cooks Transform Key Ingredients into the World's Favorite Cuisines (William Morrow, 2003). And even though her first and groundbreaking book on the Mediterranean diet sounds clinical, she really cares about food being flavorful and satisfying above all. I'm also a real admirer of Clifford Wright. His book on the food of Sicily, *Cucina Paradiso: The Heavenly Food of Sicily* (Simon & Schuster, 1992), is a stunning book—I know it's outside the scope of Tuscany and Umbria, but I can't resist mentioning it because Wright managed to take an area that already had a ton of books about it and do something that was really substantive. It deals very specifically about the enormous Arab influence in Sicilian cooking. [Sadly, the book seemed to fade away after one printing and is hard to find now, though I did locate a copy at Abebooks.com.] Wright brings a dimension to Mediterranean food that is absent from so many other books. His *A Mediterranean Feast: The Story of the Birth of the Celebrated Cuisines of the Mediterranean, from the Merchants of Venice to the Barbary Corsairs* (William Morrow, 1999) is a singular example of this: it's exhaustively researched and a very worthwhile book. Italy doesn't have quite the same tapas or meze tradition as Spain and the eastern Mediterranean countries, but Wright's *Little Foods of the Mediterranean* (Harvard Common, 2003) includes many antipasti recipes.

Matt: Alan Davidson's *Mediterranean Seafood* (Ten Speed, 2004) is a book people buy mostly for the reference information—I can't think of a single person who's ever said, "I made the stew on page twenty-two"—but it's an authoritative source for background.

Nach: Many of the fish Davidson highlights aren't found in our waters, and as he includes alternate names for the various fish, this is good for travelers. The limited number of recipes are really curiosities—he likes to say, "Here's the peculiar thing that Tunisians do with this fish: they bury it in the sand for three months and then they dig it up and roast it." That's something of an exaggeration, but Davidson, a traditional diplomat-scholar, was captivated by the exotic.

The Mediterranean is diverse enough that most general books on the region are simply too diffuse to give a very coherent picture. However, there are some good samplings of recipes in Paula Wolfert's *Mediterranean Cooking* (Quadrangle, 1977), Joyce Goldstein's *Mediterranean Fresh* (Norton, 2008), and Claudia Roden's *Mediterranean Cookery* (Knopf, 1987). And then all by itself you've got Elizabeth David's brilliant *Book of Mediterranean Food* (John Lehman, 1950—and still very much in print). David, who is interested in the ideas behind dishes, accompanies her sparse but richly communicative recipes by providing invaluable information about the ingredients and the culture that gave rise to the foods that people cook and eat.

ITALIAN

Nach: Some of the very best Italian cookbooks ever are those by Evan Kleiman and Viana LaPlace. Kleiman, restaurateur and owner of Angeli Caffè on Melrose Avenue in L.A., is also long-time host of a weekly radio show, *Good Food,* in Los Angeles. Viana LaPlace has lived extensively in Italy and has written eight books. Their *Cucina Fresca: Italian Food, Simply Prepared* (Harper &

Row 1985; William Morrow, 2001) we relentlessly recommend, and *Pasta Fresca: An Exuberant Collection of Fresh, Vivid, and Simple Pasta Recipes* (Morrow 1988, 2001), and *Cucina Rustica: Simple, Irresistible Recipes in the Rustic Italian Style* (William Morrow 1990, 1998) all have recipes that use a relatively small number of ingredients, and *Cucina Fresca* focuses on cold and room temperature dishes. Both La Place and Kleiman have spent a considerable amount of time in Italy. Later, Evan did a wonderful book on her own, *Cucina del Mare: Fish and Seafood Italian Style* (William Morrow, 1993), which, again, endorses a style which is extremely simple, with bright, fresh ideas for risotto, grilled and broiled dishes, antipasti, and stews from the sea. It's a very valuable book in the Italian pantheon, although it's out of print, of course—many of the books we recommend here at Kitchen Arts & Letters are sadly out of print. La Place also went on to do a few books on her own, including *Verdura: Vegetables Italian Style* (William Morrow, 1991; Ecco, 2000), which is one of my all-time favorites.

Matt: Cucina Fresca is not an absolutely obligatory book, but I think it is for me, and for a number of our customers it has been enormously inspiring. It's an uncomplicated, versatile, everyday cookbook in the Italian style. I pull the book out, I flip through it, and I know what to do with what's in my refrigerator. I've made many of the recipes, but often they're so simple that after I've read a recipe I don't ever really make the *recipe* again so much as I treat the food in that manner.

Nach: The books by Rose Grey and Ruth Rogers of London's River Café, *Italian Easy* (2004) and *Italian Two Easy* (2006), both published by Clarkson Potter, as well as *The Café Cookbook* (Broadway, 1998), are authentic in spirit and the recipes are terrific. The irony is that their most interesting book is one which no American publisher picked up, *River Café Cookbook Green* (Ebury, 2000), a month-by-month book of recipes organized by season. There are recipes that distinguish between early fava beans and late fava beans, and other seasonal distinctions. We import the book from England and therefore it's not inexpensive, but we still sell a lot of copies. If I told you the number of people who've walked into this store over the years and said, "I want a *Larousse Gastronomique* for Italy," you wouldn't believe me! We've heard that *Gastronomy of Italy*, by Anna del Conte (Pavilion, 2001, reprinted 2005), is a good, useful book. Her vision of it was far more encyclopedic and definitive than her publisher wanted, so while still impressive, it is not quite the achievement it could have been. Frankly, when we first learned of it, we thought, "At last! The book we've been waiting for, the book that's going to feature a comprehensive region-by-region compendium of Italian food and lengthy historical notes." That, unfortunately, has yet to be published. And speaking of reference-type books, there is a new book called *Encyclopedia of Pasta,* by Oretta Zanini De Vita, translated by Maureen B. Fant, foreword by Carol Field (University of California Press, 2009), on pasta shapes and their history. The author, a food scholar, traveled all around Italy recording oral histories, delving into family cookbooks, and poking into obscure archives to gather much of her material.

Matt: And on the subject of pasta, Julia della Croce's *Pasta Classica* (Chronicle, 1987, 1992) is a terrific book, now somewhat hard to find. It's so informative, and della Croce is so passionate and intelligent.

Nach: Marcella Hazan's *Classic Italian Cookbook* (Knopf, 1976; Ballantine, 1984) and *More Classic Italian Cooking* (Knopf, 1978; Random House Value, 1995) are extremely worthwhile. They're valuable collections of good, authoritative recipes for practically any dish that you might encounter in an Italian restaurant. But Marcella provides relatively little historical sense or regional background. Giuliano Bugialli's first and classic book, *The Fine Art of Italian Cooking* (Times Books, 1990), has much more such material. I wish it were even more systematic. And, you know, the old

Leone's Italian Cookbook, by Gene Leone (Buccaneer, 1994, originally published in 1967), of Mama Leone's restaurant fame, has some nice recipes in it, and it's just got old-fashioned Italian spirit. Among celebrity books, which often work miserably, there are those by people who really care about Italian food. Sophia Loren's first book, *In the Kitchen with Love* (Doubleday, 1972), was absolutely wonderful, as is her *Recipes and Memories* (OT Publishing, 1998). *Italianamerican: The Scorsese Family Cookbook* (Random House, 1996), by Martin Scorsese's mother, Catherine, is worthwhile and so is Dom DeLuise's *Eat This . . . It'll Make You Feel Better!* (Pocket, 1988, 1991).

Matt: Mario Batali's *Babbo Cookbook* (Clarkson Potter, 2002) is terrific, an inspired presentation of a chef's take on Italian cooking. I also like the Andrew Carmellini book that came out in 2008, *Urban Italian: Simple Recipes and True Stories from a Life in Food* (Bloomsbury), which has an Italian sensibility: open the refrigerator, see what's there, and use your imagination to make what you can with the ingredients you find. Though he is trained as a restaurant chef (A Voce and Café Boulud, both here in New York) and has extraordinary restaurant credentials, Carmellini is really talking about what he and his wife were doing during the time they were waiting for his new restaurant, Locanda Verde, to open. He has a very good chicken cacciatore recipe in the book that is very modestly updated over what you might find elsewhere, using a lot of fennel, green olives, and not a lot of tomato. I've made it half a dozen times for friends and the reaction is always eyebrow-raising surprise and delight.

Nach: Elizabeth David's *Italian Cooking* (HarperCollins, 1988) is another very, very nice book, though I do not have the impression that she had the same cultural relationship with Italy as she did with the broader Mediterranean region to which she was devoted. She writes very prosy recipes and includes all sorts of details like how you buy ingredients at the market, how the dish is made, and she's very much into the spirit of all this. I wouldn't go to her as a resource, but I would go to her for inspiration.

Matt: Another book that should be mentioned is the *Oxford Companion to Italian Food,* by Gillian Riley (Oxford University Press, 2007, 2009). This is not an Italian *Larousse Gastronomique,* but it is a very useful book by a specialist in early Italian food history. Her breadth is amazing. On one page she'll describe Tuscan agricultural practices, later she'll be talking about Michelangelo, and further on it'll be something about an Antonioni film. Inevitably, some people have found fault with some of her entries, but I think they are wading into shark–infested waters when they do that. *Delizia!: The Epic History of the Italians and Their Food,* by John Dickie (Free Press, 2008), is also a good book. Dickie is a student of Italian history, with a broad grasp of Italian culture. He doesn't swallow a lot of those old truisms that get repeated endlessly about Marie and Catherine de' Medici bringing Italian civilization to France. He can be quite a breath of fresh air. Pellegrino Artusi's *Science in the Kitchen and the Art of Eating Well* (University of Toronto Press, 2004) is also noteworthy. Artusi's range was unparalleled, and his book is filled with opinionated and erudite commentary. He has been continuously in print in Italy since 1894.

Nach: Carol Field's books too are extraordinarily worthwhile: *The Italian Baker* (William Morrow, 1985), *Celebrating Italy: The Tastes and Traditions of Italy as Revealed Through Its Feasts, Festivals, and Sumptuous Foods* (William Morrow, 1990, 1997), and *Italy in Small Bites* (HarperCollins, 2004), which focuses on midmorning or afternoon snacks known as *merende.*

Matt: One last Italian cookbook I'll mention is *Made in Italy: Food & Stories,* by Giorgio Locatelli (Ecco, 2007). Locatelli is chef at Locanda Locatelli, a London restaurant, and though you might think the recipes would be fussy and entirely too time consuming, they're actually quite uncomplicated, and his personal stories add a great deal to the book's value.

TUSCAN

Matt: We are just inundated with Tuscan material—it's an intensely published area and the designation "Tuscan" is inescapable—still, even though we can recommend a few very good books, I don't think we've yet seen the definitive volume, something similar to Lynn Rossetto Kasper's *The Splendid Table* (William Morrow, 1991), which focuses on the food of Emilia-Romagna. There's so much to choose from, but I think that most people want one general Tuscan cookbook, and after that it's a matter of burrowing in and selecting another one that's more specific. Cesare Casella did a book called *Diary of a Tuscan Chef: Recipes and Memories of Good Times and Great Food,* with Eileen Daspin (Broadway, 1998) that is about growing up in his family's restaurant near Lucca, Il Vipore, which his parents started in 1964 and which won a Michelin star in 1993. That same year he moved to New York to cook at Coco Pazzo. The book features the kind of cooking he learned there, which is a slightly more elevated Tuscan style, though it's still pretty strongly rooted in the traditional dishes that people would expect. Tuscan cooking in and of itself is not remarkably sophisticated. What you're looking for after you've absorbed the basics is somebody who's a fine cook and who has grown up with Tuscan cooking or been exposed to it. That makes Anne Bianchi's books particularly interesting. Her book *From the Tables of Tuscan Women* (Ecco, 1995) is a collection of recipes and interviews she did with Tuscan women about specific areas of cooking. The subject of beans, for example, is revealed in an interview with a woman who has strong opinions about cooking beans in the Tuscan style, and in particular in the style of Lucca. It's a book with enormous character and it gives you an amazing sense of learning from somebody who's been doing this her whole life. Bianchi's book is somewhat hard to find at this point but is very much worth seeking out.

Nach: Anne Bianchi was a literary writer who unfortunately died young. *From the Tables of Tuscan Women* also features very nice black-and-white photographs of each of the women interviewed. Another excellent Tuscan cookbook is *Soffritto: Tradition & Innovation in Tuscan Cooking,* by Benedetta Vitali (Ten Speed Press, 2001). Vitali opened Cibrèo with Fabio Picchi in Florence and is now proprietor of her own restaurant on the outskirts of Florence, Trattoria Zibibbo. What struck me about this book is that she's *really interested* in the way Tuscans do things. In her introduction, she writes, "Food is a story, and like every good story it is worth the trouble of telling. It can be told and retold, like fairy tales to children. It helps us to wander between memories and fantasy. It reveals to us our private lives." Although passionate, the book is formatted almost as if it's a manual of instructions. Vitali talks about cooking methods—sautéing, frying, steaming, whatever—and she explains what Tuscans mean when they use terms such as those and what the specifically Tuscan take is on these kitchen methods. Unlike so very many other chef cookbooks, this one is very approachable, with 125 essential Tuscan recipes, and really nothing in the book is beyond the capabilities of a devoted home cook. And, yes, the very first recipe in the book is for an all-purpose *soffritto* ("underfried"), a preparation of lightly browned, minced aromatic vegetables gently fried in olive oil—similar to a French mirepoix—which is the foundation on which many Tuscan sauces, soups, and other dishes are built. You come away with a much, much richer knowledge than you would with a simple list of instructions.★

★See page 609 for more information about Zibibbo and Vitali's cooking courses.

Matt: Leaves from Our Tuscan Kitchen, or How to Cook Vegetables is by Janet Ross, who was the aunt of Kinta Beevor, author of *A Tuscan Childhood* (Pantheon, 1999). *Leaves* was originally published in 1899 in London, and the first U.S. edition was published by Atheneum in 1974. [Note: I've seen first editions of this priced at $800 on Abebooks.com.] As old as it is, this book really holds up in terms of the Italian respect for vegetables.

UMBRIAN

Matt: Umbria isn't on most people's radar. Everybody passes through it without stopping on the way to Florence or Rome, which is unfortunate, and there have been very few books published on the region's food. Julia della Croce's *Umbria: Regional Recipes from the Heartland* (Chronicle, 2003) is excellent, with a strong emphasis on the history and the culture of the region, which one would expect from her. *An Appetite for Umbria: The People, the Places, the Food,* by Christine Smallwood and with photography by Eddie Jacob, (Bonny Day, London, 2006) is probably the best and most current book available. It's a rare combination of good and authentic recipes (all are from chefs, many never before published), beautiful color photographs, interviews, and great information for travelers. It offers recommendations not only for twenty-seven places to eat—including restaurants, *trattorie, osterie,* and *enoteche,* some high-end and others very informal places that have been family run for decades—but also for merchants offering regional specialties, such as prosciutto at Fratelli Ansuini in Norcia and olive oil at Frantoio Mancianti in San Feliciano, as well as small maps for sixteen towns.

Nach: Italian Country Cooking, by Susanna Gelmetti (Ten Speed, 1996), is an unusual book in that it focuses both on Umbria and Puglia. We think it's quite useful.

ITALIAN DESSERTS

Nach: I think in general Italian desserts have not been terribly important, and frankly there's a lot of stuff that seems to me to be more in line with what Americans seem to like, such as tiramisu, than what is actually *eaten*. In Italy the sweet course is mostly fruit or gelato, so it's not surprising that there aren't more books on desserts. There really is no tradition of highly varied or inventive desserts such as we know them, and so there's no Emily Luchetti, no Nancy Silverton, no Claudia Fleming.

Matt: You can find some desserts that resemble those in French pâtisseries, especially in Florence, but even then they're there as "sophisticated exotica," on display mostly to make an international statement. You might think that the many books on gelato would be inspiring, but they're mostly what I refer to as bait and switch. Carol Field's *The Italian Baker,* mentioned previously, *is* inspiring, but bread is really the heart of that book, although there are some desserts. [Note: I have found Field's recipe for tiramisu to be hands down the best in any cookbook, probably because it calls for chocolate *pan di spagna* and *not* the ubiquitous ladyfingers.] Nick Malgieri's *Great Italian Desserts* (Little, Brown, 1990) is one I would recommend, as well as *Desserts and Sweet Snacks,* by Viana La Place (William Morrow, 1998), which is a little more improvisational. Unique to Tuscany is Anne Bianchi's *Dolci Toscani: The Book of Tuscan Desserts* (Ecco, 1998), which includes all the Tuscan sweets you've heard of (*zuppa inglese, panforte,* and *biscotti*) and many you may not have (chestnut *timbale,* pear fritters, and *diti,* the *cannoli* of Tuscany). Bianchi's cousin Sandra Lotti coauthored the book—Lotti has continued the Toscana Saporita Cooking School they founded together (toscanasaporita.com) near Lucca. The wonderful vignettes in each chapter about Tuscan life and allure are revealing and valuable on their own.

CHEESE

Nach: Italian cheese is an underpublished category, I think.

Matt: I agree; there's really not enough to read on the subject. Steven Jenkins's great *Cheese Primer* (Workman, 1996), though it does still contain some good information on Italian cheeses, is getting rather out of date. Slow Food's *Italian Cheese: A Guide to Its Discovery and Appreciation* (Slow Food Editore/Chelsea Green, 2006) is probably the best source that comes to mind. It features 293 traditional types of cheese, mostly very obscure. It's for the really dedicated person.

ITALIAN WINE

Matt: What to Drink with What You Eat, by Andrew Dornenburg and Karen Page (Bulfinch, 2006), *The Wine Bible,* by Karen Mac-Neil (Workman, 2001), and *The World Atlas of Wine,* by Hugh Johnson and Jancis Robinson (Mitchell Beazley, 2007, sixth edition), are all good references for wine in general, and I would add to this list Matt Kramer's *Making Sense of Wine* (Running Press, 2004, revised edition), which is a very engaging and thoughtful book. He provides an approachable introduction for somebody who's probably got a generally sophisticated knowledge of Italy and Italian food. Of course, for many years Burton Anderson's books *Vino* (Little, Brown, 1980) and *The Wine Atlas of Italy and Traveller's Guide to the Vineyards* (Simon & Schuster, 1991; Mitchell Beazley, 1999) were the leading works, along with Victor Hazan's *Italian Wine* (Knopf, 1982). All are out-of-date and out of print.

A new book we like is *The New Italy: A Complete Guide to Contemporary Italian Wine,* by Daniele Cernilli and Marco Sabellico (Mitchell Beazley, 2008, revised edition), which was written by two of Italy's most respected wine journalists. There are chapters on every region of Italy—including the islands of Sicily and Sardinia—as well as maps, color photos, lists of notable producers, a grape variety almanac, and a good glossary. For somebody whose last encounter with Italian wine was Burton Anderson or Victor Hazan, this is a serious work and provides a good framework, a good overview, and decent maps. There was a point thirty years ago when Italian wine wasn't taken very seriously, and one of the reasons for this was that there was great inconsistency in the commitment of the producers. Some producers felt content with the grapes and the methods they liked. A lot of good wine was being made, but there was also a lot of plonk. However, a new generation was committed to updating and improving Italian winemaking. This book gives an accurate picture of the Italian wine scene today.

Readers may learn about many, many more great food titles by browsing the Kitchen Arts & Letters Web site, and they may also subscribe to the bookstore's newsletter.

To Matt and Nach's list of recommendations, I add the following titles:

A Tale of 12 Kitchens: Family Cooking in Four Countries, Jake Tilson (Artisan, 2006). More of a culinary memoir, this unique book takes readers to a dozen kitchens around the world in places where the author—an artist not well known in North America—has lived and visited. Tuscany is one of those places, and is one locale that Tilson knows especially well: his parents bought a farmhouse near Cortona more than thirty years ago; he spent many summers there and now returns every year with his own family. The recipes he shares are not unusual or surprising. Rather, what you read this book for are his recollections of Tuscany and how Italian gastronomy has crept into his heart. Tilson emphasizes that "when trying to re-create our Italian kitchen back in London, the results are an entirely different cuisine, wonderful but different. . . . Shops and magazines persuade you that the correct tableware will invoke the essence of Tuscany in your pallid garden or cold, wintry kitchen. Crank up the central heating for three days. It still isn't the same—ersatz Esperanto food. Go to Italy and beg or borrow a kitchen and cook. After the first bite you'll be hooked for life. You may even have to move there."

The Food of Italy: Region by Region, Claudia Roden (Steerforth, 2003; originally published as *The Good Food of Italy,* Knopf, 1990). Roden's aim with this book was to feature traditional recipes from each region of Italy, and it grew out of the "Taste of Italy" series she wrote for the London *Sunday Times Magazine.* The selection "reflects what is popular in Italy today, what I liked best, and what I feel you will most enjoy cooking and eating." Roden notes that the cooking of Italy is very varied and was never formalized the way it was in France, so that there is no equivalent of *haute cuisine* or *cuisine bourgeoise:* "It is basically country cooking for large families, a combination of peasant food and the grand dishes that belonged to the nobility and were eaten by the peasantry on special occasions—some only once a year, at carnival time. The different styles may have a city stamp but they have their roots in the land because town and country in Italy have always been closely bound." The Tuscany section includes twenty-seven recipes, while Umbria has only eight, though all are classics of the regions. Roden emphasizes that Tuscan cooking is the "simplest in the whole of Italy, but it is not poor; at its best it can be exceptional"; of Umbrian cuisine, she says, "The food here is simple, sober, and homey, but it also has great elegance. It is the incredible abundance of truffles that gives it style."

Honey from a Weed: Fasting and Feasting in Tuscany, Catalonia, the Cyclades and Apulia, Patience Gray (Harper & Row, 1986). This is one of those books I read about for years before I finally got my own copy. And it did not disappoint. There is a wealth of information in this book, and it isn't all about food, or at least it's not all about recipes. Gray reminds us that "once we lose touch with the spendthrift aspect of nature's provisions epitomized in the raising of a crop, we are in danger of losing touch with life itself." She ends her introduction with this observation: "In my view it was not necessarily the chefs of prelates and princes who invented dishes. Country people and fishermen created them, great chefs refined them and wrote them down. In Latin countries, because of inborn conservatism, the tradition is alive and we can learn from it, that is, learning from people who have never read a book."

Italian Bouquet: An Epicurean Tour of Italy, Samuel Chamberlain (Gourmet Books, 1958). This book is based on a series of articles that appeared in *Gourmet* over a period of more than two years, beginning in 1954, entitled "A Gastronomic Tour of Italy." The recipes are contributed by chefs at hotels and restaurants. Nach informed me that Chamberlain was actually an architect, and his main interest was buildings, not food (all the prints, drawings, and photographs in the book are credited to him). However, his wife, Narcissa, was the foodie between them, and she translated and adapted all the recipes in the book. One of the amazing things about an out-of-print book like this is discovering that some of the recommended restaurants are still around, such as Trattoria Sostanza (Via del Porcellana 25r); Buca Lapi, the oldest restaurant in Florence, founded in 1880, in the cellar of Palazzo Antinori; Ristorante Sabatini, though now at a different number on Via Panzani, number 9a; and Trattoria Cammillo (Borgo San Jacopo 57r), which I very much enjoyed on my last visit.

Piano, Piano, Pieno: Authentic Food from a Tuscan Farm, Susan McKenna Grant (HarperCollins, Toronto, 2006; Overlook,

2008). I had read about this book *somewhere* and wrote down its name on a scrap of paper, but when I checked at Kitchen Arts & Letters for a copy, I learned that the book hadn't yet been published in the United States. Nach and Matt kindly referred me to Barbara-Jo's Books to Cooks in Vancouver (604 688 6755/bookstocooks.com), and the staff at this wonderful bookstore sent me a copy. The title translates as "slowly, slowly, full," and if that sounds like the author is a believer in the Slow Food movement, it's not an accident: she is, and this book is filled with simple yet rich recipes that celebrate the earth's bounty (and the book is endorsed by the Slow Food Foundation for Biodiversity). But this is far more than a book of good recipes. There is much about Tuscany revealed in Grant's essays throughout the book, and readers may be interested to know that Grant and her husband own La Petraia, a fifteen-minute drive outside Radda in Chianti, which offers guests *agriturismo* accommodations and meals, as well as cooking classes and foraging expeditions. See my blog for more information.

INTERVIEW

Sergio Esposito

Italian Wine Merchants, in New York, is recognized as the foremost authority and retailer of Italian wines in the United States, and its founder and CEO, Sergio Esposito, is recognized in the wine industry as the country's premier Italian wine authority. Just as I asked Nach Waxman and Matt Sartwell at Kitchen Arts & Letters to talk with me about Italian cookbooks, I asked Sergio to do the same for Tuscan and Umbrian wines.

I'm a big fan of Sergio's weekly e-letter, which is written in an informative but very lively way (just about every week, after reading his letter, I

want to jump on the subway and buy whatever he's recommending), as well as his recent book, Passion on the Vine: A Memoir of Food, Wine, and Family in the Heart of Italy (Broadway, 2008). This wonderful book is filled with so many great passages, but one that stays lodged in my head is one relating to Italian food. He notes that ethnic restaurants—or really, any restaurant that isn't Italian—are in short supply in Italy and only survive "as a sort of proof." All the residents of a city or town have to try the ethnic food once or twice, just so they can say they have indeed tried it and can definitively say it isn't very good. "This is the true strength of Italian food. Italians don't get bored by their recipes—when something's good, why change it? The goal is not to improve on Great-Grandma's recipe; it doesn't need improvement. The goal is to replicate exactly Great-Grandma's recipe. It's almost Darwinian: the best recipes survive forever, handed down again and again and creating a historical dish that balks trends."

IWM was founded in 1999, and Sergio's partners in the venture at the time were chef Mario Batali and Joe Bastianich, co-owner of a number of Italian restaurants (some with Batali and others with his mother, Lidia Bastianich). IWM is a wonderful store with an old-world feel to it, yet a unique feature is that none of the bottles you see in the shop actually leave the store: everything is stored below in temperature-controlled rooms. There are plenty of new releases offered, beginning at about nine dollars a bottle, but Sergio has also amassed one of the greatest collections of vintage Italian wine in the world. He is dedicated to providing the highest price-quality ratio in each price point and offering the best customer service in the business. IWM has expanded, with offices in Hong Kong and Aspen, and there are currently more than fifty thousand people on its e-letter mailing list. IWM also specializes in building wine cellars and col-

lections, for beginners and connoisseurs alike, that also include non-Italian wines such as vintage Bordeaux and limited production Rioja.

Q: What are the grape varieties unique to Tuscany and Umbria?

A: Sangiovese definitely, for both Tuscany and Umbria. And interestingly, you could say that Sangiovese made Tuscany in a sense, because it's such an important part of its economy and an important part of its identity. If you think about the fact that Sangiovese is basically the grape behind Chianti, and Chianti employs a tremendous amount of people, and there's a tremendous amount of marketing used to bring people to Tuscany, and then there's also Montalcino and Montepulciano . . . well, Sangiovese can't be separated from Tuscany. Umbria has a very important role in Sangiovese as well, which is to be a supportive area for Tuscany, because most of Umbria's production of Sangiovese (and some other grape varieties) is actually transported into Tuscany.

Q: What's the definition of Denominazioni di Origine Controllata (DOC), and how many are there in Tuscany and Umbria?

A: The idea behind DOC is that the European community has to keep the authenticity of certain products, and they wanted to ensure that consumers knew where products were coming from. It's basically that the origin of the wine is checked and controlled so that unscrupulous people can't make a wine in one place and say it's made in another. And then we have Denominazioni di Origine Controllata e Garantita (DOCG), the highest level of quality control, which is also about place and also about guarantee. This is really one of the strictest regulatory systems in the world, where to have a wine be called DOCG you actually have to supply one sample every year to a tasting panel and they taste it and vote on whether it is of the quality it needs to be to be called DOCG. So you could do everything right in Montalcino and the board could say you cannot call this wine Montalcino because we don't feel it's good enough and it will ruin our name. So you'll lose 80 percent of your production because then you have to sell it as a *rosso* instead of a Brunello. There are forty-two DOC zones in Tuscany (seven of those are DOCG) and thirteen in Umbria (two are DOCG).

Q: What are some of your favorite wineries in Tuscany and Umbria to visit?

A: Without a doubt in Umbria it would be Cantine Lungarotti, founded by Giorgio Lungarotti in 1962. It's one of the best wineries in the business, and though Giorgio passed away in 1999, his daughter Teresa and Teresa's half sister Chiara are now in charge, and the family's wines are still held in high regard. Giorgio was really the one who put Umbrian wine on the map—before he came along, there was really only the white wine from Orvieto. But he had a vision, not only for wine—his red Rubesco *riservas,* made from 70 percent Sangiovese and 30 percent Canaiolo (a Tuscan grape traditionally blended with Sangiovese in Chianti but no longer required), knocked everyone's socks off—but also for tourism: he opened a hotel, Le Tre Vaselle, in Torgiano (3vaselle.it). The hotel is a beautiful country inn that's named after three seventeenth-century ceramic wine vessels (*tre vaselle*) that once belonged to an Umbrian Franciscan convent. Lungarotti is the only winery that's really equipped to take care of busloads of people (but I don't mean that in a bad way), and the family's Lungarotti Foundation also supports two fantastic museums, the Museo del Vino and the Museo dell'Olivo e dell'Olio (lungarotti.it).★

★Lettie Teague, former wine writer for *Food & Wine,* related a funny story in the May 2002 issue: Robert Mondavi met Giorgio in 1977 at a Paris wine compe-

The Antinori family, which has been making wine for twenty-six generations, does a very nice job at their properties in both Tuscany and Umbria, but they have one property called Badia a Passignano in Chianti that also has a *really* nice little restaurant, L'Osteria di Passignano, as well as a small shop, La Bottega, where all the Antinori wines are sold (both open daily 10 a.m. to 11:30 p.m.; open for tastings only Sundays 10:30 a.m. to 6:30 p.m./+39 055 807 1278/antinori.it). The *badia* (abbey) itself is really old—the archives date back to 891, but it could have been around since as early as 395. In 1049 it became home to the Vallombrosano order, a reformed branch of the Benedictines specializing in winegrowing and forestry. The order became so powerful it once owned a quarter of Tuscany. The Florentines attacked it, burned it, and razed it to the ground between 1196 and 1255. After it was reconstructed, Ghirlandaio painted one of his *Last Suppers* in the monks' refectory, and Galileo taught mathematics here in 1587. Antinori bought the vineyards around the *badia* in 1987, and though the monks still own the abbey, Antinori uses the cellars. It's a great facility to visit and it's right in the heart of Chianti and very picturesque.

Another really gorgeous winery to visit is Tenuta dell'Ornellaia (ornellaia.com), near the medieval hamlet of Bolgheri in the Maremma. It has a somewhat complicated history—it was founded in 1981 by Marchese Lodovico Antinori; Robert Mondavi Winery bought into the winery in 1999 and became full owners in 2002 while simultaneously enter-

---

tition, and a few years later Mondavi visited Torgiano. After a number of repeated visits, Giorgio started to get suspicious. Mondavi finally admitted that he'd been trying to see if he could create something like Le Tre Vaselle in California, but finally concluded that he couldn't. Teresa Lungarotti told Teague, "My father was so flattered, he sent Mondavi a pair of seventeenth-century Umbrian doors like the ones we have at Le Tre Vaselle."

ing into a partnership with the Frescobaldi family. Frescobaldi bought the remaining shares of Ornellaia in 2005, and it now owns the entire estate. It's worth noting that the Ornellaia property is adjacent to Tenuta San Guido (sassicaia.com), the premier super-Tuscan estate owned by Lodovico Antinori's cousin Niccolò, which produces the pioneering Sassicaia. The Ornellaia winery is in a modern building that's built into the hillside surrounded by forests.

Another one I have to mention that represents a combination of tremendous winemaking, history, and a beautiful setting on a smaller scale is the Montevertine winery in Chianti. They make a 100 percent Sangiovese-based wine called Le Pergole Torte, and the winery is set on a beautiful hillside around the bend where you can't see any other homes.

Q: What is La Strada del Vino?

A: This is the "wine road"—or more properly, "roads"—of Tuscany that presents visitors with organized routes taking in not only the wineries but inns, wine shops, restaurants, museums, and culinary destinations. The Strada (which, by the way, was founded by Lodovico Antinori) is a great way to plan a wine-focused visit to the region, and its Web site (lastradadelvino.com, the official site of the Consorzio La Strada del Vino Costa degli Etruschi) includes lots of information on wines, estates, roads, maps, food, accommodations, and cellar visits.

Q: Do you need an appointment to visit wineries?

A: Always. I really don't know of any winery you can just walk into without an appointment. Sassicaia does winery visits only on Tuesdays, but you still need an appointment.

Q: What are some Tuscan and Umbrian wines, both white and red, you would recommend that first-time visitors try?

A: For whites in Umbria I would say Orvieto, and also a grape variety called Grechetto, which you'll find all over Umbria—it's really the workhorse of the area. In Tuscany, hands down it would be Vermentino, which is a really spectacular, fun wine that can be a little bit salty in a sense but has great depth, great character, and is very food friendly. And for red, if you're in Tuscany, how can you not try a Chianti? Some great producers are Castell'in Villa, Villa Mangiacane, Fontodi, Falsina, and Querciabella. In Umbria, I would say the wines made from Sagrantino. The Sagrantino of Montefalco is probably the most interesting and most unique albeit of high quality.

Q: Price being no object, what ten Tuscan and Umbrian wines are your favorites?

A: I can give you one: Case Basse di Gianfranco Soldera. There's no better producer in Tuscany or Umbria or maybe the world. His wines are mind-boggling—they're exceptional in the worst of vintages, not because he makes a great wine in the worst of vintages, but because in the worst of vintages he makes truly exceptional wine for longevity. He's a true artisan. He also has a tremendous garden, with a million different varieties of roses and different types of flowers, and he's really interested in the ecosystem, so you get to see one of the region's most beautiful natural gardens along with the pond on the estate. In his cellar, you can taste wine like you can't get in anyone else's cellar. His wines aren't widely available here (though IWM receives the largest allocation) and there is very limited production, a mere 1,500 cases in good vintages.

Q: What is your buying philosophy at IWM, and how many wines from Tuscany and Umbria do you offer?

A: I don't buy wine by category. I don't say, "I need to have this because I need a Chianti in stock." Often we won't have a

Chianti in stock, and people will say, "How can you not carry a Chianti?" Well, it's because the selection here changes all the time. Most of the wine we carry is from small producers, Tuscany and Umbria included, and they're never on the shelf for more than two or three months. One thing I've been doing for a long time is tasting wine without pricing. So I taste wine without knowing what the price is. I estimate what the price is, and if I'm wrong and the wine is much less expensive, then I buy it. It's all about price for quality. I also look for authenticity when I taste wine; I don't like to be fooled. And something I prize very much is when a wine transports you, when you drink something and you think, "Wow, that really, really reminds me of that place." For me, that's what it's all about.

Q: What are super-Tuscan wines?

A: They're wines that refer to a marketing term more than anything else. Essentially, a super-Tuscan is any red wine that is made in a manner that doesn't conform to either DOC or DOCG rules for the region. It really all began with one gentleman, Mario Incisa della Rocchetta, on the Tuscan coast, who said, "I'm going to break all the rules and I'm going to make a great wine." So he broke all the rules, and in breaking all the rules, he had to name the wine something else, and he called it Sassicaia. And in doing so, when he went to market, the only way that he could categorize the wine was to call it a table wine, a *vino da tavola,* which is a category that refers to everyday wines, some of which are plonk but others are perfectly fine. But the problem was that his wine was so much higher in quality. Then the Indicazione Geografica Tipica (IGT) was created, which was nothing more than a category in between *vino da tavola* and DOCG, but it allowed the so-called super-Tuscans to enter the market in a category that more accurately reflected their quality and their nontraditional methods. The prices of wines within IGT range from a few euros to hundreds of euros, and now there are super-Tuscans that don't even need to be super-Tuscans. Take Chianti Classico, for example. At one time, you had to make it with four grape varieties, including a white varietal, or you couldn't call it Chianti Classico. Now you can make Chianti with only one. There are literally thousands of super-Tuscans today. Note that the release of the iconic Sassicaia from the 1985 vintage sold for $45. Now it has appreciated and sells for $2,500 per bottle.

Q: Do you travel frequently to either Tuscany or Umbria or both?

A: I do. I spend about three months a year in Italy, and I would say I spend a minimum of two weeks in or around Orvieto. And I also spend time in Todi. And in Tuscany I spend a lot of time in Montalcino and the Chianti area.

Q: What are some of your favorite wine towns in Tuscany and Umbria? And what are some of your favorite places to eat?

A: In Umbria the best wine town is Montefalco, because it's a very charming medieval town that's all about the wine. Then I would say in Tuscany—I mean, how can you not say, although the wine is not my favorite—the towns in and around Chianti, like Radda, and of course Montalcino, which is all about wine, with its fourteenth-century fortress that's been converted into the Enoteca La Fortezza wine shop (enotecala fortezza.it).

For places to eat: at the high end, there is no better restaurant in my opinion than Enoteca Pinchiorri in Florence (enotecapinchiorri.com), which everybody knows. It's run by Giorgio Pinchiorri and his wife, Annie Féolde, and it's been awarded two and three Michelin stars over the years. In Colle di Val d'Elsa there's a place called Arnolfo Ristorante (arnolfo.com), which is a high-end place run by a great gen-tleman—he runs the kitchen and his brother runs the dining room. It's really nice. For not so high-end, I would say a great town is Monteriggione, which is a small town outside Siena that has a wall around it that's mentioned in Dante. Right below it is a family-run place called Albergo Casalta, an un-pretentious inn with a great chef—if you go in summer you can sit outside and have a terrific meal in a courtyard. In Um-bria, I really like Ristorante Vissani (casavissan.it), just outside of Civitella del Lago, near Todi. I also really like the village of Pitigliano, which is great for anyone especially interested in Jewish history, but there's also a great winemaking and food culture there. And in the Maremma, I really like Alain Ducasse's place, L'Andana—Tenuta La Badiola (andana.it); the Michelin-starred restaurant there is Trattoria Toscana.

Q: What are some of your favorite places to stay in Tuscany and Umbria?

A: In Orvieto there's Hotel Palazzo Piccolomini (hotelpiccolo mini.com), originally built in the sixteenth century for the pontifical family (the same one for whom the Piccolomini Palace was built in Pienza). Outside of Orvieto there's a place that's a little more expensive called TodiCastle Estate (todi castle.com), fifteen minutes outside Todi, is a 250-acre prop-erty with a medieval castle in the center—the Santoro family lives in the castle, but it can be rented, along with one of the property's three restored villas, each with its own swimming pool. In Tuscany, I like Villa Mangiacane (mangiacane.it), seven miles from Florence, right outside San Casciano. The name comes from the Latin *magna cane,* for "great dog," and it's a fifteenth-century villa on six hundred acres of vineyard and olive groves. The villa was built for Machiavelli, and it's believed that Michelangelo had a hand in its design; because of the significance of the owner and architect, the original plans for the villa's improvements and enlargements are kept in the Uffizi. Also, there's a place run by a German man, Jens Schmidt, and an American woman, Ruth Dundas, called Villa Montecastelli (montecastelli.com), between Siena and San Gimignano on the old Via Francigena. It's really a thousand-year-old hamlet—they've restored the abbey and it's on top of a mountain. They even have a thousand-year-old peach tree on the property. Four apartments are available for rent. In Florence I like the Grand Hotel (grandhotel.hotelinfirenze.com), an eighteenth-century historical landmark overlooking the Arno, but the truth is I don't tend to stay in cities at all as my work takes me into the countryside. I rarely sleep in the same bed more than two nights in a row, and I haven't slept in Venice proper since the 1980s!

Q: What are some of your favorite food and wine pairings?

A: I would say in the spring in Umbria you have the most incredible selection of lettuce, the kind of lettuces you don't find anywhere else in the world. If you're at a market there, keep an eye out for these, especially cockscomb lettuce. That lettuce salad with a nice, cold glass of Orvieto is to die for. Another dish you have to have in Umbria is *cinci* with black truffles, and also *strozzapreti* ("choking priest") pasta with Umbrian Sangiovese—it's spectacular. In Norcia, there is a local sparkling red wine that's not exported and goes great with pork products. In Tuscany, *pici* pasta with boar ragù and a Brunello di Montalcino is an outstanding match. A lot of summer Tuscan dishes are, literally, brown. The famous soup, *pappa al pomodoro,* is made with tomatoes and bread, but when it's ready to eat it's basically brown. A typical Tuscan menu starts with bruschetta—you *must* have bruschetta—and then you always have sliced meats, etc. And with this classic menu you're talking about a red wine, a hearty, rich red with hearty, rich food.

Q: Can you describe some of the IWM trips to Italy?

A: In my opinion our trips are different from others because typically others are either too heavy on the wines or too heavy on something else, and I think we offer a very good balance for people who are interested in wine and for others who aren't. Also we offer a variety of restaurants. Some nights are at fancy places and others are at very simple places—you can't eat rich, filling meals every night. It's overkill. Knowing the regions as well as we do, as well as the wines, makes all the difference in the world. We also incorporate a number of cultural activities into our itineraries, such as the Palio in Siena and a Zubin Mehta concert in Florence. We work with a tour operator, and one of us from IWM always accompanies the group. When I go, I'm sometimes amazed that, as someone who spends a lot of time each year in Italy, I continue to find something unique, I always find inspiration, I find my passion, and I remember why I do all this other stuff here.

Q: What made you want to be involved with IWM in the first place?

A: I knew that the perception of what Italian wines were was a little bit negative, and so I wanted to change that. I knew this other part of Italy that people didn't seem to know, and I wanted to share that.

Q: What are the two most popular regions at IWM?

A: Tuscan wines are our number one bestselling wine—Tuscany has been referred to as "the center of the Italian wine universe," and with good reason: You have Brunello di Montalcino, Rossi di Montalcino, Vino Nobile di Montepulciano, Chianti Classico, and the super-Tuscans. The wines from Piedmont are second.

Q: What are a few resources you'd recommend to readers interested in Italian wines?

A: Of course *Vino Italiano: The Regional Wines of Italy,* by Joe Bastianich and David Lynch (Clarkson Potter, 2002). Even though I know and have worked with Joe and David—former wine director at Mario Batali's popular restaurant Babbo— I wouldn't recommend this book if it weren't excellent. They've included good background information on each region of Italy plus Sardinia, tasting notes, a glossary of Italian wine terms, resources, a bibliography; and Lidia Bastianich and Mario Batali have contributed recipes. [I can't resist adding my own two cents: this is positively the go-to book for learning about Italian wine. I especially like the background information and travel tips, and, for me, a proponent of "what grows together, goes together," Batali's remarks in the foreword are worth repeating: "Italian wine is still defined by a sense of proportion, a more moderate balance of fruit, acid, and tannin. It accentuates, rather than dominates, the food it's served with. And there's nothing quite like pairing a Roman dish with a Roman wine, or a Friulian dish with a Friulian wine. There's no substitute for that kind of elemental combination."]

Q: Is there something new that you're particularly excited about right now?

A: There's *always* something new, and I think that's why I continue to focus only on Italy, which has about two thousand grape varieties and every day they're discovering a new one. There is so much potential. In 1960 there was just one Montalcino producer—it's a very young wine region. That's what keeps me going—I always get to taste a new product. And where is our next Montalcino going to be?

Q: What wines do you recommend visitors buy in Italy and bring back?

A: The wines you bring back should be those you have an experience with on your trip, and you bring them home so you can relive the experience—but don't expect it to be the same! Everything tastes better in Italy and it's not going to be the same if you're in Dallas, Texas, and you're in your garage barbecuing. It might still be good, but it will taste different. And I'm not referring necessarily to expensive wines—remember that Italians eat and drink all the time—they drink during lunch, during dinner . . . they really take to heart an old Latin saying: "It is well to remember that there are five reasons for drinking: the arrival of a friend; one's present or future thirst; the excellence of the wine; or any other reason." So for them they need a wine that goes through the whole week, wines that can go with every dish. The important part is that they're drinking wine. Here we're programmed to think certain wines only go with certain dishes and opening a bottle is seen as a sort of special occasion. Your most favorite wine on a trip to Italy may be a *vino da tavola,* because it was good and you were having an excellent day, and that's the wine you should bring home.

🦌   🦌   🦌

Italian Wine Merchants is located at 108 East 16th Street, New York/212 473 2323/iwmstore.com. Readers may subscribe online to Sergio's weekly e-letter.

"Every time I tell people I studied art in Italy they assume I mean Florence, even when I specify that it was studio art, not art history. Maybe they have the right idea, and I would have been better off in the Tuscan capital, especially back in the days of backpackers clutching the layman's breviary, *Europe on Five Dollars a Day.* After all, the city is virtually an open museum and a never-ending stream of pleasant surprises. I'll never forget the time I was walking down the sidewalk, dragging my hand lazily along the wall to the right, when suddenly I came to a niche and realized that I had been caressing the church of Orsanmichele, and the niche held a sculpture by Andrea del Verrocchio, maestro to the young Leonardo da Vinci.

"My self-ordained destiny instead was to study at the Brera Academy in Milan, the best and most functional of the Italian fine arts academies at the time, located at the epicenter of contemporary Italian culture and commerce. Milan may have been a grim and often foggy industrial city, but all of Italy's great artists and art galleries were congregated there, and I fancied that one day I, too, would join them, by reason not only of proximity but out of a stubborn belief in my own talent.

"I finally made it down to Florence one year during the Christmas break, when I managed to put together the five dollars a day I needed for a trip. The walk from the train station to the youth hostel took me right past the church of Santa Maria Novella, with its white and green marble façade designed by Leon Battista Alberti, so I stopped in to catch a first glimpse of Masaccio's *Holy Trinity* fresco. Unless my memory fails me, the hostel was across the Arno, and not much more than a dormitory filled with bunk beds upstairs, and a common room downstairs where someone played Bob Dylan songs on the guitar while everyone else sang along in a variety of the world's accents.

"Everywhere I went—except, of course, the Uffizi—I tried to record my impressions in watercolor, doing quick sketches in cerulean blue that I filled in with generous swabs of ochre pierced by swift brushstrokes of red and green and raw umber. In my haste the medium sometimes got the better of me, especially closer to sunset, and all that was left was a big wet smear on a sheet of curling paper.

"On the afternoon of my last day, I took a public bus up to where my fellow travelers had assured me I would have the best panorama of Florence, Piazza Michelangelo and the church of San Miniato al Monte, perched atop a hill overlooking the city. The Romanesque church took me back in time, to a period that it is today unfashionable to call the "Dark Ages," long before the exuberance and pagan splendor of the late fifteenth century. Beneath the low vaults of the crypt, the muffled and serene pleasures of the monastic life still echoed all around. Yet any lingering suggestion of the Middle Ages evaporated as soon as I went back outside into the waning light and descended the steps toward Piazza Michelangelo.

"The city of Florence lay before me, slumbering beside the banks of the Arno. Brunelleschi's magnificent cupola over the Santa Maria del Fiora basilica—the greatest engineering feat of the Quattrocento and the model for countless other domes in the centuries to come, including St. Peter's in Rome and the Capitol in Washington—rose high above the tiled rooftops, a proud affirmation of human ingenuity. Not far away the tower of the Palazzo Vecchio pierced the sky, in an almost secular and feudal rebuke to the magniloquence of the cathedral. On the hillsides to either side of me, I could see the old walls of the city clinging to the slopes, a reminder of both Florentine vulnerability and the military ferocity that had safeguarded its prosperity.

"I took out my watercolor pad and tried once again to capture the beauty around me. I managed to complete two or three paintings before the night overtook me. But this time everything came out perfectly, and when the paint dried I knew that I would not have to rely on memory whenever I sought to see the world again through the eyes of a twenty-year-old."

—Michael F. Moore, Chair, PEN (poets, playwrights, essayists, editors, and novelists) Translation Committee, translator and interpreter for the Italian Mission to the United Nations, and translator of a number of books, including a new translation of the nineteenth-century novel *The Betrothed* by Alessandro Manzoni (Modern Library, 2011)

A TAVOLA!

Tutti a tavola a mangiare. (Let's all go to the table and eat.)

—LIDIA BASTIANICH,
Lidia's Italian-American Kitchen

A city's gastronomy doesn't often spread beyond the city limits, let alone into another province. Although the gastronomic landscape of Italy today can appear static, its past reveals a culinary flux of exotic influences from the early trading routes into Venice, Genoa and Messina, assimilated over centuries. . . . What might seem a culinary straitjacket fortunately allows for continual invention and improvisation at home and in restaurants, retaining an Italian feel. So although one may be worried that Italy might become the world's first Gastronomic Place of World Heritage Interest, it's still very much alive and rightfully wary of external influences whose motivations are not at all concerned with excellence of ingredients or developing national identity. Personally I don't travel thousands of miles to arrive at Florence station to eat a Magnum ice cream or a croissant.

—JAKE TILSON,
A Tale of 12 Kitchens

To know a territory, you need to eat it.

—ITALO CALVINO

CANTINETTA
DEI
VERRAZZANO

CANTINETTA DEI VERRAZZANO
VIA DEI TAVOLINI, 18/20R - Tel. e Fax 055/268590
www.verrazzano.com
e-mail: cantinetta@verrazzano.com

Florentine Trattorias

FAITH WILLINGER

✿

THIS PIECE AND the one that follows both appeared in my first edition of this book, and I wasn't at all sure that Willinger would feel the same way about the *trattorie* and *ristoranti* she'd originally recommended. But when I asked her, she carefully considered each one, and confirmed that, yes, perhaps surprisingly, she stands behind every recommendation even today, a dozen years later.

FAITH WILLINGER, introduced previously, can talk about Tuscan cuisine for many hours.

I LIVE IN Florence. So in order to write about *trattorie* in my adopted hometown I spoke to a lot of friends, noted down their suggestions, revisited places I hadn't been in years, and checked out a couple of new ones. And I looked for a good definition of "trattoria." *Webster's* says it's "a small, inexpensive restaurant in Italy." Not exactly. My Italian dictionary comes closer because it includes "a synonym of *osteria,*" a derivation of the word for host.

Notice that neither décor, cuisine, nor service is mentioned in either definition. A trattoria, more often than not a family-run establishment, is presided over by a host or hostess acting as a link between the kitchen and the dining room, or cook and diner, and has as its most important aspect its sense of neighborhood: locals dine there daily, or at least weekly, and are treated with familiarity.

Trattoria menus are composed of regional specialties and classic Italian dishes that highlight fresh ingredients and spare, unadorned preparations—the kind of cooking people eat at home (or wish they did). In other words, don't expect culinary fireworks or the showy artistry of a celebrity chef.

Meals in Florentine *trattorie* frequently begin with chicken-liver-spread crostini (toasts) or thinly sliced *salumi*—salt-cured pork products such as prosciutto, fennel-flavored *finocchiona,* or *salame toscano* (with garlic and peppercorns). Bread, baked in wood-fired ovens, is rustic, dense, and saltless—an acquired taste for most.

Typical winter *primi,* or first courses, are hearty vegetable soups such as *ribollita* (a reboiled bread, bean, and cabbage combination), *pappa al pomodoro* (a porridgelike mixture of onion, garlic, tomatoes, basil, and local olive oil thickened with bread), and *pasta e ceci* (with chickpeas), or rich, meaty sauces served on the broad, flat noodles known as *pappardelle.* Summer diners can count on *panzanella,* a refreshing salad made from tomatoes, bread, onion, and fresh basil, and on pasta sauced with vine-ripened tomatoes and basil. A few nontraditional dishes centered around seasonal ingredients generally share space on the menu with such classics as pasta with meat sauce, *bollito misto* (mixed boiled meats), and breaded and fried *cotoletta* (pork, lamb, or veal chop).

Main-course meats include chops and *bistecca alla fiorentina,* a thick grilled T-bone that's served with a lemon wedge (particularly good are those from the local Chianina breed of cattle). Poultry and rabbit are deep-fried or oven- or spit-roasted. *Arista,* roast pork loin with rosemary and garlic, is another trattoria favorite. On Fridays, fish lovers can look forward to *baccalà*—salt cod, which is either cooked in tomato sauce, stewed with leeks, or served with chickpeas—and to spicy *calamari in inzimino,* squid braised in red wine with tomatoes, spinach, and Swiss chard. Vegetables get minimalist preparations: most arrive pristine, accompanied only by a cruet of a fruity, murky local extra virgin olive oil that's called simply *olio*—a world-class ingredient that is used here not just as a cooking medium but as an everyday condiment.

The cheese of Tuscany is pecorino Toscano, not hard but a pungent product made from sheep's milk. Pecorino can be eaten *fresco* (up to a month old), *semi stagionato* (aged one month or so), or up to six months later, when it is fully *stagionato* and thus drier and sharper in flavor. Look also for fresh sheep's milk ricotta, which is far richer and more flavorful than the cow's milk variety. And, finally, the classic conclusion to a trattoria meal are *biscotti di prato,* golden, eggy, hard almond cookies that are best dipped in a glass of *vin santo,* the region's dried grape-based dessert wine. Old-fashioned *torta della nonna* (a custard-and-nut-stuffed pastry), *tiramisu* (originally from the Veneto), and *panna cotta* (cooked cream) also can be found.

The wine served in Florentine *trattorie* is usually red and probably from the zones Chianti Classico, Chianti Rufina, Chianti Colli Fiorentini, or Chianti Montalbano. Only in the hot summer months will white wine appear on the tables. Those trattoria proprietors who have graduated from offering simply the *vino della casa* or from pointing at one or another of their displayed bottles to actually printing up a wine list probably will feature nonregional or nontraditional whites as well as a wider selection of well-respected Tuscan reds.

Florence's Santa Croce neighborhood is home to the Sant'Ambrogio market, a magnet for both farmers and retailers and a prime source for two of my favorite establishments. Cibrèo, named after an old-fashioned chicken-innards dish reputed to be an aphrodisiac, comprises both a formal restaurant and, in a back room, a casual trattoria. Chef-owner Fabio Picchi carefully controls each pot on the stove and takes full advantage of local ingredients such as the hot red peppers known in Tuscan dialect as *zenzero* (his are homegrown by his dad). The trattoria décor—tiled walls, wooden tables set with paper place mats, short-stemmed glasses—is decidedly more casual than that of the restaurant. In addition, the menu is shorter, the service swift, and the seating communal. Reservations are not accepted, and lingering is discouraged. Still, prices are less than half those at the restaurant, and the food comes from the same kitchen.

A starter—usually the spicy tomato aspic or the *sformato di ricotta* (ricotta flan)—is followed by one of the four or five first courses, including the signature yellow bell pepper soup and the polenta topped with butter and Parmigiano-Reggiano. There are ten or so main-course selections, among them chicken meatballs in tomato sauce, eggplant *alla parmigiana,* sausage with Tuscan white beans, and spicy *calamari in inzimino.* Several vegetable sides—stewed potatoes, braised artichoke wedges, a cooked vegetable salad brilliantly red with beets—also are offered. A slim wedge of flourless chocolate cake or a serving of the house *panna cotta,* which is like a super-rich crème caramel, makes for a sweet finish. Bargain hunters should head to Cibrèo after ten p.m., when leftover front-room items (herb and lemon marinated lamb chops and squab stuffed with *mostarda,* a piquant candied fruit) are served in the trattoria.

Only the front room of the Osteria del Caffè Italiano, also in the Santa Croce neighborhood, feels like a real trattoria: the décor looks as though it hasn't been touched in years. The room behind it is another story. This softly lit space features terra-cotta floors, vaulted ceilings, and grand chandeliers. Black-vested waiters sporting long white aprons scurry about with an air of formality that is a bit extreme for a typical trattoria, though the menu is a standard one. The front room, on the other hand, with its dark-wood cabinets, shelves of wine bottles and glasses, display of *salumi,* and simple, place mat–covered wooden tables, feels just right. People stop in here throughout the day and into the evening for an espresso or a glass of wine, some first-rate *salumi* or equally impressive pecorino. A blackboard lists an ample selection of red wines by the glass or by the smaller, less expensive *degustazione,* or "taste." In addition, there's a much more extensive, much pricier, written list. The lunch menu is short—three first- and three main-course choices—and inexpensive. I always enjoy a walk through the dining room, with its tablecloths and brass candlesticks, to the kitchen for a glimpse of its large charcoal grill and imposing deep red enamel stove.

The aptly named La Casalinga ("the housewife") is my neighborhood hangout in the Oltrarno ("beyond the Arno") district. The food is ultra home style and the ambiance, no-frills: the two dining rooms feature white paper tablecloths, varnished pale-pine wainscotting, prepoured carafes of wine, and bright lights. Daily specials are written all over the menu, which is posted just outside the door. Begin with *fettunta* (garlic-rubbed toast, here topped with beans), bruschetta with fresh tomato, *salumi,* or herring fillets. Or skip the antipasti altogether and start with a seasonal vegetable soup, salad, or pasta. Main dishes include *bollito,* or boiled meats, served with *salsa verde* (herbs and olive oil); stewed meats; slightly over-roasted guinea hen; rabbit; and veal. Raw vegetables are served *pinzimonio* style, with a little bowl of extra virgin oil and salt for dipping. Look for such *contorni* (side dishes) as stewed beans, mixed boiled vegetables, tuna salad, and sliced tomatoes. For dessert, there's usually *panna cotta, tiramisu,* or a selection of fresh fruit. The house wine is inexpensive (and unfortunate); for more discriminating palates, a few bottles are available behind the bar in the front dining room.

There's always a crowd waiting to be seated at Ruggero, the inviting domain of Ruggero Corsi, near the Boboli Gardens in the neighborhood outside Porta Romana. Though Ruggero stays in the kitchen, his wife, Anna, and his son and daughter, Riccardo and Paola, are dynamic presences in the dining room, amid the display of seasonal produce, the homemade desserts, and the hissing espresso machine. Such Tuscan classics as chicken-liver crostini, *salumi,* and hearty soups always tempt me, but I can never pass up the perfectly cooked, spicy tomato-sauced *spaghetti alla carrettiera* (literally "teamster-style," or prepared with garlic and parsley). Other options include roast pork loin, grilled beef, and *bollito misto* with *salsa verde.* Desserts are a letdown, but no one seems to mind. And the wine selection is small, though thoughtfully chosen and well priced.

Omero, located in the gentrified countryside ten minutes from the heart of the city, may seem more like a fancy restaurant than a trattoria, but it is a popular local hangout, with the friendly ambiance of a casual eatery. Fronted by a general store where you can pick up everything from cheese, *salumi,* and bread to cigarettes and bus tickets, it also has two large dining rooms and a terrace, all with splendid views of the city below. Walk past the huge terra-cotta *orcio*—urn of extra virgin olive oil—and settle in at one of the comfortable tables for some *fettunta,* dipped, in the fall and winter months, in just-pressed extra virgin. Delicious *crostini* of chicken liver or artichoke purée keep impatient diners content as they wait for such *primi* as *pasta e ceci, ribollita, pappardelle* with rabbit or hare, and spinach-and-ricotta-filled ravioli. Main-course options include grilled steak Florentine; veal or pork chops; and deep-fried chicken, rabbit, and squab. Among the perfectly prepared deep-fried seasonal vegetables are irresistibly light, batterless artichoke wedges. The dessert cart tempts with (nontraditional) cheesecake and chocolate tart, as well as with such classics as pears cooked with prunes and marinated whole oranges. The wine list, with lots of unusual choices, also is guaranteed to please.

My favorite trattoria in the San Lorenzo neighborhood is Mario, with a tiny dining room that looks in on a glassed-in kitchen dominated by a pot-covered stove and by Romeo Colzi, the chef. His wife, Patrizia, waits on the customers, and his brother, Fabio, totals up the bills at the register. To avoid crowds at this popular lunch spot, arrive at noon; after twelve thirty there's always a line of students and market workers waiting for a

space at one of the paper-covered tables. Romeo stops ladling out food at around three p.m. The menu, displayed outside by the door as well as alongside the kitchen, features such regional classics as *ribollita,* vegetable soup, and (fantastic) pasta with hen or rabbit sauce. Regulars know there's tripe on Mondays, rabbit on Thursdays, fish on Fridays, and the town's least expensive steak Florentine every day of the week. Romeo is wild about wine and offers, in addition to the decent house Chianti, an amazing selection of heavy hitters at bargain prices. For dessert, there's biscotti and *vin santo.*

Da Sergio is the favorite trattoria of a friend of mine who lives in the San Lorenzo area. Tucked behind market stalls selling souvenirs, it is easy to miss. Two large, rather unattractive dining rooms hung with diplomas, awards, ceramics, and a Florentine soccer-squad scarf are lit by enormous iron chandeliers festooned with ugly energy-saving bulbs. This, too, is a family affair: Sergio Gozzi is in the kitchen; his wife, Grazia, is posted behind the entryway bar, where she slices bread, pours wine, and hands off the plates to her sons, Andrea and Alessandro. Seating is open, so expect to share a table with locals or tourists. My friend raved about the pasta with tomato sauce, with good reason—I no longer think of ordering anything else (though the bean-and-grain *zuppa di farro* always looks delicious). Boiled meats, tripe, breaded and fried meatballs, and *baccalà alla livornese* (salt cod with tomato sauce) are among Sergio's mainstays. Fresh fruit or biscotti are the only dessert selections; the wine list is equally spare.

Knowing the addresses and star dishes of a handful of Florence *trattorie* is just the first step to fully appreciating the peculiar dynamic of this city's warm, down-to-earth eating establishments. How can you, as a visitor, have the same—or at least a similar—experience to that of the locals? Seek out a trattoria that seems to have some promise. Dine there three times. On your first visit you'll be a tourist. On your second, your face will be recognized and your presence acknowledged. By your third visit, they'll begin to treat you like a regular.

Trattorias

Cibrèo Trattoria (Via de' Mucci 122r/+39 055 234 1100/cibreo.com). Closed Sundays and Mondays.

Da Ruggero (Via Senese 89r/+39 055 220 542). Closed Tuesdays and Wednesdays.

Da Sergio (Piazza San Lorenzo 8r/+39 055 281 941). Lunch only; closed Sundays; no credit cards.

Osteria del Caffè Italiano (Via Condotta 12/+39 055 289 020/caffeitaliano.it). Closed Mondays.

Trattoria La Casalinga (Via dei Michelozzi 9r/+39 055 218 624/trattorialacasalinga.it). Closed Sundays.

Trattoria Mario (Via Rosina 2r/+39 055 218 550/trattoria mario.com). Lunch only; closed Sundays; no credit cards.

Trattoria Omero (Via Pian dei Giullari 11r, Pian dei Giullari–Arcetri/+39 055 220 053/ristoranteomero.it). Closed Tuesdays.

Florence
A Restaurant Renaissance

FAITH WILLINGER

I AM LUCKY: I live in Florence. Built on Roman ruins in the heart of Etruscan country and the birthplace of the Renaissance, this onetime capital of Italy is home to world-class art, architecture, and artisans. Local archives are jammed with manuscripts, ledgers, etchings, paintings, and sculpture: twenty-five centuries of Florentine documentation of almost everything, notably food and wine. The Tuscan table has been chronicled in a long-gone sixth-century BC fresco of honey-glazed grape flatbread, a fourteenth-century recipe for ravioli, Michelangelo's sketched grocery list, Bartolomeo Bimbi's more-than-just-botanical paintings of long-lost fruit cultivars, Jacopo Chimenti's still-life pantries, and Ardengo Soffici's memoirs of spit roasting. Even the Mannerist architect Bernardo Buontalenti is honored not with a stone memorial but with a silky rich custard flavor of gelato called, appropriately, *buontalenti* (he invented the dessert). And many of these preparations—barely changed with the passage of time—still appear on modern menus.

Tuscan austerity is reflected in simple, unadorned dishes made with the best ingredients. The visitor to Florence should not look for formality or fussiness but should focus instead on the kind of food eaten in the home, which recently—and happily—has been appearing in restaurants. The one luxury on every table has always been local extra virgin olive oil—usually fruity and a murky, almost phosphorescent green, with an exuberant peppery bite when first pressed in early winter. Its flavors calm down after a few months of aging, and it contributes a suave, cholesterol-free richness essential to the Florentine *cucina*. Such olive oil should be thought of as a condiment, not just a cooking medium. I've found that Vino e Olio, on Via dei Serragli, has the best selection.

Bread is another fundamental element in the Florentine diet: saltless, dense, and baked in a wood-fired oven. (Mine comes from a bakery called Vera, on the Piazza Frescobaldi.) It is consumed fresh, toasted, or stale and is paired with *salumi* (salt-cured meats), pecorino (sheep's milk cheese), walnuts, dried figs, or even chocolate. *Fettunta*—the minimalist garlic-rubbed toasted bread drenched in extra virgin olive oil that was and is the snack of Tuscan olive-oil pressers—is almost always available, even if it's not listed on a menu. First-course soups such as bean and vegetable *ribollita* and tomato *pappa al pomodoro* are thickened to the consistency of oatmeal with stale bread; refreshing *panzanella* is a summery salad mixed with moist bread. All are far more delicious than they might sound.

Fresh pastas—wide strips of *pappardelle,* cheese- and greens-filled ravioli, meat-sauced *tortelli*—are often found on menus. Traditional *penne strascicate* (quill-shaped pasta "dragged" through meat sauce), spicy *spaghetti alla carrettiera* ("teamster-style"), or other creatively colored and dressed pastas are served as starters. Unfortunately, restaurants rarely get risotto or pizza right. Locals eat little seafood; what fish dishes there are—including *baccalà* (salt cod) and *inzimino* (a stew made with tomatoes, Swiss chard, and cuttlefish or squid)—are generally found on Fridays. Although sturgeons from the Arno are said to have once provided caviar with which to top white beans, this world-class dish is now executed with costly imported roe.

"Bean-eater" may not sound terribly offensive, but the term has been pejoratively applied to Florentines for centuries. And bean-eaters they are. White *cannellini* beans are still a favorite, boiled and then dressed with olive oil or served *all'uccelletto,* stewed "like little birds" with garlic, sage, and a touch of tomato. In the summer natives become addicted to the thin-skinned, pale beans known as *fagioli sgranati*. A vegetable of note is winter's *cavolo nero* (curly kale), and spring or fall brings porcini mushrooms. Best of all is the *pinzimonio* medley of raw fennel, artichokes, celery, or other seasonal *verdure* accompanied by a do-it-yourself sauce of olive oil, salt, and pepper.

🦎   🦎   🦎

Above all else, however, Florence is a town for carnivores. Don't miss the *fiorentina*, a large, lean, but well-marbled steak, optimally Chianina beef, cut at least two inches thick, grilled rare over charcoal, and dressed with salt, pepper, and a wedge of lemon. Pork products include fennel-spiked salami and fresh sausage, salt-cured pancetta (bacon), skewered livers, and *arista* (roast pork loin with rosemary).

Some of Italy's best red wines happen to be the local beverage of choice and include Chianti Classico, Carmignano, Vino Nobile di Montepulciano, and Brunello di Montalcino. Those worth seeking out include Chiantis from Castello di Ama, Fattoria di Felsina, Castello dei Rampolla, Selvapiana, San Felice, Castello di Volpaia, Isole e Olena, and Monte Vertine; Carmignanos from Tenuta di Capezzana; Vino Nobiles from Avignonesi, Poliziano, and Contucci; and Brunellos from Tenuta Caparzo, Poggio Antico, and Col d'Orcia. (Many of these fine wineries also produce top-drawer extra virgin olive oils.)

Meals most often conclude with fresh fruit or gelato (both Badiani, on Viale dei Mille, and Cavini, on the Piazza delle Cure, make wonderful *buontalenti* gelato). Many restaurants, however, now serve sweets more special than the city's not-always-easy-to-love native desserts. Smoky, unleavened *castagnacci* (chestnut tarts), *schiacciata all'uva* (grape flatbread), and the rock-hard almond *biscotti di Prato* or *cantucci* cookies tend to be acquired tastes.

For an overview of Florentine fare I recommend a visit to one of the city's food markets. Clothing and souvenir stands surround architect Giuseppe Mengoni's cast-iron-and-glass Mercato di San

Lorenzo (also known as the Mercato Centrale), one of three neighborhood markets built for the city's low-rent Camaldoli districts during an 1864 urban renewal project. Inside, ground-floor stalls are populated by vendors of bread, meat, poultry, game, fish, cheese, *salumi,* pasta, cookies, and imported out-of-season vegetables.

I can never resist stopping at the market's culinary highlight, Da Nerbone, founded in 1872 and located on Via di San Casciano (all aisles in the market are named after nearby villages) on the periphery of the ground floor. A throng of locals waits first to pay and then to hand a receipt to Alessandro Stagi while his able sandwich chef chops, seasons, and stuffs boiled beef or tripe into crispy rolls dipped in broth and dressed with *salsa verde* (herbs and olive oil). A simple menu is chalked on the blackboard—pasta, soup, a hot or cold meat dish, and a few vegetables. I usually eat at one of the marble and wrought-iron tables across the aisle. The house wine is Chianti Classico, the service nonexistent, and the ambiance pure marketplace. The boiled beef sandwich is one of the city's great gastronomic experiences and a bargain in overpriced Italy. Then, it's up the escalator (if it's working) for a look at produce stands selling wares that still smell like the country, casually piled in crates yet looking like perfect still lifes.

The Mercato di Sant'Ambrogio, on Piazza Ghiberti and also constructed in 1864, is the vegetable market for the Santa Croce neighborhood. Vendors indoors sell perishables, and those outside hustle clothing, plants, and produce. Farmers in a row at the back of the market peddle their own seasonal wares, supplying some of the area's finest restaurants. Of these dining spots, my favorite is Cibrèo, named after an old-fashioned chicken innards dish reputed to be an aphrodisiac. This culinary fiefdom was founded in 1979, when Fabio Picchi and Benedetta Vitali dropped out of college to prove a point about family-style food. They opened a trattoria and a restaurant connected by a common kitchen that specializes in the *cucina* of a Tuscan granny—Florentine comfort food rarely, until that time, found outside the home. Ristorante Cibrèo has a classic dining room with white tablecloths and sparkling stemware.

Eating at the tiny Trattoria Cibrèo, on the other hand, is like eating in a friend's kitchen. It's crowded, has communal seating, and there are no place mats. It also takes no reservations, allows no lingering, and charges far lower prices for what is, except for a few exceptions, the same food served in the restaurant. (Starters such as pecorino and raw fava bean salad; flanlike *sformati* of ricotta or vegetables; chicken liver spread on toasts, or crostini; and tripe salad are available only in the restaurant.) Pasta is never featured (it's not really Florentine, insists Picchi), but it isn't missed with such flavorful offerings as delicate yellow bell pepper or woodsy porcini mushroom soups, classic *pappa al pomodoro, ribollita,* polenta with herbs, or summery tomato aspic. Stuffed duck, baked liver, pigs' feet, fish steamed in its own juices, and mussels in butter are often on the menu, as is the city's best calamari-and-chard *inzimino. Palombo* (a small member of the shark family, it is also known as "veal of the sea") is prepared *alla livornese:* It is cooked in a sauce of tomatoes, garlic, chili peppers, and parsley. Beans are on the menu year round, joined by side dishes that include beet salad, stewed potatoes, and cauliflower with sausage. Wines are well chosen although somewhat pricey. And the desserts—all made by Vitali—are tempting, especially the intense, fudgelike flat chocolate wedge and the Neapolitan *pastiera* (ricotta tart).

Caffè Cibrèo, across the street, is perfect for sipping a glass of wine while waiting for a table at the restaurant or the trattoria or for having a sandwich, snack, cocktail, or an espresso. The menu is limited but appealing and includes fresh mozzarella (when available) and all of Vitali's desserts. The tables are cramped, but the prices are the lowest of any of the Cibrèo eateries. When the weather is warm, outdoor seating is at a premium.

La Baraonda serves homestyle Florentine food with the same

sense of whimsy that prompted the choice of its name, which is Italian for "convivial chaos." There's a handsome marble butcher's counter in the front room; three small connecting dining rooms lie beyond. For non-Italian speakers, owner Duccio Magni will expound on the unusual menu in rapid-fire English with a Scottish accent. After the decisions have been made, crostini spread with black olive paste or goat cheese are offered to the suddenly starving diners waiting for their first courses. I rarely can resist chef Riccardo Fiora's *risolata* (romaine risotto). Second courses—veal meat loaf served with *salsa verde,* for example, and grilled *tomino* cheese with cooked field greens—on the menu are supplemented by daily specials. Magni's wine of the month is usually Tuscan and always interesting. Dinner concludes with pine nut gelato with chocolate sauce; caramelized apple tart; or a few attractive, colorful fruit-shaped candies, an old-fashioned Tuscan treat. Goblets of *crema pasticciera* (pastry cream) are mixed with strawberries in the summer and with "shattered" chocolate, hazelnuts, and almonds in the winter.

With its vaulted ceilings, subdued décor, dark wood tables topped with white linen place mats, and the ambiance of the noble Antinori family (Tuscan winemakers for more than six hundred years), the Cantinetta Antinori resembles a private Florentine club. Majordomo-like Gianfranco Stoppa presides. The menu includes classic dishes and a few concessions to regulars tired of the same old *pappa,* as predictable cuisine is described in Florence. One can choose from traditional soups, fresh pastas, stewed meats, simple salads, vegetable combinations, and delicious *cannellini*. The extra virgin olive oil and sheep and goat cheeses are from the family estates. All of the Antinori wines are served by the glass as well as the bottle, a thrill for avid tasters. The desserts are unexciting, but the *biscotti di Prato* and *brutti ma buoni* cookies from the Mattei bakery are the best of their kind.

Alla Vecchia Bettola ("the old dive") hasn't really been around for all that long, and it isn't really shabby enough to be a dive.

There's one dining room, with benches and stools, marble tables, paper place mats, and rustic *cucina*. The extensive, hard-to-decipher handwritten menu of homey dishes changes daily. I look for simple starters: tomato-and-vodka-sauced *penne alla Bettola,* *topini* (potato gnocchi), and soups. Meats are the main attraction: Braised boned rabbit, herbed roast pork loin, grilled chops, and *fiorentina* steak are the stars. Except for the excellent *fagioli all'uccelletto,* vegetables and other side dishes are almost an afterthought, but desserts are homemade and always include the restaurant's lovely tiramisu. Most customers drink the house wine, although the list offers many Tuscan gems.

Trattoria Garga, with its low lighting, large plants, and an international clientele, epitomizes new-wave Florentine. A series of intimate dining rooms is adorned with swirling modern murals in muted Renaissance colors painted in part by Canadian pastry chef-hostess Sharon Gargani and her Florentine husband, chef/ex-butcher Giuliano Gargani, who sings of love as he cooks. The cuisine, unconventional and yet Tuscan in spirit, relies on the flavors of garlic, hot *peperoncino* peppers, fruity local olive oil, and fresh vegetables. Large oval platters of *"il magnifico"* pasta (the sauce is made of cream, lemon zest, orange zest, Parmesan, and mint) or piquant *vigliacca* (tomato-sauced tagliatelle) keep sophisticated diners twirling their forks. I'm always eager for spaghetti with garlic, olive oil, and barely cooked, crunchy artichokes, surrounded with a corolla of the pointy outer leaves. Veal scallops, peppery lamb, the finest *baccalà* in the city, and the house salad are good options. Mrs. Gargani's cheesecake and chocolate *torta* both win raves from dessert fans.

In 1633, Galileo was exiled to Pian dei Giullari–Arcetri. Now part of the rural but long-gentrified suburbs of Florence and only a five-minute cab ride from the city, this village is still worth a visit to check out the restaurant Omero. Its entrance-cum-grocery assaults the senses with marvelous Tuscan ingredients. Counterman Enzo trades gossip; sells bus tickets, stamps, cigarettes, and salt to locals; and slices prosciutto, *salumi,* and pecorino for restaurant diners. Host Roberto Viviani leads clients past a terra-cotta *orcio* (olive oil urn; the oil is for sale by the liter during the early winter months) and a display of Tuscan wines to the dining rooms—upstairs, downstairs, and the summer terrace, each with a view. Many diners are regulars and know exactly what to expect from this purist's menu that has barely budged from the Florentine canon. In cold months bread is toasted in the fireplace for *fettunta,* but *salumi* and chicken liver crostini are fine meal openers for the rest of the year. Chickpea and pasta soup, *ribollita,* and fresh ricotta-and-greens-stuffed ravioli are also first-rate. Chicken is flattened under a brick and grilled, or it is deep-fried Florentine-style with fried vegetables such as crispy artichoke wedges or zucchini flowers. Of course, beans are always on the menu. A dessert cart laden with the classics—among them a golden meringue-topped *zuppa inglese* (trifle)—invites indulgence; and the wine list, focusing on Tuscany and, more specifically, on the Chianti Classico region south of Florence, is a pleasure.

Palates weary of unrelievedly Tuscan cookery should hurry to Florence's Ristorante alle Murate. The logo, an empty birdcage, evokes not only a defunct nearby prison of the same name but also liberation from local tradition in all aspects. The décor is modern without a hint of rusticity, and jazz plays softly in the background. Multilingual owner Umberto Montano betrays his Campanian heritage with a warm welcome and hints of southern sunshine on the innovative menu. The cooking is light-handed, vegetables are treated with respect, and the homemade pasta is stuffed and sauced creatively. Not to be missed are the orecchiette ("little ears" of pasta) with greens and broccoli or the farfalle (pasta bow ties) with Robiola cheese, zucchini, and a raw tomato sauce. Chocolate chip cookie fans should conclude with the signature dessert called the Armstrong (named after Louis), a monster cookie served with unsweetened whipped cream. A limited menu is available in the jazz club/wine bar in the back; customers frequently stop in for a quick meal, glass of wine, or dessert. Oenophiles should ask to visit Umberto's small but packed cellar—a lovely personal selection of bottles.

🦎 🦎 🦎

Dining in Italy can be a costly, as well as time-consuming, experience. Travelers looking for less expensive possibilities will be pleased by the many easygoing, no-frills establishments packed with locals who recognize good food even without the fine appointments. (The wine choices, however, may be unfortunate.) One should remember to bring cash to these places because credit cards are rarely accepted. Budget dining on Sundays, when Florentines fulfill family obligations or escape to *trattorie* in the countryside, is difficult as most of the city's more modest eateries are closed.

Trattoria Le Belle Donne's entrance is so nondescript that it's easy to miss, although at peak lunch hours a small crowd may be waiting outside for tables. The cozy one-room trattoria is decorated with postcards from clients and an overwhelming countertop display of fruits and vegetables. Regulars—a mixture of designers, nobles, bankers, clerks, students, and shoppers—rub elbows at rustic marble tables set with paper place mats and tumblers. The service is speedy but sometimes surly. The menu (it's easiest to check out the blackboard under the window *before* sitting down) changes daily, offering traditional yet surprisingly innovative cooking. Raw mushroom salad and marinated herring starters, vegetable pastas or soups, hearty meat or poultry stews, carpaccio (paper-thin slices of raw beef), and homemade desserts like chestnut pudding or creamy *panna cotta* are frequently on the board. Vegetarians will have an easy time ordering, and there's no pressure to consume a complete meal.

Trattoria La Casalinga, "the homestyle trattoria," delivers just what it promises. It's like eating at Mamma's and is frequented by a neighborhood crowd—artists, workers in overalls, artisans, businessmen in ties, elderly women in slippers, youths in designer jackets, and students who turn up daily for the hearty food dished up in massive portions for a low price. There are no food stylists in the kitchen, just Graziella and Feruccio. Oliviero at the counter fills wine carafes while Cristina and Andrea and Paolo wait on tables. The menu offers classic first courses, traditional soups, pastas with meat or tomato sauce, a large selection of stewed and roasted meats, a few simple vegetables, and homemade tiramisu and *"crem caramel."* Specials are always a good choice.

Tranvai must surely be the city's tiniest trattoria, roughly the size of the old-fashioned Florentine cable car for which it's named. Diners may be charmed by framed pictures of trams of the past, the headlight on the bar, metal flooring, intimate seating (expanded in summer with outdoor tables surrounded by potted hedges), and swift service. Low prices keep the locals loyal. Nanda Vanni prepares those hard-to-find Florentine favorites like pasta sauced with leeks, boiled beef and onions, and stuffed cabbage and fish on Fridays. Her specialties, however (*trippa, lampredotto,* and *budellino*—different kinds of tripe and intestine), aren't for everyone.

The most intrepid gastronomes will want to visit Il Trippaio di Porta Romana, near the Boboli Gardens, not the most central nor the oldest tripe stand in the city but part of a growing trend that applies new treatments to tripe. Classic stands serve *trippa* or *lampredotto* boiled and then stuffed in a roll. But this new-wave tripe stall substitutes strips of tripe for cuttlefish in *inzimino* or for fish in *cacciucco;* it cooks tripe with beans, potatoes, and artichokes; and it also serves tripe in classic Florentine style—tomato-sauced and Parmigiano-topped. Mixed cuts of boiled beef with *salsa verde* or stewed *guancia* (cheek) are available for those with an aversion to tripe. There's no written menu, and the selection changes daily. All preparations are sold in *panino* (sandwich) form or with a plastic fork. The open-air dining options range from standing at the nearby Totocalcio soccer betting counter, sitting on a bench outside the Fine Arts Institute, or strolling, sandwich in hand, through the Boboli Gardens. Fine food and fine art are, after all, a legacy bestowed upon everyone who lives in, or visits, Florence.

Restaurants and Trattorias

Al Tranvai (Piazza Torquato Tasso 14r/+39 055 225 197/altran vai.it).

Caffè Cibrèo (Via Andrea del Verrocchio 5r/+39 055 234 5853/cibreo.com).

Cantinetta Antinori (Piazza Antinori 3/+39 055 292 234/ cantinetta-antinori.com).

Da Nerbone (Mercato di San Lorenzo/+39 055 219 949).

La Baraonda (Via Ghibellina 67r/+39 055 234 1171).

Ristorante alle Murate (Via del Proconsolo 16r/+39 055 240 618/allemurate.it).

Ristorante Cibrèo (Via Andrea del Verrocchio 8r/+39 055 234 1100/cibreo.com).

Trattoria Cibrèo (Via de' Macci 122r/+39 055 234 1100/ cibreo.com).

Trattoria Garga (Via del Moro 48r/+39 055 239 8898/garga.it).

Trattoria Omero (Via Pian dei Giullari 11r, Pian dei Giullari–Arcetri/+39 055 220 053).

Valle del Serchio and the Garfagnana

BETH ELON

THIS PIECE IS actually part of a chapter from a passionate and fascinating book entitled *A Culinary Traveller in Tuscany: Exploring & Eating Off the Beaten Track* (2006) published by one of my favorite publishers, Little Bookroom. The book appeared in 2006, and though I can enthuse about it endlessly, two other writers do so a bit more eloquently than I: Joan Didion, who says, "What Beth Elon has given us is not only a detailed and practical cookbook but also a traveler's guide—and a love letter to a place and a way of living. This is great food writing in the spirit of Elizabeth David"; and Frances Mayes, who adds, "Beth Elon not only tastes Tuscany, she savors every flavor, turns down every enticing road, and joyously reveals her long, profound, and continuing appreciation of this place of endless pleasures."

Though I'm generally not fond of featuring excerpts from books, I felt that the subject of this one, the Garfagnana, in the far western corner of Tuscany near Liguria, is very little visited and little known, even by those well traveled within Tuscany, and it deserves wider appreciation. The rest of the chapter includes recommendations for a few great places to eat as well as recipes for local specialties.

BETH ELON and her husband have lived on a little farm in a little village (population 135) in the Apennine foothills for more than thirty years.

THE GARFAGNANA, ALWAYS a fascinating place with its impressive castle ruins and precipitous hills, has lately become especially inviting for food lovers. In this area north of Lucca, the sweet plump *farro* and coarse savory polenta made from overlarge corn kernels have brought the area well-deserved celebrity. In the past, both *farro* and polenta were poor man's food, the area less alluring to the outsider.

The Garfagnana lies in the wildest part of the Apuan Alps; old fortified towns hang over narrow valleys, skinny roads wriggle their ways up through seemingly unsurpassable mountains. A few hundred years ago, the area was little more than a strategic passage, continually occupied by overbearing outsiders, robber barons, bandits, and mercenaries—a gloomy place. The poet Ludovico Ariosto, a fifteenth-century governor of the area, wrote rather grimly about "tears, voices and life in the cold white marble mountains of Castiglione . . . [where] man wins over death and disarms it."

These days the fifty-kilometer excursion into the forests and hills along the Serchio river that meanders down from the Apuan Alps to Lucca is a lot more enticing. Agriculture and small industry along the Serchio have given the area a new prosperity. Nowadays the roads are decent. It's a special pleasure to head up from Lucca along the twisting riverbank road that slowly winds into the hills. The magnificent marble mountains to the rear of Carrara suddenly emerge looking like pure snow. The softer Apennine hills curve off forever in the other direction. Within this endless forest of great green chestnuts, oaks, and pines lie not only castles and fortress towns, but a little-known wealth of local produce as well.

Its intimidating landscape kept the Garfagnana poor and isolated. Until Italian unity in the nineteenth century, the area was controlled at varying times by the warring lords of Ferrara, Florence, and Lucca. Their castles and fortresses are still there, marking the landscape, etched into the towns. Armies passing through picked up their fighters from available mercenaries along the way, and armaments too.

The right-hand side of the river Serchio is the best way to travel up the valley from Lucca (even though signs point to a bridge crossing at Ponte Moriano). On the other side, you may encounter annoying truck traffic to and from the many paper factories and other industrial plants that have sprung up indiscriminately in recent years.

As you travel up, a first worthwhile detour is at Borgo a Mozzano, and the Church of Santa Maria Assunta in Diecimo. Cross the river at the bridge indicating Borgo a Mozzano and head back toward Lucca for a few kilometers on the other side; you'll note a sign to the church on the right-hand side of the road. Follow the signs that bring you to Santa Maria Assunta, sitting on its unassuming site since the sixth century. What you actually see is the finished twelfth-century church. Its massive bell tower is one of the most impressive of the area. The simple, harmonious Romanesque church, like so many others you encounter in this area, is built of soft, seemingly pliable *pietra serena*—a deep gray travertine stone with a particular depth and beauty. Most are graced within by marble and wood sculptures of the primitive early Gothic style that is pervasive here. The Diecimo church is a perfect example. Inside—along with an early Roman sarcophagus found nearby—is a collection of early medieval wall sculptures. My favorite is *Re Pippino,* a seemingly headless horseman. There's another of the prophet Isaiah, looking sternly medieval.

(It's a matter of chance to find any particular country church open during lunch hour, or even open at all. If you find a church closed, there's usually a house nearby where you can find someone with a key; if the church is big enough as an attraction, you'll find it open even at lunchtime. Usually country churches close between noon and three. Alas, there's no way to check beforehand.)

Travel back to the right side of the river at Borgo a Mozzano. Just past the town—where a very pleasant meal can be had at Osteria I Macelli (+39 0583 762 179)—you'll soon be struck by the sight of an unusually high-arching walking bridge. It is the Ponte della Maddalena, better known as the Devil's Bridge. A feat of fourteenth-century

engineering, it spans the river in three gracefully asymmetrical arches. A first sighting takes the breath away. On a sunny day the arches are perfectly reflected in the river, making three shimmering diminishing circles. At night, it's smartly lit. There are a few parking places, and a walk over the bridge is a heady experience.

It's here, at the Devil's Bridge, that the flat Valle del Serchio begins to edge up into the Garfagnana. A few kilometers further on, a leisurely detour takes you up through nine kilometers of curved mountain road to Tereglio, a remarkably long and narrow little town, built along a steep ridge that falls off into deep gullies on both sides. I discovered Tereglio some years ago with Giovanna and Massimo Durante, Luccan friends who owned several decrepit houses and were slowly, almost brick by brick, putting together a little inn—La Fagiana—no doubt in the hope that visitors who had come so far, so high up the steep mountain, might want to spend the night, and indeed they do. Hundreds arrived for the festive opening to celebrate the new inn and enjoy the rich offering of Garfagnana special dishes, thick *farro* and bean soup, savory sausages, polenta and *funghi,* and more. The inn—during its season from May through October—is as popular as its owners.

Tereglio may strike you as one of the most unusual mountain villages you've ever seen. Once a remote mining town, it consists of a single, long, narrow lane. The meandering pedestrian walk of several kilometers begins and ends with two portals, built centuries ago to protect the place. Ancient stone houses line the way, effectively blocking a view of what lies behind them. A lovely surprise waits just beyond the halfway point. The street curves gently down to an ancient rounded staircase. Directly below is the graceful red-tiled roof of the medieval church of Santa Maria Assunta fronting a little piazza. Looking down at the church and over the rooftop at the surrounding mountains, you might believe you've reached heaven. The silence is penetrable, the feeling awe-inspiring.

From Tereglio you can follow a rather long and tortuous narrow road to another mountain town, Coreglia Antelminelli. Look right as you enter the town; there's a little ninth-century church of San Martino, a squat three-aisled rectangle. A strange lopsidedness adds to its harmony. On one of the main squares of the town, there's a delicious life-sized statue of Mario Pisani, a *figurinaio,* or figure-maker, who sculpted portraits in plaster of Paris that give Coreglia its bit of notice: from here spread the popular art of making gesso figures, little white plaster shapes to paint and decorate. A small museum nearby is dedicated to the art (Museo della Figurina di Gesso e dell'Emigrazione/Via del Mangano 17/+39 0583 78 082/June–September, Monday–Friday 9:30 a.m.–12:30 p.m., Sundays and holidays 10 a.m.–1 p.m. and 3 p.m.–6 p.m.; October–May, 9:30 a.m.–12:30 p.m.; closed Sunday and holidays).

The sculpture of figure-maker Mario is smartly dressed, ready to emigrate (which he did) in a suit and little cap, standing determinedly with a rather Egyptian-looking cat sitting on one shoulder and two saintly heads held in the other arm.

Nearby there's a little inn called L'Arcile, which, during wild mushroom season, can sate you with a full meal of *funghi. Farro* dishes are also a specialty.

From Coreglia, an almost untraveled mountain road leads you down to Barga and its majestic cathedral. This approach is special in that you come upon the majestic dome from above. Barga's

cathedral, a grand travertine-faced structure, dominates its surroundings. It sits at the top of the old town, its large porch
grandly overlooking the landscape of rooftops and the dramatic
mountains beyond. The cathedral was badly damaged in an earthquake in 1897 and later impeccably restored. The impressive
statuary inside survived intact. Most remarkable is the thirteenth-
century Romanesque pulpit by the Lombard sculptor Guido
Bigarelli, held securely in place by two serene lions.

On the road north from Barga to Castelnuovo di Garfagnana,
you pass through Castelvecchio Pascoli, named after a beloved
nineteenth-century poet who enjoyed life here a good deal more
than Ariosto. His home has become a museum. (Casa Museo Pas-
coli/Via Caprona 4/+39 0583 766 147/October–March, open
Tuesday 2 p.m.–5:15 p.m.; Wednesday–Sunday 9:30 a.m.–1 p.m.
and 2:30 p.m.–5:15 p.m.; April–September, Tuesday 3:30 p.m.–
6:45 p.m.; Wednesday–Sunday 10:30 a.m.–1 p.m. and 3 p.m.–
6:45 p.m.; closed Christmas).

Canti di Castelvecchio (Songs of Castelvecchio) evoke the landscape and aura of the Garfagnana:

> *Al mia cantuccio, donde non sento*
> *Se non le reste brusir del grano*
> *Il suon dell'ore viene con vento*
> *Dal non veduto borgo montano*

> In my corner I hear nothing
> But the rustle of the bearded grains.
> The ringing of the hour comes with the wind
> That sees not the mountain town.

Ariosto, author of Italy's great classic *Orlando Furioso,* may have
been a better poet, but Pascoli was well enough thought of to
have the town named after him. Osteria al Ritrovo del Platano, an
evocative restaurant directly on the road, is filled with Pascoli

memorabilia. The poet breakfasted here daily with his host, present owner Gabriele de Prato's grandfather.

As the road winds gently up to Castelnuovo, the Apuan Alps emerge more and more dramatically, a scene marked as well by distant spires and castle ruins. The hub of activity that is Castelnuovo di Garfagnana comes almost as a surprise. Here is the small capital of the Garfagnana, and as you arrive at its main crossroad, a fortress built by the Este dukes of Ferrara appears on the left. Inside the city walls, there is a simple Romanesque cathedral to visit. It has the usual travertine *pietra serena* façade, and an impressive thirteenth-century crucifix inside. Thursday morning is market day here; the town bustles with shoppers and visitors from all over the Garfagnana. At the edge of the market, along the main road, look for the overwhelming food shop, L'Aia di Piero. It is crammed with every sort of specialty that the Garfagnana has to offer: breads, stone-ground grains, chestnut flours and polenta, preserved vegetables, jams, honeys, *farro* tarts, and cheeses from goats and sheep grazing in the hills above. Around the corner is Andrea Bertucci's Il Vecchio Mulino, a little bar and lunch stop that overflows on every wall with specialties, wines, olive oils, photographs, posters, and everything else that speaks of Garfagnana.

From Castelnuovo, the road continues up toward Castiglione di Garfagnana. The mountains on both sides take on an awesome beauty as you climb. If there is time, a small road on the right leads to Sillico, an ancient Garfagnana hill town with a local trattoria—Locanda Belvedere (+39 0583 662 173)—whose terrace affords some of the most spectacular views of the surrounding landscape. Drive beyond Sillico to Pieve Capraia, where you'll find the lonely little church of Santa Maria. It sits in the middle of a wood. A few stones are all that's left of the castle that once stood here. The church and its little stone house adjoining became a settlement of hermitic monks; today it emanates a timeless serenity, the quiet broken only by a melodic rushing of the river below. The church gives you a surprising example of arts of earlier times:

several stunning large hand-painted Florentine wood-carved frames of the fifteenth century.

A short drive brings you back to the main road and on to Pieve Fosciana, where there is yet another simple beautiful church, San Giovanni Battista. The façade is of the usual soft gray stone, but the imposing tower was created not from *pietra serena,* but from the ancient building stones of a nearby fortress ruin. Inside is a lovely Annunciation by Luca della Robbia. At Pieve there is also the ancient water-driven mill where chestnut flour and polenta are still stone-ground. You must call first if you wish to visit (+39 0583 666 095). At Pieve, you'll also find Il Pozzo, one of the finest restaurants of the area.

The road from Pieve Fosciana continues up the mountain to Castiglione di Garfagnana, a great fortress with ramparts and watchtowers presiding over the surrounding landscape. Take the "new gate" in, walk up the ancient street to the left along the wall to find the handsomest little church of them all, Chiesa di San Michele with its sculpted twelfth-century façade of layered *pietra serena* and pink marble.

SPECIALTIES OF VALLE DEL SERCHIO AND THE GARFAGNANA

Life was hard in the Garfagnana. Each ruler in his turn extracted heavy taxes from the local population, and as a bonus forced them to keep up the defenses within the territory as well. The food specialties are those of the poor and all the more interesting be-cause of the area's isolation.

Farro is a good example. When we first arrived here, few had even heard of it. Now *farro* is being exported in greater and greater quantities. It is a hearty grain, similar to the spelt or emmer mentioned in the Bible, and given as a yearly tithe to the Roman emperors. *Farro* has been found in Etruscan tombs, but was not so long ago all but lost to the West. Were it not for a few hardy farmers of the Garfagnana, who grew it in this amenable soil, mostly as animal feed, the grain might have been lost to us completely. In this small corner of Tuscany, this mother of all grains has been resuscitated and refined to its current plump and crunchy desirable sweetness.

These days *farro* has come back into fashion. Visitors to local *trattorie* in Lucca, impressed with its earthy taste and ability to retain both shape and firm bite when cooked, carried it to the world. Garfagnana farmers took advantage of this new interest, and developed a solid export trade. *Farro* is also grown in mountain areas elsewhere in Tuscany, but the soil in the Garfagnana seems to favor it best. A puréed bean soup, in which *farro* has been cooked, is best eaten here, made with an intensely flavored bean that also has been grown for a long time in the Garfagnana. The bean is called *giallorini,* after its yellow color and small shape.

While these mountains nurture a good amount of *funghi porcini,* game, and wild berries, other interesting food products have found their way into domestic production. Early on, the farmers of the Garfagnana discovered their mineral-laden earth was perfect for the growing of grains. Alongside *farro,* a very special corn—

granturco di Garfagnana—is grown here to produce savory polenta and cornbread. The long skinny cob of this special corn was brought from the Americas in the sixteenth century and, with a certain pride, is called *otto file di Garfagnana,* "the eight rows of Garfagnana," because of its eight rows of large hard kernels rather than the usual twelve or thirteen. It is not a corn that one wants to nibble; the kernels can break a tooth. But ground into polenta, or into flour for bread, it produces a robustly flavored product.

As in other mountainous areas of Tuscany, the ubiquitous chestnut forests were once a primary means of sustenance. You can still find stone-grinding chestnut flour mills on private farms. Constant threat of war—right up until the Second World War—kept sending the local population into the forests to eke out sustenance from chestnuts. Blight after the war temporarily cut off the supply, but chestnuts are now again collected in large quantities to be roasted, boiled, and turned into flour for breads and cakes. The flour is known as *farina dolce* (sweet flour), and combined with normal grain for bread. Small pancakes called *frittelle* or *necci,* served with fresh ricotta, are a favorite finish to a winter meal. While chestnuts are also roasted over an open fire, Tuscans seem to prefer them boiled in either milk or water flavored with fennel until they are soft and the meat can just be squeezed out.

Often stone-ground chestnut, *farro,* or *otto file* flours are added to wheat flour to make a variety of other breads that in the past helped to make precious wheat go further. Mashed potatoes are often added as well, to give longer life to the loaf. Each kind of bread is delicious, and each is eaten with different specialties. Pasta too is made from *farro* and chestnut flour. In this non–wine-producing area, the local alcohol is a tasty *farro* beer.

The *salumi,* or cold cuts, of the region are diverse and spicy, going well with the different breads. The most noteworthy is the *biroldo della Garfagnana,* made with what the local population calls "the least noble parts of the pork"—head, heart, lungs, and tongue, all cooked together for hours and spiced generously with cloves and anise, cinnamon and nutmeg, a few wild fennel seeds, salt, and pepper. Blood holds the ingredients together as they are packed into the stomach lining of the beast. It sounds awful, but it's quite delicious when seasoned, aged, sliced, and eaten on a slab of one of the rough local breads, especially bread made with chestnut flour. The most elegant sausage is *mondiola,* made with the choicest pork meat, seasoned with laurel, stuffed into a broad intestinal sac, and folded in half to make a big round sausage tied with a laurel twig. The home-cured prosciutto of the area— *prosciutto bazzone*—is made from fat old pigs raised on wheat, corn, whey, and, in the last months, chestnuts; it tastes of all of them. Spiced well, *prosciutto bazzone* is more savory and succulent than the elegant prosciutto of Parma and San Daniele. I recently tried a newly concocted sausage called *linchetto,* made of beef that has been aged wrapped in a coat of dried *funghi porcini* that imbues the meat with the heavy musty perfume of the dried mushroom. All the *salumi* are made in an acclaimed artisan *norcineria*—maker of pork products—in Ghivizzano, just before Barga on the road up to Castelnuovo. If you'd like to see them at work, call Rolando Belandi at L'Antica Norcineria (+39 0583 77 008).

The cheeses of the Garfagnana come from both sheep and cows that graze in the highest mountain pastures. The most favored *pecorino,* or sheep's cheese, ripens firmly for six months to a year in a wrapping of straw. The most valued cow's cheese, *vacea,* comes from cattle that graze above 1,500 meters, on the highest peaks of the Apuan Alps. *Vacea* is available only from September through May, but another fine cow's cheese— *vaccino Bertami*—is more available and pleasingly eaten with fresh marmalade or one of the fine local honeys.

CIRCO-LO CULTURALE

TEATRO DEL SALE

Socio

CIBRÈO CITTÀ APERTA FIRENZE

RECOMMENDED READING

As Emily Wise Miller remarks in *The Food Lover's Guide to Florence,* "Someone once said that his friend gave him these directions to the best restaurant in Florence: 'Drive into the city. Park your car. The first restaurant you see, go eat there.' This is a great story, and in many ways very true; the average trattoria that you walk into in Florence is bound to be quite good. On the other hand, if you stumble blindly off the Ponte Vecchio into the nearest trattoria you also might end up in a place that is touristy, overpriced, and producing lazy and mediocre food because the proprietors know they can get away with it." I completely agree, and that's why, in addition to browsing the recommendations in the guidebooks of your choice, you should consult the experts, people who are real "foodies" and who pay attention to every detail in every type of eating establishment. The following are all terrific resources that will enlighten you as to how much great food and culinary specialties there are in Tuscany and Umbria and why you will want to make every meal during your visit count:

An Appetite for Umbria: The People, the Places, the Food, Christine Smallwood, with photography by Eddie Jacob (Bonny Day, London, 2006). This is the only book I've ever seen devoted to the culinary scene in Umbria, but that alone isn't reason to include it here; this is a very worthwhile book. Though there are many recipes (contributed by chefs), there are nearly as many recommendations for places to eat and lots of enticing color photographs.

A Culinary Traveller in Tuscany: Exploring & Eating Off the Beaten Track, Beth Elon (Little Bookroom, 2006). This wonderful, wonderful book is like no other, and Elon covers every single corner of Tuscany. As I noted in the previous excerpt, she and her husband have lived in the Apennine foothills for more than thirty years, and she says that this book is a retelling of some of her most pleasurable discoveries. She writes: "Beyond the better-known larger cities that attract ever growing hordes of tourist and souvenir and fast-food shops, Tuscany has its hundreds of small, clustered hill towns, each with a singular way of doing things. Throughout the Tuscan countryside, with its lovely churches, piazzas, and ancient architecture, you'll find a rural art that is often worthy of the finest city museums. There's also a population that clings obstinately to a sensual way of life that includes an authentic experience of food as one of its most wholesome elements. No great chefs, just great tastes." For each part of the region Elon includes an introduction to the area and an itinerary that includes a few towns or villages—don't look for big cities here—the area's specialties, and typical restaurants and their recipes.

Eating and Drinking in Italy: A Menu Reader and Restaurant Guide, Andy Herbach, with illustrations by Michael Dillon (Open Road, 2008, fifth edition). This little paperback—approximately 7½ × 4 inches—fits easily in a pocket so you won't look like a nerd in a restaurant as you look up a word. It's *really* thorough, and the menu words are presented in both Italian to English and vice versa. Methods and styles of cooking are included, which is great because these are often what trip people up the most. Plus, these guys are funny: after the entry for *trippa alla fiorentina* (braised tripe and minced beef with tomato sauce and cheese), they write, "You can put all the *alla*'s you want on *trippa* and it's still TRIPE." They also include useful related phrases and a list of their favorite restaurants around Italy (six in Florence and a few in Orvieto, Pisa, Perugia, San Gimignano, and Siena).

Eating in Italy: A Traveler's Guide to the Hidden Gastronomic Pleasures of Northern Italy, Faith Heller Willinger (William Morrow, 1998). You might be wondering why I am recommending a book on the topic of places to eat that was last updated more than a decade ago. It is not only that many of the recommended restaurants are *still* recommended by Willinger but also that her opening chapter on menus, reservations, service, tipping, when to eat, logistics, special foods and beverages, reading material, housewares, and more is second in thoroughness only to that in Fred Plotkin's book (see page 402)—so thorough that I consider this book *essenziale*. There are separate chapters for Tuscany and Umbria, with each of their culinary specialties—and related specialties, such as Deruta pottery—highlighted.

The Food and Wine Lover's Companion to Tuscany, Carla Capalbo (Chronicle, 2002). This edition is the revised, updated, and expanded version of one that originally appeared in 1998, and it sure is indispensable. Capalbo, who lives in Italy, drove thousands of kilometers all over Tuscany for several years and met hundreds of wonderful people who care about food. She shares her finds for restaurants, bars, wine bars, specialty food shops, bakeries, kitchen shops, pastry shops, trattorias, olive and flour mills, food festivals, etc., etc., etc.—this is really nothing short of a bible, for both visitors *and* residents. Best of all, there is a section on Tuscan market days, indicating weekly and monthly markets for each town. Capalbo refers to her book as "a love letter to Tuscany's food artisans" and wisely notes that "an early-morning outing to a fish market or a tour of the cellars of a stately wine *castello* may be as memorable an experience as a trip to a landmark frescoed church. They represent complementary aspects of Italian culture: one frozen in the past, the other still very much alive today." She also includes a glossary, as well as maps at the beginning of each chapter.

The Food Lover's Guide to Florence, Emily Wise Miller (Ten Speed, 2007, second edition). Miller, who lives in Florence, covers regional foods of Florence and Tuscany, wine, restaurants and trattorias, markets and shops, coffee, chocolate, pastries, pizzerias, gelato, and more in the neighborhoods of the Duomo, Santa Croce, San Lorenzo, San Marco, Santa Maria Novella, the Oltrarno, and outside the city walls. She also recommends cooking classes and features a chapter on culinary excursions in Tuscany. With maps, a glossary, and some restaurant basics.

Italy for the Gourmet Traveler, Fred Plotkin (Kyle Books, London, 2006, revised edition). Plotkin, introduced in the Tuscany section, is an all-around Italy expert and also the author of *Opera 101* (Hyperion, 1994), *La Terra Fortunata* (Broadway, 2001), and *Recipes from Paradise* (Little, Brown, 1997), among other books, first visited Italy in 1973 and has lived, traveled, studied, and worked there for much of the time since. He says he has come to think of himself as a "Garibaldi with a fork. I have slept and eaten in most of the towns he visited, and many he didn't, taking notes on everything I ate and drank." This tome—weighing in at 725 pages—is not one to bring along in your suitcase, but it *is* one you will want to peruse before you depart. Before the first region of Italy is covered, there are seventy-one pages of historical and practical information about eating out and food shopping and other topics. Separate chapters are devoted to Tuscany and Umbria, and there is an extensive glossary at the back of the book. One reviewer related that he and his friends, who had relied on Plotkin's advice on several trips to Italy, developed a credo: "In Fred We Trust." And there you have it.

Ristoranti d'Italia del Gambero Rosso. Published annually, this is one of Italy's leading restaurant guides, along with the Slow Food guides. The text is in Italian, but I figure, even if I can't read it, the establishments included have to be good, and the places I've tried were indeed quite good. The guide covers restaurants, trattorias, pizzerias, international cuisine, and wine bars. *Gambero Rosso* refers to a culinary magazine that I very much like (the English language version is available in North America). It's also the name of a restaurant in San Vincenzo, forty kilometers south of Livorno, which has frequently received the honor of best restaurant in Italy. *Gambero Rosso* also publishes an annual wine guide, *Vini d'Italia,* and both are found in bookstores and on newsstands throughout Italy.

Trattorias of Rome, Florence, & Venice, Maureen B. Fant (Harper-Collins, 2001). Fant, with Howard Isaacs, is coauthor of the *Dictionary of Italian Cuisine* (Ecco, 1998). She lives in Rome and has written many articles about eating in Italy for the *New York Times.* She writes, "It is no longer true, if it ever was, that, if you avoid obvious tourist traps, it is impossible to get a bad meal. Locals, accordingly, choose their eateries conservatively and with care." She begins her book with some background on the trattoria, and shares tips, etiquette, and an explanation of the symbols she uses throughout the book to rate establishments. There are thirty-nine pages of Florence recommendations.

"When You Go to Tuscany: Restaurants," the final chapter in *Flavors of Tuscany,* a cookbook by Nancy Harmon Jenkins (Broadway, 1998). Though the book is a dozen years old, this chapter is still a good resource as many, if not all, of the places recommended are still around and still held in high regard. It's somewhat difficult to learn of recommended places to eat outside of Tuscany's larger cities and towns, and Jenkins is a most worthy guide.

INTERVIEW

Faith Willinger

I admired Faith Willinger for years before I met her, and I thought she had one of the best jobs on earth—she authored cookbooks, wrote a book about where the best places to eat were in Italy, contributed articles about food in Italy, knew chefs and farmers and all kinds of neat people connected with food, and lived in Florence. When I met her, I realized that what she really had was one of the best lives on earth.

In addition to all of her food writing, Willinger teaches terrific weekly cooking classes called Lessons in Lunch. (They were previously known as Market to Table; the name had to change because the farmers she's known for years at the weekly market in Piazza Santo Spirito, near where she lives in the Oltrarno, no longer go there. "There were too many traffic lights," she said, so now they make special deliveries to her for her classes.) In 2005, Willinger was honored with an award from San Pellegrino and Acqua Panna waters as the Ambassador of Italian Cuisine in the World.

I have had the great pleasure of getting together with Willinger twice, in her eighteenth-century kitchen, which is a true food lover's dream: there are hundreds of books, a really big wooden table, a stove to die for, and tons of interesting things to look at, all in an especially warm and inviting room. When I last saw her, it was spring, and she put out small bowls of fresh raw peas and crumbles of fresh pecorino cheese drizzled with olive oil. She explained that the classic combination is actually with fresh small fava beans, but since these are fairly hard to find in North America, she

substituted peas. I have to say that as much as I love fava beans, this pair-
ing was equally delicious. She also enthused about two new places that
had just opened in Florence, Coccole Cioccolateria (Via Ginori 55r) and
Obika, a mozzarella bar (Via de'Tornabuoni 16; there is a U.S. location
in New York in the IBM Building, 590 Madison Avenue, at 56th
Street/obika.it). Faith's enthusiasm for all things culinary is legendary,
and more than anyone else I know, she keeps her nose glued to the culi-
nary sidewalk. Her energy for food sleuthing never stops, surpassing even
that well-known bunny in the commercials.

Q: How long have you lived in Italy?

A: More than thirty years! I first came here when I ended my marriage and my life in Cleveland, and I was traveling in Europe with my one-and-a-half-year-old son. When I got to Italy, I immediately felt at home, and you know how Italians feel about a mother and her *bambino*. Plus, my son Max was very cute.

Q: A few years ago I read an article in an issue of *Zingerman's News*, a quarterly newsletter from Zingerman's, the great food emporium in Ann Arbor, Michigan (zingermans.com). The article was entitled "Want to Improve the Enjoyment of Your Eating? Start by Buying Better Ingredients." The piece reinforced that "the finished food you prepare will never be better than the *quality of the stuff you put in*," and what followed was a list of ten ingredients to buy that would immediately improve the overall quality of our meals. With your insistence upon superb quality and maximum flavor, this piece could have

been penned by you, and if it were, what ten Italian (or specifically Tuscan) items would you put on a list of better ingredients, ideally including some items one positively cannot get in North America?

A: 1. Super-Tuscan extra virgin olive oil—my favorites are Castello di Ama and Tenuta Roccheta. 2. Real, traditional *balsamico di Modena*—not the fake stuff with age numbers on the label. 3. Quality Parmigiano-Reggiano—just can't do without it. Save the rind and toss it into a long-cooking soup, then cut into tiny cubes and serve with the soup. 4. Latini pasta, preferably Senatore Capelli. 5. Rice for risotto, preferably Carnaroli or Vialone Nano, but not Arborio. 6. Great Italian tuna. This is a bit easier to find in North America now than it was a few years ago. Read the labels to make sure it's really from Italy. The real stuff tastes very different from standard American supermarket brands. 7. *Guanciale* (pork jowl) or pancetta (belly)—both salt and pepper cured, but not smoked. 8. Super-fresh, seasonal produce, which I can't live without. Get yours from a local farmers' market or your own garden. When my favorite farmers still came to the Mercato di Santo Spirito, I had to be the first person there—my husband referred to me as the vegetable warrior. 9. Meat from a prime source—I get mine from master butcher Dario Cecchini in the village of Panzano in Chianti. You should look for a great source online if you don't have a local one. 10. *Vino italiano*—what else would you drink with Italian food? I love Chianti Classico (Castello di

Ama is an expensive but great treat) or Brunello di Montalcino for a special occasion. Or an Aglianico from Campania or Basilicata for simple, everyday drinking.

Q: On the subject of olive oil, is there any supermarket brand in the States that is better than mediocre?

A: No. Sometimes I can find something decent at Whole Foods but usually regular supermarkets (and lots of gourmet shops) have crappy oil, and most try to sell the old stuff before they put the most recent pressing on their shelves. Look for extra virgin from the most recent November. The thing about olive oil is that once you learn about it and taste a really good one, all of your food will taste better when you use it. [Readers who have never tasted quality Tuscan oil may be rather surprised by its assertive flavor and price. But quality oil is expensive to make. Two excellent mail-order sources for Italian oils are Zingerman's, which offers several from Tuscany (888 636 8162/zingermans.com), and the Rare Wine Co. in Sonoma (800 999 4342/rarewineco.com), referred to as "the best American source for fine Tuscan olive oil" by Ed Behr, editor of *The Art of Eating*.]

Q: The Shaw *Guide to Cooking Schools* (cookingforfun.shawguides .com) lists 231 cooking schools in Italy, most of them in Florence and Tuscany. What makes your classes unique?

A: My classes are a one-day commitment—or at any rate most of one day—as opposed to a weeklong course, and they're total immersion. I teach everyday Italian cooking that participants will make all the time. I believe that you don't need a lot of good ingredients, just a few, and I don't want to teach you how to make three fancy dishes you might make at home once or twice: I want to teach you how to change your life. My new class, Bistecca 101, is also quite different from what anyone else is offering. We begin cooking the beef at eleven a.m. The beef, by the way, is from Dario Cecchini's fabulous butchery in Chianti. You can only get it in restaurants, at Dario's, or here in my kitchen. I don't put the meat directly onto the heat at first—after experimenting, I've found that if I put it on a large plate and turn it around so that each side faces the flame for several hours, and then grill the meat quickly, it produces perfect results. The *bistecca* classes gave me an excuse to pour some Brunello di Montalcino, and I think that anytime you can drink Brunello is cause for celebration. Olive oil tastings and a course in coffee are part of every class. I also give my students great ingredients—expensive, like the Castello di Ama olive oil (I found these little bottles of it that pass U.S. Customs inspection for carry-on bags), Latini pasta, real *balsamico.* Sometimes I think I am out of my mind! And the gift bag is very sturdy, perfect for shopping at farmers' markets.

Q: Do you still offer culinary walking tours as well?

A: Yes, my assistant, Cristina, leads great walking tours, which include stops at places that have been around for a long time as well as new places that we think are exciting. [Cristina, too, has one of the world's best jobs. She told me that her background is actually in photography and bookmaking, but that "when you enter into the world of food you can't help but get your feet wet in the areas of architecture, archaeology, painting. . . . I see it as understanding Italian life."]

Q: Since *Eating in Italy* only covered northern Italy, and since it was last published in 1998, are you working on updating it?

A: Of course. I'm *always* working on this book, and its companion, *Eating in Southern Italy,* but there is no official date for publication yet.

Lessons in Lunch classes are offered every Wednesday beginning at noon and are limited to eight participants. The $250 fee ($225 if reserved online) includes instruction, lunch, olive oil, *granite, salumi,* pasta, balsamic vinegar, and the recipes. Usually a guest of gastronomic or cultural interest joins the group, and participants also receive a gift bag with ingredients to take home. For groups of five or six, hands-on Market to Table classes can still be arranged, though these are more expensive and begin at nine thirty a.m. Bistecca 101 classes are $225 ($200 if reserved online). The Food Lover's Walking Tours are $200. Registration is best done on Faith's Web site (faithwill inger.com); it's a great site besides, with Faith's memorable mottos, such as "Balsamic vinegar with an age in numbers on the label is a joke," "Good wine and bad wine have the same number of calories," and "Spend more time enjoying a meal than preparing it."

Faith kindly granted me permission to share a few recipes from her book *Adventures of an Italian Food Lover,* so I chose two recipes here from the Tuscany section that I think best represent Faith's philosophy of delicious, flavorful food simply prepared. (A third, a recipe given to Faith from Benedetta Vitali of Zibibbo, appears under the Z entry in the Tuscan and Umbrian Miscellany; see page 611.)

LA PANZANESE GRILLED STEAK

SERVES 4 TO 6

Contributed by Dario Cecchini, "the most famous butcher in Italy," according to Faith. Dario's shop, Antica Macelleria Cecchini, is in Panzano in Chianti and is open eight a.m. to two p.m. and closed on Wednesday (Via XX Luglio 11/+39 055 852 020/dariocecchini.com). Cecchini also operates three small restaurants in Panzano: Solociccia, which has an all meat menu, two seatings, for about thirty-two euros; Officina della Bistecca, with communal dining upstairs from the shop, steak cooked on an open grill, and all the wine you want to drink, for about fifty euros; and Mac Dario, where Dario offers his take on the hamburger with roast potatoes, for about ten euros. Mac Dario has open-air seating on an outside terrace in summer and is in the Officina space in the winter, and Faith says the turnover at lunchtime is quick.

2½–3-inch-thick steak (2–3 pounds), such as sirloin,
   porterhouse, or T-bone
1 tablespoon extra virgin olive oil (optional)
Fine sea salt (if you haven't got any Profumo del Chianti)
Freshly ground black pepper

Remove the steak from the refrigerator 8 to 10 hours before cooking. Prepare the grill, filled with red-hot coals of "noble" hard wood if possible.

Cook the steak for 5 minutes on each side, then stand the steak on end and cook for 15 minutes standing up, rotating the steak on its side every 5 minutes. Those who prefer their meat medium-rare can cook for a few minutes more—I won't tell Dario.

Let the steak rest for 5 minutes, then cut into pieces or slices. Season with a drizzle of extra virgin, sea salt (or a pinch of Profumo del Chianti), and pepper, and serve on a wooden cutting board.

CHICKPEA PURÉE WITH SHRIMP

SERVES 4

Contributed by Fulvio and Emanuela Pierangelini of Gambero Rosso in San Vincenzo, for many years rated one of the very best restaurants in Italy. The name derives from that of the *osteria* in the story of Pinocchio; Faith notes that this dish, of creamy chickpea soup topped with shrimp, has become Fulvio's signature dish, and is now found in other restaurants throughout Italy. He created it one day for winemaking cousins Marchese Incisa della Rocchetta, owner of Sassicaia, and Marchese Lodovico Antinori, owner of Tenuta dell'Ornellaia.

1 cup dried chickpeas
Sea salt and freshly ground black pepper
1 garlic clove
1 sprig fresh rosemary
16–20 ounces fresh shrimp, in shells
3–4 tablespoons extra virgin olive oil

Put the chickpeas in a large pot, cover with about an inch of water, mix in 3 tablespoons sea salt, and soak for at least 12 hours.

Drain the chickpeas, rinse them, and put them in a 3-quart pot. Cover with water by about 3 inches, then add the garlic and rosemary. Over low heat, bring the water to a boil and simmer at least 1 hour, until the chickpeas are tender. Add ½ cup boiling water if the liquid gets too low.

Purée the chickpeas with your method of choice. (Fulvio purées his through a sieve, but the fine disk of a food mill works well, too. Puréeing with a processor or immersion mixer grinds up the skins and produces a less refined soup.) Thin the soup to desired consistency (a little thicker than heavy cream is ideal) with some of the chickpea broth; add boiling water if there's not enough broth. Season with salt and pepper, and keep warm.

Remove the shells and black veins from the shrimp. Put them in a steamer basket over ½ cup boiling water in a pot, cover, and steam for 2 to 3 minutes, until they turn pink.

Put one-fourth of the chickpea purée in each soup bowl, top each with 4 or 5 shrimp, then add a drizzle of extra virgin and freshly ground black pepper. Serve.

PIAZZE, GIARDINI, E MONUMENTI

It is difficult to avoid a torrent of superlatives in appraising Tuscany and her contribution to the culture and the beauty of this world. The list of her famous sons is even now astounding, centuries after they were born.

—SAMUEL CHAMBERLAIN,
Italian Bouquet

Aaron looked and looked at the three great naked men. David so much white, and standing forward, self-conscious: then at the great splendid front of the Palazzo Vecchio: and at the fountain splashing water upon its wet, wet figures; and the distant equestrian statue; and the stone-flagged space of the grim square. And he felt that here he was in one of the world's living centres, here, in the Piazza della Signoria. The sense of having arrived—of having reached a perfect centre of the human world: this he had.

—D. H. LAWRENCE,
Aaron's Rod

To understand De Chirico well, you have to know Italy on a summer Sunday afternoon, when everything is shut up.

—DAVID LEAVITT AND MARK MITCHELL,
In Maremma

The garden in the 1930s.

Back Roads of Tuscany

WILLIAM SERTL

❧

THIS PIECE ORIGINALLY appeared in *Garden Design,* within a special section called "Global Garden." Then editor in chief Dorothy Kalins noted in the issue's introduction, "Gardens in My Suitcase"—what a great title!—that "three things go through my mind whenever I travel to someone's fabulous garden, be it Monet's or Thomas Jefferson's: How did he *do* this? How did he get it so right? What can I take from here?" I've often asked myself the same questions, and I agree with Kalins's observation that "if travel is broadening, garden travel is widening. And deepening. The way you think about your own garden is forever altered by what you behold. What can you take back from places like these? Inspiration."

WILLIAM SERTL was travel editor for *Garden Design,* a features editor for *Travel + Leisure,* and travel editor of *Gourmet* from 2000 to 2009.

"GOT A GREAT hotel in Paris for $100 a night?" That's the number one question I'm asked as a travel editor. And the answer is always no. Next is, "Any favorite places in Tuscany?" To which I have an equally terse reply: "Too many." I love this part of Italy, and while I'm not one to clip coupons, my Tuscany scrapbook is stuffed with old menus, maps heavy with annotation, and the elegant receipts doled out by garden gatekeepers. It's not the great cities of Florence or Siena that lure me. My Tuscany is more about being set free in a civilized wilderness.

Only a couple of hours north of Rome, the region is still largely rural. When I'm there, I feel compelled to get behind the wheel and bump down unpaved roads to ruinous towers and overgrown courtyards that beg to be explored. I like to stay in a fixed-up farmhouse or a small country inn, but I don't skimp on dinner. Roughing it in Tuscany means never being more than a wine list away from a fine Brunello. Though no stalker of wild game, I take my cue from the hunting parties that flock to the Tuscan hills each fall. Decked out in *bella figura* sporting attire, they sit by the roadside, feasting for hours.

Gardens give me a gentler excuse for country rambles. Some of my favorite stops on the tour mapped out here are stately land-scapes—green architecture built for the Medici, or princelings of later vintage. Other plots show the touch of humbler hands, and many are the creation of transplanted English-speaking foreigners, as much at ease in the "Chiantishire" of today as they were in the Anglo-American colony that Edith Wharton described at the turn of the century in *Italian Villas and Their Gardens*.

But, formal or freewheeling, homegrown or hybrid, these gardens rely on classic local ingredients: avenues of cypresses and lemon trees, terraces lined with terra-cotta pots and mock-heroic statues, pergolas dripping wisteria, and fountains spilling over mossy stone basins. Pursue them, and you'll travel through ancient hill towns wrapped in stone, past dusty olive groves flecked with fruit, to village hangouts where smiles substitute for English. If Tuscany's museums and churches lead back to the Renaissance, its gardens take you straight to Italy's soul.

VENZANO

As you bounce along a dirt road, six miles from Volterra, the only hint of the turnoff for Venzano is a tiny sign, not much bigger than a license plate. You may still think you've made a wrong turn when you approach the crumbling walls of what appears to be an abandoned homestead. Take heart. Signs of life soon come into view: a pergola laden with roses, crisp curtains behind windows outlined in fresh paint, plump lavender plants in clay pots, and two men in rumpled straw hats—Lindsay Megarrity and Don Leevers—conferring across a wheelbarrow.

Australian expats Megarrity, an artist who paints in watercolors, and Leevers, a former geologist, came to Tuscany in 1988 to buy Venzano (a former monastery) and to fulfill a fantasy of becoming big-time gardeners. On ten acres cradled between treeless green hills, they have not only created their own paradise, but also established a business: a nursery of aromatic plants that's the talk of Italian gardening cognoscenti. At any one time, Venzano may have ten thousand plants for sale, as many as one thousand varieties in all, from rosemary and thyme to patchouli and vetiver. A spring on the property, in use since Roman times, is a boon to growing, but both partners often work twelve-hour days, hand-watering nursery stock. Their plants are sought after for public pleasure grounds like the Boboli Garden, in Florence, as well as for private estates. "The Brits in Chianti love us," says Megarrity.

He and Leevers have done garden lovers another favor by installing three rental apartments in their five-hundred-year-old home, which also houses an austerely beautiful chapel. The exquisite flats are understated, too, yet comfortable. Waking up at Venzano, you have a privileged view of a hidden Tuscany. Only the birds demand attention as sun cuts through the mist, releasing the scents of herbs and old roses. You are also privileged to ask the gardeners for pruning tips or advice on acclimating Mediterranean natives, like cistus, to American soils. Megarrity and Leevers welcome drop-ins, but do call for directions—and caveat emptor: U.S. Customs makes it extremely difficult to bring plants into the United States.

The apartments at Venzano rent from March through November; call or fax +39 588 390 95 for information and pricing.

THE GARDEN TRAVELER

Getting Around

A detailed road map is a must (the best come from Auto Europe, Michelin, and Touring Club Italiano, all available in the United States).

Lodging

La Saracina, Pienza. The very best country inn (+39 0578 748 022/lasaracina.it).

Locanda dell'Amorosa, Sinalunga. Very romantic, with beamed ceilings and brick arches. Dine here, even if you don't stay (+39 0577 677 211/amorosa.it).

Locanda Elisa, Lucca. One of Italy's finest small hotels. (+39 0583 379 737/locandaelisa.it).

Locanda Le Piazze, near Castellina in Chianti. An inn amid vineyards and lemon trees. (+39 0577 743 190/locandalepiazze.it).

Park Hotel Siena, outskirts of Siena. A sixteenth-century manor house with a shady garden. (+39 0577 334 149/sangallopark hotel.it).

Pensione Bencistà, Fiesole. Old World, without the homogenizing deluxe veneer. A terrific find. (+39 055 59 163/bencista.com).

Torre di Bellosguardo, overlooking Florence. A glorious palace with the heart of a B&B (no TV). Huge rooms, sumptuous garden. (+39 055 229 8145/torrebellosguardo.com).

Villa San Michele, Fiesole. Luxurious but mostly small rooms in a former monastery with two-hundred-year-old wisteria (+39 055 567 8200/villasanmichele.com).

Rentals

Casa Alta, near Montalcino. This large villa rents year round (with cook and maid) for up to twelve to eighteen people (+39 040 302 655/casaalta.it). For other villas in Tuscany, call the Parker Company (800 280 2811).

Restaurants

Buca di Santantonio, Lucca. Memorable Northern Italian fare (Via della Cervia 3/+39 0583 55 881).

La Chiusa, Montefollonico. Possibly the best cuisine in Tuscany, but very expensive and rather formal. Locanda dell'Amorosa is a better deal (Via della Madonnina 88/+39 577 669 668).

Latte di Luna, Pienza. A personal favorite, for its homey atmosphere and straightforward cooking, like bread soup and roast piglet (Via San Carlo 2/4/+39 0578 748 606).

Le Logge, Siena. Excellent risotto and homemade pasta (Via del Porrione 33/+39 577 48 013).

Ombra della Sera, Volterra. Family-run. Florentine rib steak from the region's famous white cows (Via Gramschi 70/+39 0588 86 663).

To Do

Camellia Festival, held in two neighboring towns southeast of Lucca, during three weekends in March. Plus admission to private villas (camelielucchese.it).

International Iris Festival, Florence. Judging is held at Il Giardino dell'Iris at Piazzale Michelangelo, in May (irisfirenze.it). Local perfumeries extract scent from iris rhizomes.

VILLA LA FOCE

I was first drawn to La Foce by Iris Origo's stirring *War in Val d'Orcia,* a diary of her heroic struggle to shelter refugee children at her villa during World War II. An Anglo-American married to an Italian nobleman, Origo hardly mentions the garden at La Foce in her 1947 book, except as a playground for the waifs under her care, or as a target for shelling. Her reticence is tantalizing, because the landscape that she and her husband, Antonio, constructed in the 1920s and '30s (with the help of English architect and garden designer Cecil Pinsent) was famed as a fresh interpretation of Renaissance formality. You must turn to another of Origo's books, *Images and Shadows* (1970), for a thorough first-hand account of the making of the garden.

Happily, the wounds inflicted on La Foce in the forties have long since healed, and once again, eight years after Origo's death, the scene is as magical as ever. All of the classic requisites are in place—potted lemon trees framed by low box hedges, stone deities poised on plinths—but there are also stunningly original twists that few "period" gardeners would risk. Formality here slips out of the usual rigid mold: angled to fit its site, high on a hillside above the Orcia valley, the main terrace outside the house feels like the upper deck of a ship. Lower terraces descend toward the "prow" and the dizzying valley view in an irresistible surge of motion. There are also brilliant horticultural anachronisms, such as parterres anchored by evergreen magnolias, exotics imported to Italy centuries after the Renaissance had waned.

I arrived at La Foce in time to see the magnolias in bloom, having made an appointment weeks earlier with the current owner,

Benedetta Origo, daughter of Iris and Antonio. Bypassing the main gate, I pulled into a drive leading to the *fattoria,* the farmyard at the rear of the villa where once British soldiers and Italian partisans hiding from the Germans came for food. Alfiero Mazzuoli, the estate steward, was waiting for me. Although he speaks no English, he gestured graciously toward the garden as if to say: "It is all yours, signor—for a few hours."

To arrange an appointment, visit Lafoce.com or call +39 0578 69 101.

VILLA MASSEI

Nothing perks up a garden like a Renaissance grotto, or pulls together a lawn quite so well as a pair of three-hundred-year-old cypresses. Luckily for Gil Cohen and Paul Gervais, these assets came with the Villa Massei when they purchased the sixty-acre property in 1982. Not a bad starter kit for two guys who had previously lived in a New York apartment and a house in California, where serious gardening didn't enter the picture. Cohen recalls, "For us, landscaping meant clearing fallen trees with a chain saw."

It was a memorable vacation in Tuscany that prompted Cohen, then a trustee of the San Francisco Art Institute, and Gervais, an artist, to muse about buying a villa of their own—and, ultimately, to sell everything they owned in order to acquire Massei. There wasn't a stick of furniture inside the house, a medieval structure that had been converted into a hunting lodge in the sixteenth century; there were also plenty of challenges outside to keep the new owners busy. Besides those venerable cypresses and other specimen trees, they inherited a vineyard of one thousand grapevines and a sizable olive grove. Coached by the caretaker, Ugo Casapieri, who has tended Massei—as his father did—for thirty-five years, Cohen and Gervais learned to farm, and now sell their wine and olive oil to local restaurants. (Gervais also wrote a novel, *Extraordinary People,* published by HarperCollins in 1991, and a memoir, *A Garden in Lucca,* Hyperion, 2000; Cohen volunteers at a foster-care home for teenagers in Lucca.)

The four-acre garden near the villa required more than good husbandry, however. Shrubs and trees needed remedial pruning, and pavement smothered wide stretches of ground: "In the 1920s, there was a craze for putting cement in Italian gardens," says Cohen. "A lot of our 'gardening' involved pulling it out." They began adding plants to replace the cement and to connect surviving landscape treasures. Now Japanese iris line the path from villa to grotto, oak-leaf hydrangeas fill seventeenth-century terra-cotta laundry pots near a sprawling camphor tree, and new parterres expand upon the classical style of the house. A 150-year-old red camellia near the front door is a reminder that generations of Tuscan gardeners have loved glamorous exotica. "When camellias were introduced to Italy from Asia, centuries ago, they were first brought to Lucca, four miles from here," Cohen explains.

You need not be in Italy long before you learn that every detail of local history is subject to lively debate. Villa Massei is no exception. Some connoisseurs insist that the grotto dates only to the eighteenth century, not the sixteenth, though everyone agrees that its three carved masks are indeed Renaissance. If you'd like to visit Villa Massei to decide for yourself, Cohen and Gervais are glad to share the fruits of their labors, when their busy schedules allow. To make an appointment, reach them by e-mail at info@agardeninlucca.com. Ask for directions: Villa Massei sits above Massa Macinaia, a village so small it's invisible on all but the most detailed maps.

GIARDINI WORTH A JAUNT

Cetinale

The centerpiece of a baroque landscape, Cetinale was remodeled in 1680 for Cardinal Flavio Chigi, and now belongs to the English expatriate Lord Lambton. Beyond the villa, a long grassy walk runs between monumental cypresses to a theatrical gateway topped with heroic busts and obelisks. Stairs climb through ilex woods to a hilltop hermitage. (By appointment; +39 0577 311 147/villacetinale.com/open 9:30 a.m.–12 p.m., Monday through Friday.)

Gamberaia

A formal garden with heart. Romantic "water parterres" brimming with flowers soften the symmetry, and a curved topiary arcade embraces an intimate enclosure. Drive to the small town of Settignano and ask the first person you see for directions. (+39 055 697 205/villagamberaia.it/generally open 9 a.m.–6 p.m., Monday through Saturday; Sunday by appointment.)

Roseto Botanico di Cavriglia Carla Fineschi

Gianfranco Fineschi, a professor of orthopedics, has amassed eight thousand rose species and hybrids around the nucleus of three hundred antique roses that his father planted at Cavriglia in the 1930s. Even when nothing is in bloom (a rare occurrence), the meticulous labels are fascinating (+39 055 916 6237). The headquarters of Badia a Coltibuono, the well-known olive oil producer, is only a few miles away. Stop by for lunch.

Torrigiani

Lawn and *parco* typify the English-style landscaping chic in nineteenth-century Italy; surviving seventeenth-century parterres and grottoes are attributed to Le Nôtre. Open March until mid-November (+39 0583 928 041). Nearby Villa Reale, in Marlia, lives up to its name: it's a garden of regal grandeur. March through November. (Guided tours only; +39 0583 30 108/parcovillareale.it/closed Monday.) Just to the east, in Collodi, Villa Garzoni has slid into a state of disrepair that only intensifies its baroque spirit (+39 0572 429 590).

Vignamaggio

The Vignamaggio winery, near Lamole, was begun in the fifteenth century. There is also a lovely inn, Il Cenobio, on the property. (+39 055 854 661/vignamaggio.com.) Its private Renaissance garden was the location for Kenneth Branagh's film *Much Ado About Nothing.*

Villa Medici

Iris Origo grew up here, in Fiesole, amid the restored fifteenth-century gardens of a former Medici estate. The views of Florence are spectacular. (By appointment; +39 055 59 417.)

Botticelli's *Primavera*

ROY MCMULLEN

❧

ART HISTORIAN BERNARD Berenson, in *The Passionate Sight-seer: From the Diaries, 1947–56,* wrote, "The older I get, the more do I feel and appreciate Botticelli." Admittedly, that's leavened praise, and there are plenty of visitors to Florence, and Italy in general, who are rather tired of Botticelli. But I'd be telling one of the biggest lies of my life if I said I agreed with them. Occasionally, I wish I could pronounce that I prefer one of the Uffizi's more obscure works of art, but in fact, I adore Botticelli, and I love *Primavera.* And as the writer of this piece reveals, *Primavera* is far more complex than a cursory glance would imply.

ROY MCMULLEN wrote this piece for the wonderful (and sadly defunct) *Horizon* magazine in 1968. It was his second contribution to a great series entitled "Anatomy of a Masterpiece." McMullen is also the author of *Degas* (Houghton Mifflin, 1985), *Mona Lisa: The Picture and the Myth* (Da Capo, 1977), *Art, Affluence, and Alienation: The Fine Arts Today* (Signet, 1969), and *Victorian Outsider: A Biography of J. A. M. Whistler* (Dutton, 1973), among others.

SUPPOSE THAT A Racine play had survived only as notation for pantomime, or that a Monteverdi opera had come down to us without a title and with only a hint of the libretto. The resulting puzzle would resemble what faces the thousands of tourists who each summer climb the stairs of the Uffizi Gallery in Florence and halt expectantly in front of Sandro Botticelli's *Primavera*. Those who are willing to settle for a poetical tableau and a virtuoso's exercise in arabesques can of course go back to the hotel delighted. But those who want to "read" the mythology are likely to spend the rest of their holidays as art sleuths.

And staying out of the second category of viewers is difficult, for the work is obviously not just painting to dream by. It insists on looking like what it is: an allegory that has been waiting several centuries for the discovery of its original literary inner structure—its precise iconographic program. It needs that program in order to become fully coherent and expressive as visual art, much as an opera score needs a libretto to become musically coherent and expressive.

For whom and when was the picture painted? Does it contain topical allusions? What philosophy guided the artist in his striking mixture of sensuousness and idealism? Who, exactly, are the flower people on the right, the beautiful people on the left, and the young matron in the middle? Is the idealism focused on specific ideals, or is the whole affair merely a vague *quattrocento* love-in? If the return of spring, *la primavera*, is the subject, why are the trees carrying an autumnal load of ripe, golden fruit? There are still no completely satisfactory answers to these and many other questions, and I suppose there never will be, unless a lucky researcher comes across Botticelli's actual "libretto" in a Medicean coffer.

However, this is an excellent time to consider a few of the answers that can be called, for the most part, satisfactory, plus a few that cannot. On the one hand, since World War II brilliant progress toward understanding the painting has been made by professional art historians. On the other hand, this progress has not yet hardened into an orthodox interpretation. It can still be challenged by any sharp-eyed layman who feels that the meaning of a masterpiece is too important to be left entirely to specialists.

Most of the specialists now agree that the *Primavera* was ordered by, or at least for, Lorenzo di Pierfrancesco de' Medici, a second cousin of Lorenzo the Magnificent, and was originally hung in the Medici villa at Castello, on the outskirts of Florence. The Castello property was bought for Lorenzo di Pierfrancesco and his brother in 1477, and that date, or early 1478, seems about right on stylistic grounds for the execution of the picture. The drawing does not have much of the dramatic, wiry vigor that Botticelli favored a couple of years later; it shows instead the tendency toward soft gracefulness that can be seen in the Uffizi's *Adoration of the Magi,* which was probably painted in 1476 or 1477.

In fact the only reason for still worrying a little about the commissioning and the date is that Lorenzo di Pierfrancesco was only

fifteen years old in 1478. But we know that later in his short life (he died at forty) he patronized both Botticelli and Michelangelo, and we can assume that, being a Medici, he was a precocious connoisseur. Moreover, his age can help to explain the marked didactic tone of the picture. For me at least, there is something in the gesture and look of the central young matron in particular that suggests an adult instructing a child.

In 1478, according to the most reliable documents, the painter was thirty-three. He had worked with Fra Lippo Lippi and probably Verrocchio, and had apparently had his own workshop since at least 1470. Behind him lay such achievements as the *Fortitude,* the *St. Sebastian,* and the *Adoration* already mentioned. Immediately ahead lay the *St. Augustine,* the frescoes for the Sistine Chapel, the *Mars and Venus,* and *The Birth of Venus.* In other words he was in the midst of one of the most productive periods in his career, and probably the happiest period in his life—although with Botticelli happiness seems to have been relative.

Whatever descriptive label he may have given the *Primavera* has been lost, along with any other external clues about his intentions that he may have provided; and so the usual, and earliest, point of departure for an interpretation is Giorgio Vasari's *Lives,* which were published in 1550, forty years after the death of Botticelli. Vasari says that the painting is about "Venus whom the Graces deck with flowers, denoting spring (*dinotando la primavera*)," which—as a glance at the painting will show—is inaccurate enough to prove that the writer had not been invited out to Castello in quite a while. But the statement is useful because of the mention of Venus, whose presence an ordinary viewer might not suspect. Nearly everybody now agrees that she is the young matron in the middle under the Cupid, although her being fully clothed has provoked a few doubts.

What about "denoting spring"? The phrase certainly accounts for some of the personages and décor, but it leaves enough unexplained to force a conscientious investigator to look into the additional theories that have been proposed. The bulk of these fall into four categories, which can be labeled the Antitheoretical, the Simple, the Topical-Sentimental, and the Intellectual-Astringent.

An extreme example of the Antitheoretical explanation is the notion that the *Primavera* is merely a botched job—a mixture of motifs without a common denominator. A slightly more plausible and attractive example is the notion that Botticelli, who after all was primarily a painter, ignored a program—concocted perhaps by a Florentine pedant—and unified his work strictly on the basis of shapes, lines, and colors. The weakness, of course, in the "botched" notion is that the picture is not botched, and the weakness in the second notion is that dozens of Botticelli's works show that he was a thinking as well as a painting man.

Vasari's "denoting spring," if that is all he had in mind, might be listed as a Simple theory, but its historical importance really puts it in a category by itself. Anyway, there are other Simple theories. One is that the picture simply celebrates womanhood. Another is that it depicts a meeting of lovers. Still another is that it allegorizes the round of the seasons: you start with the wintry wind on the right, move through spring and summer to autumn, and back through the laden trees to winter again. All of the Simple theories are sweet and poetic, and go well with tapestries and madrigals. All, however, have the defect of being too simple to exhaust the data.

In order to follow any of the Topical-Sentimental theories, which were the favorites of our grandfathers and are still the stock in trade of tourist guides, one must have a system for referring to the cast of characters in the *Primavera*. So, accepting the designations used by the iconologist Edgar Wind, I shall call the puffing god on the right Zephyr; the windblown nymph in his grasp Chloris; the flower woman Flora; the Graces from right to left Pulchritudo, Castitas, and Voluptas; the young man Mercury; and the central figures Venus and Cupid. For this third category of theories one must also keep in mind some Florentine personages, events, and legends that fascinated the imagination of the second half of the nineteenth century (especially the English-speaking part of that imagination). The personages are Lorenzo the Magnificent; his handsome, talented, and popular younger brother, Giuliano; the beautiful Simonetta Cattaneo, a Genoese girl who entered Florentine high society as the wife of Marco Vespucci and soon became a favorite of the Medici circle; and the poet Politian, or Poliziano, famous before he was eighteen as the translator of the *Iliad* into Latin.

The first event to remember is the elaborate chivalric tournament, often referred to as The Joust (*La Giostra*) of Giuliano, which the Medici staged in the Piazza Santa Croce in 1475. Giuliano, who won the jousting prize, was dressed in silver armor and equipped with a standard on which Botticelli had depicted Pallas Athena. Simonetta was the tournament Queen of Beauty. Lorenzo's standard bore the motto *Le temps revient* (time returns), and many of the spectators must have felt that their ancient city was entering a marvelous springtime under the guidance of youth: Lorenzo was then twenty-six, and Giuliano and Simonetta were only twenty-two.

Politian, who was just twenty-one, set to work immediately on a long romantic poem, *Stanze per la Giostra di Giuliano de' Medici,* which was destined to become even more famous than the event it celebrated; and one can suppose that the legend that Giuliano and Simonetta were lovers was already in the making. But spring soon proved a treacherous season. The next April La Bella Simonetta died of consumption. April, 1478, brought the murder of Giuliano by enemies of the Medici clan.

Does it not seem reasonable to suppose that these personages and these events are somehow reflected in the *Primavera*? Many people have thought so. The motto *Le temps revient* has been proposed as a probable title for the picture. Mercury, reaching up with his staff to dispel the mists of winter (which are apparently not visible to all critics), has been identified as Giuliano. Simonetta has been presumed to be Venus, the Queen of Beauty, presiding over the return of spring and hope to Tuscany; or Castitas, the chaste Grace in the middle who is apparently about to be hit by Cupid's flaming arrow and who is perhaps looking longingly at Mercury-Giuliano; or Chloris, in the chill clutch of death or escaping that clutch—in which case the grove becomes a setting in Elysium. The atmosphere and imagery of the picture have been compared with the atmosphere and imagery of Politian's poem, and predictable conclusions drawn. There have even been suggestions that Botticelli himself was half in love with Simonetta. Unfortunately, there is no evidence to support all this lovely speculation.

We are left, then, with the Intellectual-Astringent as the most satisfactory, or the least unsatisfactory, class of theories. Here the major assumptions are that the *Primavera* is primarily a philosophical picture and that the philosophy behind it is Florentine Neo-Platonism. This system of thought mixed a good deal of eclectic mysticism and occultism with such standard Neo-Platonic doctrine as the idea of reaching the heavenly kinds of love and beauty through the earthly kinds. There are documents to support such speculation, but none so far can be called an explicit program for the picture.

One of the most important of these documents was published and analyzed by the art historian E. H. Gombrich in 1945. It is a letter written to Botticelli's patron, the young Lorenzo di Pierfrancesco, by the humanist Marsilio Ficino, apparently sometime in the winter of 1477–78 the period when the *Primavera* was probably painted. Ficino, who at this time had a European reputation as a philosophical translator and commentator, and who had been a mentor of the Medici family since the time of old Cosimo, gives the boy a moral lecture in a wildly pedantic, astrological, and mythological style, and closes with a lengthy flourish concerning Venus. She is, he says, not only "a nymph of excellent comeliness," but also the goddess-planet and allegorical figure who stands for Humanity (Humanitas) and thus for "Temperance and Honesty, Charm and Splendor."

Gombrich argues persuasively that Botticelli's fully clothed young matron is this Venus-Humanitas, a conception perhaps inspired directly by Ficino's letter. The Italian historian Roberto Salvini goes on to conclude that the *Primavera* is "an allegory of the kingdom of Venus, of an ideal world where nature and instinct, embodied by the erotic Zephyr and Flora, are ennobled by culture and civilization, embodied by Venus (Humanity) accompanied by the Graces." He accounts for the presence of Mercury by pointing out that Ficino says the god represents good advice.

This conclusion is hard to quarrel with. But where did Botticelli, or his learned programmers, find the images that convert the abstract philosophy into such a vivid tableau? Gombrich maintains—rather unconvincingly, to my mind—that the source is a passage in Apuleius's *Golden Ass* that describes a pantomime dealing with the Judgment of Paris; and his argument can lead to the conclusion that the picture was meant to be "completed" by the presence in front of it of the real Lorenzo di Pierfrancesco, playing the role of Paris being looked at by Venus. An earlier generation of scholars favored a passage from Lucretius as the source, and of course Politian's verses on the 1475 tournament. More recently, and very convincingly, Wind has argued that "Botticelli's poetical trappings are unmistakably indebted to Politian's muse and to those ancient poems (particularly the Homeric Hymns, Horace's Odes, and Ovid's *Fasti*) with which Politian and Ficino had made him conversant. . . ."

If we accept this argument, many of the details and personages—and the philosophical content as well—come into remarkably sharp focus. On the right Zephyr, as in Ovid, pursues the earth-nymph Chloris. When he touches her, flowers come from her breath, and she is metamorphosed into Flora, the herald of spring. In philosophical terms this triad shows beauty (Flora) emerging from chastity and passion. On the left the dialectic con-

tinues with the Graces: Castitas, or chastity, is about to be struck by the blindfolded Cupid's arrow and is being initiated into the mystery of love by Pulchritudo, on her right, and Voluptas, on her left. Meanwhile, still according to Wind, "Venus tempers the dance and keeps its movements within a melodious restraint," for part of the paradox in all this is that the triads of figures on the right and the left are really aspects of the nature of Venus herself.

What about Mercury? Well, one of his roles was leader of the Graces. Also, in the picture he seems to be turning from the world toward the Beyond, and touching the divine clouds through which we humans half glimpse heavenly truths. I admit that Mercury still worries me, and so does the golden fruit. To explain it, as some experts do, as simply the oranges with which Renaissance mythologists identified the golden apples of the Hesperides brings me back to a suspicion I would like to be rid of—namely, the suspicion that the *Primavera* may after all have something to do with the Judgment of Paris. Paris did give one of those apples to Venus.

None of the theories I have mentioned, including the Simonetta speculation, can be called absolutely impossible. As a matter of fact, even if we did have Botticelli's "libretto," we could not be entirely certain of the interpretation that was expounded to the young Lorenzo di Pierfrancesco. Gombrich's research makes it plain that the learned men of Florence were inclined to indulge in extremely freewheeling exegesis; we must therefore imagine Ficino improvising one explanation one day and another the next day, according to the sermon he wished to preach.

Along with the ambiguity in the allegorical meaning, there is an ambiguity in the general emotional tone of the painting. This other ambiguity can be called historical, since the dominant mood seems to vibrate between the Renaissance and the Middle Ages. But it is also a kind of ambiguity peculiar to Florence and to Botticelli.

The *Primavera* certainly qualifies as a Renaissance painting. It exhibits a Renaissance delight in sensuous experience: we can infer that the artist loved flowers with a truly Shakespearean ardor and that he enjoyed music and the dance—his arabesques, the stylized attitudes of his personages, and even their hand gestures, have a melodic and balletic quality. That he was interested in the current revival of Greek and Roman culture seems established by the ease with which scholars have found visual allusions to ancient authors, and also perhaps by the hint of a classical frieze in the draperies and in the rhythmic grouping of the figures.

On the other hand, the painting can qualify almost equally well as a medieval production. Venus-Humanitas does not look at all pagan; with the leafy arch behind her she looks much like a Madonna in a niche in a medieval church. The three Graces, supplied with wings, would make excellent Gothic angels. Mercury could pass for a Christian saint, although perhaps not as a martyr. Chloris and Zephyr have reminded at least one critic of a desperate soul pursued by a devil. Even if we rule out these recollections of the Christian art of the preceding centuries, other medieval elements can be found. The setting might be one of the allegorical gardens created by the poets celebrating courtly love, and this is a reminder that a fondness for flowers, spring, music, and dancing was by no means confined to the Renaissance. If the composition suggests a classical frieze, it suggests even more a late Gothic tapestry.

And finally, the shallow picture-space is oddly archaic in comparison with the organized deep space of such fifteenth-century avant-gardists as Uccello and Piero della Francesca. Looking at it, we understand a comment by Botticelli's Florentine contemporary Leonardo da Vinci: "Sandro, you tell us not why some things appear lower than others. . . ." Yet we know that Botticelli was capable of obeying the recently invented laws of linear perspective, for some of his paintings are almost academic in their orthodox handling of space.

We must be careful not to overdramatize the pictorial evidence and discover a spiritual conflict in what is merely a pleasant mixture of old and new styles in art. But there is plenty of external evidence that when the *Primavera* was being painted a medieval-Renaissance, or Christian-pagan, conflict was under way in the minds of many devout Florentines. We cannot suppose that the puritanical religious revival led by Savonarola arose from nothing. Was Botticelli, as early as 1478, already sensitive to the coming crisis?

About all we can say is that there are indications that in some mysterious way he was psychologically and spiritually out of tune with the cultural history he was helping to make. There is evidence, too, that his health was poor, that he was neurotic, and that during the last years of his life he was quite desperately sad and eccentric. His painting style veered back and forth between realism and antirealism to such an extent that experts sometimes disagree by ten years about the date of a well-known work. He appears to have earned large sums as a manufacturer of religious pictures, and to have spent the money recklessly. He was alternately melancholy and ecstatic, and according to Vasari, "fond of sophistry . . . and of playing tricks on his pupils and friends."

A possible conclusion to all this is that the strange charm of the *Primavera* comes from an effort to balance historical and personal tendencies that ultimately could not be balanced. Botticelli never tried to paint this kind of picture again.

The Cloisters of Florence

LOUIS INTURRISI

※

THE METROPOLITAN MUSEUM of Art has in its possession not only one of the treasures of New York but of the entire country: the Cloisters, a collection of medieval art that incorporates sections of actual European cloisters. While there, it's possible to feel a million miles away from a major metropolis, even though the Cloisters lie nearly at the tip of Manhattan.

As Louis Inturrisi notes in this piece, which was featured in the November 1995 issue of *Gourmet,* the majority of the cloisters in Florence date from the Renaissance, but no matter what their architectural style, they're all serene spots for reflection and repose.

LOUIS INTURRISI was a freelance writer and professor who lived in Rome. He wrote often about Italian culture and food for a variety of publications, including *Gourmet, HG,* and the *New York Times.*

CLOISTERS HAVE ALWAYS seemed to me the least intimidating of architectural forms. Their classical rhythms never take getting used to, and experiencing their comforting repetitions always feels like coming home to rest among the familiar folds of a mother's skirt. Moreover, because cloisters strike just the right balance between confinement and freedom, they invite lingering and encourage a childlike tendency toward indolence that is difficult to resist.

The cloisters attached to the great churches of Florence are no exception. They are blessed islands of repose amid the hurly-burly of open markets, whirlwind tours, and the noise and frustration of rush-hour traffic. And with their cool fountains, covered loggias, and open centers, cloisters make perfect places in which to curl up and while away the afternoon. Especially on sunlit days, I find it hard not to stay put and let myself be cradled by the soothing harmony of a cloister such as the Chiostro Grande (Great Cloister) at Santa Croce, with its elegant gray and white loggia echoing Brunelleschi's Pazzi Chapel around the corner.

The Great Cloister is the more remote of two cloisters at Santa Croce and is almost hidden away behind a beautifully sculpted portal by Benedetto da Maiano. Few tourists ever venture this far, so it is one of the most tranquil public places in Florence. Birds chirp, bees hum, and the monastic simplicity here is the opposite of the sensual onslaught one experiences in the church and chapel next door. Finished in the mid-fifteenth century by a disciple of Brunelleschi, the Great Cloister is a fine example of Renaissance harmony. All its measurements were worked out so that, for example, the span between the arches marching in stately procession around the center is one and a half times the height of the pillars.

Nothing detracts from these careful calculations. A few curly acanthus leaves atop the smooth columns and some floral medallions in the white spandrels between the arches are the only frills in this soberly peaceful place. It's the pleasant predictability of column and arch—repeated in their silhouettes along the pavement—that holds the attention here and makes it impossible not to stop and note how the sky framed above a cloister always seems brighter and clearer than it would otherwise.

Cloisters, of course, are nothing new. They are descendants of the Roman atrium—the heart of patrician houses at the time of the empire. The ruins at Ostia Antica and Pompeii show that the model for this type of dwelling was a series of rooms set around a large rectangle open to the sky to provide light as well as a basin for collecting rainwater.

The culmination of this plan is the House of the Vestals in the Roman Forum. There the celibate order of women lived around an open courtyard in much the same way Europe's religious orders would in the Middle Ages. The Dominican, Franciscan, and Benedictine monks and nuns adopted the Roman atrium for their abbeys and monasteries because it provided a covered walkway between sleeping quarters and chapel. This closed-in space, or *claustrum* in Latin, represented the boundaries beyond which they did not venture: outside was chaos, war, and the plague, but inside was a corner of life safely tucked away.

The impression one gets when viewing the world from the second story of the austerely simple cloister of Florence's San Lorenzo, near the Mercato Centrale and the neighborhood's street market, is almost Zen-like. Everything here is reduced to the essential: the arcade is a sweeping unadorned surface; the pillars are slender sticks; and the colors—ocher, brown, and terra-cotta—are the humble tones of the Tuscan hills. Silence is part of the architecture. You realize it whenever it is broken—by the birds hopping about the roof tiles or by the bells in Santa Maria del Fiore's campanile, its striated green and white marble soaring incongruously over the adjacent rooftops. In the garden below, rows of sharp-edged boxwood hedges converge on a miniature orange grove.

In Renaissance cloisters, which predominate in Florence, elements of the medieval cloister were modified. Before the fifteenth century, for example, the second stories of most cloisters were merely open passageways covered by roof tiles, like the one at San Lorenzo. But during the Renaissance these passageways were often walled up, windows added, and the whole converted into monks' cells. In addition, the open centers of many medieval cloisters were obscured from view by an exterior wall. In the fourteenth and fifteenth centuries this wall was gradually diminished and eventually disappeared.

Both these changes are evident in the beautiful cloister of Santa Maria Maddalena dei Pazzi in Borgo Pinti (at number 58), where the second-story loggia has been "filled in" and the dividing wall reduced to a base for a portico of Ionic columns. Moreover, instead of continuing uninterrupted around the square as it would have in a medieval cloister, the portico is broken at opposite ends by tall arches that cut into the second story and point toward the kind of monumental grandeur that typifies the Renaissance cloister.

Designed by Giuliano da Sangallo in 1480, Santa Maria Maddalena's cloister is among the most serene in Florence. Apart from the few tourists who come to see Perugino's well-preserved fresco in the lower church, this is a place where you can be alone for long periods of time, accompanied only by the sunlight and by the gray-green elegance of *pietra serena,* or "serene stone," which here, more than anywhere else in Florence, demonstrates the merit of its name.

※   ※   ※

The most refined of the Renaissance cloisters in Florence is perhaps the one called the Chiostro degli Uomini (Men's Cloister) inside the Spedale degli Innocenti (Hospital of the Innocents), in Piazza della Santissima Annunziata. Named for the biblical incident in which Herod, reacting to the birth of Christ, ordered the deaths of hundreds of innocent children, this was the first (1421) foundlings' hospital in Europe. Its cloister (visible through the gateway) is one of the wonders of Renaissance art. The noble colonnade of wide arches and smooth *pietra serena* columns echoes the elegant geometry of Brunelleschi's design for the surrounding piazza, which many Florentines consider their most beautiful square.

But there is something new here. Unlike Brunelleschi's other cloisters, where refinement and satisfaction are derived mostly from a careful consideration of "order, measure, and rule," the hospital's main cloister has a bit of decoration as well. Large white circles enclosing emblems of the other foundlings' hospitals in Florence cover the surface of the low-lying second story. And, because these were executed in white lime sgraffito against a terra-cotta background, they also give the surface depth. In addition, in the spaces where the arches meet, delicately incised medallions repeat the touching motif of babes in swaddling clothes, which Andrea della Robbia created in the 1480s for the blue and white porcelain tondos that grace the portico in the piazza.

There are a few benches here, among the potted lemon trees, where I make a customary stop. Beyond the arches the sound of children playing can often be heard because this is still a hospital and an orphanage. The babes above the arches backed by the sound of real children reinforce my conviction that cloisters are a most motherly invention. Before leaving, I always go through the little doorway on the right that leads to a second cloister—the graceful, oblong Chiostro delle Donne (Women's Cloister), also by Brunelleschi—where slender Ionic columns support a tiny cream-colored loggia like the ones so often seen in early Renaissance paintings.

The problem with cloisters, of course, is the corners. The number of arches and the span between them have to follow a precise canon or an unharmonious bunching up of columns will occur in the corners (as at the cloister at San Matteo) or a jump from columns to pilasters (as at Santa Maria Maddalena). One of the things that makes the Men's Cloister at the Innocents' Hospital so satisfying is that nothing interrupts the solemn procession of column and arch around the perfect square.

Though the hospital's main cloister is unmatchable in its serene classicism, for my money the most impressive of the Renaissance cloisters in Florence is the *chiostrino,* or "little cloister," next to the Church of San Giovanni Battista dello Scalzo on Via Cavour (at number 69). Built in 1511 for a medieval confraternity of barefoot (*scalzi*) brothers, the *chiostrino* is unique. Instead of the usual single columns, here are pairs of beautifully sculpted Corinthian columns. And they do not rest on the ground or on a wall, as in other cloisters, but are raised on pedestals, which makes them more like sculptures than mere supports. (If you look carefully at these pedestals, you will see that they are decorated with skulls and crossbones, alluding to the group's avowed mission during the Middle Ages of collecting and burying the dead from plagues and wars.)

A terra-cotta walkway surrounds the *chiostrino* and along the walls are Andrea del Sarto's hauntingly lovely scenes from the life of Saint John the Baptist, painted in pale grisaille against a dark green background. The center of this cloister is glassed over to protect the frescoes, and this feature makes it a good place to visit in the rain.

Many charming cloisters in Florence are worth visiting, yet these are my favorites. Others not to miss if you can help it, however, are the cloister next to the Church of the Carmine, with its tall cypresses so typical of Tuscany; the cloister of the Ognissanti (All Saints) along the Arno, which has an impressive *Last Supper* by Ghirlandaio; and the beautiful cloister by Michelozzo at San Marco. And Santa Maria Novella has six cloisters!

There are sixty-two cloisters in Florence in all, and it is enough to note that visitors who have strayed into any one of them know the tug to postpone tasks, stay put a while, and let themselves be nourished by this most compassionate of buildings—which shuts the world out and lets it in at the same time.

The Last Supper, Seen Six Ways

LOUIS INTURRISI

❦

WITH ALL DUE respect to Leonardo da Vinci, his painting of the *Last Supper* is magnificent, if not in pristine condition, and it's without doubt the world's most famous *Cenacolo* (Last Supper). But it's not the world's only one, and it's not the only beautiful one, either. Many visitors to Florence may not realize that there are nine paintings of the *Cenacolo* in and around the city, each of them worthy of a visit—though a tour to see a number of them, as the writer outlines in this piece, is a special journey that can easily fill an entire day. However, visitors interested in plotting out a *Cenacolo* route need to do some advance planning as not all the museums and convents in which the paintings are located are open on the same days of the week or during the same hours. It can, indeed, be frustrating to put a little tour together, and if you really want to see most or all of them, I strongly recommend hiring a guide. Art historian Alessandra Marchetti (see the Guides entry in the Miscellany, page 544, for contact information) is one of the few Florentine guides that specializes in *Cenacolo* tours, and she can arrange entry to some places even on days of the week when they are officially closed. Alternatively, you could plan on seeing some of the paintings on one day and seeing others on a following day. Either way, it will be a rewarding venture, and you may find yourself nearly alone in front of the paintings—this has been my experience on several occasions.

LOUIS INTURRISI, introduced previously, lived in Rome and was a professor of English at the University of Rome.

He also contributed a great number of articles to the travel section of the *New York Times,* where this piece originally appeared in 1997.

WHEN I WAS nine years old, I painted the *Last Supper.* I did it on the dining room table at our home in Connecticut on Saturday afternoon while my mother ironed clothes and hummed along with the Texaco–Metropolitan Opera live radio broadcast. It took me three months to paint the *Last Supper,* but when I finished and hung it on my mother's bedroom wall, she assured me it looked just like Leonardo da Vinci's painting. It was supposed to. You can't go very wrong with a paint-by-numbers picture, and even though I didn't always stay within the lines and sometimes got the colors wrong, the experience left me with a profound respect for Leonardo's achievement and a lingering attachment to the genre.

So last year, when the Florence Tourist Bureau published a list of frescoes of the Last Supper that are open to the public, I was immediately on their track. I had seen several of them, but never in sequence.

During the Middle Ages the *ultima cena*—the final supper Christ shared with his disciples before his arrest and crucifixion—was part of any fresco cycle that told his life story. But in the fifteenth century the Last Supper began to appear independently, especially in the refectories, or dining halls, of the convents and monasteries of the religious orders founded during the Middle Ages. Many of the *cenacoli,* or muraled refectories, in the brochure have been inaccessible for centuries because they were in cloistered areas or had to be restored. Therefore, they are generally well preserved, in excellent condition, with glowing colors, except for the one in the Convento della Calza, which has been poorly restored.

One reason there are so many in Florence is that the subject lent itself well to fifteenth-century Italian ideals of harmony and perspective. In fact, when Leonardo moved to Milan around 1483, he chose the Last Supper to illustrate the concept of Renaissance perspective then in vogue in Florence. The scene of Jesus and his Twelve Apostles at table did this perfectly because it allowed the artist to divide up a tight interior space harmoniously and balance it by arranging an equal number of apostles on either side of Christ so that the vanishing point was directly behind the protagonist's head.

Furthermore, Florence had major houses of all the religious orders of the day with large refectories where the monks took their meals together. The Last Supper was the preferred subject for a refectory wall not only because it represented a meal, but also because it was during this meal that the eucharist was instituted. This association of corporal and spiritual food aided the monks in meditation during their meals, which were usually eaten in silence. It was also during the Last Supper that Christ gave his apostles the mandate to "do this in memory of me," thereby establishing the priesthood of which the monks were members.

Finally, the scene of the *Last Supper,* with its startling revelation and intimation of imminent disaster, has the kind of high drama that appealed to Renaissance artists. Like Michelangelo's *David* or Cellini's *Perseus,* the *Last Supper* freezes attention on a dramatic moment just before a decisive action. In the case of the *David* it's right before he loads his slingshot; in the *Last Supper* it's the moment (derived from Matthew 26:20–23) when Christ reveals that one of his own disciples will betray him: "Now when the even was come, He sat down with the twelve. And as they did eat, He said, 'Verily I say unto you, that one of you shall betray me.' And they were exceeding sorrowful, and began every one of them to say unto Him, 'Lord, is it I?' And He answered and said, 'He that dippeth his hand with me in the dish, the same shall betray me.' "

The brochure lists nine *Last Suppers,* but by postponing three for another visit, you can easily see the other six in a day. I would postpone the *Cenacolo* of the Badia di Passignano because it is not in Florence proper, the *Cenacolo* di Santo Spirito because only a small fragment remains, and the *Cenacolo* di Ognissanti because it is almost a duplicate of the *Cenacolo* di San Marco by Ghirlandaio, described below.

Santa Croce has the earliest (1340) refectory *Last Supper* in Florence, so it is instructive as a starting point. The Last Supper is in the Cimabue Museum in the first cloister next to the church in front of the Pazzi Chapel. When you enter the former Franciscan refectory, you will see the fresco along the far wall below a crucifixion scene that spreads out like a tree. Both were painted by Taddeo Gaddi, who worked with Giotto for some twenty-five years and became the leader in fourteenth-century painting after Giotto's death.

In comparing this *Last Supper* to the others, you should remember that there is no background behind the figures, only

black space. All except Judas are lined up one after the other and face front. Each is an icon, as their halos make evident. Solid and barrel-chested, the saints are too large for the narrow table that stretches the length of the wall. Moreover, apart from a few furrowed brows, the figures communicate little psychological tension or physical movement, although they are skillfully executed. Christ has his eyes downcast in resignation, and his hand raised in a forgiving blessing; John is asleep in his lap, and the other apostles do not seem very upset by what they have heard.

All of this changes radically when you move across town to Sant'Apollonia's *Last Supper,* near Piazza dell'Indipendenza. It was painted a little over one hundred years later by one of the great early artists of the Renaissance, Andrea del Castagno. It's in the former refectory of a Benedictine convent, now the Castagno Museum, where it occupies one wall of a long, dimly lighted room.

This wall painting, through carefully calculated mathematical proportions drawn by an expert draftsman, creates the illusion of three-dimensional space on a two-dimensional surface. Rather than decorate the wall, this *Last Supper* almost replaces it, projecting the room-within-a-room so that it seems to jut out into the refectory.

There is a row of chairs in front of the painting, allowing the visitor to sit and contemplate how Castagno did this. The room where the *Last Supper* is taking place has a sloping red tile roof and inward-slanting side panels that pull the viewer in. At the same time, the black-and-white striped ceiling and diamond-shaped floor tiles push you in the opposite direction. This inward-outward movement is a bit like looking at a hologram until your eye catches on to it. Instead of Gaddi's neutral black backdrop, the background is an explosion of color from six different marble squares that stand out from their white frames and create depth behind the seated figures.

🐎   🐎   🐎

Where to put Judas is always a problem in *Last Supper* scenes. If he's with the other apostles, how does one pick him out? If he's separated, it unbalances the seating arrangement. In Castagno's conception, Judas sits alone in front of the table, but to good advantage because he interrupts the solid block of white tablecloth and forms a neat circle with Christ and Peter on the other side of the table. Behind their heads, a veined marble slab with sinister red and black flares draws Christ and the two men who will deny him into the same square.

Unlike the tranquil Santa Croce *Cenacolo,* the mood here is tense and foreboding as the dark-robed, satyrlike Judas gets ready to dip the telltale piece of bread into Christ's dish. Moreover, there is irony in the fact that the disciples, who are not paying attention—some are turned away, others are talking, and one is clearly daydreaming—seem unaware of what only Christ and Judas know is about to take place.

Castagno was one of the first to use sharp contrasts of light to dramatize mighty events, so everything is molded by a gold Tuscan light. This is the most stylized of the *Last Suppers* in Florence; it looks like a stage set that will roll off into the wings as soon as this scene is over. But it is one of Castagno's few existing works and a masterpiece of scientific realism (note the skillful transparency of the glasses and bottles on the table).

The *Cenacolo* of San Marco (1482) in the Museo di San Marco and the *Cenacolo* of Foligno (1495) by Perugino in the Conservatorio di Foligno are nearby and not far from each other. The first is in Piazza San Marco, the other near the train station. Try to see them back-to-back because both have gardens as backgrounds that open up the paintings. Ghirlandaio's garden is typically Tuscan, full of fruit trees and spindly cypresses, while Perugino's uses the feathery poplars and blue hills of his native Umbria.

These are the most elegant *Last Suppers* on the list, but there isn't much drama or excitement in either. All the figures are sober, intelligent humanists. Even the cat crouching in the foreground of Ghirlandaio's painting looks as if he knows more than we do. The apostles with their handsome tunics and neat haircuts are well-turned-out courtiers, participants at a Neoplatonic symposium rather than tired fishermen eating dinner.

Their transformation must have been more telling to the monks who could also read the Neoplatonic symbols in Ghirlandaio's garden where each flower (the lily for purity) and bird (the peacock for faith) had a meaning. The walled garden itself was a symbol of virginity and represented the monks' vow of chastity.

Both of these works are brilliant examples of the refinement and virtuosity of Florentine painters during the Renaissance. Reason is what is really celebrated here. You can see it in the regular folds of Ghirlandaio's tablecloth and in the forest of elegant pillars that Perugino has receding into the distance to carry the viewer beyond the Last Supper to the Resurrection.

Interestingly, the Perugino *Last Supper,* in the refectory of the former convent of the Franciscan tertiaries, is the only one where the apostles are actually eating anything. In all the others the menu appears to be limited to a few crusts of bread and some fruit, but here the apostles are cutting up pieces of meat (with elegant forks and knives, no less) and pouring wine. I wonder if the absence of substantial nourishment in the others wasn't intentional, given the monks' long periods of fasting.

🦎   🦎   🦎

The most famous *Last Supper* after Leonardo's is the one Andrea del Sarto painted in 1519 for the tranquil Vallombrosan Abbey of San Salvi, which is a short bus ride outside the center but not to be missed. Rather than otherworldly saints or humanist philosophers, the apostles in this painting are down-to-earth men who react with human emotions of incredulity, alarm, anger, and dismay—even John manages to stay awake. The colors of the painting and the setting are beautifully matched: the reds, browns, and tarnished yellows of the *Last Supper* blend harmoniously with the polished terra-cotta floor and cream-colored vaulted ceiling.

The amazing thing here, however, is the overall movement, which can be as subtle as the rippling of the tablecloth or as exciting as the way each hand and each shoulder points to the bread Christ is about to consecrate. In the background, as suits the most dramatic of the *Last Suppers*, two servants observe the goings-on from balconies resembling theater boxes.

I can't say which is my favorite *Last Supper*. They are all special. But the one by Franciabigio in the Convitto della Calza in front of Porta di Romana is particularly memorable because when I saw it, there were real tables set for lunch in front of it so that the diners in the painting seemed to occupy the head table in the refectory and looked perfectly at home.

There is nothing outstanding about Franciabigio's painting here, but the nun who accompanies you will tell you that it was done in 1514 and that the artist was a follower of Leonardo da Vinci. She may not tell you that it was subsequently heavily restored and badly repainted. "Don't you think it could use a little more burnt sienna?" I opined. She stopped her explanation and looked directly at me for the first time. I was about to tell her how my interest in *Last Suppers* began but decided not to. She had probably never heard of the paint-by-numbers method.

IF YOU GAZE

The brochure "Last Suppers in Florence" is available in English at the Tourist Information Offices in Piazza Stazione, at the bus depot on the right side of the train station and at Via Cavour 1r.

Following are the locations of the six paintings in the article, in the order in which they are described.

By Taddeo Gaddi: Museo dell'Opera di Santa Croce (Piazza Santa Croce 16, next to the church/+39 055 246 6105/santacroce

.firenze.it). Open daily 9:30 a.m. to 5:30 p.m.; Sundays 1 p.m. to 5:30 p.m.

By Andrea del Castagno: Museo del Cenacolo di Sant'Apollonia (Via XXVII Aprile 1/+39 055 238 8607). Open daily 8:15 a.m. to 1:50 p.m.; closed the first, third, and fifth Sunday and the second and fourth Monday of the month.

By Ghirlandaio: Museo di San Marco (Piazza San Marco 3/+39 055 294 883). Open daily from 8:15 a.m. to 1:50 p.m.; closed the first, third, and fifth Sunday and the second and fourth Monday of the month.

By Perugino: Conservatorio di Foligno (Via Faenza 42, ring the bell/+39 055 286 982). Open Tuesday, Thursday, and Saturday 9 a.m. to 12 p.m.

By Andrea del Sarto: Cenacolo di Andrea del Sarto (Via di San Salvi 16/+39 055 238 8603). Open 8:15 a.m. to 1:50 p.m. daily except Mondays. Take bus no. 6 from Piazza Antinori on the Via de'Tornabuoni in the direction of Campo di Marte; get off at Lungo Africo (about twenty minutes); backtrack to the Via Tito Speri and go down it to the first right (Via di San Salvi). Do not go straight ahead to the church; turn right before the church and go down Via di San Salvi to no. 16; press the intercom button, and someone will open the gate.

By Franciabigio: Convitta della Calza (Piazza della Calza 6/+39 055 222 287). No fixed times for viewing; ring the bell to request entry.

RECOMMENDED READING

ART

When I finished compiling the list of the many, many books in the art and architecture categories, it was so lengthy that my editor asked me if the book I *really* wanted to write was one on art history. My immediate thought was yes—I was only two classes shy of being able to declare art history as a double major in college—but I knew what she really meant was that there were so many books on the list they would fill up enough pages to equal a separate volume. Happily, I have a blog (thecollectedtraveler .blogspot.com), where I can enthuse almost endlessly about the many excellent books in these key categories, and I hope you will take a look there to read about some other great resources.

So, with limited space, I have chosen instead to focus on books that are more general and that would be of interest to readers who are new (or relatively so) to art as well as to those who would still find it worthwhile to discover art reference books and titles unique to Italian art and architecture.

GENERAL ART REFERENCE

Many visitors, even those who've taken art history courses, would welcome the following volumes, which emphasize the complexity of a great many works with which we're familiar: the *Guide to Imagery* series (*Gods and Heroes in Art, Saints in Art, Gospel Figures in Art, Old Testament Figures in Art, Nature and Its Symbols,* and *Symbols and Allegories in Art,* all published by Getty Publications); *The Museum Companion: Understanding Western Art,* Marcus Lodwick (Harry Abrams, 2003); *What Great Paintings Say,* Rose-Marie and Rainer Hagen (Taschen, 2003, in two volumes).

The Story of Art, E. H. Gombrich (Phaidon, 1995, sixteenth edition). Although Sir Ernst Gombrich has authored numerous volumes on art, this is the one that really established his reputation. To quote from the jacket, "*The Story of Art* is one of the most famous and popular books on art ever published. . . . It has remained unrivalled as an introduction to the whole subject." Though a comprehensive book, Italian artists are well represented.

History of Art, H. W. Janson and Anthony F. Janson (Prentice Hall, 2006, seventh revised edition). Still enormous, still a classic, and still a great source for Italian arts, Etruscan to modern.

Romanesque Art in Europe, edited by Gustav Künstler (New York Graphic Society, 1968). Though this book is long out of print, I think it's an outstanding volume with beautiful black-and-white photographs of a number of Romanesque structures in Tuscany and Umbria.

The Oxford Companion to Christian Art and Architecture: The Key to Western Art's Most Potent Symbolism, Peter and Linda Murray (Oxford University Press, 1996). A thorough reference guide with color plates, general background to the Old and New Testaments and Christian beliefs, a glossary of architectural terms, and a detailed bibliography.

The Metropolitan Museum of Art's Heilbrunn Timeline of Art History (metmuseum.org/toah), a fantastic creation that debuted in 2000 and includes many periods of art history in Italy. The Met has also mounted a number of exhibitions focusing on Italian artists and themes—including Painting and Illumination in Early Renaissance Florence, 1300–1450, Fra Angelico, and Painting in Renaissance Siena: 1420–1500—and accompanying catalogs were published for each.

ITALIAN ART AND ARCHITECTURE

Some publishing houses specialize in illustrated books on art and architecture and have published too many titles to mention here. A few publishers to explore are:

- Harry Abrams (abramsbooks.com), whose motto is "The art of books since 1949." Its *Masters of Art* and *Classic Art* series are noteworthy.

- George Braziller (georgebraziller.com), whose motto is "Independent publishing since 1955." I am an enormous fan of its *Great Fresco Cycles of the Italian Renaissance* series, these volumes in particular: *Piero della Francesca: San Francesco, Arezzo; Luca Signorelli: The San Brizio Chapel, Orvieto; The Brancacci Chapel, Florence;* and *Ambrogio Lorenzetti: The Palazzo Pubblico, Siena.*

- Rizzoli (rizzoliusa.com). Founded in 1929, Rizzoli has long been a leader in high-quality books, and its store on West 57th Street in Manhattan has long been one of my favorite bookstores. *Metropolitan Home* noted in its Design 100 special issue in 2006 that "Rizzoli, the famed Italian purveyor of art tomes, has over the years produced an entire library of gorgeous coffee-table books. . . . Rizzoli's editors have their fingers on the pulse of what's happening right now and next in design in the United States and abroad."

- Taschen (taschen.com). Its *Basic Art* series, with numerous titles illustrated with approximately one hundred color illustrations, each priced at $9.99, is great.

The Italian Painters of the Renaissance, Bernard Berenson (Phaidon, 1952). To my mind, this is without doubt the single best book on the subject of Italian Renaissance painters. There are, of course, hundreds of other titles, and this one is out of print, but I urge readers to check in your library or used-book stores for this edition. Berenson presents the Venetian, Florentine, central Italian, and north Italian Renaissance painters in separate chapters, which contain some color tip-ons of various works. Following a chapter on "The Decline of Art," there are more than two hundred pages of black-and-white reproductions. One of the reasons I, and many others, are so fond of Berenson is perhaps best explained by this excerpt from the preface: "Yet too much time should not be wasted in reading about pictures instead of looking at them. Reading will help little towards the enjoyment and appreciation and understanding of the work of art. It is enough to know when and where an artist was born

and what older artist shaped and inspired him, rarely, as it happens, the master or teacher who first put pen, pencil and brush into his hands. Least profit is to be got from the writings of the metaphysical and psychoanalytical kind. If read one must, let it be the literature and history of the time and place to which the paintings belong." *Essenziale.*

Looking at Pictures with Bernard Berenson, selected and with an introduction by Hanna Kiel and with a personal reminiscence by J. Carter Brown (Harry Abrams, 1974). Kiel, who translated several of Berenson's works into German and prepared the bibliography at the end of this book, here combines text from Berenson's books, diaries, and letters with 150 great Italian paintings from museums and private collections in Europe and America. I wouldn't qualify this as *essenziale,* unless, like me, you really enjoy Berenson.

The Passionate Sightseer—From the Diaries, 1947–56, Bernard Berenson with a preface by Raymond Mortimer (Simon & Schuster/Harry Abrams, 1960). Similar to *Looking at Pictures* above, this book pairs 168 works of art with Berenson's diary entries. Chapters are on various cities or regions—mostly Italian but also North African—the last one devoted to Florence and dated June to July 1956. Nearly every page in the book features a black-and-white photo or reproduction, and there are three full-page color plates. Also not *essenziale,* but Berenson fans will be glad to have it.

Architecture of the Renaissance: From Brunelleschi to Palladio, Bertrand Jestaz (Harry Abrams, 1996). This is an edition in the *Discoveries* series, originally published in France by Gallimard paperbacks, and is a terrific value. It's jammed with information; the quality of the reproductions is good; it's lightweight and easy to pack (approximately 5 × 7 inches); and the price is right.

The Splendors of Italy, Guglielmo de Angelis d'Ossat and Jacqueline Bernard, translated by Geoffrey Braithwaite (G. P. Putnam's Sons, 1964; originally published by Librairie Hachette as *L'Italie et ses merveilles,* 1960). Inexplicably out of print (but worth an enormous effort to find), this is a definitive, gorgeous, heavy volume (an oversized hardcover at about 350 pages) with hundreds of black-and-white and color reproductions and photographs of Italy's artworks and architectural masterpieces. With dozens of tip-ons, good text, some maps, and a chart of the three great schools of Italian painting (Siena, Florence, and Venice/Padua/Verona), this is a must-have, and I've not seen any other book quite like it in either quality or scope. They just don't make books like this anymore.

The Arts of the Italian Renaissance: Painting, Sculpture, Architecture, Walter Paatz (Prentice Hall, 1974). This is still my favorite book on the *quattrocentro.* I believe it was intended to be a textbook, and it is long out of print, but it remains my favorite single volume. With 301 illustrations, including sixty-one in color. A very comprehensive edition, with an excellent bibliography.

The Renaissance, Walter Pater (Oxford University Press, 1986; originally published in 1875). Pater's classic—and infamous—work is a collection of essays on those artists who to him best expressed the spirit of the Renaissance: Pico della Mirandola, Sandro Botticelli, Luca della Robbia, Michelangelo, Leonardo da Vinci, Giorgione, Joachim du Bellay, and Johann Winckelmann. No reproductions, unfortunately.

Italian Gothic Sculpture; Italian Renaissance Sculpture; Italian High Renaissance & Baroque Sculpture, John Pope-Hennessy (three-volume boxed set, Phaidon, 1950s–1960s). An absolutely gorgeous, incomparable set.

The Art of the Italian Renaissance: Architecture, Sculpture, Painting, Drawing, edited by Rolf Toman (Konemann, 1995). Also a good volume, with many color reproductions and lineage charts for the Sforza, Este, and Gonzaga families, the popes, and the doges of Venice.

Lives of the Painters, Sculptors and Architects, Giorgio Vasari, translated by Gaston du C. de Vere, with an introduction and notes by David Ekserdjian (Everyman's Library, 1996, in two volumes; translation by de Vere first published in 1912). The opening line of the introduction is the only recommendation one need ever read or hear on this masterpiece, originally published in 1550: "Giorgio Vasari's *Lives of the Painters, Sculptors and Architects* is the Bible of Italian Renaissance—if not all—art history." *Essenziale.* And a wonderful companion volume is *The Great Masters* (Hugh Lauter Levin Associates, 1986), which pairs Vasari's biographies on Giotto, Botticelli, da Vinci, Raphael, Michelangelo, and Titian with related paintings, sculptures, drawings, and architecture in 120 color plates and 127 black-and-white illustrations. There are also twenty gatefolds of selected works, including Botticelli's *Primavera.* An oversized, beautiful book worthy of your diligent efforts to find.

FLORENTINE AND TUSCAN ART

The Art of Florence, Glenn Andres, John Hunisak, and A. Richard Turner, principal photography by Takashi Okamura (Abbeville, 1989). In two enormous, hardcover volumes almost as heavy as a coffee table. You do not need to read any other books except these, which are among the most beautiful and outstanding the publishing world has ever seen. The quality of the reproductions and photographs is breathtaking, and the text is equally as superb—and it's not only about art. Volume I sets the historical stage with chapters on "Prelude to Greatness, 59 BC–AD 1200" and "Civic Pride and Prosperity, 1200–1340." It's an awfully expensive set, but I think it's a very good value for what's between the covers. *Essenziale.*

Painting in Renaissance Siena: 1420–1500, Keith Christiansen (Metropolitan Museum of Art/Harry Abrams, 1988). This is the catalog that accompanied the exhibition of the same name. Not only was this show one of the best I've ever seen, but the catalog is fascinating. As Christiansen states, "This is not mainstream Italian art, but neither is it provincial. It is, for the most part, distinctly anti-Florentine, and I truly believe it is also among the most seductive schools of painting ever created."

The Basilica of St. Francis in Assisi, Elvio Lunghi (Scala, 1996). A good paperback volume with color reproductions of the basilica, some views of the surrounding countryside, the frescoes, and artistic and architectural details. Also included are chapters on Brother Francis, the construction of the church, and the decline of Assisi, and an index of artists—including Giotto, Simone Martini, and Pietro Lorenzetti—whose works are featured in the basilica.

Painting and Illumination in Early Renaissance Florence: 1300–1450 (Metropolitan Museum of Art/Harry Abrams, 1994). Published in conjunction with the exhibit held at the Metropolitan in 1994–1995.

The Architecture of the Italian Renaissance, Peter Murray (Schocken, 1986; originally published in 1963 in different form as *The Architecture of the Renaissance*). This paperback reprint of one of the classic volumes on one of the most pivotal periods in art and architectural history contains a revised bibliography and some new illustrations. Usually such definitive books are too heavy to take along, but this one will fit easily in a handbag. Though there are a few chapters on Milan, Rome, and the Veneto, the majority of the book deals with Florence and Tuscany.

GIARDINI

Villas and Gardens of Tuscany, Sophie Bajard and Raffaello Bencini (Pierre Terrail, Paris, 1992). To quote from the historical outline, "Today, the Tuscan villa remains faithful to its fourteenth-century image as a place of rest, tranquility and privacy. . . . Only if you have an adventurous spirit will you be able to discover its jealously guarded secrets." These "secrets" apparently include addresses, phone numbers, and Web sites, which the authors do not provide; however, an Internet search successfully turns up most, if not all, of them (and others, such as I Tatti, La Pietra, and Badia a Coltibuono, are well known). This is a good resource for travelers who want to visit some of the lesser known and secluded villas near Florence, Siena, and Lucca. Some of the villas require an advance request and are not generally open to the public. Those selected for this volume collectively present an extensive survey of Tuscan art from the fourteenth to seventeenth centuries. Numerous photographs accompany each entry, and the text informs readers of each property's special features.

The Garden Lover's Guide to Italy, Penelope Hobhouse (Princeton Architectural, 1998). Hobhouse is a world-renowned gardener and writer, and she has a special affection for Italian gardens. This edition, one in the *Garden Lover's Guide* series, is divided into five regional chapters, and twenty-six gardens are highlighted for Tuscany (there are, unfortunately, none for Umbria). I was especially happy to find that Iris Origo's garden at Villa La Foce, near Montepulciano, was included, as I hadn't known it was open to the public. Many of these Tuscan gardens, including the one at La Foce, are open by appointment only, so interested readers should plan on obtaining permission well in advance. Addresses, fax and telephone numbers, hours, and brief directions are provided, as well as color photos and a map at the beginning of each chapter. A glossary of Italian gardening terms and a good selection of related biographies are found at the back of the book.

Italian Gardens of the Renaissance, J. C. Shepherd and G. A. Jellicoe, (Princeton Architectural, 1996, fifth edition; originally published in 1925). In much the same way that Wharton's book (below) is a classic, this work is, too. Shepherd and Jellicoe were fifth-year students of London's Architectural Association when they set off on a grand tour of Europe. While in Italy, they studied in great detail selected gardens dating from the fifteenth

to seventeenth centuries and produced this masterful project as a result. Reuben Rainey notes in the foreword that the gardens appear in a general chronological order, but readers are not told the criteria for the gardens chosen for inclusion. They are all significant examples; the majority of them are in the areas around Rome, Florence, and Lucca. Serious garden and Renaissance lovers will rejoice at this collection. With black-and-white watercolors, line drawings, and photographs of twenty-six major Italian villas.

Italian Villas and Their Gardens, Edith Wharton (1904). This remains the seminal work on the subject and it's available in two editions: as a paperback in the *Classical America Series in Art and Architecture* published by Da Capo Press (1976), and as a hardcover published by Rizzoli (2008). Both include illustrations by Maxfield Parrish, though the Rizzoli edition features all the original plates. Arthur Ross, in the Da Capo edition, states that Wharton's book "has stood the test of time since its original publication." The first chapters feature Florentine and Sienese villas, and the remaining cover Roman, Genoese, Lombard, and Venetian villas. Wharton also provides a bibliography of books mentioned in the text, as well as an alphabetical list of architects and landscape gardeners.

Wherever I go, I am surrounded by these beautiful objects . . . and all is Italian; not a house, not a shed, not a field that the eye can for a moment imagine to be American.

—Ralph Waldo Emerson (1832)

There is no short cut to an intimacy with Italy.

—Edith Wharton

A TUSCAN AND UMBRIAN MISCELLANY

Compiling this Miscellany is both fun and overwhelming—fun because I love enthusing about these engaging subjects and overwhelming because I could literally submit hundreds under almost every letter of the alphabet. But that's why it's so great that I have a blog! Please consult my many other recommendations, tips, and new finds at Thecollectedtraveler.blogspot.com.

A

Accademia della Crusca

Accademia della Crusca—or simply, La Crusca—was founded in Florence in 1582 and is Europe's oldest language academy, older even than the better-known Académie Française. Its founders were a group of five fun-loving Florentine intellectuals who mocked the excessive seriousness of the Accademia Fiorentina, founded in 1541 and no longer in existence. Leonardo Salviati, a man of letters and a grammarian, joined in 1583, and the group's aim became the preservation of the purity of the Italian language as exemplified by the fourteenth-century writers Boccaccio, Petrarca, and Dante. (Dante especially is credited with standardizing the Italian language.) La Crusca also sought to raise the Tuscan dialect to the status of official language. Tuscan has been dominant since the thirteenth century and was endorsed as the official language of Italy after the country's unification. Salviati interpreted the name of *crusca* (bran) in a new sense, as if to say that the academy should separate good language from bad, separate the literary wheat from the linguistic chaff. The *crusconi* (bran flakes) decided that each member should be given a nickname, a motto in the vernacular, and a symbol linked to the cultivation of wheat (Salviati's was *L'Infarinato*, "the floured one"). La Crusca published the first dictionary of "pure" words, *Vocabulario*, later used as a model by other European states.

I first learned about La Crusca because of an object I saw in the window of a wonderful Florentine art gallery, Ducci (Lungarno Corsini 24r/+39 055 214 550/duccishop.com). I relate this tale in a "Foraging" column I wrote for the travel section of the *New York Times* (September 25, 2005), so I won't repeat every detail here, but the object I refer to was beautiful—it was made of wood, it was edged in gold leaf, it bore Italian words and featured a painting of a loaf of bread. . . . I loved it, but had no idea what it was. I later learned the object is a *pala* (plural is *pale*), a baker's shovel that is the symbol of La Crusca. (In addition to the *pala* images here, you can also see a number of *pale* lining the walls at Cantinetta di Verrazzano—one of my favorite eateries in Florence, at Via dei Tavolini 18/20r—and in the pages of Elizabeth David's *Italian Cooking*.) Ducci is, to the best of my knowledge, the only place in Italy where *pale* may be purchased, and each *pala* takes three artisans two months to make: one carves the wood, another applies the gold leaf, and a third paints one of the 156 La Crusca designs. (Note that there is no official partnership between Ducci and La Crusca as the academy is a nonprofit organization.)

Ducci displays between a dozen and sixteen *pale* at any time, and a small one costs approximately 375 euros while a large one is about 560 euros. I have two in my dining room, and they are stunning—even more beautiful than the one I first glimpsed in Ducci's window—against my walls, which are a shade of red-orange like that found in Pompeii frescoes (it took me quite a while to achieve this color). Ducci also has a number of contemporary pieces of art, as well as a great selection of Florentine and

Tuscan etchings and an assortment of painted wooden boxes made to imitate marble, in the patterns of notable Florentine churches (great gifts, if you can part with them!).

With my good friend Amy, I visited the headquarters of Accademia della Crusca, located in the Villa di Castello, just outside Florence (Castello is a Medici villa notable for its gardens; Botticelli's *Primavera* and *Birth of Venus* once hung here). I'd made an appointment to see the Sala delle Pale, a beautiful room where all the *pale* are hung on the walls, and the chairs of the La Crusca members—stools with baker's shovels as their backrests—line the perimeter of the *sala*. The original dictionaries are kept here as well—Amy and

I marveled as we were shown original leather-bound volumes of all the dictionaries, as well as all the written material of the academy.

Today La Crusca is active in organizing museum exhibitions, notably the Settimana della Lingua Italiana nel Mondo (Week of the Italian Language in the World); maintaining an archive and *biblioteca virtuale;* and publishing a semiannual newsletter, *La Crusca per voi,* dedicated to enthusiasts of Italian. Villa di Castello and the La Crusca offices are not open to the public, but interested readers may contact La Crusca (accademiadellacrusca.it) to request an appointment. (The ride from Santa Maria Novella station, on bus no. 28, takes about twenty minutes; schedules are in the last office on the left at the end of the platform; ask the driver to announce the Castello stop.) Visiting the villa's gardens, however, does not require an appointment (for hours and contact information, visit Polomuseale.firenze.it/musei/villacastello).

"A language," according to UNESCO, "reflects a mentality, a world vision, and original concepts." The *pale* represent to me the beauty of the Italian language, the enviable rhythm of everyday Italian life, and the matchless respect Italians have for an exquisite object.

Accommodations

Architecture critic Paul Goldberger has written that "a good hotel is a place, a town, a city, a world unto itself, and the aura it exudes has almost nothing to do with its rooms and almost everything to do with everything else—the lobby, the bar, the restaurants, the façade, the signs, even the corridors and the elevators." Hotels like the ones Goldberger describes exist in all price categories, and they are, to my mind, the kind of places most of us seek. Italian types of accommodations include:

Agriturismi: accommodations on a farm, which may be quite nice or very basic

Alberghi: inns

Bed-and-breakfasts

Campeggi: camping—and it's important to note here that the European concept of camping is about as opposite from the American as possible: Europeans do not go camping to seek a wilderness experience, and European campgrounds are designed without much privacy in mind, offering amenities ranging from hot-water showers, facilities for washing clothes and dishes, electrical outlets, swimming pools, and tiled bathrooms to bars and cafés, telephones, television, and general stores.

Hotels

Locandi: inns that are often family run, but the word *locanda*—singular of *locandi*—can also refer to restaurants.

Ostelli della gioventù: youth hostels—a book I recommend is *Hostels France & Italy: The Only Comprehensive, Unofficial, Opinionated Guide,* by Paul Karr, Globe Pequot, 2000, third edition).

Pensioni: modest inns, guesthouses, or rooms in someone's home, where the service is similar to that of a hotel (breakfast is often offered)

Convents and Monasteries: This last category is sometimes overlooked, but it is a unique—and quiet—alternative: some good sources to consult are Monasteriesofitaly.com, *Bed and Blessings—Italy: A Guide to Convents and Monasteries Available for Overnight Lodgings,* June Walsh and Anne Walsh (Paulist, 1999), and *The Guide to Lodging in Italy's Monasteries,* Eileen Barish (Anacapa, 2007, third edition).

See my blog for more in-depth descriptions, especially for *agriturismi*.

Tuscany and Umbria have an abundance of selections in all categories and in all price ranges, and if anything it will be difficult to choose from the many appealing places! In fact, I would recommend making reservations at more than one place within the countryside of Tuscany and Umbria, and possibly even within Florence itself, depending on how long you'll be staying. In this way visitors may experience different types of lodgings as well as neighborhoods, perhaps choosing a combination of moderate inns and one very special place for a splurge. I do not buy into the idea that accommodations are only places to sleep—where you stay can be one of the most memorable parts of your trip, and the staff at your chosen accommodation can be enormously helpful in making your trip special. Deciding where to stay should not be taken lightly and deserves your best research efforts.

It is not my intent to visit dozens of hotels in Tuscany and Umbria and report on them—that is the purview of guidebooks, Web sites, and accommodation guides. But as someone who pays close attention to the tiniest details, has stayed in accommodations ranging from campgrounds to five-star hotels, is practically allergic to must and dust, has an exacting idea of the words "customer service," and has been known to rearrange the furniture in a few hotel rooms, I do think I have something valuable to share with readers. Therefore, I move around when I travel, changing hotels and arranging visits to those that are either fully booked or that I otherwise might not see. I make sure to see lodgings both moderately priced and expensive, so that readers have personal recommendations for both. Most often, I am drawn to the moderate places that also represent a good value as I've found that these sometimes receive the least attention. It's never hard to find out about the budget or luxury places to stay, but the places in between—which I believe suit the pocketbooks of the majority of travelers—are often overlooked or given cursory consideration.

I myself do not generally prefer chain hotels, especially American ones, but those who do will find a number of them, notably in Florence. I prefer to consult specialty hotel groups (assuming there is one for the destination I'm visiting), and among my favorites is Abitare la Storia (literally "to live history," abitarelastoria.it). This Hospitality in Historical Houses association was founded in 1995 and features independently owned hotels, restaurants, and historical residences in both rural and urban areas. All are in buildings of notable architectural and scenic beauty, and each is unique. I have stayed at a number of Abitare properties, and each one was memorable (and there were few, if any, North Americans). A unique aspect of the member properties is that they are run by the owners themselves—known as *appassionati proprietari* ("passionate owners")—who have renovated their homes, manor houses, *palazzi,* castles, and monasteries with care. There are ten properties in Tuscany and six in Umbria. Another Italian hotel group I like is Italy Luxury Family Hotels & Resorts (italyluxuryfamilyhotels.com), with eighteen properties in Tuscany and three in Umbria (and though the emphasis is on families, there are some properties that are perfect for couples). A group I only recently learned about is the Charme & Relax group (charmerelax.it), which represents hotels of special appeal that are small, charming, and independent, with some choices in Tuscany and Umbria.

I admit that, for Italy, I prefer these three groups above all, but international hotel groups I also like are the Small Luxury Hotels of the World (slh.com), currently with fourteen properties in Tuscany—including such outstanding places as Villa Mangiacane, La Suvera, Lungarno Hotel, and J.K. Place—but none in Umbria; the Leading Hotels of the World (lhw.com), with eleven properties in Florence and Tuscany and one in Perugia, the notable Brufani Palace; and Relais & Châteaux (relaischateaux.com), with seven properties in Florence and Tuscany and others in Orvieto and Assisi.

Other sources I consult include:

- Books by Alastair Sawday: *Alastair Sawday's Special Places to Stay: Italy* (Sawday's, 2003) and his more recent *Go Slow Italy: Special Places to Eat, Stay & Savor* (Little Bookroom, 2009). I've been a Sawday fan for years and have used his guides for other countries as well, and have discovered some very wonderful places that have not appeared in other guides. About the *Go Slow* series, Sawday writes, "This book is titled *Go Slow Italy* because it is about far more than Slow Food. It invites you to get there slowly, stay awhile, to float serenely through the days— conversing, enjoying every experience rather than longing for whatever might be over the next hill. It invites intimacy, simplicity." I feel the choices in *Go Slow Italy* are very unique and appealing—all the owners are conscious, on a daily basis, of their impact on the planet—and there are twenty-two places in Tuscany and five in Umbria from which to choose. Visit his Web site at Sawdays.co.uk.

- *Charming Small Hotel Guides: Tuscany and Umbria,* edited by Fiona Duncan and Lonnie Glass (Duncan Petersen, 2003). This series, founded by Andrew Duncan and Mel Petersen in 1986 in the UK, deserves to be better known: the inspectors "go to great pains to try to get under the skin of each hotel; to draw a word-sketch of what the hotel really is," and they are not afraid to mention any drawbacks of particular lodgings. Their Web site (charmingsmallhotels.co.uk) is also useful.

- *Hello Italy! Best Budget Hotels in Italy,* Margo Classé (Wilson, 2005, fourth edition). Classé (helloeurope.com) has traveled mostly alone to not only Italy but other European destinations as well, and she has an uncanny ability to ferret out inexpensive but clean and attractive lodgings. Of the sixteen Italian cities featured in this book, there are listings for Cortona, Florence, Lucca, Assisi, Perugia, and Siena.

- *Italian Bed and Breakfasts: A Caffelletto Guide,* Michele Ballarati, Margherita Piccolomini, and Anne Marshall (Rizzoli, 2006). Whether you reserve directly with the owners or request that Caffelletto make the reservation for you, there is no extra charge. Caffelletto (caffelletto.it) is Italy's most successful bed-and-breakfast chain, founded by Michele Ballarati and Margherita Piccolomini (Anne Marshall provides the English text for the books). The Caffelletto guides were the first high-end guides to B&Bs in Italy. There are many, many listings for Tuscany and seven for Umbria.

- *Italian Hideaways: Discovering Enchanting Rooms and Private Villas,* Meg Nolan, photography by David Cicconi (Rizzoli, 2008). This book features twelve places to stay in Tuscany and one in Umbria. Melissa Biggs Bradley, former editor in chief of *Town & Country Travel* and now editor of the travel Web site Indagare.com, wrote the foreword to this lovely and useful book. She notes that "staying in small, tucked-away hotels or renting a private villa is clearly one of the most authentic and inspiring ways to obtain an intimate view of Italy and her many-faceted charms."

- *Italian Country Hideaways: Vacationing in Tuscany's and Umbria's Private Villas, Castles, and Estates,* text by Kelley F. Hurst and photography by Stefano Hunyady (Universe, 1999). The thirty estates featured in this book—five in Umbria, the rest in Tuscany—had to meet the following criteria: the primary business of the estate must be something connected to the land, such as wine, olive oil, cheese, or horse raising; accommodations must be offered, and typically the estates are not commonly known among travelers; and each estate "must possess a special intangible quality, something that truly sets it apart: a notable history, unforgettable food, spectacular views, or some other outstanding feature so compelling that it merits particular attention."

Color photos of each property are provided, along with all the usual contact information. Prices—which now may be out of date—are quoted by the week.

• Karen Brown guides (karenbrown.com), including *Tuscany & Umbria, Italy Hotels,* and *Italy B&B* (all updated for 2009). I have found some of the most wonderful places to stay with the help of Karen Brown's guides. There are no photographs of the properties in the books (but I think the line drawings suffice), and in addition to the thorough descriptions of lodgings—some of which are in *palazzi,* old mills, and buildings of historic significance—there are a number of useful tips offered that don't appear in other guides.

Keep in mind that the Italian government's star-rating system for lodgings awards stars based on room quality and amenities, paying special attention to the number of bathrooms and toilets compared with number of rooms. The stars have almost nothing to do with charm or quality of hospitality and a lot to do with swimming pools, air-conditioning, on-premises restaurants, spas and saunas, outdoor terraces, and other amenities. All of this is to say you cannot depend on Italy's star-rating system alone. Generally speaking, a one-star establishment is equated with simple accommodations and often shared bathroom facilities. Two- and three-star places can be bed-and-breakfast or regular hotel accommodations, with a private bath. Four- and five-star hotels represent the highest standards of service and can be either quite luxurious or less so. All classified hotels, of any type, are required to display their rating on their façades, and the Italian State Tourist Board features all its rated hotels on its Web site (enit.it). You may, in your research, discover places that have no rating; this may be either because they haven't received their rating yet or because they haven't requested to be reviewed. I've stayed in a number of places with no rating, and they were all perfectly fine and

clean, some even quite deserving of two or three stars. In a nut-
shell, it's far better to read *thorough* descriptions of lodgings so you
know exactly what you're paying for and ignore the stars. And I
use the word "thorough" intentionally—I'm not a fan of Internet
forums where random people whom I don't know—and therefore don't know if they look for the same attributes of a lodging
as I do—post their random opinions about accommodations. It is
the opinions of people who understand and respect the different
types of lodgings in Italy and who've stayed at dozens, if not hundreds, of them that matter to me. Here is a selection of different
types of lodgings that I particularly like and that I believe will
make your stay in Tuscany and Umbria special:

IN FLORENCE

• Four Seasons Hotel Firenze (Borgo Pinti 99/+39 055 26
  261/fourseasons.com/florence). When the Four Seasons finished its seven-year restoration of the fifteenth-century Palazzo
  della Gherardesca and officially opened as a hotel in 2008, there
  was a lot of fanfare—and with good reason. The eleven acres of
  gardens are gorgeous, the features of the former villa—colored
  tile floors, frescoes, decorated arches, artwork, glass chandeliers—are worthy of a museum, and its spa is a standout (it's the
  only hotel in the heart of Florence with an on-site spa, and it's
  the only spa in the world to use products from the Officina Profumo Farmaceutica di Santa Maria Novella). The hotel joins a
  sixteenth-century convent and a fifteenth-century palace that
  once belonged to Lorenzo il Magnifico's chancellor Bartolomeo Scala. It was later acquired by Cardinal Alessandro de'
  Medici, who became Pope Leo XI. In his book *Four Seasons:
  The Story of a Business Philosophy* (Portfolio, 2009), founder
  Isadore Sharp notes that he and the Four Seasons visionaries
  "tried to make each hotel distinctive, give it a local flavor
  incorporating regional art and furnishings." I think if I'd had

the opportunity to stay in the hotel's royal suite—which, from the photographs I've seen, is extraordinary, and may be had for an extraordinary price of thirteen thousand euros a night—I would definitely feel I was nowhere else but Florence. (However, I didn't find Florence as much in evidence here the way the Four Seasons Sultanahmet Istanbul *really* feels like Istanbul—I believe that hotel is one of the most perfect hotels in the world.) The Four Seasons Florence is a good fifteen- to twenty-minute walk from the center of things, which is not a drawback for me but might be for other travelers. But the beauty and serenity of the hotel, its two restaurants, Il Palagio and La Magnolia, and the Atrium Bar, along with its legendary customer service—Sharp proudly states that "the one idea that our customers value the most cannot be copied: the consistent quality of our exceptional

service"—will likely ensure that "distance" is defined only by how you look at that glass, half empty or half full.

By the way, Sharp's book is a good read, presenting an insider's look not only at Four Seasons but the competitive hotel business in general and the business of customer service. It's noteworthy that the four pillars of the Four Seasons business model are quality, service, culture, and brand, and at the back of the book there's a listing of senior staff members, including general managers, and their years of service with the company. You can't help but be impressed that the average years of service for the management committee is twenty-two, twenty-one for senior vice presidents, twelve for vice presidents, fifteen for regional vice presidents, and fourteen for general managers. For more descriptive details on a stay at the hotel by writer Gini Alhadeff, see "Rooms with a View" (*Travel + Leisure,* October 2008).

• J.K. Place Firenze (Piazza Santa Maria Novella 7/+39 055 264 5181/jkplace.com). When Kathy McCabe, founder and editor of *Dream of Italy* newsletter, told me that J.K. Place Firenze was her favorite hotel in Italy, I knew I had to investigate, because Kathy is somebody who has stayed at a *lot* of Italian hotels. A short while after Kathy stayed here, I reserved a room for some colleagues, who came back raving about the hotel, for its service, the rooms, and its location on soon-to-be-all-spruced-up Piazza Santa Maria Novella. I was predisposed, therefore, to like J.K. Place, but I had some doubts—namely, that I suspected it might be gimmicky, a bit too contemporary for its own good. Yet I knew that the architect and interior designer, Florentine Michele Bönan, was quite renowned, and he'd done exceptional work for the Ferragamo family (and was also part of the team that developed the Cipriani Ocean Resort and Club Residences in Miami Beach). But when I arrived and saw the lounge filled with shelves and shelves of books, I thought,

"Wow." Anyone who places such importance on books—in this case it's owner Ori Kafri— and sees them as integral to a hotel, is someone I respect. I knew I would like it here, and every part of the hotel continued to impress me.

But to go back to that lounge: the front room is a very comfortable sitting room with a fireplace, and the books are mostly beautiful hardcover volumes about Florentine and Italian design, history, decorating, and travel. Beyond it is a larger room with a black varnished wood floor and round tables and stools—this is where guests can have a light lunch and where Florentines come in the evening for drinks. It's a great place to come to relax in the afternoon—non-guests included!—as it's quiet and practically empty in the middle of the day, and water, fruit juices, wine, hot drinks, and cocktails can be ordered, including the J.K. Lounge cocktail, consisting of vodka, Cointreau, vermouth, and grenadine. Near the door to the street there is an enormous book—three feet tall and two feet wide—featuring the photography of Helmut Newton, on its own Philippe Starck metal stand. The artwork in both rooms and throughout the public areas is a mix of framed architectural drawings and bold, modern pieces.

Back out in the hallway past the reception area (which is a library, also with a fireplace and with plaster casts representing famous writers from the 1800s) is the breakfast room, which I absolutely love, as it has an original *pietra dura* stone floor, a large walnut table, and copper lanterns from the 1800s, and it's all covered with a glass "roof." A very modern plasma TV room is farther back, and the main staircase, with gray sandstone steps (also original), is off the main hallway.

The overriding feeling here is that of a house, not a hotel, which is at least partially due to its vertical shape—the hotel is more narrow than horizontal. The twenty guest rooms—which are available in classic, double superior, double deluxe, junior suite, suite, a penthouse, and a master room—share a muted color palette, but beyond that each room is different because the building had its own quirky spaces and Bönan had to decide what to do with each one. The rooftop terrace next to the penthouse is small but terrific, with teak wood flooring and low, black cushioned seating. Black, in fact, is the signature color of the hotel, and I must say I love the J.K. Place bookmarks, the sleek pencils, and all the other monogrammed items (and my husband's initials are J.K. to boot). Kafri has also redone the Hotel Londra Palace in Venice (which I've not yet seen), and the J.K. Place Capri opened in 2009. I've heard through the grapevine that even knowing how wonderful J.K. Place Firenze is will in no way prepare me for what Kafri has achieved on Capri. Stay tuned.

• Loggiato dei Serviti (Piazza della Santissima Annunziata 3/+39 055 289 592/loggiatodeiservitihotel.it). The building that is now this lovely hotel was originally built for the order of the Servants of Mary, known as the Servites, in the 1500s. It sits directly across from the Spedale degli Innocenti—designed by Brunelleschi for unwanted or otherwise destitute children (note the swaddled babies on the façade)—on Piazza della Santissima Annunziata, considered by many to be Florence's most beautiful. Loggiato is minutes away from Piazza San Marco and the Accademia, and a few more minutes away from the Duomo and Piazza della Signoria. As the piazza is technically traffic-free—it's designated a pedestrian-only zone—a stay here is usually a quiet one (musical happenings in the piazza can be

loud, but are concluded by about midnight). In the second half of the nineteenth century the Loggiato was acquired by the Budini Gattai family, who ran the building first as an inn, then a pensione, and, in 1986, decided to convert it into a fine but not fancy hotel.

Though popular with North Americans, I didn't feel overwhelmed by the presence of my fellow continentals, and plenty of Europeans stay here, too. There are thirty-three rooms in the main building and five additional ones in the annex, which is just a short distance away. Each room is different, though all feature quality period furnishings (mine had beautiful parquet floors, a large bed with a gorgeous bedspread, and a lovely bathroom). The hotel is much larger than it appears from the outside, and it took me a good five minutes to make my way from the reception to my room, even after I learned the way (I had to walk through several public rooms

and traverse up and down small flights of stairs). There are lovely touches throughout the Loggiato, like the red rope hand-rail on the stairway to the second floor (beautiful against the yellowish wall), antique armoires, and thick Oriental rugs (though I wish the flowers in the urns were real). Breakfast is a convivial affair, with lots to choose from on the buffet as a waiter takes your order for tea or *caffè*. Rooms go quickly at Loggiato, and it's easy to see why: it offers a great price-quality ratio and it's in a very desirable neighborhood.

- Palazzo Niccolini al Duomo (Via dei Servi 2/+39 055 282 412/niccolinidomepalace.com). If a view of the Duomo is what you've always dreamed of in a Florentine hotel, you can't get any closer to it than the Niccolini; in some of the rooms (notably the honeymoon suite, Galileo, with a view all the way up to Fiesole and San Miniato), you feel you can almost reach out and touch it. The fascinating history of this unique lodging is detailed on its Web site, so I won't repeat much of it here except to say that the palazzo was originally built by the Naldini family, an important one noted for its merchants, bankers, and soldiers. In 1879, the last of the Naldini, Cristina, married Marchese Eugenio Niccolini di Camugliano, and the palazzo was brought into this other distinguished family, who still owns it today. What I find especially noteworthy is that during the building of the Duomo most of the houses in the area of what is now Piazza del Duomo were demolished—with the exception of those at the northeastern corner of the newly created piazza, some of which became part of the Palazzo Niccolini. Some of the original buildings served as workshops for Floren-tine artists, including Donatello (you can see the bust of Do-natello and an inscription on the façade of the palazzo facing the Duomo).

You might think that, being right on the Piazza del Duomo, noise would be a problem; however, to reach the guest rooms of

the Palazzo Niccolini you have to walk through a covered passageway to an inner courtyard, and from there you take the elevator up to the second-floor reception (though you may not be able to immediately grasp it, the palazzo literally wraps around the entire corner of the piazza, and all seven rooms are quiet). Guests are greeted by an antique table with beautiful fresh flowers and scented diffusers by Antica Officina del Farmacista (for more about this Florentine company, see page 511). It's a lovely welcome, and when you peek past the reception desk to the drawing room (where breakfast is served), you'll pinch yourself to make sure you aren't dreaming.

A recent renovation by the current owners, Ginevra and Filippo Niccolini di Camugliano, has really emphasized the beautiful colors on the painted ceilings and the trompe l'oeil frames around the frescoes. Every public room and every guest room is just gorgeous and very elegant, yet comfortable, too—you really feel like you're in a private home. And in a way you really are: staff members, including the wonderful and spirited Ginevra, are only there from eight a.m. to nine p.m. The guest rooms are all large and have high ceilings, and, somewhat unusually, the hotel is air-conditioned throughout. The ample breakfast includes an assortment of cereals, juice, yogurt, cheese, particularly yummy pound cake, and baked goods. Even though the palazzo is furnished in a centuries-old style, modern services are in abundance—including an Internet corner in the salon—and the resourceful staff can arrange just about anything guests desire. The Niccolini address is an elegant place to stay in an unbeatable location.

• Residenze Johanna I and II, Johlea, Antica Johlea, and Antica Dimora Firenze (various addresses, three on Via San Gallo, all in the vicinity of Piazza San Marco/johanna.it). Partners Lea Gulmanelli and Johanan Vitta are the proprietors of this quintet of charming *residenze,* all within a few blocks of each other near Piazza San Marco. Each *residenza* occupies a portion of a floor in an old palazzo, so guests feel more like residents in a building—you're given a set of keys for the portal, entrance hall, and main door, as well as one for your individual room. Bedrooms are inviting and furnished with old, quality pieces, and each *residenza* has cozy sitting rooms; Antica Johlea also has a great rooftop terrace. Johanna I and II, the originals in this family of *residenze,* are the farthest away from the city center, but with such affordable prices they are worth the longer walk or taxi ride. The newest *residenza* in the group, Antica Dimora Firenze, is the jewel in the crown. The six double rooms are painted in pastel colors and are, as Gulmanelli explained, decorated the way she would want rooms in her own home to feel—stylish and comfortable. Antica Dimora is priced a little higher but also has more amenities, such as a full and very nice breakfast (only instant coffee and packaged biscuits are provided at the other residences), direct-dial telephones, satellite television with DVD, Internet connection, and handwoven linens and silk fabrics. Guests who prefer to stay at full-service hotels may not find these *residenze* to their taste (no concierge after seven-thirty p.m.; no credit cards accepted), but they represent one of the best values in the city. And visitors who may wish to stay in the surrounding Chianti countryside may be happy to know about Antica Dimora's cousin, Villa Il Poggiale, in San Casciano in Val di Pesa, seventeen kilometers from Florence (villail poggiale.it). The fourteenth-century villa was once owned by the Ricasoli-Rucelai family, and has rooms, suites, apartments, and a swimming pool. I stay at one of these residences every time I go to Florence, and every person I've recommended these to has thoroughly enjoyed them.

• Torre di Bellosguardo (Via Roti Michelozzi 2/+39 055 229 8145/torrebellosguardo.com). Bellosguardo. I just love saying the name. And I love daydreaming about Bellosguardo. And

hardly a day goes by that I don't wish I were there (on the other days I'm wishing I were at Le Sirenuse, in Positano, which currently gets my vote for best hotel in the world). *Bellosguardo* (meaning "beautiful view") may be an understatement, as the view of Florence from up here is astonishing, taking in every single Florentine monument and without doubt the very best view of the city anywhere (Piazzale Michelangelo isn't even a contender). Guido Cavalcanti—a celebrated poet of a noble family and a friend of Dante's—chose the original fortress on this hill, above Porta Romana, to expand upon and create a hunting lodge and home. Later it was confiscated by Cosimo de' Medici, and later still it became the property of the Michelozzi family, who retained it until the end of the sixteenth century, when Galileo reportedly set up his telescope here and scanned the heavens. (After such an illustrious history, it's hard to imagine that Bellosguardo housed German officers in the *torre,* or tower, during World War II, or that it became a boardinghouse and school in the postwar years when the owner, German baroness Marion von Hornstein—who received the property after a divorce settlement from her husband, Giorgio Franchetti—couldn't afford to keep it.) This exquisite villa is still a peaceful respite from the city below, with stunning gar-

dens, a pool, and an avenue of cypresses to greet visitors. To say
it's a special place is yet another understatement. Elizabeth Barrett Browning wrote of it,

From Tuscan Bellosguardo, where Galileo stood at nights to take
The vision of the stars, we have found it hard,
Gazing upon the earth and heavens, to make
A choice of beauty.

Bellosguardo is now owned by Amerigo Franchetti, who, in
1980, decided to return what then was his run-down family inheritance to its former splendor.

When I visit Bellosguardo I am reminded of a passage in Marina Belozerskaya's *The Arts of Tuscany:* the "links between man
and nature, city and countryside, natural and man-made creations have always remained intimate in Tuscany, and endlessly
generative. The countryside is what Tuscans see just beyond
their city walls, traverse as they go to the next town, or look
forward to visiting on the weekend." For when you are looking
out at the panorama from the garden, which is really a series of
terraces that tumble down the hill, or from the second-floor ve-

randa, you see clearly that the city of Florence is encircled by green hills—there is a marked boundary between city and country. If this were a North American city, there would likely be no end in sight of the surrounding sprawl.

The Bellosguardo staff is wonderfully helpful but understands that most guests seek privacy here. Each of the bedrooms (one single, eight doubles, and seven suites) is a little world unto itself—more like a living area than just a bedroom—and each is uniquely appointed with uncommon decorative details and features, like painted wooden beams, gilded four-poster beds, or a sixteenth-century rosette-studded ceiling. Each room has a view, of the city, the garden, or the surrounding countryside. The room beneath the *torre* is the most requested, and the room inside the tower is the most magnificent, on two levels with a sitting room (perfect for a small *festa!*) and views all around. A subterranean sports center, complete with sauna, pool, gym, and Jacuzzi, is a recent addition; breakfast is served on the veranda or in the dining room and often includes seasonal fruit from the orchard. There is no restaurant (though one is being considered) but this is hardly an inconvenience as Florence is a ten-minute cab ride away (or a twenty-minute walk down the footpath). Writer Ken Shulman, in an article in *Vista,* noted

that in those ten minutes "lies all that is unique in this superb hotel. A recent visitor summed up the experience poetically. 'Staying here in Bellosguardo,' she wrote in the guest book, 'is nothing short of touching eternity.' "

At Bellosguardo, you feel from the minute you walk in the front door that you have stepped very far back in Florentine time. "You can feel the history," as one staff member told me. It's incomparable, but it's not luxurious: some of the linen napkins have holes in them, the tables wobble on the terraced veranda, and, on my last visit, outside telephone service was out and my friends didn't have a sufficient supply of hot water in the shower. (And you have to come to terms, or not, with the parrot in the ballroom lobby; on my first visit I didn't know about the parrot, and when it squawked, loudly, I nearly fell over.) But I gladly accept all these (minor) shortcomings for the opportunity to stay at this remarkable haven. In my notes from my last visit, I jotted down, "You don't come here for luxe, chic, or a restaurant. It's all about the view, the tranquility, and hearing the birds sing."

To Rent or Not to Rent?

Renting an apartment or villa might be a suitable choice depending on how long you'll be in the area and the number of people traveling together. I am constantly betwixt and between about renting—I love the idea in theory, but in my rental experiences I've discovered that I end up washing a fair amount of dishes, sweeping or vacuuming the floor, making beds, shopping for food, and generally feeling that I'm only sort of on vacation. Even when there is housekeeping service, it tends to be limited. And at breakfast, really the last thing I want is to make a mediocre pot of coffee in the kitchen and eat an inferior *cornetto* that I invariably had to buy at the local *supermercato* because the previous day wasn't the day of the weekly market or because the villa I rented is a fifteen-minute car ride away. I prefer to start my Italian day with a delicious cappuccino that somebody else made (and that somebody else will clean up) and a fresh, hot *cornetto*. All that said, renting *is* a singular experience and offers joys that can't be had by staying at a hotel. The rental companies I like best are:

• The Best in Italy (+39 055 223 064/thebestinitaly.com), founded by Count and Countess Brandolini d'Adda in 1982 (Contessa Simonetta, who is American-born, also founded the wonderful organization Friends of Florence; see page 538). When the couple began renting their own property near Siena to acquaintances from the United States, Italian friends asked them to rent *their* properties, too, and thus this most impressive portfolio of grand places to rent was born. All properties come with staff and all have pools; some have tennis courts or riding stables; and there is a minimum two-week requirement during high season. In and around Florence there are seven properties; in Chianti there are twelve; in the Siena area there are seven; in Central Tuscany there are six; around Lucca there are four; in the Maremma there are three; and there are six in the Umbria/Rome area. This is an outstanding resource if you're looking for truly exquisite and distinctive lodgings.

- The Parker Company (800 280 2811/parkervillas.com), founded in 1993 and located outside Boston and with an office in Genoa. Parker's motto once was "Italy is all we do and we do it very well," and even if the company doesn't feature it on its Web site or in its material anymore, the motto is the reason I noticed Parker in the first place: Parker has a reputation of being the cherry pickers of the industry. In addition to rentals, the company offers "Actividayz" day trips and cooking classes, a full roster of great tours in Umbria, Tuscany, and Arezzo ranging from half-day to multiday; Parker clients also receive the lowest car rental rates available in Italy.

- Villas d'Italia (509 526 4868/villasditalia.com), family owned since 1983 and now based in Walla Walla, Washington. Proprietors Nick D'Antoni and Lynn Sharp are fully committed to making sure their clients have memorable experiences, and through their partnership with Tuscan Enterprises, a tour operator and travel agent, they offer a great number of properties in Tuscany and Umbria.

"Up at the Tuscan Villa," by Christopher Petkanas (*Travel + Leisure,* June 2009), is a great source for three country properties—Il Borgo on the Castello Banfi estate; Villa Mangiacane in San Casciano; and Castello del Nero in Tavarnelle Val di Pesa—as well as five others under three hundred dollars a night, reviewed by Valerie Waterhouse, the magazine's

Italy correspondent. "The Best Country Hotels of Tuscany," by Heather Smith MacIsaac (*Travel + Leisure,* June 1999), is also worth reading online for its thorough descriptions of four noteworthy inns, plus three less expensive options in Chianti.

IN TUSCANY

• Relais Il Falconiere (Località San Martino a Bocena, Cortona/+39 0575 612 679/ilfalconiere.it). Il Falconiere was really the first country inn to open in Tuscany that lay somewhere between a rustic *agriturismo* and the high-end luxury inn Relais La Suvera, near San Gimignano. (La Suvera [lasuvera.it] is *really* old, dating from 1123, and its interior décor is very eighteenth century.) Il Falconiere is also old, built in 1600, but it's much more stylish in a way that is Tuscan country and modern, refined and simple, at the same time. Silvia and Riccardo Baracchi opened the inn, just outside Cortona, in 1989, and in

1998 it became a member of the Relais & Châteaux group. It is aptly named—the house or coop for falcons—as falcons are found in Tuscany (though they are not as numerous today as they once were) and Silvia has one of her own, named Lilo. Several buildings make up the inn, and the main villa was the *buen ritiro* (the equivalent of a country house) of poet Antonio Guadagnoli in 1848, about whom I've not been able to learn much except that he was from Arezzo. Most of the guest rooms—eleven classical rooms, two deluxe rooms, four junior suites, and three suites—are in individual buildings, which contributes to the sense of privacy, but even in the building with multiple accommodations (the *villa padronale*) tranquility reigns. The whole feels a bit like you're guests at someone's country estate, which I think is precisely what Silvia and Riccardo intend. Guest rooms are all elegantly furnished in a country style, though each is unique in color palette and décor. Some beds are four-poster, others are wrought iron with textured spreads, and other features like *cotto* tile floors, old wooden chests, antique painted cupboards, Oriental rugs, gorgeously upholstered chairs, some fireplaces, and painted stone walls combine to create an atmosphere that is very warm and sunny, supremely comfortable and informal. I especially like that there is an old family chapel sandwiched between two suites; the chapel's serene interior boasts frescoes that are quite beautiful. There are two pools on the grounds, and the Thesan Etruscan spa opened in 2009, offering a Turkish bath, sauna, hydrotherapy massages, and a full menu of facial and body treatments. In one of the rooms there is a beautiful stone tablet that was a gift from Frances Mayes.

The hotel's restaurant, in the old *limonaia,* is presided over by Chef Richard Titi and earned a Michelin star in 2002. Not only was the seasonal lunch I had here one of the best meals I've eaten anywhere in Italy, it was also among the best I've ever had. The presentation of every dish was worthy of a photograph and the service was gracious and professional, never intrusive or perfunctory—every person who served us seemed to genuinely care what we thought about each course. The miniature dessert assortment was delicious and brilliant: it solves the problem of trying to decide what to order since diners may try them all. Vegetarians are well taken care of—a kitchen garden is the source for most of the vegetables and herbs on the menu—and Titi is known for taking local ingredients and giving them a newfangled twist (one that works). In warm weather meals are served on the outside terrace, which has the advantage of panoramic views, but the two-floor interior rooms are equally lovely: the main dining room features impressive tiled and vaulted ceilings, the private room with five tables features beautiful ceramic plates displayed on the walls, and the intimate "little clocks" room has just one round table. Among the selections on the wine list are those from the family Baracchi winery, (baracchiwinery.com), which is next to the Relais and has been in the family since 1860. Astore Tebbiano, Smeriglio Sangiovese, an Ardito Syrah–Cabernet blend (50–50), and Smeriglio Merlot are made in collaboration with wine consultant Stefano Chioccioli, who was the first Italian winemaker ever to receive 100 points from Robert Parker. Chioccioli, who is Tuscan, uniquely holds degrees in both agronomy and oenology *and* has expertise in both red wine and white, notably the whites at Livio Felluga in Friuli–Venezia Guilia; he also has experience with dessert wines, notably Tenuta di Capezzana's Vin Santo. A master of wine and former sommelier at the Ritz-Carlton Boston, Bill Nesto, noted that in a conversation with Chioccioli in 2003, Chioccioli remarked that he believed the Tuscan *terroir* will become more evident in the flavor of the wines within two generations. "A suitable proverb is never far away when you are speaking to a Tuscan. Chioccioli took his right hand off the steering wheel and waved a finger, pronouncing: '*Il vino che piace al figlio, non piace al padre ed il vino che piace al padre non piace al nonno*' (The wine that appeals to the son does not appeal to the father, and the wine that appeals to the father does not appeal to the grandfather)." I don't know what former generations of the Baracchi family would make of today's newer varieties, but I enjoyed them immensely, including the sparkling Brut Millesimato (which Chioccioli does not consult on), and they are unbeatable matches with the local cuisine. All the wines (which aren't widely available in North America), plus Baracchi grappa and excellent olive oil, are available for sale in the reception office.

When I met Silvia, it was obvious that she is passionate about cuisine—our conversation turned to food so often, and her eyes lit up so brightly whenever she spoke of a particular dish served in the restaurant. She also personally supervises the cooking in the restaurant kitchen with Chef Titi, so it's no coincidence that Cooking Under the Tuscan Sun cooking classes are offered at Il Falconiere. Classes are for two to twelve people, for beginners and experienced cooks, and are taught by Chef Titi in the restaurant kitchen. Classes include Flavors from Our Countryside; Sapore di Sale . . . Sapore di Mare; Pane, Olio e Fantasia; Along the Etruscan Traces; and Wild Flavors from the Forest, which are available as single sessions (three hours with the chef, dinner with the prepared dishes, and wine tasting), three days, or six days. There is also a seven-day wine Grand Tour in Tuscany that includes not only visits to Montalcino and a number of wine estates but also a hands-on cooking lesson. I asked Silvia if she would share a few favorite recipes that are also loved by guests and cooking class students (classes are open to non-guests as well), and she was kind enough to provide the following.

PICI CON POMODORINI ED ERBETTE

Pici is a pasta shape local to the area; to make this with a dried pasta, an acceptable substitute for *pici* is spaghetti.

FOR THE PASTA:
4 gallons water
1¼ cups flour
Pinch of salt

FOR THE SAUCE:
8 tablespoons extra virgin olive oil
2 garlic cloves, chopped
1¼ cups cherry tomatoes, quartered
1 tablespoon aromatic herbs (thyme and marjoram)

Make the pasta: mound the flour on a board and make a well in the center. Into the well add water and slowly mix the flour, adding water from time to time as the dough comes together. You are aiming for a soft but not sticky mix, but don't worry if the dough is stiff, as it will relax while it rests. Form the dough into a ball, cover loosely with plastic wrap, and set aside for 20 minutes.

Cut the dough into very thin pieces. Roll each piece into a snake about ¼ inch in diameter and 30 inches long. Continue until all the dough has been cut and rolled.

Heat the olive oil over medium-high heat in a saucepan with chopped garlic until the garlic is soft but not brown. Add the cherry tomatoes and salt and pepper.

Cook rapidly, stirring occasionally. Add the aromatic herbs.

Bring a large pot of lightly salted water to a rolling boil and drop in the *pici*.

Boil the *pici* until they rise to the top, then remove them with a slotted skimmer and transfer them into the pan with the sauce. Add a handful of grated (or shaved with a vegetable peeler) aged pecorino cheese. Serve immediately.

PINZIMONIO ETRUSCO WITH BREAD, VINEGAR, AND HONEY SAUCE

10 SERVINGS

3 artichokes
5 spring onions
2 bell peppers
1 bunch of celery
5 carrots
4 pears and 4 apples
1 fennel bulb
4 tomatoes

FOR THE SAUCE:
13 ounces bread crumbs
½ cup red wine vinegar
½ cup raisins
½ cup pine nuts
2 cups olive oil
A little less than one ounce of ginger, grated
1 teaspoon honey
Salt and black pepper

Rinse all vegetables and fruit and cut them into bite-size pieces or in sizes suitable for dipping. Place them in a bowl of ice water with lemon juice added to prevent discoloration.

Meanwhile, combine bread and vinegar in a bowl and let sit for 30 minutes. In another bowl, soften raisins in lukewarm water for 15 minutes.

Combine soaked bread and raisins together with pine nuts in a mixer, gently adding olive oil, grated ginger, and honey; season with salt and pepper. Stir well until the sauce is well blended and homogeneous. [Note: I combine the bread and raisins in a blender, scrape the mixture into a bowl with a rubber spatula, and stir in the oil, ginger, honey, salt, and pepper.]

Fill a ceramic bowl with the vegetables and fruit and place it inside a larger bowl filled with ice. [Note: this will keep the vegetables and fruit crisp longer but isn't essential, I've found, if this will be eaten right away.] Fill a small bowl with the dipping sauce and place it within easy reach of the fruit and vegetables.

Il Falconiere set new trends in Tuscan hospitality in many ways, and I have included it here not because it's a secret—it has certainly received much publicity and numerous awards, including *Condé Nast Traveler's* Top 100 Southern Europe Hotels

2008, *Travel + Leisure's* World's Best Hotels 2008, and this note from *Condé Nast Traveller* UK (July 2009), with which I whole-heartedly agree: "Despite its Michelin star, Il Falconiere is not resting on its laurels; it's money well spent"—but because Silvia and Riccardo have continued to be innovative, savvy innkeep-ers. Il Falconiere has been, I believe, a model for numerous inns that have opened throughout the region and elsewhere in Italy, but its style and success are not easily imitated.

- Silvia and Riccardo also opened Locanda del Molino (Località Montanare 10/+39 0575 614 054/locandadelmolino.com), also a few kilometers from Cortona, in the spring of 2008. The property, with an old mill (*molino*), had belonged to Silvia's par-ents, who retired at the end of 2007. There are now seven guest rooms and one suite, each individually decorated by Silvia in the style of the Cortona countryside, overlooking the Esse creek. The rooms are all inviting and charming—each is filled with lots of antiques, wrought-iron beds, and wooden furni-ture; they simply lack the same level of sophistication as the rooms at Il Falconiere. The restaurant, too, is very much a country place—Silvia likes to refer to the cuisine as "simple and genuine, but never ordinary"—and features mostly traditional dishes with locally sourced ingredients. Just as at Il Falconiere, a number of cooking classes are offered with the restaurant's chefs, Nulvia and Simona (a few are Traditional Tuscan Food; Bread, Olive Oil, and Fantasy; and The Fragrance of Seasonal Vegetables). Also at the inn is La Bottega, a newly created old-fashioned country market-cum-restaurant larder. Visitors may taste and purchase culinary specialties used in the restaurant's kitchen, such as local salami, cheeses, jams, honey, olive oil, and Baracchi wines. With Locanda's garden and pool, an outdoor terrace where meals are served in warm weather, and rooms ac-commodating to both families and visitors looking for a ro-mantic stay, Silvia and Riccardo have once again established a winning inn that is a very good value.

IN UMBRIA

• Le Vigne (six miles from Perugia in the village of Colombella/+39 075 691 9307/levigne.net). Le Vigne, owned by Joan and Roger Arndt (introduced previously in the Umbria section; see page 229), is a *porzione di colonica*—a separate residence and entrance within a larger building (the Arndts live downstairs and the apartment is up a stone staircase on the side of the house)—and a lovely self-catered apartment with four bedrooms and three bathrooms. Le Vigne sits atop a hill with spectacular panoramic views all around, and in the center of the front portion of the property is a large, inviting swimming pool. The bedrooms in the apartment, all named after the color they're painted, are very appealing and stylish. The central room has a big fireplace, the open kitchen has a large table capable of seating a crowd and is equipped with every single culinary item one could possibly need or imagine—in fact, when Joan and Roger use the words "fully furnished" to describe Le Vigne, it's no exaggeration: they have thought of the smallest detail in every room. They also have employed an ingenious system for the windows, which are all screened (!) and have blinds that open and close carefully to allow for a breeze and privacy.

The Arndts will assist with planning itineraries, arranging for airport transfers, hiring guides, arrange cooking classes at Le Vigne, and just about anything guests desire. And they don't just say hello and hand you a key—they will join you in meals at local restaurants, accompany you to Umbrian locales, or take you to shops where they know the owners. Or they'll quietly disappear if you prefer to be alone.

Le Vigne is available only for weekly rentals—5,200 euros for four guests, and 6,600 euros for more than four—from the second week of March through the first week in November. Other amenities include air-conditioning, satellite TV, free Wi-Fi, a DVD player, a washing machine and dryer, a safe, and tennis and bocce courts.

A good book to buy, for about ten euros, is *Cortona: A Guide to the City*, by Enrico Aretini (Aros Comunicazione, 2008), which is widely available in Cortona and in other Tuscan towns. It's a good guidebook and souvenir as it's filled with maps, fairly descriptive text, and color photographs, but it also features some places to stay in the area that I haven't run across elsewhere. These include Alla Corte del Sole (corte delsole.com), Villa Baldelli (villabaldelli.it), La Corte dei Papi (www.lacortedeipapi.com), Corys Hotel (corys.it), Villa Petrischio (villapetrischio.it), Villa Marsili (villamar sili.net), and Portole (portole.it).

La Foce

La Foce—"the meeting place"—is aptly named as it was originally a tavern "strategically placed at the crossing of two roads that had been used continuously for many centuries. It was built in 1498 by the greatest Sienese landowner of the time, the Hospital of Santa Maria della Scala," note the authors of *La Foce: A Garden and Landscape in Tuscany* (University of Pennsylvania Press, 2001). One of the roads was the Via Francigena, the road that connected Canterbury with

Rome, which allowed pilgrims to travel between these two great sanctuaries of Christianity: Canterbury in England and Saint Peter's in Rome. The authors of this La Foce book (which is one volume in the *Penn Studies in Landscape Architecture* series and comes with a color

foldout map at the back of the book) are Morna Livingston, Laurie Olin, John Dixon Hunt, and Benedetta Origo. Benedetta Origo is the daughter of Iris Origo, author of one of the ten best books I've ever read, *War in Val d'Orcia: An Italian War Diary, 1943–1944* (David Godine, 1984; originally published 1947). So I admit I came to La Foce as an accommodation choice because of the book, and not the other way around.

In brief, Iris Origo is of Anglo-American descent; her mother was Lady Sybil Marjorie Cuffe and her father was William Bayard Cutting, secretary of the U.S. embassy to the Court of St. James. (Cutting's grandfather, Robert, was Robert Fulton's partner in the ferry operation from Brooklyn to New York, and Bayard continued to operate the ferry system of New York City and Brooklyn; today the Bayard Cutting Arboretum [bayardcuttingarboretum.com] can be visited on Long Island.) In 1910, after Cutting's death, Sybil bought Villa Medici in Fiesole, where Iris grew up, and in 1918 married Geoffrey Scott. Iris married Marchese Antonio Origo, and they bought La Foce, near Montepulciano, Chianciano, Pienza, and Sarteano, in 1924; they then hired Cecil Pinsent (whom Iris knew from work he'd done at Villa Medici and at Bernard Berenson's I Tatti) to enlarge the house and farm. Origo recounts how La Foce grew, and what happened there over the fifty years they owned it, in *Images and Shadows: Part of a Life* (John Murray, 1998) and *War in Val d'Orcia*.

In addition to my own endorsement of *War in Val d'Orcia,* I will share one that is perhaps better: I was holding a copy in my hands while on line at the Rizzoli bookstore in New York, and a man behind me asked me if I'd read the book. I replied that I had, and that I was buying this copy for my

friend Amy for her birthday. He was thrilled that I was already familiar with the book, and said, "I think Iris Origo is one of the most significant human beings of the twentieth century." It took me only a second to agree, which prompted the woman on line behind this gentleman to walk over to the

information desk and ask if the store had another copy in stock. I love when that happens, and now one more person knows about Iris Origo.

Today the nine hundred hectares of La Foce are run by Iris and Antonio's two daughters, Benedetta and Donata. Eleven farmhouses have been restored with care and are available for rent. Each accommodates a different number of guests, and each is unique. The view from almost every spot on the estate is breathtaking, overlooking undulating rows of cypress trees and the Crete Senesi (literally translated as "Siennese clays," referring to a landscape that is often described as lunar), which has the distinction of being the most photographed spot in all of Tuscany. The formal garden at La Foce is open to the general public every Wednesday from three to six p.m., but reservations are required. (La Foce, Strada della Vittoria 61, Chianciano Terme, Siena/+39 0578 69 101/lafoce.com). (See my blog for an interview with Benedetta.)

Tuscany and Umbria are filled with many wonderful, historic, and beautiful places to stay, but very few are tied so intimately with fairly recent historic events. In 1944, Origo concluded the diary she kept by saying:

> *I believe in individuals, and in the relationship of individuals to one another. When I look back upon these years of tension and expectation, of destruction and sorrow, it is individual acts of kindness, courage, or faith that illuminate them; it is in them that I trust. I remember a British prisoner of war in the Val d'Orcia helping the peasant's wife to draw water from the well, with a ragged, beaming small child at his heels. I remember the peasant's wife mending his socks, knitting him a sweater, and baking her best cake for him, in tears, on the day of his departure.*
>
> *These—the shared, simple acts of everyday life—are the realities on which international understanding can be built. In these, and in the realization that has come to many thousands, that people of other nations are, after all, just like themselves, we may, perhaps, place our hopes.*

Other books (most of them reissued editions) by Iris Origo include *A Need to Testify: Portraits of Lauro de Bosis, Ruth Draper, Gaetano Salvemini, and Ignacio Silone and an Essay on Biography* (Harcourt, 1984), *Leopardi: A Study in Solitude* (originally published in 1935; Helen Marx edition, 2000), *The Merchant of Prato: Francesco di Marco Datini, 1335–1410* (Knopf, 1957; David Godine, 1986, 2002), and *The Last Attachment: The Story of Byron and Teresa Guiccioli* (Helen Marx, 2000).

Allegories of Good and Bad Government,
by Ambrogio Lorenzetti

Iris Origo, in *The Merchant of Prato,* notes that if we want to have some idea of what merchant Marco Datini's own farms and peasants looked like—and those of every other in the vicinity—we need only look at Lorenzetti's *The Good Rule* in Siena's Palazzo Pubblico: "The Pistoiese hills, then as now, were greener than Lorenzetti's *crete senesi,* but the crops were the same: wheat, oil, and wine—the Biblical products, the food of all men of Mediterranean stock." This fresco is in a room known as Sala dei Nove (Hall of the Nine Rulers), which is adorned with a cycle of frescoes from the Middle Ages painted for the *comune* by Lorenzetti in 1337–39. The scenes depicted were chosen by the Governo dei Nove (The Nine Rulers), all wealthy merchants who wanted a grandiose work to represent the good effects of their own administration. The frescoes represent "The Allegory and the Effects of Good Government in Town and in the Country" and "The Allegory and the Effects of Bad Government." I love looking at these frescoes (as well as the Simone Martini works in the Palazzo Pubblico) not only because they are the work of the Sienese painter known as the first interpreter of landscapes as subjects for his compositions but also because the Sienese countryside in his paintings still looks remarkably similar today.

Antica Officina del Farmicista Dr. Vranjes

I notice right away when I walk into a room and it smells nice. I'm not referring to a kitchen, where you might smell something good cooking on a stove, but rooms like lobbies, foyers, bedrooms, living rooms, and bathrooms. Nice-smelling rooms are not unique to Italy—one of my best scent memories is at a lovely inn on the island of Corsica called La Signoria (hotel-la -signoria.com), where all the guest rooms smell incredibly intoxicating (but even there I was told to keep it a secret that the room fragrance was Italian, not French!). A nice-smelling room instantly puts me in a great mood, and Dr. Paolo Vranjes pioneered the idea of glass bottles filled with essential oils and bamboo reeds to diffuse the scent throughout a space. You may have seen other bottles filled with other reeds sold at various retailers in the States, but these scents have almost nothing in common with the clean, fresh scents created by Vranjes.

Though the word *farmacista* ends in an *a,* usually a feminine ending in Italian, it refers to both men and women; Vranjes is male. Originally from Bologna, Vranjes was drawn to Florence because of its tradition of artisans' workshops, and he launched Antica there in 1983. Trained as a pharmacist, chemist, and cosmetologist, he originally created room fragrances based on the four elements, *acqua, aria, fuoco,* and *terra.* Now he has many more appealing scents, including several in a recent collection named Italian Fruit and Flowers. I've tried a great number in various rooms in my house, and my favorite is pomegranate. Spray diffusers are also offered, as well as candles and body lotions.

The Vranjes showroom is located at Borgo La Croce 44r (+39 055 241 748) and the laboratory shop is at Via San Gallo 63r (+39 055 494 537). I've only been to the shop on Via San Gallo, which is very attractive. I've been able to replenish my supplies in New York at Aedes de Venustas (Latin for "Temple of Beauty," 9 Christopher Street/212 206 8674/aedes.com) and Takashimaya (693 Fifth Avenue/212 350 0100/takashimaya-ny.com); the selection in the Florence shops, however, is much broader, and the bottles are offered in additional sizes—notably small ones about three inches tall. Visit Dr. Vranjes online at Drvranjes.it.

B

Bargello Museum

The Museo Nazionale del Bargello (Via del Proconsolo 4/+39 055 238 8606/polomuseale.firenze.it/musei/bargello) is one museum in Florence I only recently visited, for the very first time. You may hear many people declare it is their favorite museum in the city, and now I finally understand why: it's a true gem. The

building has served as a police headquarters and as a prison: neither seems like a good fit for its function today, housing an outstanding cache of Renaissance sculpture. But there is nothing grim about the interior, and the inner courtyard is so beautiful I could sit in it all day long. Don't miss it if at all possible, but keep in mind its hours (which is one reason it took me seven visits to see it): it's open 8:15 a.m. to 1:50 p.m., but closed the first, third, and fifth Sunday of the month, and the second and fourth Monday of the month.

Baroni Alimentari

The Baroni counter in the Mercato Centrale was initially recommended to me by Faith Willinger, and ever since then I make sure to stop by and replenish my supplies of olive oil, balsamic vinegar, and *mostarda*—a jellylike paste that is typically spread on bread and eaten to accompany cheese—when I find myself in Florence. Baroni is a family-run business that's been in the same family since 1974 (the company was started by another family in the early 1900s). It's a great place to do some outstanding one-stop culinary shopping: there are cheeses, wines, *salumi*, pasta, condiments, sauces, fish, Amedei chocolates, and much more. On my last visit, I bought sets of small bottles of balsamic vinegar, each bottle aged for differing years, and these were a big hit as gifts (and, of course, I kept one for myself). And I stocked up on my two favorite kinds of *mostarda*, pear and red pepper. The first time I had *mostarda* was on a *panino* at Cantinetta di Verrazzano (Via dei Tavolini 18–20r/verrazzano.com); it was composed of a piece of focaccia spread with red pepper *mostarda* and topped with a slice of pecorino cheese, grated orange rind, and a few twists of ground black pepper. I make up platters of these *panini* for party appetizers and guests are always surprised at how delicious they are.

Beh

Time spent sitting at a *caffè* listening to Italians talk is always worthwhile, and in the course of listening you will likely hear the exclamation *beh!* spoken more than once. Michael Tucker, author of *Living in a Foreign Language: A Memoir of Food, Wine, and Love in Italy*, says it's his favorite Italian expression. It's pronounced very quickly, not long and drawn out as if you were saying "bey," more like saying "boo!" As Tucker says, "It means anything and everything." It could be translated as, " 'Nothing's changed; my life is the same old shit; but I'd be a fool to complain about it.' It's usually matched with a gesture; you can pick from a long list."

Biscotti

Biscotti is the generic Italian word for biscuits—or dry, crunchy cookies—and it is plural for *biscotto,* derived from the Latin word *biscoctum,* "twice baked." The origins of biscotti can be traced back to the Roman legions, who took the biscuits with them on their various far-flung missions (most biscotti even today have a long shelf life as they are still shaped into a log and baked, then sliced, and baked again to dry out). They bear a great resemblance to Eastern European *mandelbrot,* German *zwieback,* and Greek *paximadia,* but none of these others are quite as popular. According to *The Nibble,* an online magazine about specialty foods, biscotti emerged in Tuscany sometime during the Renaissance, and a Tuscan baker was credited with serving them with local sweet wine (*vin santo*). Biscotti di Prato are considered the standard from which all other versions of biscotti are de-

rived, and the company Antonio Mattei is considered the best biscotti baker in Tuscany and indeed in all of Italy (Via Ricasoli 20, Prato/+39 057 425 756/antoniomattei.it). Two other Prato bakeries—Leonardo Santi and Luca Mannori—are also reputable biscotti producers, creating versions which differ by being more or less crispy, crumbly, tender, or crunchy, and seeming to validate the ancient proverb "The Pratese alone know how to make fabrics and biscuits."

Biscotti are sometimes referred to as *cantucci* or *cantuccini*, and this can be a bit confusing, but really isn't: *cantucci* are a type of biscotti; original *cantucci* are made with fennel seeds, and once were a Tuscan farmer's breakfast. Biscotti are sweeter and heavier, made with almonds, and were traditionally served as a dessert. However, a long time ago biscotti acquired the name of *cantucci*, so the names became interchangeable. To add another layer of confusion, within Prato the biscotti are also known as *mattonelle*, which is the word for "brick" but could also be derived from *Mattei*, according to Angela Giancaterino, who showed me around the bakery.

Antonio Mattei first established himself in 1858 at an open-air stand with a sign—BISCOTTINI DI PRATO—which you can see in an old photograph that hangs in the shop, which is beautiful, with its oak counter and numerous framed medals and awards, including one from the Exposition Universelle de Paris dated July 1, 1867. Francesco Pandolfini and his sisters, whose aristocratic family dates back to the Renaissance, represent the third generation of the family that has owned and managed Mattei since their grandfather acquired it in the early 1900s. On September 8, 2008, the company celebrated its 150th anniversary—if you look through to the bakery from the counter you can see a huge

photograph of the employees in front of the shop throwing bags and boxes of biscotti up into the air in celebration!

The distinctive taste of Mattei's biscotti comes from the addition of both almonds and pine nuts and lots of egg yolks, and though the mixing and cutting of the biscuits are done by machine (they've been cut by *taglierina*—the machine—

since 1967), the shaping of the dough into logs is still done by hand, as is the packing, in those eye-catching blue bags. Staff tie a green string around the bag if it contains only biscotti, and a red one if it contains both biscotti and *brutti ma buoni* ("ugly but good"), another specialty made with egg whites and almonds with a papery wafer on the bottom. These, like a few other specialties, such as Mantovana cake and *filone candito,* are too fragile for shipping, so a visit to the shop is essential if you want to taste them! (Believe me, you want to.) Mattei also bakes crispy toasts of *biscotti della salute* and a number of terrific items in its new Deseo Toscana line, including shortbread cookies, assorted *cantuccini,* and *biscotti salati da aperitivo,* light savory biscuits made with ground almonds that are outstanding with before-dinner drinks. The Pandolfinis recommend pairing their biscotti only with Tenute Marchese Antinori *vin santo* (made with grapes exclusively from the three Antinori estates in Chianti Classico and introduced in 1987), also sold in the shop.

When you get home and your supply of Mattei biscotti runs out, I encourage you to make your own. It's not difficult—the key is to make sure your hands are very well floured as the dough is quite sticky—and excellent recipes are those found in Corby Kummer's *The Joy of Coffee* (Houghton Mifflin, 2003, revised edition) and *Biscotti,* by Lou Siebert Pappas (Chronicle, 1992).

Bookstores

General bookstores are great, but specialty booksellers are even better. Specialty booksellers understand that the best kind of travelers are interested in books about art, cuisine, and history, as well as biographies, walking guides, novels, maps, phrase books, and memoirs. So they offer all of these in one place, and more. Sadly, some of my favorite bookstores are no longer around, but here are a few that still are and that I highly recommend. All do a brisk mail-order business:

- American Book Exchange, also known as Abe Books, (abe books.com) is a great source for out-of-print books.
- The Complete Traveller (199 Madison Avenue, New York/ 212 685 9007/ctrarebooks.com). About ten years ago, the longtime owners of this wonderful store decided to stop selling current travel guides and fill its shelves with out-of-print and rare travel editions instead. Original Baedeker's guides and the beautifully illustrated A&C Black travel books—originally known as the *Twenty Shillings* series—can usually be found here, as well as volumes for under a hundred dollars and some that are worth thousands.
- Idlewild (12 West 19th Street, New York/212 414 8888/ idlewildbooks.com) is a relatively new store named after the original name for New York's John F. Kennedy International Airport. Owner David Del Vecchio, previously a press officer for a United Nations humanitarian agency, likes to say that "idle and wild are nicely associated with travel."
- Kitchen Arts & Letters (1435 Lexington Avenue, New York/212 876 5550/kitchenartsandletters.com) is one of North America's premier stores devoted exclusively to food and wine, and there are lots of hard-to-find titles here—especially those published overseas—but the store also sells titles that are food- and travel-related.
- Longitude (115 West 30th Street, Suite 1206, New York/ 800 342 2164/longitudebooks.com) is first and foremost a mail-order company, though visitors are welcome at its store-front. Visit the Web site to request its very good catalog and to see the staff's essential reading recommendations for your desti-nation.

Great English-language bookstores in Florence include: BM Bookshop, which is not exclusively English-language, but there are a lot of English and American titles (Borgo Ognissanti 4r/ +39 055 294 575/bmbookshop.com); Libreria Edison, (with four floors, one devoted to languages other than Italian (Piazza della Republica 27r/+39 055 213 110/libreriaedison.it); La Feltrinelli (various locations, including Via Cavour 12 and Via de' Cerratani 30/32r/lafeltrinelli.it); and Paperback Exchange, where owners Emily and Maurizio recently celebrated the store's twentieth anniversary (Via delle Oche 4r/+39 055 293 460/papex.it).

C

Campanilismo

This word is translated loosely as the Italian trait of trusting only that which is within view of the local bell tower. Author Dianne Hales (see Language entry, page 561) perhaps describes this attitude best when she writes that it "treats even folks on the next hilltop as out-of-towners to be viewed with a certain amount of suspicion—and sometimes derision. Northerners scoff at southerners as *terroni* (peasants who work the land). Southerners snipe at northerners as *polentoni* (big eaters of polenta, once standard fare for the *popolo magro*—the skinny or poor people). '*Non fare il genovese*' ('Don't act like someone from Genoa!') I've heard one friend chide another—in other words, don't be cheap. . . . And every time we've headed for Pisa, someone has intoned, '*Meglio un morto in casa che un pisano all'uscio*' ('Better a corpse in the house than a Pisan at the door!'). The Pisans' response: '*Che dio t'accon tenti!*' ('May God grant your wish!')"

Cartiere Miliani Fabriano

Stationer Fabriano (cartierefabriano.it) isn't based in Florence, but it has an outpost here (Via del Corso 59r) in a shop that is bright and airy with unique, colorful items. Just a few purchases I made here are sets of bookmarks with maps of Florence, Rome, Naples, and Venice on one side and matching notebook covers and notepads, as well as folding cards that are blank—for you to fill in with photographs, doodles, swatches of fabric, anything at all—tied at the top with a ribbon that says *La vita è bella*. And I *had* to buy the Fabriano Artist's Journal, even though I am no artist: with its bright red cover and soft, slightly textured pages in twelve different colors ideal for ink, pencil, charcoal, pastels "as well as for your every intellectual whim," it is hugely inspiring and ridiculously appealing.

Cassoni

Cassoni (plural for "large chests") refers specifically to painted wedding chests, which were popular in other parts of Italy but reached a pinnacle in Tuscany (notably Florence and Siena) in the fifteenth century. Marriages during Renaissance times—which were almost always arranged—had everything to do with improving one's station in life, by wealth or power, and seldom had much to do with love. A wedding that joined two prominent families called for as much opulence as possible, and thus the decoration of *cassoni,* which usually held the bride's dowry, was elevated to a task of great importance. *Cassoni* were most often made in pairs and usually painted with historical and allegorical scenes; they were paraded through the streets when the bride moved into the house of her new husband. *Cassoni* were functional as well as decorative, but they were exclusively for wealthy patrons, as a pair of chests could cost as much as a laborer's annual wage.

The first *cassone* I ever saw was one in the collection of the Metropolitan Museum of Art, *Conquest of Trebizond* by Marco del Buono, and I was completely smitten by it. This *cassone* was apparently recovered from the Palazzo Strozzi in Florence and is believed to have been made circa 1475. In the same room as this *cassone,* by the way, is a magnificent *desco da parto*—wooden childbirth tray—which derives from the custom of presenting sweetmeats to new mothers. It's called *Triumph of Fame* and was painted by Giovanni di Ser Giovanni, younger brother of Masaccio and more commonly known as Lo Scheggia. The tray dates from 1449 and celebrates the birth of Lorenzo de' Medici. The image featured on the front of the tray is taken from Boccaccio's *L'Amorosa visione* and Petrarch's *Trionfi*. The painting shows knights on horseback with their arms extended in salute to a figure of Fame, who holds a sword and a cupid while standing on a globe with winged trumpets. On the reverse side are the coats of arms of the Medici and Tornabuoni families; Piero de' Medici married Lucrezia Tornabuoni in 1444, and Lorenzo was their first son. This stunning tray is an object of unique historical importance, as befits the star subject of the Renaissance, Lorenzo de' Medici. He kept it in his private quarters in the Medici palace in Florence, and it is believed to be the largest and most opulent surviving birth tray.

In October 2008, the Isabella Stewart Gardner Museum and the John and Mable Ringling Museum of Art mounted an exhibit entitled The Triumph of Marriage: Painted *Cassoni* of the Renaissance, which unfortunately I missed, but happily there was a book by the same name published in conjunction with the exhibit (Periscope, 2008). The authors—Cristelle Baskins, Adrian W. B. Randolph, Jacqueline Marie Musacchio, and Alan Chong—note that "to look closely at *cassoni* is to see triumphal processions based on literature and history as well as on parades of the time, whether the annual Palio in Florence and Siena or Emperor Frederick III's triumphal entries into Italian cities. Considered in a historical perspective, *cassoni* resemble the sculpted reliefs of triumphal processions still visible on ancient monuments like the Arch of Titus in Rome. *Cassoni* should be recognized as indispensable to the wider revival of ancient culture that defined the Renaissance."

Children

Italy is very welcoming to younger visitors and it shouldn't be at all difficult to plan a fun and rewarding trip for kids of any age. There are many more resources available to parents now than there were ten years ago, when I was compiling my first Tuscany and Umbria edition. A few recommended sources are *Frommer's Tuscany and Umbria With Your Family,* Stephen Keeling and Donald Strachan (in the *With Your Family* series, updated regularly); *Have Kid, Will Travel: 101 Survival Strategies for Vacationing with Babies and Young Children,* Claire Tristram with Lucille Tristram (Andrews McMeel, 1997), whose best words of advice are: "Above all, don't let a bad moment become a bad day, and don't let a bad day become a bad week"; *Italy with Kids,* Barbara Pape and Michael Calabrese (Open Road, updated regularly); *Italy's Best with Kids: Extraordinary Places to Eat, Sleep, & Play,* Debra Levinson (Max Publications, 2004); and the Web site Travel With Your Kids (travelwithyourkids.com). But without a doubt, the very best resource I've ever come across is P. L. Byrne's *Italy Discovery Journal: Adventures for Kids 6–16* (KidsEurope, 2006). I wish a work like this existed for every destination on earth (happily, she also has one for Great Britain!). The journal is for kids traveling in Italy and their parents. It's filled with suggestions for small and big kids, boys and girls, and kids interested in stuff like cars or rocks or fashion. And it's just terrific, *essenziale.*

As Byrne notes in her introduction, "Our best advice is to let your vacation unfold as you discover *your* Italy, not ours, not the guidebook's, but an experience that contains things you love, ad-

ventures you have, and wonderful, warm memories for your souvenirs." Not only does Byrne offer this journal, she also sells Italian playing cards, Italy stickers to embellish the journal or a
scrapbook, euro coin sets, Italy souvenir cards, and even Italian
bingo, *tombola*. Visit her outstanding Web site (kidseurope.com),
where you can also register to receive her free travel newsletter,
read wonderful testimonials, and simply browse. Be sure to see my
blog also, as I've invited Byrne to share even more Italy travel advice and recommendations.

Chiuso

Not to be confused with *chiesa* (church), *chiuso* means "closed"
and can be one of the most disappointing Italian words you'll
ever encounter. If you have not adjusted your schedule to Italian
time, chances are good you will after seeing just one *chiuso* sign.
Chiuso per ferie (closed for the holiday) can refer to a single day or
to the entire month of August (or at least from August 15 to September 1).

Classics

Italo Calvino, in his thoughtful book *Why Read the Classics?* (Pantheon, 1999), notes that "classics are books which, the more we
think we know them through hearsay, the more original, unexpected, and innovative we find them when we actually read
them." I say, don't postpone joy, then! Reread, or read for the first
time, one of the four Italian classics I consider to be the most significant: *The Autobiography of Benvenuto Cellini, The Decameron* by
Giovanni Boccaccio, *The Divine Comedy* by Dante Alighieri, and
The Prince by Niccolò Machiavelli. Cellini's book might not be so
essential for visiting other parts of Italy, but as he was born in Florence in 1500, trained to be goldsmith there, and returned there
after some years in Rome to work for Grand Duke Cosimo in the

latter part of his life, his book seems most appropriate (and his sculpture of Perseus is in the Loggia dei Lanzi in Florence). There are several editions of his autobiography in print, but I'm partial to the recent Everyman's Library edition, a handsome hardcover with an introduction by James Fenton. Everyman's Library also published a new translation of *The Decameron* in 2009, of which I'm particularly fond. Note that Brown University has created an Internet site, Decameron Web (simply Google it), which is "a growing hypermedia archive of materials dedicated to Boccaccio's masterpiece." Machiavelli's *The Prince* is available in numerous editions, but my favorite is Oxford University Press's 2008 *World's Classics* version, translated by Italian scholar Peter Bondanella.

Regarding Dante, Dianne Hales notes in her terrific book *La Bella Lingua* that "more than seven centuries after his birth, Dante still rocks—literally. Bruce Springsteen, Patti Smith, and bands such as Radiohead and Nirvana cite him as an inspiration. They join an exalted chorus of famous fans. . . . No other single piece of literature has generated more research, analysis, commentary interpretations, or adaptations. . . . It wasn't until I spent considerable time in Italy that I realized that Dante had profoundly influenced not just literature but also Italian and Italians. Almost every day I heard echoes of his words." Modern Library has published a hardcover edition of *Inferno* (a new translation by Anthony Esolen) that features illustrations by Gustave Doré, and Everyman's Library published a one-volume edition of *Inferno, Purgatorio,* and *Paradiso* in 1995. Additionally, Anchor issued individual volumes of the *Inferno* (2002), *Purgatorio* (2004), and *Paradiso* (2008), all translated by Robert Hollander and Jean Hollander. Modern Library published a version of the *Inferno* translated by Henry Wadsworth Longfellow and edited and with a preface by Matthew Pearl (2003), whose novel *The Dante Club* (Random House, 2004), is not entirely related as it takes place in Boston, but is certainly respectful of Dante. As an aside, *Dante in*

Love: The World's Greatest Poem and How it Made History, by Harriet Rubin (Simon & Schuster, 2004), is an interesting and inspiring read.

For other classics, a book that was brought to my attention by Dianne Hales is *The Italian Renaissance Reader,* edited by Julia Conaway Bondanella and Mark Musa (Meridian, 1987), which includes excerpts from Francesco Petrarca, Leon Battista Alberti, Leonardo da Vinci, Baldesar Castiglione, Francesco Guicciardini, Michelangelo Buonarroti, Giorgio Vasari, and others. This is a superb book in all respects but is especially appealing to readers who are tentative about reading the classics in their entirety.

Color

I love how the colors of buildings are brighter and brighter the farther south you travel in Italy. (This is true in France, too—in Lyon, the colors are more colorful than they are in Paris but are in pastel shades, and by the time you reach Nice the buildings are flat-out so bold and bright you almost need shades to look at them.) In *Italian Pleasures,* Mark Mitchell describes that on one occasion when his mother visited, in the month of October, she observed that "even on the rainiest and grayest of days the warm colors many of the buildings are painted—cream, mustard, saffron, butterscotch, egg yolk, zabaglione—give the impression of sun upon them." How's that for an enticing description?

D

Dream of Italy

Dream of Italy—one of my favorite phrases—is an award-winning, subscription-only newsletter founded and published by Kathy McCabe, who is a neat person with a huge passion for Italia.

Kathy and I have participated together on panels about Italy (notably one for the Smithsonian) and she has asked me to contribute a few pieces to the newsletter, which I have happily done because I know that *DOI* readers are in love with all things Italian, as am I. Kathy has traveled many times to Tuscany and Umbria, and I asked her to share a few of her favorite things:

- **The Butcher of Panzano.** Dario Cecchini, one of Italy's most famous butchers, has a wonderful butcher shop, Antica Macelleria Cecchini (dariocecchini.com), and now a few eateries in Panzano (Chianti). The shop is usually filled with people buying *bistecca fiorentina* and pork roasts stuffed with local herbs, or standing in little groups drinking wine and nibbling bites of Cecchini's signature meat loaf. Cecchini's other passions include motorcycles and Dante Alighieri, and the charming Renaissance man is happy to discuss both with his customers.

- **Truffle hunting.** Umbrian truffles are prized throughout Italy. Saverio and Gabriella Bianconi of Tartufi Bianconi (tartufibianconi.com) offer a special way to experience these treasured tubers from start to finish, with a truffle-hunting excursion (joining the hunter and his talented dog) followed by truffle-themed cooking lessons and a delicious lunch.

- **Tasting olive oil.** You're sure to be doing some wine tasting in Tuscany; why not sample the local olive oil? My friend Franco Lombardi offers a tasting and tour every Tuesday at his beautiful farm, Pornanino, outside Radda in Chianti (oliveoil.chiantionline.com). This charming man will teach you all you want to know about the liquid sometimes called "green gold."

- **Dining in history.** The dining area of relatively new restaurant Redibis (redibis.it) occupies the curving underground ambulacrum of a first-century Roman amphitheater, so you're eating in the passageway where the gladiators entered the arena. But the setting isn't the only thing that makes Redibis in the Umbrian town of Bevagna a standout: the luscious offerings start with a delicious pecorino pudding with pear or beef carpaccio marinated in salt with a balsamic vinaigrette and Parmesan mousse. Many dishes on the seasonal menu are from the hundred-year-old recipes of the owner's great-grandmother Caterina. They're reinterpreted by an exciting young chef from Emilia-Romagna.

- **Perugia + Chocolate = Perfect Together.** One of Italy's leading chocolate makers, Perugina (maker of the famous Baci candy) is based in the Umbrian capital of Perugia, a city that has quite a reputation for chocolate. At its headquarters, Perugina offers a chocolate school where you can be schooled in *ciocolatto* by a chocolate maestro. Visit the city in October when the streets are filled with chocolate vendors offering tastings (some more unusual than others, like chocolate pasta) as part of the annual Eurochocolate Festival.

- **Another local character, Salvatore Denaro.** Denaro is the owner and spiritual leader of Il Bacco Felice in Foligno (ilbacco felice.it). He is a true practitioner of the Slow Food movement, and many of the fresh meats and vegetables at his trattoria come from Salvatore's own farm outside Bevagna. What he doesn't grow or raise himself, he sources from the very best producers local and beyond. Don't come here expecting a peaceful, staid meal (first hint—the colorful graffiti decorating the walls of this compact space). Don't even expect to choose what you will eat—there is no menu after all. Salvatore will be telling you what you are having. Don't worry: you're in good hands, even if you might be in for a bit of a wild ride.

Dream of Italy is published monthly and is available by mail or electronically. Subscribe online (dreamofitaly.com) and browse this great site—which is one of the very best resources for Italy—for a multitude of tips, stories, ideas, and information on Kathy's terrific travel-planning service, the Italian Dream Concierge.

E

Eating Establishments

An Italian proverb is "In Florence you think, in Rome you pray, and in Venice you love. In all three, you eat," which underscores the high regard in which food and drink are held. Below are a few tips for eating out anywhere in Italy, but please see my blog for a complete, descriptive list of all my recommended places to eat in Florence and throughout Tuscany and Umbria!

The different types of eating and drinking establishments in Italy include:

Enoteca: literally a "wine library or collection" and refers to a wine bar or a wine shop

Fiaschetteria: now sort of an old-fashioned word that once referred to a place both to buy and drink wine; food isn't generally offered at a *fiaschetteria,* which has as synonyms *mescita, bottiglieria,* and *cantina.*

Gelateria: shop or streetside cart selling gelato

Locanda: an inn in the countryside with a casual restaurant serving regional food and wine, dining is sometimes family style

Osteria: according to Italian food writer Maureen B. Fant, the words *osteria* and *hostaria* are both "virtually meaningless" in Italian, as nowadays they are simply another way to say "restaurant." She notes that "etymologically, this is any place with an *oste,* host, meaning landlord, innkeeper, publican, or the like.

Traditionally, this was the place where the neighborhood men would gather for conversation, card games, and wine poured into carafes from a barrel. Food was of secondary importance; often the customers brought their own (this is the origin of the 'bread and cover' charge still in use today)."

Paninoteca: a place that sells *panini* (*panino* is the word for a single sandwich and *panini* is plural).

Pasticceria: a pastry and cookie shop

Pizza al taglio: a more casual storefront operation where pizza is sold in slices (or squares, usually) by weight and is open from midmorning to midafternoon.

Pizzeria: while this may seem obvious, some readers may not know that in Italy, a *pizzeria* refers to a place that's actually a restaurant, serving made-to-order pizza, and usually open only in the evening.

Ristorante: obviously a restaurant, and almost always this will be the most expensive dining choice.

Rosticceria: a place specializing in roast chicken and meat, a *rosticceria* is essentially a deli, but many of them have tables and chairs.

Tavola calda: literally "hot table," with steaming trays filled with pasta, rice, stews, and more

Trattoria: Samuel Chamberlain notes in *Italian Bouquet* that the *trattoria* is a democratic institution that "enters into the life of almost every visitor who stays in Florence for more than a few days. A fundamental difference between a *ristorante*—where the waiters are solicitous and wear white coats, the menus are typewritten, and the tables individual—and a *trattoria* is that in the latter the waiters are in shirtsleeves and often hurried to the point of hysteria, the menus are scrawled in pencil and the public rubs elbows at the same table in a spirit of *camaraderie,* or better. The prices in a *trattoria* are sure to be lower—but the food is often better. This state of affairs explains its extraordinary popularity." This is still basically true today, though some places with *trattoria* in their name are much more expensive than one might expect.

Here are a few more tips on eating in Italy:

- The bread and cover charge noted above is referred to in Italian as *pane e coperto,* and it was originally supposed to cover the cost of bread and the rental of silverware. The fee has ranged from the equivalent of about two to six dollars, which is significant if you've just had a bowl of pasta and a glass of wine. *Pane e coperto* is no longer ubiquitous, but has by no means disappeared.

- As in other European countries, the price for food and drink is different depending on where you sit. You'll notice that Italians mostly stand at the bar, especially in the morning when they down little cups of espresso. If you sit at a table, you can expect to pay up to twice as much—although you can also expect to remain in your seat for as long as you like. In most bars and *caffès* it's customary to pay the cashier first and then take your *scontrino* (receipt) to the counter, where you usually repeat your order. It is also customary to tip the person who hands you your food or drink, usually about fifty centimes or one euro, depending on what you've ordered.

- Don't let the words *menu turistico* necessarily turn you away from a potentially great meal. Just like the *menu del día* in Spain or the *prix fixe* meal in France, the *menu turistico* in Italy is usually a good value, and nearly always includes a carafe or half bottle of wine.

- Some good words of advice from *Cheap Eats in Italy,* by Sandra Gustafson (Chronicle, 1996): "Italians believe that God keeps an Italian kitchen, and so everyone should enjoy *la cucina italiana.* . . . Dealing with Italian waiters is similar to crossing Italian streets: you can do it if you are brazen enough, showing skill and courage and looking all the time as though you own the place. A good waiter should explain the dishes on the menu and help you select the wine. But if you order coffee or tea during the meal, ask for the ketchup bottle, or request a doggie bag . . . watch out, you will be in big trouble."

• *Da portare via* is how you say you want to take food away, like when you're ordering a *panino* (sandwich) from an *alimentari* (combination store and deli also known as a *salsamentario* or *salumeria*). Often, *alimentari* are located next door to a *fornaio* (bakery), so you can count on the bread being good and fresh. Order the filling for your sandwich in two ways: either by the *fette* (number of slices) or by the *etto* (weight, an *etto* being about four ounces).

F

Fare Bella Figura

Often translated as "making a good impression" or "keeping up appearances" or literally "making a good figure," the quote-worthy author Dianne Hales informs that the phrase "goes far beyond these superficialities to describe a refined code of behavior that Italians taught the world."

Fare la Coda

This phrase translates as "to stand in line," but visitors will quickly notice that Italians do not. Ever. As Louise Fili notes in *Italianissimo*, "The concept of forming a line is tedious and boring; the etiquette of waiting has no place in their lives. In other cultures, a queue is a straight, ordered system, but *coda* (literally, 'tail') runs counter to the Mediterranean sense of *libertà*. More like a football huddle, the Italian line is a product of not only a natural desire to be first, but a curiosity about other people's business."

Faro il Ponte

This useful phrase is equivalent to the French *faire le pont,* referring to crossing a bridge, but not literally. It's used when a holiday falls on, say, a Thursday, and means that everyone who can will also take off on Friday and not report back to work until Monday (or Tuesday). It also means that if the pipes have burst at the villa you've rented, you'll have a long wait until they're fixed.

Farro

Farro is an ancient grain that, according to the Web site About Italian Food is "the original grain from which all others derive, and [it] fed the Mediterranean and near Eastern populations for thousands of years." The traditional growing area for *farro* has been Lazio, Umbria, the Marches, and Tuscany, and today Umbria is particularly known for it. (*Farro* is not spelt, by the way, which is similar but usually doesn't have to be soaked first before using.)

I love *farro,* especially the La Valletta brand (available from Gustiamo.com), which I think is a cut above most other brands available in North America. Two of my favorite *farro* recipes are the Farro Salad from *Beaneaters and Bread Soup* by Lori De Mori on page 104 and Paula Wolfert's Creamy Farro and Chickpea Soup on page 65 in *Mediterranean Greens and Grains.*

Ferragamo

The Ferragamo name is not only synonymous with shoes but is also the name of one of the first families of Florence (even though namesake Salvatore Ferragamo—the eleventh child of poor parents—was born in a village near Naples called Bonito). But shoes—oh, what shoes!—are what started it all. Even if you don't fancy yourself much interested in shoes, a visit to the Museo Salvatore Ferragamo (Palazzo Spini Feroni, Via de' Tornabuoni 2; also the home of the Ferragamo boutique) is a must. Here are displayed the original wooden lasts for all the famous women he crafted shoes for, including Ava Gardner, Audrey Hepburn, Ingrid Bergman, the Duchess of Windsor, and Rita Hayworth. You will also see a collection of magnificent shoes crafted from a great variety of materials, including gold kid leather, needlepoint lace, satin, suede, polychrome cotton thread, raffia, hemp, silk, woven grass from the Philippines, cork, crocheted cellophane, sequin, feathers, and cloth covered entirely in Venetian glass beads. "I was born to be a shoemaker," Ferragamo wrote in his autobiography. "I know it; I have always known it. I was born to be a shoemaker, but from where does my knowledge come? It is not inherited: In later years I searched the records of my ancestors through four hundred years. There was no shoemaker among them." There are also numerous movie clips shown at the museum featuring the films in which the stars wore Ferragamo shoes. (He also made all those sandals for the regulars in *The Ten Commandments.*)

Salvatore passed away in 1960, and today the Ferragamo company is still owned and run by family members. Not only shoes, but also jewelry, handbags, belts, scarves, ties, and men's and women's clothing now sport the Ferragamo logo. And naturally, when the Ferragamos branched out into the hotel business, the hotels are anything but ordinary (and it seems fitting that they are all located along the Arno):

Hotel Lungarno (Borgo San Jacopo 14/+39 055 27 261).
Lungarno Suites (Lungarno Acciaiuoli 4/+39 055 2726 8000).
Lungarno Apartments (Borgo San Jacopo 12/+39 055 27 261).
Gallery Hotel Art (Vicolo dell'Oro 5/+39 055 27 263).

All may be viewed online at Lungarnohotels.com, along with some other Lungarno properties.

An interesting read about the history of the family and the company is a book published in conjunction with an exhibit of the same name at the Museo del Palacio de Bellas Artes, Mexico, *Walking Dreams: Salvatore Ferragamo, 1898–1960* (Editorial RM, 2006). In the preface, Salvatore's wife, Wanda, notes that Ferragamo "never gave himself airs. Although he was a titan, there was not a trace of arrogance in his character, and still less of megalomania; quite the contrary. His attitude toward life was one of intense generosity." The book has some wonderful black-and-white photographs that are priceless, like the one in the Palazzo Spini Feroni workshop, 1937, with the employees—all men, except one woman—in a gorgeous room with columns and a gilded ceiling amid bolts of fabric and leather stacked all around them. "The Ferragamos' Florence," by Christopher Petkanas (*Travel + Leisure,* October 1999), is a great article featuring family members' favorite hotels, restaurants, shops, and sights in Florence. Petkanas notes that "they approached the task as if they were designing a new collection: with almost feral concentration, respect for tradition, and disregard for the obvious."

A parting quote from Salvatore that I love: "I do not have to search for styles. When I need new ones I select from those that present themselves to my mind as I select an apple from the laden dish upon my table."

Festa

A *festa* is ostensibly the Italian word for "festivity," but as Joan Arndt, in *Italian Lessons,* notes, "*festa* is a multipurpose word that covers holiday, feast day, saint's day, national holiday, festival, or party. A *festa* is a day off and no one works on a day off. There are no exceptions. . . . These days are sacred but not always for religious reasons. . . . Alfio, our extraordinary carpenter, has never worked on March 19 and never will. That's the *festa di San Giuseppe* and San Giuseppe, otherwise known as St. Joseph, aka father of Jesus, is the patron saint of carpenters." A similar word is *sagra,* which also refers to a festival—usually one in the countryside honoring a local culinary specialty—but while a *sagra* is cause for celebrating and feasting, it isn't always synonymous with a day off. Read Carol Field's excellent book *Celebrating Italy* to discover more (she includes about a dozen celebrations in Tuscany and Umbria).

Firenze

One of my favorite books—and not just for cooking—is *A Table in Tuscany* (Little, Brown, 1988; Chronicle, 1991), by Leslie Forbes. The following passage offers a good word of advice for visitors to Firenze:

> Just when you think you have cracked the system, everything shuts at one o'clock for lunch. Grey steel shutters clang down abruptly to cover all the tempting displays of goodies, leaving formerly lively shopping streets bare and bleak. For four hours nothing moves except the occasional fly and in the summer heat of Florence (one of the hottest and most humid cities in Italy) even the flies can be a little sluggish. The only solution is to follow the Florentine example. Rise early to shop and see the staggering variety of museums and churches and save the afternoon for a long, lazy lunch in a cool restaurant. Or picnic and siesta in the huge formal Boboli Gardens behind the Pitti Palace. If you can cope with the heat explore the narrow streets lined with medieval and Renaissance palaces in the precious quiet hours between one and five o'clock. During the rest of the day whining mopeds are a constant hazard, whizzing merrily down so-called 'pedestrian only' thoroughfares and missing tourists and Florentines alike only by centimetres. The city is

not now and never has been a restful place to visit. Exhilarating, yes. Restful, no.

Flood Markers

There are a number of flood markers, and evidence of floods, in Florence, but the one I like the best (for no particular reason) is the one on Via dei Neri, right on the corner with Via San Remigio. If you stand at this corner and look up a bit, you'll see a stone plaque with a hand reaching up above the waves of the river and touching the high-water mark of the flood of November 1333. The marker above it indicates that the flood of 1966 was even higher. Florence has experienced six major floods since 1177: 1333, 1557, 1740, 1844, 1864, and the most recent occurred on November 4, 1966 (note that the flood of 1333 occurred on the exact same day!). A great and dramatic book to read about the 1966 flood is *Dark Water: Flood and Redemption in the City of Masterpieces* (Doubleday, 2008), in which Robert Clark notes, "I supposed there would, of course, be more floods. Florence proved—in its squabbling and treacheries, its beauties arising miraculously from its corruptions; in all that Dante recorded and that drove him into exile as Adam and Eve went into exile; and in his descent to Hell, circuit of Purgatory, and return—that what goes around comes around." I'm a big believer in "what goes around, comes around" in life, so Clark's supposition resonated with me immediately. (And by the way, the title of this book is borrowed from a passage in Dante's *Inferno,* Canto XVI, 103–105: "So down that steep bank the flood of that dark painted water descending thundered in our ears and almost stunned us . . ." This is a book that keeps you on the edge of your seat at times, and reminds all of us who care passionately about Florence that saving artworks—or, alternatively, losing them—matters immensely.

Florence Concierge Information

This little publication is an indispensable bimonthly guide, in Italian and English, compiled by Florentine hotel concierges and published by the Chiavi d'Oro Toscana (Golden Keys Association, an international organization founded in France in 1929; guides are also available in Sardinia, Milan, Rome, and Venice). The complimentary booklets are found at the reception desks of a number of hotels, including the Helvetia & Bristol, Villa Medici, Villa San Michele, J.K. Place, Mediterraneo, Sofitel, Lungarno, and others, but you don't have to be a guest to request a copy. Each issue is jammed with updated information on exhibits, museums, markets, concerts, trains, planes, sports, nightlife, rental cars, consulates, spas, feasts, and fairs, and is more comprehensive than anything at the tourist office. Pick one up soon after your arrival and see Florence-concierge.it for more information.

The Florentine

This great newspaper, published biweekly and printed in English, is one of the best resources around for visitors to Florence. The paper covers news, events, culture, politics, business, travel, food, sports—in short, everything—and it celebrated its fourth year and hundredth issue in the spring of 2009. The paper is targeted to the Florentine English-speaking community, both residents and visitors, and it's indispensable. You'll find it all around town, and online at Theflorentine.net. It's great to browse the events listings before you arrive, and great for reading the local stories of interest when you're here. Some of my favorite columns are "The Medici Archives," "Il Fatto Bello," and "Italian Voices." The paper prints two special issues (*Florence for Students* and *Summer in Florence*) and also has a book publishing arm, TF Press.

Friends of Florence

Like the British, Americans have had a long relationship with Florence, since the nineteenth century, so it's not surprising that an organization known as Friends of Florence (FOF), devoted to preserving and enhancing the historical integrity of the arts in and around the city, was created as a U.S.-based foundation in 1998. What *is* a little surprising is that this relatively small foundation has managed to fund a number of major projects, the most significant being the diagnostic testing of the *David* that determined the course of the statue's cleaning in 2004. In just twenty-four hours, FOF raised the $200,000 needed for the testing.

Founded by American-born Contessa Simonetta Brandolini d'Adda and her sister, Renee Gardner, FOF was modeled after the nonprofit Save Venice organization, and maintains offices in Washington, D.C., and Florence. (The *contessa* also owns, with her husband, The Best in Italy, a rental and real estate agency described on page 493.) Because Italian law doesn't allow tax deductions for funding preservation, and because Italian fine arts departments can't attend to all the artistic works that need preserving, FOF really fills a significant void, especially since Florence holds more of those artistic treasures than anywhere else in Italy. Brandolini's network of noteworthy friends—including Piero Antinori, Bona Frescobaldi, Bette Midler, Franco Zeffirelli, Zubin Mehta, Sting and his wife, Trudie Styler, and Mel and Robyn Gibson—and the lure of Florence itself have aided FOF's success. One of the organization's most recent completed projects was the restoration of the Sala della Niobe in the Uffizi. I had been in this room the summer before the work began, and couldn't stop thinking about it: featured are the sculptures depicting the myth of Niobe, one of the more tragic figures in Greek mythology. (Niobe had fourteen children, and in a moment of arrogance bragged about these seven sons and seven daughters at a ceremony honoring Leto, daughter of the Titans Coeus and

Phoebe. Niobe was mocking Leto, who had only two children, Apollo and Artemis; Leto did not take the insult lightly, and in retaliation sent Apollo and Artemis to earth to slaughter all of Niobe's children.) Unfortunately, I didn't have the chance to see these restored statues on my last visit, but I remember them as hauntingly beautiful, and I urge visitors to the Uffizi not to skip this room.

For every U.S. dollar FOF receives, the organization applies 99.6 cents toward its projects. Brandolini told me that no gift is too small—see my blog for a heartwarming story about a school in Dallas whose fifth-grade students wanted to become patrons of the arts and managed to raise $2,500 for the cleaning of some of the statues in the Uffizi. However, to participate in FOF's extraordinary annual program, you must become a Founding Patron (contributing a onetime gift of $30,000) or Patron (contributing $5,000 or more annually). Patrons have an exceptional opportunity to experience programs led by renowned experts in various fields of art, historical preservation, and architecture, and they "become true citizens of Florence, seeing the city in a unique manner not possible to the casual visitor." A few past programs have been Special Treasures of Tuscany, Donatello: The Renaissance of Sculpture, and From the Classical World to the Renaissance.

To learn more about FOF's past and current projects, and its wish list, visit Friendsofflorence.org, where you can also find contact information for its offices in Washington and Florence.

G

Giovanna Garzoni

Garzoni (1600–1670) was one of the few female artists in Florence or anywhere in Italy in the seventeenth century, and though her name is hardly a household word, she was court miniaturist to the Medici. I'm a huge fan of Garzoni's still lifes, and there are a number of them in the Galleria Palatina in the Pitti Palace. Garzoni worked for the Spanish Duke of Alcalá in Naples and the Duke of Savoy in Turin before she came to Florence. In one of her earliest works, a volume of calligraphy, she decorated each letter with fruits, flowers, birds, and insects, and these were to become her trademark as a miniaturist. According to Jenny de Gex and David Fordham—authors of a wonderful book called *Florentines: A Tuscan Feast* (which includes recipes by Lorenza de' Medici, text from Giacomo Castelvetro's *1614 Fruit, Herbs, and Vegetables of Italy*, and still lifes by Garzoni (Random House, 1992)—"miniatures" refers not to size but to technique, "similar to illuminated manuscripts, of using tempera on parchment or vellum." De Gex was lucky to have the opportunity to handle many of Garzoni's original miniatures in Florence and Rome while she was working on the book, and she became "very aware of their unique quality. One stepped instantly into a world of sunshine, the more surprising, as outside, it was December, and patches of ice lay on the vast expanse of the Piazza della Signoria."

Great Fountain in Piazza IV Novembre, Perugia

I've been an enormous fan of fountains since I took my very first trip abroad, in the tenth grade, with members of my Spanish class. The fountains in Madrid and Sevilla are magnificent, and they don't really have any rivals in Italy except for those of Rome. But the fountain in Perugia's lovely central piazza is impressive. It was built as a monument to mark the success of a public works project: the completion of an aqueduct that carried water from Monte Pacciano directly into the town piazza. The marble fountain features sculptures carved by Nicola and Giovanni Pisano, a father-and-son team of sculptors and architects. According to the Web Gallery of Art database, the Piscanos were "the greatest

sculptors of their period and stand at the head of the tradition of Italian sculpture in the same way that Giotto stands at the head of the tradition of Italian painting." The fountain consists of two basins, one above the other. The larger one, on the bottom, features panels depicting the seasons and months of the year and the signs of the zodiac. The upper basin features biblical scenes, beasts, and local historical notables and places, such as Perugia, Lake Trasimeno, and Rome. At the very top are three bronze female figures, possibly representing the three Theological Virtues or, according to Carol Field, water nymphs representing "the triumphant arrival of water such a great distance from the sea." The fountain was the last great project the Pisanos created together, completed in 1278.

Guelph–Ghibelline Conflict

The Guelphs and Ghibellines were two opposing factions in central and northern Italy during the twelfth and thirteenth centuries, and their conflict is among the most significant in Tuscan history. In brief, the Guelphs supported the pope (and generally were mercantile and urban) and the Ghibellines supported the

Holy Roman Emperor (and generally were feudal, tied more closely to agriculture). The conflict was particularly intense in Florence, a Guelph city. On September 4, 1260, the Florentines raised an army of thirty-five thousand—with the support of their allies around Tuscany—and headed toward Ghibelline Siena. The Sienese asked King Manfred of Sicily for assistance and Manfred sent a German contingent, but the Sienese army numbered only twenty thousand. The battle raged all day at Montaperti, and by nightfall the Florentines were exhausted; and when the Sienese led a counterattack, the Florentines were defeated.

A few years ago, when I hired a guide to take my friend Amy and me to Siena, I asked him if he would also stop at the Montaperti battlefield, and he was surprised, because no one had asked him to go to Montaperti before—and happy—he can trace members of his family back to the battle. There is not much to see really, except for a marker in the shape of an obelisk on a small hilltop. But it was beautiful, and from the hilltop you can see Siena, and it's easy to see why it was a good place for a battle.

Of course, relations between the Florentines and the Sienese have never been the same. Matthew Spender, in *Within Tuscany,* relates a famous folktale, which, condensed, goes something like this: The Florentines and Sienese decided that the frontiers between the two should be settled by chance instead of by battle. Two roosters would start out walking from each city at dawn, and when they met, that would be the new border. The Sienese chose a young cock, fed him well, and gave him a bed of honor in church, just as they do for the Palio horses. The Florentines chose an old cock, dipped him in cold water, and put him out on the roof. He had a sleepless night, and when he saw the first light of dawn on the horizon, he said, "I've had enough of Florence. I'm going to Siena." At about midday the two cocks met, the Sienese cock having woken up late and started walking several hours after the Florentine cock. "And that," Spender's friend Vittorio told him, "is why the frontier between Siena and Florence is so much closer to us than it is to them." Spender, who'd been told this tale at the bank, took a bank slip and "subtracted the date of the Sienese victory over Florence at Montaperti from the date on the calendar on the wall, and it came to more than 730 years. A long time to nourish rancor." (P.S. The Sienese triumph was short-lived: six years later at the Battle of Benevento the Ghibellines and the House of Hohenstaufen were crushed.)

It was in Mary McCarthy's essential book *The Stones of Florence* (again, the large, illustrated edition) that I learned that architecture in Tuscany in the thirteenth century became political. She relates that the style of sacred buildings bearing black-and-white horizontal stripes came from Pisa, and wherever the Pisan influence spread in Tuscany (notably Siena, Lucca, Volterra, Carrara, Arezzo, Prato, Corsica, and Sardinia), the black-and-white stripes appear. This style did not appear in Florence, where the dark-green-and-white marble façade on the Baptistery and San Miniato and the Badia at San Domenico di Fiesole are not striped but arranged in geometric patterns, such as "lozenges or diamonds, long wavy lines like the water pattern in hieroglyphics, squares, boxes, rosettes, suns and stars, wheels, semi-circles, semi-ellipses, tongues of flame." In general, McCarthy notes that

The towns with the striped Pisan architecture were Ghibelline and the towns with the geometric patterns were Guelph, like Florence, Fiesole, and Empoli. But whatever the style, Florentine or Pisan or Pisan-Lucchese, bichromatism was prevalent throughout Tuscany in the Romanesque period, and the blacks and whites, sun and shadow, sharps and flats, recurring on the old church fronts, evoke what has been called the checkerboard of Tuscan medieval politics, the alternation of Guelph and Ghibelline, Pope and Emperor, Black and White. These were the terms, the severe basic antinomies, in which the Tuscan thought and saw.

Guides

For many years, I thought hiring a guide or joining a walking tour was a waste of money, and, worse, offended my sensibilities as a well-prepared traveler. I figured if I'd read enough and had a good map I had no need for a guide. But this was before I learned that a *really good* guide can tell you *more* than you already know, and can turn a great trip into an outstanding one.

In an article entitled "Paris at Your Feet" (*The Atlantic,* August 1998), writer Francine Prose noted that "the walking tour is, by nature, a mildly humbling experience, asking us to declare ourselves sightseers, outsiders—and to abandon all hope of passing for locals." I believe this was at the crux of my disdain for guides, but again, I was wrong. I was not only pleasantly surprised but amazed to discover that good guides are often scholars, specializing in various areas of history, art, and architecture, and they share insights into contemporary society and politics that visitors might

ordinarily miss. Guides are often discerning when it comes to food, handmade crafts, and favorite local stores and can therefore recommend great places to eat and shop. And, they can help visitors navigate locales in the most efficient way possible, allowing you to cover a lot of ground in less time.

The cities, towns, and villages of Tuscany and Umbria will all be enhanced by the expertise of a guide, and though I make no claim to knowing more than a few, I can guarantee that the following three guides are worthy of their profession:

Alessandra Marchetti (+39 347 386 9839/aleoberm@tin.it) arranges visits to well-known sites like the Uffizi and the Accademia in Florence as well as many lesser-known churches, museums, and monuments. Her rates vary and she's available for half-day and full-day tours. Alessandra is also particularly adept at arranging access to places that are ordinarily closed to the public (see the Vasari Corridor entry below for more details on how I met Alessandra).

Paolo Cesaroni (+39 347 380 3408/paolocesaroni@tin.it) is not a historian but a driving guide, and he has a passion for Tuscany in particular that is nearly unmatched (but he also knows the byways of Umbria). In the interest of full disclosure, Paolo is Alessandra's partner in business as well as in life, and he is not only knowledgeable but a ton of fun to be with and very charming. He's been an independent guide since 2003 after previously working for a tourist company in the prestigious Virtuoso network. Paolo wants his guests to see Italy through *his* eyes, to see how Italians really live, and he prefers to include smaller towns and villages on itineraries along with larger towns like Siena and San Gimignano. The most rewarding part of his job is when clients have an unforgettable trip, and he told me that at the end of each guest's journey, "I have a new appreciation of my country." (And, by the

way, Paolo's favorite part of Tuscany is La Maremma, which he refers to as "the new Chianti.")

Marco Bellanca (+39 347 600 2209/  bellsista@yahoo.it) has been a licensed guide in Umbria since 1996. When he applied, he was competing against 230 other applicants for only twelve licenses, and he told me to be a good guide you have to know everything—food, art, religion, history, the lives of the saints, etc.—and he says two major traits of good guides are the way they share the knowledge they possess and the way they assess their clients' desires ("we're a little bit like psychologists, you know"). Marco does, indeed, seemingly know everything, and he is firmly on my short list of outstanding guides in Italy. He works with tour operators as well as individuals, and he can tailor tours to satisfy all kinds of interests, such as gastronomy, architecture, Etruscan history, and more. Marco notes that a week in Umbria is ideal ("every single village in Umbria has a church with a treasure worth seeing"), and interestingly, he divides the cities of Umbria up into the following categories: the travertine towns (Perugia, Gubbio, Todi); the gentle, mild pink cities (Assisi, Spello, so named because the limestone they're built of is naturally pink); tufa stone (Orvieto); and Roman (Spoleto, which has the most important Roman buildings in the region). But, if visitors only have two days, Marco recommends including Perugia, Assisi, Orvieto, and Gubbio on their itineraries. He notes that the busiest times of year in Umbria are April, May, June, September, and October, and these are the best in terms of nice weather; but the end of June and early July are really special for festivals, events, music, and landscape (notably the many fields of sunflowers). Marco's rates are approximately fifty euros per hour, and he's available year round for half-day and full-day tours.

Guilds

In Renaissance Florence, guilds were enormously significant, and indeed were nothing less than the backbone of the entire economic system. According to author Richard Turner in *Renaissance Florence: The Invention of a New Art* (Harry Abrams, 1997), a poet in 1393 described Florence as *La Terra di Mercantatia* (The Land of Commerce) in which guilds represented everything from artisans and butchers to lawyers and doctors. There were seven major guilds, known as Arti Maggiori (Major Arts), and fourteen Arti Minori (Minor Arts), but only members of the Major Arts could be elected to public office. Members of the Major Arts included the Arte dei Giudici and Notai (lawyers and notaries), the Calimala (great merchants), the Arte del Cambio (money changers), the Arte della Lana (wool masters), the Arte della Seta (silk masters), the Arte dei Medici e Speziali (doctors and apothecaries), and the Arte dei Vaiai de Pellicciai (furriers and leather masters). Included in the Minor Arts were the Arte dei Beccai (butchers), the Arte dei Calzolai (shoemakers), the Arte dei Fabbri (blacksmiths), the Arte dei Linaioli e Rigattieri (linen drapers and used-clothes dealers), the Arte dei Maestri di Pietra e Legname (builders), the Arte dei Vinattieri (wine sellers), the Arte degli Albergatori (innkeepers), the Arte degli Oliandoli e Pizzicagnoli (oil dealers and sausage and cheese sellers), the Arte dei Cuoiai e Galigai (minor leather masters), the Arte dei Corazzai e Spadai (armorers), the Arte dei Correggiai (belt makers), the Arte dei Chiavaioli (locksmiths), the Arte dei Legnaioli (carpenters), and the Arte dei Fornai (bakers). I like that many of Florence's street names in the Centro reflect this guild heritage.

Turner notes that the guilds were also very involved in religious activities and charities. "Each guild participated in the major religious holidays of the city, and each had responsibility for the celebration of the feast day of its specific patron saint. The guilds also oversaw and had financial responsibility for the city's major churches, and for its some thirty-odd 'hospitals,' hospitals both in the modern sense and charitable foundations. Therefore to imagine a Florence without the guilds is to see a city gutted of its financial strength and philanthropic compassion."

The Church of Orsanmichele, on Via dei Calzaiuoli and one of my favorites in Florence, is a veritable monument to the guilds. The name is derived from a ninth-century church dedicated to Saint Michael (San Michele) that once stood beside several vegetable gardens (orti). The building as we know it today dates from 1284, when the Comune di Firenze approved a project for a loggia covered with a large, hipped roof with four slopes to be used for the sale of wheat. This was designed by Arnolfo di Cambio and was one of the first public loggias in Florence. This loggia was remodeled in 1367, and shortly after the appearance of a sacred image that was believed to be miraculous, it became a pilgrimage destination. At this time it was known as Orsanmichele, taken from Orto San Michele. Grain was sold on the ground floor, and the upper two floors were used for storing grain for emergencies. You can still see the holes in the ceiling where the chutes used for transferring grain from one floor to another once were.

When the government of the Signoria moved its offices to this space in the fifteenth century, it ordered each of the major Florentine guilds to decorate the exterior of Orsanmichele, so each guild commissioned a sculpture of its patron saint to fill the fourteen external marble niches on the ground floor. Rupert Scott, in his excellent book *Florence Explored,* notes that Orsanmichele has been called "the most Florentine of Florentine buildings" and "its undeniable beauty is derived from a peculiarly Florentine blend of the plain and the exotic. What might be a rather pedestrian rectangular block of *pietra forte* has a simple elegance that sets off florid window tracery of a quality not equaled in Tuscany (it is by an obscure fourteenth-century Florentine sculptor called Simone Talenti), ceramic medallions by Luca della Robbia and ornate niches, each allocated to a different trade guild responsible for their decoration." In an informative little paperback I bought in Florence called *Orsanmichele: Church and Museum,* a Florence museums superintendent referred to this arrangement as being "a unique web of religious devotion, civic pride, and flaunting of wealth and artistic excellence." This comment echoes one made by Piero Bargellini, elected mayor of Florence in 1966, who described Orsanmichele as a monument "betwixt religion and secular activity, piety and politics, work and prayer." The exterior statues today are actually copies—most of the originals are at the Bargello and some are inside being restored and not available for public viewing (though permission is occasionally granted with a guide—See entry for art historian Alessandra Marchetti under Guides).

Gustiamo.com

I first learned about Gustiamo.com (1715 West Farms Road, Bronx, New York/718 860 2949 or 877 907 2525) from Faith Willinger, and since then, over the last four years, I've been ordering and enjoying some of Italy's finest culinary specialties, a handful from Tuscany and Umbria. Gustiamo was founded by a group of native Italians with a passion for extraordinary food. They continually search Italy for small producers who craft their food products *come una volta* (in the traditional way). A few Tuscan items offered by Gustiamo are Martelli pasta, La Molina chocolate, and Tenuta Cafaggio Chianti vinegar, several olive oils, Lunardi wine jellies, and *cantucci;* and from Umbria, La Valletta farro, lentils, chickpeas, *borlotti* beans, and *fagioli del purgatorio* beans. (There are lots of other yummy items I've ordered from Gustiamo that aren't Tuscan or Umbrian, like Sant'Eustachio coffee, *colatura* from the village of Cetara on the Amalfi Coast, and Latini pasta . . . and I could go on.) The prices at Gustiamo are equal to the quality of the products—in other words, not cheap. But as Jesse Kornbluth, of Headbutler.com, pointed out in a blog post, "When inflation is driving food prices to the moon, it's shrewd to make simpler meals with fewer ingredients, and the better the ingredients, the less you need to do to make a great meal." He went on to say that none other than chef Mario Batali stocks his kitchens with Gustiamo products.

If you live in the New York metropolitan area you can visit Gustiamo's warehouse in the Bronx (by appointment), which has a few other culinary-related items available there that aren't offered online—I went a few years ago and joined an olive oil tasting and took advantage of a two-for-one special, bringing home two bottles of delicious oils from different regions of Italy. Whether you order online or in person, introduce yourself to Beatrice Ughi, and tell her I said *ciao.*

H

Hiking

There are lots of opportunities for hiking in Tuscany and Umbria. Two different mountain ranges—the Apennine Alps and the

Apuan Alps—offer two different experiences: the Apennines are more like rolling hills, round and bald at the top, and the Apuans are more of a classic range with jagged peaks, cliffs, and valleys. An important point to keep in mind about hiking in Italy is that often what you walk on is more of a pathway, not a well-groomed trail. Paths weren't created at random; they connect old footpaths which have existed for a long, long time. Routes wind through the middle of villages, sometimes cross private property where you have to open and close a gate, and are often farm tracks where you'll encounter shepherds and farmers. Walking in Italy is generally not a wilderness experience, but there are very few places in Europe—now or ever—where you can backpack into completely isolated places and not encounter roads, people, or towns. Conversely, there are few—if any—places in the United States where you can backpack and be assured of finding a place to sleep in a bed, plus enjoy a meal with wine or beer at the end of the day. Good books I recommend include *Walking and Eating in Tuscany and Umbria,* James Lasdun and Pia Davis (Penguin, 2004); *Walking in Tuscany,* Gillian Price (Interlink, 2006), which also includes Umbria; *50 Hikes In & Around Tuscany,* Jeff Taylor (Countryman, 2007); and *Village Walks: Tuscany—50 Adventures on Foot,* Martha Fay (Chronicle, 2007).

I

Istituto Italiano di Cultura

There are ninety Italian Cultural Institutes in a number of major cities on five continents, and this is a great organization to help keep you immersed in all things Italian, both before you leave and when you return. I have attended some truly memorable events at the institute here in New York; the center also has a great library (with more than thirty thousand volumes) and offers Italian language classes. Unfortunately, the ICI doesn't have one central Web site, so the best way to find out if there is a branch near you is to do a Google search (the address for the New York center is Iicnewyork.esteri.it). One part of the Web site is dedicated to events going on in Italy.

Italian Americana

A chapter in the history of Italy is the story of Italian-Americans, since, as Jerre Mangione and Ben Morreale note in their excellent book *La Storia* (see page 555), between 1880 and 1924 "there was a virtual hemorrhaging of people from Italy to America," and "a whole culture left its ancient roots to settle in the cities and towns of America. There it was transformed and woven into the fabric of American life." John Mariani and Galina Mariano, in their *Italian-American Cookbook* (see page 554), also note that 97 percent of these Italians—mostly from the Mezzogiorno, the south—came through Ellis Island and settled quickly in East Coast cities, notably New York: "By the 1920s there were more Italians living in New York than in Florence." Alex Shoumatoff, in *Westchester: Portrait of a County* (Vintage, 1990), reported that thousands of Italians were imported for the job of building a dam at the site of the New Croton Reservoir in Westchester County, just outside New York City, and that upon completion in 1907 this dam was the second-largest piece of hand-hewn masonry in the world. In Shoumatoff's original, hardcover edition in 1979, he observed that "one out of every three of Westchester's 870,000 inhabitants is likely to have Italian blood and many are descended from people whose first home in America was a shack beneath the Croton Dam."

The National Italian American Foundation (1860 19th Street NW, Washington, D.C./212 387 0600/niaf.org) was founded in 1975 and is the major advocate for nearly twenty-five million Italian–Americans, the nation's fifth-largest ethnic group. NIAF's mission is to preserve and protect Italian-American heritage and culture, and it offers a wide range of programs, such as providing grants, legislative internships in Congress, conferences, cultural seminars, and travel opportunities. Readers interested in joining NIAF may do so online (there are several membership categories) or by mail. An interesting bit of trivia I learned is that Rhode Island is the state with the highest percentage of Italian-Americans, Connecticut is second, and New Jersey is a very close third.

It's no surprise, then, that there is no shortage of works by and about Italian-Americans. Some recommended reads, including cookbooks, fiction, and nonfiction, are:

Household Saints, Francine Prose (St. Martin's, 1981; Harper Perennial, 2003). This wonderful novel, about the Santangelo family in New York's Little Italy neighborhood in the 1950s, has really memorable characters and is by a writer I particularly love—and she travels frequently to and writes about Italy.

I Loved, I Lost, I Made Spaghetti, Giulia Melucci (Grand Central, 2009). A winning memoir by Melucci, who grew up in Bay Ridge, Brooklyn, "a neighborhood that—tragically—is best known for being the setting of *Saturday Night Fever,* a movie that did about as much for Italian-Americans as the Gotti family." Melucci relates stories both laugh-out-loud funny and a little sad about the men she's dated and cooked for, and she shares lots of recipes (in one for tomato sauce, she asks that we not tell her mother that she sometimes buys canned tomatoes that are already chopped). She still lives in Brooklyn, by the way, only in a more trendy neighborhood.

The Italian-American Cookbook: A Feast of Food from a Great American Cooking Tradition, John Mariani and Galina Mariani (Harvard Common, 2000). The Marianis accurately note that Italian-American food "was born in the early twentieth century and has evolved, decade by decade, to the point where it is a legitimate genre all its own." Like other cuisines in North America, it began in immigrants' kitchens and both adheres to tradition while including ingredients found here; but unlike other immigrant cuisines, Italian-American dishes are unique to America and for the most part do not exist in Italy, or at least not in the same way. However, this is not a book full of just "red sauce" recipes and cheesecake (which when well made are among the authors' favorites); rather, the book includes recipes like Egg-Filled Ravioli with White Truffles alongside those like Stuffed Shells with Meat Sauce. As the Marianis note, "we realized the truth of the adage that there really are no bad dishes, just bad cooks." They reexamined all the old-fashioned Italian-American favorites and also collected recipes from American chefs who are using Italian ingredients to their best advantage today. Plus, they provide a number of background stories to familiar dishes that make for entertaining and informative reading.

The Italian American Reader: A Collection of Outstanding Fiction, Memoirs, Journalism, Essays, and Poetry, edited by Bill Tonelli and with a foreword by Nick Tosches (William Morrow, 2003). Some contributors to this great collection of novels, memoirs, short stories, and poems are Don DeLillo,

Mario Puzo, Jay Parini, Gregory Corso, Richard Russo, Barbara Grizzuti Harrison, Gay Talese, Victoria Gotti, Philip Caputo, and Ken Auletta; as stated on the back cover, "all their surnames happen to end in vowels, true, but that need not affect your enjoyment of this volume one way or the other." Nick Tosches writes in his foreword, "Early on, in the dark river of my youth, I wanted to become a writer. It seemed a most unlikely thing. In my neighborhood, there were few books, many bookies. I was discouraged from reading, on the grounds that it would 'put ideas in your head.' There was, of course, a certain wisdom in that." A terrific read, and I completely sympathize with Tonelli, who admits he ended up leaving out a lot of very good work, some of which he enjoyed as much as the stuff he included, as I, too, always feel there is so much more I could include in each of my own books.

La Storia: Five Centuries of the Italian American Experience, Jerre Mangione and Ben Morreale (HarperCollins, 1992). This is a definitive volume. The word *storia* means "history" as well as "story," and when published this book was hailed as being the "first comprehensive account of the Italian-American immigration," combining historical research and personal narratives. A reviewer for the *New York Times Book Review* noted, "It is a book that should be read by all Americans interested in what binds us together, despite our different backgrounds and histories." The authors have done a masterful job at tracing the Italians' journey from the Old Country to "La Merica," as many Italians called it.

Lidia's Italian-American Kitchen, Lidia Matticchio Bastianich (Knopf, 2001). Winner of an IACP Cookbook Award, this is the companion volume to Lidia's fifty-two-part public television series. Lidia notes that Italian-American cuisine was born with the immigrants from Sicily, Campania, and Apulia, and when she herself was a young immigrant (from Istria, the region of Italy that was given to Yugoslavia after World War II), she did not recognize any of this "Italian" cuisine. When she began working in Italian-American restaurants, she was puzzled at how different the food was from what her family ate at home, including spaghetti and meatballs, which was "another dish that I had not encountered. We may have had *spaghetti al sugo,* or *spaghetti bolognese,* and we ate *polpette,* flat meatballs fried and served as a main dish with vegetables, but we never had the two served together." Lidia was on a quest for many years to get to the bottom of Italian-American cuisine, and she credits the book *La Storia* with providing her with many answers. She observes that Americans fell in love with Italian-American cuisine first, then with regional Italian cooking, and concludes that "Italian-American food is a cuisine unto itself. It has become a part of us—a slice of Americana. And that is what makes America, the piecing together of a slice of every culture, which in total makes a great whole." These recipes are all winners, and interspersed throughout the book are snippets of wonderful e-mails that television viewers sent her.

Twisted Head: An Italian American Memoir, Carl Capotorto (Broadway, 2008). *Capotorto* translates as "twisted head," and as the author explains, the name was not assigned randomly, as names never are. "Our ancestors were frequently branded for a physical characteristic or personality type, trade or special skill, hometown, background, or other prominent feature. Most of the people I grew up with in the Bronx in the

1960s and '70s are good examples: the Mangialardi family (Eat Fat), Mrs. Occhiogrosso (Big Eye), or Marie Sabella (So Beautiful). They were incessant fryers, a bug-eyed doomsday type, and a dolled-up glamour queen, respectively. What else could they be? They were bound by ancestral imperative, these people, unconsciously acting upon orders issued down through the blood from generation to generation. There is a lot in a name. A name is an inheritance. Names are legacies." I laughed out loud plenty while reading this, but it's actually a substantive New York story. Capotorto played the part of Little Paulie on *The Sopranos* for six seasons.

Were You Always an Italian?: Ancestors and Other Icons of Italian America, Maria Laurino (Norton, 2000). Without revealing more, the title of this wonderful book—one of my favorites—comes from a question that former New York governor Mario Cuomo asked of Laurino, who at the time was a political reporter. Laurino shares memorable observances about her own family and many just like it, including some about Italian dialect, which she once compared to a kind of "Italian-American Yiddish. . . . But Yiddish, a medieval language once spoken by vast numbers of people from nations as diverse as Germany and Russia, became a common denominator of Jewish culture, is taught in universities, and claims its own literature. Because so few Italian-Americans openly use dialect, I could only confirm its existence by listening to my family or when randomly encountering a person who retains these words in everyday discourse." It was only when she met a scholar in Naples that she discovered the etymology of many of her dialect words.

J

Jewish History in Italy

In a country that is so overwhelmingly Catholic, it's sometimes easy to overlook the history of other faiths in Italy. Rome is home to the second-oldest continuous Jewish community in the world (after Jerusalem), and Tuscany has a great number of things of Jewish interest—the historic roots of a Jewish presence in Tuscany extend back a long way, at least to the sixth century (Umbria does not have a history of many Jewish communities). Florence's Tempio Maggiore, built between 1874 and 1882 and located at Via Farini 4, is a working synagogue and a museum (the Web site Firenzebraica.net has information on this and other topics about the Jewish community in Florence). It's also among the most beautiful I've ever seen: the exterior is constructed of alternating blocks of white and pink stone and is in a Moorish style, while the interior is a riot of painted geometrical designs on wood, in bright shades of red, orange, and blue.

Some Italian Jewish traditions are generally Sephardic, but other customs are uniquely Italian. Edda Servi Machlin in her very good book *Classic Italian Jewish Cooking: Traditional Recipes and Menus* (Ecco, 2005) notes that, for example, instead of eating *hamantaschen* (triangular pastries with fruit or poppy fillings) at Purim, Italian Jews ate *orecchie di Aman* (Haman's ears, twirls of fried sweet pastry). Likewise, Italian Jews never heard of gefilte fish, but ate jellied striped bass on the High Holidays, and at Passover they were forbidden to eat chocolate, cheese, and other milk products. (Machlin's book, by the way, is both a cookbook and an important record of life in the Tuscan village of Pitigliano, often referred to as "The Little Jerusalem" due to its large and historic Jewish population. From the fourteenth, or possibly the twelfth, century, Jews made up, at times, 25 to 50 percent of the Pitigliano population.) Joyce Goldstein, in *Cucina Ebraica: Flavors of the Italian Jewish Kitchen* (Chronicle, 1998) notes that if you take a quick look at the recipes she's gathered in this book, they may appear to be simply Italian, but a closer look reveals that they're different in how they're served, following the structure of the kosher meal and the laws of *kashrut* (kosher), so that, for example, a recipe for lasagna with meat sauce cannot contain a layer of cheese, and cheese can't be sprinkled onto a meat soup or pasta.

Great guides to consult for exploring remaining synagogues, neighborhoods, historical monuments, and markers include *Tuscany: Jewish Itineraries: Places, History and Art,* edited by Dora Liscia Bemporad and Annamarcella Tedeschi Falco (Marsilio, 1997); *The Guide to Jewish Italy,* Annie Sacerdoti and with photographs by Alberto Jona Falco (Rizzoli, 2004); and *A Travel Guide to Jewish Europe,* Ben Frank (Pelican, 2001, third edition). Wonderful books of related interest include *Benevolence and Betrayal: Five Italian Jewish Families Under Fascism,* Alexander Stille (Summit, 1991), which is unfortunately out of print but can still be found; *The Garden of the Finzi-Continis,* Giorgio Bassani (Everyman's Library, 2005), and the film of the same name won an Oscar for best foreign-language film in 1971; *When Courage Was Stronger Than Fear: Remarkable Stories of Christians Who Saved Jews from the Holocaust,* Peter Hellman (Marlowe, 1999; originally published as *Avenue of the Righteous,* Atheneum, 1980), in which one story takes place in Città di Castello in Umbria; and *This Has Happened: An Italian Family in Auschwitz,* Piera Sonnino (Palgrave Macmillan, 2006).

I finished reading this last book just a few hours ago, and found it so very, very good, and rare, as there aren't many published accounts of the Holocaust experiences of Italian Jews. This one is unique also in that the author, Piera Sonnino, wrote it as a family record, and it was only after her death that it was published. It came to light when the Italian newsmagazine *Diario* ran a special feature entitled "*La Memoria Lunga*" (The Long Memory) in 2002, and readers were invited to send a memory of their grandparents in order to preserve an episode that would otherwise be lost. Sonnino had passed away three years prior, and her daughter, Maria Louisa Parodi, submitted the manuscript. It arrived, according to Giacomo Papi, a journalist at *Diario,* as "sixty type-written pages, without an error, without a correction. Reconsidered, rewritten, refined, to be preserved for forty-two years in a red leather binder." *Diario* then published the manuscript in its entirety in a special issue the newsmagazine devotes to the Day of Remembrance, January 27.

Mary Doria Russell—author of an excellent novel I also highly recommend, *A Thread of Grace* (Ballantine, 2005)—contributed the afterword to the Sonnino book, entitled "What Went Right in Italy?" In it, she reminds us that after Germany surrendered, there were approximately forty-three thousand Jews still alive in Italy, which translates to approximately 85 percent—possibly the highest survivor rate in Nazi-occupied Europe. Russell devoted seven years of her life to writing *A Thread of Grace* and studying the Italian response to the persecution of Jews in World War II, but until she read Sonnino's account, among the many people she had encountered, "no one could recall a single Jew who was betrayed to the Germans by an Italian; in fact, many sources, published and private, specifically stated that Jews were never turned over." She believes that the reasons for this are deeply rooted in the particularities of Italian history and culture, and I won't spoil her conclusions here, but I will share some of her parting thoughts about why what happened in Italy was extraordinary: "Without knowledge of what happened in Italy any attempt to understand what went wrong in Germany, Austria, Poland, and France is stunted at best and crippled at worst. Piera Sonnino's beautifully written memoir adds significantly to that knowledge. Italy was not a nation of angels and saints. Nevertheless, it is long past time to honor those little old ladies and crippled old men, who shrug off their own deeds as 'nothing.' What such people dismiss as 'what anyone would have done' is in fact a challenge and a rebuke to all those who could have helped but didn't."

L

Language

I do not speak Italian, but I do know some key words and phrases which rarely fail to bring a big smile to the faces of my hosts and people I meet. The natives of *any* country love it when visitors try to speak their language. Italian may not be as widely spoken around the world as French, for example, but that doesn't mean you shouldn't attempt to learn some Italian vocabulary—it's a beautiful language, and if you studied Latin, you'll learn it in a snap. The Tuscan dialect is considered "standard" Italian, and though there are local dialects spoken in every part of Italy, almost everyone will recognize the Tuscan variety when you speak it and will most likely be happy to converse in it as well. You might notice that Florentines tend to turn the letter *c* into *h,* and that each area of Tuscany and Umbria has its own similar quirk; but essentially the dialect is the same across the regions.

A few good language-learning resources I like include Living Language, which has been around since 1946 and offers a number of courses that are continually updated and revised for beginner, intermediate, and advanced levels, in either audio cassette or CD editions (its Fast & Easy course was referred to as "virtually foolproof" by the *New York Daily News,* and *Italian for Travelers*—a co-publishing venture with Fodor's—is a handy, pocket-sized reference with words and phrases for dozens of situations). I also recommend *501 Italian Verbs* (Barron's), with a full page allotted to each verb showing all tenses fully conjugated; and *Better Reading Italian: A Reader and Guide to Improving Your Understanding of*

Written Italian, Daniela Gobetti (McGraw-Hill, 2003). Gobetti is an author and director of the Center for European Studies at the University of Michigan, and this book is for the advanced beginner or intermediate learner. Gobetti notes that "the first step to better reading is to read more," and to encourage beginners to pick it up, she's organized the book into sections according to eight areas of interest: travel within Italy, cuisine, fashion, customs and society, education, the family, feminism, and Italian attitudes toward America. All of the reading selections are original—not rote pieces from grammar books—because "learning to read a foreign language means learning how to understand texts that are aimed at native speakers and therefore take for granted references, context, and levels of understanding that are mysterious to foreigners. Sooner or later, readers must confront this problem if they want to understand texts that express the culture of a foreign country." Related reads are *Latina pro Populo* (*Latin for People*), by Alexander Humez and Nicholas Humez (Little, Brown, 1978), and *Le Mot Juste: A Dictionary of Classical and Foreign Words and Phrases,* edited by John Buchanan-Brown (Vintage, 1991), which includes classical languages, French, German, Italian, Spanish, and a smattering of other languages around the world. It's a great reference book I use all the time, and what I'm reminded of each time I consult the Italian pages is the great number of words we use for music and art derived from Italian.

Not a language book per se, and far more inspiring, is *La Bella Lingua: My Love Affair with Italian, the World's Most Enchanting Language,* by Dianne Hales (Broadway, 2009). I loved this book from cover to cover, and I was hooked even from the first few words of the acknowledgments: "*Grazie. Grazie tanto. Grazie mille. Vi ringrazio.* I wish there were more ways to say thank you . . ." Hales's story of learning Italian is infectious, and even if you don't have any desire or intent to learn Italian, you may very well when you've finished reading her tale. At the least, you will find her journey charming, funny, fascinating, and, of course, *bella*. As Hales notes, only four countries other than Italy—Switzerland, Croatia, San Marino, and Slovenia, and not counting the Vatican—recognize Italian as an official language, but the Società Dante Alighieri, founded in 1889, has approximately five hundred branches around the world (ladante.it). (You may also be inspired to then read, or reread, Dante's "14,233 eleven-syllable lines organized into one hundred cantos in three volumes," if only because nearly every Italian Hales knows can recite at least a few verses from the *Divine Comedy*. From a professor she learned of an anecdote from World War II, about a partisan shepherd in Tuscany who had been ordered to shoot anyone who couldn't prove he or she was Italian. The shepherd stopped a professor one night who was biking outside Pisa after curfew without any identification. The shepherd asked the professor to prove his Italian identity "by reciting the seventeenth canto of the *Inferno*. He got to line 117 but couldn't remember the rest. The shepherd finished the canto for him.") *La Bella Lingua* is nothing short of a love letter to Italy and Italian and is *essenziale*.

I caught up with Hales by e-mail recently:

Q: What prompted your first trip to Italy—the one in 1983 when you knew only one sentence: *Mi dispiace, ma non parlo Italiano*?

A: I had written my first trade book, *The Complete Book of Sleep*, and the European division of DuPont flew me to Gstaad to talk at the premiere of a new synthetic pillow fiber. Switzerland was gray and cold, so I spontaneously decided to take a train to somewhere I'd always wanted to visit: Italy.

Q: What made you want to return?

A: I was so intrigued by everything about Italy—the way it looks, the way it feels, the way it sounds. I wanted to come back and be able to speak to the wonderful people I had met.

Q: At what point were you absolutely smitten with the country?

A: It was pretty much love at first sight, but then I came back with my husband, Bob. We had traveled extensively in other countries and were particularly fond of the south of France. But we had such a wonderful time in Italy that we kept coming back. Even if Bob had a meeting in Germany or England, our routes always led back to Rome. We felt *a nostro agio* (at home) in Italy.

Q: You mention the hotel in Firenze, Palazzo Magnani Feroni, where you have stayed so many times and also at length. What specifically was it about the hotel that kept you returning?

A: The staff, notably owner Alberto Giannotti, sales and marketing director Claudia Giannotti, and key Palazzo members Annalisa Camilli, Antonella Fabiano, and Daniel Fortmann (Rita, who I mentioned in the book, has moved on). When I first went to the Palazzo, I spoke in halting Italian, but the staff encouraged me, speaking slowly, helping me find phrases. They understood how daunting the interviews I had scheduled were but offered reassurance and assistance. As I returned, they followed my progress with great enthusiasm. Above all they created an atmosphere so intimate, so supportive, and so Italian that I felt I was in a cocoon, the perfect cradle for a project like mine.

Q: What words of encouragement or inspiration would you give to someone who may be intimidated to start learning Italian?

A: Thanks to the many Latin-based words in mainstream English, you already know lots of Italian words: *ciao, pizza, lasagna, buon giorno, opera, bello,* etc. Italian words sound exactly as they're spelled, so once you know how the vowels in particular sound (they are different than in English), you can sound out phrases. Even if you feel self-conscious, try saying *grazie* or *buona sera.* Italians will compliment and encourage you so you'll want to keep talking.

There are also so many ways to acquire at least a little Italian, including great podcasts. My favorite is Learnitalianpod .com, where you can get entertaining lessons at beginner, intermediate, and advanced levels for free. Rent classic Italian films with Marcello Mastroianni or the comedies of Roberto Benigni. Read the subtitles so you can follow the plot but absorb the sounds as well. If you love opera (as I do), read the lyrics (available online) so you can listen for words and phrases. Andrea Bocelli's songs are great because he enunciates very well, and contemporary pop songs (all on YouTube) can introduce you to wonderful singers, such as Tiziano Ferro, Paolo Conte, Zucchero, Mina, among many others.

Q: You have, by your own admission, "devoted countless hours and effort" to learning Italian by studying the language every way you could find, "from Berlitz to books, with CDs and podcasts, in private tutorials and conversation groups, and during what some might deem unconscionable amounts of time in Italy." You also note that there is no English word that quite captures the word *innamoramento,* "crazy head-over-heels love, deeper than infatuation, way beyond bewitched, bothered, and bewildered," which is how you feel, "enchanted by Italian, fascinated by its story and its stories, tantalized by its adventures, addicted to its sound, and ever eager to spend more time in its company." As reading in another language often helps one speak that language, what periodicals and journals might you recommend for Italian-language enthusiasts?

A: When in Italy, I read *Corriere della Sera* or *La Repubblica* every day. Each has a glossy weekly magazine filled with interesting articles on a wide range of subjects, from Italians' sex lives to celebrities to problems like immigration and poverty. I find advertisements particularly helpful in learning idioms—and *molto divertente*. And here's my guilty pleasure: Italian adventure comic books, which have hooked generations of Italians: *Tex, Diabolik, Martin Mystere, Dylan Dog*. A teacher recommended them to build grammar and reading skills, but I got totally caught up with the characters and plots.

Q: When did you discover Porto Ercole, and what are some of the attributes you like best about it?

A: In 1990, just after the first Gulf War, Bob and I planned to drive from Rome along the coast to Nice. We found a pleasant-looking property on the coast of Monte Argentario in the Relais & Châteaux guide, and we thought we'd try it. The moment we stepped out onto a flower-lined terrace overlooking the sea, I turned to Bob and said, "I want to come back here every year for the rest of my life." And we have!

I always hesitate to recommend the Maremma to everyone since there is no art, no magnificent churches, only a few first-class restaurants, no cultural fairs, nothing of great historical note. What we love is the sea, the splendid coast (very similar to ours here in northern California, which we also love), the tranquility, the beauty that practically hypnotizes us. We started renting a villa from some friends seven years ago (where we go after our Il Pellicano stay), and the month or so we spend there every year is our annual visit to *paradiso*.

Q: What are some of your favorite places in Tuscany and Umbria?

A: In Florence, I particularly like to stay at the Palazzo Magnani Feroni [Borgo San Frediano 5/+39 055 23 99 544/palazzo magnaniferoni.it], an exquisitely restored Renaissance palazzo with just twelve opulent suites and a roof terrace with a 360-degree view of the city. I also recommend GIDEC, an extremely well-run agency that rents artfully decorated apartments in centrally located *palazzi*. Among my favorite restaurants are Golden View [Via de' Bardi 58/+39 055 214 502/goldenviewopenbar.com], on the banks of the Arno with a close-up view of the Ponte Vecchio and the Ufizzi— ignore the cheesy name, reserve a window table, and enjoy the superb *fiorentina* steak and live jazz; and Alle Murate [Palazzo dell'Arte dei Giudici e Notai, Via del Proconsolo 16r/+39 055 240 618/allemurate.it] in a restored guild hall with sophisticated cuisine and the oldest known portrait of Dante Alighieri (with a straight rather than hooked nose). My favorite places to visit in the city include Beatrice's tomb in La Badia, a church near Dante's house; the view of the sunset from San Miniato al Monte; Boboli Gardens; Masaccio's frescoes in the Brancacci Chapel of the Church of Santa Maria del Carmine; and the reading room and Michelangelo staircase in the Laurentian Library. My most unforgettable experience in Florence was watching fireworks explode above the Piazza della Signoria as Zubin Mehta conducted Tchaikovsky's "1812 Overture" for the finale of the annual Maggio Musicale concert series.

In Tuscany, my favorite places to stay include Il Pellicano [Località Sbarcatello, Porto Ercole/+39 0564 858 111)/ pellicanohotel.com], the most romantic hotel I know in the most spectacular setting; Hotel Borgo San Felice [Località San Felice, Castelnuovo Berardenga, near Siena/+39 0577 39 64/borgosanfelice.com], a small medieval hamlet surrounded by vineyards and olive groves and an ideal base for exploring the Chianti countryside; Hotel Certosa di Maggiano [Strada di Certosa 82/86/+39 0577 288 180/certosadimaggiano .com], a restored monastery at the outskirts of Siena that of-

fers a gracious setting—including a loggia for leisurely outdoor lunches—and meticulous service, including the crispest
table linens I've ever seen. Restaurants include Ristorante da
Bracali [Via di Perolla Ghirlanda/+39 0566 902 318/
bracaliristorante.it], a Michelin-starred restaurant run by two
brothers—one the chef, the other the sommelier—with innovative cuisine and a superb wine list in a sophisticated setting that mixes classic and contemporary elements; Antica
Trattoria Aurora [Via Lavagnini 12/14, Magliano in
Toscana/+39 0564 592 774], where *cinghiale* (wild boar) is the
local specialty, and you can eat it in more ways than you
might guess in this charming, rustic trattoria. The walled medieval town, particularly impressive as you drive toward it in
the evening, is itself worth the trip. My favorite Tuscan places
are La Feniglia on the lagoon of Argentario for its long beach
and shady walking trail; Pitigliano for its dramatic setting;
Orbetello for its piazza, gelato, and shops. My most unforgettable Tuscan experience was chartering a boat to explore
the pristine islands of Giglio and Giannutri and to swim in
crystal-clear waters in quiet coves.

In Umbria, we've always stayed with friends or rented
houses, so I can't really recommend any hotels, but among
my favorite places are Monte Vibiano Vecchio, a thousand-
year-old *castello* that now produces premium olive oil and
wine; Spello for the *infiorata,* or flowering of the streets on the
feast of Corpus Christi (late May or early June, depending on
the date for Easter); Spoleto for the music and dance; Assisi for
the deep sense of faith and the magnificent frescoes throughout; and other hill towns—Todi, Perugia, Orvieto—are also
worth a visit.

As for wines, here's a list of favorites my husband created
last year for my editor Charlie Conrad: Fattoria Le Pupille,
Saffredi, 2004 (our favorite local wine of the region); Mar-
chesi de' Frescobaldi, Brunello di Montalcino, Castelgiocondo

Ripe al Convento Riserva, 2001 (excellent wine!); Antinori, Toscana Tignanello, 2004 (this was our favorite—great bouquet, simply fantastic); Fontodi, Colli della Toscana Centrale Flaccianello, 2004 (we had this at Da Bracali restaurant in Massa Marittima—truly a great Chianti, on par with the Tignanello); Castello Monte Vibiano Vecchio, Andrea, 2005 (this was from a friend's vineyard in Umbria—a super-Tuscan type wine); Tenuta dell'Ornellaia, Bolgheri Superiore Ornellaia, 2004 (always a great wine); we also like the new Gaja reds from Maremma, which are modestly priced. As an aside, we also recommend the Planeta Chardonnay from Sicily, 2005—the color is quite yellow and the flavor very intense, and we've had it every year for the past decade, though I think the older vintages were better.

Q: Is there a part of Italy you haven't yet explored?
A: Yes, we haven't ventured south of the Amalfi Coast. I'm particularly intrigued by Puglia and increasingly by Sicily and the islands off its coast.

Q: When is your next trip to Italy, and where are you going?
A: We're definitely heading back to Porto Ercole next June, but I'm beginning to research my next book, and that may take me to Venice (where I haven't been in many years) and Sardinia, as well as Florence, Siena, Rome, and Naples.

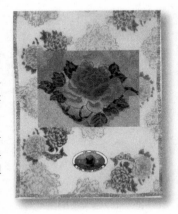

Lisa Corti Home Textile Emporium

I first discovered Lisa Corti in Positano, in the Emporio Le Sirenuse, the great gift shop of Le Sirenuse hotel. At the time, I didn't realize she had an outpost in Florence (Piazza Ghiberti 33r/+39 055 200 1860/lisacorti.com), and I'm so glad she added this city to her emporium network. (Other Lisa Corti shops are in Milan, Rome, and Madrid, while other retailers around the world carry some selected items; visit her Web site for more information and North American availability.) I am madly in love with Lisa Corti's products, and though they are all made in India, they sing with the enthusiasm and colors of an Italian spirit. The printed bedcovers and tablecloths are produced using an ancient, entirely handmade technique: a sculptor carves a series of wooden blocks, each one dyed a different color. The blocks are then pressed one by one onto the cloth, so no two pieces are ever identical. In addition to tablecloths and bedcovers, the Lisa Corti line currently includes pillows, quilted curtains, ceramics, and a few pieces of furniture.

M

Made in Italy

The "Made in Italy" tag was created to distinguish quality hand-crafted items from knockoffs in the marketplace, and though these items typically cost more, consumers know they are at least paying for something that isn't machine-made. *Made in Italy* is also the name of a wonderful and essential book whose subtitle is *A Shopper's Guide to Italy's Best Artisanal Traditions from Murano Glass to Ceramics, Jewelry, Leather Goods and More,* by Laura Morelli (Universe, 2008, second edition). This is not a shopper's guide—Morelli enhances our appreciation of (or introduces us to) the *prodotti artigianali* (most typical handcrafted products) from Italy's eighteen regions, and she has written a book that is informative, inspiring, and practical. Morelli writes that, for her, "the most impressive thing about Italian workmanship is that—even with today's sophisticated technologies—no one has improved on the hand-wrought designs of these unsung masters. Even in the twenty-first century, their work is still recognized around the world as a benchmark of quality." After the first edition of this book was published, Morelli's inbox was flooded with e-mails from readers who wanted to share stories about their own travels and the artisans and shops they'd discovered, and they asked her about how to recognize authentic goods. She believes that "people will wait and pay more for a beautiful object *when they can make a connection with the person whose labor and passion went into crafting it,*" and I completely agree.

Chapter three covers Tuscany and Umbria, and Morelli has added to this edition a special section on shopping for leather in Florence because it's been the most common request she's received. She also includes excellent information on shopping in Italy, packing, money, avoiding scams, getting your stuff home, and a phrase that is the Italian craftsman's motto: *Pochi, ma buoni* . . . ("Few, but good . . ."). Morelli loves to hear from her readers, and she may be reached through her Web site (lauramorelli.com), where readers may also subscribe to her e-newsletter, Laura Morelli's The Real Deal.

Madova

Beautiful leather gloves can be purchased many places in Florence, but I think Madova (Via Guicciardini 1r, just at the foot of

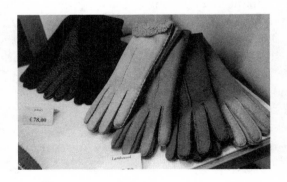

the Ponte Vecchio in the Oltrarno/+39 055 239 6525/madova
.com) is the best shop for selection, quality, size, color, and selection of linings in one place. Madova has been making gloves for
men and women since 1919, and mail orders are filled through its
online catalog (though nothing beats being able to browse the selections, and try them on, at the shop).

Marbled Paper

The art of making marbled paper, known as *ebru* ("the art of the
clouds"), flourished in Turkey in the fifteenth century. *Ebru*
served as book endpapers, mats for decorative calligraphy, decorative panels on fine woodwork, and most often as pale patterned
sheets for official documents that needed to be unforgeable and
unalterable.

Marbled paper arrived in Italy through Venice, but today the
making of it survives almost exclusively in Florence. I was surprised to read in an extensively researched book, *Marbled Paper:
Its History, Techniques, and Patterns* (Richard Wolfe, University of
Pennsylvania Press, 1990) that "Marbled decoration . . . never
became an extensive or integral part of bookmaking and book-
binding in Italy." But there are a few shops in Florence that
remain devoted to marbled paper and the book arts that I particularly like:

Giulio Giannini & Figlio, directly across from the Pitti Palace,
isn't undiscovered, but many visitors don't know that it's Florence's oldest marbled-paper maker, founded in 1856, and that it
began as a bookbinder catering to the large foreign literary colony
of the time. Elizabeth Barrett Browning's *Sonnets from the Por-
tuguese* and *Casa Guidi Windows* were published in later editions by
Giannini.

Il Torchio in via de' Bardi (via de' Bardi 17), started by Anna
Anichini three decades ago, is probably my favorite marbled-

paper shop because there are never very many people in it and its leather and paper bound books are sewn entirely by hand.

And last, is Carteria Tassotti (via dei Servi, 9/11r) steps away from the Duomo. I've included this wonderful shop on my list because, even though it doesn't stock marbled paper, its other handmade papers are beautiful. The Florence store is one of four in Italy, with the headquarters in the town of Bassano del Grappa in the Veneto. Bassano was famous between the years 1660 and 1860 for the Remondini family's publishing company, which also manufactured prints, colored paper, and decorated paper made by stamping with wooden blocks and metal plates. "Remondini papers" enjoyed an extensive reputation through-out Europe, though they were not very frequently used in book-making. The fall of the Venetian Republic marked the end of the Remondini empire, but in 1957 Giorgio Tassotti relaunched the tradition by producing hand-colored prints and now there are four thousand items in inventory. Grafiche Tassotti is a fam-ily company, and all its products are produced by the company itself.

Marbled paper is more than just a pretty product; as Richard Wolfe notes, "Few people today are aware of the considerable role that marbled paper played in the everyday life of Europe and the Western world from late in the seventeenth century until late in the nineteenth." When I purchase marbled paper—and I never leave Florence without at least one paper find—I feel I'm buying a piece of artistic heritage.

Medici Family

The Medici may be the most significant family in all of Italian history; it certainly is the most significant in the history of Florence. The family's origins are actually in Tuscany, in the area of Mugello, where the Villa Medicea di Cafaggiolo is located (the villa dates from the fourteenth century and is about twenty-five kilometers north of Florence). The villa is reportedly not very large or very grand, perhaps reflecting the family's original standing: they were farmers who only later, after moving into Florence, became merchants and bankers.

The Medici family insignia is known as Le Palle dei Medici (the Medici Balls), which may derive from the cry of *"Palle! Palle!"* used to rally supporters of the Medici, or from the representation of pills or cupping glasses, since the name Medici means "doctor." Whatever the derivation, it changed over the years, with the number of balls represented being eleven, eight, seven, and finally six. Cosimo I's version was the final one, and features six balls and the crown of the Grand Duke.

The most renowned reads on the Medici are *The Last Medici,* Harold Acton (Thames & Hudson, 1980; originally published in 1932), an illustrated edition published to coincide with an exhibit on the Medici and their world in Florence in 1980; *The Medici,* Ferdinand Schevill (Konecky & Konecky, 1949); and *The House of Medici: Its Rise and Fall,* Christopher Hibbert (William Morrow, 1975)—my edition is a beautiful one published by the Folio Society, and includes color inserts and a section called "Notes on Buildings and Works of Art," which is worthy on its own). However, on my last visit to Florence I found a new volume, *The Medici: Story of a European Dynasty,* Franco Cesati (Mandragora, 1999). Mandragora is an Italian publisher (mandragora.it), founded in 1985, that specializes in catalogs and essays in art, history, architecture, photography, guidebooks, and children's books on Florence and Tuscany. You may see a lot of books by this terrific publisher in museum shops and bookstores and will likely be as impressed as I am by their quality and title selections. I bought this at the Bargello Museum, and it's a perfect volume for travelers who want a good overview of the family but don't want to delve into larger tomes. The book is only 143 pages, packed with color reproductions of artworks and photographs, and it opens with a very good chapter, "Florence before the Medici," which presents in particular the phenomenon of the city-states that were so characteristic of Italy during the twelfth and thirteenth centuries. I admit that I was drawn initially to the cover, featuring one of my favorite paintings—*Allegory of Peace and War* by Pietro da Cortona, which hangs in the Palazzo Pitti—and I was happy to discover that the book was so substantive. (By the way, if you arrive back home and regret you didn't purchase a particular Mandragora book, contact the publisher's U.S. distributor, Antique Collectors' Club in Easthampton, Massachusetts (800 252 5231/ antiquecollectorsclub.com), and the staff will help you find a retailer that stocks Mandragora titles or arrange for a copy to be sent to you from Italy.)

A parting Medici thought from Sir Harold Acton, who contributed the foreword to *The House of Medici:* "The Medici were superlative patrons and collectors of art until their last gasp. The Rev. William Bromley's judgement in *A Philosophical and Critical History of the Fine Arts* (1793–5) is still valid: 'Perhaps on the face of the earth there never existed a family to which the fine arts, and the general interests of learning, have been so much indebted.' "

Mercati

Markets, especially outdoor ones, are one of the unrivaled pleasures of Italy: they are still one of the most important social activities, and many towns and cities have a *piazza del mercato* (especially in Tuscany). Even if you have no intention of purchasing anything, visitors should not miss walking around an outdoor (or indoor) market.

After unification in 1860, when Florence was designated capital of the new nation, an overall cleanup of the city was deemed necessary for this new honor, and three markets were built: the Mercato Centrale, also known as San Lorenzo, designed by Giuseppe Mengoni, who also designed the magnificent Galleria Vittorio Emanuele II in Milan; Sant'Ambrogio, near Santa Croce; and San Frediano, in the Oltrarno but no longer in existence. Other markets in Florence are Piazza Santo Spirito, a produce market Monday to Saturday mornings, and an antiques market on the second Sunday of the month; Mercato Nuovo, also known as Loggia del Porcellino, between the Piazza Repubblica and Via Por Santa Maria, where the legend is that if you rub the pig (*porcellino*) statue's snout it will bring good luck and ensure you return to Florence; and Piazza dei Ciompi, near Santa Croce, for antiques, open 9 a.m. to 1 p.m. and 3 p.m. to 6 p.m. daily.

A great market resource is *The Antique & Flea Markets of Italy,* Marina Seveso (Little Bookroom, 2003). It's only sixty-four pages and a paperback, so it's easy to pack, and it's indispensable, with information on market days, times, and specialties of each.

Prices for food seem to be displayed and fixed in Italy, but for other things bargaining is the accepted method of doing business (merchants will tell you if it's not; see my Istanbul book for a wealth of bargaining tips). Therefore, a visit to the market should not be an activity you try to do in a hurry. Take your time, remember to stop for something to eat or drink so your stomach (or companion) doesn't grumble, and enjoy searching for a unique *ricordo* (souvenir) while soaking up the atmosphere.

Mezzadria

Mezzadria refers to an agricultural system of labor that was not unique to Tuscany but was most firmly entrenched there and among the most defining aspects of Tuscan life. Iris Origo, in *War in Val d'Orcia,* said of *mezzadria* that "like many traditional systems handed down from father to son, the *mezzadria* compact is both very complicated and very elastic. . . . It is not quite that of landlord and tenant, nor certainly that of employer and employee— it is more intimate than the former, more friendly than the latter. It is a partnership." Yet it is a partnership that's not easily defined. I've read two accounts of the first recorded *mezzadria* contract, one dating from 759 in Lucca and the other from 821; whichever it is, more relevant is that *mezzadria* remained in place until the 1960s, when many of the old countryside farmhouses in Tuscany became vacant for the first time in five centuries.

Claudia Roden, in *The Food of Italy,* explains the background for *mezzadria* by noting that "Tuscany was different from other Italian states in that a kind of equality prevailed. All the people— noblemen, merchants, and even peasants—were citizens with political rights, and all more or less shared in public life. The landowning nobility did not live in castles. As soon as a merchant became well-off, he invested some of his money in farmland, often with a small villa where his family spent the hot summer months. The slopes of the surrounding hills were dotted with such villas and there was a perpetual two-way traffic between town and country. Everyone was tied to the land." The *mezzadria* system on the farms dictated that the landowner and the peasants who worked the land shared in the profits of the farm. But the system wasn't feudal, where vassals lived on land belonging to a noble, and it wasn't the same as sharecropping, where farmers worked the land of the noble and gave the noble part of the harvested crops as rent payment.

Isabella Dusi, in *Bel Vino,* refers to *mezzadria* as "an ugly battle for survival." The landowners didn't always have much cash at hand, but they owned enormous parcels of land. But unless the landowners could convert their land into wealth, they couldn't live in the style expected by their socially superior friends. Peasants had no land, no money, and nowhere to live, so their end of the contract was to work the land and pledge half the fruits of their labor to the landowner (*padrone*), who provided whatever the peasants needed in order to make the land produce. Dusi explains that "the crucial difference between the *mezzadria* and other medieval farming practices was the contract written as law between peasant farmer and *padrone* imposed that the *contadino*'s financial reward be reckoned according to the *profits* of his labor. As the centuries passed, the reckoning of the *mezzadria* split became a cruel battle of wits because many *padrone* believed superior social class gave them the right to reduce the *contadini* to servility." Landowners exploited the ignorance of the *contadino*, who was usually illiterate and couldn't add figures, so nearly every year the *padrone* would record in the books that the *contadino* family hadn't made a profit, making the family further indebted to the *padrone*.

By the late 1950s and '60s *mezzadria* contracts stipulated that produce harvested was to be shared half and half, but by this time farming machinery was introduced and the old ways of picking everything by hand were almost obsolete. Claudia Roden notes that "a few small farmers continue in the old archaic way of varied mixed cultivation, and their bit of landscape has remained like the background in Renaissance paintings, but the rest has changed."

Mulino Bianco

Mulino Bianco, founded in 1975 and a member of the Barilla Group, is a well-known brand of Italian baked goods. Barilla, founded in 1877 in Parma and best known for its pasta, remains a privately owned, family-run business; it also owns Wasa crispbread and sixteen other brands. Mulino Bianco crackers and cookies are found in food markets of all sizes throughout Italy, so it may seem a little odd that I am recommending such ubiquitous products. But there is something about them that is tasty and in some cases rather healthy—like the Grancereale Classico, *ricco di fibre,* my favorite—and they are great additions to alfresco picnics or for snacks while you're out and about or on the train or at the airport.

Museum of the Etruscan Academy and of the City of Cortona (MAEC)

Cortona was a wonderful town to visit before this museum opened in 2005, but MAEC's presence is now one more reason to allot significant time here (cortonamaec.org). Of most relevant interest are the finds from Etruscan tomb excavations; notable works by Pietro Berrettini (known as Pietro da Cortona), Luca Signorelli, and Italian futurist Gino Severini; and the academic library. The Diocesan Museum is a part of this complex, and nine exhibition halls hold artworks from the second century to modern art.

Olio & Convivium

Olio & Convivium (Via di Santo Spirito 4/+39 055 265 8198) is a glorious outpost of Convivium Firenze, a Tuscan *atelier gastronomico* located on Viale Europa near Porta Romana (convivium firenze.it). The Convivium emblem is a coat of arms bearing the symbol of the fourteenth-century Guild of Oil Sellers and Grocers of Florence, featuring a lion with an olive tree branch in its claws. I haven't yet been to the Viale Europa store—though I hear it's beautiful, in a restored farmhouse dating from 1300—but the Olio branch is in historic Palazzo Capponi in the Oltrarno. What makes both locations unique is that each has a restaurant (more about meals there on my blog) and a fantastic shop, where you can select provisions for a takeaway picnic (cheese, bread, salami, wine, etc.) and prepared dishes (pasta and vegetable dishes, salads, etc.), as well as a great assortment of noted Tuscan specialties;

there is also a line of Convivium's own products, including honeys, jams, pasta sauces, biscuits, and the gift wrapping and presentation is, naturally, fantastic.

Catering and cooking classes may be arranged, but to me the really special thing about Olio & Convivium is its olive oil tastings. Olio is one of the few places in Italy where you have the opportunity to taste and buy so many oils—there are approximately sixty in stock at any given time, all from Tuscany and many unavailable outside of Italy. Like wine, Tuscan oils are all about the *terra* (land), and tasting them side by side reveals their vast differences. Tasters learn that you can't tell if an oil is strong or light solely by its color, but since people tend to form an opinion based on color, the oils are poured into dark blue glasses so you can't see the color of the oil. Bites of apple between oils is a great palate cleanser, and anyone can learn to taste the difference between an artisanal oil and a supermarket oil.

Olio's oils are generally not for cooking—they're better for salads, sauces, pasta, and dips—and among the most popular here are Podere Forte and Villa Magra dei Franci. Oils that are also available in the United States are generally less expensive here and are available in different sizes. Tastings take about an hour, and reservations are required.

Opificio delle Pietre Dure

The two main types of stone in Tuscany are *pietra forte* (a yellow-brown sandstone found in the hills around Florence; many of Florence's medieval buildings are of *pietra forte,* including Palazzo

Vecchio, Orsanmichele, Santa Croce, and Santa Maria Novella) and *pietra serena* (also a sandstone, found in the Fiesole hills and of a silvery gray color; Brunelleschi was one of the first to use it, and he chose it for the columns in San Lorenzo, Santo Spirito, and the Pazzi Chapel in Santa Croce). According to Pier Francesco Listri in *The Tuscan Lifestyle, pietra forte*'s "continuing availability over the centuries meant that, fifty years ago, blocks of it were quarried to rebuild the bridge of Santa Trinità, which had been blown up by the Germans."

Pietre dure refers to the art of mosaics in semiprecious stones and colored marbles, "assembled with such precision that no joins were visible to the naked eye—one more instance of nature and art singing a duet," according to Marina Belozerskaya in *The Arts of Tuscany*. Belozerskaya also notes that the members of the Medici family loved stones—it is no accident that the Chapel of the Princes in San Lorenzo in Florence is completely lined with colored marble inlays. Ferdinando I in particular loved *pietre dure* because he also loved both natural sciences and colored stones, and it was his wish for the Chapel of the Princes (though the planning of the chapel took decades, he laid the foundation stone in 1604). The chapel took more than 250 years to complete, but before it was finished Florence had already become world famous for *pietre dure* mosaics, inset into pieces of furniture and made into ornaments, tabletops, and church altar scenes. Belozerskaya explains that in addition to the showroom and studio in front of Santa Croce, "the museums and churches of Florence are also full of *pietre dure* masterpieces. Once you are attuned to them, you start seeing them everywhere and wonder how you could have missed them before." Visitors may learn more about this detailed art at the Opificio (workshop) delle Pietre Dure (Via degli Alfani 78/opificiodellepietredure.it), which is inexplicably little visited by tourists and Florentines alike. It's referred to as a workshop because *pietre dure* mosaics are crafted and restored there (the restoration of the Duomo's cupola frescoes were handled by the

Opificio staff), but in addition there is a gem of a museum that I enthusiastically encourage you to visit. It's really beautiful, and really quiet, and really impressive.

Orario Continuato

This phrase translates as "continuous hours"—in other words, open all day, as more and more businesses in Italy are these days. Still, it's far better to assume a business will close for a *pausa* (the Italian equivalent of *siesta*) than not.

Osteria La Solita Zuppa

I stated earlier that I've devoted a corner of my blog to a detailed listing of many of my favorite places to eat and drink in Tuscany and Umbria, but I can't resist including this wonderful little *osteria* in this Miscellany. La Solita Zuppa (Via Porsenna 21, Chiusi/+39 0578 21 006/lasolitazuppa.it) is not undiscovered, but neither is it well known. I went twice during a week I was staying outside of Sarteano, during which I concluded that some mighty delicious dishes are turned out here, and I implored the owner to think about writing a cookbook. It's not only the traditional dishes—*pici con ragù di cinghiale,* bean soup, for example—that are terrific, but the unusual ones are, too, like *tagliolini allo zenzero* with a sauce of minced fresh ginger, cream, and poppy seeds, which remains one of the most memorable dishes of my life. The atmosphere is cozy and warm, the service is friendly and caring, and the tables fill up fast. I would come here for no other reason than a meal, but it happens that the upper town of Chiusi is lovely and has a small but interesting ar-

chaeological museum and a Romanesque duomo, so I recommend making a half-day journey. If you come on market day, held in the (less attractive) lower town, you can buy excellent provisions for a picnic or a villa kitchen, as well as some inexpensive practical items like kitchen linens and napkins.

P

Pane e Coperta

About a dozen years ago or so, there was a movement to try to stop Italian *ristoranti* and *trattorie* from charging a *pane e coperta* fee (supposedly for the bread and rental of the silverware; see Eating Establishments, page 528), which could range from about two to six dollars. Although the *pane e coperta* is no longer ubiquitous, some establishments do, regrettably, still charge for it. It's not really a big deal, and certainly not worth arguing over, but if you're just stopping for a plate of pasta and a glass of wine, the *coperta* could cost half as much as your meal.

Pazienza

This word, for "patience," is defined by Kate Simon in her book *Italy: The Places in Between* as "the capacity to endure with serenity"—a much better definition, I think, and very much worth remembering when traveling in Italy.

Per Piacere, Per Favore, Permesso, Più Lentamente, *and* Prego

These are some good Italian *p* words to know. *Per piacere* and *per favore* mean "please"; *permesso* means "may I" or "excuse me," and it's a polite way to ask if you may enter, sit down, take something, ask a question; *più lentamente* is useful to remember when you want to say, "please speak more slowly"; and *prego* is an all-purpose word used to mean "please," "you're welcome," "okay," "of course," "go ahead."

Pharmacies

Monasteries and convents throughout Europe have a long history of producing all kinds of elixirs, brews, remedies, and culinary specialties, and Tuscany especially has been a center of pharmacology and medicine. Historically, rooms were set aside for the care of the sick within monasteries and convents, and these rooms generally opened onto gardens of medicinal plants that were used to create remedies. According to the Louis Vuitton *European Cities* guide (volume VII, 2004), "After the turn of the first millennium, medicinal products were freely bought and sold in the public grocery stores that proliferated in Florence. The dissolution of the monastic system and the enforcement of modern sanitation norms to which hospital pharmacies gradually adhered were to outlaw counters such as these. Florence long remained the only Italian city in which these ancestral dispensaries lived on, and forty remain active today."

The most famous pharmacy in Florence is Santa Maria Novella (Via della Scala 16/+39 055 216 276/smnovella.it). The Officina Profumo Farmaceutica di Santa Maria Novella (as it's known in full) is still, after many years, the most beautiful shop I've ever stepped into in my life. Pharmaceutical activity began at the Officina in 1221, when the Dominican friars established themselves in Florence in the small church of Santa Maria fra le Vigne ("amidst the vineyards"), the old name of Santa Maria Novella. The first definitive reference to the production of an herbal potion dates from 1381, when rosewater was for sale in the infirmary—at the time, rosewater was considered to be an effective antiseptic used to clean houses during epidemics of plague, for example, as well as a mild medicine to be diluted in wine or to be used for the swallowing of pills. The monastery's ledgers over the next few centuries are incomplete, but from 1590 to the present day the pharmacy has continued its activity almost without interruption. I had the great fortune on my last visit to be given a tour of the little Officina museum, which opened in 2006, including a small section that is usually roped off to visitors. Though small, the museum is fascinating, with collections of Montelupo ceramics dating from the 1700s, distillation bottles from 1919 to 1925, a book about herbs dating from the 1600s, soap machines from the late 1800s, framed Officina logos, and huge terra-cotta pots used to make the Officina's legendary potpourri—the mixture must remain in the jars for no fewer than sixty days.

Before 1848, entrance into the Officina was through the monastery, but today visitors enter through a beautiful round-arched *pietra serena* doorway on Via della Scala. Embedded in the pediment above the door is the Dominican monks' emblem, which features a radiant sun and which has become a common emblem in this neighborhood. Once you step inside you walk down a hallway that feels a little bit like the scene in *The Wizard of Oz* when Dorothy and her pals are walking down the cavernous hall to meet the great wizard. But once you reach the end of it, there is no man behind a curtain or a wizard, just a gorgeous space that was originally one of the monastery's most splendid chapels, consecrated to Saint Nicholas of Bari, a patron saint of the Acciaiuoli, a family of rich Florentine merchants. This is the main salesroom, but I would recommend walking around the other rooms first before you come back here to linger. From the room called the old pharmacy, you can glimpse the beautiful courtyard, which is unfortunately off-limits to visitors as it belongs to a military school. My guide, Ursula Bianchi, told me that the old pharmacy room is where everything started here, and just about everything in the room is original—the wooden cabinets with glass doors, the ceiling, the sales desk. But the most precious thing of all at the Officina, Bianchi noted, is the Sacristy of San Niccolò. Since the seventeenth century this room had been used as a storeroom for distilled waters, and the walls are entirely frescoed with scenes from Christ's Passion. Though the floodwaters of 1966 did reach the Officina and did some damage (in one room you can see the watermarks, which have been purposefully retained), they didn't reach the sacristy, and the frescoes have never needed to be cleaned. The sacristy is now also a little library, and there are lots of great books about Florence there to page through (but they are not for sale).

The Officina products, for men and women, are fantastic and beautifully packaged, and some of the perfumes are made using recipes dating from 1867. Bianchi told me that the pomegranate perfume is the absolute bestseller, but my number one favorite item, which I cannot live without, is the Crema di Pedestre, almond-scented foot cream. (I can also enthusiastically endorse the Idrasol body cream, the mint bath gel, the rose-scented body lotion, the soaps, and of course the potpourri—I actually bought a package of it some years ago and keep it in my suitcase just so everything smells good for the duration of my trip.) A visit to the Officina is just as interesting, and historic, as Santa Maria Novella itself.

You can find Officina products at several outposts in the United States, notably at Lafco stores, which happily also offer other wonderful Italian products, including the Eau d'Italie products from Le Sirenuse (also one of my favorites) and products created by Florentine perfumer Lorenzo Villoresi. Villoresi customizes fragrances for individual clients as well as luxury hotels, like the Four Seasons Firenze; to reserve an appointment, visit Lorenzovilloresi.it. The flagship Lafco store is in New York (285 Lafayette Street/212 925 0001 or 800 362 3677/lafcony .com), but there are Los Angeles and Dallas locations as well.

Pom613

This nifty culinary company was founded by Jennifer Schwartz, who had previously worked with Faith Willinger. It takes its name from the many (approximately 613, according to Jewish lore) seeds in a pomegranate, long a symbol of good luck and prosperity in Near Eastern cultures. Schwartz and her team of eno-gastronomic experts arrange food lover's tours—Flash in the Pan, a one-day market and tasting tour, and Marinade, an intense four-to-five-day itinerary—as well as accommodations, transportation, guides, and exclusive visits to public and private lifestyle and cultural destinations. Though pom613 is based in Florence, the Marinade tours are offered in Emilia-Romagna, the Veneto, Piedmont, and Palermo, as well as Tokyo and Kyoto in Japan, Burgundy and Lyon in France, and in Morocco. All of this is done to support the Associazione Culturale Enogastronomica, and the pom613 staff also assists culinary professionals in what it refers to as *mise en place,* an opportunity to intern with great chefs and culinary artisans in another culture.

A pom613 experience is meant to allow guests to feel at home immediately, like they really blend in and are not viewed as just another tourist—"Walk like you live here" is a motto the company promotes. Pom city guides—unobtrusive electronic guides produced in conjunction with Digi-Guides—have also been compiled with this motto in mind (see more about these city guides on my blog). Contact pom613 at info@pom613/pom613 .com/646 502 5292 (U.S. number)/fax: +39 055 436 8108.

Prato

Prato, nineteen kilometers northwest of Florence, is a wonderful city that is often overlooked by travelers. Indeed, it was overlooked by me until my most recent visit to Tuscany and Umbria, and I was amazed at how rewarding it was—and perplexed that

I'd waited so long to visit! I admit the major reason I added it to my itinerary was that I'd recently read and very much enjoyed Iris Origo's *The Merchant of Prato*, about the real life and times of a Prato merchant, Francesco di Marco Datini. Historian Barbara Tuchman contributed a foreword to the reissued edition (the original was published in 1957; see La Foce, page 506), and she refers to it as "one of the great works of historical writing of the twentieth century." Prato was once one of the world's largest textile centers—Origo notes in her opening line that the people of Prato "are level-headed, skeptical, and practical folk whose chief concern is, and has always been, the manufacture of cloth"—and a mill on the River Bisenzio was established fifty-six years before the oldest mill in Florence. Datini was Prato's leading cloth dealer and maker, and also a banker and insurer—he invented the letter of credit for payments to banks throughout the Mediterranean world as he had agents in several ports of call. Every one of his transactions, which Origo meticulously details, was carried out "in the name of God and of profit." Origo recounts the legend— as that is what it has become—of Datini, which is a story of a merchant and a cat, but she also notes that this legend has been told about several other merchants of the time, and that in all of Datini's vast correspondence there is no mention of a cat. "But that so persistent a tradition should have continued to connect the story with his name indicates the position that he held, and still holds, in the minds of his fellow citizens."

Datini is represented by a statue in Piazza del Comune; his tomb is in the church of San Francesco; he is featured in a painting, *Prato in the Fourteenth Century,* in the Palazzo Pretorio; and the portal of the Church of Sant'Agostino features a lintel bearing Datini's coat of arms. But the best portrayal of him in Prato is his home, the Casa Datini (Via Ser Lapo Mazzei 43), now one of my favorite sites in all of Italy (admission is free). Among the many interesting facts I learned here was the clarification of the word *ceppo*. In the painting depicting Datini in the Palazzo Pretorio (Datini is the figure on the right), he is presenting his *ceppo* to the city. *Ceppo* is the word for "log," and it refers to the log of a tree that was hollowed out and in it were placed offerings for the indigent. The *ceppo* was dedicated to helping invalids, women in labor, religious men, and prisoners, and also poor people who had fallen into disgrace and didn't want their state of poverty to be known.

Prato's textile museum—Italy's largest center for the study, conservation, and exhibition of historic and contemporary textiles—is also very worthwhile (museodeltessuto.it), and there is an impressive number of open-air artworks in and around Prato, many of which are perfectly integrated in the landscape. The Agenzia per il Turismo di Prato's Web site (pratoturismo.it) offers some terrific information, including a great free download, "Prato in Tuscany: History, Art, Territory."

After I read *The Merchant of Prato,* I read a book that was quite different but equally interesting: *The Miracles of Prato,* by Laurie Albanese and Laura Morowitz (William Morrow, 2009). Though a novel, the book includes characters both real and imagined, the central one being painter Fra Filippo Lippi. It's the kind of book you start reading and can't stop until you reach the end, which is what I did over just a few days because I couldn't stand to stretch it out any longer. Then I went back and started rereading passages. *The Miracles of Prato* is a perfect companion read. I hope you'll read it, and I also hope it inspires you to learn more about the stunning work of Lippi.

Laurie's Web site (lauralicoalbanese.com) contains lots of background information on the book and stories of her friendship with Laura, as well as a section on Lippi's art. I caught up with the author team a few months after their book was published.

Q: Laurie, Laura gave you a book on the works of Filippo Lippi she bought at the Metropolitan Museum of Art for your

birthday. Were you already familiar with Lippi's paintings or were you seeing them for the first time? In either case, there are many hundreds of books published about Lippi; what was it precisely about his work or his life that led you to think of writing a novel?

A: I wasn't familiar with Fra Lippi's Italian Renaissance work until Laura made a passionate case for the dramatic narrative inherent in his art and life, and presented me with *The Library of Great Masters: Filippo Lippi* Scala/Riverside edition of his paintings for my birthday. She was very wise—the book was slim enough to tuck into my suitcase, and it's filled with more pictures than words. I took the book away with me on an autumn beach trip, and after spending only a few hours paging through the fabulous frescoes—and especially taking note of the tiny details at the edges of his paintings, where there seem to be separate dramas and mysteries being played out beyond the larger tableaux—I wrote the opening lines for our book: *There's always blood . . .*

Q: Laura, in your career as an art history professor, and as the author of a book entitled *Consuming the Past: The Medieval Revival in Fin-de-Siècle France,* when did you encounter Lippi and other Italian Renaissance artists and why were you particularly interested in delving into this subject?

A: I first encountered Lippi in an undergraduate course on Renaissance art at Brooklyn College. I vividly remember my professor telling us about this randy painter-monk who had an affair with a young nun; I thought his paintings of sensuous Madonnas with heart-shaped faces, delicious babies, gorgeous Florentine pinks and oranges and smoky greens, were beautiful. I would go to the Metropolitan Museum of Art and visit my favorite Lippis there, or to the Frick Collection. I was really smitten with early Renaissance art—precisely the period in which Lippi was working—and it became one of my areas of specialty when I went to the Institute of Fine Arts to get my PhD. I went to Florence for the first time on a scholarship in my early twenties and between the *quattrocento* paintings, the Duomo, and the gelato, I thought it was the most miraculous place on earth.

Even as a young college student I thought Fra Lippi's story would make an incredible novel or movie. When I shared my original excitement about Lippi's life and art with Laurie, we both became instantly attached to the idea of writing this story because we thought it had all the elements of a great tale—a gripping love story, against all odds, a complex and fascinating protagonist. We knew we could layer in so much about Italian Renaissance history and culture, and its politics, because Lippi himself was right at the center of what was unfolding. And we knew it would allow us to contemplate and write about some of the most stunning paintings ever produced.

Q: The three of us unanimously agree that Prato is deserving of many more North American visitors. Can you share some of your favorite things about the city?

A: Any visit to Prato should start in the old city, inside the thirteenth-century stone walls. Here, cobbled streets, small shops, and lovely cafés line the streets that lead to the Piazza del Duomo and the Cathedral of Santo Stefano, which is the cultural and religious heart of the city. The cathedral's distinctive green and white stone façade is the hallmark of Pratese architecture. The Sacra Cintola of the Madonna, a relic housed in Prato, plays a very important role in our novel, so naturally we were very excited to visit the chapel dedicated to it. Its walls are covered in frescoes by Agnolo Gaddi, from the fourteenth century, which tell the story of the miraculous belt, or girdle, of the Virgin, and the belt itself rests in an elaborate reliquary.

Directly behind the cathedral is Aroma di Vino [Via Santo Stefano 24/+39 0574 433 800/pratoaromadivino.it] where host and chef Daniello keeps an array of delicious Pratese and Tuscan specialties flowing to your table. Our kids loved the permanent "exhibit" of drawings hanging on the wall—many on place mats—by happy and sated visitors.

The Datini palazzo is only a short walk from the Piazza di Santo Stefano (in Prato nearly everything is a short walk!). This is an incredible *trecento* palazzo of the merchant of Prato, Francesco Datini. At one time his wealth was announced immediately to all passersby by a rich set of exterior frescoes. Most have been taken inside now, and what remains on the outside, the underdrawing, or sinopia, in red crayon, is a virtual lesson in mural preparation from the period. We based a family of patrons in our novel, the Valentis, on the magnanimous Datini family and loved seeing the original rooms and even a cache of letters written from husband to wife (incredibly preserved for centuries by being hidden in a little-used staircase). A statue dedicated to Datini decorates the Piazza del Comune, one of the most picturesque piazzas in the city, situated in front of the town hall. Have a cup of cappuccino or glass of wine and sit and watch the people passing by.

You don't have to stay overnight to enjoy Prato as a day trip from Florence, but there are a number of lovely small inns in the old city that are worth a visit. At the Borgo al Cornio B&B [Via Convenevole da Prato 30/+39 0574 440 222/ borgoalcornio.com], a full breakfast is served in the cheery dining room, and Massimo and his wife, Antonella, are glad to answer any questions. (Incidentally, a great thrift shop next door to the B&B proved a lifesaver when our luggage had still failed to show up two days after we'd arrived!) We recommend only staying in the old city; other inns on the cobblestone streets include the Hotel Flora [Via Cairoli 31/+39 0574 33 521/hotelflora .info] and the Giardino Hotel [Via Magnolfi 2–6/+39 0574 26 189/ giardinohotel.com].

IL PALAZZO DATINI

The Piazza Mercatale was once the thriving heart of Renaissance Prato—alive with fishmongers, butchers, vintners, and fruit sellers. Mostly quiet now, it is still thronged with numerous restaurants, such as Osteria Cibbe, and a close walk to the Porta Mercatale, the old gate that leads to the River Bisenzia crossing into a tiny section of the city, where we strolled and admired the many private mansions, many incorporating details from centuries ago.

Q: Have you received some correspondence from readers or booksellers that you felt were particularly gratifying?

A: A number of friends have visited Prato since reading our book—everyone is always very impressed with Lippi's stunning frescoes—and Odette Pagliai in the local tourism office tells us that every week she gets American visitors who come into town holding *The Miracles of Prato* or the travel piece on Prato I wrote for the *New York Times* (March 2, 2008). An art historian in Savannah even used our book to teach her students about Lippi before taking them on a guided tour of Prato. Whenever we're fortunate enough to meet a group of our readers, we hear how delighted they are to learn about Fra Lippi and his stunning works. Despite his importance in the early Renaissance and his contributions to the lifelike aspect of Italian painting, he's not nearly as well known as some of his contemporaries. After reading our novel people are inspired to learn more about the methods and even the materials that painters of that time used—a lot of it's already in the book, but there's always more to learn.

Q: As best friends and coauthors do you think you will write another book together?

A: We are at work on a new novel set in a very different time and place than Renaissance Prato, but involving the reader in an equally fascinating milieu. We are plunging into this lost time with equal gusto (even if we know the food runs more along the lines of boiled hog and rice than biscotti and *pappa al pomodoro!*).

Procession of the Magi, *by Benozzo Gozzoli*

I no longer remember the reasons why I didn't put this painting, by Benozzo Gozzoli, in the Palazzo Medici Riccardi (Via Cavour 1/palazzo-medici.it), on my short list of things to do in Florence over the years, though it doesn't really matter. I did finally see it, about five years ago, after reading what two enthusiasts wrote about it in the must-have book *City Secrets: Florence, Venice & the*

Towns of Italy (Little Bookroom, 2001). One, the poet Jacqueline Osherow, noted that she "used to find it impossible to be on the Via Cavour, or, indeed, anywhere near the Palazzo Medici Ricardi, without running into the courtyard and up the steps to spend at least a few minutes taking in" the painting. (And I am grateful to her for sharing the title of a book she found illuminating, *Benozzo Gozzoli,* by Diane Cole Ahl, Yale University Press, 1996.) The other contributor mentioned that the painting is one of her son's favorite stops in the world, "a kind of *Where's Waldo?* fresco, abundant with exotic animals and birds." Indeed, when I took my then five-and-a-half-year-old daughter there, she, too, thought it great fun to search for all kinds of things. It is a magnificent procession, and is now firmly on my short list.

R

Riposo Settimanale

This is a good Italian phrase to know as it refers to a regular day of the week an establishment is closed. You'll often see this posted on a sign, and it is often Monday.

Rivoire

I stated earlier that I've devoted a corner of my blog to a detailed listing of many of my favorite places to eat and drink in Tuscany and Umbria, but I can't resist including this renowned Florence establishment here. Caffè Rivoire, on Piazza della Signoria, is one of the world's most delightful places (+39 055 214 412/rivoire.it). It's an excellent place for people-watching, and from an outdoor seat your view includes the Palazzo Vecchio, the Loggia dei Lanzi, and the Neptune statue. And if you are outside and you feel surrounded by tourists, just step inside and you'll find it filled with locals. Many visitors who never make it inside don't realize that there is a counter with assorted Rivoire chocolates for sale. These come packaged in beautiful souvenir boxes with Florentine scenes, and there are also brightly colored small packages of chocolate squares that make great gifts and won't take up much room in your bags (neither is a suitable choice in hot weather, however). *Cioccolata con panna*—hot chocolate with whipped cream—is a popular treat here, and it is memorable (and also memorably expensive, but, remember, you can stay at your table for as long as you like, or you can stand at the counter indoors and pay far less). But *sitting* here is really what's memorable, and I would order anything for the opportunity to *be* here. Rivoire is also a great meeting place because anyone can find it.

My most recent stop there was my best yet. My brother- and sister-in-law had arranged to meet me at Rivoire but kept my presence in Florence a secret from my nieces, Caroline and Allison. On a brilliantly sunny day at noon, I walked down Via dei Calzaiuoli toward the piazza, and as I approached Rivoire, I made eye contact with my brother-in-law Gordon. At that moment, he turned to my nieces and said, "Wouldn't it be cool if we saw someone we knew here?" They rolled  their eyes and said, "Yeah, right, Dad. Dream on." Their table was only two rows in, and I stood at the Rivoire railing waiting for my nieces to notice me. Allison looked up and I was directly in her line of vision. She pointed and said, "Look, there's Aunt Barrie!" It was a special moment, and it happened at Rivoire.

La Rocca Paolina

Perugia's Rocca Paolina is, to my mind, the most extraordinary site in all of Umbria, and certainly one of the most impressive in all of Italy. It's an enormous fortress that Pope Paolo III ordered to be built after Rodolfo Baglioni (last surviving member of the family) assassinated a papal legate in retaliation for the murder of his uncle, Gian Paolo Baglioni, by Leo X. The pope decided to raise the salt tax, even though he'd previously promised not to do so, and of course the Perugini rebelled, giving the pope the excuse he wanted to gain control over the population. Very quickly papal forces moved in and, after demolishing a quarter of the city (including the houses of the Baglioni family, the Church of Saint Mary of the Servants, and the Saint Giuliana quarter), La Rocca Paolina was constructed—built by the Perugini themselves using the destroyed houses, churches, and monasteries for some of the building material. This concrete political and military symbol of authority was designed by Antonio da Sangallo the Younger, appointed by the pope, and was completed in 1543. Sangallo incorporated the beautiful Etruscan Porta Marzia into the wall structure and this is still visible.

It doesn't take much imagination to understand how much the citizens of Perugia hated this fortress, which was partially demolished in 1848 and then fully in 1860 at the time of unification. What's left today are the fortress's foundations, which were restored beginning in the 1970s (work is still continuing). The really amazing thing is that visitors can now walk through many of the underground passages of the Rocca, and doing so really conveys the fortress's size and strength. There is an ingeniously designed series of escalators that allows residents and visitors to ride from the upper part of town to the lower part while passing inside the fortifications. Inside the foundations there are some small shops and other businesses built into the fortress walls—the city has really done an impressive job of using the vast space creatively. There is a paperback guidebook available for sale at the underground museum, but unfortunately it's only in Italian; I bought one anyway because it contains a foldout colored drawing of what it's believed Perugia looked like when the Rocca was fully intact.

Rowing Clubs

The Arno may not seem like the sort of river that would support rowers, but the Florence Rowing Society (Società Canottieri Firenze) and the Communal Rowing Association (Canottieri Comunali) are very active and are credited with reviving life on the waterway. During the Renaissance, workers called *renaioli* dug sand out of the Arno riverbed, loaded it onto their boats, and pushed their way with poles to the riverbank, where the sand was transported to the city center. It was mixed into the mortar used for the construction of many *palazzi,* walls, and roads. A fascinating book to read about the Arno is *Fortune Is a River: Leonard da Vinci and Niccolò Machiavelli's Magnificent Dream to Change the Course of Florentine History,* by Roger Masters (Free Press, 1998), detailing a little-known collaboration (that was ultimately a failure) between da Vinci and Machiavelli.

If you walk to the Arno and stand between the Uffizi and the Ponte Vecchio, you'll see the manicured lawn of the Società Canottieri Firenze just below (Lungarno Anna Maria Luisa de' Medici 8). Boats and rowers are usually coming and going in and out of the river, and club members appear to be having a swell time sitting in relaxing chairs, enjoying cocktails in the evening. Only members are permitted to row and hang out on the lawn (though the club accepts temporary members, for a maximum of six months, without having to pay the lifetime membership), but visitors may have a drink at the bar or a meal at the restaurant, and from here the view is quite special. For more information about becoming a temporary member visit the club's Web site (canottierifirenze.it).

S

Saints' Days

Nearly every day of the year is a saint's day somewhere in Italy, at both the national and local levels. National saints' days fall on November 1 (Tutti Santi, All Saints' Day) and December 26 (Santo Stefano, for Saint Stephen). Offices and stores are typically closed on national saints' days, as well as on feast days honoring local patron saints. In Florence, this day is June 24, for Saint John the Baptist. Public holidays are known as *giorni festivi,* and *chiuso per ferie* (closed for the holiday, as noted previously) is a phrase you'll see often on such days, just as you will in the month of August, when Italians (and most Europeans) are on vacation for much or all of the month.

Scriptorium

This wonderfully atmospheric shop (Via dei Servi 5r/+39 055 211 804/scriptoriumfirenze.com) is one of the most distinctive in Florence. In medieval times a scriptorium was a cross between a schoolroom and a print shop. Scribes or copyists, usually monks, worked in the scriptorium, usually found in churches and monasteries, and as the fame of an abbey's scriptorium grew, so did its wealth. This scriptorium celebrates the art of writing, and offers a beautiful selection of fine note cards, stationery, silver writing instruments, inks, calligraphy pens, leather-covered boxes, and beautiful *cordoni,* blank books with leather or calfskin covers made

to look antiquated and bearing a hinge-shaped design with the Florentine fleur-de-lis at its end to resemble the city's wooden doors of the Middle Ages. I bought a notepad with a silver clip at the top that is handy and beautiful, and I will have it a long time because when the pages run out I simply replace them with another pad. Best of all is the gift wrapping: the staff will carefully wrap even your smallest purchase in a textured paper called *carta paglia,* tie it with brown twine, and then light a match to melt the sealing wax on top.

Stendhal Syndrome

Referring to the sick physical feeling that afflicted French novelist Stendhal after he visited Santa Croce in Florence, this "syndrome" describes the feeling of being completely overwhelmed by your surroundings. (My translation: seeing and doing way too much.) Stendhal wrote, "My soul, affected by the very notion of being in Florence, and by the proximity of those great men, was already in a state of trance. Absorbed in the contemplation of sublime beauty, I could perceive its very essence close at hand; I could, as it were, feel the stuff of it beneath my fingertips. I had attained to that supreme degree of sensibility where the divine intimations of art merge with the impassioned sensuality of emotion. As I emerged from the port of Santa Croce, I was seized with a fierce palpitation of the heart; I walked in constant fear of falling to the ground." Visitors to Florence especially, who arrive with too long a list of must-sees, are prime candidates for the syndrome. Organize your days, factor in how long it takes to get from place to place, and see what you want. There will be no quiz.

Street Numbers

As Louise Fili notes in *Italianissimo,* during the Risorgimento—the movement that led to Italian unification—the city of Florence went through a huge urban renewal. Many people had earned their livelihood from selling goods out of carts or market stalls, or from the ground floors of family homes, and once the big cleanup began, these vendors preferred to establish real storefronts for their shops, separate from their homes or streets. This created a problem, since now there was a need to distinguish between business and home addresses, and it was impossible to renumber the entire city. So the solution was to create a unique numbering system: red numbers would be for businesses, and the number listed would be followed by an *r* for *rosso.* Black numbers would be reserved for hotels and residences, but these wouldn't always be followed by an *n* for *nero.* Over time the little *r*'s have faded and appear to be lots of other colors besides red. The black numbers now appear to be blue. (Readers who have also visited Paris or other French cities may have noticed that some addresses are followed by letters there, too, but the French have kept up the maintenance on their numbered signs and they are much more uniform and easier to see.) In addition to the residential/business distinction in Florence, there is seemingly no rhyme or reason to the order in which numbers appear on any given street—don't expect to find buildings in numerical order, as you will often find yourself in front of, for example, 25r, which will be next to 52n and across the street from 98r. Good luck, and allow yourself plenty of time to get where you're going.

V

Vasari Corridor

For years I'd wanted to visit the Vasari Corridor in Florence, Il Corridoio Vasariano, but every time I tried it was closed for repairs, closed indefinitely, off-limits to visitors, or, when it was open, too expensive. Finally, I had my chance, thanks to Wendy Perrin at *Condé Nast Traveler*. As readers may already know, Perrin writes an annual feature called "Trips of a Lifetime," and in one of her reports she included the Vasari Corridor and the name of a guide permitted to accompany visitors on a private tour: Alessandra Marchetti, an art historian in Florence. It took me a few years before I was able to arrange for a corridor tour for myself, but in the interim I arranged for some colleagues to visit, and they couldn't have been more complimentary of Marchetti. Even when I think about it now, five months after my visit, the first word that comes to mind is "wow." What an extraordinary experience.

The Corridoio was designed by Giorgio Vasari and was completed in just five months, for the wedding of Francesco I de' Medici and Giovanna of Austria in 1565. The "urban footpath," as it's called by museum officials, is almost a kilometer long and begins in the west corridor of the Uffizi, continues to the

Arno, crosses the Arno atop the shops on the Ponte Vecchio—the original meat market that was previously on the bridge was moved so its unpleasant odors wouldn't offend the grand duke and was replaced by goldsmiths in 1593—continues to Santa Felicità and to the gardens of the Guicciardini family, and ends in the Boboli Gardens, at the Buontalenti Grotto. The corridor was envisioned as a private passageway connecting the Uffizi (originally the administrative offices of the Medici) with the Palazzo Pitti (where various members of the Medici family lived). It's amazing to look out the windows of the corridor when you're on top of the Ponte Vecchio, and more amazing when you reach Santa Felicità and realize that the corridor has been incorporated into the church, creating a private loggia for the Medici! There really is nothing quite like this anywhere else in the world. (And as an aside, the *Annunciation* and *Deposition* frescoes by Jacopo Pontormo in Santa Felicità are what I refer to as "gaspworthy.") The interior of the corridor is lined almost entirely with more than a thousand paintings, most self-portraits by some of the world's most noted painters from the sixteenth to the twentieth centuries. A few portraits stand out, but although the collection is unique, it isn't the reason you pay for the privilege to walk the length of the corridor.

Marchetti is currently working on a doctoral thesis on Michelangelo (she even lives in a house in Settignano that Michelangelo lived in) and the tours she conducts of the Vasari Corridor benefit Friends of Florence (see page 538).

Tours must be reserved in advance (Marchetti's e-mail address is aleoberm@tin.it) and the total cost is approximately 290 euros.

Villa I Tatti

Visiting Villa I Tatti, the home of historian and critic of late medieval and Renaissance art Bernard Berenson from 1900 to 1959, remains one of the highlights of my life. Even the drive from Florence to Settignano was beautiful (see more about the village of Settignano—birthplace of Michelangelo, Bartolomeo Ammannati, Desiderio da Settignano, and the poet Niccolò Tommaseo— on my blog). Upon Berenson's death, at age ninety-four in 1959, he bequeathed his estate to his alma mater, and since then Villa I Tatti has been the Harvard University Center for Italian Renaissance Studies.

Berenson, often referred to simply as BB, wanted I Tatti to be a true center of scholarship, and the center is devoted to advancing the study of the Italian Renaissance in all aspects, including art history; political, economic, and social history; the history of science, philosophy, and religion; and the history of literature and music. Each year fifteen postdoctoral scholars in the early stages of their careers are selected to become yearlong I Tatti fellows. If I had known about this fellowship in my second year of college, I would have made sure to earn that double major in art history!

BB and his wife, Mary, commissioned English architect Cecil Ross Pinsent (1884–1963) to oversee extensions and alterations to the villa and to design a terraced garden. (Pinsent also designed the gardens at La Foce.) Seeing the inside of the villa was amazing—there are 120 notable works of Renaissance and Asian art—but walking around the garden was just as much a pleasure to me, especially seeing the cypress allée (I am a nut for an allée of any kind of tree, but none more so than cypress). In order not to interrupt scholars, an I Tatti visit doesn't include a visit to the library, which holds an impressive 300,000 volumes, an archive of more than 150,000 photographs and other visual materials (the Fototeca Berenson), and 600 journals. Julian More, in *Views from a Tuscan Vineyard,* writes that Berenson "felt his time was wasted on pedantic scholarship, that art expertise was not creative, that he was just another Victorian leech on the talent of the Renaissance. It is touching, therefore, to know that he found solace in the Tuscan countryside, walking in the woods above Fiesole, coming from the glare of hot piazzas into the cool of incense-smelling churches. There was one particular oak tree, ancient as an Etruscan wall; Berenson loved to touch it. It made him feel neither Jewish, nor Catholic, but pagan. He was at one with nature." (More also relates that, somewhat remarkably, Berenson, though Jewish, was able to spend the entire war years in Tuscany as he was looked after and hidden by Italian friends. "The GI who liberated him is alleged to have said: 'What's a guy like you doing in a place like this?' ") Berenson once described a walk he took near I Tatti above Vincigliata and wrote that "every step was ecstasy. Sight, sound, smell, the nobler senses, happy. I could not help stretching my arms as if in gratitude to the Maker of it all." That's precisely how *I* felt at I Tatti and in Settignano.

BB earned his reputation as the world's greatest authority on Italian painting not only by writing numerous books, most notably *The Italian Painters of the Renaissance* (Phaidon, 1952), but also by purchasing works for Isabella Stewart Gardner, who commissioned him in the late 1800s to buy art for her in Europe. Many of the works he acquired became the core of the new museum she was creating in Boston, first known as Fenway Court and later as the Isabella Stewart Gardner Museum, one of my favorite in the world. (For more details about this beautiful collection and about the works Berenson acquired, see *Eye of the Beholder: Masterpieces from the Isabella Stewart Gardner Museum,* by Alan Chong, Beacon, 2003.) A wonderful book published after Berenson's death is *Looking at Pictures with Bernard Berenson* (Harry Abrams, 1974), which includes a great reminiscence by J. Carter Brown, then director of the National Gallery of Art, Washington, D.C., on the first time he met Berenson at I Tatti. The book opens with a Berenson quote from 1952 that seems to me to reveal the basic philosophy and passion to which he devoted his life: "We must look and look and look till we live the painting and for a fleeting moment become identified with it. If we do not succeed in loving what through the ages has been loved, it is useless to lie ourselves into believing that we do. A good rough test is whether we feel that it is reconciling us with life. No artifact is a work of art if it does not help to humanize us. Without art, visual, verbal, and musical, our world would have remained a jungle." Another good book, especially to see photographs of what's off-limits on the tour, is *A Legacy of Excellence: The Story of Villa I Tatti*, by William Weaver and with photographs by David Finn and David Morowitz (Harry Abrams, 1997).

As I Tatti isn't a museum, it isn't officially open to the general public. But scholars, students, Harvard alumni, and people with ties to Harvard or with a special interest in the Renaissance may arrange visits upon request. No more than eight visitors at a time may be accommodated; tours are offered on Tuesday and Wednesday afternoons at three and last for about an hour, and no tours are held in August, during the Christmas and New Year holiday, and on days when I Tatti is closed. However, as I write this, visits have been temporarily suspended due to construction. Contact the Villa I Tatti office in Cambridge for information about when tours will be offered again and for reservations (124 Mount Auburn Street, Cambridge, Massachusetts/617 495 8042/itatti.it). It's recommended to contact them well in advance, and to confirm your reservation after arrival in Italy.

Villa La Pietra

Florence is bursting at the seams with things to see and do, so it's hard to even consider venturing to the hills surrounding the city. But visitors who do will be richly rewarded, as it's in the hills that most of Florence's Anglo-American community once lived. In addition to Bernard Berenson at Villa I Tatti, others in this community included Frederick Stibbert, Lina Duff Gordon, and Sir Harold Acton.

This community was quite large during the first decade of the twentieth century, when everyone possessed spectacular villas with their attendant gardens. The British and American expats purchased the villas from members of the Florentine aristocracy, who were forced to sell them due to political and social upheavals resulting from the unification of Italy and the eventual move of the Italian capital from Florence to Rome. Though there is still a sizable British-American expat community in and around Florence today, it really thrived at that particular moment in Florence's history, and the opportunity to buy these villas so inexpensively has not come again. Two world wars, postwar restrictions, and an increase in the value of the land significantly reduced the size of the community. Sir Harold Acton was the last survivor of this original community after Berenson's death in 1959.

Acton was born in 1904 at La Pietra, the villa his parents had acquired the year before. At various points in his life he was a poet, novelist, historian, professor, Royal Air Force officer, and philanthropist, and he's best known to lovers of Italy for his many books, more than thirty in all, including *Memoirs of an Aesthete, The Last Medici, The Pazzi Conspiracy: The Plot Against the Medici,* and *The Villas of Tuscany.* Acton was the inspiration for the character of Anthony Blanche in Evelyn Waugh's 1945 novel *Brideshead Revisited,* and in 1985 he was made an honorary citizen of Florence. Upon his death in 1994, Acton bequeathed La Pietra to New York University, and though some very lucky students study there throughout the year (approximately three hundred per semester), the villa and its magnificent gardens are open to visitors as well.

The name of La Pietra derives from the stone pillar indicating one Roman mile from Florence's city gate of San Gallo, and is the first important milestone one encounters while heading uphill along Via Bolognese. Though the Actons re-created the Renaissance garden and formed an art collection (to become one of the finest in private hands in Florence), it was Harold himself who left an indelible mark on La Pietra and on Florence itself. Sir Harold—he was made a Commander of the British Empire and knighted by Queen Elizabeth in 1974—became, along with BB, one of the "sites" that cultivated visitors to Florence hoped to see. The La Pietra guestbook includes the names of Churchill, Charles and Diana, Lady Bird Johnson, Adlai Stevenson, and Bill and Hillary Clinton.

The villa dates from the fourteenth century and has a typical Renaissance floor plan built around a once-open courtyard where the main axis extends through the house into the gardens. In fact, as Acton once wrote, "in Italian, 'villa' signifies not house alone, but house and pleasure grounds combined: the garden is an architectural extension of the house." The grounds encompass fifty-seven acres in all, and the garden is very fragrant in spring, with roses, iris, wisteria, and herbs; some say May is the best month to visit. The villa's art collection consists of more than thirty-five hundred objects ranging from the Etruscan period to the twentieth century. La Pietra's curatorial staff has adopted a policy that emphasizes preservation over restoration, and it has presented a nice balance between the house as a former home and now as a museum. The estate also features olive groves and fruit trees, and its long avenue of cypress trees, from the main gate to the main entrance, is one of La Pietra's most memorable features. (And note that the gate doesn't accommodate the width of tour buses, one reason why La Pietra remains something of a secret.)

La Pietra is on the route of Florence's city bus no. 25 (from the Piazza San Marco stop, it's a fifteen-minute ride). Ask the driver to indicate where to get off—the stop is across the street from the villa gate, where you press a buzzer for admittance. Guided tours of the villa and garden are offered on Friday afternoons, and advance reservations are required by e-mail, phone, or fax. Tours of the garden only are offered Tuesday mornings, again with advance reservations. No tours are offered during August or from mid-December to mid-January. Villa La Pietra is located at Via Bolognese 120/+39 055 500 7210/nyu.edu/global/lapietra.

Y

Yellow Pages

Sometimes you just need the Yellow Pages, and the English Yellow Pages is what you need for Italy. Go to Englishyellowpages.it and find not only a directory of English-speaking businesses and professionals, but also a student blog, an archive of EYP newsletters, the time and weather in Italy, a converter for weights and measures, and a lot more, making it more useful than Google.

Z

Zibibbo

Zibibbo is a grape variety unique to Sicily and the island of Pantelleria, and though it can be used to make table wine and grappa, it's most commonly used in a strong wine similar to Marsala. Unlike Marsala, spirits aren't added—and the grapes are partially fermented in the sun, a process that's derived from a formula used in the Middle Ages—and dried Zibibbo grapes are often used in desserts. But Zibibbo is also a noted trattoria on the outskirts of Florence, whose chef and owner is Benedetta Vitali (mentioned previously; see pages 342 and 409). Vitali, cofounder of Cibrèo restaurant with her former husband, Fabio Picchi, had already earned her respected reputation before she opened Zibibbo, and no one—locals and visitors alike—thinks the ten-minute drive from the *centro* is prohibitive, as it's one of the best culinary destinations in Florence. In an article entitled "Choice Tables: On the Fringes of Florence, Memorable Eating" (*New York Times,* January 27, 2002), Maureen B. Fant notes that Vitali turns out some Tuscan favorites at Zibibbo but also plenty of dishes from southern Italy and the Near East, and others with no clear geographic roots. "Only a person of impeccable judgment and technical skill can pull off this sort of multicultural menu in Italy, and Mrs. Vitali has managed it."

Readers may be interested to know that Vitali offers several cooking classes, including an intensive weeklong course as well as two shorter courses, A Day in the Kitchen and An Afternoon Encounter, all at Zibibbo (Via de Terzolina 3r/+39 055 433 383/trattoriazibibbo.it or benedettavitali.com).

Vitali was one of Faith Willinger's 254 friends she included in her book *Adventures of an Italian Food Lover,* and she kindly allowed me to share Vitali's recipe for Broccoli and Cauliflower Sformatino. As Willinger notes, *sformatino* means "little unmolded," but it's neither unmolded nor little. Vitali serves it as an appetizer, in little spoonfuls on a plate, but Willinger makes it as a side dish, which is how I tried it, too. (Willinger also notes that a few jars of Zibibbo's homemade products, like orange peel in port or spicy pear *mostarda* chutney, make wonderful culinary souvenirs from the restaurant and from Florence.)

BROCCOLI AND CAULIFLOWER SFORMATINO

SERVES 6 TO 8

¾ pound head of cauliflower
¾ pound broccoli
Coarse sea salt
1 cup milk
3 tablespoons butter or extra virgin olive oil
¼ cup all-purpose flour
¾ cup grated Parmigiano-Reggiano cheese
Freshly ground black pepper

Break the cauliflower into florets. If they're large, cut each of them into bite-size pieces. Cut the tops off the broccoli, trim the stems of the tough outer parts, and cut into ½-inch pieces. If the tops are large, cut into bite-size pieces.

Bring 6 quarts of water to a rolling boil; add 3 tablespoons coarse sea salt and the cauliflower. Cook for 10 to 12 minutes or until tender, not al dente. Remove the cauliflower from the pot, place in a sinkful of cold water to cool, then drain the cauliflower.

Put the broccoli stem chunks in the boiling water and cook for 7 minutes, then add the broccoli tops and cook for another 7 minutes or until tender. Remove broccoli from the pot and place in a sinkful of water to cool, then drain and combine with the cauliflower in a large bowl. Set aside 1 cup of the vegetable-cooking water.

Preheat the oven to 375°F.

Heat the milk and vegetable-cooking water in a small pot. Melt the butter in a small pot, add the flour, and stir over low heat for a few minutes but don't let the mixture color. Add the hot milk and stir energetically with a whisk until smooth and creamy. Remove from the heat, stir in the Parmigiano-Reggiano, and season with salt and pepper.

Combine the sauce with the broccoli and cauliflower and transfer the mixture to a baking dish, smoothing to a 2-inch layer. Bake for 20 to 25 minutes, until bubbling. Cool for 5 minutes before serving.

ACKNOWLEDGMENTS

As I've emphasized previously, creating an anthology requires the efforts of a staggering number of people as well as attention to a staggering number of details. Anyone who even asked how I was progressing on this Tuscany and Umbria volume deserves my thanks—you know who you are, and I am grateful for your inquiries. But as I may very well have forgotten to mention a few names here, I offer my sincerest apologies and hope I will be forgiven. Once again, I extend my enormous gratitude to Vintage publisher Anne Messitte, Vintage editor-in-chief LuAnn Walther, and my editor, Diana Secker Tesdell. They alone are a unique trio in book publishing, but with other members of the Vintage family—notably Bette Graber, Kathy Hourigan, Florence Lui, Jen Marshall, Jocelyn Miller, Roz Parr, Russell Perreault, Nicole Pedersen, and Anke Steinecke—they are nothing less than formidable.

Sincere thanks to each of the individual writers, agents, and permissions representatives: without your cooperation and generosity there would be nothing to publish, and I would not have the opportunity to share the work of many good writers with my readers. *Mille grazie* to Simonetta Brandolini d'Adda, Laurie Albanese, Joan and Roger Arndt, Mario Batali, Marco Bellanca, Dr. Ellyn Berk, Paolo Cesaroni, Charlie Conrad, Charles Darwall, Chris Deas, Patty Flynn, Dianne Hales, Vincent La Rouche, Bill LeBlond, Amanda Lensing, Pamela Lewy, Alessandra Marchetti, Frances Mayes, Michael F. Moore, Laura Morowitz, Barbara and Mel Ohrbach, Simone Parrini, Segen Scott, Judy Sternlight, and Faith Willinger for your time, tips, and advice, and to traveling companions Peggy Harrison, Maha Khalil, and Amy Myer. I am appreciative of the kind and courteous assistance I received from everyone at the Italian Government Tourist Board office in New York, as well as from the staff at the Mount Pleasant Public Library in Pleasantville, New York, notably from Miriam Simpson, who is indefatigable in tracking down books for me—rare, out-of-print, or hard to find titles are her specialty. I remain deeply grateful to my brilliant and kind boss and mentor, Chip Gibson, who has long supported *The Collected Traveler,* and to my husband, Jeff, and our daughter, Alyssa, with whom I've spent memorable Italian moments.

PERMISSIONS ACKNOWLEDGMENTS